JAPANNED
PAPIER MÂCHÉ
AND TINWARE
c.1740–1940

JAPANNED
PAPIER MÂCHÉ
AND TINWARE
c.1740–1940

Yvonne Jones

ANTIQUE COLLECTORS' CLUB

British Library Cataloguing-in-Publication Data
A catalogue record for this book is available from the British Library

Frontispiece: One of a pair of corner cabinets which have tops and door panels veneered with papier mâché, the decoration of
which corresponds with that on door panels made by Henry Clay for Derby House, London, in 1779 (see pl. 111).
The cabinets are believed to have been commissioned by William Brummell, for Donington Grove, Berkshire; attributed to
Henry Clay, c.1785. 86 x 66 x 37cm
COURTESY OF BONHAMS

Title page: Detail from the pair to the cabinet shown opposite, painted in a style similar to decorative motifs used by
Henry Clay for four doors in the Marble Hall, at Kedleston Hall, Derbyshire (see pl. 11).
COURTESY OF BONHAMS

Printed in China
for the Antique Collectors' Club Ltd., Woodbridge, Suffolk

CONTENTS

List of Subscribers   7

Acknowledgements   7

Preface   8

Chapter I   From Imitation to Innovation: The Origins of Japanning in the West   10

Chapter II   Enter the Dragon: Tinplate Working and the Japanning Trade   16

Chapter III   A Lion of the District: Papier Mâché and the Japanning Trade   22

Chapter IV   Japanning and Decorating   38

Chapter V   Not a Bed of Roses: Workshops, Factories and Labour   88

Chapter VI   Clever Accidents? Design, Taste and Criticism   98

Chapter VII   The Decline of the Midlands Japanning Industry   106

Chapter VIII   The Birmingham Japanners   112

Chapter IX   The Wolverhampton Japanners   182

Chapter X   The Bilston Japanners   218

Chapter XI   Japanners in London and Oxford   228

Chapter XII   Products   238

Chapter XIII   Other Western Japanning Centres   270

Chapter XIV   Notes for Collectors   310

Directory of known Artists and Decorators   318

Glossary   325

Select Bibliography   326

References   326

Index   332

This book is dedicated to
Tom and Samuel Jones who gave me the courage of my convictions
and to the memory of
David Rodgers who introduced me to the subject

LIST OF SUBSCRIBERS

Amgueddfa Cymru – National Museum Wales, Library
Apter-Fredericks Ltd.
John Evan Bedford
Thomas Bennett, Charleston
Christopher Beresford-Jones
Fine English Furniture Department, Bonhams, London
John Boram
Craig R.E. Campbell
M. Janet Carlile
Dorothea Colligan
Mrs Phyllis Culley
David Foord-Brown Antiques
Robert S. Ferguson
Mrs Barbara Fogarty
Mr Robert C. Guinness
John and Leela Hardy
Linda Hynes

P.T. Kent
Peter Lang
Lauder & Howard Antiques, Fremantle Western Australia
Martin P. Levy
Sarah Medlam
Audrey and Stuart Peckner
R.G. Cave & Sons Ltd.
Jeremy C.B. Rye Esq.
Frank A. Sharman
Tim Stubbs
David Temperley
V&A Museum Library
James and Gillian Webb
Lee W. Winborne
Windsor House Antiques Ltd.
Lucy Wood

ACKNOWLEDGMENTS

In the current economic climate, this book would not have been possible without the generous financial support of Christopher Beresford-Jones, the Evan Bedford Library of Furniture History, Tom Jones, and David Temperley, for which I am inordinately grateful. Nor would it have been possible without those who so kindly subscribed, or who early placed orders in an endeavour to ensure publication. I thank them all and hope that the book lives up to their expectations.

My journey through the history of japanning was not solitary. It is not possible, here, to name the many people who, maybe only in passing, have set me on new trails of enquiry, or in some way, made my research so much simpler. Nevertheless, there are some who cannot go unmentioned, among them are my good friends, Sarah Campbell, who as former Assistant Director of Leisure Services in Wolverhampton, was more helpful than she will ever know; John Davies who, with both an eagle-eye and a knack for knowing what would especially interest me, was an invaluable scout; John Merilion who generously gave me the run of his design-library prior to its dispersal; and not least David Temperley who, with his profound knowledge of fine and rare books, led me to references I would surely not have found. Moreover, I should

like to acknowledge the late Trevor Denning who, as photographer, was a genial companion on several expeditions to photograph collections.

I am indebted to the many anonymous collectors I met, both here and in the USA, during the course of writing this book for both their generous hospitality and willingness to allow me free access to their collections. I also thank those collectors with whom I have corresponded but have yet to meet. Flavours of conversations with collectors who sadly did not live to see this book: Nigel Bingham, Judy Crawford, and Eric Hyatt, run through its pages as do those with the late Martha Wilbur, in the States, whose knowledge of the subject was formidable; each relished their collections with a quiet passion that, memorably, never got in the way of a jolly lunch.

Equally, this book has been enriched by helpful assistance and advice from specialists in museums, libraries, and other organisations. I have benefited particularly from discussions with Dr Megan Aldrich at Sotheby's Institute; Patrick Bourgeois at Le Musée de Pont-à-Mousson; Brendan Flynn at Birmingham Museums & Art Gallery; Barbara Fogarty, post-graduate student at the University of Birmingham;

Andrew Renton and Rachel Conroy at the National Museum of Wales; Pat Sanderson at Pontypool Museum; and Lucy Wood, formerly at the V&A. Dr Clare Finn (Clare Finn & Co. Ltd), and Richard Higgins (Richard Higgins Conservation Ltd), generously shared their professional expertise, and Dr Monika Kopplin at the Museum für Lackkunst, Münster, Dr Titus Eliens at the Gemeente Museum, The Hague, and the Warden and Scholars of New College, Oxford, were each helpful by sourcing images. It would be impossible to over-estimate the support and encouragement I have received from Corinne Miller, Head of Arts & Heritage, Wolverhampton, and from her colleagues, Helen Steatham at Bantock House, and Linda Ellis and Christopher Broughton; they have been behind me every step of the way, and I am extremely grateful for all they have done. Likewise, I should like to thank staff in the reference departments at Birmingham Libraries & Archives, and most especially Rob Ebbutt for his terrier-like instinct when searching obscure titles; Richard Albutt for his help and patience in digitalising images; and Fiona Tait in Archives & Heritage, who kindly alerted me to many useful references.

A quick scan of credit lines beneath the illustrations in this book, will show the extent to which I am grateful to the many antique-dealers and auctioneers who have so readily supplied images. Guy Apter (Apter & Fredericks), John Hansord, Stephen Jarrett (Witney Antiques) and Martin Levy (Blairman), have helpfully drawn important objects to my notice, and René Sattler (Kenneth Neame Ltd) gave unsparingly of his time. In particular, I would like to thank Guy Saville, Fergus Lyons and Jackie Brown at Bonhams, and Will Hobbs and Gemma Bush at Woolley & Wallis, who patiently fielded my every enquiry and request, and who also drew interesting items to my attention. Similarly, Marcus Radescke at Christie's, and Jeremy Smith and Julia Clarke, at Sotheby's, could not have been more helpful. Over the years, John Hardy, first at the V&A, and then at Christie's, has been a source of much valuable help and advice, and more recently, Peter Lang, formerly of Sotheby's New York, has been unstinting in his encouragement and support of my research. I hope that the information contained herein will provide at least some recompense.

During the writing of this book, the committee and members of the American *Historical Society of Early American Decoration*, have freely shared their knowledge, their collections, and their energies. I owe them much; would that I could name them each and every one. However, I must mention the Society's past and current presidents, Sandra Cohen and Valerie Oliver, respectively, for their support and interest, and also Shirley Baer former editor of the Society's journal, and her successor Lynne Richards, for their help in sourcing and supplying images from the Society's collection. Astrid Donellan, Joseph Rice, and Sara Tiffany, provided images at the drop of a hat, and the Society's master-craftsmen generously allowed me to reproduce their work.

I should also like to thank Andrea Allgood, Colin Benton, Richard Compton-Miller, Richard Deakin, Keith and Gill Pinn, and Anthony Phipps, for their continued interest and help, and Noël Riley, Catherine Richenburg, and Anne Stevens who, besides sharing their knowledge, ensured that I stayed the course. Not least, I thank my husband and son who have lived with the topic of japanning for so long. And finally, I offer my sincere thanks and appreciation to Stephen Mackinlay, Anna Morton and Sandra Pond at the *Antique Collectors' Club* for ensuring so painless a transition from typescript to publication.

Naturally, any errors or omissions are entirely my own.

Yvonne Jones, 2012

PREFACE

Some years ago, when cataloguing and managing the collection of japanned papier mâché and tinware at Wolverhampton Art Galleries and Museums, it became clear how few publications there were to help me. New to the subject and with none of the existing literature answering all my questions, the only way forward was to find out for myself. I had no notion of the scale of the task I had taken on nor, indeed, any idea of where my research might lead. Certainly, I did not have a book in mind; that idea came only with the realisation that museum visitors and collectors were asking questions similar to my own.

They wanted to know why it was called 'japanning' when it was not made in Japan? Why the industry developed in the English midlands, and how it differed from lacquering? Were there any links with Pontypool japan-ware and how can their products be distinguished? Was the papier mâché used in the industry, the same as we made at school? And how did the decorators paint so smoothly without showing any brushmarks? These, and many other questions, were uppermost in my mind while writing this book. In answering them, I have drawn, wherever possible, upon contemporary sources: printed, manuscript and typescript documents; and for the the period leading up to the closure of the last factories in the 1920s, I was fortunate to be able to draw on verbal accounts.

There were many gaps in the history of this industry which, though by no means insignificant, has been largely neglected in terms of research. In fact, there can be few decorative arts about which so little has been written and about which so many misunderstandings abound. And yet, in its heyday, japanners attracted important commissions from prestigious designers such as Robert Adam, and orders from fashionable society across Europe and beyond. In the 1760s, its commercial potential tempted even the astute Matthew Boulton to consider setting up a japanning workshop at his Soho Works in Birmingham.

This book, then, is a long-overdue history of the japanning industry which centred on three towns in the English midlands during the eighteenth and nineteenth centuries: Birmingham, Wolverhampton and Bilston. It is about the workers, their skills and the factories and workshops in which they laboured, as much as it is about the goods they made. It tells of matters of taste and criticism, and of how, in the machine-age, an industry which continued to rely so heavily upon hand-labour, reached its natural end in the 1880s with a few factories lingering into the 1930s. As far as possible, it illustrates mostly marked, or well-documented, examples of japanned tin and papier mâché against which readers may compare, and perhaps identify, unmarked specimens. Only three previous books have been devoted to the subject: George Dickinson's *English Papier Mâché* (1925), Jane Toller's *Papier Mâché in Great Britain and America* (1966), and Shirley DeVoe's *English Papier Mâché of the Georgian and Victorian Periods* (1971). Without these, my task would have been so much greater, but as their titles show, they focussed entirely on papier mâché. DeVoe later went on to write *The Art of the Tinsmith* which included much about English and American japanned tin, but nowhere is there a book dedicated to the midlands japanning industry as a whole. As a consequence japanned tinware is now looked upon as an entirely separate industry. To some extent the japanners themselves were to blame for this, frequently advertising as 'makers of papier mâché and japanned ware' – a distinction which still holds among the older population in some parts of the former japanning district. Nevertheless, the manufacture of japanned tin and papier mâché was so inextricably linked that to consider one without the other is to distort facts. Here, by bringing the two branches of the industry back together, it will be seen that tinware and papier mâché were often japanned in the same workshops and that their decoration was undertaken by the same painters, gilders and pearlers. If proof were needed of these close links, it is surprising how often a tray which appears to be papier mâché when viewed from a distance, on closer inspection turns out to be made from tin.

Inevitably, a number of myths and legends have developed around the trade which, over the years, have come to skew its history. Perhaps the most outstanding example of this has been the arbitrary reliance upon the firms of Henry Clay and Jennens & Bettridge, when making attributions about any good yet unmarked wares. Their reputations were justly deserved but the following pages will show that their names should no longer be used so indiscriminately; Clay was not the only maker of fine quality eighteenth-century papier mâché, any more than Jennens & Bettridge, alone, made the best Victorian products. It will be seen that both had serious rivals whose names should be brought into the reckoning when attempting attributions.

Similarly, Henry Clay is often believed to have introduced the manufacture of papier mâché in Birmingham, an honour which I shall argue belongs to Stephen Bedford. And likewise, it will be shown that not all finely painted tin trays with pierced edges were made in Pontypool as tradition has it – some were produced in Birmingham – a discovery which makes the already hazy distinction between certain types of English and Welsh products even more troublesome.

To my knowledge, no japanning factory records have survived. There are isolated examples such as Mander's *Varnish Book*, or William Highfield Jones' delightfully engaging manuscript histories of his family, which are crammed with useful details about their lives as japanners. However, the information they provide needed to be pieced together with details from elsewhere and woven into the bigger picture. I have done this as objectively as possible with the material available. As with many publications which chart new waters, maybe this book will trigger the discovery of that complete factory archive which I longed to find and fervently hope is there to be uncovered. If that happens, then I trust that any errors which may be found within my text will be overlooked in favour of the greater benefit this book will have brought to future research on the japanning trade.

The majority of papier mâché and tinware was unmarked. This book will not always enable the reader to make positive attributions, but it should prevent the making of unreliable ones. If it achieves only that, then it will have gone a long way towards recognising the contribution of the many japanners whose names have, until now, been overlooked. When the names of John Baskerville or Stephen Bedford spring as readily to mind as the term 'Pontypool' in relation to Georgian tin trays, or when a piece of Victorian papier mâché furniture is said to be 'possibly by Richard Turley', or 'perhaps by McCallum & Hodson', a significant leap forward will have been made in the understanding of this fascinating industry.

Y.J.

CHAPTER I

FROM IMITATION to INNOVATION

The Origins of Japanning in the West

'The cabinets, China, Lacquered and Japan Ware, and several other sorts of
goods that come ready made are too costly to the Nation, a great hinderance to
the imploy of our own people, and a prodigal unprofitable Expence.'
John Pollexfen, *A Discourse of Trade, Coyn & Paper Credit,* 1697[1]

Few topics in the history of English decorative arts cause more confusion than the terms 'japanning' and 'japan'. They can mean different things to different people, are sometimes mistakenly believed to be synonymous with 'lacquering', and, in the case of the majority of articles for which the term is used, have no actual connection with Japan. The term 'japanning' was first used in 1688 by John Stalker and George Parker in the title of their book *A Treatise of Japaning* [*sic*] *and Varnishing*, which together with practical instructions, included 'Patterns for JAPAN-work, in imitation of the INDIANS' (plate 2).[2] To understand this apparent contradiction we need to look to the sixteenth century and to Europe's early trade with the East. Only then is it possible to fully understand the development of japanning as an industry in the English midlands.

The Oriental Stimulus
Questions about the origin of the term 'japan' were summarised by the Reverend I. Taylor, in his epistolary book *Scenes of British Wealth* (1825). 'Why', he asked is a product of an eighteenth and nineteenth century industry 'called japan, if it is made at Pontypool, and Birmingham, and London, and many other places?' In his opinion it was 'because the first pieces of this ware, which were brought to England, came from Japan in the early part of our intercourse with the East Indies.' This was not strictly accurate since they came also from China and India, but his answer is useful for two reasons. First, it highlights a problem which arose in the sixteenth century when, through lack of knowledge and because lacquer was rarely imported direct from its country of origin, objects were randomly described in contemporary inventories as 'Japanese', 'Chinese', or 'Indian'. Second, it highlights the fact that 'East India' and 'India', had become catch-all names which stood for any Far Eastern country with which the East India Company traded. Contemporary attributions, therefore, cannot be taken too literally.

Eastern lacquer, though first brought to Europe in the sixteenth century, initially by Portuguese merchants and then by the Dutch, was not imported in any organised way until

Opposite: 1. Bureau-cabinet of black-lacquered wood with gold lacquer decoration; made in Canton (Guangzhou), Southern China, c.1730. 238 x 112 x 66.5cm

the establishment of the English East India Company in 1600[i] when trading links were set up with India, China, and Japan. Even then, most 'Japanese' lacquer continued to reach England and, indeed, the whole of Europe by way of Holland. The Dutch had engineered a virtual monopoly on imports which effectively closed Japan's ports to other European ships until the nineteenth century.

Thus, the first English ship which the Company sent to Japan in 1611, was also its last until 1854. Nevertheless, *The Clove* returned in 1614, laden with lacquered 'Scritoires, Trunkes, Beoubes [screens], Cupps and dishes of all sortes and of a most excellent varnish.'[3] The Company enhanced the rarity and monetary values of such exotic wares, by shrewdly releasing them, alongside Chinese and Indian lacquer, very slowly on to the London market. As a result, an elite clientele was assured.

This marketing ploy for Far Eastern goods remained the pattern until the restoration of the monarchy in 1660 when Charles II returned from exile in Europe bringing with him a taste for luxury and extravagance. After the austerity of Cromwell's Commonwealth, the King's new Court set the style for those wealthy enough to follow. Eastern 'lackwork', as it was often called, was richly decorated in gold and colour on black (plate 3). To a country used to dark oak furniture and wainscoting, it was a curiosity and became desirable enough to be imported in large quantities and sold in specialist 'India' goods shops. The unfamiliar shapes of the furniture and its decoration were too alien for some English tastes and so, in 1670, a number of 'artisans were sent out [to China] to introduce patterns suitable for sale at home.'[4]

Nevertheless, of the various lacquer imports, those from Japan were the most valued. 'My skill and fancy', wrote Stalker, 'induce me to believe, that Japan is more rich, grave and Majestick, and for that reason ought to be more highly esteemed'.[5] This was a view that appears to have been shared by the East India Company, as in 1699, it directed that 'none of the wares are to be sent but what are lacquered in Japan.'[6] Thereafter, it became commonplace to describe all Oriental lacquer imports as 'Japan' goods, regardless of their country of origin.

As John Pollexfen observed in 1697, the fashion for lacquered furniture was a matter of great concern to European cabinet makers. At first, English joiners, fearing they were 'in great danger of being utterly ruined',[7] petitioned against the lacquer imports, but then, like those in Holland and France, they turned the situation to their advantage. As demand for lacquer far exceeded supply, they set about imitating it and undercutting its cost. The fashion for 'japan' goods, their high prices, and the early success of European imitations are reflected in a letter written by the Duke of Hamilton late in the

seventeenth century. The Duke, when on political visits to London, was in the habit of shopping for luxuries to send home to his wife in Scotland. He admired some Indian cabinets in the City, but at forty guineas or more each, he wrote to her: 'For my part I think a counterfeit one looks as well, so let me know if you will take such a one, or give the forty guineas.'[8]

European competition was fierce. However, the imitations did not stop the flow of Eastern lacquer into the West, and by then, much of it was being designed especially for Western markets (plate 1). For example, in about 1700, the East India Company dispatched further craftsmen with 'great quantities of English patterns to teach the Indians how to manufacture goods to make them vendible in England and the rest of the European markets. After which', according to a document of c.1700, 'began the great trade in manufactured goods from the Indies.'[9]

Revered though the early imports were in Europe, the finest Japanese lacquer was reserved for home consumption and never exported. An article published in a popular English magazine many years later, in 1845, explained the position that pertained throughout the activities of the East India Company:[ii]

> *Of the lacker-work, known in this country as Japan, all writers assert that no adequate idea can be conceived from the specimens commonly seen in Europe. What is really fine cannot be purchased by foreigners; and the best ever obtained by the members of the factory[iii] are received as presents from their Japanese friends. These are mostly deposited in the Royal Museum at the Hague; and although esteemed at home [ie. in Japan] scarcely second rate are so really superior to the ordinary japan that no opinion could be given upon the beauty of the art, without having inspected that collection.*[10]

Notwithstanding, the Oriental imports continued to be admired and esteemed by connoisseurs keen to distinguish between the 'right japan' of the East and its less costly European equivalent 'japanned ware.' 'Japan' had taken on a new meaning: to 'japan' meant to decorate in Japanese style (or indeed, any Oriental style), and European articles finished in this way were said to have been 'japanned'.

By the mid eighteenth century, these terms had taken on yet another nuance.

Early Japanning in England
The earliest detailed, and best-known, account of English japanning was Stalker and Parker's *Treatise* in which they explained that Japan 'not being able to furnish these parts with work of this kind, the English and Frenchmen have endeavoured to imitate them ... if done by able hands, it may come so near the true Japan, in fineness of Black, and neatness of Draught, that

---

i. The Dutch East India Company was founded in 1602.
ii. The English East India Company effectively ceased to be important after the Indian

Mutiny; it finally ceased trading in 1947 on the passing of the Indian Independence Act.
iii. 'Factory' is here a trading station and not a manufactory in today's sense of the word.

2. A page from the book in which the term 'japanning' first appeared: *A Treatise of Japaning and Varnishing*, by John Stalker and George Parker, London, 1688. Heavily stained with japan varnish, this copy was, surely, used in a japanning factory.

WOLVERHAMPTON ARTS AND HERITAGE (BANTOCK HOUSE MUSEUM)

no one but an Artist should be able to distinguish 'em.'[11] Finding a suitable equivalent for the 'true japan', however, proved less straightforward than Stalker and Parker implied.

The ancient Eastern skill of lacquering is a long and complex procedure, requiring layer upon layer of natural varnish extracted from indigenous sources. 'True lacquer', as used in China and Japan, is a highly toxic gum or sap collected from the *rhus vernicifera* tree. In India, *lac* – a thinner substance – is obtained from the transparent dark-red resin secreted by female insects of the *lacca* family; in its various forms it was known as *stick lac*, *seed lac* and *shellac* (*qv*). Unlike true lacquer it could be dried, and the resulting flakes could be stored until required, when they could then be dissolved in alcohol prior to use.

Both types of lacquer – the true lacquer of China and Japan, and Indian resin lacquer – hardened naturally and this, together with their being natural substances, is what distinguishes them from

japan varnish. In the West, craftsmen and chemists began a long search to formulate a suitable substitute. Their enquiries show that the meeting of art and science was very characteristic of the time and ran parallel, for example, to a similar search for a European ceramic body that would equal that of Oriental porcelain.

Robert Dossie, in *The Handmaid to the Arts* (1758), wrote that 'the true Japan black laquer [*sic*]'[12] was frequently imported from China and sometimes used on snuff-boxes, cups, and other similar paper or pulp articles. It can have met with little success, however, for not only did it dry out during the long sea-voyage, but also, as Dossie himself added, 'its poisonous qualities are almost constantly fatal to those who work with it for any length of time, and sometimes even on a very slight intermeddling with it.'[13] By contrast, Indian seed lac and shellac had no such harmful effect, could be shipped without detriment, and purchased from either 'the Drugster' or ironmonger; it was upon these that early Western lacquer-substitutes were based.

Stalker and Parker gave directions for achieving a japanned surface 'as good, as glossy, and beautiful a Black, as was ever wrought by an English hand, and to all appearance … in no way inferior to the Indian'.[14] Like that of the Oriental craft they imitated, their method was long and slow. Each of the twenty-four coats of varnish had to be dried thoroughly before the next was applied and all but the first three had to be carefully smoothed. The first six base-coats were of seed lac varnish mixed with lamp-black: these were followed by three coats of varnish made from ¼ pint of seed lac, some Venice turpentine 'the bigness of a walnut'[15] and lamp-black, then, twelve hours later, a further three layers of the same. To finish, six coats of varnish made from the finest seed lac, lightly tinted with lamp-black, were applied, and left for twelve hours before another six layers were added. After five to six days, the surface was polished with water and finely-powdered rotten-stone, and left to harden for a few days; this process was repeated until the required lustre was attained.

However, there was a problem: although this gave the appearance of Indian lacquer, it lacked both its strength and density, and tended to peel off when applied to metal. Wilhelm Kick, in Holland, had gone some way to overcoming this by inventing a method for varnishing tin as early as 1619, but it was to be a hundred years or so before metal could be japanned on a commercial scale. At Major John Hanbury's (1664–1734) Pontypool ironworks in South Wales, a new japan varnish devised by two of his workmen, Thomas Allgood and his son Edward, was primarily intended to protect tinware against rust. Its distinctive ingredients were asphaltum and linseed oil which, when heated with other ingredients, yielded a sticky tar-like varnish. In order for the asphaltum to dry thoroughly and harden, articles coated with japan varnish had to be slowly baked in a stove or oven. It was this stoving that gave Pontypool japanned ware its characteristic lustre and strength of surface; it also gave it the valuable quality of being receptive to decoration.

The Pontypool Japan Works was established in the early 1730s for the decoration of domestic tinware such as trays, urns and teapots. Business was good. It was so successful that in 1734, Hanbury's son, Sir Charles Hanbury-Williams (1708–1759), Member of Parliament for Monmouthshire, and a man of fashion, wrote to his wife that 'Tom Allgood has found a new way of japanning which I think is so beautiful that I'll send you a couple of pieces of it.'[16] Decorated with imitation tortoiseshell grounds, or with oriental-style designs in gilt against chestnut-coloured grounds, these early Pontypool wares extended the market for decorative household articles to include those for whom newly-fashionable silver tewares and imported Chinese porcelain were too expensive (plate 29).

The success of these developments caught the attention of tinplate-workers in the Midlands.[iv] With good local supplies of iron-ore, nearby coalfields in South Staffordshire and the north-eastern part of Worcestershire, and plentiful supplies of wood from neighbouring forests, this region had a long history of small metal-working skills. Records show that some form of japanning was already taking place in Bilston in the late seventeenth century (see p. 18), but it is unlikely that it was anything more than a means of protection against rust. The first Midlands manufacturer to follow Pontypool's example and to use japan varnish for decorative purposes appears to have been John Taylor (*qv*) of Birmingham, a leading enameller and gilt-button-maker who, in about 1740, added japanned tin snuff boxes to his range of products.

Once perfected, japan varnish proved a suitable finish for other materials such as slate, copper, leather and, in particular, papier mâché – a material soon to be developed commercially in Birmingham. These were the roots of the Midlands japanning industry, and Birmingham, Wolverhampton and Bilston soon became its leading centres.

But what, besides their long association with metal-working, made japanning so successful in these three towns? First, the advantage of their central location was enhanced by the building of the canals which, starting in 1767, greatly extended their markets and quickened the supply of raw materials by linking them with the Thames, Severn, Mersey, Humber and Trent rivers, and thus to all major cities and ports. Second, the construction of turnpike roads improved travel across the country, and provided links with the new canals. And third, the rise of Birmingham as a manufacturing town in the mid eighteenth century attracted the rich and powerful from all over the world. Visitors were eager to see the wonders of the new factories and machines, and to purchase examples of the decorative consumer goods which they had seen in production. Among them was Faujas de St Fond,[v] who in 1784, described Birmingham as 'one of the most curious towns in England', adding that:

If any one should wish to see in one comprehensive view, the most numerous and most varied industries, all combined in contributing to the arts of utility, of pleasure, and of luxury, it is hither that he must come. Here all the resources of industry, supported by the genius of invention, and by mechanical skill of every kind are directed towards the arts and seem to be linked together to co-operate for their mutual perfection.[17]

---

iv. A term used in respect of the central counties of England, and more specifically in the context of this book, refers to Warwickshire (in which Birmingham was then situated), and Staffordshire (of which Wolverhampton and Bilston were formerly part).

v. Faujas de St Fond (1741–1819) French geologist and traveller.
vi. J.J. Quin *Trans. Asiatic Soc. Japan, 1880*, vol 9 (Reprinted London 1882). J.J. Rein *Industries of Japan*, English edn, London 1889.

After touring the factories, many visitors, in their enthusiasm, effectively became roving 'ambassadors' for the various manufactures. By this means, a demand for japanned ware was created, and the new canal networks and roads meant that it was easy to increase the speed of the supply of goods to retailers.

In Dossie's opinion, the development of japanning in the Midlands 'for ornamenting coaches, snuff boxes and skreens [*sic*], in which there is a rivalship betwixt ourselves and the French, renders the cultivation and propagation of this art of great importance to commerce'.[18] Indeed, japanning became one of the staple industries of the area and earned not only the respect of the eighteenth century architect and designer, Robert Adam, but also a worldwide reputation.

Although to a large degree, the early development of first the Welsh, and then the English japanning industries was centred on imitating Oriental lacquer, they quickly broke away from the mainstream of this tradition and developed their own processes and styles of decoration. Ironically, the heyday of japanning in Britain was well past before the method of making true Japanese lacquer became known and fully understood in the West through two studies published during the 1880s.[vi]

Though they were frequently conducted under one roof, tinplate working and the making of papier mâché were two distinct trades which, calling for very different skills, were carried on quite independently within each establishment, the products of each coming together only for the final process of japanning. It will, therefore, be historically consistent and more beneficial to the reader if the three main branches of the industry: tinplate working, papier mâché production, and japanning, are considered separately.

3. The Mazarin Chest – one of the finest pieces of Japanese export lacquer to have survived from the seventeenth century, c.1640. 59 x 101.5 x 64cm

THE TINMAN.

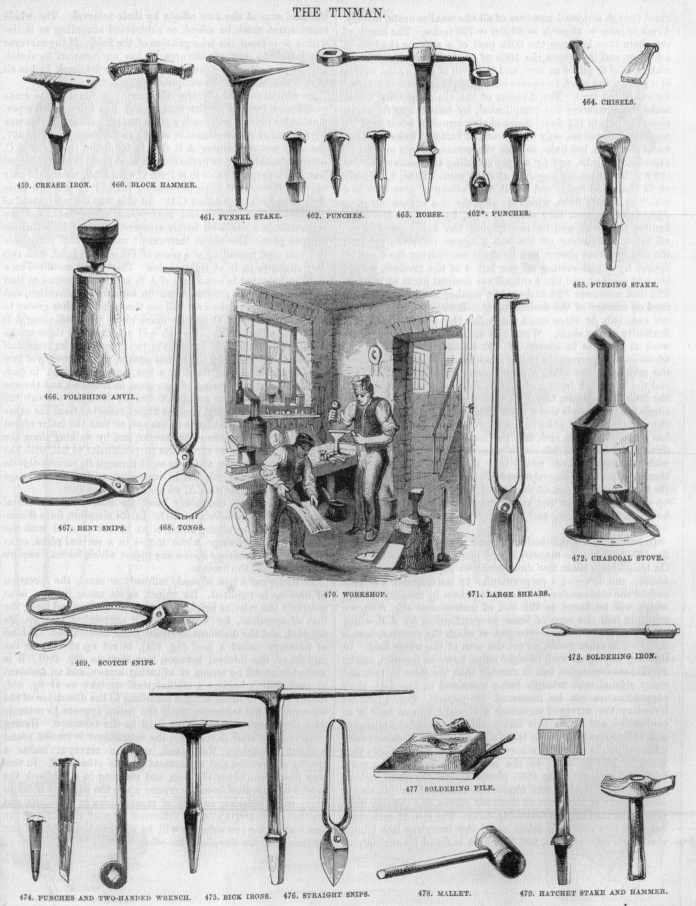

459. CREASE IRON.   460. BLOCK HAMMER.

464. CHISELS.

461. FUNNEL STAKE.   462. PUNCHES.   463. HORSE.   462*. PUNCHES.

465. PUDDING STAKE.

466. POLISHING ANVIL.

467. BENT SNIPS.   468. TONGS.

472. CHARCOAL STOVE.

470. WORKSHOP.   471. LARGE SHEARS.

469. SCOTCH SNIPS.

473. SOLDERING IRON.

477 SOLDERING PILE.

474. PUNCHES AND TWO-HANDED WRENCH.   475. BICK IRONS.   476. STRAIGHT SNIPS.   478. MALLET.   479. HATCHET STAKE AND HAMMER.

I

CHAPTER II

ENTER the DRAGON
Tinplate Working and the Japanning Trade

Tinplate

Tinplate was the earliest material to be commercially japanned in the Midlands and japanners consumed it in large quantities, but unlike papier mâché it was not made specifically for their trade. As there are many books dedicated to the iron and tin-plate industries, it is unnecessary to rehearse their manufacturing processes here. However, since tin-plate was integral to the development of the japanning industry, some consideration needs to be given to its development and use.

To begin with, it is necessary to define some terms. *Tinplate* is not to be confused with *tinned metal* – a product known since Roman times which involved dipping manufactured articles of various metals in molten tin. By contrast, *tinplate* is sheet-iron which is thinly coated with tin to make it rust-proof *prior* to being cut and fashioned into various objects. *Tin-plating* and *tinplate working* were thus quite distinct trades and it is the latter, the process by which the artisan cut and shaped tinplate into trays, boxes and candlesticks to name but a few products, that was used in the japanning industry. Although the material used by the metal-workers was strictly *tin-plated iron*, the goods they produced were commonly called *tinware* – a tradition which will be upheld throughout this book. Present-day collectors sometimes use the French terms *tôle* (meaning sheet-metal), or *tôle-peinte* (painted sheet-metal) to describe all japanned tinware, regardless of its country of origin, but since neither appear to have been used in either the eighteenth or nineteenth centuries to describe Pontypool or English goods, they will not be used here.

Experiments to coat hammered sheet-iron with tin began in Europe in the fourteenth century, but the process was not undertaken commercially until sometime between 1530 and 1550 in South Germany – a region which, for over seventy years, supplied tinplate to the whole of Europe. Andrew Yarranton (b.1616), a former owner of a small iron-works at Bewdley in Worcestershire, visited Germany during 1665–7, to discover how tinplate was made, and the first notable British attempt at production soon followed in about 1670. It is not known where, or by whom, the first trials were carried out, but they were hindered by the uneven quality of the black iron then available. This problem was partly overcome in 1697 by John Hanbury, in Pontypool, who found that passing the iron through heavy rollers, instead of hammering it, not only produced sheets of uniform thickness but produced them at a much faster rate. However, it remained for two of his workmen, Thomas Allgood and his eldest son, Edward Allgood, to perfect the tinning process, sometime between 1720 and 1728, before the industry could achieve a truly commercial footing. They were so successful that, by 1750–1760, besides supplying the home market, the Pontypool ironworks was exporting small quantities of tinplate to Europe and America.[1]

Hanbury, prompted by this success, encouraged the Allgoods to devise a durable and decorative finish for tinplate. They looked to the varnish then being used by western cabinet-makers in imitation of oriental lacquer and, with various modifications such as the addition of asphaltum, found it could be adapted to their needs. The Pontypool Japan Works

Opposite: 4. 'The Tinman', from *Illustrations of Trades*, by Charles Tomlinson, 1860.

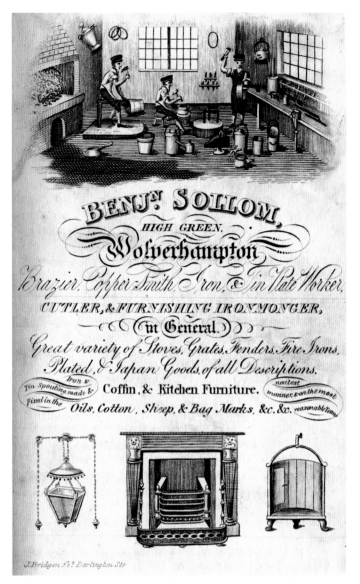

5. Advertisement for Benjamin Sollom, from Joseph Bridgen's *Directory of Wolverhampton etc.*, 1838.

was established soon after – certainly before 1734 – and while it was not the first in the field, it was the first large-scale venture of its kind in Britain.

The distinction of being the earliest known japanners of metal in the Midlands belongs to William Smith, Joseph Allen and Samuel Stone who, working independently, were recorded in the Bilston Parish Register of 1718–19. Nothing is known about the manufactures of any of these men, but if the sale of Stone's stock-in-trade some forty years later is any guide then he, at least, made a range of goods which included 'JAPANN'D BOXES, STEEL, BLACK and METAL BUCKLES with other Goods in the Toy Way'.[2] Nevertheless, operating in only a very small way, and without the benefit of Hanbury's tinplate, it is unlikely these men played as important a part in the history of the Midlands japanning industry as the contemporary developments at Pontypool.

From the 1730s, tinplate workers in Bilston, Birmingham and Wolverhampton bought most of their raw material from the Pontypool Ironworks and so were likely to have been aware of Hanbury's success with japanning. It may have been in light of this knowledge that, a little before 1740, two prominent Birmingham manufacturers, John Taylor (*qv*) and John Baskerville (*qv*), began, quite separately, to develop japan departments of their own; Taylor was even said to have employed japanners from Wales to assist his venture. Samuel Schröder, a Swedish metallurgist who visited Birmingham in about 1750, provided probably the earliest description of the type of japanned goods they produced, having seen 'tea trays, tea caddies etc. from iron sheets, lacquered with black, gold and coloured.'[3, i] Within ten years the focus of this new Midlands trade had shifted. Birmingham had become better-known for the manufacture of japanned papier mâché, and Wolverhampton took over as the leading centre for japanned tinware, specialising in the better class of goods but providing also for the middling to lower markets. Bilston, meanwhile, concentrated on largely utilitarian goods, but as will be seen, not exclusively so.

In the late 1770s, competition from japanners in the Midlands began seriously to affect those in Pontypool and to influence their styles of decoration. It also exacerbated the effects of a rift in the Allgood family which, in the early 1760s, had brought about the opening of a rival factory six miles away in Usk. Japanning had ceased in Pontypool by 1817, and after a long period of decline, it stopped in Usk in the early 1860s, and likewise in London. Henceforward, Midlands japanners were without rival in Britain.

In addition, whereas very little tinplate was made in Pontypool after 1785 – the industry having shifted to Caerleon – the combined success of tinplate working and japanning in the Midlands had prompted the opening of small iron and tinplate works to the north of the region, in Staffordshire. The earliest was the Oakamoor tinplate works near Cheadle in 1777 and others followed in the early nineteenth century but, hit by a depression in the iron trade during the Napoleonic Wars, they did not flourish until the greater general prosperity of the 1830s revitalised the japanning industry and led to increased production and demand for new products. Nevertheless, these supplies alone were inadequate and japanners continued to purchase much of their black iron plate from South Wales and tinplate it themselves;[ii] this was especially hard on Bilston japanners who were charged an extra 6d to 1/- for each hundredweight of black plate to compensate for their situation off the main supply route.

The South Staffordshire ironworks and their subsidiary tinplate factories were almost wholly dependent for their market upon the local japanning industry which they were largely set up to serve.

---

i. I am grateful to Chris Evans and Göran Rydén for permitting me to quote from their translation of Samuel Schröder's Dagbok, 1748–1751.

ii. The Patent #10,224, granted to Thomas Farmer, in 1844, included a method of coating iron trays with zinc, instead of tin, to prevent japan varnish detaching itself from the surface, and to give greater protection against rust should the surface become damaged.

6. 'Tin Plate Worker', from *The Book of Trades, or Library of the Useful Arts*, London, 1807. From *Early Nineteenth-century Crafts and Trades*, edited by Peter Stockham, 1992. REPRODUCED WITH PERMISSION FROM DOVER BOOKS

The waning fashion for japanned ware in the 1880s therefore dealt a severe blow from which they never recovered, and this, alongside the introduction of steel, brought about their decline and closure. In contrast, tinplate-making went from strength to strength in South Wales, partly because it was no longer dependent on any one industry, partly because the producers were larger and better served by major ports, and, not least, because the superiority of its tinplate continued to be recognised worldwide.

Japanned tinware

Large-scale japanners made some, if not all, of their own tinware, but from an early date, and in common with smaller workshops, they also purchased undecorated articles or 'blanks' from specialist 'blank-makers' – a practice which makes it generally impossible to identify the manufacturers of un-marked japanned tinware on grounds of shape alone. By the end of the eighteenth century, despite the huge profits made on the best quality japanned ware (p. 136), blank-making was obviously a much abused branch of the trade, as the following announcement in the *Wolverhampton Chronicle* of 1791, shows:

> *To Japanners etc. The Iron Box-makers of the Parish of Sedgley, Bilston and the vicinities thereof, respectfully inform their masters and Public in general, that they are fully determined not to allow any discount whatever in any part of their business – finding that they are totally unable to support their Families, the prices of their work being so very low...*[4]

Metal-working practices had changed little since the middle ages as may be seen in the view of a tinplate maker in his workshop, surrounded by the tools of his trade in plate 4. Though cramped, it shows an efficiently organised workshop with a charcoal stove

on the bench and an anvil close to hand, similar to the arrangement shown in an earlier engraving of Benjamin Sollom's slightly larger tinplate working premises in Wolverhampton (plate 5). In fact, in smaller workshops, such tools and working practices continued relatively unchanged until the japanning industry began to draw to a close in the 1920s.

The amount of work that had to be done by hand limited the range of early japanned tinware. A Victorian writer neatly encapsulated the problem when he reminded his readers of 'the bald and unornamental character of [tin goods] in time past; how they presented, alternately, the forms of a cylinder or a cone, or an article was built up of both united', and noted the consequent expense of 'a well-moulded, carefully-worked article in tin.'[5] Tinware constructed from these basic shapes may be seen in another engraving in which a tinplate worker is shown using a bick iron to shape a piece of tinplate into a cylinder (plate 6). A straight-sided mug, for example, would have been made up of three pieces which had been hand-cut from a sheet of tinplate: one each for the cylindrical body, the base, and the strap-handle. Straight seams were either folded into lap-joints or, like curved seams, joined with a soft-solder usually made of two-parts tin to one-part lead (plate 7). This was carried out by a solderer who, with a dish of solder in one hand and a heated soldering-iron in the other, melted drops of solder at short intervals along one of the edges to be joined and then brought the two edges together; the skill lay in having the iron sufficiently hot to melt the solder, but not so hot as to burn off the tinplate. Then he ran the heated soldering-iron along the seam to spread and fuse the solder, and cooled the work by blowing upon it.

In the eighteenth century, square-cornered boxes like those shown in plate 101, were made from a single flat sheet by folding the sides upwards, folding and hammering the tabs around each corner, and, if necessary, soldering them in position. Early rectangular tin trays were made in a similar way by simply bending the edges of the metal upwards at an angle of

7. Oval tin tea caddy, painted with views of Windsor Castle, and The Queen's Hospital, Greenwich, c.1780. H: 11cm (approx.) COURTESY OF MELLORS & KIRK, NOTTINGHAM

8. Tin cheese-cradle; early nineteenth century; a type which continued in production until the late nineteenth century. L: 35.5cm

9. Tin tea caddy painted to commemorate Lord Nelson and lettered '1805, Conquer'd & Died, Nelson'. 11 x 10.5 x 7cm

90°, or less, neatly folding their corners as if making a hospital bed, fixing them with a rivet and flattening the fold with a mallet; once japanned, the folds were less obvious. Or, like the large oval tin trays, so characteristic of the early period, their sides were simply soldered to their bases (e.g. Plate 146). Waiters, as very small trays were called, could be made by cutting a piece of tinplate to size, laying it over a mould, and beating it into shape with a mallet. For more complex objects, such as candlesticks, the tinplate was formed in a press.[iii] Whether hammered or pressed, the edges of the articles still required hand-finishing. The products made by the early tinplate workers may have been limited, but with skill and imagination, their forms were widely variable. This is borne out by the number of dies included in the sale of the stock-in-trade of a Birmingham waiter-maker, William Higgins, in 1796, which listed 'a very powerful wind-up Waiter Stamp' and a noteworthy '20 Pair of Dies'.[6]

Contemporary newspaper announcements of bankruptcy and stock-in-trade sales provide useful records of the tools and equipment found in small workshops. For instance, 'a strong one-sided Piercing Press, [and] a Quantity of Piercing Tools',[7] also included in William Higgins' sale, imply that japanned tinware with pierced lacy edges – traditionally a defining characteristic of Pontypool japanned ware – was also made in Birmingham (see also p. 124). In addition, such announcements sometimes list the range of goods which were available at the time. The advertisement of 1795, for the sale of the entire stock-in-trade of Joseph Dyke, a Birmingham tinplate worker and japanner included:

> *Large Quantities of finished and unfinished Iron Trays and Waiters, Plate Warmers, Knife Trays, Bread Baskets, Dress Boxes, Coffee Pots, Tea Pots, Canisters, Sugar Trays, Candlesticks &c. &c. a Number of Benches, Stools, Anvils, Blocks, Vices, large and small Presses, two large Japanning Stoves and Brick Work, with Racks and Pans, complete Warehouse Fixtures, and a Variety of other Articles used in the trade.[8]*

In terms of output, the notice for the bankruptcy sale of John Poolton 'Iron-dealer, Waiter-maker and Japanner' of Bilston, in 1813, is even more illuminating. His stock numbered:

> *FOUR HUNDRED & Thirty two dozen of blank TRAYS from 18 inches to 32, modern Patterns and Waiters to match; twenty Gross of Dutch Boxes; a large Assortment of Tea Pots, Coffee Biggins,[iv] Candlesticks, Bread Baskets, Knife Trays, Extinguishers, and Tin Goods; eight Dozen Coal Scopes, fourteen Dozen Cinder-sifters and Dust-pans[9]*

The amount of hand-labour involved in making tinplate goods was too intensive to support the growing demand for japanned ware. Larger factories invested in new and improved drop-hammers and screw- and hydraulic presses, but these hardly rectified matters overnight as their sheer weight and force showed up any imperfection in the iron from which tinplate was made. Other improvements followed but in practice, there was no entirely satisfactory advance until after 1842 when, at the invitation of Benjamin Walton at the Old Hall Japan Works (*qv*) in Wolverhampton, James Nasmyth adapted the steam hammer he had designed for heavy forgings, to lighter use.[v] The tinplate still had to be cut to shape by hand prior to stamping, but Nasmyth's hammer brought about a rapid rise in production and operated with a mechanical precision hitherto unknown to the tinplate workers. William Highfield Jones, an Old Hall employee at the time, recalled how Nasmyth himself, visited the factory to demonstrate the machine and:

> *Seemed amused as he looked round and saw the anxious faces watching him. He said to the workmen, "Here is a machine which will strike a blow with the force of two tons weight, or can be let fall so gently as to crack a nut without injuring the kernel." Then to the astonishment of all he showed them how to do it.[10]*

'Better results followed', said Jones, and 'no expense was spared to keep up and improve the quality and design of the tin and japan articles'.[11] An extremely large iron tray, some four feet in diameter, and made as an exhibition piece in about 1850 by the Bilston firm of Sankey & Co. shows both the supreme skill of contemporary metal workers in making and rolling sheet metal evenly on so large a scale, and how far stamping had advanced (plate 238).

At the Paris Exhibition in 1867, an American firm exhibited a pressure press capable of stamping, in one operation, a bowl 3½ in. (9cm) deep, and with which '1,000 articles could be produced in less time than 60 by the old method.'[12] It was better suited to harder metals, such as steel, than it was to tinplate, but by stamping articles from one piece of metal and at such speed, the new pressure press brought down manufacturing costs and retail prices so significantly that it opened up entirely new markets both at home and overseas, particularly in India, South Africa and the Colonies. Manufacturers had never seen its like before and they were immediately persuaded – unlike their workers who, fearful of their livelihoods, nick-named the new machine the 'Dragon'.[13]

Perhaps the 'two parallel rows of fall or stamp presses working by steam, on the principle of the pile driver'[14] seen at the factory of Henry Loveridge & Co. in 1869 were American 'Dragons'. It is certainly likely for, in the same year, Loveridge's were said to have been among the first japanners to experiment with Bessemer steel. They hoped it would provide a smoother surface than iron, but as it was hard to work under the stamp and needed frequent annealing or softening, it did not begin to replace wrought iron until the 1880s. It was said of Loveridge's display at the South Staffordshire Exhibition in 1869, that:

The variety of tin-plate and tinned iron articles now made by the ingenious combination of hand work and machinery, as shewn in their productions present a wonderful contrast to the tin-plate articles of thirty years ago. They have opened up an entirely new field for decorative art, which at that period was almost limited to the ornamentation of tea trays and kindred articles.[15]

It is likely that the author of the above, had in mind articles such as 'The Ruskin Persian Coal Scoop' (plate 219), two examples of which were placed at the forefront of their display (plate 222), and the highly decorative baths, jugs and basins which had become increasingly popular lines at both this factory and elsewhere following the Great Exhibition of 1851.

By the close of the nineteenth century, when even the most complex articles could be stamped in a single operation, the need for hand work remained. The rims of most stamped trays, bread baskets and other similarly flat or dish-shaped objects, still had to

10. Tin-plate watch-stand, in the form of St John's Church, Wolverhampton (*cf*. pl. 85); early nineteenth century. H: 25.5cm (approx.)
COURTESY OF DREWEATT NEATE, NEWBURY

be 'wired' by folding the edge of the metal over a length of wire to give the article added rigidity. This was done by setting the rim over the appropriate groove of a crease-iron (see plate 4), driving an iron wire down upon it with a mallet, and with the same tool, folding the edges over before finishing off with a punch or 'top-tool' which was specially shaped to correspond with the wired edge. Even when a 'turn-up' or 'wiring-machine', which rolled the metal over the wire in one operation, was introduced towards the end of the industry, it still required someone to operate it by hand.

Despite all these advances in production, the fashion for japanned tinware had passed. At the lower end of the market, it was replaced by newer more practical materials like vitreous enamel and aluminium. The firm making blank trays which was begun in Wolverhampton by James Fellows in the 1840s, for example, had adapted to market forces by 1902 and, under the name of S. J. & E. Fellows, exhibited as makers of 'Aluminium Cooking Utensils; Sheet Metal Stampings in Steel, Iron etc., Wrought Iron Hollow-ware; [and] Kitchen Specialities.'[16]

As for more prestigious goods, contemporary trade catalogues show that after the 1840s, if not before, these had been a relatively small part of each japanner's output; they were costly to produce and few factories could have survived by making these alone. Experienced decorators who had not, by the turn of the century, already switched their skills to the bicycle and newly emergent motor-car industries (see p. 111) were, by then, very elderly. By the early twentieth century, the industry had run its full course.

---

iii. Articles were pressed into shape by fixing a punch and a die in a screw- or fly-press.
iv. Most probably a coffee pot with a strainer as designed by George Biggin in 1803, but the term was also used for mugs similar in shape to a style of child's under-cap known as a biggin – see Daniel Fenning, *Royal English Dictionary* (1761), where such caps are described as 'covering the hind-part of [the] head, and made close, to keep the upper or

mould of it warm.'
v. A dead-weight kick stamp, introduced in the 1830s, allowed objects to be wholly or partly stamped, but as its heavy hammer had to be hand-winched and repeatedly dropped on the sheet-iron beneath, it was ponderously slow; the more easily operated steam drop-hammer which replaced it was only marginally better.

CHAPTER III

A LION of the DISTRICT
Papier Mâché and the Japanning Trade

Paper is believed to have been invented in China in the second century AD, and the Chinese art of making papier mâché objects is almost as ancient, but knowledge of paper-making spread only very slowly and did not reach Europe until the twelfth century. Paper-mills were established in France in the late fifteenth century, and soon after, French craftsmen began using paper pulp to make architectural ornaments, snuff boxes and other small articles. There were few paper mills in England until the late seventeenth century, so there was little pulp from which to make comparable articles, the paper imported from France being far too expensive to be pulped for the purpose.

By the eighteenth century, however, there were two quite distinct branches of papier mâché manufacture in England. One was allied to the making of paper hangings (see below), and the other – the one currently under discussion – to the japanning industry. Both branches took their lead from France and this, together with the name, has not only perpetuated the myth that 'papier mâché' was French in origin, but also overshadowed its ancient eastern history.

THE ORIGINS OF THE TERM PAPIER MÂCHÉ

Not only was the term *papier mâché* not recognised in eighteenth-century French dictionaries, but the *Journal de l'Agriculture du Commerce* (1778) sourced it to England and to the first edition of Dossie's book, *The Handmaid to the Arts* (1758).[1] Its occurrence,

much later, in the French edition of the Paris Exhibition catalogue in 1855,[2] may simply have been the result of the translation of texts supplied by English manufacturers. The term is, however, currently used in France today.

It has been suggested that the term derives from problems of communication between English employers and French emigré workers in the seventeenth century when 'papier mâché' was probably taken to be French for 'mashed paper' as in the instructions: 'First soak a convenient quantity of whitish paper ... then mash it in hot water'.[3,i] Literally translated, papier mâché means 'chewed paper' which explains why William Shenstone, in a letter to Lady Luxborough in 1752, told how he had 'seen a small specimen of chew'd Paper for Ceilings',[4] and why J.T. Smith, in his book *Nollekens and his Times* (1824), had Mr Twigg, a London tradesman, recall 'two old French women who came over here to chew paper for the papier mâché people'.

However, the process involved no mastication, and no elderly ladies were forced to put their teeth to work. The crux was the cachet of a French-sounding name and the penchant in some quarters of fashionable society in the late eighteenth century to look upon anything French as highly sophisticated. Whatever its origins, save for a brief fall from grace in the late eighteenth and early nineteenth centuries (see below), the term *papier mâché* was used to describe those japanned goods made from either layered or pulped paper.

---

i. 'Mash: to beat or bruise into a confused mass' (*Royal English Dictionary*, Daniel Fenning, London, 1761); to soak as in tea or brewing.

Opposite: 11. One of four doors in the Marble Hall at Kedleston Hall, Derbyshire (see p. 130); the subjects of the oval cartouches are from J.B. Boudard's *Iconologie* (1759), a copy of which was in the library at Kedleston by 1765.

PHOTO: THE NATIONAL TRUST/SIMON MCCORMACK

THE HISTORY AND DEVELOPMENT OF THE ENGLISH PAPIER MÂCHÉ INDUSTRY

The scientist Robert Boyle (1627–1691) provided the earliest reference to papier mâché manufacture in England when he wrote in 1672 that paper, 'besides its common uses, may be made into frames for pictures, fine embossed work, and other parts of furniture'.[5] By 1753, according to an entry in Chambers *Cyclopaedia*, papier mâché had developed into 'a regular manufacture' in England, though it was unspecific as to where. At these early dates, the papier mâché under discussion was almost certainly allied to the manufacture of paper hangings and architectural ornaments which, although frequently gilded, were never japanned. It was from these beginnings that the three leading London firms of Wilton, Jackson & Graham, and Charles Bielefeld developed, but they are of no concern here as the history of architectural papier mâché is a wholly separate study.[ii]

The branch of japanned papier mâché manufacture under discussion began in France in the 1740s (plate 312). 'I must inform the Reader of a late French invention of Snuff-Boxes', wrote R. Campbell in *The London Tradesman* in 1747; evidently describing something quite new, he continued:

> *These Snuff-Boxes are made of the same Materials as Paper; are to be had at Paris of any Colour, but are most commonly Black, as Ebony, and are actually as hard and durable as any made of Wood, Horn, or Tortoiseshell. They are made of Linen-Rags, beat to a Pulp, as if intended for Paper. A large Quantity of Pulp is put into a Vessel, and the Water allowed to drain off; the Pulp is dried, and coheres together in a hard uniform Lump, out of which they turn upon the Leath [lathe], Boxes or any other kind of Toys, which for their Novelty fetch a large price.[6]*

These may have been made by Guillaume Martin (d. 1749) of Paris, but the boxes for which he is known today, were made from sheets of paper glued together and pressed, while still wet, into a mould. When dry, this compacted mass yielded a firm, hard surface ideally suited to the varnish, known, eponymously, as *vernis martin*, for which he and his three brothers became so renowned (see p. 280*ff*). In principle, it was the method that had been employed in ancient China to make papier mâché vessels and even helmets, but it was also the process that japanners introduced into Birmingham in the 1750s following on from their success with japanned tinware. It is conceivable that there were experiments, contemporary with Martin's, to japan pulped paper in Birmingham, but no evidence has yet been found. What is certain however, is that

without knowledge of the more sophisticated layered method of manufacture, it is unlikely that the midlands papier mâché industry would have enjoyed the early success that it did.

It is difficult to be precise about when papier mâché was first made in Birmingham. Certainly, it was prior to 1758, the year in which Dossie briefly mentioned the town's japanning industry. Between then and the second edition of his book in 1764, its manufacture had become sufficiently important to merit a subject-heading in its own right. By whom it was first made, however, remains uncertain.

The japanner and printer John Baskerville (*qv*) has often been credited with introducing the papier mâché trade in Birmingham, but there is no foundation for this. A more likely contender was Stephen Bedford (*qv*) who, according to the Earl of Verulam,[7] was Birmingham's leading japanner. Indeed, to judge from Bedford's correspondence with the Royal Society, he was already experienced in working with papier mâché in 1759.[8] By this token, he is the earliest manufacturer of papier mâché in Birmingham, of whom we currently have record. Whether he was the first or not, it may safely be assumed that as the leading japanner, Bedford was prominent among its early exponents.

If Bedford may be said to have pioneered japanned papier mâché in the Midlands, it fell to another, Henry Clay, to give the industry a sound commercial footing. When the American, Jabez Maud Fisher, arrived in Birmingham in 1776, he went first to visit 'Clay's famous Paper Works', to see articles made according to a method which he said was invented 'about a dozen years since.'[9] By this reckoning, Clay had obviously been experimenting with paper-ware for some time prior to 1772, the year in which he was granted a patent (#1027) for making papier mâché or as he called it, 'pasteboard'. Made from layered paper, it was similar to Martin's product, but its superior strength and versatility so extended its possibilities (see p. 28), that it laid the foundations for what became a staple Midlands industry for the next hundred years or so, with Birmingham at its centre. Within five years of Clay's patent, a Birmingham newspaper had confidence enough to extol his success to the disadvantage of French manufacturers:

> *The French in this article have been, in a manner, unrivalled by other nations. But from the high esteem in which our own manufacture is held, both at home and abroad, we may reasonably hope soon to vie with their hitherto allowed excellence; and to diminish, in no very inconsiderable degree, that extensive and exclusive trade, which they have so long and so beneficially enjoyed.[10]*

---

ii. It is for the same reason that interesting and far-sighted developments such as Bielefeld's papier mâché village for Australia, which was temporarily exhibited outside Staines Station in 1853, or the manufacture of papier mâché coffins, and boats, fall outside the range of this book. A small cabinet, painted with flowers and ornamented with mother of pearl and gold leaf, which has a paper label printed for Charles Bielefeld affixed to its base, was almost certainly not made in his factory. It is more likely to have been sold via his London showrooms.

12. 'Gondola' style papier mâché chairs, impressed for Jennens & Bettridge, and with a registration mark for 1844.

Such hope was not misplaced, for while this branch of papier mâché manufacture had begun in France, it was in England that it was substantially developed and exploited.

After 1780, the term *papier mâché* was dropped, temporarily, in favour of the more accurate description of *paper ware*. Except for isolated examples like Thomas Ashwin (*qv*), 'paper [*sic*] mâché' maker, in 1791, or Richard Hipkiss (*qv*), described in 1808 as a 'japanner, papier mâché and Clock dial maker',[11] the term did not re-appear until the 1820s. And it was not until publication of the 1829 trade directory of Birmingham, that papier mâché makers were listed not only under the heading 'Japanners', but also under 'Paper tray, snuff box and japanned paper ware manufacturers',[12] making it easier, thereafter, to disentangle them from those who japanned only tin-ware. Why the name papier mâché should have fallen from favour for so long may have had as much to do with embargoes on Anglo-French trade or with xenophobia during the Napoleonic wars as with concerns for technical accuracy. Whatever the reason, it was 1839 before a section headed 'Papier Mâché Manufacturers' regularly appeared as a separate trade in Birmingham directories.[13]

In 1853, a visitors' guide to Birmingham made the exaggerated claim that the town supplied the 'whole world' with papier mâché and that it stood unrivalled by any continental makers: 'Large orders, as proof of this, are constantly arriving from the continent; and some of the most astonishing achievements in the manufacture have been accomplished in executing commissions for the crowned heads of Europe.'[14]

Papier mâché appears not to have been made in Wolverhampton until about 1810 and was never listed as a separate trade in local directories. Nevertheless, the papier mâché trade was sufficiently developed there by 1811 for the japanner Thomas Illidge (*qv*), along with several prominent Birmingham manufacturers, to have supplied paper goods decorated with patterns to match those on expensive porcelain tea-wares made by Chamberlain's of Worcester. More generally, however, and with notable exceptions like the various partnerships at The Old Hall Works (*qv*) and the Merridale Works (*qv*), the Wolverhampton japanners tended to concentrate on high quality tinware.

In Bilston, where japanners were mainly small-scale operators, they seem hardly to have concerned themselves with papier

13. *Lady Drawing: Candlelight,* water-colour and gouache, c.1840, 28 x 28cm. This painting was once owned by Joseph Gillot, a leading Birmingham pen-maker, which probably accounts for the prominence given to the pen nib, candle-snuffers, and japanned snuffers tray – all products of Birmingham industry.
COURTESY OF THE MAAS GALLERY

14. *Past and Present No. 1,* oil on canvas by Augustus Leopold Egg, 1858, in which children are seen building a house of cards on a papier mâché chair. 63.5 x 67cm
© TATE, LONDON 2011

mâché. One who did was Thomas Jones – he was granted a patent in 1805 (p. 33) for making trays, waiters 'and various other articles' from pulp (*qv*). It is unlikely that costs of outlay deterred the Bilston japanners from making papier mâché, since a report on 'The Utility of Workhouses', given by a Mr Bailey in 1778, recommended its manufacture as gainful employment for the poor in the workhouses on account of it requiring little space and 'only a very small stock and money and materials.'[15] It is curious then, that the Bilston japanners did not, at least, make papier mâche blanks alongside the tinware blanks they were already supplying to japanners in Birmingham and Wolverhampton; most probably, given the labour-intensity of papier mâché manufacture, they could not compete with larger suppliers.

In the eighteenth and early nineteenth centuries, papier mâché was largely hand-made and expensive. Employed mainly as a wood-substitute during this early period, its extraordinary potential was largely overlooked. Although the same was true of much Victorian papier mâché, it will be seen that on occasion manufacturers rose to the challenge offered by this uniquely plastic material and made objects which, at the time, would not have been possible in any other material (plate 12). Like the early tinplate worker, at first the papier mâché maker was:

> *Confined to making trays and other articles that only presented a flat surface and straight lines, but gradually the inventive principle developed itself, and expanded the manufacture into one embracing nearly every article of furniture and decoration, however intricate its shape, or recondite its ornament. Sofas, chairs, tables, work boxes, tea caddies, book covers, vases, and a thousand other articles, are now fashioned out of this fragile material, and to any one who places one of the square trays made by old Clay, the inventor [sic], beside a magnificent lounging chair – the former plain black, the latter revelling in all the glories of colour – the contrast is indeed striking.*[16]

Almost as quickly, the cost of papier mâché decreased, bringing it within easy reach of the new consumer classes. In 1850, it was written that 'few houses can now be found in which some useful and elegant trifle may not be seen made of this exquisite material'.[17] An over-enthusiastic response, perhaps, but one which nevertheless underlines the contemporary prominence and status held by papier mâché (plates 13 and14).

THE CONTEMPORARY RATIONALE FOR PAPIER MÂCHÉ

Any consideration of the subject begs the question why objects as diverse as buttons and furniture should be made from papier mâché when, as will be seen, it would generally have been quicker and, in many cases, less costly to have used more conventional materials. Today's concern for recycling cannot be imposed upon late eighteenth- and nineteenth-century manufacturers and consumers; theirs was a very different rationale – and besides, as far as the best articles were concerned, they used only new paper.

One answer perhaps lies in the prevailing spirit of invention and scientific curiosity which prompted, for example, the establishment of The Royal Society for the Encouragement of Arts, Manufactures & Commerce in 1754, and which was particularly evident in Birmingham, in the intellectual climate surrounding what later came to be known as The Lunar Society (1775–1790). The wide-ranging interests of its members, among them Matthew Boulton (*qv*), Erasmus Darwin, Joseph Priestley, James Watt, and Josiah Wedgwood, embraced the important links between science, industry and commerce. The challenge of making commercially viable household goods from paper would have fitted neatly into their thinking. As a business acquaintance of both Boulton and Wedgwood, Henry Clay must have been aware of the lively debates among Society members, and although not a member himself,[iii] his patents concerning wagons and canal locks show that he shared their breadth of vision (plate 15).

15. An advertisement for Henry Clay illustrating his patents of 1796 and 1798 (see p. 138), from Bissett's *Poetic Survey round Birmingham*, 1800 (Plate J).

16. Group of objects shown by Jennens & Bettridge at the Great Exhibition; Art Journal *Illustrated Catalogue*, p. 66.

Apart from these broad intellectual ideals, there appears to be no contemporary account of why this branch of the papier mâché industry developed in the way that it did. Its novelty as a curious invention was undoubtedly an important factor in its success and Birmingham's papier mâché manufactories were soon added to the itineraries of the wealthy leisured classes as they toured Britain's industrial towns and cities to observe the new industrial processes: 'to Clay's new paper manufactory where we saw many curiosities and purchased some',[18] 'went to see Mr Clay's manufactory for the paper buttons etc.'[19] This curiosity was sustained through the first half of the nineteenth century by the introduction of eye-catching and ambitious articles and it culminated in the extravagant displays at the Great Exhibition held in London in 1851 (plate 16).

Some of the advantages of papier mâché, gleaned from contemporary records, partly explain its attractions and may have been sufficient, at least until the mid nineteenth century, to outweigh what will be seen as its long and labour-intensive production processes. Foremost amongst its advantages, was its suitability for japanning which was much in vogue in the eighteenth century. Japan varnish (*qv*), which had proved so successful on tin, had to be stove-dried and papier mâché, unlike wood, could readily withstand the necessary heat without warping or cracking. Moreover, as it was free from grain, and closer in texture than wood, it needed no filling and only a little smoothing prior to varnishing. In addition, it was permeable to varnish, a quality which gave it a distinct advantage over japanned tin. As J. Smith noted in 1813:

Varnish cannot sink into metals, and this is the reason that japanned metal, for example a japanned tin-plate tray, is of less value than a paper one. The battering which the piece of furniture sustains in its use, soon separates the japan from it in flakes, or scales; which never happens to the paper, because the japan forms a part of its substance.[20]

Furthermore, because papier mâché could be moulded into various forms, it required no joinery and was thus incredibly strong. As solid as wood, though less hard than most, it was said to blunt tools sooner, and although heavier in mass, its strength allowed it to be used in thin sections, rendering it perfect for making small, light objects. Also it could 'if necessary, be carved or engraved in relief like the finest box-wood',[21] and by the mid-nineteenth century, it was found that it could be steam-moulded into any curve without fear of splitting (see for example, the chair-backs shown in plate 24). In short, it was considered superior to both wood and metal for 'being lighter, sounder, and admitting of a more beautiful finish'.[22] Or, as suggested in the Art Union in 1846, papier mâché was 'scarcely second to clay in means of being made subservient to art; it is singularly delicate in surface, susceptible of taking any form, and of its durability there can be no question.'[23]

It was considered superior in other ways too, for as Anne Cobbett wrote when advising couples setting up home in 1851, 'paper trays are the best, considering the small difference in the appearance; it would be better to save in many other things than to hear tea-things, glasses or snuffers, jingle on japan.'[24] In other words, paper trays were easier than tin trays on the sensitive Victorian ear.

---

iii. The ill-feeling which existed between Clay and Boulton may have prevented Clay's membership; see p. 133*ff*

THE MANUFACTURE OF PAPIER MÂCHÉ

Throughout the history of the industry, Midlands japanners worked with two kinds of papier mâché: that made from pulp by a process known as the 'common' method, and that formed from layered sheets of paper according to the 'best' or 'real method'. Henry Clay's patent of 1772 marked such an improvement in the layering process that it formed a watershed between two distinct periods of papier mâché production in England: the early years between c.1750 and 1772, and the following, much longer period, when the majority of objects which have survived to the present day were made.

English papier mâché, c.1750–1772

PULPED PAPER. Each maker almost certainly had their preferred way of making pulp, but it was unlikely to have differed much from the one described by Dossie in 1764.[25] Dossie's instructions bear remarkable resemblance to the 'The Japonese [*sic*] way of making Vessels of Paper, or Saw Dust', given in the *Gentleman's Magazine*[26] ten years earlier, which was itself a refinement of the process described by Boyle almost a hundred years before.

As Dossie's directions were intended for makers of 'boxes, frames, festoons etc.', it is clear that his recipe for pulp served makers of architectural ornaments as well. Any paper was suitable for pulping but 'writing paper' was preferred for better work. It was boiled in water until soft enough to form a paste when stirred, then drained and beaten, mixed with a strong solution of gum Arabic and water, and boiled once again, until it reached a suitable consistency for moulding – the more intricately patterned the mould, the more fluid the mix required. For simple shapes, glue or size could be used as cheaper substitutes for gum Arabic, but since they shrank on drying, they were not recommended for complex objects.

The moulds were mostly made of hardwood, but if the design of the proposed article was very detailed, then plaster moulds were better. They were made in two parts: a concave mould, and a perforated, convex one which fitted neatly inside. The difference in size between the two moulds varied according to the required thickness of the pulp – about ⅛in. for snuff-boxes, and more for larger objects. After each section of the mould had been greased, it was warmed to ensure maximum absorption of the grease, and the pulp was spread evenly inside the concave part. The convex mould was then pressed into the pulp so that any excess moisture could escape through its perforations. The moulds were removed when the pulp was dry enough to resist breaking, and the article was left until completely dry before being painted or varnished (*qv*).

LAYERED PAPER. Dossie also described how flat or shallow objects like snuff-boxes were made from layered paper. Pieces of strong brown paper were cut to shape, moistened with

gum-water – a mixture of gum Arabic and water – and laid on the convex part of a well-oiled mould. Three or four further layers were added, each was brushed with a thin paste made from eight-parts boiled flour and water, to one-part size, and covered with the concave part of the mould. It was then compressed until the layered paper article could be removed without becoming mis-shapen. When thoroughly dry and hard, it was smoothed, decorated and finally, varnished (see Ch. IV).

~

Examples of early pulp and layered paper goods have surely survived to the present day, but without documentary evidence it is unlikely that they could now be attributed to Birmingham, let alone to a specific maker. By the early 1770s however, the situation had markedly changed.

1772 and after

PAPIER MÂCHÉ MADE BY THE 'BEST' METHOD. In 1772, Henry Clay of Birmingham who, alongside Jennens & Bettridge (*qv*), is today the best known of all Midlands japanners, was granted a patent for 'Making in Paper High Varnished Pannels or Roofs for Coaches, and all Sorts of Wheel Carriages and Sedan Chairs, Pannels for Rooms, Doors, and Cabbins of Ships, Cabinets, Bookcases, Screens, Chimney Pieces, Tables, Teatrays and Waiters.'[27] (plate 11)

His invention so greatly improved the material and its potential, that a whole new class of luxury goods was born. Given its significance, it is useful to quote, in full, the relevant paragraph from Clay's specification:

> *My inventions of making paper panels for various purposes are by casting several papers upon boards or plates of regular thicknesses on each side the same, to prevent one side counteracting or drawing with superior force to the other in the state of drying; and when the same is rendered sufficiently strong for the purpose intended it is then planed or cut off at the edges until the board or plate appears, and then taken off such boards or plates. The pieces of paper are afterwards screwed or fastened on boards or plates and put in a stove sufficiently hot to deprive them of their flexibility, and at the same time are rubbed over or dipped in oil or varnish, which so immediately drenches into them as to secure them from damps, &c. After the papers are thus made they are capable of being sawed into different forms, and planed as wood. After the various articles are thus formed in the paper, they are then coated with colour and oils sufficient to make the surface even, and are then japanned and high varnished.*[28]

Although clearly a refinement of the earlier process, its advantage lay first in oiling and baking the paper which, besides making it damp-proof, bonded the various layers to produce a stronger, more versatile papier mâché than hitherto; and second, the method allowed for large sheets to be made. Objects normally made from wood or metal could now be made also from paper. It was not really papier mâché at all, and Clay seldom described it as such[iv] preferring instead to call it 'panel'[v] and advertising articles made from it as 'paper ware'. Thereafter, all the better goods were made in this 'best' or 'real' way, but being a highly labour-intensive process, the products made from 'pasteboard', as it came to be known, were considerably more expensive than those made from pulp.

It is evident from the articles listed in the title of Clay's patent that he used panel as a substitute for wood, sawing, dovetailing and joining it as in standard cabinet work. In addition, Jabez Maud Fisher noted that once the boards had been baked, they were 'sufficiently pliable to reduce to any shape [in which] state they are wrought into Form, and receive the impressions,' – an intriguing observation which he omitted to explain, but which probably referred to the manufacture of such articles as oval caddies (plate 17).[29]

However, by the early nineteenth century, Clay, and other manufacturers, saw that the methods described in the patent could be used to layer paper on pre-shaped moulds – as in the earlier period – and thus could dispense with much unnecessary carpentry. At first, the moulds or *cores*, to give them their trade name, were made of hardwood, but later ones were generally of brass, copper, hollow tin, or solid iron (plate 18). They were made in-house, or bought from specialist suppliers, but in the case of solid iron moulds, the japanners made a plaster of Paris pattern which they sent to a local foundry to be cast. As expensive precision-made objects, the moulds were expected to see many years service and few were abandoned in favour of newer types until they were either worn out or replaced by more up-to-date shapes. It is not surprising, therefore, to find that even large firms like McCallum & Hodson, or Jennens & Bettridge still used wooden moulds in the 1850s as well as the newer and much lighter hollow metal ones.

It is not known whether Henry Clay made the 'whited brown' paper used in his workshops, but for most of the nineteenth century, papier mâché manufacturers bought purpose-made and so-called 'making paper', from a few specialist suppliers, of which T.B. Crompton's Farnworth Mills, near Bolton in Lancashire, was the only one named by contemporary chroniclers of the industry.[vi] Japanners preferred machine-made paper to that made by hand as the latter became 'uneven and corrugated' with age.[30] In fact, Jennens and Bettridge regarded the adoption of machine-made paper as one of their chief

17. Oval papier mâché tea caddy decorated with a classical figure, possibly after the engraving *Abundance*, in J. Boudard's *Iconologie* (1766 edn); impressed 'CLAY PATENT', c.1780. 12 x 11.5cm
Courtesy of Woolley & Wallis, Salisbury

improvements because it yielded a smooth surface and would 'bear any climate'[31] – an important consideration in view of their export to countries like Spain and India (see pp. 151 and 157).

Like the early French makers of papier mâché, Jennens & Bettridge claimed to have used paper made only from linen rags[32] and in consequence it has been thought that this was so in all factories. However, George Dickinson, who had the benefit of speaking with a number of retired japanners when researching his book, *English Papier Mâché* (1925), said that 'making-paper' could be created from rags of any sort, including 'old bags and sacking', though it could not be produced from wool which, when stove-dried, produced an unsatisfactory surface.[33] Un-sized paper was preferred to sized or glazed paper as it absorbed the paste more readily in the layering process. Machine-made 'making-paper' resembled the best blotting paper; grey in colour (it turned brown only after oiling and stoving), it tore easily but was so strong that it resisted disintegrating when wet. It was generally supplied in sheets of about three by four feet (approx. 915 x 220mm), but sometimes larger, and it came in rolled bundles weighing 28 or 56lbs (12.7 or 25.4kg), each encircled with a broad pink paper band bearing a duty stamp (p. 36). It was expensive: £25 a ton in 1866 for example, rising to £90 a ton in 1896, exclusive of the duty, which was greatly resented among papier mâché makers, as will be shown.

iv. A rare instance of Clay using the word 'papier' is found in his bill of sale to Sir Thomas Ward, in 1774 (see p. 126).
v. A thick sheet of pasteboard for table-tops and other large articles, was called 'panel';

some articles required more than 100 layers.
vi. The paper-making firm of Spicers was also named as a supplier to the papier mâché trade, in the catalogue of the 1851 exhibition.

18. Iron 'core' covered with about eight sheets of making paper (see p. 29); Henry Loveridge & Co. Dia: 31cm
© WOLVERHAMPTON ARTS AND MUSEUMS SERVICE, www.blackcountryhistory.org

19. A papier mâché 'blank' *Octagon* tray, after removal from the 'core'; Henry Loveridge & Co. 31 x 40.5cm (*cf.* pl. 220)
© WOLVERHAMPTON ARTS AND MUSEUMS SERVICE, www.blackcountryhistory.org

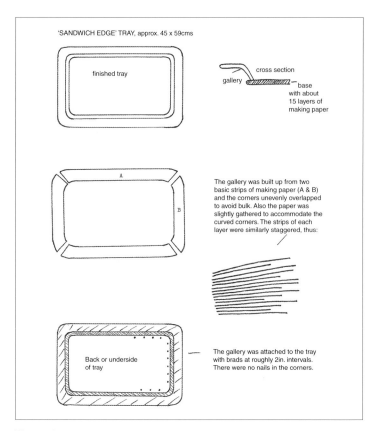

Figure 1

The paper was kept in the 'moulding' or 'pasting shop' where the work was done mostly by women and girls. To make a tray, for example, they first cut the paper to shape with the aid of a pattern, leaving sufficient margin for the paper to be folded over the edge of the mould. It was then passed to the 'pasters' who sat at tables alongside one or more large 'wash-house like coppers' containing vast quantities of paste made from roughly equal proportions of superfine flour and 'best glue' dissolved and boiled together in water. The mould was prepared with Russian tallow or a similarly salt-free grease – salt penetrated the paper and harmed the work – and the first sheet of paper, pasted on both sides, was laid on and worked over with a trowel-like tool or a cloth in order to remove any bubbles or other irregularities. The excess paper was folded tightly over the edge of the mould, by hand, and any surplus paste was wiped away. Once two or three further sheets had been added, each pasted on one side only, the article was slowly stoved at about 100–120°F (plate 18). When dried and cooled, it was returned to the pasters, its surface filed to a 'tolerable smoothness' – too

smooth, and there would be insufficient purchase for the next layer – and the process was repeated until the pasteboard was of the required thickness (plate 19). An ordinary tea-tray, about ¼in. thick, needed about fifteen layers, while thirty to forty layers was the average amount for better trays. The layers were subjected to several pressings throughout the process, so as to compact the fabric and guard against warping.

The conditions in the pasting shop were far from pleasant: the large quantities of paste housed there and the intense heat from the stoves made the atmosphere dank and humid. Moreover, the work was physically demanding. A solid iron mould for only a 12in. waiter, for example, was extremely heavy, even without its layers of wet paper, so it may be imagined how strenuous this work was, constantly lifting and turning an ever-increasing weight, and how arduous it must have been for the young boys whose job it was to load these heavy articles onto a trolley and trundle them to and from the stoves.

When these processes were complete, the article was taken to the cabinet-makers' shop. There, the excess paper that had been folded over the edge of the mould was cut away, the mould removed, and the surface of the paper smoothed and filed. This was known as 'dressing' the goods, and though apparently a more wholesome job than pasting, it had its own dangers: 'the few who are employed in "turning", inhale much fine dust. Pallor, sickness, impaired appetite, difficulty in breathing, cough and expectoration, are the results. Few men, if any, bear the employ constantly for many years.'[34]

Finally, the article was immersed in, or liberally brushed with, linseed oil, or a mixture of linseed oil and tar spirits, and stoved at 200–260°F, for twelve to thirty-six hours, depending upon its size and thickness. This turned the paper from grey to brown and made the articles so strong and water-resistant that they could be safely stored, without distortion, until such time as they were required. Known as 'blanks', these objects were then ready to be japanned.

This was how all the best papier mâché was made, but the shaping of some products requires further explanation.

TRAYS. The earliest trays and teaboards (*qv*) were made by attaching a straight edge or 'gallery', to a base cut from a sheet of pasteboard. This is seen at its simplest in an octagonal tray made by Benjamin Mander (plate 202). Other early trays, though similarly constructed, had pre-moulded rims. For example, when a 'sandwich-edge' (*qv*) tray of about 1825, was discovered by the author in a very damp state in an outhouse, she carefully took it apart, layer by layer, and found the rim to have been made as shown in figure 1. Strips of paper roughly equal in length to both the long and short sides of the tray, and slightly wider than required, were layered on a mould of the same shape as the intended rim. The slightly varying lengths of

21. Papier mâché spill vases decorated with the cross of St George; impressed 'CLAY', and scratched with pattern number E2239; c.1840. H: 13cm

the strips distributed the bulk where they overlapped at the corners, and the paper was tightly pleated to accommodate the interior corners where the edge was 'sandwiched' between the tray base and the flat rim. For added strength, the edge was secured from the underside of the tray with small metal brads at approximately 2in. intervals. Any extra thickness that remained at the points of overlap would have been levelled on a lathe. Rectangular teaboards with upright, slightly everted rims of the type made by Henry Clay, Thomas Illidge and others, as well as the earliest of the so-called 'gothic' (*qv*) trays appear also to have been made in this way.

Seamless trays were stronger than those with separately attached rims, but according to Harriet Martineau in 1851, it was still necessary to strengthen them by pasting extra strips of paper across the angle between base and rim. One writer, some twenty years later, was moved to say that trays made in this way had 'a metal ring to them'.[35]

HOLLOWARE. Vases and baluster-shaped supports for tables (plate 20) were also made on hardwood moulds, but to minimise the bulk around the narrower parts, each layer was made up of several small pieces of paper. When half the required thickness was reached, the article was stoved, and cut into two pieces from the mould – either horizontally or vertically – with great care, so as not to damage the re-useable mould beneath. The two pieces were glued together and the remaining sheets of paper were added, stoved, and oiled in the usual way. Vases with slender bases, like those exhibited by Walton & Co. in 1849 (plate 197), were weighted with lead to increase their stability, as were spill vases (plate 21). Some baluster table-legs were strengthened by the insertion of a metal tube when the table was assembled and, like vases, their bases were weighted. However, this was not always the case, for Martineau remarked upon the lightness of worktable legs and feet of other tables, which, she said, was due to their being hollow.

20. Papier mâché vase of a type made by several makers (*cf*. plates 143 and 169), c.1840. H: 31cm

22. Papier mâché tea caddy, decorated with 'bronze' landscapes (see p.74*ff*); impressed
'JENNENS + BETTRIDGE', c.1845. 20.5 x 33.5 x 20cm

RECTANGULAR OR SQUARE TEA CADDIES AND OTHER BOXES.
These were mostly made in the same way as their wooden
counterparts. If their sides were to have ogée curves, then they
were cut from a very thick section of pasteboard and shaped on
a lathe. This might involve as many as a hundred and twenty
layers of paper and forty stovings, carrying the operations over
a considerable number of days and, of course, adding greatly to
the cost of the finished article (plates 22 and 155).

Boxes of regular shape were sometimes made by wrapping
sheets of paper around a greased core of the appropriate
shape, but in addition to being cut half-way through the
process like vases, they were horizontally divided after the
final stoving to form a box and a perfectly fitting lid to which
a top and base were fitted by the cabinet maker. Card cases
were similarly made (plate 23) and Jennens & Bettridge used
this method to make tall candlesticks, though they left the
hardwood core in place for added stability.

SNUFF BOXES. In his notes to accompany the exhibits at the
Great Exhibition, Robert Hunt, a japanner, described how
some snuff-boxes were 'made by glueing pieces of paper, cut to
the sizes of the top, bottom, and sides, one on another, round a
frame or mould which is afterwards removed.'[36] This method
was much like that used for card cases (see above).

FURNITURE. Furniture was seldom made entirely from papier
mâché because, despite its strength, it was not really suitable
for the legs and frames of chairs and sofas. These were mostly
constructed from wood as in ordinary furniture-making and
chair-backs and other parts were then infilled with panels of
papier mâché. In fact to describe Henry Clay's furniture as
papier mâché is not strictly accurate, for it was merely
veneered with a thin layer of that material (p. 241).

In the 1840s or 1850s, Woodward and Midgley (*qv*) made chair
legs entirely of paper by layering it round an appropriately shaped

mould which they removed after stoving, filling the cavity with pulp. Regrettably, we know neither how successful this method proved nor whether any examples have survived to the present day, but it appears not to have been used to any great extent.

The joint between wood and papier mâché was often a source of weakness, and it is not uncommon to find that chairs have been repaired at this point. This problem was largely overcome by chair-backs made wholly from pasteboard which had been steam-moulded to curve both horizontally around, and vertically away from the sitter (plate 12). This was made possible by a patent (#11,670) granted to Theodore Hyla Jennens, of Jennens & Bettridge, in 1846, two years after the chair design was registered, which involved placing the panels in a chamber or vessel and admitting steam from a boiler. Its purpose was two-fold: once pliable, the panel could be compacted to make a stronger sheet, or it could be pressed into a pre-formed shape. Chairs made in this way stand out as being one of the few products which show any real understanding among manufacturers of the unique plasticity of the material with which they worked. No other contemporary material was capable of being used in this way, yet sadly such understanding was rare in the history of the industry.

The author of an article in the *Journal of Design and Manufactures* in 1850, went even further by suggesting that although papier mâché is 'the fittest substance for a tea tray ... [it is] most unsuitable for a sofa or a wardrobe, where its peculiar characteristics are not called for.'[37]

By 1870 ready-made panels and 'blanks' had largely replaced the labour-intensive hand-made sheet-method of making papier mâché, and firms like McCallum & Hodson which continued to paste by hand became the exception rather than the rule.

Papier mâché made from pulp – the 'common' method

The methods for making pulp changed little during the course of the japanning industry, although by the 1780s, the ingredients had extended to include a mixture of linen, silk, cotton, sail-cloth, rope (tarred or otherwise), flax, hemp, wool, and so on – in fact, any material which was commonly used in standard paper-making. The coarseness of some of these ingredients caused hard particles and 'throw up blisters, and presents, generally, an unlevelled and "curdled" appearance' in the finished articles;[38] in consequence of this, and their brittleness, pulp goods were said to have been made by the 'common method'. Their production was not confined to smaller and less prestigious makers as most larger firms, including Jennens & Bettridge, are known to have made 'common' goods.

The fragility and limitations of early pulp-based papier mâché were partly overcome by oiling and stoving pulp in the same manner described by Clay in his pasteboard patent of 1772. To judge from the details of a later patent which Clay took out in

1786, and a similar one granted to the Birmingham button-maker, Obadiah Westwood, only five days later, this had certainly become common practice, and one which, according to Westwood, brought the variety of pulp goods into line with the range of those made by the best method. As with other stovings, great skill was required of the stover. John Haddan, in one of his patent specifications prepared almost sixty years later (see below) said that it was 'well known' that the length of time required to stove the oiled pulp 'can only be ascertained by the opening and examination of a small portion of a sheet after being dried.'[39] On the whole however, he found that one minute at a temperature of 55°F was sufficient for a sheet ⅜in. thick.

In 1805, when Thomas Jones, a Bilston japanner, drew up his patent specification for new methods of making pulp articles by means of presses or stamps (#2830), he provided the earliest detailed pulp recipe to have survived to the present day.[40] His preferred recipe required the pounding and pulping of 100lbs rope and about 20lbs rags for small articles, or about 110lbs of rope to about 10lbs rag for larger objects, to which he some-times added vitriol (sulphuric acid) or something similar, to make a weak acid, though for what purpose he did not say.

The invention which Jones sought to protect was adapted from standard paper-making methods. He placed a wire sieve, the shape and size of the intended object, in a deep, neatly fitting wooden frame, poured in the pulp and covered it with

23. Papier mâché visiting-card case, the markings of its pearl decoration carefully selected for the flowers and leaves depicted (see p. 50); c.1845. 10.5 x 7.5cm

flannel and a board. After turning this upside-down, he took off the frame leaving the mass of pulp on a bed of flannel and board and covered it with another flannel and board, before pressing lightly to expel some of the liquid. When he had removed the boards, the layers of felt and pulp were placed between dies or stamps of the intended form, and stamped or pressed into shape. The dies might be made of metal, wood, stone or clay. Then, when most of the liquid had been expelled, the dies and flannels were removed and the pulp stoved at a moderate temperature. When almost dry, the article was returned to the dies, then given a further stamping and stoving – this time with a weight on top to guard against warping. Once thoroughly dry, the article was saturated in oil, stoved and 'skimmed' in readiness for japanning; skimming involved rasping the surface first with a coarse file, then with a finer one, 'floating' or smoothing the surface and planing it if necessary. Jones offered an impressive list of objects which he said could be made in this way, including 'tea trays,

24. Chair with steam-moulded motifs on apron and legs, in imitation of carved ornament; metal label stamped for Bettridge & Co. Makers Birmingham, c.1865.

COURTESY OF CHRISTIE'S

sandwich trays,[vii] waiters, bottle stands, boxes, baskets, caddies, or pannels for any coach, chaise or any other kind of carriage, tables, hats, caps, frames, etc.'[41]

Some thirty years later, in 1836, William Brindley, a Birmingham paper-maker and supplier of papier mâché blanks to the trade, was granted a patent (#7049) for 'Improvements in the Manufacture of Tea Trays and Other Japanned Ware and in the Board or Material used therein, and for other Purposes.' It was important because it was the first to show how large flat articles were made from pulp and it was this part of his invention that Brindley wished to protect. Like Jones, he made no claim to originating the pulp-making process, but included in his specification probably the most detailed contemporary description of how pulp was made: 30lbs cotton and linen rags were placed in a paper engine and when half-pulverised, 10lbs of white paper scraps were added and the mixture was beaten to a fine consistency. To this, Brindley added 6lbs of yellow soap, 1lb of alum, 3 teaspoons of white vitriol and 4 teaspoons of olive oil. He blended the mixture in a mill and transferred it to a large vat ready for use.

Brindley's improvements were simply refinements of Jones' methods, but instead of moulding articles in dies, he made them from layered sheets of pulp. 'Having prepared the pulp,' Brindley wrote, 'I proceed to make sheets of paper in the ordinary way' by laying the wet mixture on a mould, covering it with a cloth and compressing it, before adding further layers and so on until the 'board' was of the required thickness. In effect, Brindley's product was the pulp-equivalent of pasteboard and, moreover, it was the method already employed by button-board makers (see Glossary). To make a tray from this material, Brindley hand-pressed a sheet of wet pulp into an oiled mould, covered it with the second oiled part of the mould, sandwiched the whole between boards and placed it in a screw or press to expel the excess water and to take the impression. The upper mould was then removed and any cracks in the tray were filled with pulp, and its surface smoothed before the freshly-oiled mould was replaced. The tray was turned over and the process repeated on its other side. The two moulds, with the pulp between, were pressed again under increased force, and the entire process repeated two or three times according to the thickness of the tray; to save time, several moulds could be pressed simultaneously. The moulds were tightly bound with wire to compress the pulp and stoved at about 120–180°F. When dry, the tray was removed from the mould, oiled, stoved and skimmed prior to being japanned.

Both Harry Horton, in a poem about Birmingham (1853), and W.C. Aitken in 1866,[42] stated that Brindley's patent was successfully contested and 'thrown open', or made void, in 1842. By whom, or why, it was contested is not known, but with Jones' patent having expired, it is likely that Brindley's methods were not dissimilar to those already followed by many other papier mâché makers. Notwithstanding, Brindley took out another in 1845 (#10,653), this time from an address in Liverpool Road, Middlesex. Its purpose was to correct the shortcomings of his earlier method which, although claiming it had 'come into extensive use', he said was troublesome as the pulp tended to crack when pressed into the mould. He remedied the problem by using a sheet made from solid pulp instead of the layers he prescribed previously, and in so-doing he returned, in principle, to Jones' patent of 1805.

In 1848, Brindley applied, successfully, for a third patent in respect of moulding papier mâché (#12,175). Applying for a patent was a long and costly procedure so for Brindley to have made a third application suggests that blank-making was a lucrative trade.[viii] His invention this time, was the use of engraved or stamped metal moulds to produce relief-decoration on trays and other pulp goods – a process borrowed from the production of architectural mouldings made of papier mâché.[ix] As an economy, he suggested that pulp impressions when oiled and stoved, might themselves serve as moulds, and for even greater savings, articles could be moulded plain and their decoration carved with a sharp knife, although he acknowledged that this resulted in poorer definition. Neither method appears to have been much used, but a good example of relief-decoration may be seen on a chair made by J. Bettridge & Co. (plate 24). A selection of papier mâché bowls and footpans made by Brindley were included in an exhibition of 'patented and Registered Articles' organised by the Society of Arts in 1850–1.

In 1844, William Sheldon, a self-styled 'japan painter', patented a method for 'making trays and other articles of japanners' ware, or in substitution of papier mâché'. The patent (#10,064) covered both composition buttons and moulded pulp articles, but by far the most interesting of Sheldon's ideas was the one which combined sheets of making paper with pulp. The results were similar to the chair-legs made by Woodward & Midgeley (p. 32), but the process was very different. Sheldon dissolved 6lbs of glue in about 7 gallons of water and boiled them with 12lbs of flour, 6lbs of sharps [sharp-sand], 9lbs spent hops, 4lbs whiting [ground and purified chalk] and 2lbs of hair – preferably 'finely cut human hair' (this presumably acted as a strengthening agent, for which most animal hair would have been too coarse). He reduced these to a stiff paste which he rolled to the thickness of a tray, for example, covered both sides with a sheet of making paper and compressed the whole in a suitable mould. After about an hour, the tray was removed and each part of the mould was lined with a dampened sheet of making paper which, along with those already layed on the pulp, Sheldon coated with paste made from equal quantities of flour and glue. The whole was then placed between two iron moulds of the same shape, and stove-dried before being finished in the usual way (*cf.* combination trays p. 257).

Alongside these activities, there was another ingenious method of preparing pulp sheets which John Coope Haddan, a civil engineer, of King's Cross in London, patented in 1843 (#9953). Haddan proposed 'combining successive layers of wet pulp together, by winding [it] round a cylinder, afterwards cutting it off' and pressing it flat, at several points during the drying process. Although described as an improvement in making 'papier mâché and other articles', it is worth remembering that an earlier patent which Haddan shared with T.R. Crampton in 1842, showed that his real interest lay in using the material in the construction of railway wheels and carriages. Thus, any benefit which his later invention may have been to the japan trade was almost certainly a matter of serendipity.

On the evidence of these patents, there were several methods for making pulp; in all probability there were many others, though which was the one most generally used it is difficult to conjecture. Unless an object is so damaged that its construction shows through, it is unlikely that knowledge of these methods will help to identify how any given article was made. The purpose of describing these various processes is more fundamental. First, they demonstrate the perpetual search to perfect goods made in this way, and show how the challenge exercised the minds not only of japanners and paper-makers, but of a civil engineer too. From railway wheels to hats and coffins, the potential for pulp-sheets clearly extended beyond the japanned papier mâché trade – and largely beyond the remit of this book (p. 268). And second, knowledge of how pulp articles were made satisfies modern-day curiosity about a material which in many ways, and like paste-board, was ahead of its time.

The demand for pulp articles increased during the 1860s when the market for better papier mâché was declining. In 1886, wood pulp[x] was reported to have been recently imported from Sweden and employed as a substitute for paper-pulp in the manufacture of small desks, work boxes, jewel cases etc.; this enabled japanners to compete with inexpensive Chinese and Japanese lacquered goods which had begun to flood the market. The products of Ebeneezer Sheldon (*qv*) for example, while generally well-decorated, often show the coarse and grainy texture common to many papier mâché articles made from the 1880s onwards. This period also saw the rise of 'Thetford Fibre' (*qv*), a range of both decorative and utilitarian wares made in Thetford in Norfolk which, being similarly finished, is often confused by today's collectors with the products of the Midlands industry (p. 277).

---

vii. Almost certainly a reference to 'sandwich-edged' trays (see p. 252)
viii. In 1850, a patent for England alone cost £96.7.8 inclusive of the patentees living expenses necessitated by a month or more spent in London. A patent to cover the whole of the UK would have cost £300 or more.

ix. This patent also covered the moulding of basins and hats from papier mâché.
x. Wood pulp was also used for 'making so-called papier mâché parts for motor cars and telephones' and no doubt many other things besides.

Blank-making

The number engaged in making papier mâché blanks for the trade prior to the publication of the earliest Birmingham directory in 1767 cannot now be quantified, and of those who were listed from the late 1770s onwards as 'waiter makers', there is no means of distinguishing whether they made tin or paper trays. After 1805, however, producers of paper blanks began to describe themselves as such, for example John Booth, paper-tray maker, or Edmund Davis, paper-box-turner, both of Birmingham; this practice continued throughout the remainder of the history of the japan trade.

From existing records, it is difficult to assess the extent to which japanners made their own papier mâché blanks. Judging from detailed reports made by visitors to their premises, large-scale japanners like Henry Clay and Jennens & Bettridge almost certainly made all of theirs. Nevertheless, in 1794, William Barrow assured Matthew Boulton that 'J'ers do not make their own Blanks, or unjapann'd Articles, but their [*sic*] are distinct Makers of these, on which is allow'd 12 Months Credit'.[43]

Thus, it made financial sense, certainly for small-scale japanners, to purchase their blanks ready-made so as to make savings not only on time and outlay, but also on storage. And to judge from William Hutton's observation in 1835, the arrangement increasingly benefited the japanner at the expense of his supplier. At that time, Hutton wrote:

> *There are five paper tray makers in Birmingham, whose business it is to make the trays for the japanners and probably employ at least sixty persons. The returns from this business is [sic] supposed to be little short of £100,000 per annum. The nominal prices of the blanks have not varied for the last forty or fifty years, but the discount allowed has gradually increased during that time. Formerly the blank maker allowed ten per cent discount, but at the present time eighty per cent, that is, if he take to a warehouse, goods to the amount of £100, he will receive just £20.*[44]

Nevertheless, in the longer-term, blank-making would become a lucrative business, as Brindley and others clearly found. Later, several larger japanners, like Alsager & Neville, and John Bettridge & Co., were also known to supply blanks to the trade (plate 25).

In addition, papier mâché blanks could be purchased by amateur japanners. They came in the form of 'work-boxes, card racks, netting-boxes, match-cups, memorandum books, watch stands, letter racks, bellows, screens and a variety of other things.'[45] Such articles, according to B.F. Gandee, were available from 'fancy shops, both in town and country', but as they were described as 'all ready for the work',[46] it is likely that they were already japanned when purchased. Interest in japanning among amateurs persisted for, as G.W. Yapp noted

in 1878, 'those who like to try their hands at the decoration of papier mâché may purchase blanks ... for the purpose.'[47] These, he said, were 'undecorated', but it is unclear whether they were japanned.

Finishing 'blanks' in preparation for japanning

Once the 'blank' had been made, by whatever method, it was sent to the so-called 'cabinet-making shop' where all objects, from tiny boxes and trays of all sizes, to large items of furniture, were prepared for the japanning process. Here, it was turned and planed, smoothed, filed and, perhaps, fluted, and fitted with internal divisions as required. The cabinet-maker was equipped with a lathe and other standard cabinet making tools, but the plane he used for finishing the blanks was set upright, instead of reclined, and had a plane-iron with teeth like a fine saw with which to gently score the surface of the articles to provide greater purchase for the japan varnish. The regularly-spaced fine wavy lines of this scoring – evident when only a thin coating of japan varnish was necessary – may sometimes be found if the baize used to back objects, such as bottle-stands, has become detached.

After a final polish with chamois leather, the article was sent to the 'blacking shop' to be japanned. By the time it reached this stage it would have been several days in the making and already have involved several workmen to each of whom it may have been returned two or three times or more; these included pulp-makers and moulders in the case of common goods, and paper cutters and pasters for best goods, in addition to stovers, cabinet-makers and oil-dippers. On top of this, the making of moulds, the purchase of raw materials, and fuel for the stoves all had to be added to the cost of production. It is hardly surprising then, that at its best, and even before any decoration was applied, papier mâché was an expensive commodity. For example, in 1794, Barrow reckoned that a 30in. blank tray cost 3s 2d – almost 30% of the cost of the finished tray. Nevertheless, since Henry Clay is known to have made a profit of about 250% on a 30in. paper tray in the early nineteenth century, the high cost of blanks was easily reconciled.

PAPER DUTY AND ITS EFFECTS ON THE PAPIER MÂCHÉ INDUSTRY

In 1694, a duty was levied on paper mills and on all goods made from paper, and as it was not repealed until 1861, it was effective throughout the most productive period of papier mâché manufacture in England. Every maker of paper or pasteboard had to pay an annual licence fee to the Excise Office 'on pain of forfeiture',[48] hence the sign 'William Ryton and Benjamin Walton, Licensed to make paper Tea Trays' above the door to the Old Hall Japan Works in Wolverhampton. With duty levied at the rate of ½d per lb for pulp and 3d per lb for pasteboard, the effect on the better class of goods was considerable, particularly since it was further stipulated that they be made only from new and unused paper. The duty on both materials was halved in 1837.

To give some idea of the implications of this duty, in 1851 'making paper' cost 6½d per lb plus a duty of 1½d, while papier mâché made from pulp was taxed at only ¾d per lb and exempt if less than ¼in. thick. Jennens & Bettridge, concerned that this disparity caused 'a preference for the bad article over the good',[49] complained to the Excise that it was 'depraving the manufacture' and asked that 'if the duty cannot be removed from the real paper, it may be laid equally upon the paper-pulp; that the manufacturer and the buyer may have a fair chance of producing and enjoying a good article.'[50] Their argument for a quality product was echoed by Harriet Martineau when she railed: 'Official men should know that ... the humble housewife is mourning over the wrecks of her best china, smashed by the tea-tray having burst across the middle.'[51] The Excise men promised to consider the matter, but it was another ten years before the duty was repealed.

In a report compiled by the Royal Society of Arts in 1854, it is evident that Jennens & Bettridge were still raging against the iniquities of the paper duty. During a visit to their factory, a representative of the Society asked about the 'content of a number of large boxes which were being sent off to Piedmont in Italy'.[52] The response was thought to be of interest to those who were 'agitating for a repeal of the duty on paper.'[53] According to the report, the boxes contained:

> *Panelling for railway carriages – one of the most novel of the many purposes, and yet perhaps one of the most important to which papier mâché is being adapted by the firm referred to... The duty amounts to about 3d. a foot ... sufficient to prevent the order being given to the papier mâché manufacturer in cases where cheapness is the main consideration... It therefore operates in favour of an inferior quality of material being used, viz., papier mâché made from pulp – which is not subject to duty when of more than ¼" thickness – and also limits demand for an article which if generally brought into use, would give employment to hundreds of men in Birmingham alone. Even now there are said to be on hand orders amounting to some 50 or 60,000 feet, probably containing upwards of 20 tons of paper. Hitherto it has been almost solely employed upon foreign railways.*[54]

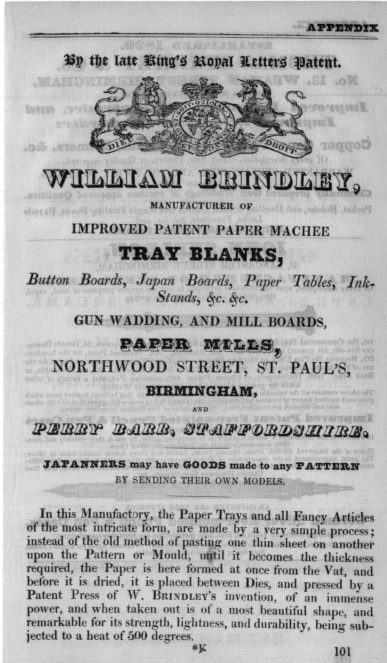

25. Advertisement for William Brindley, from Robson's *Birmingham and Sheffield ... Directory*, 1839.
Reproduced with the permission of Birmingham Libraries & Archives

Not surprisingly, it was a matter of great resentment that similar duties were not imposed in France where, in addition, manufacturers were allowed to use both scrap and soiled paper. The anomaly still prevailed in 1886, when it was noted that while there was no duty charged on German papier mâché imports, 'English papier mâché is subjected to heavy duties before it reaches the German and Continental markets'.[55] This would explain the flood of German papier mâché on to the English market at the time.

CHAPTER IV

JAPANNING and DECORATING

'The distinctive character of japan-work lies in the use of gum and spirit with the colouring agent; instead of oil and turpentine.'

The Penny Magazine, 1844

'Japanning' in the context of the Midlands industry, was the process of varnishing and decorating tin-plated iron and papier mâché in particular, but also wood, occasionally slate and, in the early period, copper.

Although so-called 'japan varnish' was used for only the first few layers, and 'mixing' and 'polishing varnishes' were employed at various stages thereafter, the decorating workshops: the blacking shop, the pearl shop, the painting, gilding and varnish shops, were collectively called the 'japan shop'. It was there that papier mâché, tinware, and any other material which was to be japanned, came together for the first time. Such distinctions were less obvious, or even non-existent, among small-scale japanners, but nevertheless, the decorative methods they employed were much the same as those used in larger workshops.

To achieve the hard, lustrous surface so characteristic of japanned ware, each layer of varnish had to be gently baked or stove-dried before the next was added and it is this which distinguishes japanning from both Oriental lacquering and other varnishing methods. During stoving, the turpentine in the varnish evaporated and left a sticky residue which fused to form a smooth surface which hardened on cooling and was capable of retaining its gloss. Moreover, stoving increased the density of the varnish and improved its adhesion to the underlying material making it more resistant to wear.

Like any varnishing process, japanning had to be undertaken in workshops which were entirely free from dust, smoke and moisture to ensure that the varnish flowed freely and smoothly; this was why the japan shop had its own stoves, quite separate from those used for drying papier mâché where the surrounding atmosphere was too humid. The stoves were a major feature of the japan shop and, with the intense heat and heady odour of baking varnish which issued from them, a defining one for many contemporary visitors.

To the inexperienced, the heat was intolerable and, even with chimneys to expel the vapours, the lingering smell of baking varnish was offensive. 'The rooms were so hot,' wrote Anne Rushout, after visiting Clay's factory in 1797, 'we could not stay to examine the process.'[1] And similarly, over fifty years later, a visitor to McCallum & Hodson's establishment, remarked that 'When the large iron doors [of the stoves] were thrown open, the temperature became very oppressive, and I found the vicinity of the opened stoves quite unbearable in some of the rooms.'[2] As for the varnish fumes, she 'was informed, that though not exactly to be compared with the "perfumes of Araby," or the spicy breezes of Ceylon, they are in no degree deleterious.'[3] This was a view shared by Charles Thackrah, a Leeds surgeon and an early commentator on health and safety in the workplace, who said that 'varnish makers [and by implication, varnishers also] inspire a strong

Opposite: 26. Papier mâché work-table, decorated to simulate walnut and embellished with brass mounts (see p. 46), c.1860. 72 x 44cm

vapour of alcohol, turpentine, gums and tar. This at first produces sickliness, and impairs the appetite; but men accustomed to the employ suffer no apparent injury.'[4] The objections made by visitors could, perhaps, be attributed to their extreme sensibilities, but it is worth noting that even an experienced japanner like William Barrow, felt it necessary to assure Matthew Boulton, the Birmingham entrepreneur (*qv*), that if Boulton took up his suggestion of establishing a japan shop at the Soho Works (p. 120*ff*), 'the varnishes could be made at some distance from the factory so that nothing in the least disagreeable would then proceed from prosecuting the other part of the business there.'[5]

Although Barrow proposed to make his own varnish, it was, by then, available from specialist suppliers. Small manufacturers like Isaac Caddick of Bilston continued to advertise as both varnish makers and japanners, but they were fast becoming the minority. Varnish making was a hazardous process which required great care, as evidenced by the tragic death of Edward Careless, of Bilston. The grim details were recorded in the parish registers of St Leonard's Church:

'On Saturday, ye 19th of January [1754], about two o'clock in ye afternoon, he went into his stove room to examine a vessel of spirit varnish that was heating in one of his stoves, and unfortunately pulling out ye cork, ye spirits took fire, and with great fury burst over him in flames, and as it was some minutes before he had any assistance, his head, neck, face, breasts, shoulders, and arms were burnt in a terrible manner. His wounds, however, digested well, and he began to heal in a kind of manner, but it is supposed that ye nerves of ye head were injured by ye fire, and that ye meringes [meninges] were inflamed, and brought on delirium on the seventh day, and upon Tuesday, January 29th, betwixt six and seven in ye evening, he died, in ye 28th year of his age.[6]

It became increasingly the case, therefore, that varnish was purchased from specialist suppliers like Thornley & Knight;[i] Gittins & Boothby, Postans in Birmingham, or Mander Bros.[ii] in Wolverhampton, who supplied not only local needs and the home market, but overseas trade also. Nevertheless, comments entered alongside some of the orders in Mander's varnish book, such as 'Extra Black for Clark',[7] suggest that every japanner had his or her varnish made up to suit their personal preference.

Each stage of decoration, from the application of the japan ground to the final polish, required very different skills and thus in all but the smallest workshops, every object was worked on by several different craftsmen and skilled artisans. The various stages involved in decorating a 30in. paper tray, and their relative costs, were listed in 'A Statement of the Cost of the different Operations of Coloured Ground Trays & Waiters with Figure and Landscape Centres' compiled by Barrow in 1794:

The Blank Tray	3s 2d
Black Grounding	1s 6d
Fire & Labour	3d
Colour Labour and Fire	1s 3d
Painting	2s 0d
Bordering	1s 4d
Varnish & Labour	1s 3d
Polishing	5d
Prime Cost	11s 2d
Profit	9s 10d
Sale Price	21s 0d[8]

No similar breakdown of costs is known to have survived from a later period. However, nineteenth-century pattern books in the collection of Wolverhampton Arts and Muesums sometimes show the cost of pearling, or gilding, for example, and a note written on a scrap of tissue paper from the Sheldon factory (*qv*) gives some idea of the time and material costs involved in making two small ladies-cabinets in the 1880s:

2 cabinets
5 hours Pearling
6 Days finishing
5 Books gold

£1	12s
	6s 3d
£1	18s 3d

[therefore] 19s 1½d each[iii]

Nevertheless, the following descriptions of the various decorative processes employed by japanners make clear why it was said of japanning that it was 'really wonderful therefore, not that this style of ornament is so dear, but that it is so cheap.'[9]

THE BLACKING SHOP

The 'blacking shop', also known as the 'black stove', was the first workshop within the japan department to receive the blank goods, and it was there that they were given their base, or ground, coats of japan varnish.

The workshop took its name from the predominance of black as a ground colour although from a very early period, varnish of every hue was applied there. In 1767, for example, in a letter to the *Birmingham Gazette*, 'a hearty Well-wisher to the Trade and Manufactories of the Town of Birmingham' said he was:

highly delighted with a new Species of Japanning lately introduced with the brightest gayest Grounds, more brilliant in their Colours than any of Nature's Productions ... nay even a stronger Red, Blue, Green and Orange, than the Rainbow or Prism afford us.[10]

In *The Handmaid to the Arts* (1758), Robert Dossie described the early method of coating iron or copper with 'common black japan grounds'.[11] After the article had been thoroughly cleaned and dried, its surface was covered with lamp-black (*qv*) or, preferably, ivory-black (*qv*) and coated with a drying oil, such as oil of turpentine. When this was 'of moderate dryness [it was] put onto a stove of such degree of heat as will change the oil black, without burning it.' Dossie assures his readers that this kind of varnish 'requires no polish having received, when properly managed, a sufficient one from the heat.'[12] It was not, however, always as durable as some would wish. In his letter, the Birmingham 'Well-wisher' had 'the Mortification to observe':

> [some articles] *which carry a very good Face, have been manifestly hurt or scratched by being rubbed with a Cambrick Handkerchief; and have been greatly marked by the Papers they have been wrapped in; whilst others with the most perfect Polish, have borne a severe but candid Scratch with my Thumb Nail, without the least Injury done them; I shall therefore make this the test of all this Sort of Goods that comes into my Hands, which if they bear, as it's an Oil Varnish, its well known that it will continually grow harder, till it becomes as hard as the Iron itself, of which I am convinced by Experience.*[13]

The problem may have arisen partly from ill-prepared varnish, but most likely it was due to haphazard stoving for it was not possible, during this period, to be precise about stove temperatures. Considerable practical experience was therefore required of the stovers who, like the blackers, were generally women. The lower the heat and the longer the stoving, the stronger the varnish would be, but if the stove became too hot, or its heat was increased too rapidly, the japanned surface might blister. Inadequate preparation of the metal brought similar results: 'I have noticed [an] Imperfection, which for some Time puzzled me,' wrote the same newspaper correspondent in 1767:

> (to wit) *the Varnish being raised in irregular Lines as fine as a Hair, and often with a small Blister in the Middle of them. This I learn proceeds from the Iron Tables*[iv] *not being freed from Rust before the first Lacker or Oil Varnish is laid on, this will in a short Time break up the whole Body of the Varnish and Painting to the Iron, as big as a Crown Piece, and will soon spread itself over the whole Body.*[14]

Clearly, there was a need for Dossie's instructive book,

though it is difficult to assess whether it ever served as a practical handbook for japanners, as distinct from being a source of interesting and curious facts for educated readers. Nevertheless, it remained a standard work of reference for many years and its section on japanning continued to be quoted, almost to the word, until the early years of the twentieth century in books such as Robinson & Swinney's *The Artists Assistant* (1770 or 1773), Rees' *Cyclopaedia* (1819), and the second edition of *A Handbook on Japanning* by W.N. Brown (1913).

Within the developing industry, the japanning process became more sophisticated and a number of detailed eye-witness reports about late eighteenth-, and more particularly, nineteenth-century methods have survived to provide a clear understanding of the new processes. No single account is complete in its detail, and while collectively they show that the methods employed in each factory and workshop were very similar, each japanner clearly had his own ways of doing things. What follows, therefore, is a piecing together of facts drawn from various sources.

Several varnishes were called 'japan' and each had a specific purpose, but only the ones known as 'black japan' and 'tar varnish' yielded the depth of colour necessary for the work under discussion.[v] Neither, however, would 'of itself, produce the jet black so greatly admired'[15] on japanned ware, and so both had to be mixed with ivory- or lamp-black. Robert Hunt, writing in the *Art Journal* in 1851, described two varnishes then in use for creating black japanned grounds on papier mâché; since he called the first 'the old form of varnish', it is to be assumed that it had been in use for many years:

> '*Colophony* [ie. rosin or gum] *or turpentine boiled down until it becomes black and friable, is melted in a glazed earthenware pot, and thrice as much amber in fine powder is sprinkled in it by degrees, with the addition of a little spirits of turpentine. When the amber is melted, the same quantity of sarcocolla* [a Persian gum] *is sprinkled in, and more spirits of turpentine added until the whole becomes fluid, when it is strained through a coarse hair bag, by being pressed between hot plates.*[16]

The second, a tar varnish, was made from 'good asphaltum or the true resin of petroleum dissolved in strong turpentine' which Hunt said, 'would appear to answer very much

---

i. A ledger from the firm of Thornley & Knight shows them to have supplied, amongst others, Jennens & Bettridge, Thomas Lane, Small & Son, and Winfield.
ii. Mander & Co's *Varnish Carriage Book* (1838+) shows that they supplied such Birmingham japanners as Charles Docker, Bill & Co., T. Small & Son, Jennens & Bettridge, Woodward & Midgley, McCullum & Hodson, Alsager & Neville, and even Thornley Son & Knight. They also supplied Henry Fearncombe of Wolverhampton, and in Bilston, Gerrard Barber, was amongst those known to have purchased varnish from Manders.
iii. The costs shown here are the author's interpretation of a confusing layout in the original.
iv. Table: any flat or level surface ... a surface on which any thing is written, or engraved; a picture from *tableau* (D. Fenning, *Royal English Dictionary*, 1771).
v. For example, cooking stoves, umbrella frames, bedsteads, bicycle spokes, sewing machines and hairpins, each had a varnish specific to its purpose: *black tar varnish* – used by holloware makers and japanners for 'common goods', and by umbrella makers, button and hairpin makers; *brown tar varnish* – as found on tin canisters for tea, sugar, etc., and on boxes (pl. 28); *Brunswick black* – a quick-drying varnish for stove grates etc.; *spirit varnish* – used by makers of paper/card packing boxes and brass-founders.

better';[17] he did not explain why, but its relative simplicity may have been significant, as may its particular suitability for japanning tin-ware. As the industry declined, so too did the quality of the ingredients used in making varnish. At a meeting held at Mander's varnish works in 1865, for instance, it was reported that all the Birmingham varnish makers were, by then, making inferior or 'common varnish' with turpentine made from petroleum spirit instead of more expensive oil of turpentine - a demise which possibly explains how in 1895, tar varnish, once held in such high regard, could be described as a bright, cheap and durable varnish for sheet metals (plate 28).

Metals were heated before any varnish was applied. Otherwise, no matter which varnish was used, and regardless of the material to which it was applied, the same blacking procedure was followed – an operation which, throughout the course of the industry, was traditionally the preserve of women. Using a large round and stubby-handled 'black stovers brush', they coated the entire surface by working from the middle to one side of the object, and then from the middle

to the other side, taking great care not to overlap the strokes. Speed was crucial and one blacker – in this case a man – said 'not even to see a good customer would he put down his job until he had finished the process and could safely pass the article to the stove';[18] to have stopped mid-way would have caused an inerradicable line across the work.

The article was then stoved at 250–280°F – the lowest temperature of all the varnish stovings – for at least twenty-four hours. Papier mâché and wood required a lower heat and usually a longer stoving than metals, and the darker the ground colour, the higher the temperature it could withstand. A patent granted to Joseph Bettridge in 1841 (#8972), explained how wood was treated at the Jennens & Bettridge factory to prevent it from warping when stoved. 'Seasoned birch, alder, or other wood' was turned in a lathe 'to a rough representation of the intended design'[19] – a chair-leg for example – and a hole was drilled through its entire length. This was placed in a japanner's stove and heated to about 120°F, rising gradually to about 250°F over a period of seven to ten days: the more porous the wood the longer it required. The article was then turned to a perfect finish prior to being japanned, or covered with paper as previously described.

When removed from the oven, the japanned surface was patchy and 'covered with small knobs, which the varnish, by penetrating the paper, has brought up on the surface.'[20] In scraping these off, much of the varnish came too, hence the need for a second application, or even a third or fourth; goods of the best quality might have received as many as twelve to eighteen coats. The articles were left in the oven until cold, sometimes for up to a day, so their surfaces could harden before the next layer of varnish was applied. The stove temperature was increased with each successive layer, rising to 300°, and since some of these stovings lasted up to twenty-four hours, each article, depending upon its quality and purpose, took from two to eighteen days to complete. For example, Henry Loveridge & Co., would have lavished many more coats on a prestigious coal vase (plate 219), than on one of 'common' iron. After so many coats, papier mâché objects became so thoroughly permeated with tar varnish as to be as insect-repellent as their iron counter-parts. Finally, the surface was smoothed with a close-grained pumice stone and water.

The method for producing coloured grounds was slightly different since the oils in japan varnish tended to discolour and affect the intensity of the pigment (plate 27). Shellac varnish – a distillation of gum, shellac, alcohol and water – answered much better. The surface was primed with two to three coats of seed-lac, over which were laid successive coats of shellac varnish mixed with the required colour. Two or three layers of varnish were generally sufficient, but Jennens & Bettridge, for instance, gave superior goods between twelve and eighteen coats. Each layer was stoved, but at the lower temperature of 230° and for a shorter time.

27. Papier mâché handscreen with a seldom-found 'white' ground, and turned gilt-wood stick, c.1840. 39 x 28cm
PRIVATE COLLECTION

The overwhelming preference for black grounds appears to have been practical rather than aesthetic. Thomas Archer, a japanner, writing about the goods displayed by J. Bettridge & Co. at the Paris Exhibition of 1867, explained that:

> 'Mr. Bettridge's efforts for some years past have been devoted to the improvement of the coloured grounds, whose perishability and liability to damage have been great drawbacks to the manufacture. The trade has been cramped through being forced except at a sacrifice of durability, to employ little else than black grounds … Mr. Bettridge, some time ago perfected a maroon ground, which has all the hardness, durability, and susceptibility to polish of the black grounds. To this he has now added a white or ivory ground, which certainly has every appearance of durability.'[21]

When a satisfactory surface was achieved, all articles, whether black or coloured, were sent to be polished in readiness for ornamenting. Or, as George Dodd wryly observed in 1854, 'Then ensue the painting and the gilding, the bedizenment with gaudy show or the adornment with graceful device, according as the goods are low or high priced or the manufacturer a man of taste or no taste.'[22]

DECORATIVE TECHNIQUES

Tortoiseshell and other Imitative Effects

'An Imitation … which greatly excells Nature itself both in Colour and Hardness.'
> John Baskerville, patent specification (#582), 1742

When japanning first began at Pontypool in the early eighteenth century, tortoiseshell was a fashionable material not only for making exquisite snuff boxes, bodkin cases and other small luxuries, but also as a veneer in combination with inlaid brass for large pieces of furniture of the type made in Paris by Charles André Boulle (1642–1732) and known generically as *boulle-work*. The mottled surface pattern of tortoiseshell was easily imitated and from about 1740 it

28. Tea/coffee canister, collar-box, and percussion box, all made of tin and thinly coated with japan varnish; late nineteenth/early twentieth century. H: 27.5cm (tallest)
WOLVERHAMPTON ARTS AND HERITAGE (BANTOCK HOUSE MUSEUM)

became a popular decorative effect among decorators of japanned ware and Staffordshire pottery alike.

Although more commonly used at Pontypool, tortoiseshell decoration was also employed by Midlands japanners. John Baskerville, for example, in his patent of 1742 (#582), had suggested it as one of several finishes for his newly invented metal-veneered picture frames and furniture (p. 115).

To create a tortoiseshell ground, the japanned surface was thinly coated with a mixture of vermilion pigment, drying oil and turpentine, left to dry, and over-coated with varnish prior to being stove-dried. Patches of varnish were then rubbed away with pumice stone until the underlying vermilion showed 'slightly through', giving an illusion of tortoiseshell. According to Dossie, the varnish used for this purpose was originally devised by Johannes Kunckel[vi] and 'revived with great success in the Birmingham manufactures,[vii] where it was not only the ground of snuff boxes, dressing boxes, and other such lesser pieces, but of those beautiful tea-waiters which have been so justly esteemed and admired in several parts of Europe.'[23] It was as follows:

vi. Kunckel, Johannes: *Ars vitraria experimentalis*, Frankfurt, 1689.
vii. As Gibbs observed, Dossie classed all japanned tinware as 'Birmingham

manufactures' unaware, probably, that some of the goods then on sale in London, were made at Pontypool. It is likely therefore, that Kunckel's recipe was used in both centres.

29. Japanned copper coffee pot, with tortoiseshell ground and gilt decoration; Pontypool, c.1760-70. H:26.5cm
© NATIONAL MUSEUM OF WALES (NMW A 50026)

30. Tin tea caddies and snuff box, with marbled grounds and Sheraton-style motifs; typical, early nineteenth century Bilston products. H: 9cm (larger caddy)

[Take] *of good linseed oil one gallon, and of umbre half a pound. Boil them together till the oil become* [sic] *very brown and thick; strain it then through a coarse cloth; and set it again to boil; in which state it must be continued till it acquire a pitchy consistence.*[24]

The result was a reddish colouring in marked contrast to the brown tortoiseshell of the earliest Pontypool goods. There the effect was achieved by covering the article with silver leaf, coating it with a golden varnish and removing small patches as described above (plate 29). 'This ware is much better than the Birmingham', observed Dr Richard Pococke, Bishop of Meath and Ossary, after visiting Pontypool in 1756, 'but is dear'.[25] This was a factor which its makers were forced to address in the 1780s and 1790s when, for reasons of economy, and against fierce competition from the Midlands, they too adopted the use of red pigment. By so doing, of course, it became less easy to distinguish English from Welsh products although Pococke – as if to help modern day collectors – noted that the early 'salvers and candlesticks and many other things' made at Pontypool were decorated 'with Chinese landscapes and figures in gold only, and not with colouring as at Birmingham'.[26]

Occasionally, Midlands workshops also used silver as a base for tortoiseshell grounds. For instance, in 1794, William Barrow, in costing the various operations involved in decorating 'Crimson Tortoise Trays & Waiters with Coloured Borders', made allowance for 'silver and colour'. Since their cost was listed separately from that for 'bordering', it is reasonable to assume that silver and colour were required for the tortoiseshell effect. Barrow's breakdown shows a clear profit of just over 70%:

	6" waiters per doz.	30" trays each
Blanks	1s 3d	3s 2d
Blacking, fire and labour	7¼d	1s 9d
Silver and colour	3d	8d
Polishing	7d	1s 0d
Bordering	6d	10d
Prime cost	3s 2¼d	7s 5d
Profit	2s 3¼d	5s 7d
Sale Price	5s 6d	13s 0d[27]

31. Utilitarian tinware photographed at the South Staffordshire Industrial and Fine Art Exhibition, Wolverhampton, 1869.
FROM THE COLLECTIONS OF WOLVERHAMPTON ARCHIVES & LOCAL STUDIES

32. A king-gothic papier mâché tray with 'malachite' ground, impressed 'JENNENS & BETTRIDGE MAKER LONDON', mid nineteenth century. 63.5cm (tray)
COURTESY OF WOOLLEY & WALLIS, SALISBURY

Curiously, among the articles that Barrow proposed making: quadrille pools (*ie.* counters trays), snuff and tobacco boxes, candlesticks, snuffers trays and so on, there was no mention of cases for pocket coin-balances which are amongst the most plentiful of tortoiseshell-decorated tin objects to have survived to the present day; nor of tri-corn hat boxes which were similarly ornamented. In fact, since neither article appears in any contemporary lists of products made by Midlands japanners, it is possible they were made elsewhere by specialist firms.

Tortoiseshell decoration slipped from favour in the early nineteenth century and save for perhaps a few isolated examples, the fashion seems not to have been revived until the 1850s or 1860s when boxes, in particular, were decorated in imitation of boulle-work.

Marble effects are known to have been used on japanned ware by Boulton & Fothergill, in the 1770s (p. 124). Nevertheless, it was Josiah Woodward (later of Woodward & Midgley [*qv*]) who is remembered for having reputedly devised a means of marbling japanned surfaces whilst employed by Ryton & Walton at the Old Hall in Wolverhampton, in about the early 1820s. It appears that 'a kind of marbled work'[28] had been sent to the Old Hall for repair or reproduction. Of all their decorators, only Woodward succeeded in copying exactly the specimen sent, creating an impression of the semi-transparency of marble by making the veins appear to extend beneath the surface. He was thought to have achieved this by beginning with a grey rather than flake-white ground, painting the veins and giving them 'depth' by washes of flake-white, and copal varnish. He is also believed to have introduced a method of imitating lapiz lazuli (see p. 168).

After the mid nineteenth century, the fashion for japanning in imitation of other materials was revived. Burr walnut was especially favoured, often in combination with ornate brass mounts (plate 26); so too was malachite (plate 32), an effect known to

have been employed by Stobwasser (*qv*) in Germany, in the early nineteenth century, and to have featured among his exhibits at the 1851 Exhibition. Nevertheless, it appears not to have been used until much later in the Midlands where it was said to have been introduced by George Harper, a decorator at the Birmingham firm of Alsager & Neville (*qv*), after seeing some gates inlaid with this rich green stone in the Russian displays at the 1862 London exhibition. It is on this evidence that malachite grounds have been traditionally attributed to Alsager & Neville, but it was a style taken up by other manufacturers like Jennens & Bettridge and their successors J. Bettridge & Co., and it frequently appeared, for example, in pattern books used by Wolverhampton japanners from the 1850s (?) through to the 1880s.[viii]

To judge from these pattern books, the range of imitative effects was considerably greater than surviving products lead us to suppose, both for all-over grounding and for enriching decorative borders. Indeed, such was their popularity that some factories had to devote workshops specifically to their production.

Besides green malachite, there was, somewhat fancifully, pink malachite as well as blue, and also noted were green and Siena marbles. Of the simulated woods, there were oak – light, dark and knotted – maple, rosewood and satinwood, as well as pine, yew and ash, but the most popular was burr-walnut. They were all used on both tin and papier mâché, but in the Wolverhampton pattern books, these effects featured mainly on tin coal boxes, toilet wares, trays and waiters – all mainstay products of the period.

Wood-grain and malachite effects were done by simply combing the pattern into a coloured varnish while it was still wet, allowing the paler varnish beneath to show through. The quality varied greatly, from closely observed, almost *trompe l'oeil* effects, to the frame of the exquisite flower painting seen here, and to the quickly executed work found on utilitarian goods (plates 31 and 33).

33. Painted tin panel, with bevelled tin frame japanned in imitation of burr walnut;
Bilston, or Wolverhampton, c.1835. 29 x 24cm

© WOLVERHAMPTON ARTS AND MUSEUMS SERVICE, www.blackcountryhistory.org

It was also possible to produce the effect of inlaid wood. Devised by a man named Hobson, this decorative finish, was achieved by 'stopping out' the design onto a japanned ground with either sugar-water or liquorice-water. When dry, the entire surface was coated with colour and again left to dry. The parts which had been stopped out peeled from the surface leaving black, or wood-grained ornaments against a coloured ground.

After the 1880s, simulated grounds were seldom used on the best goods, but wood-grain effects continued into the twentieth century as popular finishes on travel trunks, toilet sets and other utilitarian wares. Quickly produced by varnishers rather than artists, they were often crude and clumsy in contrast to earlier imitations. A description by a former workshop manager of how fire-buckets and hot-water jugs were wood-grained at the Bilston firm of Froggatt & Tyler is probably applicable to all workshops which produced these low-priced goods. He explained that when the surface had been painted with the appropriate colour it was 'daubed' with a 'special', but unidentified, powder mixed with a small amount of beer – the amount must have been very small indeed for only a pint of beer was purchased at a time.

viii. Some of the pattern books given to Wolverhampton Art Galleries & Museums by Loveridge & Co., on their closure in 1927, appear to have come originally from the Walton factory. Loveridge may have purchased them at Walton's bankruptcy sale in 1847, or at the sale of their stock-in-trade in 1883 (see Ch. 9).

34. Tin tea caddy with a hinged lid (*cf.* pl. 80), and snuffers tray, both with crystallised grounds; probably made at the Old Hall, Wolverhampton, c.1835. 9 x 13 x 11.5cm and 25cm respectively

<small>WOLVERHAMPTON ARTS AND HERITAGE (BANTOCK HOUSE MUSEUM)</small>

'BRIGHT-CUT' or INCISED DECORATION. This method of decorating japanned tinware was introduced in about 1780, and it closely resembled the patterns of contemporary 'bright-cut' silver. No records have been found which describe the technique although, clearly, it involved the use of variously-shaped gravers or burins. Since no trace of varnish is ever found in the incisions, it would appear they were made after the object had been japanned and stoved, but before the varnish had hardened, thus ensuring clean-cut edges. The absence of any protective layer of clear varnish over the cut parts begs the question of why the exposed metal has not succumbed to rust, but until such time as a contemporary explanation is discovered, the answer must remain a mystery. Bright-cut decoration appears to have been confined to workshops in Bilston and Wolverhampton; it is found on small articles like snuffboxes, tea caddies and bottle stands (plates 36, 296 and 303). It may be significant that Wolverhampton was also an important centre for the manufacture of cut-steel toys, some of which were similarly bright-cut.

CRYSTALLISED TINWARE. Crystallised surfaces were similar in appearance to the patterns made by frost on a window. The means of producing this decorative effect was patented (#4146) in 1817 by Louis Felix Vallet, who described himself as a 'gentleman' of Walbrook, in London.[ix]

As the decoration could be applied only to pure tin or tinned metals, it was undertaken prior to any other form of orna-mentation. The article, after being cleaned with a solution of

potash, soap or any other alkali, was rinsed in water, and heated 'to a temperature which the hand can bear.'[29] It was then lightly brushed or sponged with acid to create the frosted pattern; any acid was suitable, but Vallet recommended a combination of sulphuric and nitric acids. Further applications could be made until the desired effect was achieved. Andrew Ure, writing in 1839,[30] explained how, once the crystalline spangles had begun to appear, it was possible to achieve finer variegations of pattern by sprinkling the surface with water, by blowing cold air onto the surface through a pipe, or by running over it with the pointed flame of a blow pipe. Whatever method was used, great care had to be taken to avoid damaging the thin film of tin-plate.

The metal was finished with a clear varnish tinted with pigments such as verdigris, lake, blue, or yellow, which allowed the pattern to show through, and polished in the usual way (plate 34). The crystallised effects were generally enhanced with touches of gold leaf, sometimes with border stripes, and later, with printed decoration (plates 35 & 181).

In 1827, Ryton & Walton of Wolverhampton advertised as 'manufacturers of Vallet's chrysalised [*sic*] articles', they were 'the chief if not the only makers'[31] of such goods – at least during the first half of the century. Snuffers trays bearing the mark of the Birmingham retailers, Mapplebeck & Lowe, were perhaps made in Wolverhampton, and together with tea-caddies, are among the objects most frequently found with crystallised decoration.

---

ix. A similar, but slightly more complex method had earlier been patented in France, by M. Allard in c.1814, where the effect was known as Moiré Métallique.

35. Tin tea canister with lift-off lid, printed in black over a yellow crystallised ground, lettered above the foot-rim 'J Bartlett & Son, Bristol, Tinplate Decorating Co., Neath, Gowers Patent'; late nineteenth/early twentieth century. 14.5cm

PRIVATE COLLECTION

36. Tin tea caddy with incised decoration; made in Bilston or Wolverhampton, 1780–1800. 12 x 14 9cm

PHOTO © VICTORIA AND ALBERT MUSEUM, LONDON (Museum No. W.72-1919)

Pearl decoration

'A *favourite material for ornamenting papier mâché is mother-of-pearl, and the artist cannot certainly be accused of want of liberality in the use of it.*'

Cyclopedia of Useful Arts, Charles Tomlinson, 1854

The earliest mention of pearl in connection with the Midlands japanning industry is found in a patent (#1180) granted to Henry Clay in 1778, for making papier mâché buttons which amongst other things, might be 'inlarged [*sic*] with pearl, stones, mettal and various other ornaments.' In other words, the paper buttons were set into pearl mounts as distinct from later products in which pearl formed part of the decoration of the japanned surface. Eight years later, Obadiah Westwood suggested that his paper buttons might be 'inlaid with pearls',[32] but was unclear about whether he meant beads rather than decorative motifs cut from flakes of pearl. Whatever Clay and Westwood intended, neither patent appears to have much in common with the more familiar form of pearl decoration – introduced in the 1820s – which became almost synonymous with Victorian japanned ware (see plate 41).

A dusting of tiny pearl pieces, in imitation of Japanese *makii* effects, is sometimes found on late eighteenth/early nineteenth century goods such as tea caddies and trays (plate 37), but except for those items, pearl was seldom used by early Midlands japanners. This is surprising on two counts: first, English

japanners had used it in the late seventeenth century to decorate furniture made in imitation of eastern lacquered goods, and second, Birmingham, as the centre of the English pearl industry, had several shell-dealers and a number of established pearl-workers making buttons, ornaments and other luxury goods

37. Oval papier mâché tea caddy, the surface powdered with pearl-dust in imitation of ancient Japanese lacquer; probably Birmingham, late eighteenth century. H: 11.5cm

COURTESY OF SWORDERS, STANSTEAD MOUNTFITCHET

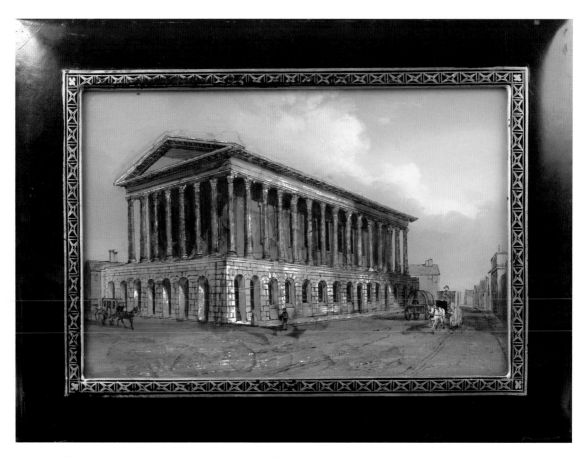

38. A 'patent pearl glass' panel printed and painted with a view of Birmingham Town Hall, in a papier mâché frame, c.1850. 22.5 x 30.5cm. (According to legend, the Town Hall was built on a foundation of waste shell from the town's pearl-working industry.)
© Birmingham Museums & Art Gallery (450'29)

(plate 38). In Wolverhampton (save for an isolated reference in 1751[33]), and Bilston, there is no evidence of a pearl-working tradition, and shell decoration was not used in the japan workshops of either town until several years later than in Birmingham.

At first, the shell sold in Birmingham came mostly from New Zealand, and some from Guernsey, but by the 1860s, japanners and button-makers were using pearl from the East Indies, South America and many parts of the Pacific. The three types of mother-of-pearl seen in use at McCullum & Hodson's factory in the mid nineteenth century: aurora, snail, and white, were those used by the japanning industry as a whole; 'aurora' and 'snail', for example, were noted alongside a design in a contemporary pattern book from a Wolverhampton factory.[34]

The pearl employed on the best goods was selected for its marking (plates 23 and 39). According to one anonymous author, aurora shell was preferred for 'the various and brilliant colours it displays', but its wavy markings, though good for 'vine leaves, oak leaves and even for some flowers', made it unsuitable for roses as it 'cannot convey the idea of a globular form.'[35] Instead, roses, 'convolvuluses, and other flowers which have an apparent centre' were best done with snail shell on account of it being concentrically marked 'in the way that water is, when a large stone has been thrown into it';[36] it was also useful for delineating fruit. White shell, with its lack of markings, was especially suitable for tulips and other large flowers and for landscape views (plate 40).

The scaly layers of the shell were separated with a small cutting-engine, or by being dipped in nitric acid, before they were cut into flat sections with nippers and ground by hand. This was usually done by boys and girls who filed the shell on both sides until it was even and of the required thinness; to steady the pearl, they sometimes stuck it to the work-bench with wax. It was a slow and tedious method but less hazardous than the mechanical one which replaced it. This required the workers to press the shell against a rapidly rotating grinding-wheel with the palms of their hands, until it was anything between one-fortieth and one-hundredth of

39. Writing slope – the lower drawer from the lady's cabinet shown in Plate 199.
Wolverhampton Arts and Heritage (Bantock House Museum)

50

an inch thick – the finer the article to be decorated, the thinner the shell. Since they used only a small piece of corduroy to protect their hands and wore no protective masks, the dangers and health risks were many. The problems suffered by pearl button-makers, and described by Thackrah in 1832 would have applied equally to pearl-workers in the japan trade. 'The pearl dust', he said, 'produces often bronchial irritation and this excites pulmonary consumption in individuals predisposed to the disease', moreover, he continued, these workers were 'generally intemperate, devoting two days a week to the impairment of their health!'[37] Any possible link between the dusty atmosphere in which they worked and their excessive drinking seems to have been overlooked.

Once ground, the shell was ready to be cut into decorative motifs. Very thin shell could be cut with ordinary scissors if it was first softened in hot water, but it flaked easily and was difficult to handle; neater edges were achieved by using thicker pieces and a fine frame-saw and file. Both techniques were rather slow but George Souter, a decorator at Jennens & Bettridge, devised several faster methods which his employers patented in 1825 under the title: 'Certain Improvements in the Method or Methods of Preparing and Working Pearl Shell into various Forms and Devices for the Purpose of Applying it to Ornamental Uses in the Manufacture of Japan Ware and of other Wares and Articles to which the same can be applied'.

This patent (# 5137) has generally provided the date for the introduction of pearl decoration into the Midlands japanning industry, and quite reasonably so, for while it almost certainly marks the culmination of a period of experimentation, there is no evidence of local japanners using pearl much before then. It is most likely, therefore, that Souter's so-called 'improvements' were based upon traditional methods borrowed from craftsmen in the general pearl trade. His patent covered four methods of cutting ground-pearl:

1. The intended shape was drawn, or 'stopped-out' on a piece of shell, with a very fine brush, known as a 'camel-hair pencil', dipped in a solution of asphaltum and either oil or spirits of turpentine. When dry, the surface was brushed with nitric acid to corrode the unprotected parts, and the asphaltum removed from the remaining motif with a solvent.
2. The pearl was painted all-over with a similar stopping-out fluid, and the design drawn into the dry, painted surface with an etching needle. The surface was brushed with acid which, because it attacked only the shell exposed by the etched outline, left the drawn shape intact.
3. Thicker pieces of shell could be decorated in relief by stopping out those parts which were to remain prominent and brushing the surface with acid to eat away the unprotected parts. It was a technique seldom used in japanning.
4. Six to twelve pieces of shell, no thicker than ⅟₈₀in., could be cut simultaneously by cementing them together and drawing the intended design on the top layer. The pearl-stack was fixed in a vice, filed, drilled and sawn into shape, and the pieces separated with solvent.

Notwithstanding these improvements, the old methods still prevailed: in 1850 for example, at McCallum & Hodson's, workers were seen cutting pearl with scissors, and by eye, into leaf, fruit, and flower shapes. In other cases quick alternatives were resorted to, which involved stamping or saw-piercing the pearl; they were clumsy by contrast, but as Aitken observed, they avoided infringing Souter's patent.[38] Possibly one of the most bizarre attempts to evade the patent was made by the Birmingham japanners Woodward and Midgeley, who tried gluing pearl to thin sheet-copper, marking the outline of the motif on the mounted shell and then sending it to the saw piercers to be cut; it was so impractical they gave it up.

Thus, it was customary for the larger japanners to engage several boys to grind and flake pearl. However, a man named Morgan, himself once a pearl-filer in the japanning industry, saw the potential in developing the craft as a separate trade. He set himself up in business in Aston, near Birmingham, cutting pearl into various forms which could be readily combined for ornamental work. This saved japanners both time and money, and thereafter many bought ready-cut pearl from Morgan and other specialist suppliers.

40. Papier mâché blotter cover (detail) showing delicate washes of colour over white pearl; mid nineteenth century. 30.5 x 23cm
PRIVATE COLLECTION

Contrary to appearance, pearl was not inlaid into the japanned surface in the generally accepted sense, but attached to the article, either before or after the first coat of varnish and prior to any further decoration. Even so, the manufacturers themselves, and most contemporary commentators, referred to it as 'inlaid pearl', as do most collectors today. It is nevertheless, a misnomer.

Before commencing the pearl-work, the design was drawn, full-scale, on paper and the outlines of the parts to be pearled were pin-pricked. The paper was laid on the surface which was to be decorated, pounced (see glossary, p. 325), or dusted with fine whiting, gently brushed and lifted off to reveal dotted outlines of white powder where the pearl was to be positioned; these areas were painted with gold size or with copal varnish and left until tacky. Each piece of pearl was taken up with a thin stick or a sharp iron instrument tipped with sticky gold size and carefully placed in position. Little of the pearl was wasted; tiny off-cuts were used to create decorative, so-called, 'scrap-pearl' designs (plate 41) and its dust was sprinkled on wet varnish to give a sparkling powdered effect (plate 63). When all the shell was in

41. Papier mâché blotter-cover, showing the use of both carefully selected pearl to convey form, and the use of scrap-pearl in the border; mid nineteenth century. 23 x 15cm

place, the article was stoved to fix the varnish. The entire surface, including the pearl motifs, was then coated with tar-varnish and given another stoving, after which the article was 'placed in the hands of a woman'[39] who, using the finest pumice-stone dipped in water, removed the varnish from the face of the pearl and smoothed any roughness elsewhere. This was a delicate operation as too much pressure would crack the thinner films of pearl, particularly on curved surfaces where they were applied in small sections to accommodate the rounded form. This process was repeated until the level of the varnish was flush with that of the pearl. The surface was then polished with chamois leather.

Occasionally, pearl served as the only ornament, but at other times gold leaf might be used for discreet embellishment (plate 42), or in the case of scrap-pearl, to outline and give shape to an otherwise indistinct pattern. Mostly, however, it was used in conjunction with painted decoration and incorporated into the overall design by being brushed with thin washes of transparent varnish colours to allow the marking of the pearl to show through. At its very best, the effect was stunning, giving iridescence to the feathers of an exotic bird or to the delicate wings of a butterfly; at worst, it could be clumsy.

A style of decoration in which the pearl was picked out in mauve and grey, was known as 'ceremonial ware'. It was produced during the period following the death of Prince Albert in 1861, but as George Dickinson dryly observed in *English Papier Mâché* (1925), it was so subtle that, 'had it not been suggested it is unlikely that one would recognize that it was intended for mourning ornament.'[40] Blotters, inkstands, paper-racks and work-boxes were decorated in this manner.

Frequent use, combined with over-rigorous cleaning has damaged the overlying varnish colours on many objects found today, and parts of the pearl are exposed. There have been misguided attempts to disguise this by removing all remaining varnish from the pearl, and the unhappy results are often taken to be the decorator's original intent. Such treatment is easily detected not merely by the starkness of the pearl within the overall design, but by the jagged, slightly raised edge of the surrounding japan varnish. In all but the cheapest pearl-decorated goods, it was not possible to feel where the shell and japan surfaces met – a test which many pieces still pass today. Sometimes, however, oils in the japan varnish have dried out and caused its surface to shrink below the level of the pearl; this is an irreversible ageing process and probably results from a deficiency in the original varnish, but it is not how the article would have left the factory.

Contemporary opinion was divided on the merits of pearl decoration. One saw it as 'by far the most chaste style of decoration',[41] while another lamented that 'Flowers and fruit do not shine and glitter; but tinfoil does: and there is too much of a tinfoil look about this method of ornament.'[42] Even the pearl decoration on a papier mâché piano for which Jennens & Bettridge were awarded a Prize Medal at the Great Exhibition, received muted reaction from one exhibition juror who thought 'the ornaments ... in good taste and well executed', but 'scarcely suitable in style for the materials employed, which being necessarily in small pieces, would have probably told with better effect if arranged in the form of a mosiac'.[43] The public appeared to like pearl decoration, however, and its popularity continued unabated for several years. By the 1860s, some manufacturers began to display 'a morbid taste for ... placing great blotches of pearl upon articles made of pulp, and finishing them in the gaudiest of colours',[44] with the outcome, it was said that 'trained workmen had the painful alternative either to pander to a depraved taste or leave the trade.'[45] 'It will be a great benefit', George Wallis wrote in 1862, 'when it is once seen that the more difficult the piece is to cut in the pearl the worse for the effect of the work when it is done.'[46]

Towards the end of the 1860s, pearl was in short supply because of the failure of fisheries on the coast of Central America; inevitably, its price rose, reducing its consumption among the various Birmingham trades by about a third to 300 tons per year. New supplies were found off the Australian coast, but whereas in 1865 pearl had cost £20-30 per ton, by 1886 its price had more than doubled to £50-70. Thus, economics rather than aesthetics, probably played the greater part in the demise of pearl decoration on japanned goods.

Polishing

'The finest of aristocratic ladies, whose hand is seldom out of her glove, could not polish a pen-dish, or door-plate. She might possibly find that she had scratched it.'
Harriet Martineau, *Household Words*, 1851

When the various imitative effects and pearl work had been done, and the final japan varnish had been applied, the article was polished in readiness for further decoration. This, its first polish (as distinct from smoothing), was perhaps the most important of all, providing the painters and gilders with a flawlessly smooth, shiny surface upon which to work. All subsequent polishing between the various stages of decoration, was done in exactly the same way.

Many pieces of eighteenth- and early nineteenth-century papier mâché and tinware now have matt and crazed or sometimes lightly pitted surfaces. This is because the oils in the varnish have dried out – it is not how articles appeared when they were first made. Contemporary diarists, after visiting Henry Clay's factory, frequently commented upon the high varnish of his goods and Robert Adam went further by praising some of Clay's door panels for being 'so highly japanned as to appear like glass'[47] (pp. 128-130).

42. King-gothic papier mâché tray sprigged with pearl flowers and birds and highlighted with gold leaf; impressed: 'JENNENS & BETTRIDGE / BIRMM' beneath a crown, c.1840. 47 x 63cm
COLLECTION OF ANTHONY PHIPPS

This high polish we are told by Richard Warner, a visitor to Clay's workshops in 1801, was given by a 'party of ladies who polish [the tray] with sand and water to take off every roughness, and give one uniform smooth surface. The fine polishers then take it, who give it the beautiful brilliancy of its appearance, with rotten stone and rubbing of the flat hand.'[48]

To judge from later accounts, these methods changed little over the years, and the work continued to be the remit of women. They worked at a thick smooth bench in the 'polishing shop' where, after removing every speck of dust from the varnish with pumice stone and water, they rubbed the surface first with a 'bob' – a piece of chamois leather, wool or cotton containing pulverised pumice-stone – and then with another containing pulverised rottenstone. Except for being cleaned with a soft duster, this was usually sufficient for inexpensive goods. There are no records of how they polished the interior surfaces of small boxes, so it must be assumed they used their finger-tips and a cotton bob for the interior corners.

If a very high gloss was required, the article was given a further polishing, this time with the bare hand. The polisher, or 'hander' as she was known, rubbed a little finely powdered rottenstone and a few drops of oil on the ball of her hand and worked over the surface, sometimes for upwards of half an hour, frequently cleaning her hand on a piece of leather. Finally, 'daubing the work with little touches of oil, which she [had] smeared upon her left wrist',[49] she removed any dust from the surface, and all traces of oil with a piece of silk which she kept pinned to her apron.

Their hands became conditioned to this gruelling repetitive work and, with the help of salt-water, it was said their palms, although remaining soft and smooth, became as tough as leather. When they were not polishing, the handers wore

43. Round tin box with lift off lid, containing the seal of the Grant of Arms to Sir George Lyttleton of Frankley, Worcestershire, in 1757. The central reserve is thinly painted to allow the underlying silvery, tinned surface to show through; London, or Birmingham, c.1756/7. 7 x 2cm REPRODUCED WITH THE PERMISSION OF BIRMINGHAM LIBRARIES & ARCHIVES (HH BOX 76 No. 357406)

Thus, not only did some early japan artists paint to a standard worthy of attention from a prestigious London manufacturer, but their skills were readily transferrable despite their unfamiliarity with the colour changes which took place when ceramics were kiln-fired. Although there is now no way of knowing whether it was made in the Midlands, London, or Wales, the box shown here, in (plate 43), is a good early example of japanned tin.

With the Staffordshire potteries to the north of the Midland japan centres, and the Worcester china manufactories to the south-west, the shift of painters between the two industries, and at every level of competence, was probably more frequent than can now be proved. In addition, there were other local trades from which artists might be drawn or with which, as journeymen painters, they might be shared. Similarities of decoration between japanned goods and enamel boxes made in Birmingham, Bilston, and South Staffordshire in the eighteenth century, and between canal-boat painting in the nineteenth century, are often too close to be coincidental and are surely indicative of the peripatetic employment of at least some decorators (plate 44). Indeed, some of the earliest Birmingham enamel box-lids are fitted onto japanned iron or copper bases.

Moreover, it seems reasonable to suppose that when the Birmingham enameller, John Taylor, added japanned tinware to his manufactures in about 1740, he would have deployed the skills of his existing enamel painters for the purpose. If contemporary accounts are to be believed, Taylor paid 'one servant', or workman, £3 10s 0d per week (£3.50p) for painting boxes; at the rate of a farthing each, that amounted to a staggering weekly total of three-thousand, three-hundred and sixty boxes. Whether they were japanned or enamelled is unclear and in this instance immaterial, as the significance here is the speed with which run-of-the-mill boxes were painted. The rapidity of the japan artists was not lost on Wedgwood who in 1770, wrote to his partner Bentley:

> You certainly judge very right when you say we must have a second and a third sort of painting... I would have what quantity I could get done in the best manner, to please the nicest eye, and shew what we can do; but at the same time I would get all I could done in such a manner as Mr Wilcox, a Japaner [sic], Fan, or Waiter Painter could do them, and I think I may venture to assert that if all your present stock of plain vases were done in that way they would be sold in a few days, and more money got <u>in the same time</u> by these common paintings, than by the very fine ones, and <u>no credit lost to us</u>, as we shall have <u>very fine ones</u> for <u>very fine Folks</u>.[55] [Wedgwood's underlining]

This was less of a sleight to japanners than it may seem for decoration of a 'second' and 'third' order at the Wedgwood factory almost certainly represented painting of the first quality from lesser potteries.

gloves by way of protection, prompting one factory visitor to note a 'degree of gloved carefulness not usual in their rank in life.'[50] Moreover, they took care never to 'wield the scrubbing brush or handle the broom',[51] a fact endorsed by the daughter of one of the last hand-polishers to be employed at the Loveridge factory in Wolverhampton during the 1920s, who said that her mother would never wash dishes, not from laziness, but from fear of losing her livelihood.

A clumsy but no doubt well-meaning commentator said of the best trays, 'it is pleasant to know that it is to the fair sex, who have made the graces of the tea-table so peculiarly their own, that we should be indebted for the lustre of its most indispensable accompaniments.'[52] How sad then, given the 'unrivalled polish' they gave to the finished goods, that each hander, a 'hard-working, poorly dressed woman with long, bony, turned up fingers, skinny and yellow'[53] was looked down upon by others in the factory as a lowly, unskilled worker.

Painted Decoration

An early indication of painted decoration on Midlands japanned goods is found in an advertisement in Aris's *Birmingham Gazette* in 1753, for the Bow China Factory, in London:

> This is to give Notice to all Painters in the Blue and White Potting way and Enamellers on China-Ware, that by applying at the Counting-House at the China-Works near Bow, they may meet with Employment, and proper Encouragement, according to their merit. Likewise Painters brought up in the Snuff-Box Way, Japanning, Fan-painting &c. may have Opportunities of Trial.[54]

This movement between japanners and potters continued throughout the nineteenth century. Two who made the transition from ceramics to japanning were Richard Steele, who was lured from The Potteries to 'improve the painting of natural flowers'[56] at the Old Hall in Wolverhampton; and William Bourne who, with a particular aptitude for painting verbenas, moved first to Wolverhampton and then to Birmingham. Moreover, since the japan and enamel painters in Bilston between 1800 and 1839 are known to have had an artists club at the Angel inn, where they freely discussed their crafts, it is likely that a similar bond existed between workmen in the two trades in Birmingham. In terms of painted styles, therefore, the history of japanning had much in common with other contemporary decorative industries. However, in terms of painting methods, the processes used in japanning were very different.

PAINTING METHODS. Though styles of decoration varied according to fashion and caprice, the methods used to paint japanned ware changed little during the course of the industry.

Prepared pigment was increasingly available from specialist colourmen in the eighteenth century, but some japan painters continued to grind their own or, as at Ryton and Walton (*qv*) had them prepared 'under their own eye' by the 'grinder'[57] who was employed especially for the purpose. Obadiah Ryton, for example, anxious to expedite orders taken during a particularly successful selling trip to Liverpool in 1792, wrote to his brother at the factory asking him to 'order Sall the Grinder' to prepare some blue pigment and to ask for 'Ester to mix it with oil Varnish and [to] strain it well.'[58] Benjamin Mander (*qv*) still had a colour-grinder in his employ in 1817, though obviously the work did not fully engage her as she was said to have 'filled up her time in picking gum'.[59, x] There is now no way of knowing the extent to which painters continued to prepare their own colours. As late as the 1850s, there were artists at Woodward & Midgley's factory in Birmingham, with stone slabs for grinding their own colours, but elsewhere the habit was likely to have diminished concomitant with the rising demand for japanned goods. According to George Wallis, an influential advocate of art education and once a tray painter himself, the practice had virtually died out by 1880. He looked wistfully back to when japan artists ground their own pigments and 'knew exactly what they were using'. This, he added, 'is more than can be said of nine-tenths of the painters nowadays.'[60, xi]

Like all workshops in which varnish was used, the painting shop was kept at an evenly warm temperature to allow the paint to flow freely, and it was also draught-free to prevent any particles settling on the work. A photograph taken at the

44. Travellers' flat tin samples of snuff boxes. Bilston, or Wolverhampton, c.1820-30. Average meas. 7 x 5cm
WOLVERHAMPTON ARTS AND HERITAGE (BANTOCK HOUSE MUSEUM, LP334)

McCallum & Hodson factory in the early twentieth century shows a typical decorating shop with painters seated at benches around the edge enabling them to make maximum use of daylight.[xii] Artists who were seen working at easels at Jennens & Bettridge in the 1850s were the exception rather than the rule, and were probably engaged in painting ship and other panels. These were much in demand at the time and because of their size and format, would have been more easily painted on an easel (plate 146).

Each painter worked with a range of camel hair pencils of various sizes, using at least one for each colour. The smallest, with hairs ¾in. long and only about six in number, was used for delicate details like flower stamens or tiny droplets of dew on a petal; it was very difficult to control except in the most practised hands as too much paint, or too fluid a mix, soon resulted in clumsy lines and splodges of colour. Such accidents could be quickly wiped off, but time equalled money for both the painter and his employer. Also close to hand were palette knives, tins or cups[xiii] of turpentine and copal varnish, a rest for

x. Picking gum: the best gums were those which contained the largest, palest, and most transparent pieces of gum; the pieces were picked out by hand.
xi. This was obviously a widespread problem; the Pre-Raphaelite painter, William Holman Hunt had delivered a lecture to the RSA in London on a similar theme in April 1880 (*Colour*, V. Finlay p. 16).

xii. The present whereabouts of this photograph is not known, but it is illustrated in Shirley Spaulding Devoe's *Papier Mâché of the Georgian & Victorian Periods*, London 1971, fig. 50.
xiii. Cups were specially made for the purpose by firms like Albert Potteries Ltd., Burslem which amongst more domestic wares, made 'every description of China used by brassfounders, tinplate workers, japanners etc.'

45. Tin waiter, the foliage skilfully worked with a thin wash of asphaltum varnish over 'bright' gold-leaf; c.1850-60. Dia: 25.5cm

WOLVERHAMPTON ARTS AND HERITAGE (BANTOCK HOUSE MUSEUM, LP379)

however, this method proved to be 'too slow, and that of painting in the whole flower with white, and then tinting it as a whole', was soon adopted.[63]

The final operation in the painting department was the drawing of the thin stripe or 'filet' which is often found at the edge of japanned trays, boxes, and so on (plate 232). It was carried out by the liner, striper or fileter as he was variously known. These workmen frequently possessed remarkable skill and dexterity; George Dickinson wrote of one in particular, Mr Sadler, a workman at the Old Hall, who was remembered for his ability to hold a 30in. oval tray on the fingertips of his left hand, and with a single sweep of the brush, paint a continuous and even line round its edge.

When all the painting was done, the article was slowly stoved until the mixing varnish was thoroughly dry and hard. It was then sent to the gilding shop to be finished or, if no further decoration was required, it was sent for its final polish prior to packing and despatch.[xiv]

the hand to protect the work whilst painting, so-called 'fudge rags' on which to wipe brushes, and a candle and candlestick (presumably to extend the working day).

One of the most striking characteristics of the painting found on japanned ware is its smoothness and freedom from brush-marks. This was achieved by binding the pigment with transparent 'mixing varnish' – a mixture of copal varnish, oil and gum animi – which, when thinned with spirits of turpentine, allowed the colours to be laid evenly on the japan or pearl surface. Applying colour in this way was evidently a specialised skill to judge from an advertisement placed in Aris's *Birmingham Gazette*, in 1790, by Strickland of London, for 'Japanners and transparent painters'.[61] Besides aesthetic considerations, the use of mixing varnish kept costs down, since the smoother the colours, the fewer coats of varnish were needed which, in turn, reduced the amount of hand-polishing required.

Subtle colour gradations might be obtained by applying pigment in powder form. For example, the 'mysterious softness' of detail observed on some handscreens at Jennens & Bettridge was done by an artist who, after painting 'various flowers in white or cream colour', was seen to apply 'some colouring powder; depositing it in the darkest centre, and wiping it thinner and thinner towards the lighter edges.'[62]

A small tin waiter by an unknown maker shows this means of decoration to good effect (plate 45). As may be imagined,

THE PAINTERS. It was written in 1801 that there were essentially two sets of japan painters, 'one employed in delineating the little fancy patterns, the other in the more beautiful and difficult line of landscape and figure painting.'[64] Within these 'sets' was a distinct heirarchy of master painters, copyists, and apprentices who usually came to the industry by one of three routes. Some were minor easel painters in search of extra employment, generally as journeymen; some, as already shown, transferred from other decorative arts industries, and others were trained in the factory under the apprenticeship scheme.

There was no institutional art training available to eighteenth-century japanners or, indeed, for artists in any of the decorative arts industries. Although this was recognised as a problem as early as 1754, almost a century passed before schools of practical art were set up to address the problem, and even then the apprentices attended only part-time. In the meantime, japan artists and, by implication, designers of japanned ware also, received some art tuition in private academies as did Obadiah & William Ryton (qv) or, like Henry Clay (qv), they were apprenticed to easel painters. The majority, however, learned their skills by being apprenticed to the trade.

George Wallis, believed that japanning offered 'a very sound practical school'[65] for apprentice painters. George Lindsay, writing in 1878, shared this conviction and observed that he knew of:

46. Oval tin tray decorated in the style of George Morland, and initialled 'SR' – perhaps for Samuel Raven (see p. 322); probably made in Birmingham, c.1810. W: 65cm (approx.)
COURTESY OF CHANTICLEER ANTIQUES

several gentlemen of high position as artists, obtaining almost fabulous sums for their paintings, who owe their introduction to fame and more than that, their rapidity of execution at the easel – as important to the japanner as to the painter - to the systematic training and instruction which they obtained while practically employed as workmen in the japan shops of Birmingham and its neighbour town.[66]

Nevertheless, japan artists were not without their critics, and this prompted one writer in 1851, to rise to their defence:

It is an ignorant spirit that sets down iron and paper articles ornamented and painted as at "Birmingham"... The spirit referred to has many times characterised the beautifully executed pictures of Maclise as "Tea-tray Painting". Many men who have been honourably mentioned in connexion with Art have spent much of their time in painting tea-trays, and have not been ashamed of their occupation.[67, xv]

He may have had in mind two earlier Wolverhampton japan artists who were often cited in this context. The first was Edward Bird (*qv*), an apprentice tray-painter at the Old Hall, who rose to become Court Painter to Queen Charlotte in 1813 and a Royal Academician in 1815. The second was Joseph Barney (*qv*) who, by 1827, was described as a 'painter in fruit and flowers to His Majesty'; as the son of a japanner of the same name, he is thought to have occasionally painted japanned ware.[68] However, the term 'tea-tray painter' had obviously become one of abuse and the jibe at Daniel Maclise (1806-70) was loaded with the same derision as the term 'chocolate-box painter' in more recent times. However, the industry continued as a source of employment for skilled painters and, in 1878, artists of 'the highest available talent' were said to be still attracted to paint japanned ware.[69]

Collectors today like to attribute styles of decoration to specific artists, but it will be seen that the practical arrangements of the workshop dictated against this. The master painters produced the original designs from which copyists and apprentices worked and seldom repeated their design themselves; in some instances, the master never painted on actual objects. George Neville, a renowned painter of flowers, parrots and birds-of-paradise, was a case in point; as painting foreman, or workshop-manager, at Jennens & Bettridge, with a number of pupils working under him, 'his work at the time was mostly designing for copies and after about 1850, he did few, if any articles for sale'.[70] This was perhaps because, by then, he was co-partner in his own firm, Alsager & Neville (*qv*). There were of course exceptions like the decorator at Jennens & Bettridge who, in 1851, was seen painting a work-box and had 'a convolvulus in water before him'[71] as his point of reference. Until the introduction of the Copyright Laws in 1842, the 'original' itself might have been taken from a well-known painting (pl. 105), but this, like

xiv. The La Rochefoucauld brothers who visited Henry Clay's factory in 1785, observed that the final stage in making a papier mâché tray was 'to rub them with soft-soap and pieces of cloth and dry them in drying-stoves.' However, their comment is ambiguous and could refer to the final stage before trays were painted (Norman Scarfe, *Innocent*

Espionage, 1995, p. 113).

xv. Birmingham was used as an umbrella-term for the midlands manufacturing area and should here be taken to include Wolverhampton and Bilston.

47. Tin tray with convex-edge, painted after George Morland; made in Wolverhampton, or possibly, Birmingham, c.1820–1830. 57 x 77cm

COURTESY OF KEITH PINN

copies of the master-painter's own originals, was regarded as the master's work and he received a royalty on every one sold. Master-painters were usually employed full-time at the factory and the most senior, with workshops of their own, enjoyed positions of considerable prestige and privilege. It is easy, then, to see how an artist like Edwin Haselar, with six apprentices working alongside him at the Old Hall, could afford to be 'something of a dandy [who] impressed his fellows by riding to and from his work on a big white horse,'[72] and how in the 1870s, master-painters were regarded as 'the aristocrats of the workers ... going to work in top hats and frock coats.'[73]

Some master painters were outworkers, as at McCallum & Hodson where the original 'oil painting' was done 'by properly qualified artists, who work at their own home.'[74] They too, were said to:

> earn large sums weekly; and all have what may be considered as excellent wages [with] one man who, having great skill in designing, earns at least £10 a week, and has done so for many years – sometimes he doubles that sum, but of course, such lucrative employment is the exception and not the rule.[75]

These outworkers were unlikely to have painted actual objects for, as George Wallis, who had over fifty years experience of the japan trade, emphatically stated, they had neither the stoves nor the varnishing equipment to do so. No more would the celebrated designer Owen Jones, who supplied designs for Walton & Co (qv), have decorated japanned objects, or John Heaviside of London, formerly Master of Birmingham School of Design (from August 1845 to March 1846), who exhibited 'designs for China and Papier Mâché amongst other things'[76] at the Great Exhibition in 1851. Nevertheless, there were journeymen, or peripatetic decorators like John Thomas (qv) who clearly undertook the painting of actual objects outside the more organised workshop environment.

Since an original work might have been copied over several years by a number of apprentices and copyists, it is clear why so few examples of painted tin and papier mâché were signed – notable exceptions being an oval iron tray signed 'SR' (plate 46), a small papier mâché panel signed by Richard Tyrer (qv) (plate 85) and two items from the Jennens & Bettridge factory: a table signed 'AE' (plate 137) and a toilet box decorated with an accomplished painting of Warwick Castle, which bears the interesting signature 'J Bettridge' (plate 139). It also explains why two paintings of the same subject can vary so much in artistic skill. But most importantly, perhaps, the practice of copying highlights the futility of attempting to attribute objects on the basis of subject matter alone. In their day, individual artists inevitably became linked with particular subjects or styles of ornament and George Dickinson provides a long list of these in his book: Davis with copies of George Morland's paintings (plate 47), William Bourne with verbenas, William Jackson with lilies-of-the-valley, Luke Amner with tulips, and so on, but with so many copyists, some of whom would have acquired considerable facility through practice, it is of no help today in identifying the work of these specific artists. Moreover, flowers and birds are perennial favourites for surface decoration and no artist or factory could possibly have had exclusive rights to them.

The apprentices and copyists worked either alongside their master, or in an adjoining room, copying perhaps from one of his finished articles, but mostly from designs he had painted on paper. A series of small designs, sold in London in the 1980s, had been used for this purpose at Jennens & Bettridge in the 1830s; each painting of a small spray of flowers, suitable for a tray-centre or for a box-lid, was mounted on thin card with a loop of string at the top so that it could be hung in front of the copyist. This was the practice at McCallum & Hodson also, where, in 1850, many painters were seen 'with painted groups of flowers before them, from which they were copying.'[77]

It was too costly for novice apprentices to paint directly onto japanned objects, so they practised on sheets of making-paper coated with several layers of japan varnish until they were sufficiently competent to work on actual articles alongside the copyists. Once apprentices had reached this stage, their employment was open to an abuse which severely threatened the livelihoods of experienced journeymen painters. 'Bystander' who was 'well aquainted' with 'those in the Japanning and Painting Business', drew attention to this as early as 1767, in his column in the *Birmingham Gazette*:

> *Some of the Masters seem to think, if they can have their Business done by 'Prentices for their Board, they have no Occasion to pay Wages to Journeymen, and it is well known one Master has had Eleven 'Prentices at one Time, and that the Number of Apprentices among Six Masters has amounted to upwards of Fifty.*[78]

In consequence, some journeymen, although regarded as 'good hands', found themselves in long-term unemployment. Was the deception 'not plain to see?' the article continued:

> *A Man that has served a regular Time, who perhaps has taken a Wife, and perceives a growing Family, and to his Parent also, who 'tis likely strained a Point to give him a Sum of Money, that his Son might support himself by an ingenious Art,*

because it would require no Capital to begin his Profession.[79]

Under a good master, however, the apprentice learned more than how to paint. William Highfield Jones apprenticed to work under John Perks at the Old Hall in the 1840s (and later a japan-master himself, see p. 212), fondly recalled his master's 'steady work':

> *He kept his eye on me during working hours, and urged me on whenever I flagged, to persevere. He taught me a lesson which was most usefull [sic] – for by him I learned to keep pegging away, and not be afraid of constant application to the work in hand. I have never been affraid [sic] of work since and could stick to it, under all circumstances ... And this faculty has been the making of me and largely been the cause of my success.*[80]

48. Gothic-shaped tin waiter, with unwired edge (see p. 21), painted decoration, and cork-stencilled border (see p. 66); Star Japan Company, Bilston, late nineteenth /early twentieth century. 26 x 19.5cm

WOLVERHAMPTON ARTS AND HERITAGE (BANTOCK HOUSE MUSEUM)

49. One from a pair of tin plaques with reed-moulded edges, depicting the *Flight into ...* (shown), and *Return from Egypt*, believed to have been made in Bilston; early nineteenth century. 24.5 x 33.5cm

<small>WOLVERHAMPTON ARTS AND HERITAGE (BANTOCK HOUSE MUSEUM)</small>

Not every apprentice was destined for such success: 'The painting requires close application and a good knowledge of drawing; and many persons after an apprenticeship of seven years, turn out but very indifferent workmen.'[81] Nevertheless, with their mechanical copying skills, there was a role for these less talented workmen in painting goods for the middle and lower ranges of the market, not only in small firms, but in large factories like Jennens & Bettridge which, as we have seen, catered for the middle market as well as the luxury one.

In 1866, it was said that 'A skilled artist can paint with ease two gross of small landscapes per day'.[82] This was not equal to the rate of Taylor's men (see p. 54) but it is impressive nonetheless. To work efficiently and competetively at this rate, artists would devise their own short-cuts. In order to paint a rose for instance, Mr Franklin, a decorator at Smith Armstrong (*qv*), of Bilston, in the early 1900s, would place some red paint alongside some white on his palette, run his brush through the two, simultaneously, and with one sweep, effortlessly paint a petal which subtly blended from red into white; in such expert hands, a spray of flowers was soon painted (plate 48). Thus, with constant practise, and a combination of speed and dexterity, many hack-painters achieved simple, yet charming effects, the earlier examples of which, today, are as keenly sought by collectors as some of the finer specimens (plate 48).

PAINTED DECORATION AND ITS STYLES. Samuel Schröder had drawn attention to gilt and coloured ornament on Birmingham japanned ware in about 1750 (p. 18), but the form and content of early painted decoration remain largely matters of conjecture.

A small tin box, made in 1756 to contain the seal of a Grant of Arms, and decorated with flowers on a green ground through which the tin surface is clearly visible, offers some clues (plate 43), but there are, besides, other pointers to serve as guides.

Dr Pococke,[xvi] for example, noted in 1756, that the Midland painters used colour, though his comments are too ambiguous to tell whether this was to create chinoiserie designs like those from Pontypool. However, in view of the influence of seventeenth and early eighteenth century japanned furniture, and of Pontypool tinware itself, it is probable that at least some Midlands products were decorated in oriental style. In addition, the anonymous correspondent to a Birmingham newspaper, in 1767, who wrote of the 'new Species of Japanning', commented upon its painted decoration, and noted a variety of ground colours upon which were painted 'a vast Variety of elegant Designs in Landskip, History, Pastoral, Conversation, Fruit, Flowers, &c.'[83] A description which, demonstrating the influence of *vernis Martin*, might well have included birds and chinoiseries. These were exactly the subjects which, alongside engravings of animals, shells, boats and rococo swags and borders, appeared in *The Ladies Amusement* (1758) – a popular design source for decorators of enamels, ceramics, textiles and silver, and a repository of all that was fashionable in contemporary decoration (plate 50).[xvii]

By the 1760s, records show that waiters, bread-baskets and other tin-ware made by John Baskerville were painted with fruit or flowers, with pastoral scenes, or with classical subjects such as the one he fulsomely entitled 'Agamemnon sacrifising his Daughter Iphegenia who is carryed away in a cloud by Minerva

---

xvi. Dr Pockoke was Bishop of Meath & Ossary.
xvii. *The Ladies Amusement or the Whole Art of Japanning Made Easy* was published in at least two editions between 1758 and 1762. With over 1500 engraved designs, it quickly became popular as a design source for the decoration of enamels, ceramics, textiles, silver etc. Some of the gold leaf ornaments on Pontypool japanned ware have been traced to this

volume and likewise, many designs on contemporary Birmingham, Bilston and South Staffordshire enamels. In view of the close links between enamelling and japanning in those centres, it seems likely that japan decorators in the midlands also looked to it for ideas.
xviii. Georg Christof Lichtenberg: German physicist and Professor of Mathematics at Gottingen University who visited Birmingham and its industries in 1775.

50. Engraving by Jean Pillement: plate 52 from *The Ladies Amusement or the Whole Art of Japanning Made Easy*, (see p. 60, and *cf.* pl. 189).

and a Hind left upon the altar' (see p. 117). As in other workshops, such pictures were probably copied from engravings of popular contemporary paintings or from Old Masters, the works of Raphael being especially favoured (plate 51).

These styles of painted decoration were thus in place by the time that Henry Clay, soon to become the most prominent japanner of his time, entered into partnership with John Gibbons in 1767. There is no proof that they were the styles they adopted, but as a former apprentice-painter and potential rival to Baskerville, Clay would have been very familiar with them. He was a man of great independent spirit who, when he set up in business on his own in 1772, wasted no time in introducing a style of painted ornament wholly new to papier mâché: the 'antique'. In so doing, he shrewdly captured a corner of the rich and fashionable market for neo-classicism alongside two of its foremost proponents: Josiah Wedgwood, and Robert Adam, with both of whom he would subsequently collaborate.

In 1766-7, Sir William Hamilton, Envoy Extraordinary to the Court of Naples, published a four-volume *Catalogue of Etruscan, Greek and Roman Antiquities*, with engravings and text by the French art-historian, Pierre Francois D'Hancarville, with the intention that they should serve as design sources for Britain's new manufactures. Drawing upon the current enthusiasm for classical excavations, Clay looked to these engravings for some of his antique designs: 'coffee trays and all sorts of vessels' were, according to Georg Lichtenberg, a visitor to Birmingham,[xviii] 'made and decorated in black with orange

51. Papier mâché panel in a japanned tin frame, the painting probably derives from a Renaissance original; Bilston, or Wolverhampton; early nineteenth century. 34.5 x 28.5cm

52. Papier mâché tea caddy stencilled with classical figures after d'Hancarville's drawings of Sir William Hamilton's antique vases; attributed to Henry Clay, c.1770–1775 (see p. 61). 10.5 x 12 x 9cm
MADRESFIELD COURT, WORCESTERSHIRE

colour figures in the manner of Etrurian vases',[84] much in the style of the small caddy illustrated in plate 52. But one of the most notable examples of Clay's work, which drew on D'Hancarville's engravings, is a japanned mahogany pembroke table made for Robert Child at Osterley Park, Middlesex (plate 110). However, these volumes were not the only source of classical ornament, as Robert Hunt noted many years later, in 1851. Some of the earliest papier mâché trays, he said, were decorated 'with polychromatic borders from the decorations in the Vatican and in the centres were painted monochrome groups of figures copied from the antique.'[85] In fact, Clay used contemporary engravings from a variety of sources. For example, a table from a set of six made by Henry Clay for Lord Bristol, and a fine oval paper tray in Birmingham City Museum, are both painted after a sixteenth-century painting by Beatrice Cenci which is in the Palazzo Barbarini, in Rome (plate 113). As Jabez Maud Fisher was later to observe, 'the Warehouse in which [Clay's] goods are exposed to Sale is like a Nobleman's Room hung round with paintings: Flowers, Landscapes, Fruit Pieces, Beasts, Portraits and History'.[86, xix]

Clay continued with the antique style for many years, but he did not hold a monopoly. In 1794, for instance, when japanner William Barrow proposed setting up a japan manufactory at Matthew Boulton's Soho works in Birmingham (p. 40), he intended mainly to make goods such as 'Roman Waiters &

Trays', similar to those he had made whilst employed by Francis & Guest (qv) between the years 1784 and 1789.
In the 'Statement of the Japan Trade' which Barrow prepared for Boulton, he described the other 'most prevailing' styles of painted decoration at Francis & Guest and, in so doing, usefully rehearsed the ranges which were popular across the industry in the last quarter of the eighteenth century. They were figure and landscape subjects, striped trays and waiters (plate 108), and articles with black, crimson or tortoiseshell grounds with coloured borders. This is borne out by an advertisement in the Birmingham Gazette in June 1788, which read: 'Wanted, painters that can execute figures and landscapes in a masterly manner.'[87]

Antique painting had had its day by the turn of the century, but 'history painting', usually copied from contemporary engravings of the Old Masters, continued as a favourite subject on trays and waiters until well into the nineteenth century. This category of painting – which included classical and mythological subjects as well as biblical and literary themes – was regarded by contemporary art connoisseurs as the highest art form of all. Also carried over into the new century, were scenes of topical interest commemorating a famous battle, for instance; the death of a prominent person; rural subjects; flowers, birds, butterflies; and all the other perennial favourites of decorators and public alike. Some of these were copied from well-known paintings but many were designed specifically for japanned ware.[xx]

xix. I am grateful to Peter Jones for his permission to use this quote.
xx. George Wallis cited Angelica Kauffman (1741–1807), Francis Wheatley (1747–1801), Giovanni Battista Cipriani (1725-85), Gavin Hamilton (1723-98), and John Singleton

Copley (1738–1815), as artists whose work was copied by japanners, and noted that the 'Woodman', by Thomas Barker of Bath (1767–1847), was especially popular.

In addition, the painters worked from a variety of other sources. These included topographical books of both British and Continental views published in the early nineteenth century which, though intended primarily for the libraries of gentlemen, became popular design sources for contemporary decorative artists, as did books of ornaments like Knight's *Gems*, or his *Fancy Ornaments*. Prints by James Gillray, Thomas Rowlandson, and others were much copied by painters of papier mâché snuff-boxes, and the paintings of Edwin Landseer and George Morland were thought especially suitable for copying onto japanned trays, tables and the like (plate 47).

If the painters were to keep up not only with fashion and taste, but with an increasing demand for japanned goods from the new middle class, styles of decoration had to change. New styles of painting, in keeping with developments elsewhere in the decorative arts, were introduced.

One of the most dramatic changes came in 1832, when Jennens & Bettridge introduced an 'improved' style of naturalistic flower painting. 'Until then,' it was noted, 'flowers were not painted in imitation of nature, but a sort of Chinese impasto'[88] (plate 53). The new style, characterised by sprays of flowers centrally placed against a plain background and framed by a

53. Straight-edge papier mâché tray decorated in variously coloured bronze powders in imitation of Oriental impasto decoration; umarked, though similar trays are stamped 'CLAY'; c.1810. 28 x 35.5cm

COLLECTION OF SARA TIFFANY, PHOTOGRAPH BY DON NELSON

border pattern 'was regarded by the trade as a bold step, but it seemed to hit the public taste, and the patterns put into the market continued to sell freely for nearly thirty years'.[89] George Lindsey, writing about papier mâché in 1878, named Edwin Haselar as the originator, although elsewhere the credit is given to George Neville (see p. 177), a fellow painter and rival at Jennens & Bettridge. Whomsoever it was, its exuberance was a radical departure from the earlier, more restrained styles of flower painting, and it continued as a recurrent theme both at this factory and others for the remainder of the industry.

There were other changes too. Hitherto, painted decoration had stood alone, or been highlighted with gold leaf, but with the introduction of mother-of-pearl into the design, as well as more florid gilded borders, painting often played only a small part in the overall decoration. This was not thought to have demeaned the painters – as one commentator wrote, the men who applied colour to the surface of the pearl motifs could 'certainly be termed *artists*';[90] and unquestionably, at its best, their work showed remarkable delicacy (plate 23). Moreover, there were other opportunities for painters to exercise their more traditional skills, notably on fine quality hand-screens and snuff boxes, and in the small, decorative vignettes found on the best boxes, caddies, and trays (plate 54). Yet, despite the quality of the painting, and with the exception of a number of snuff-boxes, these pieces, like earlier examples, were rarely signed by the artist. In the 1840s, a revived interest in all-over painted pictures in the form of panels for furniture, rooms, and ships saloons gave artists the chance for magnificent displays of virtuosity, but even they remained unsigned by the painter. Made mostly by Jennens & Bettridge, these panels were generally so competently painted that when a ship was broken up, they were salvaged and mounted in gilt frames; to this day they are frequently mistaken for traditional oil paintings on board (plate 146).

Inevitably, the quality of the painting reflects the original cost of the object – a fact touched upon in the following extract from the December 1844, edition of *The Penny Magazine*:

> *As in most other branches of art, there are manufacturers who serve the cheap as well as the good and for 3d or 4d the centre of a large tray is bedizened with fine staring flowers or ornaments by a process midway between painting and stencilling. But in the kind of work under notice at Jennens & Bettridge, the painters are really artists, competent in the landscapes, portraits and other specimens of the pictorial art, the minuteness and high finish of which are made to depend on the costliness of the article.*[91]

Every japan master knew his market and operated accordingly. When Edward Jones left the Old Hall to set up as a japanner in his own right, he believed it would have been foolish to continue with the style of decoration to which he was accustomed. It 'was rather too expensive to sell',[92] he said, so he compromised by devising a style that fitted between that, and so-called 'Bilston work'. The decoration of Bilston goods rarely rivalled that on Birmingham and Wolverhampton wares because, we are told, it was intended for export to Spain and South America etc., 'where brilliance of colour and cheapness is preferred to quality.'[93] As a result, japanners in Bilston were less affected by changing tastes and fashions – a situation which allowed several of them to outlive more prestigious firms in the neighbouring towns.

Thus, from the beginning of the industry until its close in the early twentieth century, the quality of painting found on papier mâché and tinware was as varied as the objects upon which it appeared.

Printed decoration

There were three types of printed decoration employed by japanners: transfer-printing, stencilling, and chromo-lithography.

TRANSFER PRINTING. The need to find quick and efficient ways of decorating japanned goods in order to meet growing demands, was evidently a matter of concern, even for the very earliest japanners.

As early as 1752, the engraver John Brooks had recognised the suitability of transfer-printing as a means of decorating japanned ware,[xxi] and advertised in *Aris's Birmingham Gazette*:

> *Such Gentlemen as are desirous of having WAITERS printed, may apply to John Brooks, Engraver, in the New Church-Yard, Birmingham, who is willing not only to treat with them on reasonable Terms, but also engages to execute the work in the most elegant Manner, with Expedition... N.B. He also recommends that his Work may not be spoil'd by committing it into Hands of unskilful Daubers.*[94]

And a few years later, in 1759, Stephen Bedford (*qv*) was granted a patent (#737) for:

> *impressing in imitation of ingraving* [sic] *upon varnish laid upon copper, iron, paper, and other bodys, to be used in coach pannels, snuff boxes, and other kinds of merchandize, and impressions of foliages, figures, decorations, ornaments, and other devices.*

---

xxi. Brookes' transfer prints are known to have been used on enamels made in Birmingham and elsewhere, but in this instance the reference to 'waiters' almost certainly alludes to japanned tinware for it was not until after 1780 that articles of that size could be enamelled.

xxii. This figure which is taken from W.H. Jones (p.126), seems inordinately high. A weekly aggregate of 5000 seems more realistic especially when compared with the 2000 tea-caddies which were said to have been produced weekly in Bilston (*Birmingham & the Midland Hardware District*, ed. Samuel Timmins, 1866, p. 122).

The part of his invention that he sought to protect was the substitution of a very thin sheet of rolled lead in place of paper which was used for transferring an inked impression from an engraved copper plate. Since paper transfers adequately met the needs of both the contemporary ceramics and enamelling industries, it is difficult to see the purpose of this innovation. Whatever Bedford's thinking, it was not a very practical idea; as Richard Prosser observed over a century later, 'the lead would certainly stretch and thus produce a blurred impression, and the metal would not yield up the colour very readily, but we have the principle of transferring clearly indicated.'[95] Indeed, it is as the earliest endorsement of transfer-printing specific to the japanning industry, that Bedford's patent has any value today.

The extent to which transfer printing was employed by japanners in the eighteenth century was greater than hitherto believed. Much of the decoration on Henry Clay's paper goods made in the 1780s, for example, was printed using a method adapted from Francis Egington's so-called 'mechanical painting' (pp. 319-320). Indeed, Egington's process appears to have formed the substance of a patent (#3219, see below) granted to London japanner Charles Valentine in 1809, which provides the earliest account of how prints were applied to japanned surfaces.

Notwithstanding, it is unlikely that transfer printing had not been employed for decorating more run-of-the-mill products in the intervening years. We know for example, that when Lady Shelburne visited John Taylor's enamel and japan factory in 1766, she was given an enamel box, *printed* with a landscape taken from a copper-plate engraving, and it seems not unreasonable to suppose that Taylor would have decorated his japanned tinware similarly.

Valentine adopted the standard method of copper-plate engraving, but instead of employing just one plate, he used four, shaded from dark to light respectively. On one sheet of gummed paper, he first transferred an impression from the darkest plate, then one from the second darkest, and so on. After about a week, when the print had thoroughly dried, it was evenly coated with the intended background colour mixed with copal varnish, left until tacky and applied to the japanned surface. The paper was peeled off and the printed article was stove-dried. If required, the print could afterwards be enhanced with transparent colours.

There followed another long silence on the subject until Gerard Barber of Bilston 'adapted the art of tranferring designs to japan waiters' some time after 1834, 'and this method has been generally adopted in the trade ever since.'[96] The method, though not explained, was suitable for a 'great variety' of designs, mostly of fruit and flower subjects, and had the effect of producing 'the smartest and most brilliant effect with the smallest amount of labour'.[97] By about 1860, it

54. Handscreens, lettered in script 'Warwick Castle' (left), and the 'Suspension Bridge, Yarmouth', decorated on the reverse with floral motifs in gold leaf; turned wood sticks, c.1840. 42 x 28cm
PRIVATE COLLECTION

was estimated that fifty-thousand[xxii] of these brightly coloured waiters were exported weekly from Bilston: the cheaper kinds to Russia, Norway, and to South America (where it is understood that the Brazilians favoured designs incorporating either a shield and crown or coffee berries), and to the Spanish colonies where birds and pagodas were especially popular. Large numbers of jugs and basins transfer-printed with thistles in red, blue and green and lettered 'Wallace' or 'Bruce', were apparently sent to Scotland.

Previous accounts of the japanning industry have alluded to a style of printed decoration which has come to be known as 'the Goodman Method', but viewed in the wider context, George Goodman's patent of 1852 (# 14,099) was essentially a reworking of Valentine's earlier one, and thus less significant than hitherto believed. Described in the title of the patent as a Birmingham 'manufacturer', Goodman was a japan artist who had been apprenticed to Jennens & Bettridge, and was noted for articles painted with church interiors. His patent was concerned, straightforwardly, with the transfer of copper-plate engravings and did not, as once asserted, involve attaching printed paper designs to the japanned surface and painting over them to conceal the print beneath. Nevertheless, the latter means of decoration had been in use since at least the 1820s on lids of papier mâché snuff-boxes, of both English and Continental manufacture, but the prints are sometimes so densely overpainted that it is difficult to discern the line engraving beneath. These have no more in common with Goodman's patent than the view of 'Scot's Grave' seen on a tray by B. Walton & Co., the scratched surface of which, showing white, suggests that like the above snuff boxes, it was painted over an applied print (plate 281).

STENCILLING. Henry Clay appears to have used stencilling, in the 1780s, on both large pieces of furniture, and on smaller products like trays and tea caddies (plate 17). However, stencilling was most commonly used on wares for the popular market. It was done in one of two ways, either with cut-paper shapes or, to a lesser extent, with cut-corks. Stencilling over shapes cut into paper, or 'paper cutting' as it was sometimes known, was widely adopted by japanners in about 1820 and continued in use until the closing years of the industry in the 1920s. It is seen to very good effect on a rectangular tin tray decorated with a scene depicting the *Gathering of the Unions on New Hall Hill Birmingham May 1839* (plate 55), in which some of the stencils have been repeated in different colours, to create, with the greatest possible speed, a crowd scene. Other, and sometimes more complex designs might involve multiple layers of paper stencils, one for each colour.

Cuthbert Bede, writing in 1880, said:

Such painted tea-trays are still hawked about country villages, and I frequently see them in cottages, reared up against the wall on a side table. Battle scenes are favourites, and are painted cheaply. Plenty of smoke is the formula, for the painter of these tea-trays could not afford to supply battles of Waterloo at one shilling each (thirteen to the dozen) if he did not stencil his figures through punctured forms, and then, with a liberal brush, throw in plenty of smoke. The misty wreaths afford evidence, to the bucolic mind, of the hotness of the conflict, and testify to the courage of the brave general whose cocked hat is surging above the sea of gun-powder.[98]

The stencils were cut from any scrap of paper provided it was thick enough. In fact, those used in the early twentieth century at the Star Japan Works in Bilston (*qv*), were cut from pages torn from old accounts ledgers (plate 240).

The second method, which involved the use of corks, was used mainly for repetetive border patterns; it is described later in relation to gilding (p. 74). Clumsy by contrast with the cut paper method, it was not much used until about the middle of the nineteenth century.

It was lamented in *The Visitors Guide to Wolverhampton*, in 1871, that paper and cork stencilling, together with transfer-printing, had 'revolutionised the trade' with the effect that 'japanning, which was formerly an art, has now become little more than a mechanical trade.'[99]

Nevertheless, stencilling in particular, lent the decoration of articles an immediacy and simplicity which today, along with their often topical subject matter and lively colouring, make them highly prized examples of English popular art from the nineteenth century. Curiously, they are found in greater numbers in America than in England, but this probably has as much to do with their earlier appreciation by mid twentieth century American collectors as with contemporary export (plate 56).

CHROMO-LITHOGRAPHY. The first known mention of chromo-lithography in the decoration of tin and papier mâché wares, appeared in 1851; it was heavily critical:

Some of the views upon papier mâché, sold at low price, have the details of buildings transferred from lithographic prints. However well they may be filled in, they look worthless; the distant objects looking so far as the details are concerned, as near the eye as those at the base line![100]

Notwithstanding, five years later, Samuel Tearne and George William Richmond[xxiii] of Birmingham, took out a patent for printing the design on to thin tissue paper from a series of litho-stones, one for each colour. Although used in 'the general japan trade',[101] chromo-lithography seems to have been particularly favoured by the bedstead manufacturers Peyton & Harlow of Birmingham (*qv*) for ornamenting 'the posts and other parts ... with scrolls, wreaths or flowers, either in gold or colour'.[102]

Gilding

'I have had infinite trouble with the gold leaf. I think it is the most fidgetty thing I ever used in my life. I have wasted a quantity. I could not make the knife separate it, and it stuck to my fingers, and then to the tip, and when I had it just over the drawing to put it down, away it flew half across the room; and I really could not place it down smoothly, it would fall so much in a heap.'
Gandee B. F., *The Artist or Young Ladies' Instructor in Ornamental Painting, Drawing etc.*

The exuberant gold leaf decoration, now almost synonymous with Victorian papier mâché and tinware was, like other aspects of the japanning industry, rooted in the decorative traditions of eastern lacquer. But gold leaf is only one of several types of metal ornament found on papier mâché and tin-ware. As in the East, there were other kinds of metal leaf

---

xxiii. Richmond was a lithographer who was, at one time, employed by one Thomas Underwood.

55. Convex-edge tin tray stencilled with the '"Gathering of the Unions" on New Hall Hill Birmingham May 18 1832', from the engraving by Henry Harris; Birmingham, c.1832. 54.5 x 7cm

© BIRMINGHAM MUSEUMS & ART GALLERY (1965f509)

56. Convex-edge tin tray with stencilled decoration; probably Bilston or Wolverhampton, c.1830. 46 x 6cm

PRIVATE COLLECTION, USA

available and a colourful variety of metal powders to offer the gilder a rich palette and an even richer range of decorative possibilities (plate 60).

The earliest gilding in the English midlands and, indeed, at Pontypool and other European japanning centres was, predictably, mainly oriental in style, but as japanners became more adept in their craft, so they felt less constrained by these influences using them instead as springboards from which to devise wholly new techniques and styles more in keeping with prevailing western taste. These stylistic changes are important in dating papier mâché and tinware, not least because regular revivals of some gilt patterns, and most particularly of traditional Eastern designs can be a source of confusion for modern collectors (plates 57 & 58). Therefore, while the various decorative metals used by japanners, and the methods by which they applied them, were similar to those used in other contemporary crafts and industries, it is appropriate to describe them here.

A wholly chronological survey of gilding would necessitate darting from one type to another. As this would serve only to confuse, each type of gilding will be taken in turn, starting with gold and other metal leaf, moving on to 'bronze' decoration, then to the so-called 'inlaying' of aluminium, and ending with what the japanners called 'raising'.

GOLD AND OTHER METAL LEAF. Metal leaf was made by rolling and hammering gold and other metals into sheets thinner than the finest tissue paper. Although japanners purchased some of their metal leaf from gold-beaters in Birmingham, their supplies came mainly from Germany in small books containing twenty-five sheets of metal each measuring about 3½ x 4in. (85 x 100mm) and interleaved with thin paper. The colour and quality varied according to the metal, or alloy of metals, from which it was made, but in skilled hands this variety allowed for extraordinarily rich effects and colour combinations.

In 1782, the retail cost of gold and silver leaf rose for the first time in thirty-six years 'since which' the gold-beaters pleaded 'every Necessary of Life is considerably increased in Price.'[103] Pure gold leaf (bright gold) was the most expensive, and in the 1920s, Samuel Loveridge, of Henry Loveridge & Co., was known to have kept his factory's supply locked in his office. No doubt earlier factory owners did likewise. Not surprisingly, a low carat second quality, at only one-twentieth of the price, was much more widely used. Even some alloys were

57. Sandwich-edge papier mâché tray decorated in Indian-style in 'dead' gold (see p. 69); impressed 'CLAY/KING S^T/COV^T GARDEN', c.1810 W: 66cm

58. Concave-edge papier mâché tray decorated in variously coloured metal leaf, in 'Old India' style; impressed 'Henry Loveridge & Co.', c.1860-70. W: 42cm

too expensive for anything but the best work; early nineteenth century japanners in Birmingham favoured a leaf made from the palest alloy by Robert Warner (*fl.* c.1803-c.1835) a local japanner, and from about 1829, a bronze-powder manufacturer also, but it cost two guineas an ounce (ie. £2.10p per 28 grammes troy). By contrast, so-called 'Dutch' gold (a corruption of 'Deutsch' and therefore really German gold) – a much-used substitute for all types of gold leaf – was only two-shillings and sixpence per thousand leaves (ie. 12½p per 12 grammes troy). By 1835, Hutton said 'the borders of the articles were usually painted with various devices' using 'yellow and Dutch metals' – by which, of course, he meant German – and coated with 'a spirit lacquer ... to make them look more like gold and silver leaf.'[104] Made from alloys of copper, brass and zinc, Dutch gold came in several colours and shades, but had one major drawback – it quickly discoloured if it was not varnished soon after application. Similarly, pure silver-leaf also tarnished, so alloys of tin or zinc were used in imitation.

Specific tools were necessary for laying metal leaf: a leather pad on which to cut the leaf, a palette knife, a plentiful supply of cotton wool, a burnisher, and a range of brushes: fine camel hair ones with which to draw the intended design, a broad, soft hogs-hair brush known as a 'gilder's tip' for lifting the leaf, and a smaller hogs-hair brush, or a cotton swab, to remove any excess leaf when the work was done. Dickinson, drawing upon conversations with retired japanners, told how the brushes were made by only two or three specialist makers and how, before using a new brush, a gilder would hold it up to the light, spread its hairs between his finger and thumb, and remove any that were coarse and likely to scratch the work.

The lament of a novice amateur japanner in 1838 – quoted at the head of this section – demonstrates that applying metal leaf was a delicate operation and, in the case of pure gold, an expensive one too. But for the commercial japanner, gold leaf was far too precious to waste and any 'sweepings' which adhered to his swabs or brushes, and any off-cuts, were 'carefully collected and sent to the refiners of whom the leaf was again bought'.[105] In 1758, for example, John Cox, a 'sweep washer' advertised in the *Birmingham Gazette* that he 'Buys and sells gold and silver sweeps, and refines for silversmiths.'[106] Swabs which contained metal leaf other than gold were sold to bronze powder manufacturers who, like the gold-refiners, burned them to extract the metal. A japanner could receive as much as six or seven pounds a year for recycling waste metal in this way.

The finished appearance of gold and other metal leaf depended upon the method by which it was attached, but essentially, oil-gilding produced a matt effect, and water-gilding, a burnished one. This was so for all types of metal leaf, whether pure or alloyed, and so for simplicity, and with

59. Oval papier mâché tea caddy with gilt *mapwork* borders (see *fn. vii*, p. 275). 11.5 x 12.6cm
Courtesy of Woolley & Wallis, Salisbury

few exceptions, the terms '*gold leaf*' or '*leaf*' will be used here to describe them all.

Oil Gilding. Robert Dossie wrote in 1758 that oil-gilding was the only method used for gilding japan work,[107] a fact which held true for the greater part of that century. The matt or 'dead gold' finish was entirely due to the oil-based gold size with which the leaf was attached. This was made from gum, asphaltum, umber and linseed oil, thoroughly blended to eliminate any coarse particles which would otherwise show up in the finished work, and mixed with a little vermilion to ensure that it remained visible on drying. It was thinned with oil of turpentine or, for a slightly brighter finish, with fat-oil – a term for concentrated linseed oil – and used, very sparingly, to paint the parts of the design which were to be gilded – too much gave the gold a pitted texture.

Henry Clay's mastery of gilding glossy japanned surfaces led the potter Josiah Wedgwood to seek his guidance on 'gilding in oil upon glazed ware'. Fortunately for us, Wedgwood noted the advice he was given in his *Common Place Book* and it shows how Clay had perfected the method described by Dossie. 'To secure the gold with a copal varnish', Clay recommended that:

> *It should be first covered with seed lac varnish, and then lay on the oil copal varnish; for if the copal varnish is laid on first, it destroys the lustre of the gold instantly.*

> *The same precaution is still more necessary in silvering; but instead of spirit varnish, use a solution of isinglass in water, filtered with a very little spirit of wine, a teaspoonful to two tea cups of the isinglass solution – the solution must be perfectly clear.*[108, xxiv]

---

xxiv. I am indebted to Anne Stevens for drawing this document to my attention and allowing me to quote from it, prior to the publication of her own book, *English Tea Caddies*.

60. Detail from plate 120, showing the use of variously coloured bronze powders.
WOLVERHAMPTON ARTS AND HERITAGE (BANTOCK HOUSE MUSEUM)

of oil which he had smeared on his wrist for the purpose. He pressed the leaf down and smoothed it with a pad of cotton wool wrapped in fine linen. When the work was dry, he gently removed any excess leaf with a swab or brush.

Two early nineteenth century tea-boards made in Henry Clay's workshops show how the process could be varied to produce different results. In the first example, the fine details of its chinoiserie design were painted in size and the metal leaf was attached according to the method described above (plate 60). By contrast, although the leaf was attached to the second tea-board in the same way, it was laid in larger patches and the detail of its 'Indian' style ornament was afterwards picked out or, to coin the workmen's terms 'etched' or 'pencilled', on the surface of the gold leaf with a camel-hair brush dipped in asphaltum varnish (plate 62).

GILDING WITH METAL POWDERS. Metal powders were used from the late eighteenth century until about the mid nineteenth century, and usually in combination with metal leaf (plate 63). They were not really powders but tiny flakes of metal leaf which were strewn over a sized surface and brushed or rubbed in to create a speckled or glittery effect similar to the *maki-e* or 'sprinkled pictures' of twelfth-century Japanese lacquer.

61. Straight-edge papier mâché tray sprigged in gold leaf, the underside lettered *India* in red script, c.1810. 59.5 x 78cm
WOLVERHAMPTON ARTS AND HERITAGE (BANTOCK HOUSE MUSEUM)

There were three types of powder: 'true' or pure gold powder, Dutch or 'counterfeit' gold powder, and *aurum mosaicum*. True and counterfeit powders were made by grinding the metal leaf in honey and leaving it to

Timing was crucial, for if the leaf was laid on when the size was too wet, it would wrinkle, and if the size was too dry, any joins in the leaf would show. When the size was sticky, but too dry to leave any trace on the finger, the leaf was picked up on the gilder's tip, or with a ball of cotton wool, and laid on the work. To avoid the leaf curling up on itself or wafting away on his merest breath, the gilder sometimes gave the tip, or cotton wool, greater adhesion by running it lightly through his hair or across a patch

stand in water until the particles had separated from the honey and settled; the water was poured away and the glistening flakes were left to dry on a sheet of paper. The method for making *aurum mosaicum* was altogether different and involved adding quicksilver (mercury) to melted tin; when cool it was ground with *sal ammoniacus* (ammonium chloride) and sulphur. The result, however, after further re-heating and cooling, was similarly, a 'mass of bright flaky gold powder'.[109]

62. King-gothic tray decorated in dead-gold with pencilled details; impressed mark: 'CLAY/KING Sᵀ/COVᵀ GARDEN, c.1825/30. 28 x 38cm

COLLECTION OF ASTRID DONELLAN

63. Concave king-gothic tray painted with exotic birds on a bronze ground, their wings highlighted with fine flakes of metal leaf, c.1835. 46.5 x 65cm

PRIVATE COLLECTION

WATER GILDING. Water-gilding is distinguished by its 'burnished' or 'bright' finish and yet the metal used to create this effect was exactly the same as that employed in the earlier oil-gilding technique. Its brilliance was the result of it having been applied with isinglass – a water-based semi-transparent adhesive obtained from the viscera of fish. 'Bright gilding', as it was most commonly called in the industry, was said to have 'caused a revolution, not only in the manner of working, but also in the patterns and the artistic treatment of the japanned ware',[110] and articles gilded in this way certainly bear testimony to this (plate 64).

It is difficult to be precise about when japanners first used bright gold. A small tray lent by the japanner John Jones for exhibition in Wolverhampton in 1884 was described in the accompanying catalogue as 'one of the first japan trays on which burnished gilding was introduced'.[111] If, as claimed, it was painted by Edward Bird at the Old Hall (*qv*) then its date of manufacture, and thus the introduction of this type of gilding, was some time in the late 1780s or early 1790s when Bird was employed at that factory. However, Mr Hobson, a journeyman at Jennens & Bettridge, was credited with its introduction in the 1820s and all surviving evidence in the form of decorated objects, supports this as the more likely date, if not of its introduction, of its widespread use. Save for minor idiosyncracies, Hobson's gilding method was widely adopted for the decoration of the better class of tin and papier mâché goods; it was seen in use at McCallum & Hodson some thirty years later, and there is no evidence of any marked divergence elsewhere either then, or later.

To create a bright gold pattern around the edge of a tray, for instance, 'the whole or nearly the whole'[112] border was washed with a weak solution of isinglass and water or, if the gilder preferred, wetted with his tongue. This trick, which some believed gave better adhesion, had to be exercised with caution since any acid in the saliva following meals or during illness was likely to discolour the leaf. Sheets of gold leaf were laid down until the edge of the tray was entirely, or nearly, covered. When the water had evaporated, the border pattern was painted onto the gold with thin asphaltum varnish to protect or 'stop out' those parts of the pattern to be saved. The asphaltum showed up as a dull yellow, enabling an experienced gilder to work by eye with 'freedom and correctness',[113] adding 'perhaps a leafy wreath, or an arabesque or scroll ornament'[114] as the work dictated. Bordering in this free-hand manner required considerable skill, much experience, and a good eye if the spacing of the pattern was not to go awry. Once the asphaltum had dried, the exposed gold was rubbed off with damp cotton wool and the protective varnish was removed with turpentine to reveal the bright gold border pattern. Subtle and complex motifs were achieved by using several different shades of metal together, though such extravagance was generally reserved for only the best quality goods.

As in the earlier period, thin washes of coloured varnish were sometimes applied over bright gold leaf to heighten the effect of a flower, or to give iridescence to the feathers of an exotic bird or the wings of a butterfly. In addition, sheets of metal leaf made from silver alloys were laid over a large part of the surface and washed with coloured varnish to create the golden skies which would become a popular background on japanned goods (plate 65). This gave a 'peculiar gorgeousness of tint', as one admirer of the technique wrote in 1850, 'which can be obtained by no other method'.[115] Details such as leaf veins were sometimes etched or pencilled in asphaltum onto the shiny gold surface; this, and the previous technique, may be seen in combination on the tray illustrated in (plates 45 and 63).

By slightly modifying the method for applying bright-gold, it was possible to achieve other effects. For a dead-gold finish, for example, the design was painted in gold size, as it was in the early period, but instead of leaving it until it was sticky, it was left until thoroughly dry, and then brushed with a solution of isinglass prior to the leaf being laid. The size had the effect of dulling or deadening the gold, while the isinglass, it must be presumed, aided adhesion. It was a method which C.J. Woodward (son of Josiah Woodward of Woodward & Midgeley [*qv*]) said, in a paper he gave to the Birmingham Society of Artists in 1926, allowed for very lacy work.

64. Papier mâché tea caddy and blotter-cover, the latter painted by Richard Stubbs, and gilded by his son Edwin (decorators at Shoolbred, Loveridge & Shoolbred, and its successive partnerships), c.1855–1865. 13.5 x 18 x 9.5cm and 23 x 30cm
WOLVERHAMPTON ARTS AND HERITAGE (BANTOCK HOUSE MUSEUM)

In addition, extravagant patterns were made possible by combining the effects of bright- and dead-gold, especially if several colours of gold were used together. To achieve this variation, the parts of the first layer of gold which were to be shiny were stopped-out with asphaltum, and those which were to appear dead were painted with size. A second layer of gold leaf was then applied over everything. This, of course, added considerably to the cost, particularly if areas of contrasting gold abutted, since this necessitated the whole border and, in some cases, the entire surface of the object, being covered with two or more layers of gold. Once the excess gold had been rubbed away, and the stopping-out fluid removed with spirit, the contrasts of bright- and dead-gold took on the appearance of rich damask or brocade.

Another technique credited to Hobson at the Jennens & Bettridge factory, was 'embossing'. This was a variant of the combination effect described above. First a 'plain dead ground of bronze'[116] powder was laid on a japanned and sized surface, and the intended design was drawn on in oil. The oil caused the size beneath the bronze powder to soften, making it possible, after a while, for the oil and the underlying bronze to be rubbed off, leaving the design in black within a bronze ground. The whole was then brushed with isinglass and water and covered entirely with gold-leaf. Where the leaf touched the exposed black outline, it shone brightly, and where it touched the sized bronze parts, it appeared dead, creating a glistening pattern against a field of dead gold. It is a technique that appears to have been rarely used.

Hobson was also said to have introduced the technique known as 'spangles'. This involved gilding a glass surface, such as a bottle, varnishing it, and when the varnish was dry, scraping off the gold onto a tacky japanned surface. The effect was very similar to that achieved with metal powders (plate 63).

PRINTED GOLD AND OTHER METALS. Charles Valentine's patent of 1809 included a method for printing japanned and other goods in gold – a development which appears to have been a topical concern among contemporary decorators. For instance, a similar patent, in respect of porcelain, was granted the following year to Peter Warburton of Staffordshire. Even so, the process was not new, for it had been used on enamel plaques and boxes at Battersea in London in the mid-1750s, and on Staffordshire salt-glazed stoneware in the 1760s. It is possible, therefore, that there were earlier attempts to print in gold onto japanned surfaces, but if Valentine's method was typical, it is equally as possible that the time involved outweighed any saving of skilled labour. It was thus not until many years later that this form of decoration was widely adopted by japanners.

According to Valentine, the whole of the surface to be decorated was gilded twice (it is not clear why), coated with copal varnish and left to dry. An engraved copper plate was inked with a mixture of printing ink and 'virgin's wax' (ie. fresh beeswax)

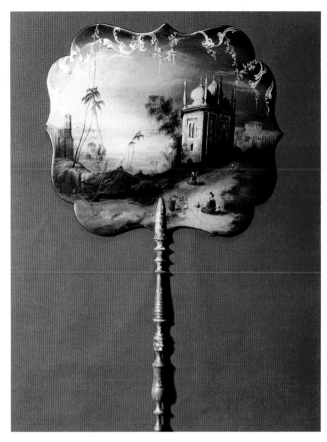

65. Handscreen with late bronze decoration of Musjid at Ghazipore, India, from an engraving by W. Finden (1838); turned-wood sticks, c.1845. 20.5 x 24.5cm
PRIVATE COLLECTION

and an impression taken from this, on gummed tissue paper, was transferred to the gilded surface. After what he described as 'a few days', the work was coated with the proposed ground-colour which he mixed with a little copal varnish. When this had dried, the object was warmed to soften the waxy ink beneath the ground colour, making it easy to rub off to reveal the gold-printed image. The result, Valentine said, was 'the same as if the gold size had been applied by the pencil.'[117] It is possible that the finely-worked background pattern on a pair of vases made by Jennens & Bettridge for Lady Hertford in about 1830, was done in this way (plate 133).

To judge from Thomas Farmer's comments some thirty-five years later that *painting*, as opposed to *printing*, designs directly on to gold leaf with stopping out fluid was still the norm, it seems that transfer-printing in gold was not commonly used. In all probability this was not through lack of interest, but for want of efficient means. Farmer himself pursued the problem in a patent of 1844 (#10,224), but as it made only slight changes to Valentine's method and was concerned mainly with the preparation of copper plates for printing, it is of little relevance here.

Of greater interest was the 'negative process' of gold printing. This is understood to have been patented by George Haselar of Wolverhampton in 1852/4, but no specification has yet been found. It is necessary therefore, to rely upon the description given by Prosser in 1881. An inked impression of those parts

66. *Premier*-shaped papier mâché tray, impressed for Henry Loveridge & Co., with a design Registration Mark for 1868. 30 x 41.5cm

What was needed of the transfer printer was not aesthetic judgement, but care, a good eye for accuracy and, above all, practice. A number of border patterns introduced in the 1860s – largely facilitated by Breese's patents – shared many characteristics with those favoured by the electro-platers whose success was beginning seriously to threaten the japanning trade (plate 66). The downside, however, was that these 'chaste' styles, encouraged by critics, led to unemployment for many skilled men.

Stencilled gilding also required accuracy and practice. Although 'stencilling' was the contemporary name for this type of decoration, it is somewhat misleading. The patterns were applied with corks in a manner similar to potato-printing rather than stencilling as we understand it today. It was introduced as a faster, less expensive means of applying gilt borders to goods made for the lower end of the market and it was especially popular among japanners in Bilston (plate 48).

of the design *not* to be gilded was transferred to the object, and the whole surface was brushed with a weak solution of isinglass and water. Gold leaf was applied all over and rubbed with spirits of turpentine to remove, in one operation, both the unwanted gold and the underlying negative impression. Areas not touched by the transfer were left sharply defined in bright gold. It is difficult to see how this was an improvement, but Prosser asserted that it 'was worked satisfactorily for some years by one of the leading houses in Wolverhampton',[118] by which he must surely have meant either the Old Hall, or Loveridge's Merridale Works (*qv*). However, it would not now be possible to identify goods decorated in this way.

Two patents, issued in 1853 (#361) and 1854 (#1714), to Charles Breese, a japanner at Breese and Hayward in Birmingham, were almost identical to each other, and described yet another method for transfer-printed gold decoration. By printing the design onto gold leaf with a stopping-out fluid instead of painting it, Breese's idea was an obvious development from Hobson's free-hand methods. It quickened and standardised the decorating process and was welcomed for having brought in its wake 'plain black centres, and simple gold or metal borders' and 'almost entirely banished the tasteless and loaded ornamentation formerly in vogue'. The description also explains that 'patterns designed by skilful artists can, by this method, be multiplied to an extent that enables the manufacturer to put on the cheapest articles a style of ornament only used a few years ago upon the most expensive.'[119]

Thus, besides speed, gilding with transfer prints brought with it other savings and benefits. Instead of requiring experienced hands, articles could be 'gilded by young boys who, in another sphere of life would probably fancy themselves incompetent to drawing a tree or a scroll with any degree of taste or correctness'[120] – or so it seemed to one visitor to McCallum & Hodson's factory in 1850.

An account of how a tray border was stencilled at the Bilston factory of Smith Armstrong in the early twentieth century, may be taken as standard across the industry. At so late a date, the work was as likely to have been done by women as by men, since this would have reduced labour costs. The corks were about 3.5cm long; one end was shaped, if necessary, to fit the curved profile of a tray's rim, and cut away to leave a pattern-motif in relief. On all but the simplest tray shapes, a separate cork was necessary for printing corner-motifs. The gilder dipped the cork in gold size and, using the little finger as a spacing-tool, printed a repeat-pattern round the edge of the tray – a little lemon-yellow mixed with the size ensured that the motif remained visible. When the size was sticky to the touch, Dutch gold – or a similarly inexpensive alternative – was laid on, and the excess wiped away.

'Cork-cutting' was listed as a separate trade in local directories and most japanners would have ordered their 'stencils' from these specialist suppliers rather than cutting their own. Each pattern was given a name so that as corks became worn with use, new sets could easily be ordered.

Bronzing

Notwithstanding Dickinson's regret that 'some really weird iron trays are to be met with in bronzes picturing apocryphal beasts in savage poses',[121] some of the finest examples of papier mâché and tin-ware were decorated by this means. 'Bronzing' was carried out with bronze powders which, being ground from various metals, gave the decoration a slight sparkle. It produced very different results from the earlier method of gilding with metal powders, and its outcome was more subtle.

There were two distinct periods of bronzing; each had its own techniques and distinguishing features, but both lent themselves to strangely atmospheric and dramatic effects.

EARLY BRONZING. According to William Hutton, writing in 1835, bronze decoration was introduced by Henry Clay. In its simplest form, it was arranged in bands interspersed with stripes of painted colour like the trays and waiters with 'single' and 'double bronze' borders which Charles Docker, a Birmingham japanner (*qv*), supplied to Chamberlain's porcelain manufactory in Worcester, between 1804 and 1806. Bronze decoration was at its most popular between about 1812 and 1820 when, besides formal borders, an entire tray-base might have been decorated with a figure subject, a scriptural theme, or rustic landscape, wholly carried out in bronze powders (plate 67). With their subdued colouring, these pictures frequently resembled Old Master paintings mellowed by ageing varnish, and this may have been part of their contemporary appeal.

The bronzing technique was described by two Londoners, Thomas Hubball (*qv*), a japanner, and William King, a tin-plate worker, in their patent of 1812 (#3593). This patent, although wrongly believed to mark the date when bronze powders were introduced, is useful for being the earliest known detailed specification of the process. The powders could be made from various metals, but Hubball and King preferred to use pulverised iron ore. First, they prepared the japanned surface with size; when this was nearly dry, they laid over it a cut-paper or parchment stencil of the proposed bronze ornament, and applied the powders with a soft material such as leather or cotton. Once dry, any superfluous powder was removed and the work given two or three protective coats of copal varnish and polished, first with pumice, then with sand and, finally, with rottenstone until it acquired 'the appearance of damask.'[122]

This was essentially the method used by other japanners, but there were slight variations which are worthy of comment in so far as they shed light on how some of the finest work was achieved. For example, bronze powders were available in greater variety than Hubball and King suggested. They were made not only from mineral ores (either in their natural colours or chemically stained), but also from finely ground metals like brass, copper, zinc, silver, and gold. In addition, they could be made from Dutch metal in its several alloys. This enabled decorators to work with up to eighteen differently coloured powders, and often with striking effect. In place of stencils, some work was drawn free-hand with gold size, using a camel-hair pencil for fine details and what were described as 'stump-like tools'[123] for the bolder parts. The powders were then scattered over the sized parts and worked in with a bob which, in this instance, was a small stick wrapped at one end with chamois leather, wool, or cotton. For very fine work, the bobs were made by tying a tiny piece of leather to a length of string and pulling it through the shaft of a quill to form a small pad at the end. When the bronzing was complete, the work was buffed with a soft cloth to give a shine to the metals in the powder.

Bronzing was evidently deemed suitable for amateur japanners, presumably on account of it not having to be stoved. At least, not according to B.F. Gandee in his, or maybe her, book *The Artist or Young Ladies' Instructor* published in 1835 and written as a series of letters to a young lady. Gandee gave particularly clear directions which may be usefully quoted here because they describe also how bronzing was carried out in the japanning workshops:

> *I begin with the pale gold bronze for the middle and larger parts, and at a little distance, add orange, green or copper bronze... To Strengthen and brighten the colours, I add more of each with a little cotton. Sometimes a pleasing rocky effect is obtained by cutting a piece of writing paper into a waved form, and rubbing the bronze over the edge of it with the cotton, and removing it a little further add more bronze and again to as many as five or six rows... Another very good effect is obtained by putting the dark colour over large flat leaves or other surfaces, and spreading the bronzes over to produce a varied effect. They may be put on bright all over the edge of a leaf, and left dark towards the middle, and when this is dry, a few gold veins over the shaded part, will produce a particularly good effect... By scattering bronzes thickly over a dark ground also, a comparatively distant effect may be given.*[124]

An example of the 'pleasing rocky effect' described above, may be seen on a teaboard made by Henry Clay (plate 120). Some of the finest examples of bronze-work came from the Wolverhampton workshops of Thomas Illidge who seemed to have specialised in these effects.

67. Straight-edge papier mâché tea-board decorated with an Arcadian landscape in bronze powders; impressed mark of Thomas Illidge, c.1815 W: approx. 70cm
COURTESY OF STOWE ANTIQUES

68. Gothic papier mâché tray with bronze, gold leaf, and painted decoration. The details of the central leaves were 'drawn' by wiping away parts of the surface while still wet (see p. 80); impressed 'CLAY/18 KING Sᵀ/COVᵀ GARDEN', c.1840 (*cf.* pl. 279). 51 x 69cm

69. Sandwich-edge papier mâché tray to which leaf-details were added *after* the bronze surface had dried (*cf.* pl. 68); similar decoration appears on trays by Jennens & Bettridge, and McCallum & Hodson; 1840/50. 57 x 76cm

There is scant information about the bronzers themselves. William Aitken wrote in 1866, of two examples of bronze decoration which he attributed to an artist named Davis. The first represented the Goddess of Earth in a chariot drawn by two chained lions and driven by two cupids, and the second showed Daniel in the Lions' Den. Davis, he said, 'gained some celebrity by his copies in the same style of subjects by Morland, in which he carefully reproduced the touches of the original artist.'[125] This has led many collectors to believe that Davis was responsible for all the bronze pictures copied from, or in the style of George Morland (1763–1840). But to judge from the quantity and varying quality of those which have survived, this is unlikely and the most that can be said, in the absence of any firm evidence, is that they were *perhaps* from the workshop of Davis.

Unlike these handsome bronze pictures, some bronze decoration was applied by stencilling. This 'half-mechanical method',[126] as it was described by an anonymous contributor to the Birmingham *Weekly Post*, allowed it to be undertaken by apprentices. Writing retrospectively in 1877, the author took as an example a tray decorated by Woodward & Midgley (*qv*) which was stencilled with 'a shepherd boy in a storm':

70. Gothic-shaped papier mâché handscreens decorated in bronze, and each lettered *Jennens & Bettridge*, in script at lower right; gilded turned-wood sticks; c.1835–1840. W: 23.5cm

Holes of the shape of the hat, head, coat, breeches, stockings, boots, dog, &c ., were all cut in different pieces of paper. The article to be ornamented was then covered with a coat of gold-size and allowed to get nearly dry, when the artist proceeded to his work... He first took the paper containing the hole representing the coat, laid it over the gold-size, and dipping a dry camel-hair brush in the orange bronze, dusted it through the hole until the gold-size would take no more. The paper was then lifted off and the coat showed as orange on a black ground. The dog and the hat being white bronze, were next done in a similar manner. Then through another paper the face was dusted in with "flesh" bronze, and so on, the most solid parts being done first. The bronzes might be stained or shaded with colour afterwards, though, as they are themselves very varied in colour and shade, this was not absolutely necessary.[127]

LATE BRONZING. Although the earlier bronzing method continued, two new styles emerged c.1830 which combined bronze powders with painted, and sometimes pearled, decoration. These styles form what is now called 'late bronzing'.

The first of these styles is seen to particularly good effect on a tray made by Henry Clay (plate 68). The leaves at its centre were individually bronzed all over, using the same cut-paper stencil for each. While the underlying size was still wet, the details were, in effect, 'drawn' in with a fine bob by lifting or wiping away the bronze – in some places, down to the japan varnish – until every vein, leaf-marking, and tonal contrast was in place. Even the shadowy background leaves which show more black than gold, were done in this way.

In a less sophisticated variant of this style, the motifs also began as large blocks of gold-coloured powder, but their details and contrasts of light and dark were obtained either by adding darker bronze colours, or by drawing them in thin

asphaltum varnish. Adding details, rather than removing them, was obviously much quicker (plate 69). Comparable effects were achieved even more quickly by strewing white metallic powder, made from silver, lead, zinc or other white metal onto painted motifs while they were still wet – another development from the sprinkled pictures of old Japanese lacquer.

In the second, and concurrent, style of late bronzing, the same methods were employed but to radically different ends. Here the bronze formed a background to the overall design. A typical example may be seen on a slate-topped table (plate 71), where a painted and pearled Italianate landscape with plashing fountain and exotic birds, is set against a heavy and turbulent bronze sky. Golden scenes bathed in sunlight were equally as characteristic. The style enjoyed such long and widespread popularity that Verdant Green, the eponymous hero of Cuthbert Bede's satire on life as an Oxford University freshman, disparagingly dismissed it on account of 'those offensive cockatoos, in an arabesque landscape, under a bronze sky, which usually sprawls over everything that is papier mâché.'[128] A jaundiced view, but otherwise accurate in its detail.

71. Slate-topped table, with a wooden support, the base of which is covered with papier mâché; painted and pearled with an Italianate garden against a bronze sky; c.1845. H: 72cm Dia: 94.5cm

Alongside these landscapes was another equally distinctive, but short-lived style for which late-bronzing was well-suited. It came to be known as the 'Wolverhampton Style', having been introduced there in 1845 by Benjamin Walton at the Old Hall Japan Works and was 'much sought after for seven years', but by 1851, 'had nearly gone to rest.'[129] It was defined by a 'selection of interior and exterior views of the old baronial halls of England, and the various cathedrals,'[130] which with their narrow slit windows, or stained glass, allowed for a play of dramatic shafts of light across the surface of the picture. The pictures were executed on so-called gothic-shaped papier mâché trays (plate 72), and some of the best were said to have been from the hand of Frederick Perks, a decorator at the Walton factory, about whom little else is known. In spite of its Wolverhampton associations, the style is known to have been adopted also by Jennens & Bettridge (plate 150). There were two ways of achieving this bronzed effect. One, according to George Dickinson, involved using paper stencils to correspond with the patches of sunlight, as in early bronzing. The other, George Lindsey wrote, resulted from 'the judicious use of transparent colours upon pure gold and silver',[131] although given the tendency of silver to tarnish, he may not have meant pure silver, unless, of course, the colour washes protected it from discolouring. Landscapes, he added, were similarly treated and their 'skies in particular being singularly effective and natural'.[132] Hunt, too, noted the popularity of 'stained silver, in the shape of birds', but it is difficult to imagine his meaning when he added that this style, when used in combination with bronze skies, made paper trays look like iron ones'.[133]

Another decorator at the Walton factory, known only as 'Brown', gave his name to a style of bronze and silvery-brown floral borders. They enjoyed so long a run that in about 1850, 'Mr Walton was in favour of dropping "Brown's borders"',[134] but when his travelling salesmen declared them best-sellers, he quickly agreed to their continuation. Contemporary with these was a pattern of 'sea-shells in brown and gold bronze in a row round the margin of a tray, and sometimes on the tray itself in regular pattern.'[135] This design has been attributed to both David Sarjeant and Charles Neville. Dickinson believed such trays were made in great numbers as they were still commonly found when he was writing in 1925; they are less profuse today.

DECORATING WITH ALUMINIUM. In 1865, J. Bettridge & Co. (*qv*), successors to the Birmingham firm of Jennens & Bettridge, were said to have:

> *patented an invention for the inlaying of aluminium and its alloys in their goods, which adds a richness … which can only otherwise be achieved by the use of precious metals, and being covered over with a coat of transparent varnish, will retain their brilliancy for any length of time.[136]*

On this evidence, it might be supposed that this form of 'inlaid' decoration is out of context here. However, the extract is

misleading. First, no such patent exists; second, it is probably wrong to impute too much accuracy to the use of the term 'inlaying'; third, and most important here, the varnishing of the aluminium would suggest results not dissimilar to the 'Wolverhampton Style' of bronze decoration (*qv*). This last is borne out by Aitken's brief but probably accurate statement that, in 1864, Bettridge & Co. applied aluminium 'and bronze formed from it, to the decoration of envelope cases, card trays, binding for albums, &c.'[137] Certainly, this was how Dickinson interpreted it in 1925, when he described it as a 'silvery bronze [made] from aluminium [which] was pretty and effective, especially with flowers and foliage', adding cryptically, that 'it has no association with early bronze pictures'[138] – a rider which implies that visually, one may be forgiven for thinking that it did.

However, commenting on Bettridge's display at the Paris Exhibition of 1867, David Sarjeant provided yet another equally baffling interpretation. He described 'a white casket, inlaid with metal in the form of a border, relieved with pale green. This style', he continued, 'is capable of development, although it has been neglected in England.' Was he thus likening it to the inlaid metal ornaments used by Stobwasser in eighteenth-century Germany, for example, and to those used later in France by maker's such as Adt Brothers (see p. 281*ff*)? By going on to observe that 'the inlaying may be assisted by the electrotype process patented, some twenty years ago, by Mr. Farmer' (see pp. 73 and 169), this would indeed seem to have been the case, for the patent included a method of attaching electro-deposit medallions to japanned surfaces. But then Sarjeant confused matters by adding that 'bisque work, Persian lac, and enamelling … may furnish suitable patterns for this kind of work; but there is no necessity', he said, 'for such voluntary humility as to call it imitation ivory.'[139]

In short, unless a marked specimen of so-called inlaid aluminium comes to light, it seems we are never going to fully understand this style of decoration.

Such decorative use of aluminium was made possible by a reduction in its cost due to the work of a Frenchman, H. St Clair Deville in 1855. His research was published in England in 1859, and by 1860, aluminium was being produced there. Nevertheless, it appears to have been a further fifteen to twenty years before aluminium was generally adopted by japanners, and by then, as Dickinson said, 'most of the glory had gone out of the trade.'[140]

GILDED IMPASTO OR RAISED-WORK. With descriptions of gold leaf and bronzing now in place, it is nececcsary to return to the early nineteenth century to consider a style which was often used in combination with both of these techniques, namely gilded impasto work.

Given the influence of both Oriental lacquer and its early Western imitations on the Midlands japanning industry, it is

72. King-gothic papier mâché tray, the base lettered in white script 'Southam Hall' and '1196'; the painting is from *The Mansions of England in the Olden Time*, by Joseph Nash, published between 1839 and 1849; impressed mark: 'B WALTON & Cᴼ/WARRANTED', c.1850 (see p. 78, and *cf.* pl. 150). 37 x 45.5cm

surprising that impasto decoration was not adopted by japanners in that region until about 1820. The style is characterised by quasi-oriental landscapes in which the main parts – figures, birds, animals, flowers, trees, pagodas, etc. – were highlighted in low relief. It was known in the trade as 'raised-work' or 'raisin[g] colour'.

Raised-work is thought to have been introduced by Joseph Booth – the gilder who may have decorated Lady Hertford's magnificent vases (*qv*) – when he was employed by Jennens & Bettridge between the years 1821–1825. The style was widely copied in other workshops and factories, but it was Booth who became 'justly celebrated for his exquisite imitations of Chinese and Japanese ornament,'[141] and who, in 1824, was apparently called upon to decorate a tray in this style for the Prince Regent. Fine examples of this style are popularly attributed to Booth, but without documentary evidence and at this distance in time, no-one can be really sure of the accuracy of so-doing.

There were various receipts for making 'raising composition', but the one given by Gandee and described as 'Birmingham raising', may reasonably be presumed to have been the formula favoured in the local industry. It consisted of flake white, vermilion and gold size and took longer to dry than other compositions, but had the advantage of being easier to apply and more durable.

Gandee's instructions were aimed primarily at the amateur; nevertheless, raised-work cannot have been an easy undertaking. The proposed design was traced onto the japanned surface and its outline lightly painted with the tip of a medium-sized brush which was dipped into the composition to only half the length of its hairs. The brush had to be frequently replenished, but not so fully laden that the composition dripped on the work in hand, and nor should its point 'be rested on so heavily as to bend the hair'[142] for that would have resulted in blots. It was a tricky and skilful operation.

If any of the composition was allowed to overlap, the surface would dry unevenly; Moreover, unless the work was kept absolutely level, the composition would 'flow' or run. Once an area was covered, further raising was added around its edge. Gandee's instructions seem perverse when it was the centre that was to be prominent, but it was a measure designed to counteract the tendency of the composition to sink in the middle as it set. By this means, the extra composition flowed to the middle, and retained its level as a skin formed. Any mistakes could be removed with spirits of turpentine, but as this dulled the japan varnish, Gandee advised that its gloss could be restored by first rubbing a little lard into the surface and then rubbing it with a little flour to absorb the grease – a point not mentioned in any other contemporary account, but almost certainly the principle by which all decorators worked – amateur and professional – for mistakes there must surely have been. In the industry, the

73. Straight-edge papier mâché tray with 'raised work' decoration, and thin washes of colour over gold and silver-coloured leaf. It belonged to William Cope, an employee at Henry Loveridge & Co. (from c.1869–1920); c.1875. 32 x 40cm

WOLVERHAMPTON ARTS AND HERITAGE (BANTOCK HOUSE MUSEUM)

completed raised work was hardened in a stove, bronzed or gilded in the usual manner, and the details 'pencilled' in colour onto the raised parts. A particularly fine example of this type of decoration, in combination with early bronzing, may be seen on a tea-board made by Thomas Illidge (plate 206). Sometimes, raised work was carved with a fine tool to create the effect of folds in drapery for example, or the gnarled trunks of trees and occasionally, it was used in combination with pearl decoration. This style of decoration was not much used after the 1830s, but it enjoyed a short revival in the 1860s, notably on goods made by Henry Loveridge & Co of Wolverhampton (plate 73).

~

It is ironic that despite their considerable talent, gilders were generally regarded as *skilled workmen* rather than *artists*. Nevertheless, whether their work was left to stand alone without further embellishment or, as was more usual, formed only part of the overall decorative scheme, it was often the most eye-catching aspect, and thus the quality of the gilding was integral to the success of japanned goods.

Patent Pearl Glass

This was the term used to describe designs and pictures painted on the underside of glass panels and highlighted with thin flakes of pearl. Made as inserts for both papier mâché articles and tinware, their style of decoration is easily confused with 'patent gem inlay' and 'Patent Crystal Trays'(*qv*).

'Pearl glass' was patented in 1844 (#10,046) by Birmingham japanner Joseph Gibson as a suitable embellishment for 'buttons, panels for articles of furniture, or for decorating rooms, door or finger-plates, table tops, fire-screens, chimney pieces, work boxes, and cabinet work generally.'[143]

In his patent, Gibson claimed 'exclusive right' to two methods of

fixing pearl to glass. In the first method, after any necessary gold leaf had been attached to the back of the glass, the entire surface was thinly coated with copal varnish and the cut pearl pieces were gently pressed on by hand before the panel was stoved for six to seven hours at about 120°F – anything higher would have discoloured the varnish. After a second coat of varnish and a further stoving, the same side of the glass was painted all-over with the intended background colour. The second method involved tracing an outline of the design on the back of the glass and any gold leaf ornaments that were required were attached at this point. Then, save for those parts to be pearled, the back of the glass, including the gilded parts, was painted with the intended ground colour. When the colour was quite dry and hard, the whole surface was coated with copal varnish, sheets of pearl were pressed into position, and the panel stoved as above. When viewed from the front, the shell, in both cases, was set off against a single-coloured ground enriched, perhaps, by gold or silver leaf.

Few, if any, examples decorated in this restrained manner have survived and 'patent pearl glass' is now mostly associated with the colourful pearled, and sometimes gilded, glass pictures which appeared some time around 1849 on blotter covers, box-lids, in the bases of cake-baskets, and as glass brooches. The colours were usually painted over transfer-printed outlines and mostly depict views of famous buildings and prominent landmarks (plate 74). Although executed according to Gibson's patent, these glass pictures are largely associated with Thomas Lane (*qv*), proprietor of the Royal Papier Mâché & Patent Glass Works in Birmingham, where Gibson had been employed since 1846. Examples of pearl glass were included in Lane's displays

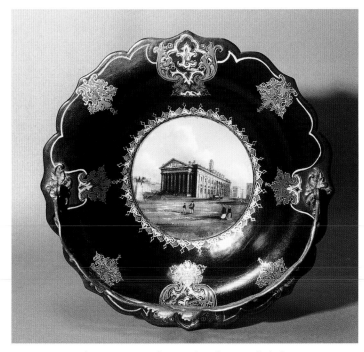

74. Papier mâché visiting card tray of gothic octafoil shape, inset with a foil-backed glass panel printed and painted with the 'Royal Exchange', London; c.1850. 25.5cm

PRIVATE COLLECTION

75. Blotter cover inset with a *Patent Pearl Glass* view of Joseph Paxton's building for the Great Exhibition, from which it was purchased as a souvenir, in 1851.
Approx. 15 x 22cm
THE BODLEIAN LIBRARY, UNIVERSITY OF OXFORD (A Nation of Shopkeepers, no. 24)

76. A pearl-decorated papier mâché frame, inset with a printed, painted and foil-backed glass panel showing Buckingham Palace; mid nineteenth century.
16 x 23cm
PRIVATE COLLECTION

at both the Birmingham Exposition of Art & Manufactures in 1849, and at the Great Exhibition of 1851 (plates 75 and 165).

After Gibson's patent expired in 1858, pearl glass pictures were taken up by other manufacturers, particularly in Wolverhampton where they became especially popular for ornamenting the lids of tin coal vases, scoops and purdoniums.[xxv] But even before its expiry, Woodward & Midgley, mindful of its success, resolved that Gibson's patent 'had to be rivalled or imitated', and 'soon turned out representations of every picturesque ruin or building in

England'.[144] They neatly evaded any infringement by using 'tin-foil of many colours instead of pearl' which, according to Woodward's son, writing some years later in 1877, was not only cheaper, but 'sufficiently near enough in effect to the patent to spoil its sale',[145] and moreover, better for moonlight views. In Woodward's opinion, had his father and Midgley patented their idea 'it would have paid better than the one it was meant to rival'[146] (plate 76). But in time, it too was copied by 'other and lower houses, and acquired a vulgarity' which Woodward was pleased to note was 'of little use to its introducers.'[147]

---

xxv. Purdonium or purdonian: a tall cylindrical vessel, generally with a sloping lid, for holding coal.

Both pearl glass and tin-foil pictures were vulnerable styles of decoration. The glass, being 'as thin as is compatible with sufficient strength',[148] was, nevertheless, very fragile, and deterioration of the copal varnish has often caused the paint, gold leaf and pearl to detach themselves from its surface. Today, damaged examples abound, giving an impression of tawdriness, but in a pristine specimen – albeit vulgar to some tastes – the picture appears very much at one with the richness of its japanned and gilded frame.

Gems and other Inlays

In 1786, John Skidmore, a Clerkenwell maker of stove-grates, patented a means of ornamenting 'all sorts of Japan Wares' with imitation gems (# 1552).[149] Besides the japanned 'stove grates, fire stoves, stove fronts, fenders, shovels, tongs, and pokers' for which he proposed such ornament, he also suggested that japanned coaches and carriages could be 'made to look very elegant'[150] if their doors and panels were bordered with gems, and their arms, crests, devices, and initials embellished likewise. In addition, he said that the interiors of houses and ships could be decorated in this style. The gems were attached to the article, either before or after it was japanned, by one of two methods: they could be glued onto a flat surface or into grooves and crevices, or they might be set into bezels which had been fixed to the japanned surface.

77. Papier mâché firescreen, inset with paste gems, and painted with Keith Hall, Inverurie. It was part of a suite of furniture, ordered from Jennens & Bettridge in 1850, by the 8th Earl and Countess of Kintore, who are shown with their dogs, Flush and Bruno. 128.5 x 89cm

Photo © Victoria and Albert Museum, London (Circ.168-196)

A large gilded pine chimneypiece, richly embellished with rhinestones and imitation diamonds embedded in peacock-blue painted copper panels was sold in America in 1999. It dates from about 1790, and though it is not japanned, it strikes a chord with Skidmore's patent. Nevertheless, while no japanned articles decorated in this way are known to have survived, Skidmore's patent is interesting for the way in which it foreshadowed developments at the Jennens & Bettridge factory over sixty years later.

Whether or not Benjamin Giles, an employee at Jennens & Bettridge, had this patent in mind when he introduced decorating with 'inlaid gems', his idea was remarkably similar, not least in the stones he used: 'glass, gems, jewels, real or fictitious pearls [ie. imitation], glass cut and "quicked" [ie. mirrored with quick-silver or, as it is known today, mercury], or otherwise, paste, enamel, coloured or marbled, wax, ivory, tortoiseshell, steel and other beads, and the glass beads commonly called pearl beads.'[151] Alert as ever, to the need to protect ideas, Theodore Hyla Jennens patented it in 1847 as 'a New or Improved Method of Ornamenting Papier Mâché Articles [and for] Ornamenting Purposes generally' (#11,670). It also had much in common with Gibson's earlier pearl glass, upon which the 'improvements', claimed in the title of Giles' patent, were no doubt based.

Giles proposed two methods of attaching the gems. The first was like Skidmore's in that the stones were set into 'suitably formed cavities'[152] either before or after the article was japanned. If the latter procedure was followed then the gems were occasionally backed with foil to increase their brilliancy and stuck flat-face down, so that their faceted side projected above the surface (plate 77). In his second method, the gems were attached to the underside of the glass by exactly the same means as Gibson used when fixing pearl (plate 78).

Just as Skidmore had recommended his jewelled panels for decorating ships, so too, in 1854, Jennens & Bettridge made just such a set for the saloon of the *Imperador*, a steam-ship built by John Laird for the South American & General Steam Navigation Company. The set was made up of 'glass panels of peculiar brilliancy and effect, embracing gold tracery and spangled borders',[153] highlighted with gems and their centres alternately painted with 'groups of fruit, flowers, and views of Madeira, Rio de Janeiro, Lisbon and Bahia'[154, xxvi] – places which almost certainly represented the ports most frequented by the ship. The effects were deemed to have been 'at once chaste and gorgeous.'[155]

Others were less enthusiastic. After visiting Jennens & Bettridge's factory in 1851, Harriet Martineau, writing in *Household Words* mustered only qualified praise: 'We saw some panels – such as might form the doors of small cabinets, or the top of jewel-boxes – splendidly inlaid with pearls, rubies, amethysts, emeralds, and turquoises. Two of these

78. Papier mâché writing box, with a panel of *Patent Inlaid Gems* (see p. 85); impressed
mark of Jennens & Bettridge, c.1850. W: 34.5cm

were designed for the Queen of Spain's jewels' but, she said,
they were not 'half so pretty as the convolvulus in the wine-
glass, or the half-open lily, or drooping fuchsia, on many a
screen or paper-knife'[156] in the colouring room.
Nevertheless, at the top end of the market, 'inlaid gems'
enjoyed a fairly long run to judge from the Official Guide to
the 1862 London Exhibition, in which it was reported that
Jennens & Bettridge had made a pair of vases for Prince
Albert, 'in this style of ornamentation, from designs by
Ludwig Gruner.'[xxvii] 'No work, we have seen', the writer said,
'could compare with the recherché effect produced by this
combination of gems, glass and metal'[157] (see p.145). The style
was continued by Jennens & Bettridge's successor, John
Bettridge (*qv*) until the closure of his factory in 1866.

Soon after Giles' patent was granted, Woodward & Midgley,
as seemed to be their custom, devised a way of circumventing
it by attaching coloured tin-foil beneath cut-glass in place of
paste gems. But otherwise, inlaid gem ornament seems not to
have been taken up by other manufacturers, probably on
account of its manufacturing costs and the soaring price of
pearl (see p. 53).

See also 'Patent Pearl Glass', and 'Patent Crystal Trays'.

Varnishing and finishing

When each stage of the decoration was complete and, if
necessary, stoved, the article was sent to the varnishing shop
where, because japan varnish was 'apt to become dull and
acquire a sort of mouldy appearance, especially when
subjected to a change of climate',[158] it was given one or more
coats of 'copal varnish (*qv*), as pure and transparent as the
finest olive oil.'[159]

Each coat was stoved at 100–160ºF. For extra protection, a
further coat of copal varnish might be applied, but only over
the decorated parts of the article, and this also required
stoving. The edge of this final, transparent layer is often
discernible if the article is held up to the light. Such
protection had its downside, as Thomas Archer observed in a
report on the Paris Exhibition of 1867: 'this last coating of
varnish soon gets a film over it that is highly injurious to
light coloured grounds',[160] causing white grounds to appear
today as cream-coloured.

After a final stoving, the 'handers' polished the article with
pumice-stone, then with pounce, 'thirdly with rotten-stone
and oil, rubbed on with very fine rags, and lastly with the
worker's hand'[161] to give it 'the beautiful glass-like polish so

xxvi. Bahia: a seaport in Ecuador, South America.
xxvii. Ludwig Gruner (1801–1882) b. Dresden. He came to London and served as an art

advisor to Prince Albert. His book Specimens of Ornamental Art (1850) was widely
infuential among contemporary manufacturers.

obvious on all well finished papier mâché,'[162] and tin-ware. The more expensive the work, the greater the number of polishings it received.

The goods were then sent to the 'cabinet makers, liners and fitters, when locks, hinges, and all the other parts [were] added to make each thing complete.'[163] During the early period, these 'other parts' would have included, silver or ormolu mounts, enamel plaques (plate 101), jasper cameos (plate 116), gilt medallions, ivory knobs and other fittings. After the 1820s, when more complex shapes became available, boxes were lined with silk, velvet, or printed paper, and fitted with hinges, pearl, ivory, bone, brass or silver knobs and other ornaments; if required, they were given ormolu mounts or handles. All these parts could be made locally,[xxviii] and any glass bottles for placing in toilet boxes or upon ink-stands, would have been readily available from glass manufacturers in either Birmingham or the nearby glass-making centres at Stourbridge and Brierley Hill.

Finally, the articles were packed ready for despatch. Trays, for example, were packed with tissue paper between each, and wrapped in brown kraft paper. At Loveridge's in the 1920s, these parcels were then packed in saw-dust in tea-chests which the apprentices collected from local grocers, or packed in large basket-ware crates, for despatch by rail. In earlier times of course, the goods left the factory in covered horse-drawn wagons.

Copyright
As George Wallis lamented, 'an artist's works were no sooner engraved than the tray painters seized upon them, for it must be remembered no copyright existed to restrain this kind of publication even down to the time when Landseer's subjects became popular, and the revival of tray painting about 1837-8, made his engraved pictures common property on papier mâché.'[164, xxix]

This wholesale copying of pictures by manufacturers was curbed by the Copyright Act of 1842. Thereafter, decorative artists were supposed to rely entirely on their own inventions or pay a copyright fee. It was, however, print-sellers, as distinct from artists, who benefitted mostly from the Act. In 1846, in answer to a query about 'how far manufacturers are justified in copying prints, the copyright of which is vested in the publisher', the Art Union was ambivalent. While recognising its illegality, they considered it would increase rather than lessen print sales and defended it on the grounds that widely circulating a print in this manner 'cannot fail to improve the taste of those by whom it is seen.' Unsure of their stance, however, they sought legal advice and were forced to advise readers that copying a published print 'on a pocket-handkerchief, a tea-tray, a china plate, or other fabrics' without permission, would indeed be an infringment.[165] On this evidence, it would have been a foolhardy japanner

79. Travellers' samples of 'premier shaped' tin counters-trays, each showing two distinct patterns; Bilston or Wolverhampton, c.1830-1840. 10.5 x 16.5cm
WOLVERHAMPTON ARTS AND HERITAGE (BANTOCK HOUSE MUSEUM)

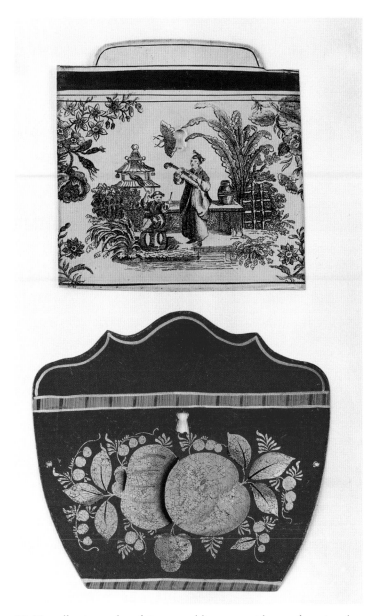

80. Travellers' samples of tin tea caddies, one with transfer printed decoration; Bilston or Wolverhampton, c.1835–1840. H's: 11.5cm and 12.5cm

<small>WOLVERHAMPTON ARTS AND HERITAGE (BANTOCK HOUSE MUSEUM)</small>

At Mr Walton's papier mâché stall there was Mr Horsley's picture of Malvolio, only exhibited a few months ago, copied on a waiter. I should like to ask if Mr Walton obtained leave from Mr Horsley to use his thought and labour in this way, or sought any permission from the proprietor of the picture. If I do Mr Walton injustice, perhaps he will say so.[167, xxx]

Whether or not the question was justified, the fact that the writer felt obliged to draw attention to the matter indicates that widespread copying of an artist's workwithout permission, was still a matter of concern. Evidently, and nothwithstanding the advice of the Art Union, some japanners were prepared to take the risk.

The above issues relate to copying easel paintings, but the situation regarding decorative painting is less clear. Consider, for example, the bronzed decoration seen on gothic-trays by both Henry Clay and B. Walton & Co. (plates 68 and 279). This was unlikely to have been piracy – more a case, perhaps, of Clay's firm having recently closed in the early 1850s, and their decorators seeking work elsewhere. Moreover, since there are no records to show that journeymen decorators were obliged to confine styles of decoration to specific manufacturers, it is possible that such duplication was not infrequent.

Commercial Travellers and their Samples

When the goods were finished they had to be sold to retailers. In the eighteenth and early nineteenth centuries, this entailed the japan master embarking on an annual journey for the sale of his goods. Having carefully planned his route, he set off on horseback, his workforce giving 'him a hearty send off [and] wishing him a successful journey and a safe return',[168] to visit London, Bristol, Liverpool and other large towns and ports with a view to sales and export.[xxxi] His saddle-bags, tightly packed with '*specimens* of the various articles, if practicable; or pictured representations, where too bulky or too numerous', served as his 'portable *show rooms*'.[169] As Hawkes Smith observed in 1836, 'now a tolerably complete set of "patterns" will weigh 5cwt [hundredweight]. And, with their exhibitor, forms a full and ample load for a one horse carriage.'[170]

Among items lent by John Jones to the Wolverhampton Exhibition in 1884, was a 'Japan tablet, ornamented in the Italian style on both sides, date 1775', which served as a pattern and of which it was said: 'This represents the bottom of a tea tray'[171]. Given that Jones was the grandson of Edward Jones who

who showed articles in breach of copyright at public exhibitions, and yet the readiness of critics to doubt that permission to copy a picture had been sought indicates otherwise. Expressing surprise at 'the price at which the japanners are able to produce really excellent paintings', a reporter in the *Journal of Design & Manufactures*, in 1849, continued 'at the Birmingham Exposition we noticed a table manufactured by Messrs McCullum & Hodgson [*sic*] with a very fair copy of a Landseer (copied we fear, without leave) for the top, the price of which table and picture, was only nine pounds!'[166] He went on to explain that:

---

xxviii. For example, Paul Moore & Co., a 'General hinge-maker', of Great Lister Street, Birmingham, showed at the Great Exhibition of 1851: 'German silver and embossed electro-plated hinges for ornamental articles of furniture, whether of timber or papier mâché' (Spicer's *Official...Catalogue*, p.624, no. 274).

xxix. By 'tray painting' Wallis was referring specifically to the painting of pictorial scenes.
xxx. John Callcott Horsley RA (1817–1903): historical genre painter.
xxxi Scotland and Ireland were rarely visited on account of their relative inaccessibility.

worked at the Old Hall, this may well have been a sample from that factory. Flat examples of tin-plate snuffers trays, and tea-caddies, the origins of which are uncertain, are shown in plates 79 and 80. Examples of papier mâché tray-edges and border patterns may be seen in plate 81.

In 1794, William Barrow was at pains to inform Matthew Boulton how important it was that 'Travelling Setts of Patterns should be completed and circulated' and moreover that 'at the

same time a London Agent should be supplied with a general Assortment of Patterns. – While these were in circulation', he said, 'till the return of orders, two or three Hands might be employ'd in finishing some full size'd different pattern Trays, and one of every other Article to match, so as to form Setts for the purpose of being exhibited [*sic*] at Soho'.[172] In fact, it was customary for the japan master to write weekly to his factory in order that work could begin on the orders he had received; a letter sent by Obadiah Ryton to his brother in 1792 is an instance of this practice (p. 55).

81. Travellers' samples of borders for sandwich-edge papier mâché trays; c.1830–1840. 13 x 35.5cm
DONATED TO THE HISTORICAL SOCIETY OF EARLY AMERICAN DECORATION BY THE CHILDREN OF THE LATE DR EDWARD STANNARD

Finished goods then had to be despatched, taking weeks, sometimes months, to reach their destination by wagon. The advent of the canals and then railways brought about a sea-change in methods of distribution. Commercial travellers, as distinct from the japan master, began to take responsibility for selling the goods, and because they were not confined by how much a horse could carry, their samples were 'packed closely in large square japanned cases, fastened with strong leather straps.'[173] Hotels in most towns provided overnight 'commercial rooms' for such men. Mindful of how easily business may have given way to pleasure, Charles Mander, the varnish maker (see p. 196*ff*) felt it necessary, in 1839, to prepare a list of 'Regulations' for his travellers, and it is unlikely that he was the only manufacturer to take such precautions. 'Travel in those hours least suited for the transaction of business', he advised, 'if you stop the night, see your room and have all you wish carried into it – as your packages are otherwise soon known by others and advertise your presence... Never ... at ... dinner sit more than 1 hour – taking care to notice the wine... Dinner bills are often swelled by those who state good will to the house.'[174] If, as was still the case, men travelled by horse, then Mander strictured that the horse be tended to first. In fact Mander left nothing to chance, giving instructions for payment, advising on gratuities, and generally cautioning his traveller about his personal conduct.

After 1840, commercial travel by rail was considerably faster and more efficient. Larger quantities of samples, or finished articles were packed in huge wicker crates and conveyed in the

82. Travellers' samples of tin and snuffbox lids with incised decoration; first quarter of the nineteenth century (*cf.* pl. 36).
WOLVERHAMPTON ARTS AND HERITAGE (BANTOCK HOUSE MUSEUM)

goods-vans which were linked to the rear end of most passenger-trains. By then, it was usual for complete, but small-sized trays to serve as samples; these were generally backed with hessian or other soft fabric to prevent any damage when stacked for transit, and often had paper labels attached, on which were printed the costs of the various available sizes. Sometimes, such labels were applied directly on the japanned surfaces (plate 83). At their destination, the wicker crates were transferred to a horse-drawn wagon and taken by the commercial traveller to the various retailers in that town.

Printed and illustrated trade catalogues from which retailers might place orders appear not to have been used by japanners until about 1840. They are now comparatively rare and keenly sought by collectors of such books.

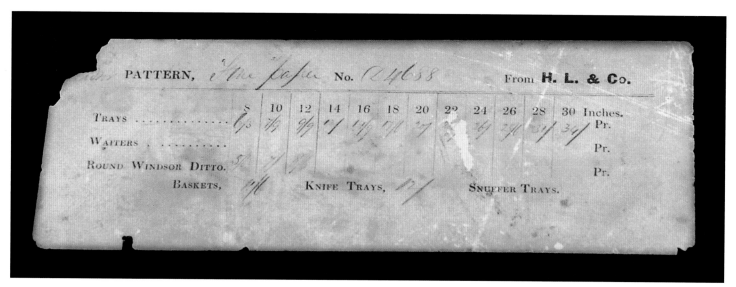

83. Price-list attached to the underside of an oval papier mâché tray – a travellers' sample for Henry Loveridge & Co.; the advent of the railway made it possible for travellers to carry such bulky samples; c.1860. 7.5 x 20cm
COLLECTION OF SHIRLEY BAER

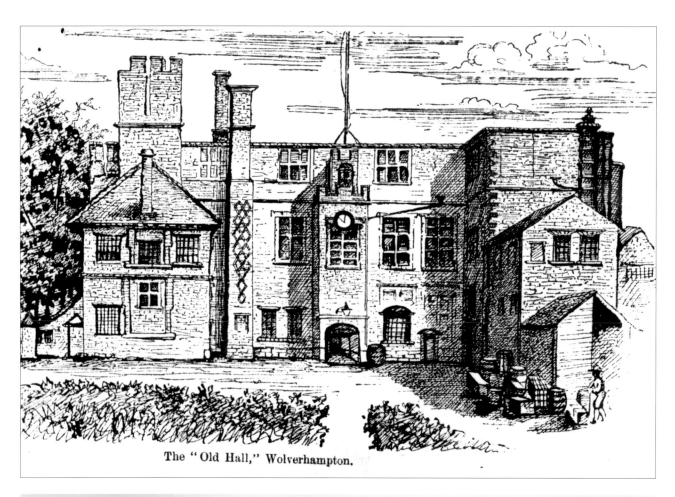

The "Old Hall," Wolverhampton.

NOT A BED OF ROSES

Workshops, Factories and Labour

'Apprenticeship in the japanning and papier mâché trade was not a bed of roses, and one gasps with astonishment at what the boys were expected and required to do.'

George Dickinson, *English Papier Mâché*, 1925, p. 103

There are no known detailed accounts of how japan workshops and manufactories in the eighteenth and early nineteenth centuries were organised; instead, there are isolated snippets of information which, if pieced together, provide some insight. The opening of Matthew Boulton's Soho Manufactory just north of Birmingham in 1765, heralded a new age of factory production and hitherto unknown opportunities for other local and like-minded entrepreneurs. Its processes and organisation, its size, and the sheer elegance of its neo-classical façade, made it a national spectacle. It aroused such curiosity among the rich and fashionable, from both home and abroad, that a whole new craze for visiting workshops began.

This openness was, of course, double-edged and manu-facturers were understandably wary of some visitors. Reinhold Rücker Angerstein, for example, on a mission to spy on trade and industry for the Swedish government, obviously aroused suspicion during his visit to Birmingham in 1754, for

he wrote of having 'to use many tricks and much effort before I could get to see everything I wished to.'[1] It was clearly an ongoing problem. In November, 1785, an announcement in the Birmingham Gazette warned of:

> *Foreigners now in this town and neighbourhood who act as spies upon our machines and manufacturers, and are using every means in their power to procure full information on the subject. Therefore it is earnestly recommended to the manufacturers, to be very cautious what persons they admit into their works, in order to frustrate as much as possible the intentions of their visit.*[2]

And in the same newspaper the following January, manufacturers published their resolve 'not to admit any strangers whatsoever.'[3] Nevertheless, the practice of visiting factories continued, along with its concomitant dangers. For example, one visitor to Henry Clay's workshops, Count Otto Cronstedt, a Swedish mineralogist, showed more than passing

Opposite: 84. The Old Hall, Wolverhampton, when it was a japanning factory; photographed from a nineteenth-century etching.
<small>FROM THE COLLECTIONS OF WOLVERHAMPTON ARCHIVES & LOCAL STUDIES</small>

85. Painted papier mâché panel, inscribed 'Bond Street Wolverhampton. March 26. 1811', and initialled 'RT', probably for Richard Tyrer (see p. 324). St John's Church, is in the distance (*cf.* pl. 10). 20.5 x 29cm
<small>PRIVATE COLLECTION</small>

interest in the technicalities of papier mâché manufacture. Writing from Stockholm upon his return in 1788, he implored William Withering, his Birmingham host, to ask 'Mr. Clay ... some few questions about his Paper manufactuaria', thinly veiling his professional interest with the assurance that it was 'for nothing else but only my own plaisure'.[4]

Enamellers, glass-makers, pearl-workers and japanners, in fact everyone in Birmingham who made luxury goods on any significant scale, threw open their doors to take advantage of the flow of carriage-trade through the town. Visitors – benign and otherwise – assiduously recorded their 'discoveries' in their journals, and it is largely from these, and from rare accounts written by some of the workmen, that a picture of an early large-scale japanning factory begins to emerge. Likening Clay's cabinet-making shop to a 'timber yard', for example, conjures up a vivid image of large stacks of pasteboard sheets and a hint of disarray, while a description of Charles Mander's japan and varnish works in Wolverhampton, ranged round a large square yard with cherry trees and flowers, conveys a sense of the relatively informal, almost domestic mode in which some successful concerns were still operating in 1817. However scant such records are, when matched with later, more detailed accounts left by William Highfield Jones, for example, it becomes clear that the organisation of early workshops, based as they were upon practical necessity, set the pattern for those that followed. What did change was the scale of operations: the shift from small workshop to factory, the replacement of people with machines, and the concomitant rise in industrial hazards. Machinery was seldom fenced before 1850, and many a woman's shawl or long hair was ensnared; likewise a man's loose apron or sleeves. These factors, together with successive legislation, and increased production, resulted in the larger workshops becoming rigidly departmentalised factories with each section strictly supervised by a foreman.

The earliest tin-plate workers and japanners had workshops in, or adjacent to, their dwelling. If trade prospered, they built a further workshop at the back of the property and continued to extend in this way until they had a row of workshops, or 'shopping', which almost filled their back yard.

This practice was common-place. In about 1740, John Baskerville, when he 'entered into the lucrative branch of japanning',[5] both lived and worked at the premises he rented in Moor Street, Birmingham. And in the 1820s and 1830s, when larger premises were built specifically as factories, their layouts maintained a similar plan. Substantial dwellings for the japan masters, offices, and showrooms fronted onto the road, but instead of one, there might have been two transverse blocks of workshops at the rear – one storey high, or more – which, as trade increased and extra space was needed, were often linked by further workshops to create a completely enclosed yard. With windows overlooking the yard on every floor, the decorators were able to benefit from natural light, and the stovers were ensured some respite from their hot ovens. A wagon entrance for deliveries and despatch connected the yard to the road outside. Jennens & Bettridge's factory on Constitution Hill, Birmingham, with its impressive neo-classical domestic façade, was developed on this principle (plate 129), although, like most major factory proprietors whose business prospered, neither Mr Jennens nor Mr Bettridge continued to reside there.

This, basically, was the plan upon which Shoolbred & Loveridge's large new factory was built in Wolverhampton, in 1848. As a purpose-built factory it was obviously designed to accommodate the latest machinery and new levels of output (plate 88). Most workshops, however, were adapted from existing premises to keep up with increasing levels of demand and to house new machinery, none more so than the various partnerships which occupied the Old Hall (qv). An outwardly picturesque moated Elizabethan manor house in Wolverhampton (plate 84), the Old Hall still had a green paddock in 1839 and a 'nicely kept garden laid out with flower beds, and fishponds filled with gold fish.'[6] A small part of the Hall was used as a dwelling house, but elsewhere the interior was completely transformed:

> *The grand oak staircase with its dark balustrades, instead of leading to the state ball-room, now led into warehouses where women and girls were employed wrapping up goods, and the bedrooms were used as storerooms... The large open kitchen fireplace, instead of providing feasts for the great personages who resided at the Hall, was utilised for tinning the goods; vats of molten metal and grease stood under the great fireplace, and the kitchen floor was strewn all over with pans and dish covers in the process of tinning. All the other rooms ... were degraded to trade purposes of one sort or another.*[7]

Not all japanners aspired to expansion on such a large scale. At the end of the nineteenth century, there were those who still clung to eighteenth century practices, making and japanning everyday utilitarian wares such as tin oil-cans, lamps, and canisters for local consumption and very meagre returns. Working alone in tiny premises adjacent to their dwelling or within the home itself, and with only the simplest of hand-tools at their disposal, they would have carried out only one or two of the allied trades, usually tinplate working and a crude form of japanning – sometimes no more than a coat of quickly applied brown tar varnish. In view of their workaday nature, it is unlikely that many of their wares have survived to the present day, and if they have, it is equally as unlikely they could be confused with the similar, more robustly made utilitarian articles which, from the 1840s, featured prominently in the printed trade catalogues issued by more prestigious firms.

The deprivation which these men and women suffered can be gauged by the experience of Mary Smith who was, in fact, comparatively better placed than most. In about 1850, Mary succeeded to her family's tray trade which occupied a workshop behind the Japanners Arms tavern in Bilston; although this probably meant that she supplied trays – blank or japanned – to the bigger firms, still she was 'very poor' and her life 'a pathetic struggle'.[8] Her link with licensed victualling was not uncommon among japanners and tin-plate workers for, in order to make ends meet, several small firms occupying the 'shopping', or small workshops, at the rear of inns and taverns, were run by the licensees themselves. Secondary occupations were particularly characteristic in Bilston, where even owners of the more successful of the smaller businesses like James Caddick and Enoch Fellows – regular suppliers of blanks to the leading japan houses – found it necessary. Caddick boosted his income by being both licensee of The Blank Makers Arms and a tea-dealer, while Fellows doubled as a licensed victualler. A company which was to become a household name in the twentieth century, GKN Sankey developed from equally humble beginnings in the shopping behind the Golden Cup where Joseph Sankey, amongst others, had been employed by the licensee, Mrs Birch, to make and japan tea trays.

Benjamin Mander (*qv*) continued as a baker and maltster for some years after setting up as a japanner in Wolverhampton, in 1792. However, the incidence of japanners and tin-plate workers holding two jobs was generally less prevalent in Wolverhampton, where there was a greater number of large firms to provide steady employment. In Birmingham, where the focus was mainly on papier mâché for the fashionable market, the workers were better paid and less likely to need, or indeed have time for, other employment; there were, of course, exceptions like Edward Lunn who, in 1770, worked as a 'japanner and helmet maker',[9] and Samuel Chandler who, in 1808, was both 'japanner and victualler'.[10]

Not surprisingly, the close proximity of japan workshops to taverns was sometimes counter-productive. Daniel and Tom Caddick had 'learned too well the art of copious drinking'[11] at their father's bar and were said to have brought about the collapse of his business. Mrs Birch's sons, whom she employed alongside Sankey, were also said to have 'dissipated the family fortune' by their heavy drinking. Notwithstanding, there is no evidence that drinking was any more of a problem for japanners and workers in the allied trades than for those in other industries, though clearly it was a matter of some concern to their masters. To some extent the problem was job-related – as it must have been for those who worked all day in the vicinity of hot stoves (see below) – but it also stemmed

from want of anything else to do outside work. Theatrical entertainments, and institutions like the Tradesmen's & Mechanics Library[i] set up in Wolverhampton in 1827, to offer 'evening education and enlightenment'[12] to the working classes as counter-attractions to the beer shops may have been suitable diversions for some – provided they were not 'too much fatigued'[13] to attend. However, for those whose social lives were entirely work-centred, an evening spent drinking in the company of their workmates was the more tempting prospect. Moreover, such camaraderie among the drinkers bolstered a sense of much-needed solidarity and served as a sort of unofficial 'union' in the troubled years following the Napoleonic Wars. It was also the source of much tension. Workmen at the Old Hall, in 1839, were said to have divided into two classes, the 'sober God-fearing men' and the 'free and easy sort' who were given to 'a good deal of sneering and petty persecution' towards their tee-total workmates.[14] Henry Loveridge, writing about Wolverhampton tinplate workers and japanners in 1866, noted a marked improvement:

> *Many of the men who were most intemperate have become sober. The public house is less frequented than formerly. Sobriety has brought in her train economy and propriety; order reigns where brawls were frequent.[15]*

He gave no explanation for this change, but the enduring hardship engendered by the Corn Laws, the deprivations of the 'hungry Forties', and the feared closure of one of Wolverhampton's largest japan shops, B. Walton and Co., in 1848 (p. 188*ff*), compounded by the generally depressed state of trade in the 1850s which saw many men out of work, must all have played a sobering role. The setting up of a branch of the Tin-plate Workers Union in Wolverhampton in 1845, cannot have come too soon for these workers.

Repetetive and tedious tasks had for long been meted out to women in the industry, and with few exceptions, they undertook most of the unskilled work in each of the three trades. Decorating – by far the largest department – which called for manual dexterity and training, was almost exclusively carried out by men, at least until the decling years of the industry:

> *WANTED PAINTERS that can execute Figures and Landscapes in a Masterly Manner. Also experienced Workmen in the Japan Business, and a Woman that has been accustomed to Stoving of Waiters may have constant Employ.[16]*

This state of affairs continued at least until the industry was at its peak. A newspaper report on female labour in Birmingham in 1850, shows that it was by no means peculiar

---

i. The japanners William Shoolbred, Benjamin Walton, and Edward Perry, were all involved in establishing the 'Tradesmen's & Mechanics Library' in Wolverhampton.

to this particular industry:

> *From the tender age of seven to sixty and upwards, females may be found in the larger or smaller workshops and factories engaged at work which is not always consistent with the notions elsewhere entertained of womanly strength, or even decency and propriety.*[17]

A visitor to Jennens & Bettridge's factory in 1851 was similarly bemused by the situation:

> *The decorative parts of this manufacture seem to suit women's faculties of head and hand; and it looks strange at first sight, that only about a fourth of the three hundred people employed in this establishment are women; and that the women do the coarser parts of the work – having necessarily, lower wages than the men.*[18]

She went on to explain why:

> *Women do not learn the business and stick to it as men do. A boy serves an apprenticeship of seven years; and then regards the employment as the main employment of his life. Girls come for months, or years, as it may happen: and it never does happen that they look upon it as the one settled business of their lives. They marry, or they think of marrying. They are sooner or later,*

more or less unsettled; and it commonly happens that a home and a baby call them from the manufactory, as soon as they have become thoroughly trained to their work.[19]

The introduction of machinery exacerbated their position, reducing not only the number of female workers required, but also any need for manual skills. However, if the sisters Emma and Rose, who worked as polishers in a japan factory in Worcester in the 1860s, were typical, then unskilled work had its advantages – for some women at least. It enabled them to rear large families and to hold down jobs, since as piece-workers, they could easily return home to see to their children between batches of work and this, they thought, 'made for a very happy relaxed atmosphere in one's working life.'[20] More generally, however, such choice was not available to women. In 1874, when asked to consider evening classes for females, the Committee of Birmingham School of Art approached those manufacturers 'whose trade seemed to indicate them as probable employers of women in artistic decoration'[21] and found there was insufficient demand:

> *At present no such work is assigned to women; the operations in which they are chiefly employed being varnishing, polishing, handing, transferring, and such painting or simple operations in metal work as require manual dexterity only without the aid of any artistic education.*[22]

86. Premier-shaped tin bread basket, its edge made from two pieces of metal joined by folded seams at its narrowest point; c.1830s. 22.5 x 36cm

To the educated classes, women who worked in factories were deemed neglectful of both their children and their menfolk and were thus accorded much blame for the frequently depraved morals of both. This attitude, and the lowly status of women in the workplace, can only have worsened their sense of drudgery.

Until the passing of the first Education Act in 1870, children also were engaged as unskilled labour. The pitiful tale of Edward Jones illustrates their unhappy lot: in 1810, aged only ten or eleven, he 'could be seen a shoeless lad, trudging from "Barber's Japan Factory" [qv] at Bilston with bundles of cheap Japan Bread Baskets on his head'[23] to the Old Hall in Wolverhampton, a distance of about two miles (plate 86). His situation improved slightly when his uncle, a foreman at the Old Hall, felt sorry for him and took Edward on as an apprentice, but his hours were very long: 7am to 8pm on weekdays, and Saturday, 'instead of being a half holiday, was the heaviest in the week,'[24] ending at 9 or 10 o'clock at night. On top of this, and to help his parents in their struggle to feed their large family, Edward took on extra work 'painting Tin Toys, rising at 4 o'clock in the morning and working till "the Old Hall Bell" summoned the people to labour at 7.' His 'good Mother', he said, 'always placed a piece of bread on the table for me overnight, so I should not begin work fasting.'[25]

According to Charles Thackrah, the hours of work had somewhat improved by 1832:

> *Japanning, at least as carried on at Birmingham, is remarkable for the comparatively late periods at which the day's labour commences. The operatives begin at eight and end at seven and have the usual intervals of an hour and a half for meals.*[26, ii]

There were exceptions of course; small factory owners themselves, especially if their businesses were new, might work inordinately long hours to meet orders and thus ensure the success of their venture. Overall, however, the introduction of a factory inspectorate in 1833 brought with it much-needed regulation. A Government Report of 1864, was thus able to state:

> *In larger tin-plate and japan factories in Wolverhampton, the employers are opposed to all overtime, and it is scarcely ever resorted to. In some of the smaller factories at Bilston, overtime to 9 and even 11 p.m. is occasionally resorted to for one or two nights in the week, but generally speaking the hours of work in this trade are less than in the other trades of the district.*[27]

As both the century and the industry drew to a close, the working day steadily reduced, so that by 1926, a japanner, or

'blacker' at Scott Harris in Bilston, for example, worked from 8am-5.50pm on weekdays, and 8–12.50 on Saturday mornings – a total of 49 hours per week, excluding breaks.

In 1791, Arthur Young thought wages in Birmingham were 'in general very high'; boys aged ten to twelve were paid from 2s. 6d. to 3s. per week, women from 4s. to 10s., and men from 10s. to 25s., 'and some much higher.' These were 'immense wages', he said, 'indeed they are so great that I am inclined to think labour higher at Birmingham than in any other place in Europe.'[28] Young was referring to the Birmingham trades in general, but if his figures are compared with wages at the Old Hall Japan Works some fifty years later, it appears they are likely to have been typical of the contemporary japanning industry.

In about 1812, 'first class men' at the Old Hall, received 24/- per week (£1.20), and others 18/- to 20/- (90p – £1.00); the weekly rates for apprentices were 4/- rising to 7/6 in their seventh and final year, aged twenty-one.[29] There is no record of how much Walton paid unskilled females, but if women's wages in the Birmingham japanning trade in 1866, may serve as a guide – and bearing in mind that wages were higher there than in Wolverhampton – then it would have been less than half the amount paid to men. In Birmingham, the weekly rates for women were 12/- to 16/- as best 'handers', 10/- to 12/- as blackers, and girls, regardless of job, 6/- a week – considerably less than male decorators who by then received 30/- to 50/- a week, and more if they were 'superior hands employed on special work'.[30] Wages in Bilston were even lower; there, in about 1855, Jackson & Sankey (qv) paid their apprentices 3/- per week in their first year, rising annually by 1/- per week until, in their tenth year, they received 12/-. These rates were considerably in excess of those paid, in Bilston in 1864, to children painters aged eleven to thirteen, who received only 1/6 to 2/-, or if girls, aged fifteen, 3/-. By the 1890s, when demand for japanned goods had declined and there was little work for the best decorators, the average pay for men aged 18 and over, in Birmingham and district, had dropped to 12/4d per week, and by the 1920s, Scott Harris paid their blackers a weekly wage of 26/5d (£1.32).

In selecting where boys should be apprenticed, families remained loyal to specific firms, sending their sons to factories in which they or their siblings already worked. Occasionally, lads were sent further afield – a move which could prove expensive if the master demanded an apprentices fee since on top of this, there would be costs for board and keep. To judge from the large sum of £31 paid for Charles Valentine's seven year apprenticeship with the London japanners Strickland & Wilton in 1791, for example, all these costs were included.[iii]

---

ii. These breaks would have been staggered throughout the day.

Writing in 1837, and despite the assurance that 'nothing is more common ... than for apprentices to be received without any fee whatever',[31] N.Whittock nevertheless considered it necessary to prepare a price-guide to the cost of apprenticeships across the various trades. He thought £40-£60 an appropriate fee for apprentice japanners and varnishers, and £50-£70 for those seeking an apprenticeship at a 'Japan and Tea-tray warehouse'[32] – the distinction being, perhaps, that the latter was concerned wholly with the decorating processes. Fees for apprentice tinmen were pitched significantly lower at £20-£30, presumably to reflect the lower wages available to them at the end of their seven years. Although Whittock had intended to include apprenticeship costs for papier mâché makers, he forgot – an oversight which leads to the deduction that his first category was wholly concerned with making and japanning tin-plate ware.

Although indentures represented a two-way contract, it has already been shown that the scheme was open to considerable abuse by unscrupulous employers who saw these young lads, only two or more years into their apprenticeships, as cheap labour and a means of avoiding the need to pay qualified men at the full rate. This contentious practice had been the subject of a letter to the *Birmingham Gazette* as early as 1767 (p. 59). In addition, apprentices, in all trades, were 'often subjected to rough and cruel treatment.'[33] With this in mind, the following advertisement published in the same newspaper some years earlier, in 1759, is more interesting for what it implied than what it said:

> *Parents and parish officers who have healthy boys not under the age of 11, to place out apprentice, may hear of proper masters ... as will treat their apprentices with humanity and instruct them thoroughly.*[34]

The boys were required to work sixty hours per week, and 'liable to twenty more';[35] any apprentice who neglected his work or absented himself without leave was 'dragged before the magistrate, and as a matter of course, sent to prison for a month.'[36] As a former apprentice-japanner, William Highfield Jones observed: 'It is sad to think that many well-meaning boys, for a slip of this sort, were degraded as common criminals.'[37] The influence of newly formed societies, such as the National Education League, afforded greater protection – not just for apprentices, but for all young factory workers – and required, amongst other regulations, that each factory should keep a register of its child workforce. The fines for ignoring this ruling could be high as John Groves, a Wolverhampton japanner, was reminded by magistrates when he failed to register the name of a young girl in 1869; he was fortunate on that occasion to be fined only £1 plus costs, but as penalties were cumulative, they could run up to £200.

The apprentices were placed under the watchful eye of an experienced worker who taught by example. One of the first things apprentice decorators were taught 'was the power to use a camel hair pencil effectively by what was called in the trade "feeling the point of the pencil". This power', we are told, was gained only by 'long practice.'[38] After seven years spent learning their trade, they might emerge as skilled workmen but their futures were far from secure. James Bissett, who was apprenticed to Thomas Bellamy (*qv*) in Birmingham, in about 1776, in recalling his fellow-apprentices and what became of them on completion of their training, poignantly conjured a sense of atmosphere in the workshop. They were an odd mix; there was Peter Holland from Knutsford in Cheshire who became a drawing master in Liverpool and a Royal Academician, then there was James Green from Wolverhampton who apparently 'died of a broken blood vessel by excessive exercise at Fives',[39] and Charles Maloney 'a very worthy youth'[40] who, having read letters from Bissett's devout mother, was converted and became a Baptist preacher. The fourth was Thomas Sheppard, 'an industrious man with a large family and a rather unthrifty wife',[41] for whom life was a struggle. Bissett encountered him again in 1817 when, as 'a poor meagre-looking old man',[42] Sheppard called on him wishing to dispose of a dozen japanned waiters; Bissett, who by then was very prosperous, bought them all, and Sheppard, overjoyed, declared him to be just 'what you always was'[43] – a generous man. Bissett himself went on to become an 'author, royal medallist, poet, and inventor',[44] and compiler of the lavishly illustrated *Poetic Survey round Birmingham*, accompanied by a *Magnificent Directory* (1800). Thus, out of five apprentices, only one pursued the trade and even then he met with little success. Or, as William Jones, a skilled and competant decorator, found when he received his indentures from the Old Hall in 1851, there was not necessarily a job waiting for trained apprentices if 'trade was bad'.[45]

With little or no education, the lives of the apprentices and other child employees 'would be spent in the limited outlook of the workshop';[46] in this respect, they were worse off than pauper children in work-houses to whom at least some education was freely given. It is all the more remarkable then, that Jones and others like him were able to rise to become masters themselves. Determined to overcome his weaknesses, Jones resolved that during the temporary lull which followed the setting up of his own workshop in 1853, 'I could profitably employ my time by learning the multiplication table correctly, so I paced up and down doing mental arithmetic for I knew I should not have a moment to spare after I began to work'.[47] That any business could prosper with such limited knowledge at its disposal seems incredible to us today, and yet as 'Jones Brothers', this firm flourished into the twentieth century and became a limited liability company.

---

iii. Until 1767, apprenticeships lasted 7 years until the age of 24; thereafter, boys were apprenticed, for a similar period, at the age of 14.

There was a steady exchange of apprentices and specialist workmen between Birmingham and Wolverhampton, and to a lesser extent between these towns and Bilston, and it was evidently worthwhile for japanners in both Pontypool and London to advertise for workmen in the *Birmingham Gazette*. To allay any concerns about moving to a strange and distant town, Allgood of Pontypool assured would-be applicants when he advertised for a tin-plate worker in 1788, that 'Pontipool has a very cheap and plentiful Market, is supplied with Coals at a very moderate Price, and House Rent is remarkably low.'[48] A newspaper announcement to the effect that James Fellows and his wife, formerly of Bilston, and Susannah Compson, formely of Willenhall, had absconded from Allgood & Edwards, in Pontypool, serves to demonstrate that such advertisements were taken up.[49] Similarly, there were several occasions when the japanners Strickland & Co. (*qv*), of Tottenham Court Road, London, widened their search to Birmingham to attract skilled and specialist workmen.

In addition, many Midlands workshops, large and small, were owned or run by men trained in one of the larger establishments in Birmingham or Wolverhampton. Alsager & Neville and McCallum & Hodson are just two of several firms run by men who had worked at Jennens & Bettridge in Birmingham, while in Wolverhampton, the factories of Edward Perry & Co. and Henry Fearncombe were amongst those owned by former employees of the Old Hall. Not all such ventures were successful, as Jones' father, Edward, had found to his cost. After twenty-seven years spent at the Old Hall, fourteen of them as superintendant of the japan department, he set up in business on his own account in 1838 and built 'shopping with Drying Stoves'[50] at the back of his three houses in Melbourne Street, Wolverhampton. Yet despite his considerable experience, Jones sadly underestimated the amount of capital involved and within two years had returned to his former employer.

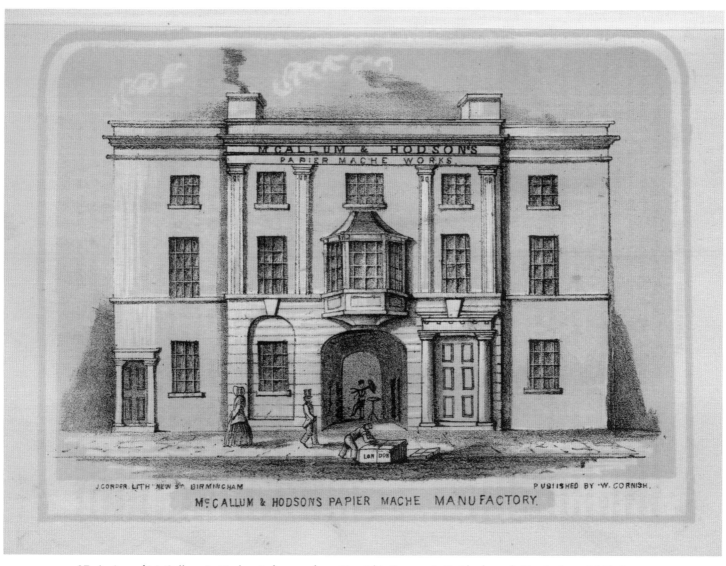

87. A view of McCallum & Hodson's factory, from Cornish's *Stranger's Guide through Birmingham*, 1852–5.

It is difficult to quantify the amount of capital required to set up a japanning factory. A newspaper advertisement from 1778 would seem to provide the answer: 'Wanted a partner in the japanning business that can advance five to six hundred pounds',[51] but was this sum towards setting-up costs, or simply to bail out a financially failing firm? Apart from securing premises and having sufficient funds to pay suppliers and allow credit to customers, it appears from contemporary accounts that the greatest outlay in setting up as a japanner or papier mâché maker was the provision of stoves. William Barrow drew attention to their cost in his offer to set up a japan factory for Matthew Boulton in 1794, and suggested that 'if there are a few vacant shops, about £150 will be sufficient to Build the Stoves etc.'[52] Significantly, this was his only reference to cash requirements. Barrow clearly had a large concern in mind, since most japanners appear to have managed with far less. When Whittock estimated, in 1837, that a small-scale japanner or varnisher required £50–100, and a tinman £100–500, to set up in business, he posed as many questions as he answered: had there been a drastic reduction in the cost of stoves? Had he in mind a japanner who bought ready-made blanks and applied only the thinnest varnish to his goods thereby reducing the number of stoves required? And were the tinman's costs so much greater because he would have to purchase tools and presses? Sadly, there is no way of answering these questions, but by Whittock's reckoning, Jones did very well when he branched out on his own in 1854, for he was able to rent an 'old Japan Factory' for £20 per annum and a cash payment of £20 secured both the japan stove and some old work benches.[53] He was clearly more fortunate than his father, Edward, had been in 1838.

In small workshops, the ovens were like large sheet-metal boxes, with a small door opening into a chamber fitted with wire shelves and hooks from which to suspend some of the articles. In larger firms, the stoves were like small rooms, about ten feet square, with large iron doors through which the stovers pushed their trucks heavily laden with articles to be dried. The goods were stacked on tiered shelves of transverse horizontal iron bars giving the appearance of animal cages – the ovens at McCallum & Hodson's prompted an analogy to 'the dens of the lions and tigers at the Zoological Gardens.'[54]

The earliest brick-built ovens, being heated by underground fires and stoked from outside, were warmest near the outer wall where stoking was easier – this was where chairs and and other large objects were dried. Gas-fired ovens, introduced in the mid-nineteenth century, were so much 'cleaner, more easily regulated and freer from dust',[55] and greatly improved conditions for those factories which could afford to convert; for smaller concerns, however, the stoves continued to demand constant attention. It was uneconomical, for instance, to allow the stoves to cool completely and one man, writing of his father's factory as it was in Bilston in about 1915, recalled that each Sunday morning – their one day of rest – he

and his father walked to the factory to stoke the boiler in readiness for work the following day. Whatever type of oven was used, it was vital to the success of the work that the atmosphere in the painting and varnishing shops be kept as free from dust, smoke and moisture as possible.

Apart from helping to meet the cost of premises and equipment, working under the auspices of a successful manufacturer like Boulton was for some the only means of patenting their ideas. 'Having saved a trifling sum whilst a Journeyman', and having conducted his own 'small manufactory of Japan goods'[56] in Birmingham for three years, Thomas Ashwin (*qv*) sought Boulton's financial help in 1778, to promote what he considered a very advantageous discovery, though he carefully avoided saying what it was. Such applications, while financially necessary, were not without risk as Ashwin was only too aware: 'shou'd it not in your opinion be likely to answer [I] rely upon your honour in keeping the discovery secret'.[57] A further risk, as explained in an article published many years later, in 1853, was that the patentee had to discuss the viability and practicality of his idea with whichever major manufacturer he approached, some of whom, it was said, were known to put the idea into production long before a patent was granted. But what alternative was there for men with ideas but no capital, when, inclusive of living expenses necessitated by having to spend a month or more in London, it cost £96.7s.8d to secure patent protection in England, and a staggering £300 or more for wider protection?

Financial anxieties aside, japanning was a relatively healthy occupation according to Thackrah who wrote, in 1832, that 'Japanners have varied and moderate muscular exertion, in rooms not crowded, and generally well ventilated.'[58] Even so, the conditions in which they worked were far from pleasant. The heat from the stoves was overbearing, according to both Anne Rushout and a later visitor to McCallum & Hodson's factory, and records show they did not exaggerate. Thackrah noted temperatures between 100°F to 110°F outside the stoves, where the operators, for reasons which he did not explain, sat with their backs to the stoves, perspiring profusely, with the result that 'they are subject to head-ache, giddiness, and loss of appetite';[59] in addition, as mentioned previously, 'restricted in their drink while at work, they are said to indulge in the use of spirits at night.'[60] As Harriet Martineau observed, stoving 'must be unwholesome work'.[61]

W.H. Jones, recalling his apprenticeship at the Old Hall in the 1840s, wrote of 'foul-smelling whale oil' burning in tin oil lamps during the winter months, and of 'dense clouds of black smoke'[62] issuing from them. By the mid nineteenth century, most large factories had installed gas-lighting, which although cleaner, still created a smoky atmosphere and hardly provided adequate light for intricate decorative work; tallow candles provided back-up when the gas failed. Improved lighting and the introduction of gas-fired stoves removed many evils from the industry and by 1864, a Government report, almost echoing Thackrah's report over thirty years earlier, noted that 'most of the factories of this class, both in Wolverhampton and Bilston, are well built and the rooms properly ventilated. As a rule they are not overcrowded.'[63]

Conditions in 'the dark japanning shops'[64] were no worse, and the hazards often a good deal fewer, than those that attended other industries, but it is useful to remember the environment in which these goods were made and decorated.

The hot, murky atmosphere, the ceaseless noise of hammering and stamping, and the constant risk of fire posed by the many inflammable substances stored on the premises,[iv] combined with the 'disagreeable' smell of varnish, the long hours and the health risks attendant upon specific processes make it abundantly clear why George Dickinson believed that being apprenticed to the japan trade was 'not a bed of roses'. In general however, the industry offered relatively secure employment and the decorators, in particular, were highly esteemed workmen, both within the factory and beyond.

iv. Barney & Ryton's warehouse was destroyed by fire in Dec.1790 (see p. 184), and a fire in premises adjoining Henry Clay's factory caused minor damage to his factory in September 1792. These are but two examples of a perennial hazard.

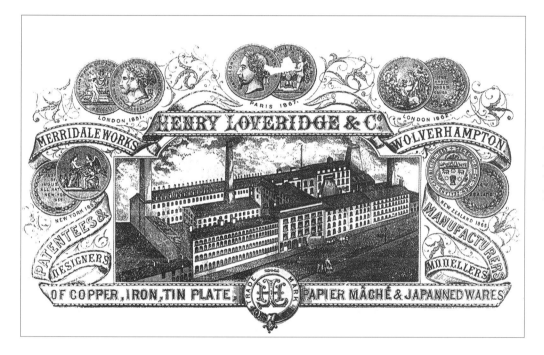

88. The Merridale Works of Henry Loveridge & Co., from their catalogue of 1869, showing one of their trade marks.

WOLVERHAMPTON ARTS AND HERITAGE (BANTOCK HOUSE MUSEUM)

89. Convex-edge tin tray, painted with *A View of High Street, Birmingham*, from the aquatint by J.C. Stadler, published 1 July, 1812, by T. Hollins; Birmingham; c.1815. 56 x 77.5cm

COLLECTION OF DAVID AND ROSEMARY TEMPERLEY, PHOTOGRAPH BY COURTESY OF JOHN MARKS

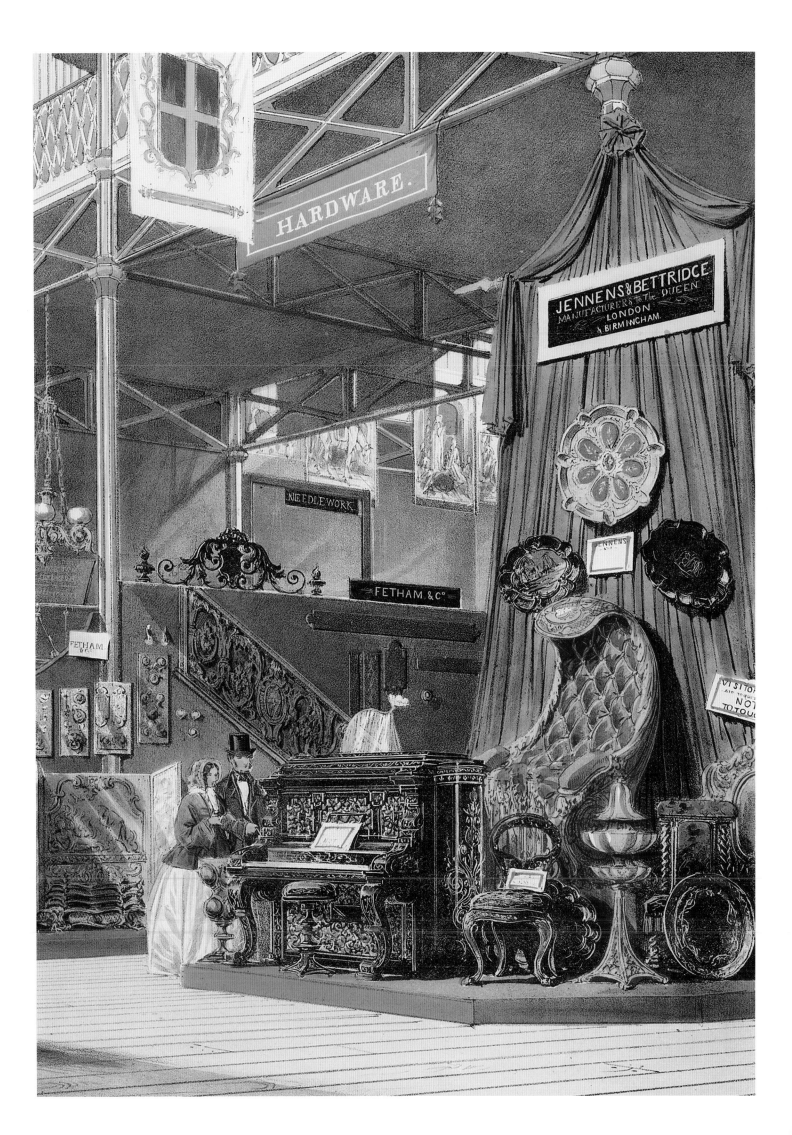

CHAPTER VI

CLEVER ACCIDENTS?
Design, Taste and Criticism

'Papier mâché articles ... are shams – we know that. They wriggle themselves into society under false pretensions. They pretend to be mosaic or marqueterie or arabesque... Why talk severely of styles, or taste, or schools...? What although a man combines arabesque with renaissance, and byzantine with early Christian? Would you enlarge upon anatomy to a dollmaker, or upon comparative anatomy to a hobby-horse manufacturer?'

The Morning Chronicle, 14 May 1851

The ambivalence that characterises the above view is indicative of reservations held by contemporary critics about 'the redundancy and inappropriateness of much of the ornament'[1] on japanned goods at the Great Exhibition, and highlight in particular, current concerns about papier mâché which, being usually more fashion-led and less functional than japanned tin-ware, received the greater derision (p. 90).

While admitting that 'very beautiful work of this kind is to be found', critics generally shared the view that 'the florid decoration of common papier mâché goods, paint and gold upon mother-of-pearl and tinfoil, without art, or taste, or even cleverness, must be classed amongst the most wretched instances of misspent labour.'[2] Their patrician jibes, of course, did not reflect public opinion at large since the standards by which quality and value were popularly judged were mostly based on technical expertise and thus very different from those employed by the artistic intelligentsia.

Such criticism was rarely heard before the 1830s, but by 1886, papier mâché, once admired for its intrinsic qualities, was 'condemned by fashion and Art-priggery as lacking in "truth"'[3] – in other words, designers were not true to the possibilities of the materials with which they worked. And, to this day, there are those for whom japanned papier mâché and tinware continue to symbolise the worst excesses of High Victorian taste. So, what had gone wrong, and when?

The earliest articles on which Midlands japanners worked followed established design traditions. Iron-tray and snuff-box makers took their lead from those in Pontypool who themselves had looked to familiar silver shapes. Similarly, early papier mâché box-makers emulated the highly esteemed articles made from the same material by the Martin brothers in Paris who, in turn, were mirroring shapes used by contemporary goldsmiths. Even after Clay's 1772 patent, the resulting flat sheets of pasteboard were

90. Detail from 'The 1851 exhibition stand of Jennens & Bettridge'; a lithograph from *Dickinsons Comprehensive Pictures of the Great Exhibition of 1851*, published London, 1854. 43.5 x 59cm

91. Detail from the lid of the box surmounting the cabinet shown in pl. 171, decorated with a painted view of Osborne House, after Thomas Allom (see p. 173).

employed mainly as substitutes for wood or metal, and were sawn and fashioned into trays, caddies and other boxes in shapes traditionally associated with those materials. Despite its potential, therefore, Clay's patent did not immediately bring about any significant change in the range of objects available.

The same was true of early decoration; oriental subjects which featured prominently on Pontypool tinware and the 'picture' trays for which that town was later renowned were both adopted and adapted by Midlands japanners, and continued for some time after (plate 92). So too, were the delicate floral motifs and pastoral scenes found on *vernis Martin* and, indeed, on most European porcelain of the period. In short, the shapes and decoration of early japanned goods accorded with what was generally perceived as 'good taste' among the fashionable society for whom they were made.

By the early nineteenth century, when production was faster and the trade had expanded to meet the needs of more popular markets, papier mâché and tinware became available in a wider range of qualities. New, less sophisticated styles of decoration were introduced. Writing in 1851, Harriet Martineau recalled how:

Forty years ago, one of the things we were most sure to see on entering the parlour of the farm-house, lodging house, or shop-keeper's back room, or the kitchen of the best sort of cottage, was a gaudy tea-tray, set up against

the wall on the top of the bureau, or the side table, or the dresser. On the tray might be painted a yellow tiger, or a scarlet lion, or a pink shepherdess with a green shepherd; or a very yellow sheep beside a very red cow; or flowers and fruit, not particularly like anything that ever was really seen. (plate 94)

'Those were the war-days', she added, 'when the English taste had no opportunity of being improved by intercourse with foreign countries.'[4] Nor, of course, was there any desire for contact with France, as their fashions were at that time a subject for mockery in both the political press and popular cartoons. Martineau was not alone in her thinking. Since the eighteenth century, decorative artists in France and Germany had received formal tuition in design which gave them a leading edge over their English counterparts. The disadvantages of there being no comparable instruction for English artisans was the subject of much discussion in London and led to the founding of the Society for the Encouragement of Arts, Manufactures and Commerce (later styled the Royal Society of Arts). No doubt prompted by the on-going debate, the same concern was aired in a Birmingham newspaper by one, 'A.B.' in January, 1754 – just two months prior to the Society's establishment:

If a Deficiency in the Art of Drawing and Designing is the great obstruction to our making a more considerable Figure in the Iron, or any other Manufactory, than what we have hitherto done, why is it not some Method fix'd upon for improving that Art amongst us?[5]

92. Papier mâché tea-board with a deep sandwich-edge, and narrow rim, decorated with early bronze chinoiseries in variously coloured metal powders; c.1825. 39 x 51cm

93. Tin tray painted with the *Death of Wolfe*, after Benjamin West; Birmingham or Wolverhampton; c.1795. 58.5 x 76cm

94. Convex-edge tin tray with stencilled bronze decoration incorporating tigers (see p. 100); Birmingham or Wolverhampton, c.1830. W: 78.5cm

It was in this climate that private academies were set up in manufacturing towns to teach the art of drawing to artisans. In 1760, for example, James Eagle, a Birmingham chaser and steel engraver, informed 'mechanicks in the Toy Trade that he intends to open a drawing school to teach the art of drawing'.[6] This and other similar academies evidently had some influence, for in 1818, 'toys' made in Birmingham were said to have been 'formed with the utmost taste, and admirably finished' – qualities which, it was suggested, were due chiefly to the establishment of 'a seminary for drawing and modelling'.[7] In general however, these private initiatives were beyond the means of the average artisan who had to wait another twenty-five years before any affordable and professional design teaching became available in the region. In the meantime, japanners in all branches of the industry, acquired their skills through working as apprentices alongside their masters.

Continued concern about how far England lagged behind France and Germany in matters of design resulted in the Board of Trade setting up a School of Design at Somerset House in London in 1837. By 1843, a branch School of Practical Art was established in Birmingham, with teachers trained at Somerset House, and a similar school opened in Wolverhampton in 1854. For a small sum, manufacturers could enrol their artists and designers as part-time students at these schools in the hope that they would 'carry out of them, into their workshops, ideas, which prevent them from tolerating things in positive contrast to the perfections of the antique'[8] – an aspiration wholly in accord with critics of the japanning industry.

The Report of the 1844 Annual General Meeting of Birmingham School of Art, made clear that japanners were among the School's major targets for student recruitment. 'The Papier Mâché Manufacturers', it noted, 'will be enabled to combine good and correct drawing (often a desideratum), with the gorgeous colouring the late improvements in this branch of manufacture has enabled the artist to use and render permanent.' Out of a total of 143 students from local manufactories, there were twenty-six from japan workshops in 1845 (by far the largest single group of artisans in attendance), followed by eighteen die sinkers, and fourteen architects. Predictably, they were drawn from the most prestigious factories: Jennens & Bettridge, Thomas Lane's Royal Papier Mâché Works, McCallum & Hodson, and the bedstead manufactory of R. Winfield – all were firms whose masters were actively engaged in supporting the School. In Wolverhampton there were forty-two japanners out of a total of 347 students at the School of Art. Although this was less than half the number of 'schoolboys' in attendance, it was, again, the largest single group of local tradesmen to take advantage of the classes. That only one tin-plate worker (as distinct from japanner) was recorded, indicates the extent to which form came second to surface decoration in the minds of local manufacturers.

By the 1840s, further improvements in stamping and moulding iron and papier mâché, together with new decorative techniques, had allowed for ranges of japanned goods unlike any that had preceded them. In effect, a wholly new industrial art had been invented and the then unique properties of papier mâché were exploited to create forms which, at the time, could not easily have been made from any other material (plate 141). Unfortunately, since most factories were 'managed by warehousemen and shopmen, who are as a body ignorant of the elements of drawing and design',[9] these new forms and decorative techniques were mainly matters of trial and frequent error. 'The besetting sin of the papier mâché artist', reported the *Art Union* in 1846, 'is a tendency to excessive fulness [of decoration]. There seems to be a kind of fascination in the material, which lures him on and on, almost in spite of himself.'[10] It was a failing which George Wallis still fulminated against ten years later:

The facile power of hand displayed by our japanners is often very great, but this is too frequently directed by nothing more than the merest tradition of the workshop. The inventive power, too, of some of the most talented is also very great; but being undisciplined by a knowledge of the laws which govern composition in ornament, they are rather the producers of clever accidents in arrangement, than designers in the full sense of the term.[11]

Thus, the setting up of the art schools, while a step in the right direction, had not improved matters overnight. When 'a manufacturer of a superior class to the average' – though not a japanner – could say 'with perfect *naiveté*' in 1849, that 'a designer's ability is quite a gift, like an instinct, but an artist's is quite mechanical!',[12] he, and others like him, would take a lot of convincing before they believed otherwise. As Wallis expostulated:

So long as this state of things exists employers may calculate upon little improvement in their manufactures; and with a beautiful material, great facilities in production, almost boundless variety in pigments, gold and silver powders, gold leaf, and pearl, the higher qualities of design will remain dormant for want of educ[ated] power in the worker.[13]

Despite the apparent contradiction of his having written, only a year before, that the same 'facilities' were 'stumbling blocks'[14] in the pursuit of purer design, Wallis and his fellow critics were simply saying that there was nothing intrinsically wrong with the materials employed by japanners, only with the way in which they frequently misused them. They had no problem, for example, with papier mâché being used for chairs, couches, tables, or cradles, as long as it was 'considered purely for itself '[15] and not as a substitute for other materials.

However, such arguments were becoming academic as the market for high quality papier mâché had begun to decline. At the same time, and perhaps not coincidentally, the number of japanning apprentices attending classes at Birmingham School of Art had also fallen significantly. By 1858, they had dropped to twenty-four and no longer represented the largest group, that distinction having shifted to engravers who outstripped japanners by more than two to one – a clear sign of the threat posed by the success of electro-plating. Ten years later – after the closure of Jennens & Bettridge – the number of japanners in attendance had fallen to two. In Wolverhampton, only eleven japanners and no tinplate-workers attended the school in 1858 – a disappointing return, especially in view of a renewed interest in japanned iron goods following the succesful introduction of toilet sets (plate 229). The japanner, Henry Loveridge, himself chairman of Wolverhampton School of Art, neatly summed up the situation in 1866:

The great and valuable benefits to be obtained from a School of Practical Art are not yet thoroughly understood in this locality, or we should most certainly see more of the artisan children there, where for so trifling a fee sound knowledge may be obtained from thoroughly qualified teachers; but the lack of knowledge is not felt by many of the men, and their children, of course, lose the advantages which are so nearly at hand.[16]

Nevertheless, their influence was felt, albeit indirectly and somewhat negatively. Questions concerning the design and decoration of japanned ware increased noticeably around the time of the opening of the art schools. Simultaneously, and

not unconnectedly, a number of critical articles about British decorative art industries began to appear in newly-introduced journals devoted to art and design. Though many reviews were complimentary, from then on, the critics had a regular public forum and no amount of novelty would protect the trade from its detractors – their knives were out and they were braced for 'the attack'. 'The sooner [papier mâché] has a thorough revision the better,' said a juror at the 1851 Exhibition, 'since at present it is a mass of barbarous splendour that offends the eye and quarrels with every other kind of manufacture with which it comes in contact.'[17]

A tray made by McCallum & Hodson, and painted with Irish views, was taken to task in the *Art Union* in 1846, for having the landscapes painted partly over its edge:

Every object became distorted; a "round tower" was bent "two double;" and the trees were made to assume most unnatural twists. This is an unpardonable error on the part of the designer, or rather the arranger, and one we pray him in future to avoid. The evil is the greater, because the landscapes referred to were wrought with considerable skill.[18]

David Sarjeant, a juror at the 1851 Exhibition, and a japanner himself, recalled in 1867 how 'it became a favourite practice with art critics and lecturers to point to the papier mâché trade as a shocking example of the untaught condition of English art-workmen.'[19] The errors which especially outraged its critics were catalogued in a critique entitled *A House full of Horrors* published in 1852. They included a papier mâché tray which had been selected as a specimen of poor design for the Department of Practical Art's museum at Marlborough House. Painted 'with a bit of one of Landseer's pictures', it was described as:

An example of popular but vulgar taste, of a low character, presenting numerous features which the student should carefully avoid:– First, The centre is the piracy of a picture; Second, The picture on which the most labour has been bestowed, is thrown away. It is wrong to hide a picture by putting a tea-pot on it: if a picture is wanted it should be placed where it can be seen, and will not be destroyed by use; Third, the scroll lines of the ornament, instead of following the form, are directly opposed to it, and are scattered, as if by chance, anywhere; Fourth, the glitter of the mother-of-pearl is the most prominent feature of the whole, and being spread about, creates the impression that the article is slopped with water.[20] (plate 95)

The rationale for this attack was provided by guidelines laid down for designers by the Government School of Art. One guideline, which must have come as a shock to japanners, was 'that flat surfaces should not be ornamented with imitations of objects in relief',[21] thus ruling out flowers and other favourite subjects for the decoration of trays, table-tops and their like. Another, somewhat unrealistic recommendation was 'that each article of furniture should "tell its own story", from a coal scuttle to a piano! That the one should be decorated with a scene from a coal-mine, and the other with the Muse of Harmony and singing birds!'[22] Since the commercial viability of luxury articles decorated with industrial views was likely to be somewhat limited, this, together with other guidelines, was manifestly ignored.

The criticisms and debates, however, had positive results in the run-up to the Great Exhibition, when distinguished designers were consulted about the composition and decoration of goods intended for display: Jennens & Bettridge looked to John Bell (1811–95), for example, and Walton & Co. to Owen Jones (1809–74).[i] However, due to a lingering air of mistrust about whether the new and 'somewhat severer style' could survive the temptation to revert to "startling effects",[23] any impact made by these authorities tended to be overshadowed by continuing tirades against the excesses of japanners' other manufactures.

The critics were at their fiercest during the national and international exhibitions of trade and industry which, since the late 1830s, had become strategic showcases for major producers of all classes of goods, both at home and abroad. In a new climate of conspicuous consumption, firms competed to produce ever larger, more elaborate and eye-catching products. Sarjeant, writing in 1867 of japanned ware exhibited in 1851, said it was as if 'the public conceived a notion that the quantity of material was the test of value and began to ask for more pearl and gold.'[24] Again, Harriett Martineau spoke for many when she objected to the 'tinfoil look' of such decoration,'[25] but more stoically, George Dodd saw it as a passing fashion and predicted that 'something more sober, will probably live longer.'[26]

By 1856, according to Wallis, though there 'appeared' to be greater restraint generally, he saw little evidence of it among Birmingham's japanners. He believed progress would come only as 'the result of improvements in other departments of ornamental industry being taken up from time to time, and adapted to the wants of the japanner and his employer'.[27] To some extent events proved him right, for as we have seen, several border patterns introduced in the 1860s had much in common with those found on electro-plated goods. Even so, while conceding there were exceptions, Wallis generally lambasted the decoration of the japanned ware shown at the 1862 exhibition in London.[ii] Had the schools of art had no effect on drawing, he wondered, and why did 'brainwork' not

count for as much as 'handwork'? And perversely, designs which concurred with his own preference for minimal decoration did not escape criticism since he saw them as proof that japanners did, in fact, know better.

Part of the problem with papier mâché was its popularity both at home and abroad. Aitken, writing in 1866, laid the blame for deteriorating standards squarely on export goods:

> *Besides the ordinary articles for house-consumption, large quantities of panels for steam-boat cabins, dining room furniture, &c, are made for the export trade to Canada, North and South America, Russia, Spain, &c., besides an immense variety of large pieces of household furniture, wardrobes, loo and other tables, dressing glasses, sofas &c., decorated to suit the taste or the want of taste of purchasers in the countries to which they are exported.*[28]

Cruelly, the mounting production costs incurred by the overseas liking for 'over-elaboration' were met by a reduction in the amount paid to each workman. Decorators unprepared to lower their standards left the trade and were replaced by inferior workers, or in some cases children. But as Aitken shrewdly observed, while well-designed goods appealed only to those 'of educated taste', it was 'too much to expect that producers should deliberately shut themselves out of the more extended and profitable market'.[29] Somewhat disparagingly, Sarjeant believed this bothered neither those buyers at home who could not 'discern between the qualities of good and bad work', nor those in America who, anyway, 'had a decided liking for the latter kind'.[30] Thus, despite the setting up of the art schools, public taste had shifted little since the time when Sam Wiley, an employee at Jennens & Bettridge, lamented in 1835 'I could frequently sell bad articles, bad in execution and design, for the same money as I could sell the best.'[31, iii]

Having invested so much in the American market, many japanners were caught out, first by the Morrill Tariff Act of 1861, which all but ended that country's trade with England, and then by its taxation on British manufactures which, by 1867, had risen to 80%. The result was that a surplus of 'rubbish hitherto made for America'[32] was sold very cheaply on the English market. The tawdriness of these goods, together with 'a morbid taste' which had developed 'for placing great blotches of pearl upon articles made of pulp, and finishing them in the gaudiest of colours', plunged the standing of japanned goods to yet lower depths. 'Nothing in worse taste could possibly be conceived.'[33]

i. It has been suggested that Henry Loveridge engaged Christopher Dresser to design some water jugs in the 1860s (see Everett, A., 'Wolverhampton Japanned Ware', in Lyons H., *Christopher Dresser: the People's Designer, 1834-1904*, p.216). Evidence for this is based on designs found in a pattern book held by Wolverhampton Art Galleries & Museums (patt. Bk no. LP 154), the numbers of which are prefixed 'D' which are tentatively taken to stand for Dresser. However, it is worth noting that patterns in another book are prefixed 'A' and 'B'.
ii. See George Wallis, *The Art Manufactures of Birmingham and the Midland Counties in the International Exhibition of 1862*, London, Virtue Bros., 1863, where the decoration of the bedstead makers, Peyton & Peyton, and the japanners, J. Bettridge & Co., Griffiths & Browett, R. Turley, and McCallum & Hodson, was severely criticised.
iii. I am grateful to Clive D. Edwards for permission to quote from his book, *Victorian Furniture, Technology & Design*, Manchester University Press, 1993, p. 129.
iv. G.W. Yapp was Assistant Commissioner and Compiler of the Official Catalogue of the 1851 Exhibition.

95. Concave king-gothic tray painted with a detail from Sir Edwin Landseer's painting, *Bolton Abbey in the Olden Time*; indistinctly lettered, in script, for Jennens & Bettridge, c.1850, 35.5 x 48cm. This is probably the tray criticised by the Department of Practical Art, in 1852 (see p. 103).

By 1876, Grecian, Etruscan and Persian designs, 'chaste and decided in character'[34] had become the fashion of the day. Their symmetry, although often incorporating motifs of extraordinary intricacy (plate 219), lent itself to transfer printing and thus removed the need for the dextrous brush-work which had been such a feature of earlier painted and gilt ornament. Similarly, the intricacy of early pearlwork was replaced by 'neat narrow pearl lines and ornaments'.[35] In effect, these styles which had been encouraged by the critics, brought with them unemployment for those decorators engaged in work of the highest technical order. As to form and shape, those 'that were popular half a century ago, are in renewed demand ... and stranger still, the ornamentation on these trays has once more reverted to the old Japanese style of enrichment (plate 73).[36]

'The want of artistic education in the public as well as in the manufacturers of such goods ... happily has at last been nearly annihilated by its own extravagance',[37] or so G.W. Yapp[iv] said of the japanning industry in 1879, choosing to ignore the important part played by the retail buyer who 'practically decides not what the taste of the public may really demand, but that which in his judgment will best suit it.'[38] However, enthusiasm for a revived interest and regard for surface decoration totally overlooked the fact that the materials from which the articles were made, were fast becoming outmoded and that, sadly, no amount of art education would permit the industry to survive.

Given the vociferousness of critics, it is not surprising that neither japanned tin nor papier mâché feature in contemporary books on household furnishings, unless as targets for derision. Writing in 1850 for a readership with more conventional tastes, an anonymous author was probably nearer popular opinion in stating that 'among the many beautiful arts ... not one occupies so conspicuous a position as that of Papier Mâché work, which has during the last few years become so popular'.[39] At the same time, the author acknowledged that 'in this, as in everything else, there are infinite varieties of quality, and value'.[40]

No.213. LETTER BOX.

No.1807. NEW KNIFE TRAY.

No.930. ROUND SPICE BASKET.

No.931. OBLONG SPICE BASKET.

No.922. ROUND TEA CANISTER.

No.936. SPICE BOX.

No.937. OBLONG SPICE BOX.

CINNAMON | ALLSPICE | NUTMEGS
CLOVES | MACE | GINGER

No.921. ROUND CANISTER.

No.1806. SINGLE-KNIFE TRAY.

No.1809. DOUBLE KNIFE TRAY.

No.1810. DOUBLE KNIFE TRAY.

TAYLOR, LAW & CO., BIRMINGHAM.

96. A page of utilitarian domestic goods from the catalogue of Taylor, Law & Co., Birmingham; c.1890.

PHOTO BY COURTESY OF DAVID TEMPERLEY

CHAPTER VII

THE DECLINE of the MIDLANDS JAPANNING INDUSTRY

'Fashion and caprice have done much to vary the form and quality of japan ware; and competition has reduced the profits of the trade to mediocrity.'
The History of Birmingham, William Hutton, 6th edn., 1860

In 1899, the *Journal of Decorative Art* published an article entitled 'The Rise and Fall of an Art Industry', in which it was remarked that:

> The art of japanning declined from the year 1851. At the present day there is but a small demand for fine work, and but few good men work at it ... whilst art is more of a fashion than a necessity in our daily life, there is little hope that the applied art of the japanner may revive.[1]

Whilst the anonymous author went on to identify some of the major factors in the demise of the industry, the underlying causes were more complex, not least because the two branches of the industry (papier mâché and tinware) declined at differing rates and for different reasons. Not surprisingly, the papier mâché trade, reliant upon a fickle luxury market, succumbed sooner than the japanned tin trade which provided for more utilitarian markets, and showed no significant drop in demand until the 1860s. The demise of each branch therefore, is best considered separately.

According to David Sarjeant, writing in 1867 'the sudden decline of the papier mâché trade' was not due to the product having 'been superseded by any materials possessing more desirable qualities', but rather it was the result of 'a period of unhealthy prosperity, which', he said, 'culminated some thirteen years back.'[2] In short, like the above author,

he blamed the influence of the Great Exhibition of 1851, and the years leading up to it, for encouraging manufacturers in many decorative industries, to vie with each other to produce elaborate showpieces, and in the case of japanners, to upstage and literally outshine their rivals. Before then, Sarjeant said, japanning 'had been a steady and improving trade, but now it began to attract undue public attention, and at length it became *fashionable* both here and abroad, and now', he concluded, 'the seeds of disaster were sown.'[3] Maybe he was alluding, like Aitken a year earlier, to the bouyant international market for large showy pieces of furniture. Curiously, this growth was not matched by a corresponding rise in the production of trays and other small articles.

Although contemporary critics had predicted a downturn of interest if manufacturers did not pay greater attention to matters of design and decoration, their influence was minimal. Not only were the goods they favoured more expensive than the general but their more severe styles had less appeal to the wider public for whom lavish quantities of pearl and gold ornament equated with value. With too few skilled workmen still in their employ by the 1860s, many manufacturers found it more profitable to produce 'gaudy and meretricious decoration, to the neglect of better and more studied work'.[4] Cost-cutting had became the order of the day although, as Aitken shrewdly observed:

97. Round-gothic tin cake basket, thickly painted and highlighted with gold leaf; Henry Loveridge & Co., c.1880. Dia: 27cm

The leading manufacturers fully understand the errors of the style ... but so long as ... show and glitter [are favoured] and articles decorated in accordance with true principles are only selected by buyers of educated taste, it is too much to expect that producers should deliberately shut themselves out of the more extended and profitable market.[5]

Tawdry decoration and the introduction of ready-made stamped pulp blanks to reduce costs in the 1860s soon made papier mâché 'totally unworthy of the name'.[6] Pulp trays which sold in the last quarter of the nineteenth century at 6s 6d per set of three were a far cry from the paper tea-boards which, one hundred years earlier, Henry Clay had sold for upwards of three-guineas each. In short, 'good work did not pay, and after a time bad work did not sell.'[7]

Besides declining standards of workmanship, there were external factors which adversely affected the japanning industry and papier mâché in particular. Caroline Martineau, during a visit to Birmingham, foreshadowed the serious impact of electro-plated goods in her journal on 16 August, 1850. 'After dinner', she wrote, 'we visited Jennens &

Bettridge's papier mâché factory & were taken round to see the different processes ... We were a long time among the beauties in the show-room all of which', she lamented, 'were far beyond our means.' By comparison, three days later in Elkington's 'magnificent show-rooms' she saw the most splendid looking plate', the cost of which she observed was 'reduced to the means of everyone.'[8] Thomas Archer, commenting on the 1867 exhibition, also pointed to 'powerful rivals', explaining that:

Embossed leather has gained great hold on public favour; and in higher walks, articles with panels of enamel or porcelain, mounted in ormolu or ebony, or with other combinations, take the position once occupied by papier mâché.[9]

In addition, the taste for Japanese (as distinct from japanned) artefacts that had developed in artistic circles in the 1850s, had been bolstered by the Japanese displays at the International Exhibition in London in 1862. Firms like Farmers & Rogers, and later Liberty & Co., both in London, began to specialise in the sale of exotic eastern goods, particularly to artists, designers, architects and aesthetes who bought not only a screen or the odd piece of lacquered furniture, but occasionally furnished entire rooms in the Japanese style. Although famously parodied by Gilbert & Sullivan's *Patience* in 1881, 'Japonisme' continued as a major design influence until the end of the century, and midlands japanners were dealt a severe blow by the flimsy but competetively priced lacquered goods made in the East to suit popular Western tastes which soon flooded the market.

Moreover, the fiscal anomaly which allowed large quantities of inexpensive German papier mâché articles to be imported free of duty, while similar English products were subjected to heavy fees when exported to the continent, further dented the already vulnerable Midlands japanning industry. These German goods, made by the firm of Adt Frères (*qv*), were widely exported across Europe and the USA, and frequently advertised in late nineteenth and early twentieth century shopping catalogues issued by firms like Harrods, and Gamages, in London, and by Sears and Roebuck in Chicago (1908). They have survived in large numbers, most notably in the form of trays, string boxes, dressing-table sets, and other small articles. Mostly, they are transfer-printed in gold with oriental scenes, or all-over star patterns, or they are painted with daisies and chrysanthemums (plate 313).

Another influx was Swedish wood-pulp, introduced as a substitute for paper-pulp in the 1880s. This allowed English papier mâché manufacturers like Ebeneezer Sheldon in Birmingham (*qv*) and 'Thetford Pulpware' (*qv*) in Norfolk to make similarly small, inexpensive articles. Both firms are known to have decorated their wares with oriental-style prints, and some of the Thetford shapes and designs in particular, bore a close resemblance to Adt products. By now, oriental lacquer and German imports were so freely available and low-priced, that no amount of imitation would allow English japanners to compete favourably. Firms like Henry Loveridge & Co. and McCallum & Hodson continued to produce good quality wares until the 1920s and 1930s respectively, but they were the exceptions rather than the rule. Had it not been for the loyalty of their ageing workforces, the elderly proprietors would probably have closed their factories sooner. Over and above these factors, was the instability of the American financial markets brought about by over-speculative trading and unsustainable development during the prosperity of the early 1850s. The commodity market collapsed, there was widespread depression, and, in 1861, just prior to the start of the American Civil War, the Morrill Tariff was introduced to prohibit all external trade. The export of foreign goods to America all but ceased until peace was restored in 1865.

98. Tin tray with transfer-printed decoration; made by Henry Loveridge & Co., c.1910. Dia: 46cm

WOLVERHAMPTON ARTS AND HERITAGE (BANTOCK HOUSE MUSEUM)

While the papier mâché trade began to decline around 1850, the vicissitudes of japanned tin-ware followed an altogether different path. Wolverhampton's japanned tin trade was said to have doubled between 1849 and 1862, partly, it was thought, on account of the expansion of existing firms and the entry of new ones. Its growth was all the more remarkable for coinciding not only with the Great Tin-plate Workers Strike of 1850, but a concurrent depression in the iron trade, and the impact of the recently-developed electro-plating industry.

Japanned tin had held its own against papier mâché until the 1830s when improved production methods allowed the latter to dominate the luxury market. In contrast to papier mâché, tinware was less durable because its surface soon rusted once damaged. Nevertheless, at the lower end of the market, it remained popular for colourful, everyday utilitarian trays – the 'bread-and-butter' lines of most japanners and the 'cheap tin trays' of John Masefield's poem *Cargoes* (1910).

The following list of japanned tinware shown at the 1851 exhibition by Edward Perry of Wolverhampton – a firm badly hit by the Tin-plate Workers Strike – is worth quoting in full to show the range of goods made by the largest japanners. Although long, it is by no means exhaustive:

> *baths; bread and cake baskets; boiler fillers; bonnet boxes; botanical boxes; candle boxes and safes; candlesticks; canisters, round and square; cash-boxes; cheese trays; agar trays; coal scoops, shovels, and [coal] vases; date cases; dressing cases; ewers and basins; fire*

baskets and screen; gunpowder canister; hearing trumpet; inkstands; jugs; knife trays; lamps, lanterns; leg bath; letter cages; music stand; nursery lamps; plate carriers and warmers; sandwich and spice boxes; spittoons; snuffer trays; sugar-boxes; tables; tea caddies; toast racks; toilette sets; trays; umbrella stands; vegetable warmers; ventilators; waiters; water cans; wax boxes and writing boxes.[10]

Away from the context of a major international exhibition where 'showiness' was paramount, the majority of these articles, intended for everyday household use, would have been simply decorated, usually with no more than bands of colour and dutch-gold. Articles which were more lavishly decorated were intended for use in family rooms 'above stairs', rather than in the servants' quarters below.

By the 1860s, japanners had begun to feel the effects of the electro-plating trade. Competetively priced trays, looking for all the world like real silver, began to displace demand for japanned tin trays. Utilitarian goods like lamps and shovels, were not affected, but it prompted japanners to focus upon their newer products – coal vases, boxes and purdoniums, toilette sets, and baths – for which no improved substitutes were yet available. A few japanned coal receptacles date from earlier periods, but mostly the elaborately decorated examples

which have survived in large numbers (and in varying states of repair), were made around this time. In practical terms, no contemporary material rivalled japanned iron for such products and it thus outlived the fashion for papier mâché, albeit by only a few years.

Between 1870 and 1875, the japanned iron trade enjoyed two further and final fillips. The first was the opening up of foreign markets following the Franco-German War (1870), and the second, a new demand for japanned iron travelling trunks, not only for overseas travel, but also to provide for the developing trend towards seaside holidays on the homeland. 'Output and prices soared',[11, i] but the introduction of the power press at much the same time greatly reduced the cost of tin-plate blanks and saw the trade through the Great Depression which gripped the nation in 1878-9.[ii]

Having, to some extent, overcome competition from electro-plated goods, japanned iron was beginning to be replaced by other materials like steel which, being more ductile, yielded better under the pressure of the new presses. By the early twentieth century, vitreous enamel ware and aluminium had taken over from japanned metal. Not only was the material itself outmoded, but so too were some of the staple products which had been fashioned from it; shopkeepers for example, had replaced japanned cash-boxes with more efficient check-tills.

99. Oval tin footbath from a toilet set (*cf.* pl. 221), with a brass label stamped for the retailers Wilson & Smith, Late Barron & Wilson, King William Street, Strand; 1900–1910. W: 53cm
Courtesy of Duke's Auctioneers, Dorchester.

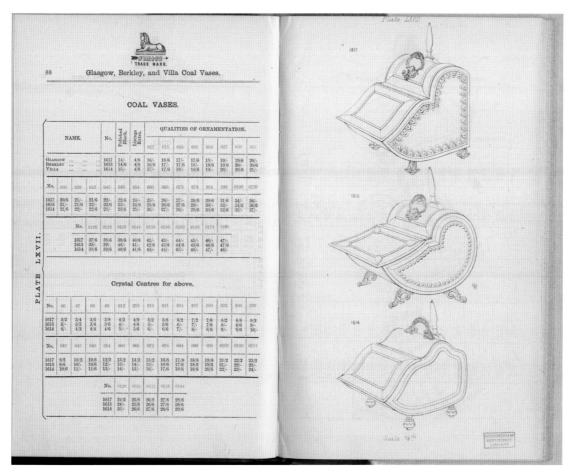

100. Pages from the *List of Prices* issued by J.H. Hopkins & Sons, 1874.

A few workshops survived into the 1930s, but most of their metal workers had already turned their skills to other industries like the copper, aluminium and sheet-metal goods trades of the region. Likewise, some of the 'blackers' or varnishers, and filetters turned to the bicycle and newly-emergent motor-car industries: the workforce itself had come to see no future in the trade.

An industry which had begun in a blaze of glory had come to an ignominious end. Sadly, today, the industry is too frequently judged by specimens which are much the worse for wear, or by the tawdry products which were made in large numbers and have consequently survived in quantity. But as explained in *The Visitors Guide to Wolverhampton* in 1871:

> *Critics are apt to forget that there is little room for the display of art where a gross of waiters is a common stint for a day's work, and the selling price two shillings a dozen; and also that the art education of the buyer has more to do with the character of the work than the art education of the manufacturer. Until the people of Spain, South America, and Russia demand a higher class of goods, and are willing to pay for it, it is useless to cry out against the 'hideous daubs and animal abortions' which adorn the productions of the japanner.[12]*

The disrepute into which the industry had sunk was a source of bitter regret to accomplished japan artists. Writing optimistically in 1889, one of them agreed that, though japanning had come to be regarded as 'cheap and trashy', it still had merits: 'it is a process ... which gives great opportunities for artistic excellence; and fitness for the refined adornment of the English home; and it is possible, may again, as many another decayed industry, rise, Phoenix-like, from its ashes.'[13]

It is unlikely that his hopes will ever be fulfilled in the way he envisaged, but in a world of dwindling resources and in which the need to recycle is an urgent issue, then the return of some form of mass-produced papier mâché, if not of japanned tinware, is not completely unrealistic.[iii]

i. By 1872, the cost of japanned ware had risen by 30%.
ii. By the mid-1880s, intense competition, particularly from overseas, forced the cost of iron to unprofitable levels and brought about the closure of several Midlands iron-works. To compound matters, the McKinley Tariff, introduced in the United States in 1890 to tax and control imports of tinplate, prompted the closure of another two Staffordshire tin-plate works. By the mid-1890s, the japanning industry was in a thoroughly depressed state.

iii. Two examples of 'new' uses for paper recently appeared in newspapers. According to the first report, 2.5 millions copies of romantic novels from the publisher Mills & Boon were pulped and incorporated into the surface of the newly constructed M6 toll road in the English Midlands; the pulp served as a binder to help prevent the surface from splitting (*The Guardian*, 'G2' supplement, 19 December, 2003). The second report highlighted the potential use of waste from paper mills in house-building materials (*The Independent on Sunday*, 3 June, 2007).

CHAPTER VIII

THE BIRMINGHAM JAPANNERS
(in chronological order)

'Birmingham is literally a repository of trade. There is hardly a single inhabitant that is not engaged in some lucrative concern. Everything wears the air of industry and commerce.'
A Tour through the South of England, Wales and part of Ireland, Edward Daniel Clarke, 1791

JOHN TAYLOR (later **Taylor & Pemberton**)
fl. **c.1738–c.1760** (as a japanner)
Dale End, Birmingham

The story of John Taylor (1710/11–1775) is a curious one, for while contemporary accounts accord him great prominence as the first japanner of any significance in Birmingham, they give little information about either the man or his manufactures. 'To this uncommon genius', William Hutton wrote in 1783, 'we owe the gilt button, the japanned and gilt snuff-boxes, the numerous race of enamels'[1] and yet as William H.B. Court observed, 'the traces of his activity remain exasperatingly slight'.[2] Although it is unlikely that Taylor's japanned ware could be identified today, his early influence and prestige should not be overlooked.

Taylor, who was of humble birth, began work as a journeyman cabinet-maker. He appears not to have commenced japanning until about 1738 – a date which supports the belief that it was Taylor's success as a japanner that prompted John Baskerville (*qv*) to follow suit in about 1740.

It is not known if Taylor was engaged in any other of the trades by which he was to make his fortune[3] when he began japanning, nor are there any details about the precise nature of his japanned ware and its decoration. The artist and drawing master, Charles Fenn, a contributor to Sayer's *Ladies Amusement* (p. 60), lived next door to Taylor's factory, but while it is feasible that he was employed as a decorator, there is no evidence to this effect. Lady Shelburne, who visited Taylor's factory in 1766, explained how she had seen some enamelled boxes being transfer-printed and it seems highly probable that he used a similar process for the decoration of at least some of his japanned boxes. The first person to make a clear distinction between Taylor's japanned and enamelled ware was Thomas Henry Ryland, in the 1880s, but since he was reminiscing about tales told him in his youth he was reliant upon distant memories of hearsay evidence. He told how John Taylor first undertook japanning at his house and shopping in High Street,[i] Birmingham, and how, with his wife, he would work late into the evening checking and packing goods ready for sale. It was after such a day that Mrs Taylor was reputed to have fallen asleep over her work and allowed a lighted candle to fall among some boxes or tea-caddies.

---

i. This was in Crooked Lane in the Dale End area – a continuation of High Street.

Opposite: Plate 101. Set of tin toilet boxes with deep red japanned grounds, gilt chinoiserie borders and inset enamel panels showing Italian scenes; Birmingham c.1755/60. Large casket W: 25.5cm
COURTESY OF CHRISTIE'S

Instead of his stock being ruined, Taylor found that 'a curious and new pattern' had emerged, 'a sort of curled pattern such as would be made by holding a piece of metal or glass over a smoky wick',[4] and he quickly set about copying the effect. This may have been the 'mystery'[5] process which Taylor was said to have carried out in a locked room and kept secret for many years until, with much amusement, he divulged the simplicity of his methods. According to Samuel Lloyd, Taylor had imitated these wavy patterns on brightly coloured and variously shaped boxes, by working his 'unusually broad and coarse-grained thumb'[6] into their second coat of colour while it was still wet. Boxes decorated in this way were said to have 'sold in immense quantities' and reaped Taylor 'a wonderful profit'.[7]

By 1751, the combined success of his various enterprises had enabled Taylor to purchase a substantial house – Sheldon Hall, about six miles east of Birmingham – and given him sufficient financial status to be elected Low Bailiff of the town in 1752, and Sheriff of Warwickshire in 1756.

Although by the mid eighteenth century Taylor's output of japanned ware was a matter of serious concern to japanners in Pontypool and Usk, whose prices he undercut, japanning appears to have been a relatively short-lived venture for him and only a minor part of his trade. A visitor to his factory in 1755 omitted any mention of japanning and noted instead that Taylor was 'the most considerable Maker of Gilt-metal button and enamell'd Snuff-boxes'.[8] The account of his visit dwelt upon these two branches of manufacture but, more importantly for this book, it shows the scale of Taylor's operations, and identifies him as one of the leading pioneers of the factory system that became a staple of nineteenth- and twentieth-century industry: the division of labour. The incredulous visitor commented:

> We were assured that he employs 500 persons in those two Branches, and when we had seen his Workshop, we had no Scruple in believing it. The Multitude of hands each button goes thro' before it is sent to the Maker, is likewise surprising; you perhaps will think it incredible, when I tell you, they go thro' 70 different Operations of 70 different Work-folks; but so we were inform'd; whether it be exactly true or not I cannot affirm ... tho' from what dwelt on my Memory afterwards ... I could not find so considerable a Deficiency as to raise a Doubt of the Truth of it.[9]

It was in this throbbing factory, against the noise of hammers and presses, that Taylor's japanned boxes and caddies were made. Taylor himself, in a petition to the House of Commons in 1759, claimed to have a workforce of 600, but whatever the precise number, it appears that not all the workers were employed simultaneously, for as Thomas Hall and John Mulford observed a few years later, in 1765, 'Mr. Taylor employs daily not less than 300 persons.'[10] Since by then Taylor had abandoned the practice of 'putting out' work, this fluctuation in daily employment suggests that people worked in the factory only when their particular skills were required.

Lord Shelburne, who visited Birmingham in 1766, named Taylor among the town's hardware men who 'are now worth three or four hundred thousand [pounds]'[11] and attributed his wealth to two factors: his use of a ductile alloy to facilitate machine stamping, and the breaking down of the production process enabling each employee to become highly adept through constant repetition of the same operation.[ii]

Nevertheless, Taylor also owed his success to his understanding of the fashionable market and not least because he himself had become part of it. Lady Shelburne who accompanied her husband when he visited Birmingham, affords a glimpse of his lifestyle in a diary entry on 16 May, 1766 describing how she had taken tea at Taylor's 'handsome house with a dairy and garden about it', also mentioning that afterwards his daughter 'played on the harpsichord and sung [*sic*] to us.'[12] As J. Drake observed of Taylor, in 1825:

> No source of profitable speculation, connected with ornamental manufacture, seemed to escape his attention. He appeared to possess an exhaustless invention, combined with the rare faculty of an almost intuitive perception of the final acceptableness of any novelty which struck his active mind.[13]

Having introduced the industry to Birmingham, Taylor appears to have ceased japanning in the 1760s, though why he should have abandoned the trade when others were taking it up is not apparent. He may have foreseen, when Stephen Bedford (*qv*) began his experiments with papier mâché in the 1750s, that the fashionable market for japanning in Birmingham was vested in that material. Whatever, his reason, unlike Baskerville and, later, Matthew Boulton (*qv*) who fashioned extravagant and costly japanned articles, Taylor appears to have focused on japanning only small metal boxes.

Prior to the publication of Birmingham's first trade directory in 1767, Taylor was evidently joined in partnership by John Pemberton for it was as 'Taylor & Pemberton, button-makers', that the firm was listed with premises in Queen Street.[iii] Taylor died in 1775, but the firm continued as Taylor & Pemberton until about 1780;[iv] Pemberton carried on as a button-maker at the same address until about 1787.

John Taylor died in Bath and was interred in his family's vault in St Philip's Church (now the Cathedral), Birmingham. At the time of his death he lived at Bordesley Hall, a house which he rebuilt at a cost of £10,000, and he also owned much property on the eastern side of Birmingham. James Watt, in a letter to his business partner, Matthew Boulton, wrote scathingly that 'John Taylor died the other day worth £200,000 without ever doing a generous action'[14] – an amount not borne out by his will. An obituary in Aris' *Gazette* on 3 April, 1775, was altogether kinder, being testament to the important part that Taylor had played in the development of industrial Birmingham and the high esteem in which he was generally held, both personally and commercially: 'a cheerful companion and a steady friend, a man to whose extraordinary ingenuity and indefatigable diligence, the trade and manufactures of this town are much indebted for their increase and estimation.'[15] (plate 101)

JOHN BASKERVILLE
fl. c.1738–c.1773 (as a japanner)
22 Moor Street (c.1740–1745)
Easy Hill, Birmingham (1745+)

John Baskerville (1706–1775) is best known today as a printer of fine books and a paper-maker; hitherto, only token acknowledgment has been made of his contribution to the development and commercial success of the Midlands japanning industry. To a large extent, this is because no documented examples of Baskerville's japanned goods are known to have survived. Nevertheless, to judge from contemporary descriptions of his trays and waiters, many may indeed have survived to the present day but are now, perhaps, mistakenly attributed to Pontypool in South Wales.

Baskerville was born in Wolverley, Worcestershire. He is believed to have been apprenticed to a stone-cutter, although he himself said: 'I was brought up to no kind of business; but had early in life a great fondness for print characters.'[1] According to William Hutton, he had also a talent for painting – an accomplishment which would serve him well as a japanner. By 1726, Baskerville had moved to Birmingham where, to enhance his income as a writing master, he also cut gravestones. He was still teaching in 1737, but by then John Taylor (*qv*) had introduced japanning into Birmingham with such obvious commercial success that Baskerville saw an alternative direction for his artistic leanings.

There is no precise date for when Baskerville commenced japanning, but there are clues. In 1738, he moved to a larger house, in Dale End, Birmingham, possibly in order to experiment with japanning; within two years, this property had become too small for him and he leased a house and workshops nearby, at 22 Moor Street, where he remained until 1748 'retaining his old school house in Edgbaston Street as a shop or stores until 1757'.[2] It was from Moor Street that Baskerville applied, in 1742, for the first patent ever to be granted in respect of japanning (#582). The patent was for making metal mouldings which, when japanned or varnished in 'fine glowing mahogany colour', in black, or in imitation of tortoiseshell, could be used as veneers on picture frames and large pieces of furniture. If, as he said, his Petition, or

patent application, had followed 'many Essays, made by him for the space of several years, last past',[3] there can be little doubt that Baskerville took up japanning some time around 1738 or 1739. He evidently intended operating on a fairly significant scale for he emphasised, by way of strengthening his application, that if it were successful, 'a great number of Poor Persons will be employed in the working and finishing the said metal plates ... who', he added, 'are now under the most pressing necessities for want of business'.[4]

An unlikely tale of Baskerville resorting to low cunning and deceit in order to discover the secrets of Taylor's japan varnish probably said more about its author, Mark Noble, than it said about his subject. By whatever means Baskerville learned the art of japanning, the several years he spent perfecting the technique were rewarded by early success. In 1747, having outgrown his premises once again, he secured a lease on eight acres of land to the north-west of Birmingham. There, he built a house and workshops which, under the terms of the lease were to cost no less than £400, but upon which, by the time of his death, he had actually 'laid out little less than £6000.'[5] He named it 'Easy Hill' and moved there on its completion in 1748. Intriguingly, a wholly separate lease, dated 1747, described Baskerville as a 'boxmaker' rather than a japanner.[6]

Over and above his patent, the earliest description of Baskerville's japanned products appears in Angerstein's diary. He visited Baskerville on 6 April, 1754, 'to see his type-foundry and factory for tea-trays and other household goods made from thin iron sheet'.[7] There, he observed 'semi-finished sheets from Bristol[v] pickled, scoured, dried and primed and varnished, and then painted with birds of all kinds, some pictures and flower arrangements', and noted that 'such a tray is sold at a half to 2 guineas according to size and quality of painting.'[8]

By default, Angerstein's report, following his visit to the Pontypool Japan Works, in June of the same year, sheds further light on the nature of Baskerville's japanned goods:

In Pontypool there are two brothers by the name of Edward and Thomas Allgood, who from black sheets fabricate bread baskets, tea trays, snuff boxes, and various kinds of sheet-metal work that is cut and embossed in rings,[vi] and then scoured, dried, varnished and painted in the same way as at Mr Baskerville's factory in Birmingham.[9]

This is the first indication that the earliest japanned goods from Birmingham were not so very different from those made at

---

ii. There was another contributory factor to his wealth. In 1765, in equal partnership with another Birmingham man, Sampson Lloyd, Taylor co-founded Birmingham's first bank under the name of Taylor & Lloyd; it became Lloyds Bank in 1852. Taylor's primary concern, however, was manufacturing and he largely devolved his banking interests to his son.

iii. One, Edward (Ned) Pemberton (b.1762) of Birmingham, worked for William (Billy) Allgood at Pontypool from c.1780–1794, and is believed to have worked also at Usk. Robert Stephen (1909–1946), a local authority on Pontypool japanned ware, was of the opinion that Pemberton was a general factotum and not, as often asserted, 'the best decorator of the day'. Any link between Edward and John Pemberton has yet to be established (see p. 114).

iv. It is believed that Henry Allgood, son of Thomas Allgood of the Pontypool Japan Works, joined Taylor & Pemberton in 1779, following his disagreement with his brother Billy (see p. 275), and that he may have moved to Wolverhampton, where a branch of

the Allgood family was established by 1804.

v. The iron sheets used by Baskerville would have been made in South Wales and shipped to Bristol across the Severn estuary and thence up the River Severn to Bewdley in Worcestershire, an inland port which served Birmingham, Wolverhampton, Bilston, and many other manufacturing towns in the Midlands. It was yet another link between the Pontypool and Midlands japanning industries.

vi. R. Nichols, in his book *Pontypool and Usk Japan Ware* (p. 13), quotes an earlier translation which describes this as 'cut out and designed in circular shapes'; a comparison of the two translations suggests that Angerstein was referring to the punched border patterns which are traditionally associated with Pontypool japanned goods. The same translation interprets, although less plausibly, 'butter dishes' in place of snuff boxes.

Pontypool – an idea to which we will return shortly. Within four years of his move to Easy Hill, Baskerville had made sufficient money from japanning to set up a printing press and thereafter, ran the two trades in parallel; he did not, as some have suggested, relinquish japanning in favour of printing. Indeed, the second Lord Palmerston confirmed as much following his visit to Easy Hill in 1760: the printer, he said 'deals likewise much in japanning and painting teaboards, waiters etc.'[10, vii] In fact, in a letter of 1762, sent to Horace Walpole as 'Patron & Encourager of Arts, & particularly that of printing', Baskerville went so far as to say that printing was not commercially successful, that he was 'heartily tired' of it and moreover, regretted ever attempting it.[11] Five years later, and despite his 'reputation for excelling in [printing] the most useful art known to mankind',[12] he wrote in a letter to the American statesman, Benjamin Franklin (a printer by training who twice visited Birmingham, first in 1758, and again in 1760), 'I cannot even get bread by it. I must starve, had I no other Dependence'.[13] Japanning then, financed his printing venture and he continued to be closely concerned with it until at least 1770.

Japanning also supported a comfortable and somewhat ostentatious lifestyle. As a man of obvious substance, he rose to positions of high office in Birmingham, being appointed Overseer of the Highways in 1749, and High Bailiff in 1761.[viii] He purchased 'a most gorgeous chariot' or coach, the panels of which were 'in the nature of a picture "got up in the japanware fashion"', and drawn by two, if not four, 'cream-coloured horses'.[14] Hutton described it as the 'pattern-card of his trade',[15] although there is evidence which implies that the coach was both made and painted in York.[16, ix] Whatever the origin of his chariot, Baskerville must have cut quite a dash driving around Birmingham, fashionably attired in his favourite green coat, scarlet waistcoat and small round hat, all edged with gold lace. These were the clothes he wore for his portrait by James Millar in 1774, which Samuel Raven later copied on a papier mâché snuff-box (plate 102).

In order to maintain the two branches of his business, he depended upon the practical support of his wife, Sarah. During a visit to Easy Hill with her husband in May, 1766, Lady Shelburne noted that while he and Mr Baskerville discussed books, she was shown the japan workshops by Mrs Baskerville 'which business she has chiefly the management of.'[17] Easy Hill was 'in its way, handsome and elegant', according to Dr Alexander Carlyle who visited in 1758[18] or, in the eyes of Lady Shelburne 'a pretty place out of the town'.[19] The Baskervilles received many distinguished visitors over the years on account of both their printing and japanning workshops. Among them was Franklin, whose visit in 1758, although primarily linked to his position as a senior partner in a Philadelphia printing firm, provided the opportunity for him to buy 'a selection of Baskerville's japanned goods for which he paid £2.4s.';[20] sadly, there are no details of what the selection included.

However, a description of Baskerville's japanned goods provided by two later visitors, Thomas Hull and John Mulford,

in 1765, observed that Baskerville had quit printing 'for Waiter making being Iron japan'd, pierced and some beautifully painted'.[21, x] The significance of this description is two-fold. First, it describes the waiters as 'pierced' – a style of decoration hitherto wholly associated with japanning in Pontypool rather than the English midlands (see also W. Higgins, 1796, p. 20). Second, as far as is known, it is the only contemporary evidence that Baskerville was, in the 1760s, japanning iron – as distinct from papier mâché. Several authorities have described Baskerville as a 'pioneer' of the commercial manufacture of papier mâché in the mid eighteenth century and, given his knowledge of paper-making, it is tempting to concur with them.[xi] However, to date, there is no contemporary evidence to support this notion. The idea that he made papier mâché might stem from a misreading of an entry in Lady Shelburne's diary on the day *following* her visit to 'Easy Hill', when she 'went to see the making of buckles, papier mâché boxes, and the melting, painting, and stamping of glass.'[22] There is nothing here that suggests she returned to Baskerville's premises to observe these processes; the implication is rather that her visit was made elsewhere. Equally, in view of the relative novelty of papier mâché at the time, Hull and Mulford would surely have commented had they seen it being made by Baskerville.

Further details of Baskerville's products are found in a Birmingham directory of 1767, where he is described as a 'japanner of Tea Tables, Waiters, Trays &c.'[23] And more vividly, in the same year, Samuel Derrick writing to the Earl of Corke, said of Baskerville and his goods:

> *This ingenious artist carries on a great trade in the japan way, in which he shewed me several useful articles, such as candlesticks, stands, salvers, waiters, bread-baskets, tea-boards, &c. elegantly designed, and highly finished. Baskerville is a great cherisher of genius which, wherever he finds it, he loses no oppportunity of cultivating. One of his workmen has manifested fine talents for fruit-painting, in several pieces which he shewed me.*[24]

The artist in question was almost certainly Amos Green (1734–1807) who, besides being 'esteemed inferior to no one in England for fruit' could also paint 'flowers, insects and dead game very well'.[25, xii] Indeed, one of Baskerville's strengths was that 'he was apparently able to select just those men who were best fitted for their particular occupation'.[26] Regrettably, however, there is little information about other talents in his employ. It has been suggested that the ceramic painter John Giles[xiii] worked for Baskerville, but other than being a decorator, also living and working in Moor Street, there is no hard evidence that he did. All that is known for sure is that, in 1767, three of Baskerville's apprentice painters – Samuel Clayton, James Pinfield and Samuel Jackson – absconded, and that the latter, going on to become a 'Tortoiseshell-worker and Japanner'[27] in his own right, was listed in local directories from 1797 until c.1812. Tradition also has it that Baskerville apprenticed the young Henry Clay (qv) but this is not borne out by contemporary records. However, since this idea was first mooted in the 1840s when many japanners would still have remembered Clay, the possibility of some early commercial involvement between the two, should not be overlooked.

Along with Taylor's japanned tin-ware, Baskerville's products not only competed favourably with articles from Pontypool, but also provided a lead for Welsh japanners in terms of painted goods.[xiv] His standing as a japanner was acknowledged in a letter sent, in 1771, by the prestigious Birmingham manufacturers Boulton & Fothergill to one of their clients, Mrs Mary Stovin, a London 'Toy Shopkeeper': 'your order for Jappand [*sic*] Goods we have given to Mr Jno Baskerville who is one of the most imminent [*sic*] Jappaners in Birmingham & we doubt not is capable of serving you'.[28] Of the goods she ordered: plate warmers, candlesticks, candle-snuffers and extinguishers, inkstands, tea kettles, coffee pots and bread baskets, Baskerville said he made only the latter so, unless it simply suited him to say this, he had presumably given up making candlesticks in the four years since the Earl of Corke's visit. In addition to promoting Baskerville's wares in this way, Boulton & Fothergill also took them on a sale or return basis, although, to judge from a note sent with a tray to one of their customers, William Matthews, in 1771, they reaped no profit from this: 'Count Scarafis bought a Tray of Baskerville the same as this sent and gave £2.2.0 for it – for w[ch] reason we can charge it no more altho' B. will not allow us Dis.[ct].'[29]

It is difficult to see what benefit this arrangement held for Boulton & Fothergill when they were themselves setting up japan workshops at Soho. If Bennett, in his biography of Baskerville, was correct in conjecturing that he was winding down his japanning interests, then perhaps Boulton was simply repaying the kindness of an old friend who had helped him financially in the mid 1760s, while at the same time building a reputation for Boulton & Fothergill as purveyors of fine japanned goods. Whatever the reason, there must have been some incentive as they were still taking goods on a similar basis two years later, as this letter from Baskerville shows:

> Easy Hill 20th July 1773
>
> Dear Sirs,
> I consider the prices below less than Value of the Goods, but act discretionally, but without Disct.
> Y[rs] &c John Baskerville

102. Papier mâché snuffbox painted with a portrait of John Baskerville, signed 'S Raven'; the inside lid lettered in red 'S Raven pinxt. Patronised by H.R.H. the Duke of Sussex and Prince Leopold of Saxe-Coburg', c.1820 (see p. 322). Dia: 15cm

© BIRMINGHAM MUSEUMS & ART GALLERY (1965f 215)

No.1 & 2	2 trays oval fruit	6. 6. -
No.3	A 32 Inch fine tray fruit (oval)	5. 5. -
No.4	an oval Flower piece 30 Inch	2.12. 6
No.5	a pastoral 34 Inch oval	3. 3. 0
No.6	A fine Fruit piece	£5. 5. -
No 7	Agamemnon sacrifising his Daughter Iphegenia who is carryed away in a Cloud by Minerva & a Hind left upon the Altar	£6. 6. 0

NB. On sale or return[30]

It will be seen from this list that Baskerville's prices had risen considerably since Angerstein's visit in 1754.[xv] But in addition, it provides a sufficiently clear image of Baskerville's japanned trays to suggest, once again, that at least some of the fine, early oval tin trays which today are often indiscriminately attributed to Pontypool, could in fact have come from

---

vii. 'Teaboard' is a term generally associated with large paper trays. Might this suggest that Baskerville did make paper trays, or could it be that they were blanks decorated in his workshops?

viii. The duties of High Bailiff included inspection of the market, the maintenance of justice, and the checking of weights and measures. The japanner Stephen Bedford (*qv*) was Low Bailiff at the time.

ix. Thomas Horner to Matthew Boulton, from Ripon, 11 May, 1766, about a chariot he was making and decorating for Boulton, ended his letter: 'I hope to be so fortunate as to merit the good opinion of Mr. Boulton as also Mr. Baskerville having taken some extronory [*sic*] pains in making the body in a smart new and tasty form and of as good material as could be picked out' (see Bennett, vol. II, pp. 115-6). A highly decorated carriage found on the Baskerville estate at Manton, near Marlborough, Wilts., was not the vehicle in question since there appears to be no obvious link between this family and the Baskerville's of Wolverley (see Strauss & Dent, 1907, *Baskerville's Carriage*, p. 108).

x. Baskerville had not quit printing but was experiencing difficulties when Hull & Mulford made their visit. Thomas Hull, an actor, managed the King Street Theatre in Birmingham from 1759-62, and was later the stage manager at London's Covent Garden Theatre (see Shenstone Letters, p. 483, n3).

xi. For example, N&Q vol. C p. 192/3, 1839. *Mogg's Handbook for Railway Travellers*, "To Baskerville [we are] indebted for the introduction of papier mâché or paper-board work."

xii. Green had also painted boxes and other 'trifles' for Matthew Boulton, although there is nothing to suggest they were necessarily japanned.

xiii. Any link with James Giles, a painter at the Worcester porcelain factory, has yet to be established.

xiv. 'Even the ardent supporters of Pontypool do not dispute that they found it necessary to obtain black-plate workers, japanners, varnishers and painters from the Midlands, particularly in the later part of the century.' Gibbs v.9, 1953, p. 207

xv. *cf.* Angerstein's note that in 1754, Pontypool 'tea trays cost from 4 shillings to 18 shillings'.

Baskerville's workshops at Easy Hill. It would seem, therefore, that current attributions within a whole class of painted tinware, may be due for revision.

John Baskerville died in 1775. In compliance with his wishes, he was buried in his garden at Easy Hill, but during excavations for a canal in 1825, his remains were exhumed and transferred – after much deliberation on account of his atheism – to 'Mr Knott's vault at Christ Church',[31] nearby. Sarah Baskerville died in 1788, having discontinued her husband's japanning interests, and printing only two books after his death. Easy Hill, with its 'spacious Warehouses and Workshops suitable for Mercantile Business or any extensive manufactory',[32] was sold.

STEPHEN BEDFORD
fl.1755–1773
48 Moor Street, Birmingham (sometimes given as number 135)

The only surviving object known to have been made by Stephen Bedford (d.1781) is a fine rectangular japanned iron tray in the National Museum of Wales (Plate 103). It is significant on three counts.

First, and unusually for this period, it is stamped with the maker's mark. Second, its pierced edge and style of decoration provide irrefutable evidence that many articles which have hitherto been attributed to the Pontypool Japan Works were, indeed, made in the Midlands. And finally, when considered alongside contemporary evidence, it endorses the important part that Bedford played in the early history of the Midlands japanning industry.

Bedford was described as a japanner in a document relating to Birmingham in September 1755,[1] but otherwise there are no details of his activities until 1759, the year in which he was granted a patent in respect of transfer printing. As Prosser has shown (see p. 64), the patent was unlikely to have met with much success, but nevertheless, it is noteworthy for being only the second (after Baskerville's in 1742) to be granted to a japanner and, more importantly, for its tacit suggestion that Bedford envisaged manufacturing japanned goods in a quantity that necessitated the expedience of transfer-printed decoration.

It may have been Stephen Bedford who pioneered the manufacture of papier mâché in the Midlands (p. 24), but even if subsequent research refutes this, it was almost certainly he who made it commercially viable by devising a clear and durable varnish with which to finish both japanned paper and metal goods. In March, 1759, two years after the competition was first advertised, Bedford rose to the challenge from the Society of Arts which had offered a premium of twenty pounds to anyone who could make:

One Quart at least, of the best, most transparent and colourless varnish, equal in all Respects to Martin's at Paris, commonly called Copal varnish; the properties

whereof are great Hardness, perfect transparency without discolouring any painting it is laid over, being capable of the finest polish and not liable to crack.[2]

The competition was a very protracted affair but the surviving correspondence between Bedford and the Society bears close scrutiny as it sheds light on both his activities and the contemporary japan trade.

Since Bedford complied with the rules laid down by the Society in 1757, his delayed application suggests that the intervening time had been spent perfecting a suitable varnish, rather than ignorance of the original competition. But in 1759, with a varnished copper panel and a quantity of varnish ready for submission, he found that the rules had changed, and candidates were also required to produce a wooden panel large enough for a coach-door. He enquired of the Society:

> Birmingham 29 March 1759
>
> Sir
>
> ... the advertisement I saw in the papers was for a coach pannell but Did not mention wood Iron or Copper and as of Late I have made many Setts of Pannells for Coaches and Chariots of Copper So thought the Newest fashion would be most acceptable but now I shall Vastly Excell that because I have Several Setts making in paper which will be Exact the Same as Martins in Paris please to favour me with a Line Soon if the Gentlemen would choose to have the next pannell on paper I should Like Better to do it on that because it is the Height of the french which in this affair we are Endeavouring to Rivall otherwise Shall be Done in Wood by your humble Servt; Stephen Bedford
>
> P.S. I hope to be in London in the Easter week then will Shew you something Curious.[3, xvi]

The Society stood its ground and, in September 1760, Bedford wrote again, somewhat impatiently:

> I ... hope you will favour me with what encoragements [*sic*] you think I deserve for what I have done in the makeing of a fine varnish a specimen of which you hold at the office more than twelve months and as I live so farr from Town had not an opportunity of [hearing?] whether it pleased or not till ... Mr Box told me the objection was not against the varnish but its being done on copper.[4]

By way of explanation, and with a hint of exasperation, he added 'as I was then concerned in the article of making copper pannells for coaches I laid it on copper'.[5] But evidence of Bedford's breadth of vision and enterprise are found in his concluding lines, and it was surely these capabilities which placed him in the forefront of the developing Midlands japanning industry. If his varnish was approved, he wrote:

[it] would be of great service to our country as well as myself in stopping the importation of French Paper Boxes in the manufactury of which articles I am largely concerned. The Common objection is that our English Varnish was not so good as the French and formerly there was a reason for it but for some time past I have by trying so many experiments brought it to such perfection that I undertake to make it as good as theirs.[6]

He finally made his submission in 1761, but the Society postponed its decision until the following year because of 'the difficulty of getting it properly polished.'[7] Bedford was belatedly called before the Society's Committee of Chemistry in March 1763, and when asked about the differences in quality between his varnish and Martin's, he confidently replied 'None at all'.[8] In May, after the panel had been 'exposed for three months to the severity of the weather', and been found capable of 'receiving a good polish',[9] it was resolved that while it was the best varnish ever made in this country, it failed to meet all expectations. Bedford was thus awarded only fifteen guineas of the premium which, by then, had been raised from £20 to £30.[xvii]

Although Bedford's dealings with the Royal Society concerned only panels for carriages, it is evident from the announcement of his award in a Birmingham newspaper, that he made also 'Paper Boxes and other Articles in Paper and Japanned Wares'.[10] Along with the one surviving tray from his workshop, their quality may be judged from Stephen Bedford's own endorsement of his rivalry with the French, which surely conveys some idea of the class of goods he was making.

Dossie, who had been one of the judges of the competition, drew on this national rivalry to construct a curiously ingenious logic with which to temper the Society's criticism of the varnish. He argued that 'more ought to have been ascribed to the very rough state of our streets at that time, compared to those of

103. Tin tray with pierced edge, the base impressed 'BEDFORD' and 'BHAM', for Stephen Bedford of Birmingham; wooden battens to the reverse suggest that it may have been a table-top – hence, perhaps, the orientation of its decoration; c.1765. 76 x 56cm
© NATIONAL MUSEUM OF WALES

Paris' adding that if coaches varnished in France had been subjected to British roads, then they too would have been 'found to be nearly as soon cracked and spoilt by the jolting and shocks.'[11] Be this as it may, for the prize to have been advertised from 1757 until 1763 without a successful candidate, shows the order of the challenge and the improvements needed before England could rival France in this respect. Bedford's varnish therefore not only enhanced his own reputation, but would have significantly benefited the home industry.

---

xvi. This intriguing post-script may have referred to his papier mâché panels which, on the above evidence, he must have commenced making no later than 1758.
xvii. Algernon Graves, in *A Dictionary of Artists*, 1760-1893 lists a 'B. Redford' (surely a mis-spelling of S. Bedford), a Birmingham painter who exhibited 'a coach pannel of papier mâché, being the first ever in England', at the Free Society of Artists in London, in 1764 (Cat.no.204).

Despite the acknowledged superiority of vernis Martin, the Earl of Verulam, in his role as overseer of British exports, wrote in 1769, that Bedford exported to France, as well as to Russia, Holland and Denmark, but noted that his sales to America had dropped ninety per cent on account of Towsnhend's taxation (ie. the taxation which led to the separation of the American colonies).[12]

At home, in his warehouse in Moor Street, Birmingham, Bedford looked to visits from 'the Nobility and others, who may depend on being served, if they please, with the highest Pieces of Work, ever finished in their kinds, and down to the lower Sorts'.[13] This announcement, placed in the *Birmingham Gazette* in 1772, was to assure the public that he had not 'left off the Japanning Branch'[14] as rumoured during a month-long absence in London. Rather, Bedford affirmed, he had been 'on an Affair to serve the Public'[15] – a curious assertion in view of the following advertisement in the same newspaper less than two weeks later:

> To be LET and entered on immediately, That large commodious House, Warehouse, Shops &c. in Moor-Street, Birmingham now in the possession of Mr. Stephen Bedford.[16]

The move appears to have been triggered by the death of his landlord – an event which may have necessitated his London visit – but whatever the cause of this turn-around, Bedford sold 'his general Stock of Japanned Goods'[17] to Thomas Bellamy (*qv*) in 1773, and retired from the trade.

Bedford's success as a japanner gave him the status and wealth necessary to be appointed Low Bailiff of Birmingham in 1761 – an office which, besides requiring him to call a jury and select the town's officers, also required that he 'treat his friends to the tune of £70 or £80'.[18, xviii]

Having made one, if not two, of the most important contributions to the success of the Midlands japanning industry, Stephen Bedford died from gout in 1781. Other examples of his wares, in addition to the tray, have no doubt survived to the present day, but sadly, unless they bear a maker's mark or are accompanied by sound documentary evidence, there is now no means of identifying them. All that is known for certain is that he japanned tin and paper goods for both the higher and lower ends of the market, and that he made papier mâché coach panels, boxes and, on the evidence of his patent, snuff boxes.

THOMAS FLETCHER
fl. **1764–1791**
Lionel Street, Birmingham

The earliest mention of Thomas Fletcher, 'japanner and painter' of Birmingham, is found in Aris's *Gazette* in 1764

when he announced that his apprentice, one John Mills, had absconded.[1, xix] He was evidently a japanner of some esteem for it was he who, together with Henry Clay, was recommended by Boulton & Fothergill to one of their clients as a maker of 'Tea Kitchins' and other japanned ware (see p. 121).[2]

He joined forces with a man named Dean and they traded as Fletcher & Dean until 1791 when their partnership was dissolved. Soon after, and in the same year, the business was revived by Fletcher's son, also Thomas, who announced to the public that:

> *He carries on the Business of Japanning in general, and ornamenting of Buttons, on the same Terms as formerly (under the Firm of Fletcher and Dean) on his own account, at his Shopping, near the Top of Lionel Street, Birmingham, where their Favours will be carefully attended to.*[3]

There may have been a link with this firm and the partnerships of Fletcher & Hicks (*fl.*1781–1800) and Fletcher & Hunt (*fl.*1805–7), but unless any of these japanners marked their wares, it is unlikely that it will ever be possible to identify their products, least of all to tell them apart. Nevertheless, if the credentials lent to Thomas Fletcher by Boulton's recommendation may serve as a guide, in its day, his workshop was clearly significant.

BOULTON & FOTHERGILL
fl. **1765–1779** (as japanners)
The Soho Works, Birmingham

Matthew Boulton (1728–1809) was one of the leading manufacturers of his age and a pioneer of the Industrial Revolution. He is inextricably linked with James Watt (1736–1819) and the development of the steam engine, and he engineered radical advances in the minting of the world's coinage, as well as having introduced the first ever insurance scheme for factory workers. Indeed, Boulton's achievements were many and diverse, but it is his partnership with John Fothergill (1730–1782) which is of concern here.

Soon after he inherited his father's toy-making business in 1759, Boulton purchased land at Soho (then on the outskirts of north-west Birmingham) where he erected a large factory: The Soho Works. There, together with Fothergill, he produced silver, Sheffield-plate, ormolu and other metalwork of such quality that it quickly attracted the patronage of celebrated clients across Europe and beyond.

Fothergill had considerable experience of the toy trade, both at home and across mainland Europe, but besides his substantial financial input, he played a less colourful, but nonetheless important role of overseeing trade at the Soho warehouse. Boulton, by contrast, was a flamboyant entrepreneur and

---

xviii. John Baskerville was High Sheriff at the time.
xix. Mills was obviously an incorrigible recalcitrant since he ran away again in 1767, together with fellow-apprentice Richard Delves.

dynamic innovator. He was also a central figure among Birmingham's intellectual elite and a founder member of the 'Lunar Society' (p. 26). Like his great friend, the potter Josiah Wedgwood, Boulton was always ahead of the market. For instance, he was quick to pick up on interest sparked by recent classical finds at Herculaneum and Pompeii, and made magnificent 'antique' vases of polished marble and 'Blue John', offset by fine gilt metal mounts. He was equally alert to the commercial possibilities of Birmingham's new japanning trade, and in this – as in other branches of manufacture – Boulton's achievements were founded on his understanding of science, and of chemistry in particular.

Boulton's many notebooks testify to his inquisitiveness in these fields.[1] The earliest, compiled between 1751 and 1759, was filled with recipes for waxes, ink, and solders, and for enamels and many other things besides.[2] Most importantly here, it also includes receipts for japan and imitation tortoiseshell varnishes. Less than a decade later, by 1765, decorative japanned ware was in production at Soho, and by 1769, the firm was making vase- and urn-shaped cutlery cases of 'japanned and varnished'[3] iron (plate 104).

Wedgwood saw a similar case 'of Black Japan'd Iron, richly ornamented with Gilt Festoons &c.',[4] when he visited Soho in 1776, and was especially impressed by the cutlery-drawers in its mahogany pedestal – a great improvement, he thought, upon more conventional cases in which spoons were placed, handle-first, into slots, for they dispensed with the 'indelicacy' of footmen 'taking hold of the bit of the Spoon ... which you are immediately to put into your mouth'.[5] Another advantage, in his opinion, was that japanned iron was relatively light. Cases made from heavier materials tended to topple backwards when opened – a problem Wedgwood had experienced with ceramic vases of his own making, but with 'a Vase Knife Case of this Sort', he noted, 'the top is a light japan'd one and is thrown up by touching a Push which sets a Spiral Wire at liberty for that purpose ... a Cover of our Ware will be much too heavy.'[6]

The magnificent cutlery cases to which Wedgwood referred are indicative of the prestigious market upon which Boulton & Fothergill focused. A customer who, in 1772, required more commonplace goods was politely directed elsewhere: 'If you want Jappand [sic] Tea Kitchins or any other kind of Jappand Wares, Mr Thomas Fletcher or Mr Henry Clay ... are very capable of serving you upon the best terms.'[7] And similarly, while pleased to accept an order for '6 paper Snuff boxes rather small, inside tortoiseshell, mounted in Silver', Boulton informed the client 'that such parts of this order as

104. Japanned iron cutlery urns with ormolu mounts; Boulton & Fothergill, c.1770. H: 56cm
COURTESY OF MALLETT, LONDON

are not manufactured at Soho must be omitted', namely '48 Common paper Snuff boxes of Sundry sorts ... all intended as patterns', which 'must be in general at low prices'.[8]

Nevertheless, by 1779, the Soho japan department had closed down; thus, Boulton & Fothergill's involvement with japanning lasted fewer than fifteen years. Given the firm's general pre-eminence, it is remarkable that apart from the existence of important objects like the cutlery caddy described above, and of two surviving departmental inventories, there is no known evidence of what form Boulton & Fothergill's japanned ware took. The reasons for this anomaly were several, and they are best explained before any consideration be given to the inventories and what they tell us about Boulton & Fothergill's japanned goods.

Crucially, the firm's finances were precarious. Besides debts incurred by the building of the new factory, there were serious management flaws which undermined the profitability of the toy department in which tortoiseshell, cut steel, japanned ware and other small articles were made. Fothergill, as overseer of the department, flagged his concerns as early as

1773, and suggested the partnership cease trading. But it was not until about 1776 that any positive action was taken. At the time, Boulton was too involved with Watt and the steam engine to be much concerned about the decorative branches of his manufactory, and as Wedgwood's biographer, Eliza Meteyard, observed, it may have been that which led Boulton to invite Henry Clay (*qv*) – then an established and highly regarded japanner by whose 'exceeding taste and ingenuity'[9] he was greatly impressed – to join him in partnership. Clay, evidently ruffled by such interest in his area of expertise, declined, and Boulton looked instead to Francis Egington (1737–1805), a talented decorative artist who numbered japanning among his several skills.

Two years later, Egington (*qv*), with his brother, John, and Edward Jee, set up in partnership with Boulton & Fothergill, and took responsibility for the Soho japan shop. This was a curious arrangement, given that Egington had proved a very inefficient manager, but it may have been designed to galvanize him into taking greater care; it may also have been intended to lessen Boulton & Fothergill's financial liabilities. John Hodges, manager of the factory's silver and plate department, alerted Boulton to Egington's poor management in May 1778: 'No – Japan'd Wares are sold to signify – I learn Mr E– has a large quantity of fresh ones nearly finished … which will only increase the Stock if no Orders can be procured to take them off.'[10] A few months later, William Keir advised Boulton of a 15% loss in some branches of trade at Soho, including japanning:

> *I think some effectual steps ought to be taken to sell your stock of tortoiseshell, steel watch chains, and japanned goods, & everything else that is not likely to be ordered. The method that has been taken of lowering the price of the species of goods is not sufficiently effectual to get off the old stock & it ruins the trade for the time to come. The only method would be to expose these individual goods to sale at such prices as can be got for them, but not to take orders for any to be made but at a gaining price. The question is, how to sell them? Would it be prudent to … try to sell them in London, by offering them to the Shopkeepers and by putting them in Sales?*[11]

The problem of Egington's over-stocked stores would continue for several years. After inspecting the closed Japan Shop in 1780, prior to compiling an inventory, Hodges informed Boulton that he was 'astonished and sorry to see what quantities of your property there are that lay buried almost in oblivion', and feared that unless 'vigorous' sales methods were adopted, there was 'little or no probability' of shifting such 'large quantities of Japan & Paper Trays'.[12] Like Keir, Hodges looked to London for a solution: 'would it not be well', he asked, 'if some person could be found in London to take the charge of 'em and sell them by auction or any other advisable means? …for they now lye [*sic*] Year after

Year (few sold) getting worse & more out of date.'[13] Hodges explained that he had dispatched 'several trays with plated borders for the inspection of Monsieur Cavalli', ruefully adding that 'no doubt many of these kind of trays might be sold if with good paintings and well executed – some dozens of borders as well as plates are finished, but very few will fit or match owing to improper management.'[14] Five months later, rather than hold on to stock any longer, Boulton & Fothergill accepted £102.10s for a quantity of japan trays and waiters of various sizes, designs, and qualities. This left them with 'upwards of six dozen of the best, which … with the common paintings',[xx] Hodges believed, would 'still make a large shew, and be the more likely to sell.'[15]

In view of Boulton's business acumen, it is curious that japanning should have floundered at Soho, when a little over a mile away Henry Clay was enjoying such phenomenal success with japanning. Hodges, as we have seen, put it down to Egington's 'improper management' by stock-piling finished, or near-finished articles, which, once out of fashion, became difficult to sell, or were so ill-assorted that it was impossible to match tray-bases with plated galleries of the right size.

However, the relatively high cost of Boulton & Fothergill's products may also have played a part. While it was their 'desire to sell as cheap as any body', they argued that 'the goodness of some of the figure paintings &c.'[16] necessitated higher prices than those charged by others – a stance that failed to convince at least one customer, a Mr R. Preston of Liverpool, who could see no 'striking difference' between japanned goods from Soho and those made by Clay, Fletcher, and others who, he said, charged only one shilling extra 'for painting of figures in a good stile.'[17] Moreover, difficulties caused by the number of middle-men involved in this branch of business, should not be overlooked; in a letter to the Countess of Craven, for example, Boulton & Fothergill despaired 'of ever getting [her] knife cases done by Mr Clay' and advised her to 'no longer wait in expectation of them,'[18] – though given the apparent rancour between Boulton and Clay at the time, there may have been other issues at work here (p. 133*ff*).[xxi]

Boulton's disillusionment with japanning explains why, in 1794, he declined William Barrow's well-considered proposal 'to Conduct a Japan Manufactory' on his account (p. 40). In any case, the time was hardly suitable to make such an approach for, later that year, Boulton would write to Lord Lansdown:

> *Our Manufactures at Birmingham are in a deplorable state from the conduct of the Russians as well as the French and I fear Peace could not suddenly restore our trade to the state it was in 3 years ago.*[19]

Such a turbulent background to Boulton & Fothergill's experiments with japanning, certainly makes it clear why the venture was so relatively shortlived.

The Inventories

It is mainly because of the closure of the workshop and the two inventories which were drawn up at the time that we know anything about Boulton & Fothergill's japanned ware. The first inventory, dating from 1779, was compiled by Francis Egington, the department's manager and by then, joint-partner in the business.[20] This was followed by a second, made by John Hodges in 1782.[21]

To judge from the earlier inventory, the department had separate workshops for painting, polishing, varnishing and stoving. This implies that it was set up for decorating, rather than manufacturing, iron blanks or sheets of pasteboard. There was also a 'Little Room' which, with items like '1 Book of [Pliny's] Anatomy', '7 Books of Dutch Mettal' and '8 Quire of brown paper'[xxii] together with '1 large Book of memorandums of Waiters', a 'large Day Book', and a 'Cash Book', appears to have doubled as a store and general office.

There is no evidence that iron blanks, or pasteboard – as distinct from articles made from that material – were ever made at Soho, and with specialist suppliers in Birmingham, it is unlikely they would have been. The second inventory details a large store of pasteboard, numbering twenty-nine and a half sheets of 'best' pasteboard, more than 2,300 sheets of 'common' boards, and, somewhat surprisingly, 720 sheets of a 'comoner' [*sic*] type. This was a considerable number of sheets to have held in stock, and it gives some idea of the level of output intended. In addition to the pasteboard, there were various other types of paper, including 2¼ reams of 'large white brown Paper',[xxiii] which may have been required for making into strips for reinforcing the joints, or seams, of articles cut from pasteboard (p. 31), or which Egington may have needed for other decorative purposes, such as mechanical painting (pp. 319-320).

Boulton & Fothergill's letter to Lady Craven, concerning her knife caddies, shows that some iron goods, at least, were japanned elsewhere, though mention of blank-waiters and trays in both inventories implies that others were indeed japanned at Soho. As for their papier mâché goods, it is unlikely, having made their own blanks from pasteboard, that Boulton and Fothergill would have sent them elsewhere to be japanned.

The later inventory provides more detailed descriptions of individual pieces, but neither this, nor the earlier one, should be read as anything more than indicative. By their very nature, the inventories include only those items in stock immediately prior to, and after, the department's closure and, thus, do not speak for articles sold. Moreover, piecing together the evidence they provide in light of what is known about other japanners prompts caution. For example, there is nothing in the 1782 inventory, to prove that an 'oval Iron Tea Table richly painted with Fruit and Flowers', and measuring 32 x 23½ in., was not in the Soho warehouse on

sale-or-return as per the deal with John Baskerville (p. 117), though the following entry of '1 oval top for ditto', similarly decorated, suggests that such tables may have been assembled there. Nor can we now be sure of the source of several '24" iron trays with pierced border & Etruscan Figures' for they, too, could have been part of the deal with Baskerville. The presence of an oval paper tray by Henry Clay raises further questions – was it waiting to be fitted with a plated metal gallery before being returned to Clay, was it there as a model of its type, or did Boulton & Fothergill retail Clay's ware? And should the inclusion of 'Pontipool painted Waiters' be taken literally, or be read as japanned tin waiters decorated in Pontypool-style (p.272*ff*)?

Nevertheless, mindful of these provisos, the inventories begin to reveal the range of Boulton & Fothergill's japanned products. The majority of their japanned goods were oval, round and rectangular iron and copper 'plates' or panels. Those made of iron – for example a '24 Inch oval Japan Tea Tray painted with plated Borders' – were designed to be fitted with silver- or gilt-plated galleries or rims. The copper panels, meanwhile, were made as decorative inserts for furniture, chimney-pieces (*cf.* plate 112), or for general interior decoration. In some cases, the intended purpose is not entirely clear – '1 painted Door Pannel on Copper with an antique Painting in the Middle & with Or Moulu Ornamts.', could, for example, have been a door for either a cabinet or a room.

The decoration on all copper plates is misleadingly described as 'painted', rather than japanned. This was probably because these panels, being decorated all-over, had no need to be coated with japan varnish as a background to any ornament. However, since they were painted with varnish colours, they had to be stove-dried, and were thus, japanned. Stephen Bedford (*qv*), a leading Birmingham japanner, had already established the benefits of japanning, rather than cold-painting, copper, some years earlier, and Boulton & Fothergill, with their overriding concern for high quality products, are likely to have used the same process (*cf.* George Brookshaw, p. 240).

The inventories also record iron snuffer pans, and an iron bread basket, as well as buttons. On the evidence of those listed in 1782, the buttons were mainly of solid wrought iron, variously japanned in green, yellow, or black; less expensive ones were simply described as 'Tin Plates painted blue'. But curiously only one 'Japand Tea Urn', and no japanned and ormolu-mounted cutlery cases, were recorded – the two articles which feature prominently in any discussion of Boulton & Fothergill's japanned products. This absence is most likely explained by their high cost, and their being made, generally, only to order. For example, when in 1778 Boulton & Fothergill held a sale at Soho, to dispose of excess stock, lot number 92, 'An elegant japan vase on a mahogany pedestal, mounted in or moulu to contain knives, forks and spoons',[22] sold for £19.19s. – one of the higher prices realised.

---

xx. This may have been Egington's so-called 'mechanical painting'.
xxi. Lord and Lady Craven did eventually receive their knife case; it cost £36.

xxii. Quire: twentieth part of a ream (1 ream = 516 sheets of paper).
xxiii. *cf.* the 'whited brown' paper used by Henry Clay (see p. 28).

The second inventory also includes brief descriptions of '8 Paper Tea Caddees unfinished and unmounted'. These were valued at 2/6d each, while '1 finished old Paper Tea Caddee', was valued at 7/6d, but most intriguing of all, are two paper tea caddies with 'gilt mounts', which were rated more highly at 21/- each. Their presence raises the possibility that Boulton & Fothergill may have made the exquisitely painted, gilt-encaged papier mâché caddies which date from the 1760s. But while the quality of surviving examples, complete with their equally fine enamel tea canisters (plate 105), supports this theory, further evidence is needed before we can be sure.

Also among the paper articles made at Soho, were round, oval, and rectangular trays and waiters. Their bases were cut from pasteboard, which when japanned and decorated, were set into silver or gilt-plated borders, or galleries, to which plated handles were sometimes fitted – a style revived by Henry Loveridge, in 1860, for trays with similar metal edges which he called 'combination trays' (p. 257). Other papier mâché objects found at Soho, in 1782, and most likely made there, were pairs of bottle stands, '3lb of old Paper Boxes, mostly lined with Tortoise[shell] & imperfect', 48 'round Paper Japan Boxes', several 'Paper Toothpick Cases', one of which appears to have been combined with a 'Smelling Bottle', snuffer pans, four 'small Paper Quadrille Dishes' (ie. counters trays), and a 'Paper inkstand, painted'.

The inventories shed light on decorative styles, though in places, the earlier one is frustratingly ambiguous in this respect. For example, entries like '3 Andromaches finished' or '1 Bacchus & Areadny Dead Colord', could as readily refer to Egington's mechanical paintings on canvas (see pp. 319-320) as to japanned objects. But since subjects like 'Turkish Heads' are variously found on square[xxiv] paper panels, small oval iron plates, and canvas, it is reasonable to assume that the same was true of other subjects listed.

The 1782 inventory provides more detailed information about decoration. The familiar fruit, flowers, birds, dead game, and landscapes, all featured on Boulton & Fothergill's japanned ware, as did antique heads and figures – both singly and in groups – mythological and allegorical subjects, and topical subjects like a 'Profile [of the] Empress of Russia'. Also listed are copies of popular paintings such as Angelica Kauffman's Calypso and Penelope. The colours of their japanned grounds included blue, chocolate and white, as well as marbled effects; black appears to have been used only on iron goods, some of which were edged with 'laurel borders'. Egington, himself, probably undertook much of the artistic work, though mention of '2 Turkish Heads done by Haughton', or 'Dead Game by Orton' (probably a misspelling of Haughton [*qv*]), and of 'Simmons the painter' (about whom nothing more is known), implies the involvement of others; the artist, Amos Green (*qv*), although named in neither inventory, is known to have decorated japanned ware for Boulton & Fothergill.

Overall, the conclusion to be drawn from both inventories, and from contemporary correspondence is that Boulton & Fothergill were not interested in japanning in its own right, but looked upon it as a complementary adjunct to their ormolu ornaments. They were neither concerned with extending the boundaries of japanned iron nor with developing the possibilities of papier mâché manufacture. Instead, they sought to exploit the rich effect of combining lustrous japanned surfaces with ormolu, and by so doing, created objects of exceedingly fine workmanship.

By virtue of their original cost and prestige, examples of this firm's japanned goods have, surely, survived to the present day. However, it is likely they are mistakenly attributed to other manufacturers, and, probably, to a greater extent than can now be proved. It is to be hoped, therefore, that while the foregoing information does not allow for positive identification, it should ensure that the partnership between Boulton and Fothergill is not forgotten in any assessment of high quality japanned iron or papier mache articles made during the third quarter of the eighteenth century.

105. Papier mâché tea caddy with gilt-metal mounts, painted with Italian scenes, including views of Venice from prints by Visentini, after Canaletto; lined with green velvet and containing three enamel canisters; Birmingham, c.1765. H: 21.5cm, W: 24cm
COURTESY OF WOOLLEY & WALLIS, SALISBURY

HENRY CLAY
fl. 1767–1812
Newhall Street, Birmingham

'Clay died worth 80,000.l, made entirely out of his papier mâché enterprise'

> Joseph Brasbridge, *The Fruits of Experience*, 1824

Henry Clay (1738–1812) was one of the most important figures in the history of English papier mâché and japanning (plate 106). His foresight and flair placed him ahead of his rivals, and his products won the respect of the designer Robert Adam, and the admiration of fashionable society at home and abroad. Success brought him great wealth and, in 1788, election as High Sheriff of Warwickshire – an office which he evidently enjoyed to the hilt. 'Few gentlemen', it was said, 'have made so brilliant an appearance or been so numerously attended in the high office which he holds, as Mr. Clay,'[1] when he opened the Commission for the Assize at Warwick two years later. In a procession, almost half a mile long, and cheered, alledgedly, 'by upwards of forty thousand'[2] people, Clay rode from his home in New Hall Street, Birmingham, in a coach striped in chocolate and dark green, and drawn by cream horses. Accompanied by javelins[xxv] and servants 'in rich liveries of white faced with red, silver epaulettes, buttons and capes' and by 'postillions in jackets of scarlet and silver, with black caps and silver tassels',[3] he provided a spectacle to match any the town had ever seen, and ample proof of his commercial success. The local newspaper marked the event with a poem which included the lines:

> *In Europe's Grand Toyshop with lovers of trade,*
> *The scene what great pleasure must crown,*
> *Deserved respect to the Arts had been paid,*
> *And honour it does to the Town.*[4]

Clearly, Clay was not a man who did things by halves. In many respects, he was to papier mâché what his acquaintance, Josiah Wedgwood, was to ceramics. His commercial acumen and determination to stay ahead in his field never caused him to lose sight of the principles of taste on which his designs were based and, despite their comparative restraint, his products and manufacturing processes laid the foundations for the exuberant papier mâché and tinware industries of the Victorian period. Today, although all good examples of eighteenth or early nineteenth century papier mâché are popularly, but often erroneously, attributed to Henry Clay, surprisingly little has hitherto been written about this enterprising man.

Apprenticeship records of the period belie the popular belief that he was apprenticed as a japanner to John Baskerville (*qv*) and show, instead, that on 28 February 1753, he was apprenticed for six years to John Allport,[5] a Birmingham 'painter in general and drawing master',[6] for the sum of £10.00.[xxvi] There is even a

106. Portrait of Henry Clay (1738–1812), oil on canvas, believed to be by a painter named 'Williams' or 'Williamson', and exhibited in the 1790s. 76 x 61cm
PRIVATE COLLECTION

suggestion that Clay began as a painter of enamels. The notion that his apprenticeship was served under Baskerville first appeared in an article in the Art Union in 1846.[7] This was sufficiently close in time to be based on hearsay reports, but distant enough for the story to have been distorted in the telling. Maybe it was for Baskerville, that 'cherisher of genius', that Clay first worked after completing his apprenticeship, and in whose workshops he honed his japanning skills, but this is mere speculation.

In about 1767, Clay entered into partnership with John Gibbons, an 'enamel manufacturer' and 'Paper-Snuff Box Maker'.[8] As Clay & Gibbons, they traded from Charles Street in Birmingham until 1770, when they moved a short distance to 7 New Hall Street – the premises at which Clay was to make his mark. Their products appear to have been largely utilitarian. Amongst other things, they made 'Royal Marine Candlesticks and Nossels [nozzles]' according to the patent of 'Mr Pinchbeck of Charing Cross, London',[xxvii] who had transferred to them 'the whole Power of making them in iron or Brass, japann'd or not japann'd, and polished Steel'.[9] They endeavoured to make japanned tea urns, but on filling them they found that 'the room they are in becomes likes [*sic*] a Jappaners Shop from the disagreeable smell the hot water causes',[10] and after much experiment, they 'partly' gave up.

---

xxiv. Here, 'square', also stands for rectangular.
xxv. Javelin: an armed member of a sheriff's retinue, or judge's escort at assizes.
xxvi. There is the possibility that this John Allport was uncle to the painter David Cox

(1783–1815).
xxvii. Christopher Pinchbeck (*fl.* 1695–1732), a London watchmaker, who gave his name to 'pinchbeck' – an alloy made in imitation of gold.

Gibbons died in 1772, and 'the Japanning Business [was] continued in all its branches by Mr. Clay'.[11] By then, the problem with tea urns appears to have been overcome, for as we have seen, Boulton & Fothergill, upon receipt of an order for a similar vessel, advised their client to go to either Henry Clay or Thomas Fletcher.[12] For what better recommendation could Clay have wished?

Fewer than three months after Gibbons' death, Clay took out a patent which was to have far-reaching effects for the papier mâché industry (p. 28). Besides embracing panels for coaches, carriages and sedan chairs, as Stephen Bedford had done earlier, the title of Clay's patent shows that he envisaged a wholly different range of objects from any previously made from papier mâché of this type. He proposed using paper panels for rooms, doors and ship-cabins, and foresaw that, if treated like sheets of wood, they could also be employed to make cabinets, bookcases, screens, and chimney pieces, as well as tables, tea-trays and waiters. Within months, he was assuring the public that not only would his japanned goods 'endure all Weathers and Climates', but also that they could be 'painted to any design'.[13] Indeed, the decoration of much furniture and other prestigious articles was, most likely, a matter for consultation between himself and his client as, for example, his negotiations with Lady Craven over a cabinet (see below).

Clay's Birmingham factory soon became an important venue for the carriage trade as both a curiosity and a showroom from which visitors might purchase. In fact, the letters and journals of such visitors provide much of what we know today about Clay and his manufactures. Dr Johnson who lived in Lichfield, only about fifteen miles north of Birmingham, took his old school-friend, Edmund Hector, and the indomitable Mrs Hester Thrale to visit Clay's factory in 1774 – 'we saw many curiosities and purchased some', said Mrs Thrale. 'The hardness of the paper is really astonishing and the ware equally elegant and durable. I like it extremely.'[14] Clay obviously valued such visits and saw them as precursors to sales, taking it upon himself to conduct visitors round the whole of his factory with an 'obliging civility'[15] which, according to the Reverend Richard Warner, 'enabled us to observe at our leisure the ... process for preparing this elegant article of furniture'[16] – a civility which, as we have seen, proved too much for the Hon. Anne Rushout.

Besides the Birmingham showroom, Clay had advertised in 1773, that his work 'may be seen at their Majesty's Sedan Chair Maker's in Coventry Street, Piccadilly,[xxviii] and at Mr. Wright's, Coach-maker to his Royal Highness the Prince of Wales, in Long-Acre, London,'[17] firms to which he may have supplied paper coach panels, and whose showrooms would have attracted the rich clientele for whom his goods were intended.

A bill of sale sent to Sir Thomas Ward (1717–1778) of Northamptonshire, in 1774, provides an interesting overview of Clay's business at the time, both in terms of retail costs and of the goods he stocked.[18] For example, he supplied Ward with what appears to have been an easel-painting: '1 fine square Picture of two Misers from a painting in Windsor Castle, on Canvass with Gilt Frame – £3.3.-', which was almost certainly one of Egington's so-called 'mechanical paintings. More predictably, he also supplied '1 pair of fine oval Pictures, the Senses of hearing & Smelling, on paper high Varnishd with Gilt Earthen Frames' at three guineas each. And while we cannot now be sure if the remainder of the pictures which Sir Thomas ordered were on canvas or on japanned panel, it is useful to list them since they may, in future, provide important points of reference:

> 12 fine square Pictures with Gilt Frames at £2.12.- each of the following subjects Viz.
> Shylock & the Venetian Merchants, a Turkish Lady Reading by Candlelight, a Lovely Lass & Fryer, Portia, Shylock, Leonora & Diego, Leonora & Leander, Iachimo, a Philosipher [sic], an Indian Family, Venus, Dænea & Jupiter

In addition to these, there were pictures of 'a cat' at one guinea, and of 'a Squirrel' priced at fifteen shillings. These may belong in the same category as 'An Owl' painted by Moses Haughton on a japanned paper panel which is multiply-stamped 'Clay' on the reverse (plate 107).

Besides pictures, Clay also supplied Ward with:

a fine Dutch[xxix] Tea Urn with Silver[d] Furniture	3. 10. -
a fine Japand Tea Chest of papier [sic]	3. 3. -
1 30 inch Carton Tray trebble gro[d, xxx]	2. 10. -
1 16 inch ditto ... imperfect	10. -
1 Japand Bread Baskett	6. -
1 ditto Knife Tray	4. -
2 6 inch round Waiters ... at 9[d]	1. 6
1 22 inch Iron Tray	1. 0. 0

From this, it is clear that although Clay's paperware achieved instant success and became his main focus, he evidently felt it wise to continue japanning metal. A letter sent by Georg Lichtenberg after he visited the factory in 1775, further endorses this:

> *Here most excellent lacquered tinware is made which is now imitated in Brunswick, also paper boxes, caddies, panels for coaches and sedan chairs... Coffee trays and all sorts of vessels are made and decorated in black with orange colour figures in the manner of Etrurian vases – they are beautiful beyond words.*[19] *(plate 52)*

---

xxviii. This was the firm of Vaughan, Holmes & Griffin.
xxix. Whether this was Dutch in style, or made in Holland, is not known.

xxx. 'gro[d]' – perhaps 'ground', ie. 3 coats of varnish.

107. An owl, painted (perhaps mechanically – see p.320) by Moses Haughton (*qv*), on a papier mâché panel which is stamped 'CLAY'; c.1775. 42 x 33

© Birmingham Museums & Art Gallery (1935 P76)

Nevertheless, one year later, in 1776, it was Clay's papier mâché that caught the eye of another overseas visitor, Jabez Maud Fisher from Philadelphia, who recorded in his journal, the 'Trays, Waiters, Decanter Stands, Snuff Boxes, Dressing Boxes and an hundred other Articles',[20] he had seen in the workshops . By 1781 paper goods appear to have taken over, and it became less usual for Clay to japan metal. He wrote to Josiah Wedgwood of some goods which had been ordered from Dresden and explained, almost apologetically, that 'the reason of those not being done on paper was that they were expressly order'd on Tin or Iron.'[21]

Among his clients for paperware was Horace Walpole, the aesthete and collector who, between 1778 and 1779, purchased the following goods at the prices shown:

To a waiter and Card Rack	14. 6
To a Tea Cade	3. 3. ..
To a waiter	19 ..
To a table	9. 9. ..
	£14. 5. 6[22]

Walpole displayed the 'Tea Cade' and 'table' in the 'Beauclerc Closet' at Strawberry Hill, his gothick folly in Twickenham, in the county of Middlesex. He described them in the inventory he prepared for visitors, as: 'A tea-chest of Clay's ware, painted with loose feathers', and as 'a writing table … highly varnished [in] black with blue and white ornaments in a gothic pattern, designed by Paul Sandby.'[23] When sold with the contents of the house in 1842, the same table, described as 'A curious japanned and painted writing table … in imitation of the old India Japan, with flap and drawer', despite its provenance, realised only £2.5s.[24] (*cf.* sale of 'antique' papier mâché in mid nineteenth century London, p.137).

Because of its novelty, Clay's paper furniture was more often recorded or written about than smaller articles like trays and waiters and, as a result, our knowledge of his earliest goods is somewhat skewed in its favour. Only a few examples of his furniture are known to have survived but, given the original cost of such articles, and the care which would therefore have been lavished on them, it is likely that there are others which simply await identification. It is therefore worth rehearsing what is known about Clay's early furniture in the hope that it may trigger the discovery of further specimens.

One of the earliest existing items of furniture known to have been made by Clay is a japanned mahogany pembroke table which stands in the Etruscan Dressing Room for which it was designed for Robert Child at Osterley Park House, London (plate 110). Decorated in white and gilt on black, it picks up the Etruscan theme of Robert Adam's room and shows a 'Scene in the Garden of the Hesperides', painted

from D'Hancarville's engraving of William Hamilton's finest vases. The table was made some time between 1776, when D'Hancarville's engravings became available in London, and 1782, when it was included in the inventory of the house. It was therefore not part of Adam's original designs in 1773, and there is nothing to suggest that he played any part in its commission. However, in 1774, Adam is known to have employed Clay's panels for the doors to the third drawing room at Derby House in London (demolished in 1862), which Adam described as 'beautifully

108. Straight-edge oval papier mâché tray, decorated with a classical motif against a printed, striped ground, impressed 'CLAY/PATENT' beneath a crown, c.1780. 27 x 36cm
COURTESY OF SOTHEBY'S PICTURE LIBRARY

109. Writing box, oak, veneered with papier mâché; tentatively attributed to Henry Clay, c.1780/90. 15 x 28 x 56cm
COURTESY OF KEITH PINN

Opposite: 110. Pembroke table, mahogany covered with papier mâché, made by Henry Clay for the Etruscan Dressing Room at Osterley Park House, Middlesex; c.1780. H: 74cm
THE NATIONAL TRUST. PHOTO BY COURTESY OF FRITZ VON DER SCHULENBURG/THE INTERIOR ARCHIVE (O.P.H 25-1949)

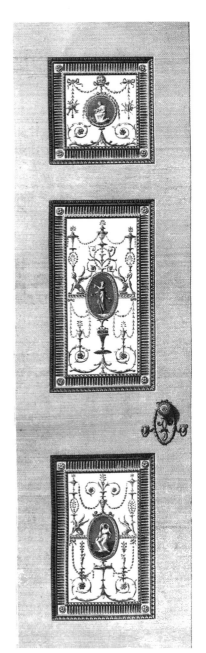

111. Design for a folding door for the third drawing room at Derby House, London, to incorporate papier mâché panels by Henry Clay; Plate VIII, from *The Works in Architecture of Robert and James Adam Esquires*, vol. II part I, 1779.

112. Chimneypiece from Hams Hall, Warwickshire, with copper panels painted after Angelica Kauffman; attributed to George Brookshaw, showing ornaments of the type Clay would have made for chimneypieces; 1780s. 155 x 209.5 x 30.5cm

painted by Zucchi ... on papier mâché and so highly japanned as to appear like glass'[25, xxxi] (plate 111). Similar panels, veneered with papier mâché and painted in the style of Angelica Kaufmann (1726–1795), are still to be seen in Adams' Marble Hall at Keddleston Hall in Derbyshire (plate 11). According to Charles Burlington and David L Rees in 1779, they were made by 'Mr Clay', and the panels were 'highly varnished, and the paintings well executed',[26] though like most of Clay's surviving wares, their original gloss has now dulled with age.

Akin to these door panels were 'chimney pieces' and 'panels for rooms' which Clay also included in the title of his 1772 patent.

A description of such a chimney-piece occurs in another of Robert Adam's decorative schemes. This time, in his proposed designs for the Great Drawing Room at 20 Hanover Square, the London house of Sir John Hussey Delaval, where, in 1780, the 'ornaments' of a white marble chimney-piece were 'to be done by Mr. Clay according to the design'.[27] To judge from Adam's drawings, the ornaments comprised variously-shaped japanned panels attached to the marble (*cf*. plate 112). However, on the evidence of François Rochefoucauld, a visitor to Clay's workshop in 1785, some such ornaments may have been painted directly onto the marble. Clay, he said 'has the secret of painting on marble in a manner more durable [*solide*] than is commonly done. He showed us a white marble chimney piece, painted with

---

xxxi. Antonio Zucchi, RA, (1726–95) decorative painter, married Angelica Kauffman, 1781.

113. Pier tables from a set of six made by Henry Clay, for Lord Bristol in 1791 (see pls. 114 and 115). 74.5 x 92.5cm

114. The tops of two tier tables from the set made for Lord Bristol (see pls. 113 and 115).

medallions and garlands of laurels and roses', which, after commenting on its charms, he noted 'cost 250 guineas.'[28, xxxii] And he noted too, Clay's boast that Catherine the Great had recently ordered from him 'a superb chimney piece painted with furnishings the most noble that any sovereign ever had ... her expression,' Mr Clay assured him 'word for word'.[29]

In addition, Rochefoucauld made the interesting, if somewhat ambiguous, observation that Clay made 'a considerable quantity of the most expensive papers for furniture [ameublement]' and that he had 'made several of them for the Empress [Catherine]'[30]. Sadly, since The Hermitage Museum in St Petersburg has no record of any such orders from Henry Clay, we cannot now be sure whether the 'papers' in question arrived as integral parts of pieces of furniture, or were supplied as panels for use by cabinet-makers at the Russian court.

A few years later, Clay made a set of six pier-tables for the 4th Earl of Bristol, two of which were in Clay's workshop when the traveller and collector, Edward Daniel Clarke, visited in the summer of 1791. Noting that they were made from papier mâché and 'painted after some designs brought purposely from Rome',[31] Clarke declared them 'by far the most beautiful things of the kind I ever saw'.[32] All six have hinged tops which open to form circular tables with highly polished black japanned surfaces encircled by gold-leaf borders (plates 113–115). The gilt motifs on their friezes and square tapering legs correspond to a pattern by Johann Tischbein (1751–1829), Director of the Royal Academy of Paintings in Naples who, from 1791, supervised the engravings of Sir William Hamilton's collection of Greek, Etruscan, and Roman vases. It was said that Clay presented another pair of pier-tables, painted after Guido Reni, to Queen Charlotte, together with a sedan chair. As with Wedgwood, such gifts were made with an eye to royal patronage. Clay was assiduous in such matters as the London silversmith, Joseph Brasbridge, hinted when he observed that Clay's shopman 'often attended upon the King'.[33] By 1780, Clay was reputed to have supplied 'several pieces of superb furniture which now adorn the royal residence',[34] so his ruse evidently paid off.

When Gibbons & Clay started out, there were only nine japanners in Birmingham; by 1800 there were thirty-one,

115. Pier table (one from a pair) from the set made for Lord Bristol (see pls. 113 and 114). Present whereabouts unknown.
PHOTOGRAPH BY COURTESY OF CHRISTIE'S, LONDON

several of whom were producing articles very similar to Clay, including 'tables, cabinets, tea-trays, caddees, pannels for doors, coaches, chaises and sedans, snuff-boxes, &c. &c.'[35] This competition may explain why Clay's workforce was said to have dropped from 300 in the eighteenth century, to only 100–150 by 1802, although improvements in production may also have reduced the number of hands needed. In relation to japanned tin goods, Clay had at least one early rival in Thomas Fletcher (qv) but, in theory, his papier mâché patent should have offered protection for fourteen years. However, in only three years, he considered it necessary publicly to threaten legal action against any infringment:

> Intimation hath been given to the said Patentee, that (notwithstanding his exclusive Right by virtue of such Letters Patent) other Persons have begun, or intend to make, upon the Principles of his Invention, some of the Articles stipulated therein. Notice therefore is herby given, that if any Person or Persons whomsoever, shall presume to infringe the said Patentee's Right, they will be proceded [sic] against according to Law.[36]

At this early stage, his threat was likely to have been directed towards Matthew Boulton (qv). Eliza Meteyard, in her biography of Josiah Wedgwood, tells us:

---

xxxii. Certainly, George Brookshaw who decorated similar chimney-pieces, is known to have employed both methods.

116. Oval papier mâché single-compartment tea caddy with pearl-dusted ground, and glazed silver mounts containing Wedgwood jasper tablets of the *Sacrifice to Hygeia* (front), and *A Seated Warrior*; c.1785. 12 x 12 x 8cm

During 1775 and the early part of 1776, Boulton seems to have been too occupied in his negotiations with Watt, and with business relative to the steam-engine, to take a very active part in his ornamental manufactory. But a man named Clay, a most ingenius cabinet-maker of Birmingham, was at this time doing much for Wedgwood's fame, by inserting the cameos in tea-caddies, writing desks, dressing cases, and similar articles; and so much were these admired, that he soon began to make small dressing and other box lids entirely of one cameo. These signs of Clay's exceeding taste and ingenuity induced Boulton to suggest a partnership, but Clay for some reason declined.[37] *(plate 116)*

At this point, and on the evidence of other surviving documents, it becomes necessary to read between the lines of Meteyard's account. It appears that, fearful of Boulton's interest in japanning, Clay spoke with Francis Egington, the overseer of the japanning workshops at Soho, with a view to luring him away. Boulton, 'very much offended',[38] felt obliged to take Egington into partnership as a japanner in order 'to keep him easy and in his service in other branches where he cannot very well do without him'.[39] 'So,' Wedgwood wrote to his partner Bentley in 1776, 'Mr B. and Mr. C. do not see each other.'[40] The rancour did not end there; the extent of their rivalry is perhaps best understood in light of a letter Wedgwood sent to Bentley later in the same year, informing him 'Mr.Clay was just gone to Lord Craven's, to shew Lady Craven some drawings of Cabinets. The Panels of which are to be of his painted Cartoons, perhaps inlaid with W[edgwood] & B[entley]'s Cameos', and predicting that 'Mr. C. will get the start of Mr. B. as a Cabinet Maker, and I apprehend we may furnish a good many Cameos etc.'[41] Soon after, Boulton 'added

the business of cabinetmaking to the already multifarious works at Soho, and introduced painted cartoons and cameos into various kinds of decorative furniture.'[42] It is small wonder that Clay was so concerned, but as Wedgwood shrewdly observed, 'His manufacture will give him fame before Rivals can interfere essentially.'[43] And rivals they certainly were, as is evident from Boulton's punning reference to Clay in notes he made when considering a London showroom. 'If my plan was adopted', he wrote, 'we should at once stride over the heads of all others and totally eclipse both the Staffordshire burnt clays and the Birmingham varnished clays.'[44]

His disagreement with Boulton might explain why Clay, who was eligible in so many respects, had little or no dealings with the Lunar Men (see p. 26), a group in which the former was so prominent. Instead, Clay belonged to The Bean Club, a conservative institution closely associated with the development of Birmingham and a useful meeting place for both town and county. Among its members was Samuel Aris, founder of the *Birmingham Gazette*, the paper in which Clay had announced his threat to his 'imitators'. Nevertheless, the ill-feeling cannot have lasted long, for Clay appears to have sent trays to Boulton, to be fitted with plated rims in 1780 (p. 123).

From 1791–1797, Wedgwood & Bentley had a Birmingham warehouse for 'Cameos, Intaglios &c.'[45] in Great Charles Street, conveniently close to Clay's factory and home in New Hall Street and his adjoining workshops in Little Charles Street. Whether or not this was coincidental, or whether the existence of one attracted the other, Clay had clearly been an important customer for their cameos for several years. So much so that, in a letter to Bentley in 1776, Wedgwood had referred to 'white Cameos the same of [*sic*] those we sell to Mr. Clay etc.' and, he continued, 'We cou'd make several other very pretty large Cameos for this purpose, and for bracelets if we had half a doz[n] more Hackwoods'.[46] This implied that Clay used cameos by William Hackwood, one of Wedgwood's finest modellers. A further letter from Wedgwood to Bentley, written only twelve days later, draws attention to broader issues by highlighting the interdependence of leading eighteenth-century manufacturers in creating design or fashion trends, and by underscoring their continued competition with France:

I told you I would endeavour to push the Cameos into a wholesale channel whilst I was in Birmingham, but I had very little time there. However, I mentioned to Mr. Boulton, and Mr. Clay the idea of Suiting the Cameos for the different Markets by making the Heads of their eminent Men – But they both told me that the French are so much superior to us, both in Paper and Tortoiseshell Boxes, that they have not much expectation in those articles (unless in very cheap paper Boxes) from any market where they have the French for their Rivals. So you must do what you can in this line with the French box makers.[47]

By 1783, Clay had opened a 'Birmingham Warehouse' at 18 King Street in Covent Garden, London, where his tea-trays, snuff boxes and other small articles attracted royal and aristocratic patronage. For some, like Joseph Brasbridge, this dealt a devastating blow. Looking back on his days as a silversmith at 89 Fleet Street, London, he recalled how Mrs Piozzi (formerly Mrs Thrale):

> *was a great admirer of the tea-trays, then just come up, of papier mache adorned with figures from the Etruscan vases, at that time newly-discovered amidst the ruins of Herculaneum; these tea-trays were invented by a Mr. Clay, and I, admiring the ingenuity and taste displayed in them, endeavoured to promote their sale to the utmost of my power, but by this means I did myself as much injury as I rendered him service; for encouraged by his success, he open-ed a warehouse in King-street, Covent Garden, which operated as a net to intercept my customers.[48]*

117. Papier mâché shuttles, both impressed 'CLAY' on the short inter-connecting shaft; c.1780. L: 13cm

COLLECTION OF DAVID AND ROSEMARY TEMPERLEY (ABOVE), AND PRIVATE COLLECTION (BELOW).
PHOTOGRAPHS COURTESY OF BONHAMS

The La Rochefoucauld brothers provide, in their journal, an informative list of articles they saw being made in Birmingham: 'tea-caddies, ladies' work-boxes, little coffers, snuff-boxes, bread-baskets, buttons etc., and even paintings of the greatest perfection (see Francis Egington).'[49] Snuff-boxes, although not generally associated with Clay's manufactures, were, of course, seen in his workshops by Jabez Maud Fisher in 1776. And Clay's friend, Mrs Papendiek – Keeper and Reader to Queen Charlotte – credited Clay with having 'greatly improved' them by introducing hinged lids, and much enhanced them by 'miniatures being introduced or settings of hair'.[50] He is also known to have made papier mâché shuttles and miniature frames, although marked examples are now rare (plate 117).[51]

Equally as elusive are Clay's paper buttons. To judge from contemporary accounts, they were made in such large numbers as to make it extraordinary that none are known to have survived to the present day. It is to be expected that they might be found attached to contemporary garments in major costume collections, but with their japanned decoration and sometimes rich colouring, they perhaps defy identification and are now mistakenly thought to be made from other materials such as wood or jet. Clay 'had for some time been perfecting'[52] the making of paper buttons when, in 1778, he filed the first of his two patents in this respect. From then on, visitors to his factory emphasised this branch of his trade. The Hon. John Byng described button manufacture as Clay's 'most flourishing trade',[53] while in 1796 Hatchett wrote: 'went to see Mr Clay's

Manufactory for the paper buttons',[54] and the following year Anne Rushout saw 'a great many women employed making buttons'.[55] The patent was for 'buttons, japanned, with or without shanks or catgut, or set in cups or sockets of various metals', which could be 'ornamented with painting, gilding and so forth, or inlarged with pearl, stones, mettal, and various other ornaments.'[56] As may be inferred from Parson Woodforde's diary entry for 24 April, 1793, they were widely known by name: 'To 11. Dozen of Buttons Coat and Waistcoat, some Italian, some Clay's Paper ones, all Black, at Bakers [Norwich] pd. 0.9.6.'[57] Mrs Papendiek noted how Clay's buttons, intended for 'gentlemen's mourning attire',[58] improved by wear and lasted many years.[xxxiii] It was she, also, who relayed the oft-told story about George III who, a keen button-maker in his youth, requested that Clay send 'several sets of buttons, for as I am called George the button-maker, I must give a lift to our trade.'[59] Yet as François Rochefoucauld rightly observed 'I mustn't give the impression that they make only smooth flat buttons. I've seen them being figured and even made in bas relief.'[60]

The second of Clay's patents for buttons, filed in 1786, was for a type 'much more useful and ornamental than any now in use'.[61] They were made from pulped natural fibres and 'all kinds and sorts of raggs and stuffs',[62] dyed to the required colour and formed into flat sheets from which buttons could be cut or die pressed. These buttons were not, apparently, japanned.

He also made buttons from slate which were said to look 'uncommonly rich' and to resemble 'the finest silk'.[63] Their manufacture was a direct result of another patent (#1918)

---

xxxiii. If this was their intended purpose, then it may explain James Woodforde's need, as a parson, to purchase so many black buttons. Rochefoucauld observed that Clay's buttons were 'all black when intended for the clergy'.

granted him in 1792 for slitting slate, blue stone and portland stone into thin panels which could be veneered to wood, paper, cloth, or other strengthening material, and finished by japanning, painting, gilding, varnishing, or other appropriate decoration. He considered the panels suitable for decorating coaches and carriages, tables, and cabinets, or 'for putting on or setting in miniature paintings, prints, drawings, cameos, or other ornaments'.[64] He proposed their use 'also for picture pannels or plates for painting thereon in oil colours, water colours, crayon or otherwise,'[65] and it was probably these that Clay introduced to the royal family in 1793 as 'infinitely superior to any substance hitherto used'[66] for painting upon.

Notwithstanding the success of his furniture and buttons, Henry Clay's reputation today, rests on his paper waiters, trays and 'tea-boards' (plates 118-120). The latter, too large to be carried as trays, were placed under the tea-kettle, teapot and china, to protect the table beneath when tea was served in the drawing room; they were so decorative that, when not in use, they were frequently propped up for display on side tables. Like the smaller trays, teaboards were generally oblong or oval in shape, made in two pieces with a base and separately attached, slightly everted sides. Clay's profit on trays and teaboards was so 'enormous' that, when interviewed in 1846, one of his former apprentices likened it to 'coining money', giving as an example 'a 30" paper tray' which retailed at £5.8.9 and yielded a profit of £3.18.2.[67] Among his distinguished clients for trays and tea-boards were the Duke of Northumberland at Syon House, the Earl of Jersey (grandson by marriage of Robert Child) at Osterley Park, and King George III who, in 1800, commissioned four large paper tea trays to be finely painted from four views belonging to the Langrave of Hesse-Cassel, at 25 guineas each. An oval tray in the Royal Collection, which is painted with *Schloss Wilhelmshöhe and the Great Fountain at Kassel*, appears to be from this set. It was this commission which thereafter entitled Clay to

118. Straight-edge oval papier mâché tea-board, painted with *The Death of Captain Cook*, after George Carter (*fl*.1769–1784); impressed mark of Henry Clay, c.1790. 60 x 78cm (approx.)
COURTESY OF CHRISTIE'S AUSTRALIA

119. Sandwich-edge papier mâché tea-board, with gold-leaf chinoiserie decoration, and gilt-metal handles; impressed Clay/King St/Covt Garden, c.1810. 67.5cm
COURTESY OF SOTHEBY'S

120. Papier mâché tea-board, the straight edge decorated on both sides with flowers and 'rocky effect[s]'; impressed mark 'CLAY/KING ST/COVT GARDEN', c.1810. 55.5 x 77cm
WOLVERHAMPTON ARTS AND HERITAGE (BANTOCK HOUSE MUSEUM)

impress his goods with a crown above his name.[xxxiv] Their cost was exceptional, even for Clay. Much more representative of his prices, was a tray decorated with broad gold borders, for which Wedgwood paid four guineas in 1808 (plate 121). On this reckoning, the person who, six years later, bought second-hand, but only six-months old, 'two handsome Clay's paper tea trays, 3 waiters and a bread basket'[68] for only 8s 5d in total, should have been well satisfied.

Trays were available in matching sets, like the one Clay gave Mrs Papendiek as a wedding gift in 1783 which comprised a 'tea-board, waiter, bread basket, snuffer-tray, and four little stands [probably bottle-stands], all alike'[69] (*cf.* plate 122). Or, like the table designed to match Adam's decorative scheme at Osterley Park, trays could be decorated to match the customer's porcelain. For example, an order book kept by Chamberlains, in Worcester, shows them to have ordered '1 paper tray from Clay's exactly to match'[70] the china they supplied to Lady Eley in 1802.

It has often been said that Clay sold his Birmingham factory in 1801 or 1802, but the Birmingham Rate Book for the years 1810–1813 tells a different story and shows 'Henry Clay Esq.' still paying rates on the property in Newhall Street; moreover, his firm continued to be listed in Birmingham directories until 1812. Henry Clay died that year, on 28 April, aged 74, and was buried in St Martin's Church in the Bullring, Birmingham. Three weeks later, the following announcement appeared in Aris's *Birmingham Gazette*:

TO JAPANNERS AND OTHERS
Any Person desirous to treat for the Good will of the Concern lately carried on by HENRY CLAY, Esquire, are requested to apply by Letter addressed to Hyla Holden,[xxxv] Newhall-street, Birmingham.[71]

By whom, if anyone, this invitation was taken up remains a mystery. The firm of Henry Clay, japanners and makers of 'paper tea-trays', continued to be listed in London trade directories until 1823, but little else is known about this period of its history. However, it is likely that the following advertisement in the same edition of the above newspaper was for the sale of part of Clay's stock-in-trade:

TO JAPANNERS, FACTORS &c

TO be SOLD by AUCTION, by KAY and HODGSON (removed for the Convenience of Sale, to their Rooms,

121. Invoice from Henry Clay to Josiah Wedgwood for the sale of a paper tea tray dated 11 April, 1808.
<small>IMAGE BY COURTESY OF THE WEDGWOOD MUSEUM, BARLASTON, STAFFORDSHIRE (L112-2211)</small>

122. Oval papier mâché bread basket and bottle-stand, decorated with gilt oeil de perdrix and 'mapwork' (*cf.* pl. 309); impressed 'CLAY' (the mark on the bottle-stand is inside the base), c.1810. 23 x 35.5cm and 10 x 3cm
<small>PRIVATE COLLECTION</small>

55 High-street, Birmingham) on Wednesday, May 27, 1812, upwards of 20 Dozen elegant Bronze, Flower, and other Border Trays, Part with Centers [*sic*], and Waiters to match, and will be sold without the least Reserve.[72]

Another frequently cited anomaly in Clay's history is that when his patent of 1772 expired, 'the manufacture was then extensively carried out by Small & Son, Guest, Chopping and Bill, and subsequently by their sons.[73] This statement first

<hr>

<small>xxxiv. Clay styled himself variously: 'Japanner to the Queen' from 1777; 'Japanner to his Majesty' from 1781; 'Japanner to her Majesty' from 1790; 'Japanner in Ordinary to his Majesty, and his Royal Highness the Prince of Wales' from 1800; and 'Manufacturer of Paper Tea Trays to their Majesties and the Royal Family' from 1816.
xxxv. Hyla Holden (1776/81-1842) married Clay's third daughter, Rebecca, in 1805. Described in Clay's Will, as a 'merchant', Holden may have been the coach and saddlers ironmonger of that name, who, in 1808, had premises in Livery Street, and Newhall Street, Birmingham – very close to Clay's own workshops. However, he is described elsewhere as a 'solicitor'. The name 'Hyla' can be sourced to the marriage of William</small>

<small>Holden, of Wednesbury, South Staffordshire, to Elizabeth Hyla of Newport, in 1687, since when it has been used by successive generations of that family. Therefore, It may be significant that Theodore, eldest son of Aaron Jennens co-founder of the Birmingham firm of Jennens & Bettridge, and his first wife Ann Phillips, was also named 'Hyla': Theodore Hyla Jennens. The occurrence of this highly unusual name within two important Birmingham japanning families, suggests a possible link between the Clay and Jennens families. If so, Messrs Jennens & Bettridge (*qv*) could well have been recipients of the 'Good Will' of the firm of Henry Clay, when it was advertised in May, 1812 (see above); certainly the date of their establishment accords with this notion.</small>

appeared in an article published in 1846 which has since been mis-read as not only giving the names of the successors to Clay's factory, but as the name of one firm. In fact, the names are those of three distinct concerns: Small & Son; Guest and Son; and Chopping & Bill, and if read carefully, the statement does not imply that any one of these manufacturers actually took over from Clay, but rather that they each developed along similar lines. Prosser was therefore correct when, in 1881, he wrote of Clay's factory that 'we are unable to trace its descent',[74] at least, not between 1812 and 1823.

The firm re-appeared in London directories in 1830 when 18 King Street (and number 17 also, from about 1840) was shared by another trading under the name of Henry Clay, and Thomas Small (*qv*), a Birmingham japanner – a fact which gives some credence to a possible link between the two makers. It is uncertain under whose ownership the Clay firm was continued although, according to Prosser, it was that of 'W. Clay & Son, of Fenchurch Street, London, who claimed to be the representatives and descendants of the first inventor'.[75] If this was so, then he may have been the W. Clay who had acted as London agent to the earlier Clay. As Henry Clay & Co, 'designers', the firm exhibited a range of typically Victorian papier mâché articles at the Great Exhibition in 1851. It included a chiffonier decorated in pearl and gold with painted fruit and flower panels, a toilet-table and glass with matching chair and footstool, fire-screens with needlework panels, 'multiformias', and a chess-table, the centre of which was 'glass, enamelled with mother-of-pearl'.[76] In addition, they exhibited 'The Regency writing-desk', trays – including a 'Lady's work-tray' – pot-pourri jars and a tea-caddy.[77] From 1853, Henry Clay & Co. took a showroom in Pall Mall, a prestigious London thoroughfare, but the fashion for high quality papier mâché was soon to wane and the firm finally closed in London in 1855.

Returning to the originator of the firm, Henry Clay's inventiveness emerged in two further patents which, though not directly concerned with japanning, must surely have come about as a result of his position in that trade. The first, granted in 1796 (#2092), was for a wagon designed to speed up unloading by shedding two loads simultaneously; the second, granted in 1798 (#2213), outlined a method of saving water at canal locks (plate 15). Although ingenious, the latter was too expensive to be put into operation. Nevertheless, what both these inventions record is a breadth of vision which defines Clay as very much a man of his time.

With his bold spirit and enquiring mind, it is neither surprising that Matthew Boulton sought his partnership in business, nor that Henry Clay, perhaps confident of his own commercial flair and secure future, refused. By 1784, he had accumulated sufficient wealth to purchase Maxstoke Hall in Warwickshire though it appears he never lived there; the house and its 320 acres, were sold on his death. He was said to have died worth £80,000 'derived soley from the profits of his manufactures,'[78] although his Will, divided between his surviving daughters,

gives no hint of anything approaching this amount.

That 'Clay's Ware' is as keenly sought today as it was some two-hundred years ago is testimony to its strength, durability, and prestige. Indeed, as if to bear witness, Mrs Papendiek observed of her wedding gift from her friend, Henry Clay, that 'the tea-board is only just now, some fifty years after, worn out.'[79]

See also, Henry Clay & Co., London (p. 232).

R. WATSON
fl. c.1770–1786
76 High Street, Birmingham

Robert Watson first appeared as a papier mâché maker in a Birmingham directory in 1770, but in the same year, he joined forces with another and began trading as Watson & Kindon. An advertisement in Aris's *Gazette* shows them to have been makers of 'all sorts of Papier Machee [sic] ornaments and paper hangings from their original manufactory on Long Acre, London.'[1] Their work was, therefore, allied to the manufacture of architectural mouldings, as distinct from the type of papier mâché under discussion here. However, by 1779, Watson had entered into a new partnership with John Rayney (or Rayner), in New Street, Birmingham, and they described themselves as japanners. This arrangement lasted only until 1786 when Rayney was declared bankrupt. The contents of the sale of his stock-in-trade give some idea of the nature of Watson & Rayney's business: 'finished and unfinished Tea trays, waiters, bread baskets etc. [and] an assortment of oils, varnishes, colours and other effects.'[2]

THOMAS BELLAMY (later T. & J. Bellamy, and S.T. & J. Bellamy, and finally S. Bellamy)
fl. c.1773–c.1825
Edgbaston Street, Birmingham

In 1773, Thomas Bellamy (d.1823), a japanner of Edgbaston Street, Birmingham, purchased Stephen Bedford's (*qv*) 'general Stock of Japanned Goods' and advertised soon after, 'that he makes and sells ... all Manner of Japanned Goods, in either Copper, Iron or Paper, as Mr. Bedford, the original Patentee, has enabled him to embellish his Paintings with a superior Varnish to all others.'[1] It would appear from this that the protection offered by the patent was transferred to Bellamy, and from what is known of Bedford's workshop at the time, Bellamy's purchase could have included coach panels, boxes, and perhaps snuff-boxes.

A colourful account of Bellamy's business, written many years later by James Bissett,[2, xxxvi] one of his former apprentices, provides rare detail about a hitherto neglected firm and leaves little room to doubt the scale of its operations.

Bissett had come from Scotland in 1776 to assist in the warehouse and counting house of his brother, George, a Birmingham merchant. 'But having been sent on an errand to a japan manufactory' and taken 'such a liking to the profession of painter', his brother paid forty guineas for him to be apprenticed to Thomas Bellamy, 'with whom [he] happily resided in bonds of intimacy and friendship for five years. During my apprenticeship', he recalled:

I was chiefly employed in painting neat devices of flowers and fruit, landscapes and general fancy work, on waiters and snuff boxes. My daily task was two gross of snuff boxes, or six dozen of small painted waiters, but I have very frequently painted three gross of boxes in a day, or, when we have been much hurried to get up orders, I have, in the course of twelve hours per day, painted upwards of twenty gross of snuff boxes in one week, with roses, anemones, and various coloured flowers, with three tints to every flower, and three to every leaf.[3]

123. Advertisement for S.T. & J. Bellamy, from James Bissett's *Grand National Directory*, 1800.

One apprentice, then, if pushed, could paint up to 2,880 boxes per week; given that Bellamy had four other apprentices in his painting shop, besides Bissett, it is a good indication of the scale of his trade. Also working in the painting shop was a young man named John Brook,[xxxvii] who, for reasons which Bissett did not explain, struggled and 'barely subsisted.'

From about 1788, the firm was styled T[homas] & J[ohn] Bellamy and by c.1798, it was re-named S.T. & J. Bellamy. Two years later, the Bellamys moved to nearby Freeman Street, where they made tea-urns and clock dials in addition to japanning, and according to an advertisement in Bissett's *Grand National Directory*, had a 'showroom open from 10. to 5. o'Clock' (plate 123).[4] After a further change of name, the firm finally ended, as S. Bellamy, in 1825.

It is evident then, that while no objects can as yet be attributed to this firm, in its early days, it operated on a significant level and was as likely as any of its contemporaries to have manufactured some, if not many, of the snuff-boxes, trays, and other boxes which have survived from this period.

OBADIAH WESTWOOD
fl. c.1774–c.1808
20 Great Charles Street, Birmingham

Obadiah Westwood is often cited alongside Henry Clay as a manufacturer of papier mâché buttons. However, Westwood's involvement with this material appears to have been exaggerated.

Westwood was a button-maker, who joined in partnership with John Westwood[xxxviii] (a dye-sinker and engraver) in about 1774 for the business of dye-sinking and coffin-plate furniture

making; by 1785, they appear to have diverged. John, who became a 'roller and seller of metals in general',[1] moved to neighbouring premises, while Obadiah continued at the same address, as a button-maker and manufacturer of 'the new invented Coffin Furniture, Borders for Rooms, Picture Frames, and Ornaments for Chimney Pieces'.[2] As such, it is Obadiah Westwood who is of concern here.

In 1786, he was granted a patent (#1576) for making, from pulp:

Tea and other Trays, Waiters, Card Pans, Caddees, Dressing Boxes, Bottle Stands, Ink Stands, Coat, Breast, Vest, Sleeve, and other Buttons, Frames for Pictures, Looking Glasses, and other Things, Mouldings, Cornices, and Ornaments for Rooms, Ceilings, Chimney Pieces, Doors, Pannels and various other Purposes.

Notwithstanding, the detail of the specification was concerned solely with making buttons from pulp. Westwood obtained the pulp by grinding materials such as silk, linen, rope, and sail-cloth, and binding them with glue, flour, and water. The buttons were formed in metal moulds, and after being stove-dried, they were either fitted with shanks, or drilled with holes. They were then varnished, painted or gilded, or were 'inlaid with gold, silver, metals, stones, pearls, foils, or other things.'[3] Although reported in Aris's *Birmingham Gazette* as 'a construction never attempted before',[4] as Prosser later observed in 1881, Westwood's patent bore 'a very suspicious resemblence to Clay's' (*qv*),[5] which was granted only five days earlier.

This seems to have been the main thrust of Westwood's trade until c.1808 after which he was no longer listed in local directories.

---

xxxvi. Bissett went on to become an 'author, royal medallist, poet, and inventor', and compiler of the lavishly illustrated *Poetic Survey round Birmingham*, accompanied by *A Magnificent Directory* (1808).

xxxvii. Not to be confused with John Brooks, the printer.
xxxviii. The relationship between Obadiah and John Westwood is not known.

THOMAS ASHWIN & Co.
fl. 1775–1791
Paradise Row, Birmingham

Thomas Ashwin had been apprenticed 'to Mr Neale Painter and Japanner in Park Street',[1] Birmingham. After working for a while as a journeyman japanner, he set up a small business of his own in about 1775, and soon advertised in the *Birmingham Gazette* for an apprentice. His approach to Matthew Boulton in 1778 for help in financing a patent application shows Ashwin to have been ambitious even without our knowing the idea he wished to protect (p. 96). However, since Ashwin was largely concerned with japanning buttons at the time, and would almost certainly have been aware of Clay's button-patent earlier in the same year, it is possible that Ashwin's proposed patent also concerned buttons. By 1791, the business had expanded to include other products and, trading as Thomas Ashwin & Co.,[xxxix] was listed in a local directory as makers of 'Paper [*sic*] Mâché, Clock Dial, Composite and Japanned Iron Buttons, Copal and Coach Varnish, and Japan Manufacturers in general.'[2]

Ashwin died in 1791 from 'a wound he received on the head from one of the rioters during the late unhappy disturbances' in Birmingham.[3]

JOHN WARING
fl. c.1779–1801
5 Edmund Street, Birmingham (and later at **Church Street**)

The first mention of John Waring, japanner, appeared in Aris's *Birmingham Gazette* in 1779, where he announced 'WANTED. An ingenious Lad, of a reputable and industrious Family as an Apprentice in the Japanning and Painting Business; also a steady Person who would chuse to become a Partner in the above Business', adding that 'a large Capital will not be required.'[1] The advertisement implies that he made decorative japanned articles. He evidently operated on a fairly extensive scale for when his stock-in-trade, was advertised in 1786, it included 'six large Japanning Stoves'.[2] Although the sale was necessitated by Waring's bankruptcy, he appears to have recovered from this set-back, since a record in the Chamberlain archives shows that a letter was sent him, as a japanner, in 1791,[3] although this, in itself, is no proof that Waring supplied Chamberlains with japanned goods. He continued to be listed in local directories until 1801.

FRANCIS BYRNE
fl. 1790–1803
Paradise Street, Birmingham

Francis Byrne[xl] was first listed as a painter and japanner at Coleshill Street, Birmingham, in 1767, and by about 1790, was trading as both a japanner of clock dials, and as a factor. By 1792, he was the most regular supplier of japanned tin and paper goods to Chamberlain's porcelain manufactory in Worcester, for re-sale in both their factory and London showrooms. Although no marked specimens of Byrne's products are known, contemporary Chamberlain stock-lists, held in the archives of Worcester Porcelain Museum, provide some clues to his output. Byrne supplied mostly tea-trays and, to a lesser extent, waiters, snuffers trays and bottle stands. Their costs, if compared with John Baskerville's trays in 1773, suggest that they were decorated with borders only. In 1796, for example, Chamberlain's expenditure on Byrne's japanned goods was as follows:

May	For one 26 inch Tea Tray, gold border 12/- [retail price 17/-]		
July	For Four paper quart bottle stands 7/-[retail price 7/- a pair]		
August	For one 32 inch paper tray Octagon[xli]	No.149	35/-
	one 22 inch		20/-
	one 32 inch .. .. .. Grapes		35/-
	one 22 inch		20/-
September	For one 32 inch octagon paper tray.	No.89	£1/19/-
October	For one 32 inch paper tray and 22 inch waiter, oval		
		No.149	£2/15/-
	one 32 inch paper tray & 22 inch waiter, oval		
		No.156.	£2/15/-
December	For one 32 inch octagon paper tray.	No.152	£1/19/-
	one 22 inch 152		£1/5/-
	one 32 inch 1571		
	one 22 inch 1571		£3/4/-[1]

Today, in the absence of marked examples, there is no practical means of judging Byrne's wares against those of his better-known contemporary, Henry Clay, from whom Chamberlains also ordered trays, but the inference from the above list is that they would have compared favourably as otherwise a firm like Chamberlains, with its high profile clientele, would not have stocked them.

Francis Byrne appeared in local directories as a 'japanner and factor' until 1803. A firm which styled itself 'Ashwin & Byrne', also situated in Paradise Street and listed in the Birmingham Directory of 1798, was probably the result of a merger between the survivors of Thomas Ashwin & Co. (see above), and Francis Byrne.

JOHN GUEST
1797–c.1818
Foredrough Street, Birmingham (and later at **Navigation St.**)

First listed as a japanner in 1791, John Guest was joined by his son James in c.1797 after which the firm was styled Guest & Son. It ceased to be listed after 1818. There are no records of the type of products they made and the firm is mentioned here only to demonstrate that it existed in its own right as distinct from being linked to the workshops of either Small & Son, or Chopping and Bill (*qv*), as earlier authors have implied (see p.137).

124. Concave king-gothic papier mâché tray; impressed mark of Smalls & Hipkiss of Birmingham, c.1825. 41.5 x 56.5cm. Taken from Godden, G., *English Paper Trays* ('Connoisseur', August, 1967, p. 254).

REPRODUCED BY KIND PERMISSION OF GEOFFREY GODDEN

125. Papier mâché bread basket with painted and bronze decoration; impressed 'SMALLS & HIPKISS' beneath a crown; c.1825. 21.5 x 35cm

COLLECTION OF JOYCE HOLZER

HIPKISS & HARROLD
1797–c.1803
Suffolk Street, Birmingham

This firm was begun by John Hipkiss (d.1797) who was first recorded as a japanner at 6 Newhall Street in about 1777, near to Henry Clay who occupied number 7. On Hipkiss' death in 1797, his son Richard entered into partnership with a man named Harrold about whom nothing is known. There is, in a private collection, a long-case clock made by John Holmes of Wolverhampton which has a japanned dial stamped on the reverse with the names Hipkiss & Harrold. The partnership ended some time after 1803. Richard Hipkiss continued to be listed as a japanner in his own right until at least 1809, but he subsequently merged with Thomas Small (see below) for what must have been a very short time as the partnership was dissolved in February, 1811, a few months before Hipkiss was declared bankrupt.

THOMAS SMALL (later Small[s] & Hipkiss, then T. Small)
c.1797–c.1845
Paradise Street, Birmingham

The history of this firm is complex for it appears there were two workshops, run separately, and concurrently, by two men who shared the name Thomas Small.

The first workshop, recorded in 1797, was in Suffolk Street, Birmingham, and the second, established shortly after, in about 1800, was in nearby Bristol Street; both were given over to button-making. It is the earlier of these concerns, which later became involved with japanning, that is of interest here. In about 1809, its owner, Thomas Small, was joined in partnership by Richard Hipkiss – a japanner, papier mâché-

and clock-dial-maker – and on the evidence of the few surviving articles bearing their impressed mark 'Smalls & Hipkiss'[xlii] beneath a crown, their products were of the highest quality as the objects seen here, testify.

Notwithstanding two announcements in the *Wolverhampton Chronicle* in 1811, first on 27 February, to the effect that the partnership had been dissolved, and the second, on 17 July, declaring Hipkiss bankrupt, it was as 'Small, Hipkiss' of Paradise Street, to where the firm had moved in 1815, that the business was impressively advertised in 1825, as:

> *Manufacturers of Papier Mâché and Japanned Gothic, Convex, Concave, Silver form and Round Corner Tea Trays, Sandwich Trays, Bread Baskets, Knife Trays, Snuffer Trays, Quadrilles, Bottle Stands, Snuff Boxes, India Cabinets, Work Boxes, Card Boxes, Fire Screens, Hand Screens, Table Tops, Highly finished and ornamented in the most fashionable taste, or plain for ornamenting. In this establishment is a handsome Show Room, where specimens of the various articles produced in this manufactory are exhibited for inspection and sale.*[1]

It is difficult to establish whether Hipkiss had any active involvement in the firm after 1811, especially as from about 1815, the concern was listed in local directories in the name of only Thomas Small.

Before moving to Paradise Street, it is possible that the two firms sharing the name Thomas Small had merged. The likelihood is that they were father and son, for in 1829, both Suffolk Street and Paradise Street were the addresses of one firm, Thomas Small & Son, and as such, they were described, in 1830, as makers of papier mâché and japanned articles at their 'extensive manufactory'.[2, xliii]

---

xxxix. See Francis Byrne, p.140.
xl. He may have been be one and the same as Francis Braine/Brane, also listed as a painter and japanner in Coleshill Street in the 1760s and 1770s.
xli. 'Octagon' most likely refers to a rectangular tray with canted corners (see pl. 220).

xlii. Papier mâché articles marked for this firm show the name as 'Smalls' while in contemporary records it is given as 'Small'.
xliii. One, T. Small, was appointed to the Committee of Birmingham School of Art in 1825, and thus was involved in its early years.

126. Advertisement for Robert Winn, from Wrightson & Webb's *Directory of Birmingham*, 1833.

127. Advertisement for Richard & George Bill – note the gothic tray at centre right; c.1830.

Not long after this, they opened a London showroom at 18 King Street, Covent Garden, where Henry Clay also had a showroom (from c.1840 they also occupied number 17). The firm of Thomas Small & Son, was listed in the London Post Office Directory of 1830 as a 'Manufacturer of Paper Tea Trays to his Majesty and the Royal Family' – a clear indication of its standing among contemporary japanners, as was their continued royal patronage by Queen Victoria and members of her family.

T. Small & Son ceased trading in about 1845.

CHOPPING & BILL
1797–c.1818 (see R. & G. Bill)
Great Hampton Street and Henrietta Street, Birmingham

There were three factories linking the Choppings and the Bills but precisely how they interconnected is unclear. It would seem, however, that two factories, one situated in Henrietta Street, and another in Caroline Street, were both offshoots of an earlier firm run by Thomas Chopping between 1797 and 1815, at Great Hampton Street.

The first of these was Chopping & Bill[xliv] in Henrietta Street, only a few streets away from the original firm, who were listed as 'paper tray makers' from 1801 until 1825, before becoming known as either Thomas Chopping & Son, or John & Thomas Chopping & Co. This partnership continued at Henrietta Street until 1831.

A second factory, also run by Thomas Chopping & Son, had commenced making papier mâché at Caroline Street in 1828

and continued until c.1831. In the meantime, another change of partnership saw Messrs Chopping & Cooper listed, concurrently, at the same address for the three years between 1828 and 1831. These details are of no great importance in themselves, but they do show where Chopping & Bill belong in the history of the japanning industry (see p. 137).

R. & G. BILL
c.1818–c.1843
12 and 13 Summer Lane, Birmingham

Richard (b.1793) and George Bill (b.1796) began as japanners in about 1818 and later subsumed the business of Chopping & Bill (*qv*).

An engraved trade card for R. & G. Bill describes them as 'Japanners and Manufacturers of Paper Trays etc.', and shows a tray of gothic shape nestling at the foot of a floral arch (plate 127). It also mentions that they produced snuff-boxes, although some, if not all, of these were decorated outside their workshop. One of their former apprentices, reminiscing in 1886, recalled how he used to be sent to deliver large snuff boxes to be painted by an artist in Stafford Street who, he believed, was Samuel Raven (*qv*).[1] In 1840, Raven and R. & G. Bill showed at the Halifax Exhibition in Yorkshire – the only Midlands papier mâché makers to have done so – a fact which lends credence to the above story. Raven exhibited snuff boxes, and R. & G. Bill some trays and a pearl-decorated table. Interestingly, they were displayed in a section of the exhibition called 'Curiosities'.[2] The firm closed in about 1843 or 1844.

xliv. See R. & G. Bill.

T. WATSON
fl. c.1803–c.1820
101 Snow Hill, Birmingham

Thomas Watson, formerly apprenticed to Henry Clay, was listed in local directories as a japanner and 'paper-button-maker'. He stated on his trade card that he was a 'Royal Patent, Paper Button manufacturer',[1] but since there is no record of him as a patentee, he may have been operating under license from his former employer.

CHARLES DOCKER
fl. c.1804–c.1856
134 Great Hampton Street, Birmingham

If it were not for the Chamberlain archives (see above), Charles Docker's significance as a japanner would, almost certainly, be overlooked. A wholesale price list of trays which he supplied to Chamberlain's between 1804 and 1806 shows that he made waiters in five sizes (from 10–18in.) and trays in eight sizes (from 18in. upwards in 2in. steps to 32in.). Although their decoration was limited to only four basic designs – single or double gold border, and single or double bronze border – their quality evidently met Chamberlain's exacting standards since an order was placed in 1805; sadly, records do not show whether it was for paper or iron trays. Docker's wholesale prices for double bronze borders ranged from 3/6 for a 10in. waiter, to 24/- for a 32in. tray less 10% if payment was made within six months, 15% discount for cash[1] – slightly lower than Francis Byrne's prices shown above.

Less is known about Docker's later productions although he continued to be described as a japanner and manufacturer of japanned goods throughout his operative period. A trade directory of 1849 shows there to have been a Charles Docker junior at the same address in Great Hampton Street; although an artist, he was not a japanner.

ROBERT WINN
fl. 1808–1847
25 Henrietta Street, Birmingham

Robert Winn was a blank tray, waiter, and clock dial maker, for many years before adding papier mâché goods to his trade. The first evidence of this appears in an advertisement placed in a Birmingham trade directory in 1833 where it will be seen that he made a wide range of products, including vases and 'paper pannels'[1] (plate 126). An example of such panels may be seen in the folding screen, shown here (plate 128). It is the only known article to be marked for Robert Winn and if the quality of its decoration is typical of his work, then his products were, undoubtedly, on a par with those made by better known makers.

128. Three-fold screen with two papier mâché panels, one of which is signed in gold leaf: 'Robert Winn, Birmingham'; c.1840. Each papier mâché panel measures 89 x 70cm

© WOLVERHAMPTON ARTS AND MUSEUMS SERVICE

On the evidence of an advertisement in a London trade directory in 1837, there is little doubt that his product range was also on a par:

Papier Machee [*sic*] and Wood Cruet and Liquor Frames, Paper Pannels
Watch Stands, Wax Tapers, Quadrille Pools, Time Pieces
Ink Stands, Paper Weights, Chimney Ornaments

Tea chests, Caddies, Snuff Boxes, Cigar Cases
Miniature and Picture Frames
Table Tops, Cabinets, Ladies Dressing Toilet,
Work and Card Boxes
Pole and Hand Screens, &c &c

And General Iron and Tin Plate Worker[2]

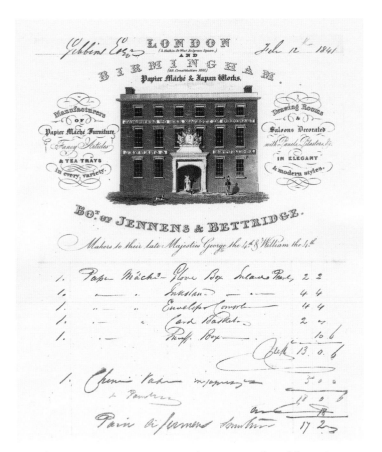

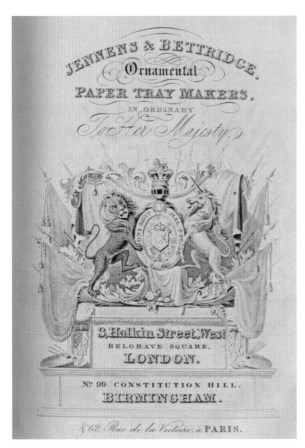

129. Invoice for various papier mâché items purchased from Jennens & Bettridge in 1841.

130. Advertisement for Jennens & Bettridge, from Wrightson & Webb's *Directory of Birmingham*, 1839; note their Paris address.

JENNENS & BETTRIDGE
fl. c.1810/13–1860/1
99 Constitution Hill, Birmingham

'The stranger who visits this establishment cannot fail to be struck with the gorgeous and truly regal display of richly elaborated structures, embracing every purpose of utility and luxury, which in crowded and dazzling profusion adorn the show-rooms. Here the light and plastic paper is seen to assume every variety of form suggested by the imagination of the artist, while at the same time it is shown to be susceptible of every species of ornamentation that can be applied to manufacture.'
'Birmingham and her Manufactures, IX Papier Mâché',
The Leisure Hour, no. 62, 3 March,1853

The partnership between Aaron Jennens (1788–1868) and John Bettridge (b.1790) is one of the of the best-known in the history of the English papier mâché industry. It first appeared in the Birmingham Rate Book for the years 1810–13 when, trading as Jennens & Bettridge, they occupied premises in Lionel Street, where one of their varnish suppliers, Messrs Thornley & Knight, was also situated.

They evidently enjoyed considerable early success because between 1821 and 1823, they were able to take out a lease on 99 Constitution Hill,[xlv] an imposing three-storey building with a late Georgian/early Regency façade, and a rateable value three times higher than their previous premises. By 1823, they advertised as

'japanners and paper tray makers to his Majesty in ordinary'[1] – an honour allowed regular suppliers of goods and services to the royal household – and continued to enjoy royal patronage for the remainder of their partnership, displaying a magnificent Royal Coat of Arms on the front of the building where it may still be seen (plate 129). The business went from strength to strength and by 1828, they had a London showroom at 12 Bell's Buildings, Salisbury Square, Fleet Street; within five years, they had moved to a smarter address at 3 Halkin Street West, Belgrave Square. An advertisement of 1839 shows them to have had a showroom in Paris at 62 Rue de la Victoire (plate 130), and, between 1851 and 1852, when they were described as the largest manufacturers of papier mâché in England, they had an office in New York possibly in anticipation of the Exhibition of the Industry of all Nations, held there in 1853.

Though there is now a popular tendency for any unmarked yet good examples of Victorian papier mâché to be attributed to Jennens & Bettridge, there is no doubt that their reputation is justly deserved and of long standing; in their day, they were judged to have 'no rivals, or anything approximating to an equality'.[2] But to continue to make arbitrary attributions, based only on their reputation, is to overlook the serious competition they received from firms like the Old Hall (*qv*) and Merridale Works (*qv*), both in Wolverhampton, or from McCallum & Hodson (*qv*) and Thomas Lane (*qv*) in Birmingham. So, what was it about Jennens & Bettridge that ensured the endurance of their name above all others?

To some extent, it had to do with what is now called 'brand image'. They were shrewd and astute businessmen who recognised the importance of maintaining a high profile. To this end they protected their ideas and improvements in three highly significant patents and introduced 'a greater number of varied articles in the material, than any other house'.[3] As leaders, they also took 'risks which have not been incurred by those who followed their example, and have the benefits of their experiments and experience.'[4] Their factory, with its showroom, was one of the curiosities of Birmingham industry and, more than any other papier mâché establishment at the time, it attracted visits not only from leading journalists and design critics, but also from their readers – the buying public. A.W.N. Pugin, the architect and designer, was sufficiently interested to visit in April 1839, when he was in Birmingham overseeing the building of St Chad's Roman Catholic Cathedral; he appears, however, not to have made a purchase, nor to have engaged in any subsequent collaboration with Jennens & Bettridge. In 1849, it was observed that:

131. Corner detail from a straight-edge papier mâché tea-board by Jennens & Bettridge – a shape not usually associated with this firm; c.1820.
PHOTOGRAPHED WITH PERMISSION, AT BONHAMS, OXFORD

> *This manufactory has, during the last three reigns, been patronized by royalty, and was honoured by a visit from the present Queen prior to her accession, by the Duchess of Kent, Prince Albert, the Duc de Nemours* [2nd son of Louis Philippe], *the Duc de Bordeaux, and indeed, by almost every one of distinction who has passed through the town.*[5]

With visits from such eminent clients, the papier mâché goods of Jennens & Bettridge were bound to stay in the public eye.

Moreover, in the 1840s, when it was said they employed three to four-hundred workers, their output would have exceeded that of their rivals and this, together with the fact that they marked their wares more consistently than any other firm, means that theirs is the name most commonly found on goods today. But their policy on marking was selective. This has skewed modern-day thinking for, while Jennens & Bettridge is now almost wholly associated with papier mâché of the 'best' sort, they also made 'common' or pulp-goods to which they did not affix their names 'because they cannot warrant the wear, and cannot be proud of the workmanship';[6] the same policy seems to have been applied to their japanned tinware, although a handsome trio of marked, gothic-shape tin trays, in the collection of Pontypool Museum, is a rare exception. As a result, there is now no means of identifying anything but their best goods.

These factors have served to perpetuate the notion that Jennens & Bettridge were without rival, and made only the finest goods. That neither claim is true, does not detract from their pre-eminence: their large and progressive factory served as a training ground for the proprietors of many smaller firms, and the expertise of their

132. Concave king-gothic papier mâché tray decorated in various bronze colours; impressed Jennens & Bettridge, c.1825–1830. 47 x 64cm
COURTESY OF SWORDERS, OF STANSTEAD MOUNTFITCHET

decorators and workmen was keenly sought by other workshops.[xlvi] By these means, their influence filtered through the whole of the Midlands japanning industry, and in itself, this adds to the difficulty of attributing unmarked articles to a specific factory.

Jennens & Bettridge began by making 'ornamental' paper trays (plate 131). They claimed to have been the inventors of the gothic-shaped paper tray (perhaps adapted from similarly shaped Chinese export trays).[7] It was to become one of the most popular forms for papier mâché trays and it was the judicious gift of such a tray to George III which led to Jennens & Bettridge being appointed 'Makers in ordinary to the King'.[8] Some of Jennens & Bettridge's earliest trays were Oriental in their style of decoration and were often ornamented with impasto, or 'raised work' by Joseph Booth; a gothic-shaped tray of this type, though not necessarily by Booth, is shown in plate 132. Their early history was so

xlv. Now nos. 60 and 62.
xlvi. Their influence was not confined to the japanning industry; painters at Messrs

Hardman's, of Birmingham, ecclesiastical furnishers, were said to have been trained by Jennens & Bettridge.

134. Papier mâché snuff box, painted with *St George Slaying the Dragon*; lettered inside: Wm. Pickin George Hotel Stafford, and impressed Jennens & Bettridge; c.1820-30. Dia: 15cm

COLLECTION OF JÜRGEN GLANZ, HAMBURG

133. Papier mâché vases with gilt-metal mounts, made for Lady Hertford's Blue Drawing Room at Temple Newsam House, Leeds; impressed mark: 'JENNENS & BETTRIDGE' – the mount-maker has not been identified; c.1830. 95.5cm

COURTESY OF TEMPLE NEWSAM HOUSE, LEEDS MUSEUMS AND GALLERIES.
PHOTO COURTESY OF CHRISTIE'S LONDON

inextricably linked with the manufacture of trays that it was said in 1851 that 'forty years ago, [they] set to work to improve the national tea-tray, and ... have since carried their improvements into every sort of dwelling – from the cottage kitchen to the state rooms of Buckingham Palace',[9] a clear sign that Jennens & Bettridge supplied every market.

They advanced from trays to other basically flat forms like screens and tables, and by the 1820s, had successfully introduced papier mâché hollow-ware such as vases, and advertised as makers of 'Japan Wares of ... every variety of European, Indian, and Persian style.'[10] The extraordinarily large and handsome vases shown here (plate 133) date from about 1830, and are believed to have been commissioned by Lady Hertford for the Blue Drawing Room at Temple Newsam House, Leeds, which she was furnishing with a mixture of chinoiserie and French Régence pieces. Influenced by Chinese porcelain vases, they are decorated with birds,

animals, butterflies and landscapes, in reserve panels edged with mother-of-pearl. Their decoration so closely resembles the style of Joseph Booth that it may indeed be his work, for as an acknowledged expert in chinoiseries, it is unlikely that such an important order would have been given to any other artist. When the vases were sold in London in 2003, their fine mounts were attributed to Edward Holmes Baldock of London, but the possibility of a Birmingham mount-maker should not be discounted. There was for example, Matthew Boulton's Soho Works which after his death, were maintained by his son who continued making high quality gold and silver plate, and ormolu, until 1846. The combination of papier mâché and gilt metal is one which features on several of Jennens & Bettridge's best pieces, like the fine table shown here (plate 135), a ewer in the Victoria & Albert Museum, and on a vase they decorated for Prince Albert in 1856 which is known to have been fitted with mounts of Birmingham manufacture (plate 145).

Opposite: 135. Papier mâché table-top showing skilful use of gold leaf to create the effect of iridescence in the birds' feathers. It is impressed Jennens & Bettridge, but the maker of the fine gilded brass pedestal has not been identified; c.1830/5.

COURTESY OF OTTO VON MITZLAFF

136. Sandwich-edge papier mâché tray; impressed mark JENNENS
& BETTRIDGE beneath a crown, c.1835-1840. 26 x 32.5cm
COLLECTION OF SHIRLEY S. BAER

Among Jennens & Bettridge's greatest contributions to the
industry was their patent of 1825 for improvements in preparing
pearl for use in japanned ware. The simplicity of the pearl
borders on Lady Hertford's vases therefore, suggests they may
have been made prior to this since Jennens & Bettridge would
surely have been keen to show off their expertise in cutting
elaborately shaped pearl motifs, particularly on such extravagant
articles. Certainly, by 1830, their pearl designs were considerably
more complex, being based in 'Natural History, Botany, and
Entymology, as well as in the luxuriant designs of fancy'.[11]

An advertisement of 1830 shows their range of products to have
included 'Table Tops, Cabinets, Ladies Dressing, Toilet, Work and
Card Boxes, Pole and Hand Screens; Ornaments for Chimney
Pieces, Quadrille Pools &c; Tea Chests, Caddies, Snuff Boxes
&c.',[12] in fact, as was said later, 'almost every variety of household furniture and trinkets without number'.[13] As their products
developed, so did their decoration. Chinese, Japanese and Indian
styles gave way to a greater realism in 1832, when one of their
decorators, was said to have introduced natural flower painting in
the centre of articles 'to which was given a border of light ornamental gold-work, at once chaste and beautiful'.[14] It was quickly
taken up by other manufacturers and sold so well that it is today
the style most closely associated with japanned papier mâché and
tinware; a similar trend was apparent in the ceramics industry

In 1846, a visitor to the factory described being:

> *gratified to find many successful copies of good
> paintings and engravings, made by artists on the
> premises, which exhibited considerable freedom of
> touch and accuracy; we may allude in particular to
> some of the animals of Landseer, introduced on the
> sides of portfolios and upon fire-screens.*[15]

137. Papier mâché tilt-and-swivel-top table (see also pl. 262); the
brass swivel mechanism stamped 'J&B/PATENT' (for Jennens &
Bettridge); c.1840. 72.5 x 51.5cm
PRIVATE COLLECTION

A fire-screen was especially commended for being painted after
Watteau 'whose style is peculiarly suited for decorations in
objects of this character; and has been at all times largely used.'[16]
The same visitor also praised the factory for standing 'almost
alone in the application of Art to the articles of their produce'.[17]

At the height of their success, Jennens & Bettridge employed
sixty-four full-time decorators.[xlvii] Many had been trained in
London, or at Birmingham School of Design where, as noted
earlier, in the mid nineteenth century, japanners were the largest
single group of craftsmen in attendance, and where, in 1843,
Aaron Jennens' two younger sons, Aaron (b.1825/6) and
Benjamin (1828–1905), were awarded prizes for their work.
Benjamin became a japanner, artist and traveller, but Aaron

xlvii. In the 1851 Census, Aaron Jennens listed a total workforce of 160.

xlviii. For details about the name 'Hyla' see fn. xxxv, p. 137.

chose not to enter the trade, taking up portraiture instead. It appears also that John Bettridge (father or son?), was also engaged in decorating the firms products, and on the evidence of a signed view of Warwick Castle painted on a box-lid, he was a talented artist (plate 139).

Jennens & Bettridge exhibited at all major provincial and international exhibitions, both at home and abroad, and won many medals and awards. In 1840, they showed at both the Glasgow and Nottingham Exhibitions, taking to the latter, a range which included a box, an ink-stand, a card case, folios, vases and panels. The following year, their display at the Dumfries Exhibition included 'a collection of Vases, Tea-Trays, Ink-stands, Fire Screens, Finger Plates'.[18] They were the largest exhibitors of papier mâché at the Exposition of British Industrial Art held at Manchester in 1846 from which the Art Union selected two of their articles for illustration: 'a cabinet of excellent form, good ornamentation; and very admirably painted'[19] and a richly decorated chair which, given its curved form, could have been a prototype made by a process of steam-moulding which Theodore Hyla Jennens (1810–1882)[xlviii] – eldest son of Aaron senior and half-brother to Aaron junior and Benjamin – patented the following year (#11, 670), some three years after they had registered the design of these chairs.

138. Papier mâché inkstand; imressed mark: 'JENNENS & BETTRIDGE/BIRM[M] &/LONDON', beneath a crown, c.1835-1840. 30 x 15cm

Chairs of this shape were truly innovative and could not have been made from any other material at this time. According to the Art Union in 1847, this firm showed greater improvements in chairs than in any other product, but ironically this was not because of their novelty of form, but because the manufacturers had:

so subdued the ornamentations as to render the objects refreshing to the eye instead of, as they used to be, painful from excess of glaring decoration. This advance in the right direction influences, more or less, all their later works; their light greens, and gaudy reds, and staring blues, are, in a great degree, displaced from their

139. Papier mâché toilet box, the hinged lid painted with Warwick Castle, signed in white script 'J Bettridge', and in red script, for the makers, 'Jennens & Bettridge'; the base impressed 'JENNENS & BETTRIDGE', and the silver fittings hall-marked for Henry Manton, Birmingham, 1845–1846. 14 x 28 x 21cm

140. Papier mâché two-compartment tea caddy; impressed: 'JENNENS & BETTRIDGE/MAKERS TO THE QUEEN', c.1840 11.5 x 21 x 15cm

fabrics; or are so skilfully and ingeniously brought into harmony with more sober colours, as really to place objects in Papier Mâché among the most desirable acquisitions in Industrial Art.[20]

Nowhere, the author argued, were these improvements 'more obvious, or more beneficial than in the drawing-room and boudoir chairs, of which they have recently manufactured a large variety, and which are rapidly making way into mansions where refinement keeps pace with fashion'[21] (plate 141). The article continued in similar vein, reporting that Jennens & Bettridge had recently sent two open-back chairs to Queen Victoria for inspection, and approving their combination of 'elegance with solidity, and lightness with strength'.[22] The shapes of these chairs had , it said, 'been contrived with a view to the ornamentation: one decorated on a dark ground in arabesque style after Mr Gruner,'[il] and the other, 'borrowed from the Alhambra', was done on grounds of either 'delicate pink, or French white.'[23] It is not known whether the chairs remained at the Palace. An entry in Jennens & Bettridge's Visitors Book in 1838, suggests that if customers wished, they could arrange to have chairs upholstered themselves; the Reverend H. Jackson of Holt Rectory in Norfolk, for instance, asked that a chair he had purchased be sent 'to the care of Mrs Ling, upholsterer'[24] in Bridewell Alley, Norwich.

141. One from a pair of papier mâché sofas reputed to have belonged to the Spanish Royal family; possibly part the suite which Jennens & Bettridge exhibited in London in 1849. H: 85cm W: 166cm De: 71cm
COURTESY OF BONHAMS

142. A range of goods made by Jennens & Bettridge, and illustrated in *Art Union*, 1846 (p. 60).

143. Papier mâché vases, impressed 'JENNENS & BETTRIDGE' beneath a crown; c.1840. H: 27cm

In 1849, Jennens & Bettridge exhibited several items of furniture at the third, and last, annual exhibition of British Manufactures & Decorative Art held at the Society of Art in London,[l] where they were presented with the Gold Isis Medal by Prince Albert, for the pearl ornament on a table-top. The Society had reservations about the suitability of pearl 'for the expression of the more delicately graduated scale of light and shade', but congratulated the artists in overcoming these difficulties 'as far as is possible'.[25] This must have been the table, seen prior to the exhibition, by a reporter at their London showroom and described as 'a large and magnificent loo table', richly pearled and painted with a group of flowers encircled by a wreath of flowers 'in a style that would bring no discredit on some Dutch masters.'[26]

It was perhaps at the same exhibition that Isabella II, Queen of Spain (1830–1904), ordered the suite of drawing room furniture which Jennens & Bettridge supplied in that year. A pair of sofas, sold in London in 1996, and reputed to have once belonged to the Spanish Royal family, may have been from the suite in question being similarly 'richly emblazoned in mother-of-pearl and burnished gold'[27] (plate 141). Queen Isabella's purchase prompted the Journal of Design and Manufactures to comment:

> *We are delighted to recognise* [papier mâché] *acquiring a European reputation. We are glad to see even in these revolutionary times, the continued dropping of a shower of good fortune on these enterprising manufactures, and if their subsequent works maintain the character for grace and brilliancy this must acquire, we have little doubt that such "articles de luxe", will find an extensive market abroad.*[28]

---

il. Ludwig Gruner (1801–82) born in Dresden. He came to London and served as an art advisor to Prince Albert. The 'renaissance' and 'grotesque' designs in his book, *Specimens of Ornamental Art* (1850), greatly influenced manufacturers and were much in evidence at the Great Exhibition.

l. The Society of Arts held three Annual Exhibition(s) of *Select Specimens of British Manufactures & Decorative Art*, in London from 1847 to 1849.

144. Chairs, with a panels of 'Patent Inlaid Gems' inset in the papier mâché backs (see p. 82); made by Jennens & Bettridge, c.1850.

Over the years, Queen Isabella purchased several extravagant items from Jennens & Bettridge including a dressing case in 1849 which was considered 'one of the most costly and sumptuous articles which has been issued from their establishment.'[29]

Also intended for the luxury market was a range of goods decorated with 'inlaid gems' or 'gem-enamelling' – a style introduced in 1847 by Theodore Hyla Jennens (1810–1882), and protected by the same patent as his method of steam-moulding papier mache (#11,670, see above and p. 33). It was first used on a cheval screen shown at the Society of Arts in 1848:

> the outer portions are of white and gold pierced; the inner parts solid, containing the "gems", set in groundwork of light blue, pink white, &c.; the centre may have either a looking-glass, or a painting of any kind, for each of which it is equally well adapted.[30]

Attaching the gems was tricky and the difficulties of achieving the effect 'were indeed so great as for some time to deter the manufacturers from any further attempts'.[31] Nevertheless, they 'persevered' and besides screens, introduced this style of decoration on articles such as writing-desks, work-boxes, portfolios, finger-plates, and even on chairs (plate 144).

A curious sidelight on gem-enamelling was offered by a pair of glass vases that Jennens and Bettridge decorated for Prince Albert, as a birthday gift for Queen Victoria in 1856, with

designs by Lewis Gruner (plate 145).[li] There is no known record of where the vases were made, but the likelihood is that it was at one of the leading glass-works in Birmingham or in the important glass-making centres of nearby Stourbridge or Brierley Hill. Richly encrusted with diamonds, emeralds, rubies and topaz, and incorporating the national flower emblems (rose, thistle and shamrock), the vases were set in fine pierced electro-gilt metal mounts made by Elkington & Mason of Birmingham, and stand about 17in. high (43cm). These vases become less surprising when it is remembered that the original patent for this type of decoration was not confined to papier mâché goods but included 'other articles' too; nevertheless, these are the only glass vases which Jennens & Bettridge are known to have decorated in this way.

As already seen, the firm supplied papier mâché panels for the SS Imperador (p. 82). Such decorative panels for rooms and ship saloons were not a new idea; Henry Clay had suggested a similar use in his patent of 1772, and Jennens & Bettridge themselves advertised on a bill-head of 1841, that they could provide 'Drawing Rooms & Saloons Decorated with Panels, Pilasters &c. in elegant & modern styles' (plate 129). The advertisement is, of course, ambiguous. The pilasters could have been like the architectural mouldings made by firms such as Charles Bielefeld, and Jackson etc., but as there is no other contempory evidence of Jennens & Bettridge having made such goods, it could be that the panels were japanned and decorated in their usual manner. No rooms fitted out with their decorative panels are known, but by all accounts their painted ship-panels proved a very lucrative line and to judge from those which have survived, they were worked on by their very best painters. Just how profitable they were may be judged by Jennens & Bettridge's eagerness to engage John Thomas (qv), a japan artist, to paint ship-panels, offering him an advance of fifty per cent on the fees he was currently receiving as a painter of book covers etc. We do not know whether he accepted, but it is known that he later went to Glasgow to paint similar panels for a Mr T. Laurie (p. 323).

Panels of this type, made mostly between the 1830s and early 1850s, were a much more important branch of the trade than has hitherto been understood. In 1847, Jennens & Bettridge made a set painted with copies of frescoes which a Mr Townsend had painted for Buckingham Palace; these panels, we are told, were copied from woodcuts published in the Art Union, with full encouragement from Townsend himself who,

---

li. Interestingly, John Allgood (fl. 1779–90) had 'experimented with japanning on glass' at Pontypool, but nothing is known of the outcome (see R. Nichols' p. 37). Thomas Archer, reporting on the Paris Exhibition of 1867, noted that 'Prussia, represented by

Stobwasser and others, sends [amongst other things] japanned glass.'
lii. W.S. Lindsay was author of The History of Merchant Shipping (1874-6).

when Jennens & Bettridge sought his permission, 'at once and readily, supplied them with such information as sufficed to act as guides for colouring the copies'.[32] As the *Illustrated Birmingham Times* announced in 1854: 'This firm has just completed some of the finest specimens of Paper Machee [*sic*] that it is possible to conceive, for panels in ships saloons.'[33] Among them was a set for the *Robert Lowse*, a ship built by Scott & Co. of Greenock for W.S. Lindsay Esq.,[lii] which included four large panels, each 183 x 122cm, painted with 'clever transcripts of London, Constantinople (plate 146), Venice and the Lake of Como',[34] a smaller set painted with views, and some door panels painted with 'groups of running and twining flowers'[35] against a light cream-coloured ground. These were felt to be 'quieter in tone than is often found in works of this class',[36] by which was meant quieter than papier mâché in general. A further set, painted for the *Parana* – a ship belonging to the Malcolmson Brothers Line – showed South American views, 'the vessel being intended for that quarter of the world'.[37]

145. One from a pair of glass vases decorated with 'inlaid gems' by Jennens & Bettridge (see pp. 83 and 152), and illustrated in the *Art Journal*, 1856 (p. 184).

These japanned and painted panels were generally marked Jennens & Bettridge in tiny red-painted script in their lower left corner, as indeed were some of the paintings found on handscreens and box-lids. Many panels were salvaged when the various ships were broken up, and subsequently placed in gilt frames. As a result, their original purpose was forgotten and for many years they appeared in sale rooms as 'oil paintings on board'. Some, like the Constantinople panel, are extremely heavy on account of having been constructed by

compressing pulp between layers of making paper, to a thickness of 1cm (*cf.* Sheldon's patent, p. 35ff).

Another development, more or less contemporary with inlaid-gems and the production of ship-panels, was the introduction of parian bas-reliefs to decorate papier mâché (*cf.* Clay and his use of Wedgwood medallions). Few examples seem to have

146. Papier mâché panel made in 1854 for *SS Robert Lowse*, and painted with *Constantinople, from the entrance to the Golden Horn*, from an engraving of 1838, by J. Couzen, after Thomas Allom (1804–1872); impressed Jennens & Bettridge. 122 x 183cm

147. Engraving of a papier mâché and wood chiffonier, made by Jennens & Bettridge, from the *Art Journal*, 1849 (p. 306).

survived, perhaps on account of few having been made after the disappointing criticism which they received in *The Journal of Design & Manufactures* in 1850 where a workbox, decorated with 'Penelope and her maids spinning', was felt to be 'more suggestive than successful'.[38] This particular parian relief was by the sculptor John Bell (1811–95) who, from 1845 to 1860, worked as a modeller for Minton's, in Stoke-on-Trent – a firm renowned for making parian figures and portrait busts. However, since the Minton factory archive has no record of having supplied Jennens & Bettridge, John Bell may have supplied them directly.

Increasingly during the mid nineteenth century, and in response to published criticism, the manufacturing industries looked to established and respected designers and artists to improve both the form and decoration of their goods. Jennens & Bettridge was no exception. Like many others, they had relied upon popular paintings, both old and new, to copy onto their products, but following the Copyright Act of 1842, they were thrown back on their own resources. In addition to John Bell, Jennens & Bettridge commissioned eminent designers like Richard Redgrave, and Hugh Fitz-Cook to work on prestigious 'exhibition' pieces, and they looked to the published designs of Ludwig Gruner. Conversely, the Act also served to protect a manufacturer's own designs and many of Jennens & Bettridge's 'gondola' shaped chairs for example, show a design registration mark for 1844. However, originality and plagiarism were separated by only a very thin line. A reporter for *The Journal of Design and Manufactures* condemned a wine tray shown by McCullum & Hodson at the Birmingham Exposition of 1849 for being 'obviously a plagiarism' of one by Messrs. Jennens & Bettridge. 'I submit', he wrote, 'that some direct poaching has been going on'.[39] Nevertheless, when they themselves had sought the opinion of the editor of the same journal a few months earlier, Jennens & Bettridge were advised not to pursue the matter. Had they been 'the first to introduce a shape on this principle', said the editor, 'then we think they have reason to complain that the principle has been pirated.'[40] In other words, 'parlour maid's trays', as their general shape is popularly called today, were first introduced by another manufacturer and Jennens & Bettridge might themselves have been accused of piracy.

One of the most improbable objects that Jennens & Bettridge made was a papier mâché easel. They sent details to the *Art Journal* for comment and it was featured in 1849: save for the polished mahogany support for the picture, it was made entirely of paper ornamented with gold and pearl, and its upper part took the form of a 'sort of scroll-pattern'.[41] The journal was almost certainly correct in judging that it 'must only be intended for a library or drawing room, as it is far too elegant an object for an artist's studio';[42] as such, it is unlikely that it was a standard line and this may have been the only one ever made. There is no record of anyone purchasing such an easel, but like so many obviously expensive papier mâché articles, it was probably hidden from sight as fashions changed, and may, even now, await re-discovery in an attic or out-house.

148. Papier mâché wine-tray, designed by Richard Redgrave, in 1847, for Felix Summerly's Art Manufactures, and made by Jennens & Bettridge, in 1865. 40 x 72.5 x 4cm

149. Papier mâché wine-tray (*cf.* pl. 148); impressed 'JENNENS & BETTRIDGE/MAKERS TO THE QUEEN', beneath a crown, and printed mark of Richard Redgrave, c.1850s. 37.5 x 72.5 x 4cm

Following their success at the Society of Arts in 1849, Jennens & Bettridge mounted a sumptuous array of goods at the Birmingham Exposition later in the same year, where they once again displayed the gem-inlaid cheval screen, last seen at the Society in 1847, and the table for which they had received a Gold Isis medal. They also showed a wide range of small articles in Birmingham, but it was the larger, more spectacular pieces of furniture which attracted the most interest: a chiffonier (plate 147); a seven-leaf folding screen painted with flowers; a Ladies Robing Glass with matching Dressing Table; an 'Alhambra chair' to match the cheval screen; and a copy of the sofa they had earlier supplied to the Queen of Spain. In addition, they showed a new shape of wine tray designed by Richard Redgrave in 1847, under the aupices of Felix Summerley's Art Manufactures, which the Art Union had featured the year before (plate 148 and *cf.* plate 149). Decorated with 'vine and grapes' and incorporating 'compartments to receive the decanters and prevent their shifting among the glasses', the tray was shaped to fit

150. King-gothic papier mâché tray, decorated with a painting entitled *Grande Salle a Manger Chenonceaux, Temps Francois I*; Jennens & Bettridge, c.1850 (*cf.* pl. 72). 60 x 80cm

155

comfortably round the waist when carried, and thus provided 'the convenience of horse-shoe tables. Instead of the painful sight of waiters holding trays of wine and cake at a long stretch ... we shall now see them in a state of ease, if not an attitude of grace.'[43] Their display in Birmingham also included a cabinet inlaid with pearl figures in 'Watteau' style – an enlarged version of one they had made at the request of the Lord Principal and Council of the Queen's College and Hospital, Birmingham, for presentation to Jenny Lind in 1848 (plate 151).

This exhibition had served as a 'practice run' for the Great Exhibition held in London two years later, when, according to the 1851 Census, Jennens & Bettridge employed 160 people. Furniture played a similarly prominent part in their display at this huge event, but this time functionalism came second to stunning visual effects. The 'most conspicuous'[44] of their exhibits was a cottage piano with matching stool and canterbury (plate 90). The piano – made by Dimoline of Bristol, and constructed of 'the best white Archangel deal', with a sound-board 'of the

151. Ladies' cabinet of papier mâché, with a silver tablet inscribed 'To Mademoiselle Jenny Lind from the Lord Principal and Council of the Queen's College and Hospital Birmingham as a small testimony of their sense of obligation for her very noble and gratuitous services at a concert held in the Town Hall on behalf of the funds of the Queen's Hospital, December 28th, 1848.' Nightingales are included in the decoration, in recognition of Lind's reputation as 'The Swedish nightingale'. Made by Jennens & Bettridge, whose name appears in a band of gold leaf at the back of the cabinet. 29 x 37 x 35cm

Photographed while in private ownership, and since acquired by the Theatre Museum (S.276.1987)

152. Engraving of an Elizabethan chair by Jennens & Bettridge, from the *Art Journal Illustrated Catalogue of the Industries of All Nations*, 1851 (p. 66).
REPRODUCED WITH THE PERMISSION OF BIRMINGHAM LIBRARIES & ARCHIVES

153. The Day Dreamer's Chair made by Jennens and Bettridge from the *Official Descriptive & Illustrated Catalogue* of the Great Exhibition (Vol. II p. 369); 1851.
REPRODUCED WITH THE PERMISSION OF BIRMINGHAM LIBRARIES & ARCHIVES

154. The Victoria Regia Cot made by Jennens & Bettridge from the *Art Journal Illustrated Catalogue of the Industries of all Nations*, 1851 (p. 65).
REPRODUCED WITH THE PERMISSION OF BIRMINGHAM LIBRARIES & ARCHIVES

finest Swiss pine'[45] – was encased by Jennens & Bettridge in papier mâché and decorated in 'Italian style' in variously tinted mother-of-pearl on a black ground. *The Illustrated London News* had nothing but praise for the piano, but its report was at odds with the verdict of the exhibition jurors who, conceding that the decoration was 'in good taste and well executed' nevertheless thought it 'scarcely suitable in style for the material employed, which being necessarily in small pieces, would have probably told with better effect if arranged in the form of a mosaic'.[46] As to 'its merits as a musical instrument',[47] the *Morning Chronicle* declined to comment on account of not having had the opportunity to judge,[liii] but since the piano appears not to have sold it was, perhaps, not a wholly successful product.

Jennens & Bettridge took a number of chairs to the exhibition, including a prie-dieu of 'Gothic' style upholstered in painted velvet and an 'Elizabethan chair' (plate 152) which was considered 'a favourable specimen of the success which may attend the manufacturer who fearlessly carries out his conceptions in any material, however discouraging it may appear in the outset.'[48] But the chair which attracted most comment was the one Jennens & Bettridge had named the 'Day-dreamer' (plate 153). Of 'curious and novel appearance',[49] it was designed by H. Fitz-Cook in the 'Italian' style with winged figures personifying dreams, both sweet and otherwise. Curiously, the preposterous gilt throne which overshadows everything around it in Dickinson's print of Jennens & Bettridge's display at the Great Exhibition (plate

90), appears to have been overlooked by contemporary critics, and it is difficult to match it to any article described in the various published lists of exhibits. It may have been the so-called 'Oriental chair' which was said to be 'unique',[50] and to have been very difficult to produce – as surely this object would have been. If this was the chair in question, its unique status was short-lived, as 'orders from Eastern potentates [were said to be] flowing in fast.'[51] Similarly, it is possible only to conjecture that the gilt tray, seen hanging above this chair in the same print, was 'The Pacha's Tray' which, measuring 58in. (147.5cm) in diameter, was 'made to receive the filigree saucers on which great Oriental dinners are served.'[52] Birmingham had a long-standing tradition for supplying India with costly goods and both this large tray and the Oriental Chair were almost certainly made with an eye to attracting the many eastern dignitaries who were expected to visit the exhibition. It was after all, an exhibition representing the Industry of all Nations, and included courts devoted to India, Persia, Greece, Egypt, and Turkey, as well as to Spain, Portugal, Madeira and Italy – in fact over thirty countries took part.

Other eye-catchers which appealed to contemporary writers were the nautilus-shaped 'Victoria Regia Cot' and the 'Lotus work-table', an extraordinarily impractical device in spite of its adjustable height, which was intended for the boudoir (plates 154 & 90). Both articles were designed by the sculptor John Bell whose papier mâché chess-board and Parian chess-men were also exhibited.

---

liii. The likelihood is that this piano has survived, but its present location is unknown.

155. Papier mâché tea-caddy displayed at the Great Exhibition; impressed 'JENNENS & BETTRIDGE, makers to the Queen' beneath a crown, c.1850. 22 x 23 x 15cm

PHOTO © VICTORIA AND ALBERT MUSEUM, LONDON (Museum No. 37:1, 2-1852)

156. Papier mâché finger-plates and door-knobs; impressed 'Jennens & Bettridge', c.1850. 25.3 x 7.5cm (plates) 5.5 x 6cm (knobs)

© WOLVERHAMPTON ARTS AND HERITAGE (BANTOCK HOUSE MUSEUM)

It is impossible here, to ennumerate all that Jennens & Bettridge showed at the Great Exhibition. There were many exhibits which were neither described in detail, nor illustrated, but which are, nevertheless, worthy of singling out, not least to give a more balanced view of Jennens & Bettridge's output at this period. These included a set of toilet furniture, a bachelor's sideboard, a Redgrave wine tray decorated in pearl with the Royal Arms, ink-stands, reading stands, sofa-tables, writing desks, albums, portfolios, finger-plates, and so on. In complete contrast, they also showed a range of papier mâché trays 'for hotels', and four papier mâché trays of the second quality which were 'exhibited for their cheapness.'[53]

Many of Jennens & Bettridge's exibits at the Great Exhibition were anathema to educated mid nineteenth-century taste, and critics rightly observed that 'the style of work of some of the large objects ... however well designed and ingeniously executed, did not appear suitable to the material'.[54] Notwithstanding, recognising 'the great merit due to this house',[55] the Exhibition Jury awarded Jennens & Bettridge the only Prize Medal in their Class.[liv]

They also received a medal at the New York Exhibition in 1853 where they exhibited what, by then, had become their usual array of goods: 'tables, chairs, trays, inkstands and other articles'.[56] A similar range was shown that year at the Dublin Exhibition by William Mansfield, a retailer and Jennens & Bettridge's representative in that city. It included tea chests, dressing cases, work tables, portfolios, pole screens, and writing desks.

In the same year, 1853, the Department of Practical Art published a catalogue of decorative articles which it had purchased or been given for their Museum intended 'for the use of Students & Manufacturers and the Consultation of the Public'.[57] Among them were two items presented by Jennens & Bettridge which, in terms of their decoration, harked back to the early design influences of the Midlands japanning industry. The first was a tea caddy 'somewhat after the Indian principle'; although effective, it was judged its 'harmonies of colour might have been better',[58] and the second, a papier mâché panel, exemplified the revival or 'successful repetition of Japan work in England'.[59] The other objects by Jennens & Bettridge – a chair and a work-box, decorated with mother-of pearl – were purchased by the Museum as examples of 'good workmanship; decorated on just principles and with greater simplicity than has heretofore been the case in this manufacture.'[60] They cost £2.10s and £3 respectively.

liv. This medal, the present whereabouts of which is unknown, is housed in a purpose-made papier mâché case, the lid decorated with the royal arms in mother-of-pearl.

157. King-gothic papier mâché tray with pearl, painted and gold leaf decoration;
impressed 'JENNENS & BETTRIDGE' beneath a crown, c.1850. 48 x 64cm

Despite their success in the luxury market, Jennens &
Bettridge continued to produce goods of every class. This
was evident from the second quality trays they exhibited in
1851, and was made plain in the following announcement of
1854:

Their PATTERN ROOMS & SHOW ROOMS,
contain every variety of Article manufactured in Papier
Mâché suitable for Exportation, Presentation and
Domestic Use, viz:- Tea Trays (Best Paper, Second
Quality, and Japan,) Chairs, Tables, Work Boxes,
Inkstands, Folios, Writing Desks, Door Plates etc.[61]

To this list might have been added bagatelle and other gaming
boards, miniature frames, snuff boxes, paper knives, door
knobs (plate 156) 'and even rosaries, for Catholic or
Mahomedan use; the beads of which are black and polished,
and light as jet, while less liable to fracture.'[62] Their list of
products seemed endless.

Jennens & Bettridge exhibited at the Paris Exhibition of 1855
where they were awarded two First Class Medals. Obviously,
they had heeded the severe criticism which followed their
display at the Great Exhibition in 1851, since the *Art
Journal*, now noted 'that most of the specimens sent by this
firm show less of the gaudy colouring than we have been
used to see from this establishment,'[63] adding elsewhere, in
the same report:

*There is a tendency to a somewhat severe style of
decoration, but we fear that the very facilities for
producing "startling effects" is a common temptation for
what in theatrical phrase, may be called terrific contrasts.*[64]

A good indicator of Jennens & Bettridge's prices is found in the
catalogue of goods they took to the Edinburgh Exhibition in
1857. Here, not only are the descriptions sufficiently detailed to
provide a clear idea of each article but, very unusually, their
individual costs are also given. The most prestigious of the goods
exhibited were described and priced as follows:

Patent Green Enamelled Vase in the style of a pair Jennens & Bettridge had the honour of making for the Queen	£42.10s
Secretaire, Patent Pearl, Italian style	£50
Writing desk, 18 inches, pearl and gold	£10
ditto 13 inches, pearl and mosaic	£5
Papeterie, 14 inches, Patent Gems	£7
Chair with gem panel	£6.10s
Table, 22 inches	£10[65]

Prices of the smaller goods varied considerably according to their
styles of decoration. For example, a quarto folio embellished
with gems cost £3, while a similar folio painted with a copy of
Landseer's picture 'The Queens Favourites' was £2.10s. (£2.50),
and one with a 'Pearl fountain', £1.15s (£1.75); a flower-painted
folio of 'post size' was £1.6s (£1.30), and an octavo folio in

159

158. Cabinet on wooden stand, with papier mâché door panels, and six graduated
drawers each faced with papier mâché; raised-work decoration (*cf.* pl. 270); impressed
'JENNENS & BETTRIDGE/LONDON'; c.1850–1860. 157 x 97 x 57.5cm

© WOLVERHAMPTON ARTS AND HERITAGE (BANTOCK HOUSE MUSEUM)

'mediaeval' style, only 6s. (30p). A plain black inkstand retailed at £1.10s. (£1.50) but one with 'pearl, mosaic and coloured' ornament was £2.5s. (£2.25). Two guineas (£2.10) would have secured a 24in. tray with 'pearl all over', and £5, a graduated set of three trays with maroon grounds. Of the other items listed, the most interesting were a spill cup painted with a dog's head at 8s. (40p) and a pair of hand screens painted with a scene entitled 'Highland Music' which sold for £2.10s. (£2.50).

These prices show little, if any, increase on those which Jennens & Bettridge charged for comparable articles almost twenty years earlier to judge from entries in their Visitors Book for that period. On 21st September, 1839, for example, the individual cost of each of three items purchased by Mr & Mrs Hole of 27 Baker Street, London, was as follows:

Chess Table with Pearl	£18.18.0	(£18.90)
Round Table Flowers	£10.10.0	(£10.50)
Pole Screen Lake	£10.10.0[66]	

NB. A *List of Articles Manufactured by Jennens and Bettridge with prices attached*, c.1851–1852, is available to view at http://library.winterthur.org (Library call no: NA 3680 J54 TC).

For some, the ostentatious luxury of Jennens & Bettridge's papier mâché goods became more acceptable when new and faster methods of manufacture brought down the prices of their more everyday goods:

From end to end of the show-room ... there is a refinement of convenience as well as of beauty, which would make one ashamed, but for the evidence presented throughout, that luxury is not confined to the rich, even now, and that it is likely to descend more and more abundantly into humble homes... If we can but see this, we shall willingly let unique Oriental chairs go to Persia, and sixteen guinea chess tables to India, satisfied with our humbler share in the improvements of the arts of life.[67]

Jennens & Bettridge's interests were wider than are generally supposed. They saw alternative and far-ranging uses for the very strong and plastic papier mâché which they produced, and in 1854, manufactured:

panelling for railway carriages – one of the most novel of the many purposes, and yet perhaps one of the most important, to which papier mâché is being adapted by the firm referred to ... their appearance, a mere compact slab of brown paper, contrasts most strangely with the chef d'oeuvres of the japanners art and ornamentists: but the material is superior to wood in many respects – in non-liability to contract, warp or split.[68]

Three years later, T.H. Jennens successfully applied for a patent for making 'calico printing rollers with a core of papier mâché on a mandril of iron, the copper shell being subsequently drawn over the core to compress it.'[69, lv] Whether these ideas were put into practice is of small concern here, but what is important is the breadth of vision they displayed – the same breadth of vision which ensured that Jennens & Bettridge led the field in the manufacture of high quality japanned papier mâché goods for the luxury market.

The partnership ended in 1859[lvi] on the retirement of Aaron Jennens, one of the founding partners, at a time when the industry was beating off the effects of newer, highly competetive materials like electro-plate. Theodore Hyla Jennens appears to have continued alone until at least 1861, selling first class goods from the firm's London showroom at 6 Halkin Street West, Belgrave Square. The parent company, Jennens & Bettridge, continued for a short time under the direction of John H. Bettridge at 19–21 Barr Street (see below).

JOHN BETTRIDGE & Co. (late Jennens & Bettridge)
fl. 1859–c.1869
Constitution Hill
1865+ Royal Papier Mâché & Japan Works
19–21 Barr Street, St George's, Birmingham

On taking control of the former Jennens & Bettridge Works in 1859, John Bettridge (b.1818), son of one of the firm's founders, and formerly London Agent for the parent company, informed the public that he would maintain the high standards of the old firm and promised 'ARTICLES OF NEW AND ELEGANT DESIGNS including MEDIEAVAL, MALACHITE, and PATENT GEM ENAMELLED GOODS, at unprecedently [*sic*] low prices.'[1]

He then began preparations for the sale of the premises on Constitution Hill. The sale, to be held in November 1859, included Jennens & Bettridge's 'spacious showrooms, offices, warehouses, stores and numerous ranges of well-lighted workshops, fitted with 12 japan stoves.' Evidently the sale was unsuccessful for, in 1861, only a few months before the premises were finally sold, all but the front of the factory and the first floor show-room was destroyed by fire.[lvii] Bettridge moved to premises on Hockley Hill, Birmingham, occupied by the japanner Charles Swann with whom he continued in business as John Bettridge & Co. By 1860, they had moved to nearby 19–21 Barr Street and had secured wholesale showrooms at 97 [or 76] Cheapside, London.

Like Jennens & Bettridge, they also made goods of 'a Commercial kind' decorated in a style that was 'more chaste

---

lv. Robert Fuller of London, was granted a patent, in 1684 (#238) for making paper and pasteboard for the 'hot and cold Pressing of Cloath'; it was wholly associated with the woollen cloth trade.
lvi. Theodore Hyla Jennens appears to have continued alone for a short time after the partnership ended, selling high quality papier mâché goods from 6 Halkin Street West, Belgrave

Square. It is possible, therefore, that his 1857 patent was taken out on his own account.
lvii. The fire-damaged parts were subsequently rebuilt and the premises adapted for use by an iron-founder. Fortuitously, both the neoclassical frontage and the early nineteenth-century royal coat of arms survived.

159. Piano, its wooden carcass encased in papier mâché and inset with panels of 'inlaid gems'; made by John Bettridge & Co., and exhibited at the International Exhibition, London, 1862.
COURTESY OF BLAIRMAN, LONDON

160. Half-tester bedstead with papier mâché head and foot-boards, and iron posts, designed by 'Mr Fitz-Cook' for John Bettridge & Co.; from the *Art Journal Illustrated Catalogue of the International Exhibition* (p. 60), London 1862.
REPRODUCED WITH THE PERMISSION OF BIRMINGHAM LIBRARIES & ARCHIVES

than is common in the trade'.[2] Indeed, it was for high standards of design and manufacture that J. Bettridge & Co. received Honorable Mention at the London Exhibition of 1862 where, together with a predictable array of papier mâché and iron goods, they exhibited a half-tester bed. Designed by H. Fitz-Cook, it was said in the *Art Journal* catalogue of the exhibition to be their 'piéce de résistance ... being as elaborate as is usually looked for in articles of this fabric, yet sufficiently subdued and in very good harmony'[3] (plate 160). George Wallis, however, took a different view, believing it to have been 'unhappily based upon so decided a wooden type as to practically contradict the material of which it was made,'[4] and although looking favourably upon the decoration of their other goods, he nevertheless criticised their flower painting for falling short of their usually high standard. In the same year, and possibly at this exhibition, J. Bettridge & Co. sold 'a magnificent assortment of articles in Papier Mâché'[5] to a Russian nobleman, and had sold so many pieces of furniture to the East that they could justifiably claim that 'Oriental Princes repose in Sofas and Couches'[6] made at their factory.

A report in *The Stationer and Fancy Trades Register* in 1865, described their factory as 'extensive' with over 100 employees; some were engaged in transfer printing, but 'a large proportion' of the workers were artists. 'On passing through the artists' room', the author could not help but notice a set of panels for the Pacha of Egypt 'ornamented with gold and elaborately inlaid buhl, with a richly painted medallion centre' and six dozen chairs for the Nizam of Hyderabad, which were deemed 'superb specimens of artistic workmanship'.[7, lviii]

According to Wallis, the firm continued to be 'remembered as Jennens & Bettridge'.[8] This is hardly surprising given the extent to which John Bettridge & Co. perpetuated the trade of the parent company. For example, in an advertisement of 1867, besides describing themselves as makers of 'papier mâché and japanned iron tea trays, coal vases, tables, chairs, sofas, bedsteads, desks, inkstands, photo-albums', they also advertised as 'ship decorators with papier mâché and glass panels and pilasters.'[9] In the same year they showed, at the Paris Exhibition, several articles ornamented with their new method of aluminium inlay (p. 78) and once again, were awarded a Bronze Medal. Among their exhibits was a papier mâché piano which was evidently more successful than the one taken by Jennens & Bettridge to the 1851 Exhibition, for at least two were sold and both have survived to the present day (plate 159).

Soon after their return from Paris, J. Bettridge & Co., the then premier makers of papier mâché in the Midlands, finally closed their doors. Whether they looked upon the Paris Exhibition as a fitting swan-song, or whether their decision to close was sudden we cannot now be sure – although the appointment, in 1868, of Bettridge's younger brother, Joseph (b.1825), as London agent, suggests the latter – but the heyday of the industry was certainly past. The business, and its London showrooms, were taken over by McCallum & Hodson some time between 1867 and 1868. Links with the old firm continued when McCallum & Hodson appointed John Bettridge as their London agent, and Benjamin Jennens (half-brother of Theodore H. Jennens) as a commercial traveller – a position which he had previously held together

162. Papier mâché chairs, steam-moulded to create the effect of studded ornament; stamped brass label of John Bettridge & Co. c.1860.

COURTESY OF SWORDERS, OF STANSTEAD MOUNTFITCHET

161. Papier mâché chair, stamped 'BETTRIDGE & CO/MAKERS/BIRMINGHAM', on a brass plate; c.1860. H: 83cm

COLLECTION OF ANTHONY PHIPPS

with Joseph Bettridge, whilst at the parent company. However, Benjamin's appointment was very short-lived as he emigrated, almost immediately, to Denver, Colorado.

The Sale of Papier Mâché Goods from the estate of Messrs. J. Bettridge & Co, 1870

On August 8–10 1870, J. Bettridge & Co's remaining stock of 'finished specimens'[lix] of papier mâché was sold, without reserve, by the auctioneers Thomas & Bettridge, at the Royal Hotel in Temple Row, Birmingham.[lx] There were 720 lots, some of which comprised up to four, and sometimes five, items, as for example: 'Small inkstand pearl, 8vo. Blotter, and three neck-chains'.[10, lxi]

The catalogue is interesting on a number of levels, and not least because of the number of large pieces of furniture in their remaining stock. If, as was likely, J. Bettridge & Co. had disposed of the greater part of their stock before they ceased trading, then their previous stock-levels of furniture must have been very high indeed – even allowing for their spread across both the Birmingham & London showrooms. For example, there were 124 chairs (including twenty-five paired sets) (cf. plates 161-2), among them a replica of the 'massive arm chair' (Lot no. 308) originally

sold to the Nizam of Hyderabad; a pair of chairs decorated with Wedgwood medallions which had recently been exhibited at the Paris Exhibition (Lot no. 99); twelve tables ranging from a 'small coffee table with chess squares on top' (Lot no. 127) to a large circular table (Lot no. 575a) which Jennens & Bettridge had shown previously at the Great Exhibition in 1851; several work-tables and chess tables; and five so-called multi-formia.

Of particular interest among the smaller articles was 'a four pack card box' (Lot No. 89) decorated with mother-of-pearl and gold 'similar' to one supplied to Queen Victoria, and two 30" trays, one scarlet and the other black, of a pattern 'invariably supplied to the Queen' (Lot nos. 113 & 114), which suggests that this was a regular order from the royal household. The most surprising were the lots which included 'sets of dinner mats'. Lot number 468, although not a set, is interesting for being the most descriptive entry for such items: 'two 16in. [41cm] dinner mats, maroon and gold' – a size that suggests these particular mats were intended for use in the centre of the table. There was also a folio inset with a view of the Crystal Palace beneath glass (Lot no. 36) – an article not usually associated with the firm, it may, of course, have been made by Thomas Lane (qv), and kept by Jennens & Bettridge out of curiosity or competetive interest.

lviii. A chair of this type is in the Victoria & Albert Museum (W.21-1971).

lix. It is not known whether the blank and unfinished articles were auctioned separately or if, as seems probable, they were purchased by McCallum & Hodson when they took over the business.

lx. There were other tradesmen of this name in Birmingham at this time eg. the silsversmith

Thomas Bettridge, and the likelihood is that they were all, in some way, related.

lxi. There were forty-two 'plain black' neck chains included in the sale. Invariably sold in groups of three, they bore no relevance to other items within the same lot appearing, rather, to have been make-weights. Since they were described as chains, it is unlikely that they were the same as the rosaries made by Jennens & Bettridge in the 1850s (see p.159).

With few exceptions, the catalogue makes no distinction between old and new stock, so there is now no means of deducing whether articles designed by Richard Redgrave and Christopher Dresser (1834–1904) were made by Jennens & Bettridge or their successors. However, unlike some earlier references to papier mâché articles designed by these men, the objects in question were described, albeit cursorily:

Lot 77	Very handsome inkstand, large cut glass, and two wafer boxes, designed by R. Redgrave R.A.
Lot 107	Extra large portfolio, designed by Dr. Dresser
Lot 400	4to. folio, designed by R. Redgrave R.A.

To judge from the catalogue, the most popular ground colours in use at J. Bettridge & Co. were black and maroon. Simulated walnut and malachite surfaces also featured prominently on both large and small pieces; these were decorated mostly with gold leaf, but often with 'gold' or gilt mounts. There were examples of imitation buhl, the most spectacular of which was a 'Very handsome CHEVAL SCREEN, tortoiseshell and gold buhl, with exquisitely painted fruit and flowers in the centre, as supplied to H.H. the Viceroy of Egypt' (Lot no. 91).

The sale included many articles decorated with Bettridge's special 'inlaid aluminium' but, once again, their descriptions are too vague to shed light on the true nature of this style. Articles decorated in this way included dinner mats, tea-caddies, trays, chairs and much else besides, and mostly they had ivory coloured grounds – a combination which may help in their positive identification.

Although advertised primarily as a sale of papier mâché, it also included a number of iron goods. There were iron trays of both the 'commercial kind' and of 'best quality' some of the latter being richly gilt and pearled or, as in the case of one tray, painted after Landseer (#286). In addition, there were iron bread-baskets and coal vases, including one decorated with inlaid gems and the Prince of Wales' feathers (#90). A number of plate-glass ship panels were also offered for sale, several of which were painted with views or, like the one 'supplied to the yacht Napoleon 1st', with fruit or flowers and measuring 24 x 18in. (#96).

In summary, the catalogue greatly extends our knowledge of the range and quality of the products of this firm and it shows J. Bettridge & Co. to have been worthy successors to one of the best-known Midlands japanning factories. As the auctioneers stated on the title-page:

The public should note the superiority of design, excellence of material, and perfection of workmanship in these goods; and that no such opportunity of purchase can ever again occur, the Firm now becoming absolutely extinct.

THOMAS LANE
fl. c.1821–1855/6
Royal Papier Mâché Works
91 Great Hampton Street, Birmingham
also **20 Upper Hockley Street** (off **Gt Hampton St.**)

Thomas Lane (born between 1797 and 1801) occupied workshops first on Constitution Hill and then in Mary Anne Street, before moving in 1828 to the 'Royal Papier Mâché Works', a handsome building behind a small garden on Great Hampton Street, not far from Jennens & Bettridge (plate 163). In addition, he had showrooms in London, first at Brownlow Street, then at 506 New Oxford Street, and then at 3 Hart Street, Bloomsbury.[1]

Today, as in his own time, Lane is best known for papier mâché articles inset with designs and pictures painted and highlighted with thin flakes of pearl on the underside of glass, which he called 'patent pearl glass' (plate 164). Though this style of decoration is generally known as 'Lane's Patent' – and indeed, some products are marked as such – the patent was actually taken out in 1844 in the name

163. Trade-card of Thomas Lane, showing his Birmingham manufactory, c.1830–1840.
THE BODLEIAN LIBRARY, UNIVERSITY OF OXFORD (Shelf mark JJ Trade Cards 21 [5])

of Joseph Gibson, a japanner, two years prior to his being employed by Thomas Lane (p. 80).

On the evidence of goods shown by Thomas Lane at the Exposition of British Industrial Art held in Manchester in 1846, these pictures must have been introduced at his Great Hampton Street Works soon after Gibson commenced work there. Among the exhibits, for example, was a patent pearl-glass picture of 'the Palace of Francis I from a drawing by Müller'[2] set in a table similar to one which Lane had presented to Prince Albert, and copies of a pair of pole-screens, also containing pearl-glass pictures, which he had presented to the Queen. Presumably it was through the acceptance of these gifts that the firm was allowed to advertise as the 'Royal Papier Mâché & Patent Pearl Glass Works, by special appointment to her Majesty & his royal highness Prince Albert'.[3]

Cornish's *Visitor's Handbook through Birmingham* urged its readers to visit Lane's show rooms so they could:

> examine the brilliancy of his inlaid Pearl Glass, and other tasteful works which he exhibits for household decoration, and as panels for furniture for which the application seems well fitted, and it is but justice to say that much time, money, and no little care has been expended in bringing the invention to its present state of perfection.[4]

An article published in the Art Union in 1846, although describing Lane's factory as one 'which ranks high in popular estimation, and one of considerable merit in the application of Art to the material',[5] was not wholly uncritical. The anonymous author believed him – and Jennens & Bettridge – guilty of perpetrating 'a great number of errors in the selection of mal-shapes', which was held 'scarcely pardonable'[6] in a material such as papier mâché. Why this was less acceptable in papier mâché than in other materials was not explained. Whatever the reason, it was observed that, with Lane's son[lxii] being 'one of the most assiduous pupils of the [Birmingham] School of Design ... a better and worthier system is making rapid way into his establishment.'[7] To demonstrate, several objects decorated with patent pearl-glass were singled out for praise: these included some fire-screens – 'exquisite specimens'[8] of their type – and a chess-board which the Art Union considered the most effective of all their products.

The emphasis in contemporary reports on the success and popularity of Lane's patent pearl glass was at the expense of his other manu-

164. Papier mâché writing box inset with a painted, patent pearl glass panel; impressed mark 'LANE/BIRM$^{M'}$ beneath a crown, c.1845. W: 34cm

factures, and collectors today are generally unaware of their extent (plate 166). In the 1850s for instance, he advertised on a trade card as a 'Manufacturer of Paper, Iron & Tin Japan Goods. Tables, cabinets, desks, inks, pole & hand screens'.[9] Moreover, because (like so many japanners) he was inconsistent about marking his wares, Lane's goods are now mostly impossible to identify.

However, engravings and lithographs of goods made during the 1840s and 1850s and the breadth of his display at the Birmingham Exposition of Arts & Manufactures in 1849 (plate 165), show Lane to have been a prominent maker of general

165. A range of papier mâché articles, made by Thomas Lane, from a *Portfolio of Lithographic Drawings of Principal Manufactures at Birmingham Exposition* 1849 (pl. 19).

lxii. This may have been Joseph Lane (b. about 1832) who became a clerk in his father's factory.

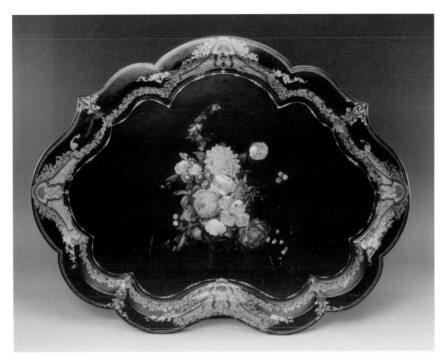

166. Papier mâché breakfast tray – a shape popularly known as a parlour maid's tray, impressed 'LANE/BIRMᴹ' beneath a crown, c.1845. W: 82cm
COURTESY OF TRING MARKET AUCTIONS

japanned goods. For instance, despite the furniture he had exhibited in Manchester three years earlier, Lane's focus in Birmingham was on smaller yet more showy goods like the small and 'beautiful cabinet which occupie[d] the centre of his stand', and the 'Louis Quatorze' inkstands.[10] By far the largest group of objects, however, consisted of, 'portfolios for drawing room tables',[11] inset with patent pearl-glass and variously decorated with views of historic buildings such as Warwick Castle, Stratford-on-Avon Church, Windsor Castle, Eaton Hall, and Bath Abbey, or famous London landmarks like the Houses of Parliament. Other exhibits included finger-plates, several pearl-glass panels of different sizes including one decorated in the style of the French eighteenth-century artist, Jean-Antoine Watteau, and a pair of cabinet doors, inset with panels of 'birds, flowers, etc.'[12] against white grounds. Alongside these were trays, candlesticks, pole screens, decorative paper panels for ships' cabins, and boxes of every description – in short, a display of goods typical of most leading japanners at the time.

Lane also showed his wares at the Great Exhibition in London in 1851, where he received a prize-medal for his pearl glass. It was the most ambitious of all his exhibition displays, and included, once again, some large pieces of furniture. A selection of the articles he exhibited is sufficient to show that his output was in every way similar to that of say, Jennens & Bettridge: a 'table with inlaid border of mother-of-pearl and landscape and figure centre',[13] a cheval screen decorated with flowers on a white ground, pole screens, a reading table, cabinets on stands, and a chess table, as well as 'panels for ship cabins, rooms and other decorations'.[14] Also listed in the catalogue of Lane's exhibits were 'specimens of patent gem painting on glass invented by

Miss E. Tonge, Boston, Lincs.'[15, lxiii] – items which were almost certainly included as a means of evading Theodore Hyla Jennens' patent of 1847, for so-called 'inlaid gems' (p. 82). Today, blotter-covers inset with views of Paxton's glass building in which the exhibition was housed, are among the most frequently found examples of patent pearl-glass. They were probably made by Thomas Lane and sold at the exhibition as souvenirs, although the possibility that some were made by Jennens & Bettridge cannot be ruled out (plate 75).

Along with Jennens & Bettridge and other prominent English papier mâché manufacturers, Thomas Lane also showed at the Paris Exhibition in 1855.

Lane was, and rightly remains, best-known as the leading maker of japanned goods inset with pearl-glass panels, but similar panels were also produced by other makers. Soon after their introduction, Woodward & Midgely (*qv*), for example, had found a means of imitating them without infringing Lane's patent. And many years later, at the Paris Exhibition in 1867, the firm of L.J. Nooyen of Rotterdam, showed a large folding screen inset with twelve large glass panels which Thomas Archer, in his Artisans Report on the exhibition, maintained was the work of one of Lane's former employees (p. 304).

The Royal Papier Mâché Works should not be judged by its glass pictures alone. Thomas Lane was an all-round japanner whose name should be included in the reckoning when any good, but unmarked, example of japanned tin or papier mâché is under discussion (plate 166).

RICHARD TURLEY
c.1828–1874
381 Summer Lane, Birmingham

Richard Turley was first listed as a japanner in partnership with one, [J.?] Harrison, in 1825, but when he took part in the 1849 Birmingham Exhibition he did so in his own name (plate 167). His display included hand-screens painted respectively with the singers [John] Sim Reeves (1818–1900) and Jenny Lind (1820–1887), ink-stands, writing desks and dressing cases, all decorated in the style of the period. In addition, he showed three vases painted with landscapes and flowers, and a miniature table painted with 'The Queen'. Unusually, however, almost half Turley's exhibits were relatively large pieces: a pole-screen, octagonal and rectangular needlework tables, a chess table, a table with a view of Tintern Abbey in 'raised gold', and two further tables painted with 'Wellington's Shield' and 'Byron's Dream'.

lxiii. A Miss Eliza Tonge, of Red Lion Street, Boston was listed as a 'music professional' in the History, Gazeteer and Directory of Lincolnshire, in 1856.

Similarly, he took several items of furniture to the Great Exhibition where he showed a large folding screen ornamented with landscapes, fruit and flowers, a large loo-table, a selection of smaller tables including one painted with 'The Round Tower of Oberwesel' – possibly with an eye to Prince Albert's German relatives who were expected to visit the exhibition – and a range of large and small cabinets. Interestingly, even in 1851 when the manufacture of papier mâché was well-established, Turley thought it appropriate to demonstrate 'the beauty and durability of … papier mâché',[1] by exhibiting a tray over thirty years old.

When George Wallis criticised a small, pearl-decorated folding screen which Turley displayed at the 1862 exhibition in London, he did so, he said, because he was compelled by 'the very excellence of the work as a whole'.[2] Indeed, he was so generally complimentary about Turley's other exhibits – trays, tables, and a chess-table (the last two of which both received an Honorable Mention by the jurors) – that it may be safely assumed many good examples which are now attributed to hitherto better known factories, were made in his workshops.

WOODWARD & MIDGLEY
c.1829–c.1857
George Street, Birmingham

Josiah Woodward (b.1804) and Charles Midgley (born sometime between 1794 and 1801) commenced business in about 1829 at the 'Old Shell Warehouse',[1] a former pearl-shell depot in 'smoky' George Street, only two streets away from Jennens & Bettridge. They erected a sign in large gilt letters over the door announcing its change of use to a 'Japan Manufactory'.[2] From this near-ruin of a building with bulging walls, came an array of typically exuberant papier mâché articles. Both men were competent artists, but neither was an innovator. Their success rested almost entirely upon their ability to pick up on the ideas of other manufacturers and to cleverly adapt them in ways which would avoid charges of plagiarism.

An idea of the scale of Woodward & Midgley's enterprise is found in Charles Midgley's entry in the 1851 Census which reads 'japanner and papier machi [*sic*] manufacturer employs 7 men, 6 women and 11 boys in partnership with J Woodward.'

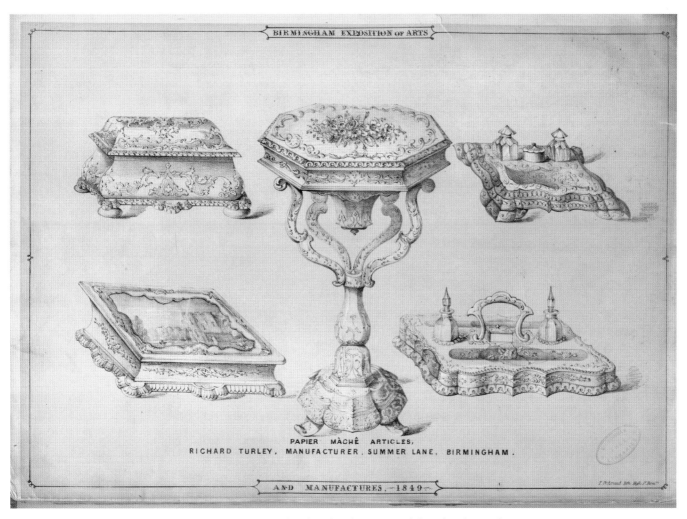

167. Papier mâché goods by Richard Turley, from a *Portfolio of Lithographic Drawings of Principal Manufactures at Birmingham Exposition* 1849 (pl. 6).

However most of our knowledge about this factory comes from the writings of Woodward's son, Charles Joshua Woodward (b.1839)[3] who had himself been apprenticed there. Unsurprisingly therefore, rather more is known about Woodward than Midgley.

Josiah Woodward would have been among Jennens & Bettridge's earliest apprentices having joined them in about 1812, when only 8 or 9 years old. From there he went to work for Ryton & Walton at the Old Hall in Wolverhampton where he developed skills as an expert copyist. One of his first successes was a copy of a tray painted with a scene of rush-gatherers by the well-known japan artist Joseph Booth. Ryton & Walton resented the high prices that Booth charged as a decorator and set Woodward to work on a copy; the result so pleased them that they displayed it at the Old Hall as a *chef d'oeuvre*. His other notable achievements at the Old Hall were the effective copying of marble surfaces and the development of a technique for imitating the sparkle of lapiz lazuli on a japanned surface (see p. 46).

There were two japanners by the name of Charles Midgley – they were father and son (b.1831), and both were very able decorators. The only known reference to the work of the older man is found in the catalogue of an exhibition devoted to the history of the papier mâché trade held in Birmingham in 1926.[4] Among the exhibits was a card-table painted 'with a fine group of flowers' by Charles Midgley. The exhibition also included several papier mâché articles painted by his son, a journeyman painter, who, besides working for Alsager & Neville (*qv*), decorated for Jennens & Bettridge and others, though not, apparently, for his father's firm.

Thus, both partners possessed decorative skills of a high order, but it was Woodward who had the business flair to ensure they kept abreast of developments in the trade. Nevertheless this did not prevent them from making mistakes. For example, their attempt to evade Jennens & Bettridge's patent of 1825 for pearl decoration was too cumbersome to pose any threat to the originators (p. 51), and similarly, their imitation of Farmer's patent for electro-gilding japanned ware was no more successful than the patented method itself (see below).

The firm's real turning point came after the mid-1840s when Woodward & Midgley found ways of rivalling two highly successful patents. The first was to substitute tinfoil to achieve effects similar to Thomas Lane's popular Patent Pearl Glass (*cf.* plate 76). Many examples of such work are found today but as the style was quickly taken up by others, it should not be supposed that they were all made by Woodward & Midgely. Their second success was the imitation of Jennens & Bettridge's patent for 'inlaid gems' for which tin-foil gems were placed beneath glass in substitution of more expensive paste. This led Woodward & Midgley to experiment also with ivory, amber and egg-shell inlays though the lack of any examples today, suggests that they met with little success.

Woodward & Midgley made a wide range of papier mâché articles which included chairs with hollow paper legs filled with pulp (p. 32). But like other japanners, their output was not confined to that material alone and they are also known to have decorated cast-iron chimney pieces with pearl and simulated marble grounds.

The factory closed on the death of Josiah Woodward in 1857.

ISHERWOOD SUTCLIFFE
fl. c.1833–c.1881
27 Great Hampton Street, Birmingham

The contemporary significance of this firm may be judged by the fact that it was among a select few japanning factories included in the Birmingham section of the Art Union's Illustrated Tour of the Manufacturing Districts in 1846. Isherwood Sutcliffe (b.1811) concentrated chiefly on the manufacture of tea-trays, which, according to the Art Union, he 'brought to a very great perfection ... in the quality of the material as well as the design.'[1] It was for these qualities that a tray, almost identical to the one shown here (plate 168), was chosen to illustrate the article, though it was conceded that the border decoration 'would be better for judicious weeding'.[2]

Sutcliffe showed a more varied range of papier mâché at the Great Exhibition. In addition to trays, there were, for example, a loo table painted with the 'Ruins of Carthage', and smaller objects like folios, boxes and inkstands. Most interesting of all, perhaps, were some 'Chinese papier mâché vases with figures and gold ornament';[3] being listed among his other exhibits, these were surely made by Sutcliffe in oriental style and were not Eastern specimens as their ambiguous description might imply. A similar array of goods was taken to the New York Exhibition in 1853.

Writing in 1900, W.H. Jones[4] observed that after the 1851 Exhibition, Sutcliffe along with other japanners, found it necessary to focus on less expensive articles. Indeed, by the 1850s, Sutcliffe was describing himself as a varnish manufacturer, as well as a japanner, a papier mâché maker and a manufacturer of blank trays and waiters. The varnishing branch of this business gradually eclipsed its other commercial interests until, by 1883, it had completely taken over as, indeed, had his son, also named Isherwood (b.1845).

THOMAS FARMER
fl. c.1835–c.1850
11 Summer Lane, Birmingham

In 1841, in Pigot's directory of Birmingham, Thomas Farmer (b.1801) was described as a manufacturer of papier mâché, iron and tin japanned goods, and of patent papier mâché and other trays. As there is no record of a patent in Farmer's name prior to that date, the trays in question were likely to have been made under license from the patentee. Farmer's factory was of sufficient standing to have been among those visited in Birmingham, in preparation for the *Illustrated tour in the Manufacturing Districts*, published by the Art Union in 1846. 'The only matter that here requires report',[1] the visitor wrote, was Farmer's use of electro-deposited metal for decorative purposes, and some portfolios and card-baskets incorporating electro-coated medallions and even these, they thought were not wholly successful (Pat. # 10,224, p. 73).

The fourteen papier mâché articles which Farmer showed at the Birmingham Exposition of Arts in 1849, fell into the usual categories for such goods: pier glasses and toilet mirrors, ladies cabinet and work tables, a music stool, an 'Elizabethan' chair, and a clock. In addition, there was an inkstand and a portfolio, and an oval patent papier tray of 'improved composition, produced at one pressure from the pulp.'[2] Variously decorated in pearl and gold, and sometimes painted with flowers or landscapes, the *Journal of Design & Manufactures* considered Farmer's goods to be 'a little over-ornamented'.[3]

McCALLUM & HODSON
fl. **1835–1920**
147 Brearley Street (and **Summer Row** from 1855)

'*Manufacturers of papier machee [sic], consisting of all the elegancies in ladies' work tables, work boxes, cabinets – patent multifarious portfolios, pale and handsome writing desks, wine trays, chairs inlaid with pearl, trays, card racks, envelope boxes, and cabinet work tables, and other articles of use and elegance, in great variety.*'
  Cornish, *Stranger's Guide through Birmingham*, 1849, p. 79

Although in its day, McCallum & Hodson was considered one of the leading papier mâché factories in Birmingham (employing 128 people according to the 1851 Census), its significance has since been greatly underestimated. The partnership was first listed in Birmingham directories in 1835 at premises in Brearley Street. They described themselves initially as japanners, but by 1841[1] they advertised as makers of papier mâché trays and made such a name for themselves in

168. Papier mâché tray; impressed 'Nº806/REGISTERED BY/ISHERWOOD
SUTCLIFFE/BIRM'; c.1846 (*cf*, a tray, by M[?] Sutcliffe, *Art Journal*,1846 (p. 62).
W: 70cm
COURTESY OF P.F. WINDIBANK, DORKING

this branch of manufacture that it was predicted, in 1846, they would 'ere long ... lag behind no competitor in a pursuit for which Art may do so much.'[2] Between 1852 and 1855, McCallum & Hodson marked their success by moving to larger and more prestigious premises in Summer Row (plate 87).

James McCallum (born about 1810), the senior partner, was the less artistic but commercially more astute of two brothers who had been apprenticed to Jennens & Bettridge.[lxiv] Edward Hodson (born about 1809/10), was a businessman with the benefit of 'outside experience'.[3] Together, they built up a factory which became renowned for both its extensive foreign and home markets and its supply of 'blanks' or undecorated articles, to the trade.

McCallum & Hodson were not innovators, but according to an article in the *Art Union* in 1846, they possessed an 'obvious determination to keep pace with the best of their competitors in the race for public favour' (plate 169).[4] On the evidence of a challenge by Jennens & Bettridge concerning the design of a wine tray, one of the ways in which they kept abreast was by imitating the successful products of their rivals (p. 154). In addition, they employed skilled workmen and were said to have consulted 'the safest authorities for artistic guidance'[5] although to judge from the following observation, this simply meant copying the work of established artists and designers:

> *As usual, in the showrooms connected with manufactories of this description of goods, we found a few meritorious copies of celebrated pictures, or rather engravings, well and carefully executed – the most successful of them from a French print of Paul and Virginia, appeared to show that the artist had taste, and 'a good eye' for colour.*[6]

It has already been shown that pictures, as distinct from borders and other painted patterns and motifs, were not executed in McCallum & Hodson's factory, but by artists who worked at home, and for handsome returns. These were probably the master-paintings from which copies were made by lesser artists employed in the factory, for as George Wallis observed, it is unlikely that outworkers ever painted directly on japanned articles. He did not say why it was unlikely, but the want of suitable conditions for the application of varnish colours was almost certainly a major factor.

A visitor to their workshops in 1850, saw a table which 'looked more fit for a Queen than for any less distinguished person',[7] and a range of drawing room furniture which surpassed anything they ever imagined. In fact, by then, McCallum & Hodson had established a reputation for making large, showy pieces of household furniture and, increasingly, this was reflected in the goods they showed at major exhibitions. Here, for example, are some of the items which were among an extensive range of 'best' papier mâché which they took to the Birmingham Exposition in 1849:

> *Boudoir looking glasses, work-tables, loo-tables, work-boxes, cabinets, writing-desks, &c; together with the usual productions of minor size and importance, such as card-cases, card-trays, albums, blotting-books, ladies companions, &c.*[8] *(plate 170)*

It was one of these tables that a critic took to task for plagiarising a painting by Landseer. However, the *Art Journal* was less guarded, and considered their exhibits 'highly to their credit'[9] and praised especially, their pearl-work and painting of flowers, landscapes and figure subjects.

McCallum & Hodson showed a similar mix of large and small articles at the Great Exhibition in 1851. It included a gothic work-table painted with a view of Kenilworth Abbey, and a round loo table which was four feet across and decorated with pearl and flowers. Also shown was a flower stand which converted to a table, various workboxes and jewel cases, a pier glass, a girandole, inkstands, portfolios, and 'a beautiful little tea chest in the Alhambra style'.[10] But the centrepiece of their display must surely have been the 'royal cabinet' which, although unmarked, can be identified from an engraving in the 1851 exhibition catalogue. This cabinet, 'partly Elizabethan and partly Italian'[11] in style, with its paintings, extravagant pearl and gilt borders, and gem-encrusted finials, shows virtually every surface decoration then fashionable, and represents a virtuoso performance of McCallum & Hodson's decorative abilities and their expertise as makers of complex papier mâché objects (plate 171).

Likewise, the moulded acanthus leaves which embellish its cabriole legs show a familarity with new technical developments such as the recently perfected process of steam-moulding. As one of the few articles which can be reliably attributed to this firm, it leaves no doubt that McCallum & Hodson should be considered, along with others, as possible manufacturers of high quality, but unmarked, Victorian japanned goods. For this reason alone, it is useful to examine the cabinet in greater detail.

Despite its obvious royal interest, the cabinet was no more likely to have been commissioned by royalty than the gothic table painted with portraits of 'the princesses of England',[12] or the dressing-case painted with a view of Windsor Castle which McCallum & Hodson also exhibited in 1851. It was anticipated that Queen Victoria, Prince Albert, and their European relatives, would be frequent visitors to the exhibition and many firms sought to attract their patronage by decorating goods with royal subjects.[lxv] For their part, McCallum & Hodson showed two new styles of tray which they named 'Queen's shape' and 'Albert shape', although in the absence of further detail, they cannot now be identified. Tsar Alexander II, who presented the 'royal' cabinet to his wife's relatives in Hesse, in 1873, is known to have visited the Great Exhibition and it is plausible that he may have purchased it on that occasion.

169. Papier mâché vase by McCallum & Hodson, from the *Art Union*, 1846 (p. 61).

170. Articles, exhibited by McCallum & Hodson, at the Birmingham Exposition of Art Manufactures, in 1849, from the *Art Journal* of the same year (p. 309).

The contributions of Messrs. M'CALLUM & HODSON (147, Brearley Street), who hold a very prominent position as manufacturers of the best order of Papier Mâché, are numerous and excellent. they consist of boudoir looking-glasses, work-tables, loo-tables, work-boxes, cabinets, writing-desks, &c.;

together with the usual productions of minor size and importance, such as card-cases, card-trays, albums, blotting-books, ladies' companions, &c. We found much to praise in the works of these gentlemen; they have made liberal, but not injudicious, use of the mother-of-pearl shell, and their imitations of

flowers are very successful; the landscapes and figure subjects, too, which adorn many of the articles, are painted with very considerable ability. Their "show," indeed, is altogether highly to

their credit; they effectually help to sustain the repute which Birmingham has hitherto obtained and kept almost exclusively, for a class of productions which finds admirers everywhere.

Described as 'a multum in parvo', the cabinet contains a writing desk, a needlework box, and drawers for jewellery, coins, writing materials, envelopes, deeds etc., and is mounted throughout with silver-plated hinges, locks and escutcheons. The stand, which is largely of japanned wood and richly decorated with flowers, doubles as a work-table and incorporates chess and backgammon boards. On the front of the cabinet is a portrait of Queen Victoria after the American artist Thomas Sully, and one of Prince Albert.[lxvi] On the sides are likenesses of Queen Victoria's eldest daughters, copied from *The Four Princesses* painted by Winterhalter in 1849, which is in the Royal Collection. In the double-cushioned top are two boxes. The lid of the uppermost box is painted with a view of Osborne House, the Isle of Wight home of Victoria and Albert, after a water colour by Thomas Allom. None

lxiv. James McCallum's elder brother, Philip, was an accomplished japan painter (see p. 321); he entered into partnership with Philip Nock (see Nock & McCallum).
lxv. Exhibitors were so keen to sell to royalty and to attach large 'sold' labels to this

effect, that exhibition officials had to ask them to refrain.
lxvi. The original from which this deceptively familiar likeness was taken, remains unidentified.

of the painted copies are signed and cannot be reliably attributed, but among artists known to have been employed by McCallum & Hodson were James Hinks who specialised in landscapes and copies of well-known pictures, and a man called Berks, a figure and portrait painter, who painted many royal portraits on papier mâché, 'principally for loyal subjects abroad'.[13]

There is no record of the original cost of this cabinet and stand, but since it was a specimen upon which neither time nor expense was spared, it may be imagined that it exceeded the 50guineas (£52.50) charged by Jennens & Bettridge for a cabinet which, although of similar form and size, had only one painted view.

Not surprisingly, contemporary opinion was divided over McCallum & Hodson's opulent displays. On the one hand they were accused of having 'materially injured the trade, by fostering a taste for exuberant decoration opposed to all true principles of design'[14] while the official exhibition catalogue applauded them for their 'excellent design and great richness in the variety of colours introduced'.[15]

An article in the *Morning Chronicle*, about the papier mâché shown at the 1851 Exhibition, drew attention to McCallum & Hodson's extensive export trade,[16] so it is somewhat surprising that they did not exhibit at the International Exhibition held in Paris four years later. They showed a representative range of japanned and papier mâché goods' at the London Exhibition in 1862, but no descriptive details appear to have survived. Nevertheless, it is safe to assume that furniture would have been among their exhibits. Their advertisements, more than those of any other general japanner, focused upon this branch of the trade and indicate that they were responsible for much, if not the majority, of papier mâché furniture found today. In 1860, for example, they advertised as:

Manufacturers of Ladies' Wardrobes, Papier Mâché Bedsteads, Chairs, Tables, Couches, Etageres, Davenports, and ladies writing desks; Work boxes, work tables, dressing cases; and all kinds of Fancy Cabinet Goods. Drawing Room Furniture, &c.[17]

172. Secretaire, papier mâché and wood, with mother-of-pearl borders, painted with views of Windsor and Kenilworth Castles; McCallum & Hodson, an identical cabinet made for presentation, is dated '1879', c.1865. H: 60.5cm, W: 72.5cm
COURTESY OF THE CANTERBURY AUCTION GALLERIES

A little later, McCallum & Hodson styled themselves 'papier mâché and black ornament manufacturers',[18, lxvii] and by 1870, their range had extended to include iron bedsteads, and 'fancy cabinet goods' in pearl and tortoiseshell.[19]

Opposite: 171. Papier mâché cabinet on stand, made by McCallum & Hodson, and exhibited at the Great Exhibition, in 1851 (see p. 170*ff*). 134 x 667 x 60cm
COURTESY OF OTTO VON MITZLAFF

---

lxvii. Others listed as 'black ornament manufacturers' made glove fasteners, spring sleeve links etc., which suggests that this term covered a range of wholly utilitarian japanned metal articles.

173. Papier mâché articles made by McCallum & Hodson, an engraving from *The Ladies Library*, 1850.

174. A papier mâché breakfast tray made by McCallum & Hodson, an engraving from *The Ladies Library*, 1850.

Like so many japanners, McCallum & Hodson rarely marked their goods. With the exception of the cabinet shown in plate 172, we have to rely on contemporary engravings to help identify their products (plates 173-4), and partly upon a surviving group of objects painted by one of their decorators, Reuben Neale (*qv*). Nevertheless, on this evidence alone, it is clear that this partnership was responsible for many more of the unmarked articles than has hitherto been allowed.

By the 1860s, Edward Hodson's three sons – Edward (b.1840), Charles (b.1842), and Frederick (b.1844) – had all joined the firm as clerks, and in 1866, McCallum & Hodson took over the business of John Bettridge (*qv*), and appointed him their London agent. In 1887, they absorbed the business of Alsager & Neville (*qv*) whose old sign, over-painted with the names McCallum & Hodson, was shown in an exhibition of papier mâché held in Birmingham in 1921. When it closed in 1920,[lxviii] McCallum & Hodson was one of the last japanned papier mâché factories in Birmingham; very little business had been done for years but no-one, it seems, was discharged on account of age or quality of work, thereby ensuring a dignified exit for everyone.

FOOTHORAPE, SHOWELL & SHENTON
c.1845–c.1885
25–26 Church Street, Birmingham

Foothorape, Showell & Shenton,[lxix] manufacturers of japanned papier mâché and iron goods, is another of those factories which, though their showroom housed 'a vast display of tables, chairs, screens, envelope boxes, blotting cases, cabinets, tea caddies, trays, &c.',[1] has since been overlooked (plate 175). It is unlikely that their products can now be distinguished from those by other makers, but from the scant information which survives, it is evident that they were manufacturers of some significance.

They exhibited in Manchester in 1846, and in Birmingham in 1849. The *Art Journal* noted 'some remarkably elegant

tables'[2] made by Foothorope, Showell & Shenton for the Birmingham exhibition but, these apart, and with the exception of a snuff box painted with a dog – an article seldom included in japanners lists at this time – they displayed an otherwise typical range of papier mâché goods (plate 176). Variously painted with flowers, birds, figures and landscapes, and embellished with burnished gold and mother-of-pearl, the *Journal of Design & Manufactures* considered their papier mâché 'elaborate' and its decoration 'hap-hazard' finding praise only for 'a very pretty'[3] writing box.

They showed similar articles at the Great Exhibition in 1851 where, like other manufacturers, they pandered to the interests of visiting royals. A ladies work-table for example, was decorated with a picture of Buckingham Palace, and a jewellery box with a view of Windsor Castle. An advertisement of 1849 included quadrille pools[lxx] and card cases among their products, and at the Paris Exhibition in 1855, they showed furniture and small, decorative articles of papier mâché.

Showell ceased to be a partner in 1858. Foothorape and Shenton continued until 1875, when Shenton also ceased trading. The business continued as Charles Foothorape & Son until its closure in about 1885.

J.H. HOPKINS & Sons
c.1840–1899
Granville Street Works, Broad Street, Birmingham

John Hopkins (b. about 1795) began by making 'Patent Teapots', which he quickly followed with candlesticks and other articles. Described in 1855 as 'Japanners in General',[1] Hopkins' workshop specialised in the cheaper type of metal goods, making also 'Copper, Zinc, and Iron Goods, all kinds of Tinmen's Furniture, and Tinmen's and Braziers Tools.'[2] Some, if not all, their japanned articles were named 'Sphinx Ware', and were stamped with a sphinx, as seen in plates 100 & 177, or sometimes the logo was encircled by the letters 'J H Hopkins & Son, Birmingham'.

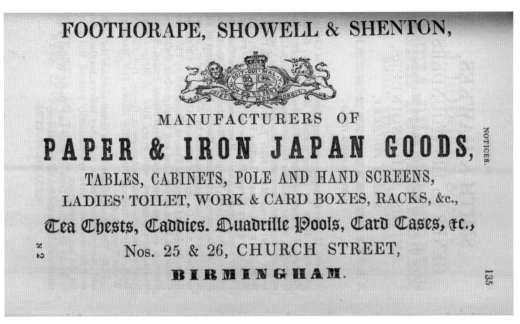

175. Advertisement from Cornish's *Stranger's Guide through Birmingham* (1849).

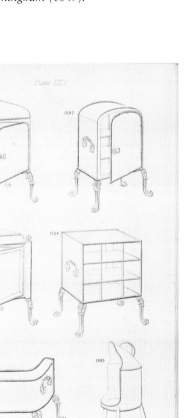

176. Papier mâché work-table and box, by Foothorape, Showell & Shenton, from the *Art Journal*, 1849 (p. 314).

177. Pages from the trade catalogue of J.H. Hopkins & Sons, showing plate and vegetable warmers, and their prices, 1874.

The firm showed japanned goods at both the 1855 Paris Exhibition and the 1862 Exhibition in London. From 1872, they replaced stencilled decoration with transfer-printing and the use of highly polished black grounds was said to have been superseded by Alfred Hopkins'[lxxi] invention of 'a dead, morocco-like surface, in low tones of pleasing appearance'.[3]

The business and the sphinx trade-mark were sold to J. Sankey of Bilston in 1899 (*qv*).

---

lxviii. It is likely that the firm was continued by the sons of both McCallum and Hodson.

lxix. Frederick Foothorape (b.1823) was listed as an apprentice japanner in the 1841 Census, and Charles Showell (b.1812) as a japanner. There is no indication of any partnership at that date.

lxx. An early name for counters trays; quadrille was a card game.

lxxi. Alfred W. Hopkins, b.1837, the second son of J.H. Hopkins. His brother, John L. Hopkins, b. about 1828, was also involved in the firm as a tin-plate worker and japanner.

HALBEARD & WELLINGS
c.1846–1908
116 Constitution Hill, Birmingham
(and from c.1852, 45 St Paul's Street)

George Halbeard (b.1817) was first listed as a japanner in his own right in 1845, and was joined by Wellings the following year; in five years, they had a workforce of thirty-five people. On the evidence of their display at the 1851 Exhibition, Halbeard & Wellings specialised in making large items of papier mâché (plate 178). Among their exhibits were tables painted with flowers and decorated with mother-of-pearl, large cabinets with painted vignettes, and 'a handsome toilet table in the Elizabethan style inlaid with mother-of-pearl'[1] with corresponding mirror, for which they received an Honorary Mention from the jury. To judge from the official catalogue, they were the only exhibitors to illustrate the manufacture of papier mâché from the raw material to the finished product.

178. Engraving of a papier mâché work-table, made by Halbeard & Wellings, from the *Art Journal Illustrated Catalogue of the Industries of all Nations*, 1851 (p. 251).
Reproduced with the permission of Birmingham Libraries & Archives

Among their apprentices in the 1840s was John Breakspear who became a distinguished painter of flowers and birds on japanned ware (p. 319). After two further changes in partnership – to Morris, Halbeard & Stamp (1854), and then to Perman & Stamp (1867) – the firm which began as Halbeard & Wellings was finally subsumed by McCallum & Hodson in 1908.

ALSAGER & NEVILLE
c.1843–1892
111 Upper Tower Street, Birmingham

Some time in the early 1840s, John Alsager (1805/6–1870) and George Neville (d.1887) left Jennens & Bettridge, where they had been apprenticed many years earlier, to set up in business on their own account. It is difficult to give a precise start-date for their partnership, but it was as Alsager & Neville that they ordered varnish from Charles Mander of Wolverhampton, in 1843.

By tradition, and upon documentary evidence, their names are almost wholly associated with papier mâché goods decorated with either oriental scenes in mother-of-pearl, or painted in imitation of malachite, yet these were only two styles among many that they produced. Their output was typical of papier mâché goods of the period but since they seem rarely to have used a factory mark, their firm, like several of its rivals, has been overlooked in favour of the better-known firm of Jennens & Bettridge.

Much that is known about Alsager & Neville is based upon an interview between Charles Neville, then aged ninety, and George Dickinson, author of the book *English Papier Mâché* (1925). As a former japanner with the firm, Charles' information is largely reliable, but as George's brother, his memories were inevitably biased in favour of the latter. Consequently, there is less information about Alsager, although it is known he came from Manchester.

However, a pair of papier mâché hand-screens, attributed to Alsager while working for Jennens & Bettridge, and illustrated by Dickinson,[1] show him to have been an artist of considerable talent. Though they were painted with classical landscapes, it is for his 'Indian' and 'Chinese' designs in mother-of-pearl that he is remembered today (plate 179). Alsager was not a slavish copier from Oriental originals; his intention was that his characteristic clustering of temples and pillars should convey only an impression of the East. Whether the pearl was allowed to stand alone or, as was mostly the case, it was complemented with gold leaf, the overall effect was always restrained. Alsager had begun working in this style while still at Jennens & Bettridge but executed most of this decoration in his own workshops.

George Neville was also a highly skilled artist. Jennens & Bettridge had transferred him to their London workshops, but finding it impossible to make ends meet in the capital, Neville abandoned his apprenticeship and fled to Paris. No more was heard of him until three years later when he returned to Birmingham in search of work. Jennens & Bettridge re-engaged him on condition that he made good the outstanding two years of his apprenticeship, and he quickly proved himself one of their most distinguished flower painters. Charles Neville credited him with having introduced a new style of decoration in which naturalistically painted flowers were set against black rather than pale or bronze grounds as hitherto, but as a similar claim was made for Haselar (*qv*) – his close rival at Jennens & Bettridge – this cannot now be confirmed. Neville described it as 'painting down to the black'[2] and it involved softening colours at their edges in order to avoid harsh and unnatural contrasts. Transparent rose leaves were said to have been particularly characteristic of his work, as were painted convolvulus 'always with a folded or turned-up edge showing a morsel of the reverse in another colour'.[3] Parrots and birds of paradise also featured prominently in his designs. Towards the end of his employment at Jennens & Bettridge, Neville was mostly engaged in designing, and painted few, if any, articles for sale.

Thus, both men brought very high standards of pearl and painted decoration to the partnership. Neville, in addition, had several years experience as a foreman at Jennens & Bettridge where he had overseen many pupils who, themselves, later became accomplished japanners.

Alsager & Neville built up a large business and took on many apprentices. They employed several artists who had trained at Jennens & Bettridge, among them George Goodman, Charles Neville, Robert McCallum, Peter Jones, and John Thomas. Goodman, whom they employed as a painter prior to 1852, is known to have painted landscape vignettes on the doors of a small cabinet otherwise decorated by Charles Neville,[4] while Robert McCallum, though described as 'a fair workman',[5] was better known for his military skills than his artistic ones. Peter Jones, having worked in a slate-marbling firm before joining Alsager & Neville, introduced marbling as a new surface decoration for their papier mâché, but his secrecy about his technique and his insistence upon locking his workshop in his absence, so angered his employers that they soon dismissed him. After careful examination of Jones' workshop, their foreman finally discovered his methods, and marbling became one of their standard lines.

John Thomas had two brief spells of employment at Alsager & Neville, the second of which was highly successful. The first, which followed his apprenticeship at Jennens & Bettridge and his attendance at classes in figure drawing and landscape painting at the Birmingham School of Practical Art ended when he left to seek better pay as a journeyman painter. It is likely that it was in this capacity that he returned to Alsager & Neville to execute a large and urgent order they had received from a London publisher. The order was for

papier mâché book covers for luxury editions of works by Burns, Byron and Walter Scott, and they were to be painted with Burns' Cottage, Newstead Abbey and Abbotsford respectively. Thomas completed the painting on time and was paid '60s. the gross – about 5d. each'.[6] The covers were so fine that Jennens & Bettridge were said to have offered him 'an advance of 50 per cent on the prices he was then getting',[7] to return to their employ to paint ship panels. It appears, however, that Thomas declined and went to Glasgow instead to undertake 'ship decoration'.[8]

Another of their decorators was Charles Midgley (later of Woodward & Midgley (*qv*) who, whilst in their employ, circuited Jennens & Bettridge's patent for inlaid gems by using gold and silver foil in place of pearl. Then there was George Harper who was said to have introduced the imitation malachite grounds which became almost synonymous with Alsager & Neville, after seeing the Russian gates inlaid with

179. Piano stool of wood and papier mâché; impressed 'ALSAGER & NEVILLE', c.1845. Dia: 38cm
© Christie's Images Limited

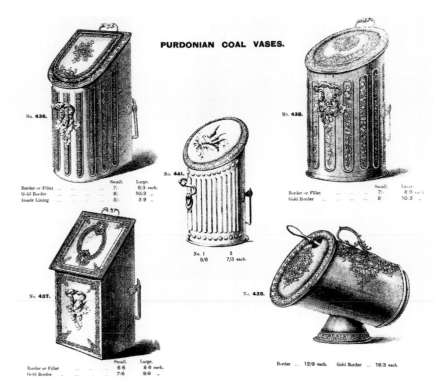

181. Tin waiters with crystallised decoration (see p. 48), from a catalogue of Griffiths & Browett, c.1885.

COURTESY OF JOHN MARKS

180. Iron purdonian coal vases from a catalogue of Griffiths & Browett, their type was common to many contemporary japanners, c.1885

COURTESY OF JOHN MARKS

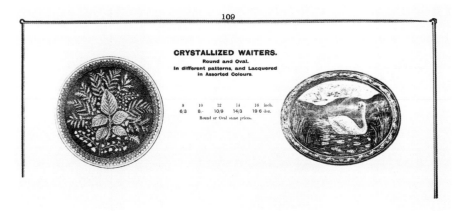

decorating their goods, and with no apparent marking policy in existence, it is almost certain that many papier mâché articles which are today attributed to the better-known firm were actually made by Alsager & Neville.

GRIFFITHS & BROWETT
fl. c.1846–c.1894 (as japanners)
68 Bradford Street, Birmingham

Griffiths & Browett were prominent iron and tin-plate workers and japanners who specialised in inexpensive goods. Theirs was a large factory which kept up-to-date with the latest machinery. In 1835 they took out a patent for metal-stamping and burnishing, and in the mid-1840s, it was they who unsuccessfully attempted to sue Benjamin Walton of Wolverhampton (*qv*) for infringing their patent for spinning tin teapots. Though primarily metal-workers, and later enamellers, they began japanning in about 1846, and by 1862, were said to have made a name as japanners:

Their Toilet Services and Baths of all kinds, Tea-Trays and Coal-Boxes, their Grocer's Show-Vases [for shop-display] and Canisters, are produced and decorated in every variety of style. In several of these articles we find evidences of correct taste, and a good feeling for art as applied to decorative sense.[1]

They also patented a very inexpensive method of transfer-printing coloured landscapes and flower groups. And in 1867, they were granted a licence to use the type of pressure presses used in France, and covered by a French patent, which were far gentler than the heavy blows delivered in the English stamping process.

malachite at the 1862 exhibition in London.[lxxii] However, this style soon became popular throughout the industry, so not all malachite ornament can be attributed to their workshops.

James Neville, another of George Neville's brothers, was a die-sinker, and he too had worked for Jennens & Bettridge. He made dies for Alsager & Neville and also for other papier mâché manufacturers, but some decorators believed his designs were too elaborate and spoilt the effect of their work. Nevertheless for a period, Alsager & Neville made all the papier mâché blanks for Spiers of Oxford (*qv*) and occasionally supplied them part-decorated.
John Alsager died in 1870, and George Neville in 1887. Although their factory had dropped from sixty to fifty hands in the ten years following 1851, the firm continued as Alsager & Neville until c.1892 when it was taken over by McCallum & Hodson (*qv*). With so many former Jennens & Bettridge employees involved in

A catalogue which although undated, appears to date from the 1880s, shows Griffiths & Browett to have made baths with japanned oak exteriors and marbled interiors, and the usual gamut of other toilet wares, Persian coal scoops, and every other type of vessel for holding coal (e.g. plate 180). Of greater interest, however, is the illustration of a Georgian-style tin tea-caddy which, if based on appearance alone, could be mistaken for an early nineteenth century example. To judge from other objects illustrated in this catalogue, many articles made by Griffiths & Browett have survived in large numbers to the present day. For example, they made light-weight tin bread baskets with printed decoration, and stronger specimens with printed borders, stars, Japanese designs, or with filleted edges, and also 'Unique' iron trays with black edges and imitation wood-grain or malachite centres. The catalogue also includes a range of waiters with crystallised grounds (plate 181).

182. Papier mache articles made by Harris & Crick (not Creke, as shown), from a *Portfolio of Lithographic Drawings of Principal Manufactures at the Birmingham Exposition* 1849 (plate 19).

However, many of the goods shown in Griffiths & Browett's catalogue appeared also in catalogues issued by other local firms. A fine set of grocer's shop display vases, for instance, featured also in a catalogue produced by W.H.B. Wood of Birmingham, the only difference being that the catalogue illustrations were drawn by different artists (plate 299). After about 1894, Messrs Griffiths & Browett no longer advertised as japanners focusing their attention, instead, on enamel ware.

CHARLES RESTALL HARRIS
fl. 1849–1850
Summer Lane, Birmingham

This short-lived firm of japanners and manufacturers of papier mâché goods began as Harris & Cricke, but when their partnership was dissolved, Charles Restall Harris continued alone. The list of goods that they showed at the Birmingham Exhibition in 1849 reads like that of any other japanner at the time. Among the smaller articles were trays, and portfolios painted with flowers or scenes such as the interior of a baronial hall. His larger exhibits included a dressing glass with a papier mâché frame and stand, and two flower-painted tables one of which was enriched with pearl (plate 182). Harris was declared insolvent the following year.

NOCK & McCALLUM
c.1854–c.1858
29 St Paul's Square, Birmingham

Stephen Nock[lxxiii] joined Philip McCallum[lxxiv] in partnership in about 1854. Although the firm lasted only about four years, Nock & McCallum made for both the home and overseas markets, and produced a 'great variety of ladies' cabinets, desks, work boxes, album writing cases, tea caddees [*sic*], ink stands, tea and wine trays, and drawing room and boudoir furniture',[1] which they advertised as 'suitable for Domestic Use or Presentation and at Moderate Prices'.[2]

KNIGHT, MERRY & Co.
c.1854–1870
129–131 Bradford Street, Birmingham

Beginning as Knight & Exley, within a year this firm was listed in a Birmingham directory of 1855 as Knight, Merry & Exley: 'general japanners, tin and iron-plate workers, manufacturers of every description of baths, carriage, railway lamp and lantern makers' and so on.[1] Exhibiting as Knight, Merry & Co. at the London International Exhibition in 1862, they won a medal for the excellence of

---

lxxii. The German firm of Stobwasser & Son (see p. 290), had introduced malachite effects in about 1800, and included examples among the japanned goods which they showed at the Great Exhibition in London, in 1851.

their lamps, but it was by three papier mâché trays that they were represented in the illustrated catalogue. The trays, described as 'good in design, and of great excellence in finish and workmanship',[2] were variously shaped and, to judge from engravings (plate 183), were richly decorated with deep border patterns in gold leaf.

From 1868 until its closure in about 1870, the factory was styled Knight, Merry & Davies.

GEORGE DAVIES
fl. 1851
7 Brearley Street, Birmingham

In the Official Catalogue of the Great Exhibition, Davies was described as a 'designer and entire producer'.[1] His small display of papier mâché at that exhibition included a work-box and a panel, both inset with decorative glass 'tablets'. On the evidence of their catalogue descriptions, these involved neither imitation gems, nor flakes of pearl, and thus neatly evaded the patents for similar styles of decoration belonging to Jennens & Bettridge and Thomas Lane respectively (*qv*). The work-box, decorated in Elizabethan style, incorporated 'glass tablets of the monarchs from the Conquest'[2] which were part-painted, part-transparent, and given added brilliance by the use of stained metal leaf. By contrast, the 'glass tapestry panel' which he exhibited as 'a new style of decoration for rooms, furniture &c.'[3] although painted in transparent colours, was backed with white and coloured satins.

Since there is no trace of George Davies as a japanner, and unless he was later in short-lived partnership with Knight and Merry (see above), it appears that his foray into the design and production of papier mâché was solely for the purpose of this prestigious exhibition.

EBENEZER SHELDON
1881–1950
Bradford Street and Caroline Street, Birmingham

The products of this factory, so typical of their period, demonstrate well the number of makers of papier mâché and japanned tin-ware who, if it were not for a quirk of history, would otherwise have escaped notice. It is the loan of objects and associated artefacts to Birmingham Museums & Art Gallery by descendents of Ebenezer Sheldon (1827–c.1902) which provide the necessary information to ensure that his part in the history of the industry is not overlooked. While the loan includes only examples of papier mâché, Sheldon also produced japanned tin-ware.

Although the firm was not listed in local directories until 1881, several sheets of designs, included in the collection, show earlier dates. A design for a cabinet, for example, was dated 1872, while designs for another cabinet, writing boxes and inkstands were executed in 1878; a sheet of designs, identified as the work of Hinks (*qv*) and variously painted

with 'Building and River', 'Building', 'Figures' and 'Building and Domes', was dated 1879. There is now no way of knowing whether these earlier designs originated during Sheldon's employment prior to his setting up on his own account (the 1841 Census shows him to have been an apprentice iron-roller, and a japanner from 1861), or whether his own business was established earlier than records show.

Be that as it may, as examples from the later years of papier mâché production, the collection is significant insofar as it represents a range of objects which have survived in large numbers to the present day; without this evidence, many such wares would be attributed to an earlier period. Take, for example, the ladies cabinet, painted with rustic landscapes and evidently made for his wife, which contained a note reading: 'To dear Annie, asking her acceptance of the accompanying, as a tribute of the sincere love and good wishes of the donor', which he signed and dated 'E. Sheldon, July 19 / [18]80'.

Among the sheets of designs was a reference to inkstands with imitation walnut and malachite surfaces, and another marking the position of 'pearl in [a] building', which featured in a painting of a 'Landscape by Goodman' who was also responsible for a 'windmill design'. It is likely that this was George Goodman (*qv*) who had worked previously for Alsager & Neville and who was no doubt grateful to be still employed when the industry in which he had worked so long was nearing its end. Other decorators whose names appeared alongside designs for Sheldon's japanned ware were Ward who was to paint a '20 inch Round table [with] flowers [in the] centre', and a man named Hill about whom nothing more is known.

It is unlikely that Sheldon made papier mâché himself; he would have bought it in ready-made sheets or panels which could be steam-moulded or, if sufficiently thick, turned on a lathe, to make a variety of goods: table-tops, mirror frames, blotter covers, book-slides, 3- and 4-fold screens, bellows and trays, including what were described as 'card plates 8', and spectacles cases. Even the cabinets, bread baskets and crumb-trays which he is known to have produced, would have been made in this way. Many objects in the Sheldon loan show the textured surface which is common to articles of late manufacture, and none are marked with his name. Nevertheless, to judge from a yellow paper label centrally printed with the royal coat of arms and lettered for a 'Regd. Eugene Tray' which was found among his papers, he clearly marked at least some of his goods.

Sheldon was among the last in Birmingham to make papier mâché goods of this type. Although japanning continued to feature in his advertisements until 1936, if not later, his trade shifted towards making mud-guards for the cycle and motor trades and to commercial enamelling, nickel-plating and polishing.

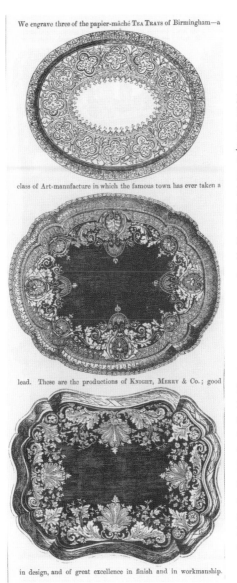

We engrave three of the papier-mâché TEA TRAYS of Birmingham—a

class of Art-manufacture in which the famous town has ever taken a

lead. These are the productions of KNIGHT, MERRY & Co.; good

in design, and of great excellence in finish and in workmanship.

183. Engravings of papier mâché trays by Knight, Merry & Co., from the *Art Journal Illustrated Catalogue of the International Exhibition*, 1862 (p. 282).

184. One of several pages of tin trays from the catalogue of Taylor, Law & Co., Birmingham, which includes also baths, deed boxes, coal vases, and many other utilitarian goods; c.1900.

TAYLOR, LAW & CO., BIRMINGHAM.

It should not be assumed that all such late pieces of papier mâché may be attributed to Ebenezer Sheldon's factory for there were probably several other lesser-known workshops producing similar wares in Birmingham at the time, and it will be shown that there were still several makers of japanned tin trays in Bilston. Instead, the collection stands as a sobering reminder of this fact.

NB. Because of their loan status, these objects cannot be illustrated. They may be viewed at Birmingham Museum and Art Gallery, and they are illustrated in Shirley DeVoe's earlier book, *Papier Mâché of the Georgian and Victorian Periods* (plates 159, 160, 167, 168 and 173).

~

The japanners listed above represent either the best-known makers of japanned papier mâché and tin-ware, or those about which sufficient details are known to provide a clear idea of the nature of their goods. There were besides, many others who were contemporarily significant, but whose products, for various reasons, are unlikely to be identified today (plate 184). Among them were firms like Allen & Moore of which it was said in 1853: 'there is a very spirited and enterprising firm, lately commenced in the manufacture of papier mâché... They have recently added to the area of their premises a considerable range of very superior shopping, which is appropriated to the manufacture of trays and other articles in papier mâché.'[1] Also there was for example, the company of Dewson & Sons who, we are tanatlisingly informed, made 'a fine tray with bronze ornamentation', which was considered one of 'the more interesting' exhibits in an exhibition in 1926, devoted to the 'extinct' Birmingham papier mâché industry.[2]

Until such time as more information becomes available, there is nothing to be gained by providing a list of names, not least because as has been shown, many of those listed as 'japanners' in local directories, were as likely to have been employees rather than manufacturers in their own right. Or, like John Simonite who exhibited at the Great Exhibition, they japanned goods of a very utilitarian nature such as shovel handles.

lxxiii. Although George Dickinson cites Philip Nock as the partner in this firm, local trades directories point to it having been Stephen Parker Nock who was listed as a japanner from 1846–1850.

lxxiv. It is not clear whether this was Philip McCallum senior (b. about 1800) who, in 1861, was described as a foreman in a japan factory, or his son Philip (b.1825), a painter of papier mâché.

185. Papier mâché table-cabinet with cushion-top, decorated in Moresque style; unmarked, but
reliably provenanced to the factory of F. Walton & Co.; c.1850. 37 x 45.5 x 48.5cm

CHAPTER IX

THE WOLVERHAMPTON JAPANNERS

(in chronological order)

THE OLD HALL JAPAN WORKS
Wolverhampton

For over one hundred years, and under various partnerships, the Old Hall (plate 84) was one of the most prominent japanning factories in the Midlands. Known originally as the Great Hall, it stood near the site of the present library on Snow Hill in Wolverhampton. It was built between c.1563 and 1575 by the Levesons, a family of rich wool merchants, in whose possession it remained for almost two hundred years. At the end of the seventeenth century, when virtually a ruin, the hall was leased to John Turton, an ironmaster, but by 1750, Turton's Hall, as it was then known, was again untenanted and remained so for several years.

By 1767, and possibly sooner, the Hall was occupied by japanners: first by Jones & Taylor, then by Taylor, Jones & Badger, and from c.1790, by Barney & Ryton whose factory continued there, under various partnerships, until its closure as F. Walton & Co. in 1882. Despite each partnership having a distinct name, the factory was generally known in Wolverhampton and beyond, as the Old Hall Works. Such was its influence that in a report of the Children's Employment Commission in 1862, it was observed that many Wolverhampton firms had been founded by men who had trained there.[i] In fact, the Old Hall Works was said to have been the only effective competitor to Jennens & Bettridge in training men for the japanning industry. In this light, it is curious that its history has been so overlooked in earlier accounts of the industry.

Jones & Taylor
pre 1767–1784/5

According to local trade directories, Jones & Taylor (sometimes styled Taylor & Jones) commenced their trade at the Old Hall sometime before 1767.[ii] They were the first japanners of any importance in Wolverhampton.

Their partnership began in Pontypool[1] where Jones had been a foreman japanner, and Thomas Taylor, a businessman. It is likely that they were attracted to the Midlands by the success of Baskerville's japanning venture in Birmingham. An advertisement placed by Jones & Taylor in Aris's *Birmingham Gazette* in 1774 for 'good workmen at screw candlesticks, 2 or 3 barrel filers, [and] a good hand at Steel Post Coffee Mills',[2] is the only clue to their early products. A local directory of 1780 listed them as as 'japanners and merchants,'[3] and as they were said to have employed 23 apprentices,[4] theirs was by no means a small concern.

By 1784 or 1785, they had taken on the already talented Edward Bird (*qv*) as an apprentice painter,[5] a clear indication that they were producing finely painted tin trays at that date. Bird was taught to copy the engravings of their master painter, Mr Gower, and quickly earned a reputation, both at home and abroad, as a highly skilled tray-painter.

There is, for example, a story about how Bird and several companions visited Boulogne, and were served tea on a tray so beautiful that it excited his friends' notice and praise. They

---

i. Edward Perry & Co. (*qv*), and Henry Fearncombe & Co. (*qv*), are but two examples of japanning firms owned by former Old Hall workmen.

ii. The Wolverhampton Directories for 1871 & 1884 both give a start date post 1740/45.

186. Japanned tin portrait of John Ryton (1736–1788), proprietor of the Old Hall Japan Works, painted by John Hughes, c.1780. 28 x 23cm
PRIVATE COLLECTION

doubted such an article could have been made in France, upon which Bird smiled and said: 'It was not made here, it was made in Birmingham,[iii] for I painted it.'[6]

His employment at the Old Hall is the only evidence of the likely quality of Jones & Taylor's output.

Taylor, Jones & Badger
c.1784/5–c.1795

If, as believed, the firm was styled Taylor & Jones when Edward Bird was apprenticed in 1784/5, then Badger must have joined as a partner some time between then and 1789 when, as Taylor, Jones & Badger, the firm advertised for several experienced japanners.[7] Nothing is known of the goods they made, nor is there any evidence that their output differed in any way from that of the earlier partnership. It is therefore likely that they, too, made the type of oval and rectangular painted tin trays which were so characteristic of this period (plate 187). They appear to have vacated the Old Hall by 1790. Thomas Taylor, although he had entered the partnership as a businessman, was described as a japanner on his death in 1795.[8]

Barney & Ryton
c.1761–1791

In 1791, the Old Hall was under the new tenancy of Joseph Barney (b. c.1725–1799) and Obadiah Ryton (c.1771–1818). Barney was already a japanner in Wolverhampton when

Obadiah's father, John Ryton (1736–1788), the son of an Oxfordshire yeoman, moved there in search of work in about 1754, having completed an apprenticeship as a tinplate-worker in Oxford. The two men, Barney, and John Ryton (plate 186), entered into partnership in about 1761. By 1780, they had moved to Tin Shop Yard where the firm, described as 'japanners, merchants &c.',[9] remained until its move to the Old Hall in 1791 – a couple of years or so after Ryton's death.

John Ryton's elder son, Obadiah (c.1771–1818), joined Barney in full partnership at the age of seventeen. In the same year, 1788, Obadiah's brother, fifteen year old William Lott Ryton (1773–1847), informed his mother by letter that he, too, was preparing to join the firm: 'Knowing the time is short', he wrote, 'I shall endeavour to make the best use of it I can by applying close to business. I am sensible I shall be of use in the Compting House.'[10]

Both boys were educated at Barr Academy, near Birmingham, where, according to a later advertisement, 'Drawing being not only a polite Accomplishment to the Gentlemen, but absolutely useful to the Manufacturer, [was] taught scientifically by Mr BARBER of Birmingham, whose abilities, as a Drawing Master, stand unrivalled in this Neighbourhood.'[11] This training would have stood them in good stead for the industry upon which they were to embark, but the partnership between Joseph Barney and Obadiah Ryton was a turbulent one.

Their first set-back occurred in December 1790, when their warehouse was destroyed by fire:

> *The flames had burnt through the roof, and spread over the adjacent buildings, before the watchman had discovered the accident. Nothwithstanding the assistance of the engines, and the exertion of a number of people, it was a considerable time before the fire was extinguished; among their books, which were thought to be entirely lost, has been found the ledger, though much injured, yet in a state sufficient to reinstate their accounts.*[12]

Their landlord was inadequately insured and tried to make good his loss by increasing the annual rent. Barney & Ryton refused to meet his demand and looked instead for alternative premises, but the search triggered a bitter dispute between them. Feelings ran so high that Barney issued a printed statement in October 1791, detailing the 'ill treatment'[13] that brought his thirty-year partnership with the Ryton family to an end. According to Barney, new premises were soon found, but owing to his unwillingness to accept a twenty-one-year lease, he was informed that, in future, only six months notice would be required, by either party, to dissolve the partnership. Sensing trouble, Barney refused to agree to the move. In the meantime, not only had their existing landlord discovered their removal plans and served notice for his property to be vacated, but Obadiah Ryton had also agreed an advance rent on the new premises at the Old Hall. As Barney had feared, Ryton wished to dissolve the partnership.

187. Straight-edge tin tray, painted with *Rebecca at the Well*; traditionally attributed to Edward Bird, and the factory of William & Obadiah Ryton; c.1800. 56.5 x 71.4cm © WOLVERHAMPTON ARTS AND HERITAGE (BANTOCK HOUSE MUSEUM)

188. Tin roundels painted by Edward Bird (see p. 312), c.1800 Dia: 23cm © WOLVERHAMPTON ARTS AND MUSEUMS SERVICE, www.blackcountryhistory.org

Obadiah Ryton, on the other hand, felt that Barney had not 'acted with that Candour we had a Right to expect', and informed him in a letter dated 19 June 1792, that:

> *Our Manufactory will be carried on in future in the same Buildings,[iv] as usual, in the Firm of OBADIAH and WILLIAM RYTON ... where we shall be glad to receive your Orders, which shall be executed on the most just and honourable Terms; and shall take the Liberty of waiting on you in about a month. – Your Orders in the mean time, addressed as above, may depend on having executed with Goods of the best Quality and immediate Dispatch...[14]*

It is apparent from this that Barney continued as a japanner on his own account, and evidently with considerable success

since he had sufficient means to become one of the proprietors of Wyrley & Essington Canal in 1795. Barney died in 1799, leaving his japanning business to his son and namesake, Joseph. The younger Joseph is next mentioned in a newspaper in 1812,[15] as a partner in Barney & Bevans – a firm which, to judge from a local directory, continued japanning and tin-plate working until at least 1818–20;[16] he died in 1827.

Edward Bird's employment at the Old Hall continued despite the changed ownership and this fact is the only evidence that remains of the quality of Barney & Ryton's output (plate 188). Notwithstanding its troubled history, the firm of Barney & Ryton was important for having ensured the future success of the Old Hall Japan Works which, under various partnerships, grew into one of the leading japanning factories in the Midlands.

---

iii. There is no evidence for Bird having worked as a japanner in Birmingham; the error probably stems from the anecdote being reported by a non-local.

iv. It is unclear whether this was the Old Hall or the fire-damaged building, though the date suggests the former.

Obadiah & William Lott Ryton
c.1790–1818/20

Obadiah and William Ryton were probably responsible for the manufacture of some of the finer pieces of japanned tinware to have survived from the late eighteenth and early nineteenth centuries. The brothers moved to the Old Hall in about 1791, soon after their premises in Tin-Shop Yard, North Street were destroyed by fire and their partnership with Barney had ended. Residing in a small part of the Hall, they devoted the remainder of the building to their business as japanners, tin-plate workers, and iron-workers.

Large oval tin trays were an important part of their trade. Many of these were were painted by Edward Bird who continued to be employed by the new partnership at the Old Hall. According to George Wallis, Bird painted trays in the style of Gainsborough and, by the age of eighteen, it was said, that he 'excelled in Shakespearean compositions and depicted scenes from *Don Quixote* and *Hudibras*'.[17] A tray made by O. & W. Ryton and exhibited at the 1884 Wolverhampton Exhibition, where its decoration was attributed to Bird, was thought to be one of the first examples of burnished gilding on a japanned tray. Also exhibited in 1884, and made at the Old Hall during this period, were two small papier mâché trays each measuring 13.5in. (34cm) by 11in. (28cm). They were decorated with extremely fine 'pencilling' by Edwin Booth whose signature appeared on one of the trays, and whose work, the catalogue said, was unrivalled; he specialised in fine gold work in the Indian style. He was also known for 'his impetuous temper'.[18] In a guide to Wolverhampton, written many years later in 1871, Booth was described as a decorator of snuff and tobacco boxes which 'fetched extravagant prices'.[19] He was said to have emigrated to America.

A letter written by Obadiah to William, in early 1792, during one of his promotional selling trips around the country, suggests that trays were a lucrative line for the Rytons. It also shows how useful these expeditions were, and sheds light on other goods which were currently made at the Old Hall:

> *I shall go off tomorrow for Chester I have taken several good orders since I wrote to you last particularly from Preston of L'Pool [Liverpool] who behav'd exceeding civil to me ... you will ... see after the Trays from Abraham as I have Sold a good many and most of the sort that get the most Money tell your Uncle[v] I shall make the Orders taken £200 and upwards before I come Home remember and get 2 Dz Sett of Quadrills [counter trays] from Evans and one Dz oval candleks [candlesticks] from Abraham.[vi] Fairclough the Merchant inform'd me this morning that I might depend upon having one half of his Jack Orders...[20]*

Clearly, alongside decorative japanned articles, the Rytons also made utilitarian objects such as cooking-jacks. Moreover, it is evident from the letter that some, if not all, of their counters-trays and candlesticks were bought as blanks from different suppliers, and not made on the premises. Whether these blanks were already japanned, we cannot be sure, but certainly, some years later, the Rytons were known to have purchased bread-baskets from Barber's of Bilston which were japanned ready for decorating (see p. 93).

Besides the home market, Obadiah & William Ryton also looked to supply the world market. Accordingly, they were among the signatories to an open letter to the Constables of the town which was published in the *Wolverhampton Chronicle* in 1812:

> *We the undersigned, request you to call a meeting of those inhabitants of this town, who are interested in the Manufactories & Commerce of the United Kingdom to consider the Propriety of Petitioning Both Houses of Parliament to Discontinue Such parts of the East India Company's Charter, which exclude British Merchants from trading to the East.[21]*

In about 1800, as a result of an industrial dispute, the Rytons lost many of their workmen and decorators to other firms. Obadiah died in 1818, and William was later joined by Benjamin Walton.

Ryton & Walton
1820–1842

Following the death of his brother, Obadiah, William Ryton was joined in partnership by Benjamin Walton in 1820. Walton, was an imposing man, 6ft. 4in. (193cm) tall, and of gentle disposition, whose infectious energy and enthusiasm were matched by so great a business flair, that the Old Hall rapidly progressed under his direction:

> *The style of decorating tea trays changed. The old-fashioned Indian work gave way to the advance in ideas, and crystallising tin tea trays and other articles came into fashion ... But the most important advance was the introduction of paper tea trays.[22]*

If this was so, and Ryton & Walton were the first to manufacture papier mâché trays at the Old Hall, then in this respect, they lagged behind Thomas Illidge (*qv*) who is known to have made such goods in Wolverhampton at least as early as 1811. Nevertheless, when Ryton & Walton erected a sign above their workshop-door to the effect that they were 'Licensed to make Paper Tea Trays' (see p. 36), it marked the start of a large and important new branch of their trade, and they were so successful that by 1823, they had offices in London, at 51 Kirby Street, Clerkenwell.

Besides decorative articles, the larger part of Ryton & Walton's trade was in very functional objects, as shown by their entry in a directory of 1827, which lists them as:

Japanners of all kinds of Pontipool goods, also general japanners on paper, tin and iron, tin and iron-plate workers, manufacturers of Vallet's chrystalised articles,[vii] also of steel saddle trees and panels, complete for Thompson's patent saddle.[23]

Notwithstanding, it is for their decorative ware that they are remembered today – a legacy of their determination to employ the best available artists (plate 189). It was probably this policy which prompted Joseph Booth to approach them when he left Jennens & Bettridge, but if Dickinson's account is accurate, it is unlikely the artist was impressed by their deceitful methods. Booth offered to sell them a tray, perhaps for use as a future pattern, but Ryton & Walton, believing it to be far too expensive, suggested he leave it with them while they considered the matter. They gave him a small sum of money 'to relieve his immediate appetite for beer' and as soon as Booth left, had one of their workmen copy it. The original, decorated with a chinoiserie scene entitled *The Rushcutters*, was returned to Booth on the grounds that it was too costly and the copy was hung in Ryton & Walton's warehouse as an example of their fine workmanship.

Not all artists faired so badly. W. H. Jones whom Ryton & Walton apprenticed in 1839, later wrote a book in which he recalled some of the artists they engaged. An artist named Voss, for example, was brought from Dusseldorf, to paint trays with scenes which included the Vale of Llangollen, Dovedale, the Conway Falls and Conway Castle, while Richard Steele was brought from the Potteries to paint flowers. Between 1827 and 1832, George Wallis (*qv*) was engaged to paint the centres of their best trays. These artists were among the most accomplished in the factory and would have been responsible only for superior examples of the styles described. Less well-painted examples were almost certainly the work of copyists.

Trays painted in the style of the popular artist George Morland are particularly associated with the Old Hall during this period. The best examples were the work of William Davis, a decorator at the Old Hall, who was so expert in copying Morland's rustic subjects that some years later, George Wallis was asked if all such trays were painted by Morland himself; he confirmed they were not.

Ryton & Walton appear to have been the first firm at the Old Hall to have marked their goods. The most commonly found objects bearing their mark are rectangular sandwich-edged trays which, together with small waiters and bread baskets, were among the earliest of their papier mâché products; the style of these goods was carried on by their successors (plate 192). Under Walton's influence, the range soon extended to include 'inkstands, ladies work-boxes, tea-caddies, hand fire-screens,

189. Covered vase, with chinoiserie decoration in the style of Jean-Baptiste Pillement; made from relatively thin papier mâché – hence its stabilising foot (*cf*. later, and thicker, weighted vases eg. pl. 143); c.1820, 31.5cm. Until recently, this vase was part of a small collection of japanned ware begun by Obadiah and/or his brother William Lott Ryton, but this is insufficient evidence upon which to reliably attribute it to the Old Hall, since the collection also included examples from elsewhere – perhaps as models for copying. However, the painted and gilded figures share characteristics with those found on a tray by Ryton & Walton (pl. 193).
COURTESY OF BONHAMS

v. Richard Ryton had been apprenticed as a tin-plate worker by his elder brother John Ryton.
vi. This may have been John Evans, a Wolverhampton japanner and tinplate worker, who was declared bankrupt in 1796; Abraham remains a mystery.
vii. See p. 48. Vallet's crystallised tin.

folio cases, card cases, cake baskets and jewel boxes.'[24] To mark the coronation of Queen Victoria in 1838, the firm produced a 'queen-gothic' tray – a shape which they named 'Victoria' – decorated with designs by George Wallis. They were not alone in making this gesture, for there were other manufacturers who gave this name to their new trays (p. 254).

There was similar progress in their tin-shop. This was due to the foresight of John Pinson, foreman of the stamping department, who suggested that Nasmyth's steam hammer might be adapted to suit their purposes (see p. 20). After visiting the Old Hall to assess their needs, Nasmyth designed a lighter version which 'ultimately revolutionised the trade [and] beautifully shaped tea and coffee urns were made; [and] an almond shaped tea kettle which was artistic in form, was deservedly admired.'[25] Due to the amount of manual labour which it replaced, the hammer struck a blow to the workers as well as the tin, but in terms of piecework payments, they soon found they were amply compensated by its increased output.

191. King-gothic papier mâché tray, the scene described on the underside in painted letters *Cork River*; impressed mark B. WALTON & CO, c.1845. 65cm
COURTESY OF BONHAMS

190. Iron coal vase with lift-off lid, bearing a brass label, stamped: 'Registered by Benjamin Walton & Co. No. 862 Wolverhampton 7th October 1841'. H: 61cm, W: 56cm
COURTESY OF APTER FREDERICKS, LONDON

Trade also increased once Mr Walton abandonned the annual selling tour of the country in favour of quarterly journeys. Instead of travelling with a heavily laden pack-horse, he rode in a high dog-cart, which had been fitted to carry samples of complete objects as well as flat, travellers samples as patterns. In this way he not only offered a more comprehensive selection of goods and saved much time, but also rapidly increased the rate at which orders were received.

The partnership ended in 1841 with the departure of William Ryton who, at the age of sixty-eight, and in partnership with another, embarked on a wholly unsuccessful venture to manufacture iron bedsteads. A disappointing outcome for a man whose principle 'to manufacture a good article, pay a good price to his workmen, and to expect a reasonable return from his customer',[26] had served him so well at the Old Hall. When Ryton died in 1847, The Old Hall closed for a day as a mark of respect for an employer in whom his 'workpeople in sickness and misfortune ever found ... a steady friend.'[27] Over one hundred and twenty of his workmen attended his funeral at St John's Church, close by the Old Hall – a testament to his benevolence, and an indication of why the firm of Ryton & Walton had become so successful.

B. Walton & Co.
1841–1847

By 1841, Benjamin Walton had become sole proprietor of the Old Hall Japan Works (plate 190). He oversaw one of the stormiest periods in the history of the factory and, through no fault of his own, witnessed its slide from flourishing prosperity into bankruptcy during the general depression of the late 1840s.

He approached his new role with the same energy and enterprise that he had shown when he first arrived over twenty years earlier. He brought in artists from other trades and introduced a new and distinctive form of decoration which came to be known, as the 'Wolverhampton style' (see p. 78) – though this was somewhat misleading since it was not confined to that town. 'Gothic' trays decorated in this manner, with dramatic interior and exterior views of cathedrals, castles and baronial halls became almost exclusively associated with his factory (plate 72).

Also associated with this firm is a series of gothic-shaped papier mâché trays, usually between 20–25in. (51 x 63.5cm) wide, and well-painted with all-over landscape views, or figures in landscapes. They are generally lettered on the reverse with evocative descriptions of the scene depicted, such as *Crusader's Castle,* or *Crossing by a Sangha Near Jumnootree* (plate 191). Perhaps the 'three or four finely-painted tea-trays'[28] which constituted the Old Hall display at the 1846 Manchester Exposition were of this type. Although seldom, if ever, signed by the artist, these trays are generally impressed 'B. Walton & Co.', or 'B. Walton & Co. Warranted'. The fact that most have survived in very good condition suggests that they were rarely pressed into service as tea trays, but were more commonly looked upon as decorative pictures. Alongside these, Benjamin Walton also made the older style sandwich edge trays as shown here (plate 192).

Today, the firm of B. Walton & Co. is best known for its fine trays because it is those articles which commonly bear the factory mark. However, besides these luxury goods, they made functional black japanned tin articles as well as 'common', or un-japanned, tinware. An example of the latter is shown by a large dish-cover held by one of their tinplate-workers in a photograph taken at the Old Hall, in which he is seen wearing the 'uniform' of his trade – a square, folded paper hat and leather apron. This branch of their trade was equally as competetive as japanning. In 1845/6, for example, Griffiths & Browett of Birmingham brought an action against Walton for allegedly infringeing their patent for spinning tin teapots. To the joy and delight of the factory, Walton won the trial. Flags were hoisted over the Old Hall clock tower, and a banquet for his friends and workmen was held in a local theatre bedecked 'with flags and banners, and with various devices in gas lights, in the centre of which was a design of a large teapot, crowned with laurels, and in letters of light the

192. Sandwich-edge papier mâché trays, impressed with the mark of B. Walton, c.1845. Ws: 46cm and 35.5cm
COURTESY OF MORPHETS OF HARROGATE

193. Sandwich-edge papier mâché tray with fine chinoiserie decoration (*cf*. pl. 189); white printed mark of Ryton & Walton, c.1825. 54 x 71cm
COURTESY OF BONHAMS

word "Victory".'[29] Fittingly, beer was served in large japanned tin beer-cans.

By now Walton's health was failing, and the strain of the trial was exacerbated by the downturn in the economy when bad wheat and potato harvests in 1845, and the crippling effects of the Corn Laws, not only forced up the price of food and filled the workhouses, but made it impossible for traders to get credit. Japanners competed fiercely for orders. As 'a thorough-going Liberal', who had spoken up 'for Reform, the Repeal of the Corn Laws, and did much by force of character to push forward Free Trade',[30] it must have hit Walton very hard when he was impelled to stop payment, had to lay off many of his men, and was declared bankrupt.

PAPIER MACHE VASES.—BY MESSRS. WALTON AND CO.

These vases, in *papier maché*, by Messrs. Walton and Co., are generally of classic form ; the devices varied and elegant, and the colouring extremely rich.

194. Papier mâché vases made by Frederick Walton & Co., from the *Illustrated London News*, 6 Sept. 1851 (p. 308).

He died in 1847, and was thus spared the sadness of seeing his stock-in trade being sold in December of that year. For his workers, however, 'it was with intense sorrow and with tearful eyes [that they] saw wagon-loads of articles of real artistic merit carried out of the Old Hall to the auction room'.[31] The sale lasted twenty-one days and attracted buyers from far and wide. Rival japanners in the town, like the recently established firm of Shoolbred & Loveridge (*qv*), seized the opportunity to take the Old Hall trade, not only by buying up their pattern books and 'blank' articles, but also by taking on their workmen. As a result, Walton's shapes, patterns and decorators, not to mention a large number of blank objects, stamped for B. Walton & Co, were taken up by other makers – a possible source of confusion today. But the japan trade was highly specialised, and speculators like Samuel Griffiths, who hoped to make a quick profit by setting up a factory near to the Old Hall, offering high wages to its former workmen and selling Walton's patterns at reduced prices, soon floundered against competition from rival firms which had been established for longer.

Many of the younger workmen found employment elsewhere, taking with them the skills and standards acquired at the Old Hall, but for older men the prospect was bleak, especially during such hard times. 'I have been here all my life', said one,

'now I am old and my eyes are dim, what is to become of me?'[32] Not a plight that his former employer, the philanthropic Benjamin Walton, founder member of Wolverhampton Mechanics Institute, opponent of Church rates and other 'crying abuses',[33] would have wished to behold.

With cruel irony, the sale was unnecessary as Walton was subsequently found to have had sufficient assets to pay his creditors. His son, Frederick, obviously cast in the same mould as his father, wasted no time in re-establishing a japan factory at the Old Hall.

Frederick Walton & Co.
1847–1882

After the closure of B. Walton & Co., the firm was re-established by Walton's eldest son Frederick (b.1791–1861) who 'obtained financial help, and secured the tools and machinery to start with.'[34] He added new workshops, converted old barns and took on a workforce which by 1850, was said to have numbered two-hundred and fifty.[viii] In just three years, and with as many as forty-eight stoves in operation at any one time, the Old Hall had not only restored its flourishing and lucrative trade but, as will be seen, its products

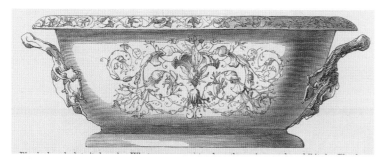

195. An iron footbath and coal-box, made by Frederick Walton & Co, from the *Art Journal*, 1849 (p. 317).

reached their highest perfection. With his new-found wealth and social standing, Frederick Walton built a large house for himself at a cost of £15,000 and was made a magistrate.

No sooner had he revived the firm, than he successfully applied for a patent (#11,592) for enamelling (see Glossary) wrought iron and other metals, and decorating them in the style of japanned goods. Since it was said to have been the result of 'considerable expenditure of time and capital',[35] it may have been a project carried over from his father's factory but, nevertheless, the invention was notable for being the first enamelled sheet iron made in England. Known in the Wolverhampton trade as 'light iron ware',[36] it could withstand atmospheric changes and sudden alterations in temperature – a matter of long-standing concern to hardware manufacturers. There were two qualities available, each distinguished by its surface colour: pure white and colours for better goods such as toilet wares, trays and so on, and black for 'commoner' articles like 'stable buckets, water-cans, &c.'[37] Enamelling was sometimes used in combination with japanning, so an iron tray, for example, may have had an enamelled top and a japanned underside. Light ironware was a sufficiently

important part of Walton's trade to be shown at major exhibitions and, together with the showers and baths which were highly regarded by the medical profession, serve as a reminder that japanned tin and papier mâché were often only two of several allied products made by any one of the larger firms.

Notwithstanding, Walton & Co.'s reputation among collectors today rests upon their highly decorative paper goods and tinware. A clear picture of the range and quality of Walton's output emerges from contemporary descriptions of their displays at major exhibitions, both at home and abroad. These leave little doubt that Walton & Co. were as likely as any of their contemporaries to have been responsible for many fine but unmarked examples of japanned tin and papier mâché which have survived to the present day.

At the Society of Art in 1848, Walton & Co. exhibited 'a beautiful tray ornamented in arabesques of excessively tasteful design.'[38] The following year, their impressive display at the Birmingham Exposition of Art prompted a prediction that 'Messrs Walton will make Birmingham look to its laurels',[39] and showed them to have been serious rivals in quality, if not output, to firms like Jennens & Bettridge. Their exhibits included a large campana vase decorated with vine leaves, ten smaller vases (plate 194), an 'Elizabethan' style inkstand, and a cabinet with pearl and gold arabesque ornaments. Among the trays was a '30" Elizabethian [*sic*] Paper Tray' painted with an interior scene at Penshurst Park in Kent, entitled 'Bringing in the Yule Log', and a set of three painted with seasonal landscapes: 'Spring' with a border of hawthorn blossom, 'Autumn' edged by a border of oak leaves, and 'Winter' framed by holly and ivy. In addition, there were oval paper trays measuring 16in., 24in. and 30in. (40.5cm, 61cm and 76cm), decorated with ornamental borders or 'Elizabethian [*sic*]' ornaments. Their light ironware was represented by two patent enamelled baths and hand-basins ornamented with lithographs, and their japanned tinware by a foot bath and coal box which were admired for both their 'simplicity and purity'[40] (plate 195).

> *The brilliant execution of the painting* [seen on their exhibits in Birmingham] *and the great cleverness and judgement with which the ornamental lines and patterns are adapted in the forms of the objects they decorate, are admirable, and testify that in this branch of manufacture, at least, that great and most desirable consummation is ariving in which the workman becomes the artist himself ... in most of what Mr Walton exhibits, the artists hand and mind are developed, working in fresh and healthy unity of purpose.*[41]

This was by no means fortuitous, as Walton, like his father, set great store by employing the best artists available: Edwin Haseler, Richard Steele, George Hicken and James Voss, and

---

viii. G. Bernard Hughes said 600 were employed, mostly on trays (Old English Picture Trays – I, *Country Life*, 12 March, 1948).

he was said to have given trials to many who had just completed apprenticeships with Jennens & Bettridge. In fact Walton & Co. were consistently praised 'for their endeavours to free themselves from the old style of ornamentation applied to papier mâché goods'[42] and to this end, commissioned designs from Owen Jones, some of which they later exhibited at the Great Exhibition (see below). The painter and celebrated photographer, Oscar Rejlander, who worked in Wolverhampton during the 1850s, was also associated with the Old Hall, although his involvement may not have extended beyond painting a miniature portrait on ivory of Frederick Walton himself (plate 196).

However, as already shown, Walton's display at the Birmingham Exposition had its detractors, not least in the report written for the Journal of Design & Manufactures which questioned his moral integrity in relation to the possible piracy of Horsley's recent picture of Malvolio, copied on a waiter (p. 85).

Nor were Walton's high-minded ideals always in tune with the buying public – witness his unsuccessful attempt to discontinue 'Browns borders' (see p. 78). On occasion, however, he stood his ground. In the 1860s, a painter by the name of Newman, who had learnt his trade at the Old Hall, took to painting peacocks 'which for their unfailing appearance in environs suitable and unsuitable, became something of a joke in the workshops.'[43] He was no favourite of Walton's foreman who, 'at a weekly show-up of work for payment, roughly told Newman that he had "had enough of him and his damned peacocks" and forthwith rubbed off the painting on the articles.'[44] Newman took his employers to court and won the case 'on the ground that, however suitable

or unsuitable his decoration may have been, the foreman had destroyed the evidence by rubbing out the work.'[45] The painter had won, but so too had Walton, for Newman left the Old Hall and went to work for Loveridge and Co., before moving on to Alsager & Neville in Birmingham.

The set of trays depicting 'The Seasons' which had attracted much attention in Birmingham, was shown again at the Great Exhibition alongside a set showing views of Windsor Castle, Holyrood House, and Glengarry Castle, and a set painted after Retzsch's *Outlines of Faust*,[ix] 'which a local reporter thought clever but otherwise unpraiseworthy.'[46] Other exhibits were decorated with 'various Louis Quatorze ornaments and figures after Watteau',[47] and there were trays painted with marine views and shell and seaweed borders, besides other articles variously embellished in the Byzantine, German gothic, Renaissance, Alhambresque and Elizabethan tastes which were so popular among japanners, and indeed other decorative artists, at the time.

Alongside these, they showed everyday articles like enamelled trays, toilet wares, and sponging and milk pans which were designed by Alfred Finley, and painted with figures by Henry Stanier, and flowers by Edwin Haseler. In addition, they exhibited a range of 'bronzed' metal-ware which included coal vases, dish covers, and kettles and stands. These goods were varnished in imitation of bronze, and their finish was wholly different, therefore, from the decorative technique known as 'bronzed gilding' which is described on p.74*ff*.

However, the centrepiece of Walton's stand at this huge international exhibition must surely have been the papier mâché vase with handles 'made rather in the style of the Warwick vase,'[48] and measuring 4½ft. (137cm) high and about 3ft. (91.5cm) wide. Apart from the practical skill needed to make such a piece from papier mâché, by far the most difficult part of its manufacture was the preparation of a mould or core so large that it required a tree trunk to be cut and slowly turned on a lathe.

The Old Hall is not generally associated with the manufacture of japanned furniture, so it is surprising to find loo tables listed among their exhibits at the 1851 exhibition. The following anecdote tells of the preparation of one these tables and sheds interesting light on the haphazard timing involved in decorating:

196. Portrait miniature of Frederick Walton, proprietor of the Old Hall Japan Works from 1847 until its closure in 1882, painted on ivory by the photographer, Oscar G. Rejlander, in 1851.

198. Papier mâché tray, painted by Edwin Haselar for presentation to Queen Victoria; F. Walton & Co, 1852. 51 x 66cm
PRIVATE COLLECTION

197. Papier mâché vases on weighted tin pedestals, one painted with the number '21' on its base; provenanced, by descent, to the factory of F. Walton & Co. (*cf.* pl. 194), which exhibited ten similar vases in Birmingham, in 1849.

© WOLVERHAMPTON ARTS AND HERITAGE (BANTOCK HOUSE MUSEUM)

[It] *was an unusually large one, and took much longer in the mechanical making than was anticipated, so much so that when the borderer had taken a long time in working out an exquisite gold margin, the head of the firm had doubts as to whether it could be got ready in time. The master sent for his principal painter, Haselar ... and asked him how long he would take to paint a bunch of roses in the centre. "A day – or two hours if necessary", was the confident reply.*[49]

In the event, it was completed in a day. Haselar had painted the centre with roses, and across them 'from side to side of the table' was painted 'a single stalk of canary creeper that appeared to be laid over.'[50] It was much admired. Another table, of papier mâché and iron 'in the form of a grape vine and grapes',[51] was less admired, at least by Dickenson writing some years later, who described it as 'a quaint and ugly object, and one which few people would care to see outside a museum.'[52]

Upon receipt of an important commission the next year, Frederick Walton turned again to Haselar. The train on which Queen Victoria was returning from Balmoral to London, was scheduled to refuel at Wolverhampton. The stop was to last only three minutes, but local worthies chose to mark the event by giving the Queen a papier mâché tray as a symbol of the town's manufacturing riches. Mr Walton suplied some specimen roses for Haselar to work from, and

other national flower emblems were incorporated in the gilding (plate 198). The plan was that Haselar himself should make the presentation and, being by all accounts a kindly man, he decided to offer the tray together with a bunch of hot-house grapes which Walton had agreed to supply from home. On the day, the mayor and mayoress, councillors and other town dignitaries assembled on the platform to await the arrival of the train, at which point Haselar would step forward and present the tray through an open carriage window. All went to plan until the presentation itself when the Queen, very graciously, accepted the grapes and left poor Haselar holding his tray. He was distraught, but some very quick-thinking member of the assembly rushed forward, seized the tray and presented it to the mayoress as if that had been the intention all along. Thus, in large white painted letters on the back of the tray is the inscription:

This Waiter was used
on the occasion
of HER MAJESTY'S VISIT to Wolverhampton
Oct[r].14th 1852
W[M]. WARNER JUN[R]. ESQ[R]. MAYOR

———

PRESENTED TO M[RS]. WARNER
by the Manufacturers
FRED: WALTON & CO.

---

ix. Friedrich August Moritz Retzsch (1779–1857), German painter and engraver.

199. Papier mâché lady's cabinet decorated with mother-of-pearl, and lined with purple velvet. Gifted to Wolverhampton by a daughter of the japanner Joseph Jones, it is perhaps the cabinet he decorated for Walton for display at the Great Exhibition (see p. 213); c.1850. 34 x 40 x 39cm

© Wolverhampton Arts and Heritage (Bantock House Museum)

The fiasco 'afforded much chaff and amusement, but it embittered Haselar's life for a long time ... He was consequential in manner, and took himself very seriously.'[53] These details apart, the tray has significance as the only example of japanned ware which is known to have been painted by Edwin Haselar and is thus among the very few articles of papier mâché and tinware which can be reliably attributed to any one painter.

Despite Walton's comments in 1853 that 'Materials were high, Trade was bad and the Competition fea[r]full',[54] his firm showed a range of goods – albeit somewhat limited – at the Dublin Exhibition of that year. A more varied range of paper and tin goods, including trays, screens, vases and tables, was sent to the Paris Exhibition in 1855.

Later in the same year, Walton was granted a patent (#2717) for improvements in papier mâché trays. The object of his invention was to prevent japanned surfaces from being 'readily scratched and injured by hot bodies placed thereon,'[55] – an interesting aim in view of similar claims made by earlier manufacturers concerning the strength and durability of japanned surfaces (see p. 27). He did this by making the upper surfaces of trays, urn- and teapot-stands of glass or enamel. Curiously, despite the vulnerability of the glass-topped and so-called 'Patent Crystal Trays' (plates 200 & 201), they appear to have survived in greater number than their enamel counterparts.

Despite her deep mourning for Prince Albert from 1861 onwards, Queen Victoria was touched by an invitation from the 'widows' of Wolverhampton to unveil a commemorative statue of her late husband, and agreed to perform the ceremony in 1866. The town was thrown into a flurry of decoration, and three temporary triumphal archways symbolising Wolverhampton's trades were built along the processional route. One arch was hung with iron tubes, edge tools and ropes, 'but the most prominent and important part' was bedecked with 'coal-vases, baths, papier mâché-goods, and general hardware ... arranged in a very artistic design',[56] from the Old Hall and Loveridge factories – the two leading japan houses in the town.

200. Walton's Patent Crystal Tray, one from a graduated set of three, with a papier mâché rim, wooden base, and a painting inserted beneath glass; the trays are numbered '522 F864', '1576 F864', and 'F523 F864'; c.1850. 79.5 x 61cm
© WOLVERHAMPTON ARTS AND HERITAGE (BANTOCK HOUSE MUSEUM)

201. Engraved paper label on the base of a Patent Crystal Tray (see above).
© WOLVERHAMPTON ARTS AND HERITAGE (BANTOCK HOUSE MUSEUM)

Clearly then, Walton & Co. were still a dominant force in the town in 1866, yet after showing in Paris in 1855, they did not take part in any further international exhibitions. They were not even represented at the South Staffordshire Industrial and Fine Art Exhibition held in Wolverhampton in 1869. It is difficult to establish why, particularly since the Old Hall was described that year as 'the most interesting, if not the most extensive manufactory'[57] in the town. Maybe Walton & Co.

withdrew from the market as their local rivals, Henry Loveridge & Co.(*qv*), gained ground. Or, possibly, they were responding to the effects of electro-plating which, since the 1850s, had seriously reduced demand for the better class of japanned tin and papier mâché goods. It could also have been because Mr Walton had died in 1861, aged 75. Whatever the reason, they were noticeable by their absence from all major exhibitions after 1855.

The Old Hall Works closed in 1882: 'At present there is but a small demand for fine work and but few good men work at it',[58] said one of their former employees. High quality papier mâché had long gone out of fashion, and japanned tinware was being replaced by more up-to-date materials. On 24 January, 1883, an advertisement in the Wolverhampton Chronicle announced the four-day sale of finished and unfinished stock to be held on the premises; it gives a clear idea of the nature of their trade at the time (plate 203). On 6 February, the first day of the sale, it was reported that satisfactory prices were realised. The building was demolished in the same year.

MANDER BROTHERS
1792–1840
John Street, Wolverhampton

In 1792, Benjamin Mander (1752–1819), baker and maltster, in partnership with Thomas Shepherd, established a japan shop in John Street, Wolverhampton. Trading as Mander & Shepherd, they quickly advertised for 'Tin-plate workers and Japanners in general.'[1] Their premises were adjacent to those of Mander's brother John who, as a chemist, druggist, and varnish maker was able to supply them with varnish and other materials at cost price: in 1794 for example, they 'Payd Mr Mander ... for Paint, Oil, Turpentine, etc., etc., £2 8s 6d.'[2]

Records of Mander & Shepherd's early wares – which included trays, firescreens, wine coolers, clock cases and ornamental cupboards – suggest that they were japanners of some significance, but little is otherwise known about their products. The only example known to have survived to the present day is a fine rectangular papier mâché tray with canted corners and a deep border of chinoiserie figures in a landscape. It was illustrated in The Connoisseur in 1967, but its present whereabouts are sadly unknown[3] (plate 202).

When Shepherd left the partnership in 1799, Benjamin Mander's sons, Charles (1780–1853) and Benjamin (1785–1835), who had worked briefly as japanners and tin-plate workers, became more involved in their father's firm. By 1803, Charles was making and supplying varnish to other japanners, including Obadiah & William Ryton at the Old Hall (*qv*), and it was the varnish-making branch of the trade which he and his brother would ultimately pursue in favour of japanning (plate 204).

It is not clear precisely when Benjamin took his eldest son Charles into partnership, but in 1811, and as Benjamin Mander & Son, the firm supplied a papier mâché waiter and other japanned wares to Chamberlains china manufactory in Worcester for sale alongside their fashionable tea and other wares. This alone would be sufficient indication of the quality of Manders's papier mâché goods, but further evidence is found in a letter sent them in 1815, which shows that export was a possibility:

> *Mr. J. Shore called yesterday; he admires the wine coolers very much, also the plate warmer, which he thought very elegant and quite suitable for the American market ... He says his friend (an American) will want some trays for the Spring trade, and hopes he will be able to do something with us.*[4]

Like so many japan masters, Benjamin Mander was a staunch non-Conformist. Although it was not common practice in the trade, he fined any worker who did not join him in prayers before work and he ensured that each working day ended with hymns. However, as his business increased, the habit was quietly dropped. On his death in 1819, the factory was inherited by his son Charles; though he continued to be listed in a local directory as a japanner and tin-plate worker, his main focus was varnish making. To this end, he made his chief manager and invoice-clerk, William Wiley, a partner in 1835, and gave him responsibility for the japanning department on the understanding that the firm should decorate paper trays made only in their workshops. This allowed Mander not only to focus on varnish-making, but 'to barter with the paper tray makers and others varnish for paper trays and other things as he has heretofore been accustomed to do.'[5] It proved an unworkable arrangement, largely because of Wiley's dishonesty, and the partnership was dissolved two years

202. Straight-edge papier mâché tray with chinoiserie decoration in variously coloured gold powders; the only known tray marked for Benjamin Mander & Son, c.1790s; 76 x 56cm. From Godden, G., 'English Paper Trays' (*Connoisseur*, August, 1967, p. 251).
REPRODUCED BY KIND PERMISSION OF GEOFFREY GODDEN

THE OLD HALL TIN AND JAPAN WORKS,
WOLVERHAMPTON,
IMPORTANT TO JAPANNERS, TIN-PLATE WORKERS,
IRONMONGERS,
GENERAL DEALERS, AND OTHERS.
SALE OF THE VALUABLE FINISHED STOCK, &c.

MESSRS. SOLLOM and BARNETT are instructed to continue the SALE by AUCTION, at the OLD HALL, WOLVERHAMPTON, on TUESDAY, WEDNESDAY, THURSDAY, and FRIDAY, February 6, 7, 8, and 9, and on TUESDAY, February 13, 1883, when they will SELL, absolutely without reserve, the valuable and extensive STOCK of FINISHED PAPIER MACHIE, IRON, TIN, JAPANNED, BRASS, ENAMELLED, and other GOODS, and the remainder of the UNFINISHED STOCK.

On the FIRST FOUR DAYS the Sale will consist almost entirely of FINISHED GOODS, in great variety, including coffee and tea pots, fish and asparagus kettles, beer, canton, and fancy jugs, cake tins. chop covers, drip pans, cheese toasters, moulds, cash, letter, jewel, and housemaids' boxes, Scarborough and other trunks, sitz, sponging, and other baths ;

VALUABLE PAPIER MACHIE GOODS.

comprising trays in sets, waiters, inkstands, &c., japanned toilet sets, ale cans, iron and tin saucepans, stewpans, nursery lamps ; ship, railway, police, and other lanterns ; letter boxes and racks, candlesticks, sugar and spice boxes, bacon broilers, tinned bowls, coal vases ; a quantity of

ENAMELLED IRON GOODS,

including dishes, plates, basins, bowls, spittoons, saucepans, &c. ; a quantity of BRASS, COPPER, and NICKEL GOODS. railway and other footwarmers, pudding, melon, and other moulds, &c., &c. The Sale on

TUESDAY, FEBRUARY 13,

will include principally unfinished goods, fittings, patterns, contents of colour paper and lithographing rooms, &c., comprising a very large quantity of papier machie, pasted pulp and japanned goods, wood and japanned coal vases, tea caddies, inkstands, knife, bread, and crumb trays ; crystal waiters. large lot of coal vase glasses, coal vase bodies, linings, handles, and feet ; a valuable lot Japanese-painted wood lids, candlesticks, knobs, locks, a very large quantity of patterns for coal vase lids, candlesticks, caddies, &c. ; a quantity of varnishes and colours, lithographic press, with stones, plates, &c. ; 25 cwt. various paper, 50 japanned and wood traveller's boxes, &c., &c.

Sale Each Day at Eleven.

Catalogues (gratis) upon application to the AUCTIONEERS, 89, Darlington-street, Wolverhampton.

N.B.—The Sale will be strictly unreserved, and arrangements for viewing the bulk may be made.

203. Notice of the four-day sale of the stock-in-trade of Walton & Co., *Wolverhampton Chronicle*, 24 January, 1883 (p. 8, c.1).

FROM THE COLLECTIONS OF WOLVERHAMPTON ARCHIVES & LOCAL STUDIES

204. An advertisement for Charles Mander from Bridgen's *Directory of Wolverhampton*, 1838.

FROM THE COLLECTIONS OF WOLVERHAMPTON ARCHIVES & LOCAL STUDIES

later. By 1838, Wiley, together with Mander's chief decorator, Hancher, had set up in business on their own account as japanners, tin-plate workers and varnish makers, but it was a short-lived venture and lasted little over five years.

Notwithstanding the departure of Hancher, Mander submitted two papier mâché vases to an exhibition of local manufactures held in Wolverhampton in 1839, where a prize of one guinea was offered for 'the best piece of Japan Ware, the ornamental part being an original design'.[6] The vases – one claret, the other green – both over two feet high, and decorated by Mr Stockwin (another of Mander's artists), came second to an entry from Edward Perry, a rival Wolverhampton japanner (*qv*).

Despite his obvious abilities as a japanner, it had long been

Mander's plan to close that branch of his business if varnish-making went well. Accordingly, in 1840, he sold his japanning interests to William Shoolbred (*qv*). Some of Mander's workers were retained by Shoolbred, among them Jemima Cox, who in 1871, at the end of her working life, wrote a vivid account[7] of her association with the japanning industry, first in the employ of Mander and then at the Merridale Works. As suppliers of varnish to many leading japanners, however, the Mander firm retained close links with the industry. Among japanners named in their 'Varnish Carriage Book',[8] for example, are the Birmingham firms of Jennens & Bettridge, Thomas Lane, Woodward & Midgley, Alsager & Neville, and McCullum & Hodson, and in Wolverhampton, the Merridale Works, and Henry Fearncombe (*qv*), while in Bilston, they supplied Gerard Barber (*qv*).

205. Papier mâché tray with a deep sandwich-edge with early bronze decoration; made by Thomas Illidge, 1810–1820; 41 x 56cm. From Godden, G., 'English Paper Trays' (*Connoisseur*, August, 1967, p. 251).

206. The floor of a straight-edge papier mâché tea-board with raised work decoration; impressed 'ILLIDGE … ANTED' (probably Warranted); 1810-20. 57 x 77cm

THOMAS ILLIDGE
fl. c.1810–1820
St James' Square, Wolverhampton

Some of the finest decoration on papier mâché is found on articles impressed with the name 'ILLIDGE', or sometimes 'ILLIDGE WARRANTED'. These were the marks of Thomas Illidge (1771–1824) of Wolverhampton – a short-lived concern about which surprisingly little is known.

At the time, Illidge's japanned ware was sufficiently regarded for Chamberlain's of Worcester to place orders for papier mâché in 1811 and 1813. Detailed entries in Chamberlain's order book of 1813 show that in both styles of decoration and wholesale prices, Illidge was a maker of considerable significance:

As Flint Ink, the firm of Manders Ltd. continues to the present day manufacturing paints, printing inks and varnishes.

NB. Nicholas Mander, in *Varnished Leaves* (2004, p. 19), cites several japanned objects which were included in a family probate inventory in 1930. While some are tentatively linked to Mander Brothers, they are mostly unidentified; in view of their provenance, however, it is worth listing them here as they may be indicative of Mander's general range of goods:
- Mahogany pole fire screen with square base and papier mâché oblong banner with Nubian figures in coloured lacquer, decribed as a 'Mander heirloom'
- Six landscape plaques (possibly painted by Benjamin Mander)
- Oval plaques of 'Lord Nelson', 'two children and a dog', 'a girl with a basket';
- water cans, snuffer stands
- Also in current Mander ownership is a 'music stand with bulbous support c.1840' and various items of late Georgian japan work.

One 30 inch paper tray, rich double border, flowers etc,			42/43		£2/16/-
24 inch	..	..		42/43	£1/18/-
30 inch	..	..	..	ruins	£2/16/-
24 inch	..	..	..		£1/18/-
32 inch	..	India (Japan pattern) border No.70			£2/10/-
24 inch	..	..	..	..	£1/15/-
32 inch	..	Medallion border No. 84/85			£3/-/-
24 inch	..	..	..		£2/-/-
30 inch	..	Dead game all over			£3/16/-
30 inch	..	Single border, landscape centre 86/7			£3/5/-
24 inch	..	..	..		£2/-/-[1]

Moreover, he clearly had an eye to export. In 1812 for example, he (and other prominent Wolverhampton manufacturers) undersigned an announcement in the *Wolverhampton Chronicle* urging the discontinuation of the East India Company's monopolies and promoting British trade with the East.[2]

Illidge was last listed, as a japanner and tin-plate worker, in a local directory covering the years 1818–1820. Marked examples of his products are rarely found, but their quality may be judged from those illustrated here (plates 205–7).

EVANS & CARTWRIGHT
c.1810–c.1870s/1880s
Whistle Hall, Dudley Road, Wolverhampton

John Evans, who began business in the first decade of the nineteenth century, was listed in a Wolverhampton directory of 1816, as a japanner and 'children's toymaker'.[1] By then, his 14-year-old stepson, Sidney Cartwright (1801–1883) was working as a traveller for the firm, and by 1827, at the latest, he had joined him in partnership.

Described in Langford's *History of Staffordshire & Warwickshire* as 'probably the largest toy factory in the kingdom, where are made whistles, popguns and a thousand and one painted gimcracks',[2] their manufactures mostly fell outside the mainstream japanning industry of Wolverhampton. Nevertheless, a very rare snuff box, marked for Evans & Cartwright, shows the type of boxes they made, and serves as a reminder that many similar surviving boxes may also have been made at Whistle Hall (plate 208).

207. Straight-edge papier mâché counters-trays, with bronze decoration; the largest tray is impressed 'ILLIDGE', 1810–1820. 13 x 9.5cm and 10 x 7.7cm

PRIVATE COLLECTION

208. Tin snuff box with hinged lid, decorated in imitation of tortoiseshell and mounted with a cat motif in white metal, the inside lid stamped with the rare mark 'EVANS & CARTWRIGHT'; c.1830. 6.5cm

PRIVATE COLLECTION

209. Japanned tin wash-stand for a dolls-house, impressed with the mark of Evans & Cartwright, c.1840. 11 x 11cm
PRIVATE COLLECTION

Since the recent discovery by a collector of japanned dolls' house furniture marked for Evans & Cartwright, many such miniature toys, previously thought to have been made in France and Germany, can now be reliably attributed to this firm (plate 209). It is for this furniture that Evans & Cartwright are now best known. Large quantities were exported to America and elsewhere, and every conceivable article of domestic furniture was made in miniature, as Charles Dickens evocatively showed in his story *The Christmas Tree*:

> There were rosy-cheeked dolls, hiding behind the green leaves; there were real watches (with movable hands, at least, and an endless capacity of being wound up) dangling from innumerable twigs; there were French-polished[x] tables, chairs, bedsteads, wardrobes, eight-day clocks, and various other articles of domestic furniture (wonderfully made, in tin, at Wolverhampton).[3]

JAMES PEDLEY
fl. early nineteenth century
Wolverhampton

Between 1813 and 1816, James Pedley supplied papier mâché goods to Chamberlain's of Worcester:

May 31st, 1813	one paper tray, pheasants etc.	£5. 5. 0
Sept. 29th, 1813	one pair paper trays, shells etc.	£7. 7. 0
June 16th, 1816	one large paper tray & waiter, Roman bridge & Ruins	£6. 6. 0[1]

Pedley does not appear in local records as a japanner, but described himself as such when he offered to sell his business to Matthew Boulton in 1814 – a situation necessitated, he said, by 'pecuniary motives'.[2] Thus, Pedley's involvement with japanning may have been very shortlived which could explain the fact that he was not listed in local directories.

He explained to Boulton that his 'first commencement in business was in the regular Japan line', but that he had since 'introduced the manufactory of Chinese Screens – to great size and magnificence',[3] and also cabinets fitted with drawers of various sizes. To judge from the costs and descriptions of the papier mâché trays he had supplied to Chamberlain's, Pedley's boast to Boulton that he had 'the patronage of Lord Holland and many of the Nobility',[4] was probably well-founded. Nevertheless, since he was still trading with Chamberlain's, in 1816, it appears that Boulton did not take up his offer.

The subject matter of the trays described above sound much like those found on trays stamped for another Wolverhampton japanner, Thomas Illidge & Co. (*qv*), a firm which also supplied Chamberlain's. It is therefore possible, though purely speculative, that Pedley had worked or trained with Illidge. Either way, he was one of the earliest papier mâché manufacturers in Wolverhampton

HENRY FEARNCOMBE & Co.
c.1827–c.1902
Phoenix Works, Dudley Road, Wolverhampton

Originally from Taunton in Somerset, Henry Fearncombe (1791–1856) had worked as a journeyman tinman at the Old Hall before establishing his own workshop in about 1827. W.H. Jones described him as a 'first class workman ... known as a keen buyer and an active pushing commercial man ... in the front rank.'[1] Like many other businessmen in the town, he was a Congregationalist and a subscriber to Snow Hill Church.

Fearncombe was first listed as a japanner and tinplate-worker at Walsall Street, Wolverhampton in 1827, but by 1833 he had taken over the japan factory of J. Langston in Dudley Road where he remained for the rest of his working life. An advertisement of that year shows the wide range of utilitarian and decorative tinware that he produced, and the relatively small range of papier mâché articles, namely bread baskets, knife trays, snuffer trays, and tea trays (plate 210) – goods which would not reappear in his advertisements for another

x. This is a reference to their being japanned in imitation of wood. Many articles were decorated with crystallised effects (see pp. 46-8)

210. Advertisement for Henry Fearncombe from Bridgen's *Directory of Wolverhampton*, 1833; it shows him to have produced mainly tinware, but includes also some paper trays.

are very elegantly designed, especially in their pedestals. The last represents a nautilus shell set on a piece of coral rock; the handle of the lid represents a sea-horse. The novelty and beauty of this design must challenge approbation; indeed, the entire set quite merits being devoted to a more honourable, though not more useful, purpose than that for which each is intended. They are designed and modelled by Mr. F. Wright. Wolverhampton has long been celebrated for its japanned iron ware: such works as these must tend to increase its reputation.

211. Iron coal boxes by Henry Fearncombe, from the *Art Journal Illustrated Catalogue of the Industries of all Nations*, 1851 (p. 110).
FROM THE COLLECTIONS OF WOLVERHAMPTON ARCHIVES & LOCAL STUDIES

twenty years or more (see below).[xi] He took part in the 1851 Exhibition, where his display focused on ironware as shown by the following selection: wash-stands decorated in imitation of mahogany or marble, a 'flat-top' coal vase painted with a hawking party, and another in the shape of a nautilus shell, and tea-trays both painted and with Elizabethan-style ornaments (plate 211).

The emphasis of Fearncombe's trade was always on utilitarian ironware, though in 1855, he added 'fine Papier Machie [sic]

and Fancy Pontipool [*sic*] goods' to his entry in a local directory.[2] According to Dickinson, papier mâché articles were not made in the Fearncombe workshops but purchased as blanks from McCallum & Hodson and other specialist suppliers.[3]

Fearncombe died in 1856, leaving his business, jointly, to Ann Dalton (a daughter by marriage) and his nephew, John Oaten, who was already in his employ. During the 1860s, the firm became Henry Fearncombe & Co., and a japanned iron 'curfew' bearing an oval brass plate stamped with this name, may be seen in plate 212; a tray, with a registration mark for 1880, is shown in plate 213. By 1884, the factory had become known as the 'Phoenix Works'. Fearncombe & Co. sold out to Orme Evans & Co. Ltd. (manufacturers of enamelled and japanned iron, brass and copper coal vases etc.) in about 1902.

RICHARD, GEORGE & EDWARD PERRY
fl. 1827–1890s (as japanners)

Richard Perry (b.1781)[xii] was first listed in 1827 as a japanner and tin-plate worker in Little Brickkiln Street, then on the outskirts of Wolverhampton.[1] By 1833 he had moved, more centrally, to Queen Street.[2] Although nothing is known of his early products, he and his sons were to become, for close on one hundred years, major producers of japanned tin and papier mâché goods in Wolverhampton. Richard's son Edward (b.1801) established a factory of his own, while his brother, George (b.1806) later joined their father in partnership. The two factories successfully ran in parallel until Edward's death in 1871, when they merged to become one company.

While it will never be possible to identify all that the various Perry firms made, it is clear that between them, they were responsible for the manufacture of huge quantities of nineteenth-century japanned tin and papier mâché articles. Moreover, some of these products, certainly in the early years, were decorated to a very high standard.

The Perry story is a tangled one and is best understood by considering each phase of its development in turn.

Edward Perry, b.1801
Having spent 'his youth and early manhood'[3] at the Old Hall Japan Works as a japanner and tinman, Edward Perry had presumably served his apprenticeship there and was, therefore, accustomed to work of a very high standard. When starting his own workshop in Queen Street in about 1827, he laid the foundations of what became one of the largest japanning and tinplate-working concerns in Wolverhampton.

By 1833, Edward had moved his business to Temple Street (not far from the Old Hall), and expanded his trade to include pasteboard-making. It was obviously a flourishing concern, to

212. Iron curfew, with a curved reverse-glass painting; marked on the back with a brass label stamped H. Fearncombe & Co., c.1850. 57 x 58cm

COURTESY OF MELLORS & KIRK, NOTTINGHAM

judge from a notice in *The Times*, in 1836, advertising the lease of two substantial factories – one to accommodate two-hundred workers, and the other a workforce of eighty – which were 'lately occupied by Edward Perry'.[4] By 1838, he had moved to Paul Street where, besides japanning and tinplate-working, he announced himself a 'Manufacturer of Fine Paper Goods, Fancy Pontipool Work &c',[5] a description which suggests he was producing highly decorative japanned goods.

Known as the 'Jeddo Works',[xiii] Edward's factory appears to have been the most prestigious of the Perry concerns. There can be little doubt that at least some of his papier mâché ranked among the best of its day since, in 1839, he won first prize of one guinea at a Wolverhampton exhibition of local manufactures. Perry had submitted a table painted 'with a bouquet of flowers surrounded by landscapes',[6] by one of his employees, Richard Stubbs, a gifted decorator who later became a master painter at the Loveridge factory (*qv*).

A trade catalogue issued by Edward Perry in 1849 contained 180 lithographed pages of common and japanned tin and papier mâché. Trays, baths, coal vases, scoops and purdoniums were all illustrated, as were lamps, boxes of every

description, trunks, and many other everyday objects too numerous to mention. Besides these, he also produced a huge range of copper jelly moulds. The size and range of the catalogue shows the Jeddo Works to have been a serious rival to both the Old Hall and Merridale Works.

'A tall, thin, wiry man, with restless fidgety habits',[7] Perry was endowed with common-sense and a steely determination – strengths upon which he needed to draw during the Great Strike of tinplate workers in 1851. The strike was caused by the issue, in 1850, of a standard book of prices which listed the amount each tinplate worker should receive for the various objects he made. Edward Perry, along with other Wolverhampton factory owners, refused to accept its recommendations, instead entering into two-year contracts with those of his workers who were willing.[xiv] A man called Preston incited his fellow-workers to resist Perry's scheme, and was instantly dismissed – an action which prompted an ultimatum from the Trade Association: reinstate him or a strike would be called. Perry stood his ground. The Jeddo Works were picketed, and abuse – sometimes even dead vermin – was hurled at the 'rats'[8] who crossed the picket line.

Some of Perry's men who had found employment at the Old Hall were induced to return to the Jeddo Works by the offer of good wages and a £5 bonus, but this only served to enrage their Old Hall colleagues who were contributing to the strike fund. Others of Perry's men were moved or 'spirited away' by the unionists to Scotland, Ireland and remote villages in England, and Perry responded by importing workers, first

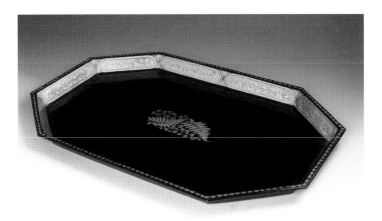

213. Straight-edge tin tray, impressed 'H.F. & Co.' for Henry Fearncombe & Co., and printed with a diamond registration mark for 6 November, 1880. 22 x 38.5cm

COURTESY OF WOOLLEY & WALLIS, SALISBURY

---

xi. Fearncombe's occupation in the 1841 Census is given as 'japanner 200'; it is possible this figure represents the size of his workforce.

xii. There may have been a link with an early nineteenth century Bilston japanner, James Perry, and with the Perry family of enamellers of the same town, but such connections are difficult to establish because of the number of Perry families living in and around Wolverhampton at the time.

xiii. Whether the name 'Jeddo' derives from 'Edo' – the old name for Tokyo – is pure speculation, it could equally be a play on 'Edward'.

xiv. Frederick Walton and Loveridge both accepted the prices.

The three COAL-VASES, or, as such articles of domestic use are generally called, coal-skuttles, are from the establishment of Mr. PERRY, of Wolverhampton, who has, with much good taste, endeavoured to give a character of elegance to these ordinary but necessary appendages to our

"household hearths." Hitherto, in whatever room of a dwelling-house one happens to enter, the coal-scuttle is invariably thrust into some obscure corner, as unworthy of filling a place

among the furniture of the apartment, and this not because it is seldom in requisition, but on account of its unsightliness. Mr. Perry's artistic-looking designs, though manufactured only in japanned iron, may, however, have the effect of drawing them from their obscurity, and assigning them an honourable post, even in the drawing-room. It is upon such comparatively trivial matters

that art has the power to confer dignity; and, notwithstanding the absurdity—as we have sometimes heard it remarked—of adopting Greek and Roman models in things of little importance, they acquire value from the very circumstance of such pure models having been followed.

from France and then from Germany. This allowed him to complete outstanding orders, but otherwise the employment of unsuspecting foreigners had little long-term benefit as they were deeply unhappy on every level.

Throughout the agitation, Perry compiled sufficient evidence to take the conspirators to court. Arguing that he only appeared to pay less than the recommended rate, he produced in his defence:

> *Two tin colanders; one was made by hand in the old fashioned method...* [using] *seven pieces of tin, raised, punched, and jointed together by the tinman; for this article 12s. per dozen was the book price paid.* [The other colander] *was made by machinery in one piece, the tinman had only to fix the handles, for which he was paid 1s. per dozen.*[9]

Thus, Perry concluded, his men could earn more by the second method than the first, and having installed lathes, stamps, presses and other modern machinery to make this possible, the old prices were not applicable.

Dragging on for eighteen months, the strike coincided with the period leading up to the Great Exhibition – a factor which made Perry's impressive display at that exhibition all the more remarkable (see p. 109). In addition to common tin articles, it included a multitude of japanned tin goods showing him to have been a japanner of some importance (plates 214 & 215). He exhibited again in London, in 1862, where his goods received mixed reviews: an Honorable Mention from the Jury, for the excellence of his design and manufacture, and sleighting criticism from George Wallis, for both over-decoration and a frequently poor standard of draughtsmanship.

Edward Perry died suddenly in 1871 and his trade transferred first to his nephews, Messrs Lees, and then to Richard Perry & Sons which, by then, was styled Richard Perry, Son & Co. (see below).

Richard Perry & Son

By 1838, Richard Perry (b.1781) had taken his son George (b.1806) into partnership and moved to the Temple Street Works, probably the same buildings as those recently vacated by his other son, Edward. They traded as Richard Perry & Son, describing themselves first as 'wholesale manufacturers of block tin and japan wares',[10] and then, in 1847, as 'japanners, iron and tin-plate workers'.[11]

214. Iron coal vases by Edward Perry, from the *Art Journal Illustrated Catalogue of the Industries of all Nations*, 1851 (p. 32).
REPRODUCED WITH THE PERMISSION OF BIRMINGHAM LIBRARIES & ARCHIVES

They exhibited at the 1851 Exhibition, where they focused on a range of domestic, common tin goods that was standard for all but the smallest japan workshops: dish covers, baking dishes, stomach warmers, and other similarly utilitarian articles. Nevertheless, as japanners, it is likely that their display also included at least a few decorative wares. It is not apparent from the exhibition catalogue which of their exhibits were japanned, but by their very nature, it was probably the following: 'inkstands, [an] almanack case; knife, spoon and cheese trays; card racks; date cases; spice boxes; toast racks, tea caddies; bread and cake baskets; [an] envelope and paper box; tea-trays &c.'[12] To judge from an advertisement four years later, they were certainly making highly decorative articles, for in addition to iron and tin-plate goods, they were described as makers of 'fine Papier Machie [*sic*] and Fancy Pontipool goods.'[13]

As with many factories, it is now difficult to identify the products of the Temple Street Works, but it is highly probable that many of the japanned tin goods surviving from this period, would have been made by R. Perry & Son.

Richard Perry, Son and Co.

The change in the firm's name had taken place by 1869 when, as Richard Perry, Son & Co., it exhibited at the South Staffordshire Fine Art and Industrial Exhibition. Although they showed the usual tin and iron wares, 'decorated articles prevailed'; these included 'iron and papier mâché tea-trays and waiters, breakfast trays, flower vases, cash and deed boxes, tea caddies, inkstands and card stands, toilet ware, dish covers etc.'[14] Their products were praised for being 'generally well designed', with well-drawn decoration and 'tasteful' gilding.[15] A pair of japanned shop-display vases in the collection of Wolverhampton Arts and Museums is unusual for showing the stamped mark of this factory – a Staffordshire knot incorporating the name of Perry, Son & Co.

In 1871, the firm absorbed Edward Perry's Jeddo Works. New lines continued to be added to existing ones, and by 1891, their output had expanded to include brass and copper articles, and wooden equivalents of rectangular japanned metal coal vases. The Temple Street factory at that time had a frontage of 260 feet, was three storeys high and was equipped with the latest machinery. 'Upwards of 200 hands' were employed in its general tin and japan departments, and by retaining well known 'art designers',[xv] theirs was said to have been a factory 'as well known as any in the trade'.[16] The Jeddo Works were sold to the Bilston japanner, John Marston,[xvi] a former apprentice of Edward Perry.

Richard Perry, Son & Co. ceased japanning in the 1890s.

215. Iron coal vase, similar to one shown by Edward Perry, at the Great Exhibition (see pl. 214), c.1850. 76 x 52.5cm
COURTESY OF WOOLLEY & WALLIS, SALISBURY

HENRY LOVERIDGE & CO.
1840–1927

The Wolverhampton firm of Henry Loveridge & Co. is today one of the better-known among collectors of papier mâché and tin-ware. It had its roots in the factory set up by William Shoolbred, in about 1840 or 1841.

As a young man, Shoolbred (1796–1882) moved from Scotland to Wolverhampton to join his brother, a woollen-draper, tailor and hatter. This trade held little attraction for the ambitious Shoolbred and he soon secured employment with the japanner, Edward Perry, (*qv*) where he was quickly joined by his son, also called William, who was keen to learn the trade. They stayed with Perry until 1840, when the elder Shoolbred purchased the japan department of Charles Mander (*qv*) and set up as a japanner in his own right. The japan trade was bouyant, so with his business acumen and his son's practical skills, Shoolbred had a most propitious start.

---

xv. The Perry firm commissioned Christopher Dresser to design a range of brass and copper ware; he was not employed full-time as this would imply.

xvi. Better-known today as the maker of Sunbeam Bicycles.

He engaged Henry Loveridge (c.1811–1892) as a commercial traveller – a jovial man whose tact and persuasiveness were such assetts to the reserved Shoolbred, that he took him into partnership. A footbath made by 'Shoolbred & Loveridge', as they styled themselves, is shown in plate 216.

A condition of Mander's sale was that the japan department be moved from his premises in John Street. Accordingly, Shoolbred & Loveridge secured land in Merridale Street on the outskirts of the town, where, 'surrounded on all sides by fields and gardens',[1] work commenced on a large new factory. The site was so rich in clay that 'several brick kilns were put up and plenty of good cheap bricks helped them along'.[2] With an anxiety that was characteristic, Shoolbred appeared every morning at six o'clock to check its progress.

However, Shoolbred and Loveridge soon found that it was not the best time to have commenced business. The beginning of the depression of the mid-1840s brought about a sharp downturn in trade and in 1847, forced even a long-established firm like B. Walton & Co., to close, albeit temporarily (see p. 189). To some extent, however, Walton's misfortune worked to the advantage of Shoolbred & Loveridge who, besides taking on some of his best workmen, enjoyed a brief period without competition from the Old Hall. To judge from material that their successors, Henry Loveridge & Co., passed to Wolverhampton Arts and Museums many years later, Walton's alleged bankruptcy also enabled them to acquire some, if not all, of Walton's pattern books at the sale of his stock-in-trade. The acquisition of these books would explain why a tray, marked for Henry Loveridge & Co., which

appeared some years ago in a London sale-room was painted with a still-life similar to one shown in a Walton pattern book (see plate 283 for an unmarked yet identical tray).

Shoolbred's son was made a partner in 1847 and under the name of Shoolbred, Loveridge & Shoolbred, they advertised as 'Manufacturers of Paper and Japan Tea Trays, General Japanners, Iron and Tinplate Workers.'[3] The following year, the firm moved into its new premises, 'The Merridale Works'. Equipped with the most modern and efficient machines, and under various partnerships, the works became one of the leading japanning and tinplate-working factories in the Midlands. As contemporary accounts vary so much, it is difficult to judge the size of the labour force at the Merridale Works,[xvii] but at its peak in the 1850s and 1860s, it appears to have been on a par with both its main rivals in Wolverhampton: the Walton and Perry factories (*qv*).

The move to the Merridale Works was marked by the publication of a catalogue in 1848, which included a bird's eye view of the large new factory (*cf.* plate 88) together with two-hundred and twenty-five engravings of their products which ranged from the utilitarian to the luxurious. According to its introduction:

a leading feature in their business is the manufacture of Paper and Japanned Tea Trays, Bread Baskets, Snuffer Trays, Round Waiters, Coal Vases, Albert Coal Scoops etc., in all their varieties... The trays varying in style and quality from 4s.6d [22.5p] per set of three, japanned, to 100s. [£5.00] each, the thirty inch papier mâché.[4]

Somewhat surprisingly at this late date, it also featured a range of bottle stands of various shapes including gothic, fluted and straight.[xviii] But by far the greater part of this catalogue, and of two later and enlarged editions of 1855 and 1869 (see below), was devoted to utilitarian japanned and common tin goods reflecting the general balance of their output. Their display at the Birmingham Exposition of 1849 had a similar emphasis and included a range of japanned shower baths, sponge baths and other toilet ware, as well as coal vases and scoops which, although well-made were not judged 'by any means equally well-painted'.[5]

This problem had to be addressed if they were to succeed in this competetive market and there is little doubt that they looked to poach skilled decorators from rival firms. Two leading artists who are known to have moved to the Merridale Works from

216. Iron footbath with transfer-printed decoration; marked for Shoolbred & Loveridge, c.1845. L: 46cm (approx.)
COURTESY OF WILKINSON'S, DONCASTER

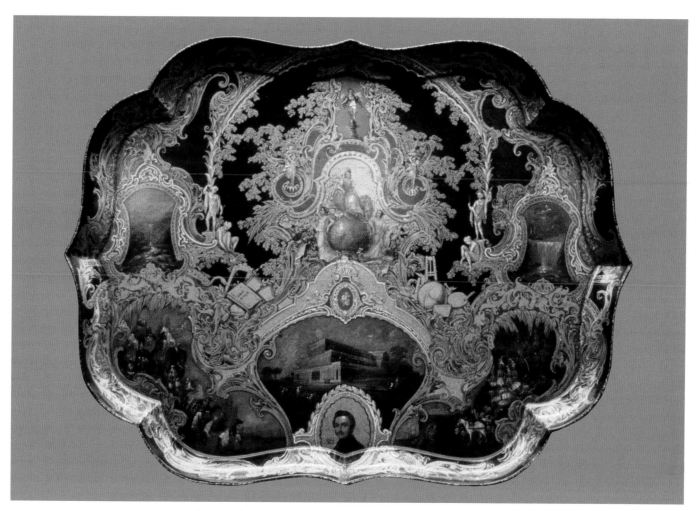

217. Concave king-gothic papier mâché tray, made by Shoolbred, Loveridge &
Shoolbred for display at the Great Exhibition, 1851. 78.5 x 60.5cm

the Old Hall were Newman, whose 'damned peacocks' had so irritated Mr Walton, and George Sadler, a highly skilled filetter (p. 232). This movement of workmen between the two firms continued until the closure of Walton's in 1882 and is likely to have been more frequent than can now be proved.

In the run-up to the 1851 Exhibition, the Merridale Works received a delegation from the National Trades Association to investigate unrest among Wolverhampton tin-plate workers about their rates of pay for piecework. But Shoolbred, Loveridge & Shoolbred, like Walton at the Old Hall, agreed to pay according to the book of standard prices and so avoided the long-running strike which had such devastating effect at Perry & Co. They were thus able to focus on preparations for the exhibition and won a prize medal for a range of japanned iron goods similar to those they had shown in Birmingham:

Papier Mâché trays in various styles. Coal-vase, and scoops. Shower bath, Windsor hip-bath. Sponge-bath with various ornaments and improvements. Nursery hand-shower bath... Sets of toilet ware. Wine cooler. Dish covers. Teapots, coffee pots, and tea-kettles. Cash, deed and writing boxes. Date Dials for libraries, counting houses etc.[6]

Amongst the papier mâché exhibits was a gothic-shaped tray bearing the mark of the Shoolbred, Loveridge & Shoolbred partnership (plate 217). Richly decorated in gold leaf, the tray is painted in commemoration of the Great Exhibition with a portrait of Prince Albert beneath a view of Paxton's 'crystal palace' and views from the Empire, an allusion to the event's status as an 'exhibition of all nations'.

As a demonsration of technical skill, the tray cannot be faulted, however, it also exemplifies the excessive ornament that many manufacturers believed was necessary to impress the public, and which elicited much criticism from contemporary critics.

xvii. In the 1850s and 1860s, they were said to have employed 250 workers – a figure which brought it in line with both the Walton and Perry (qv) factories, although it is stated elsewhere that between 1850 and 1870, they employed sixty japanners and a hundred tinsmiths, while in 1869 it was alleged that their workforce was larger than

Walton's and that 400-500 hundred men were employed.
xviii. Gothic, here, would refer to the flange of the bottle-stand; fluted refers to horizontal flute-moulding; and straight describes conventionally shaped stands like those seen in plate 287.

218. Iron coal vase, by Loveridge & Co., decorated with a portrait of William Shakespeare after the statue in Westminster Abbey, from the *Art Journal Illustrated Catalogue of the International Exhibition*, 1862 (p. 262).

220. Octagon tray, with a border influenced by contemporary silver patterns, on a pink ground described as 'carminette' by its maker Henry Loveridge & Co.; c.1870 (*cf*. pl. 19). 30 x 40cm

Although continuing to advertise as makers of papier mâché it was, again, japanned tinware that Shoolbred, Loveridge & Shoolbred took to both the New York Exhibition in 1853, and the Paris Exhibition of 1855. That same year, the senior partner, William Shoolbred, a man 'much respected for his integrity and kindliness',[7] retired through ill health, and the firm continued as Loveridge & Shoolbred. Following the death of the younger Shoolbred, some time after 1860, Loveridge became sole proprietor. It is not clear precisely when the firm became known as Henry Loveridge & Co., but it was under this name that it showed at the next major international exhibition in London in 1862, where, once again, they focused on practical and useful goods.

Henry Loveridge fully understood the importance of drawing and design to his manufactures and was, by then, chairman of Wolverhampton School of Practical Art. A coal vase made from japanned iron by Loveridge & Co. and decorated with a portrait of William Shakespeare, was chosen by the *Art Journal* to illustrate their guide to the 1862 exhibition (plate 218), but it was the paper trays and other wares from this factory which were praised for their 'excellent design and manufacture'[8] and awarded the only medal in their class – a far remove from their position in 1849. He showed at the New Zealand Exhibition in 1865, and returned to Paris in 1867 where, again, he received the only silver medal awarded for papier mâché.

While papier mâché seems to have featured more significantly than hitherto, under Loveridge's proprietorship of the Merridale Works, japanned iron continued to account for the greater part of their business. This decision proved shrewd on two counts. First, although the decoration of some utilitarian articles may have been extraordinarily rich, they were less subject to fashion than papier mâché goods. Certainly, the writer of the following statement was of this opinion:

> *Since the decay of the fancy portion of the papier mâché business, the energies of the trade have been directed towards the development of the useful, especially in connection with coal vases of great variety of shape and decoration; baths and toilet requisites, grocer's canisters, show bowls, and numerous other articles of utility and ornament.*[9]

219. The Ruskin Persian Coal Scoop. Iron, printed in gold leaf and colour; stamped with a design registration mark for 1869, above the impressed mark 'H.L. & Co./RUSKIN', for Henry Loveridge & Co., exhibited in 1869 (see pl. 222). H: 46cm L: 50cm

Second, Loveridge had more-or-less carved a niche for himself in this market. No other Wolverhampton japanner was represented at the Paris exhibition by these or any other goods, and it was noted that the Birmingham trade was 'entirely unrepresented' in these 'important branches'.[10] It was not that

Iron toilet wares photographed in 1869, at the South Staffordshire Fine Art & Industrial Exhibition, Wolverhampton, and probably made by Henry Loveridge & Co. (*cf.* the Octagon tray, pl. 220).

Loveridge's were the only makers of such articles, for firms like Walton and Edward Perry also made them, but Loveridge appears to have specialised more than most in baths and other toilet wares – at least at the higher end of the market.

The position that Henry Loveridge & Co. held among the japanners of Wolverhampton may be measured by the fact that it was they, together with Walton & Co. at the Old Hall, who were invited to decorate the triumphal arch, dedicated to the town's japan trade, which was erected in 1866 for Queen Victoria's visit (see p. 195). It was also Colonel Henry Loveridge[xix] who, as President of Wolverhampton Chamber of Commerce, in the same year, wrote a chapter on 'Wolverhampton Trades' for Samuel Timmins' book *Birmingham & the Midland Hardware District.*

In spite of such recognition, it was a solitary coal vase, soberly decorated 'with a green diaper pattern, and gold lines', that was commended among Loveridge's contributions to the Paris

Exhibition in 1867. The same critic harshly denounced the remainder of their exhibits (notwithstanding the praise they received in the illustrated catalogue of the exhibition), for having disregarded the Government School of Art's guidelines against the realistic painting of objects in relief on flat surfaces; he reserved particular condemnation for 'the ornamentation of a hip-bath, painted on the bottom and sides with imitations of sea shells and corals, which, though pretty to look at, are suggestive of uncomfortable things to sit or stand upon.'[11]

Photographs of Henry Loveridge's stand at the South Staffordshire Exhibition held in Wolverhampton in 1869, show their so-called 'Octagon Range' which, besides toilet wares (plate 221), included trays such as the small papier mâché example shown in plate 220. Also displayed was 'The Ruskin Persian Scoop' (plate 219), presumably named after the critic John Ruskin, in an attempt to curry favour following his earlier disparaging remarks about the decoration of japanned ware.

---

xix. In 1860, Loveridge joined the newly formed and patriotic Volunteer Movement, hence his military title.

222. Japanned ware by Henry Loveridge & Co., photographed at the South Staffordshire Industrial & Fine Arts Exhibition, in Wolverhampton, in 1869.
FROM THE COLLECTIONS OF WOLVERHAMPTON ARCHIVES & LOCAL STUDIES

In the same year, Loveridge published his sixth catalogue. Like his earlier catalogues, it reminds us that articles all too frequently attributed to the Regency period could as easily have been made as late as 1869. Bottle stands and vegetable warmers, for example, were made, uninterruptedly and with few modifications, over many years and thus defy dating on grounds of shape alone, their construction and the quality of their japanned surface being of much greater importance to the equation.

A breakdown of the 508 illustrated pages in the 1869 catalogue shows not only the main thrust of Loveridge's output, but is also representative of the contemporary japan trade. In particular, it puts papier mâché production into perspective. Despite the many fine articles Loveridge made from this material, only a few pages of trays, bread baskets and knife boxes, as well as one showing a cast-iron table, available with either a tin or paper top, had any relevance to this branch of their trade. Thirty-six pages were devoted to various iron receptacles for coal, one-hundred and twenty-three pages to elborately shaped copper jelly-moulds, forty pages to pastry cutters, tart and patty tins, and several pages of handles and other fittings for kettles, dish covers and saucepans. The remainder of the catalogue covered all manner of everyday tinned iron goods ranging from small oil cans to large japanned travelling trunks.

Concurrent with these utilitarian articles, and notwithstanding the criticism levelled against their exhibits in 1867, H. Loveridge & Co. produced decorative japanned ware of a very high order. Examples of such work may be seen in a group of papier mâché and tin-ware which, although unmarked, is known to have been gilded by Edwin Stubbs and painted by his son, Richard Stubbs,[xx] master decorators at the Loveridge factory. Only rarely is it possible to reliably attribute decoration in this way. The trays and baskets which form the greater part of the collection date mostly from the 1860s and are variously painted with landscapes, flower groups, still-life subjects, and a copy of a Landseer painting, or they are simply embellished with formal gilt borders (plates 223 and 224). Their quality is such that, without their impeccable provenance, they would probably be attributd to a Birmingham maker. Unfortunately, however, they cannot be used as a guide to attribution. Not every Loveridge article decorated in these styles was the work of these men: the Stubbs' were master craftsmen and their work would have provided the originals from which less experienced decorators might copy.

223. Round gothic tin waiter painted by Richard Stubbs, and gilded in two shades of gold leaf by Edwin Stubbs, at Henry Loveridge & Co., c.1865. Dia: 27cm
© Wolverhampton Arts and Heritage (Bantock House Museum)

224. Convex-oval tin bread basket, gilded by Edwin Stubbs with two large, and two small floral 'principals', as these parts of the border were known; Henry Loveridge & Co., c.1865. 34 x 27cm
© Wolverhampton Arts and Heritage (Bantock House Museum)

Under Henry Loveridge & Co., the firm marked its goods more consistently than previously, but as the Stubbs' collection shows, their policy was still fairly erratic. Sometimes however, marks are there to be found, but are so submerged beneath layers of japan varnish that they are discernible only in certain lights. Two of the most commonly used marks were the

---

xx. There was no known link between Edwin and Richard Stubbs and the celebrated earlier equestrian painter George Stubbs.

impressed initials 'H.L. & Co.' found mostly on metal-ware, or an impressed monogram, with or without an encircling ribbon (plate 225). The latter is found mainly on small rectangular papier mâché trays, moulded in one piece and usually with rounded or canted corners, which Loveridge & Co. made in abundance during the 1860s and 1870s. Many of these trays were decorated with surfaces imitative of wood grain or semi-precious stones such as malachite (plate 226). Others, which were decorated with raised-work chinoiseries, Indian sprigged designs or restrained formal borders, are sometimes mistakenly believed to date from an earlier period (plate 58), but the satin-smooth finish of their varnish is distinctly different from that found on earlier examples. On some trays, the firm's monogram may be accompanied by the term 'Club Fine', the precise significance of which has still to be identified although it is likely to indicate a superior quality (p. 271).

In 1882, Henry Loveridge & Co registered the design of a new tray. Like the trays described above, it was rectangular with rounded corners, but its base was cut from a flat sheet of pasteboard and mounted in a plated metal gallery, often fitted with carrying handles. These trays were usually stamped or printed with a diamond Registration Mark and the description 'The Combination Tray' (plate 286).

Another rectangular tray produced by Loveridge in the 1860s and 1870s had a 'straight edge' (plate 73) similar to those found on tea-boards by Henry Clay and other early manufacturers. This can cause confusion when attemping to date them, but close inspection of their smooth japanned surfaces will soon distinguish them from the pitted or crazed textures of their earlier counterparts.

225. The monogram of Henry Loveridge & Co., one of several marks used by this firm; the cross was a tin-plate worker's mark used for calculating his weekly output and payment.
© WOLVERHAMPTON ARTS AND HERITAGE (BANTOCK HOUSE MUSEUM)

Besides the initials H.L. & Co., the method used to mark toilet ware and coal boxes often took the form of oval metal labels which were attached to the article either before or after it was japanned. Centrally stamped with a diamond registration mark, the legend 'H. LOVERIDGE & CO., WOLVERHAMPTON' runs round their edges. These labels can be so discreetly placed as to be easily overlooked, and since it is not always easy to upturn a heavy iron coal-box, it is advisable, first, to see if such a mark may be located by touch – an important precaution if the lid is inset with a vulnerable, decorated glass panel (plate 227).

By 1871, with 420 hands, the Loveridge factory was a major employer in Wolverhampton. The firm became a joint stock company in 1903 but continued as Henry Loveridge & Co., under the control of H.W. Wildman until 1917, when he was succeeded by H.F.W. Taylor. Although Samuel Loveridge continued to be involved with the firm after his retirement in 1908, he was by then little more than a figure-head. The firm continued to make good quality tin and paper wares until its closure in 1927; a tin crumb-tray and brush, and a round iron tray decorated with an applied print, both polished by Sarah Cadman, one of the last 'handers' employed at the Merridale Works, are typical of the japanned goods made in the closing years of the factory (plate 98). But the focus of Loveridge's trade had shifted to the manufacture of japanned articles like cash, deed and despatch boxes, brass and copper goods, and art metal work; it was they, for instance, who supplied a range of copper pans, hot-plates and other catering goods to the Savoy Hotel in London.

The fashion for japanned goods had passed and by then John Marston was employing all the best metal workers in the town for the manufacture of 'Sunbeam' bicycles – with their varnished frames and striped embellishments, they called for the skills of a japanner. According to one of the last men to be apprenticed at the factory, Loveridge's closure was due in part, to a refusal to mechanise and modernise – a sad end for a factory which, in its early years, had been renowned for its up-to-date methods. The Merridale Works was auctioned in 1927 and was finally demolished in 1973.

JONES BROTHERS
1854–c.1923/4
Ablow Street, Wolverhampton
(later **Jones Brothers & Co., The Graiseley Works, Ablow Street**)

This firm had the unique distinction of having its history written by its founder, William Highfield Jones (1829–1903), in two unpublished family histories which he compiled in 1899.[1] In describing the growth of his business from a small workshop into a medium sized factory, Jones gave flesh not only to his own highs and lows, and the various obstacles he encountered, but almost certainly, to the experiences of all japanners who, like himself, branched out on their own.

Jones, like his father Edward Jones (b.1799), had been apprenticed at the Old Hall. He was a talented artist whom Walton had entrusted to decorate articles for display at the Great Exhibition (plate 199), but despite this, he was unable to find work on completion of his apprenticeship. Trade was bad, his foreman said, but if he made some patterns to serve as traveller's samples, Jones could have any work that resulted. With orders enough for only three days work per week, Jones took additional employment making drawings of a cabinet-maker's designs, and was willing, if necessary, to undertake house-painting.

He continued in this unsettled way until 1853 when an old japan factory, occupied for fifty years by a maker of tin toys, became available in Cleveland Street. With a little equity from the sale of five cottages in which Jones had invested, and a few other savings, he leased the workshop at an annual rent of £20, and for a further £20, purchased the japan stove and some work-benches. After painting 'W. JONES Japanner' in white letters on the front gates, he was ready to commence business.

Undeterred by a note from Walton about it being an inauspicious time to start such a business, Jones rolled up his sleeves and pre-pared the run-down factory for work. 'To do menial work went against my notions',[2] he wrote. 'I had been a superior kind of Japanner, who had never been called upon to soil my fingers with rough work. But on taking this step I had, I found it necessary to put my pride in my pocket. I must "Stoop to Conquer".'[3]

Leading suppliers were reluctant to deal with new japanners. Whitehead, a well-known Bilston blank-maker, refused to supply Jones for fear of losing Walton's custom, and Mander having 'lost money by fellows like you',[4] would not, at first, supply varnish. Jones looked instead, to James Fellows who, himself, had just started in business as a blank-maker and would have been glad of his custom, and he looked to varnish makers in Birmingham.

Anxious to get some sample trays ready, Jones took on a woman polisher and a young lad, but unable to find a stover and blacker, he varnished and stoved the trays himself. Believing it would be a mistake to emulate the expensive work of the Old Hall, he 'introduced a new style, and succeeded in doing cheap work without following the style of the flashey [*sic*] and coarse work done at Bilston for the Foreign Market, and known as Bilston work.'[5]

Carrying his patterns in a blue bag, he hawked them among the Wolverhampton merchants. He called first upon Samuel Cope, a fellow-worshipper at Queen Street Chapel, who advised 'there are so many in the Trade, there is no room for another. You had better go back to the Old Hall, as it is utterly useless to begin business in these bad times', impatiently brushing aside Jones' business card: 'Cards, cards, we have a bushel of cards. We should never find yours. It would be like looking for a needle in a bottle of hay to search for it. No, no, don't leave it.'[6]

226. Concave-edge tray and oval bread basket: papier mâché, with imitation burr walnut grounds. The tray, with gold-leaf printed border, is by Henry Loveridge & Co., c.1870. The basket, decorated for the Worshipful Company of Fishmongers of the City of London, is numbered on the base '8206', and printed in red for the retailer, Benetfink & Co., the City depot of Gamages; 1870-80. 42.5 x 32cm and 33.5 x 26.5cm

© WOLVERHAMPTON ARTS AND HERITAGE (BANTOCK HOUSE MUSEUM)

227. Coal vase and shovel, the hinged lid containing a painted curved glass panel; marked Henry Loveridge & Co on a stamped oval metal label; c.1865. 36 x 30.5 x 43cm

© WOLVERHAMPTON ARTS AND HERITAGE (BANTOCK HOUSE MUSEUM)

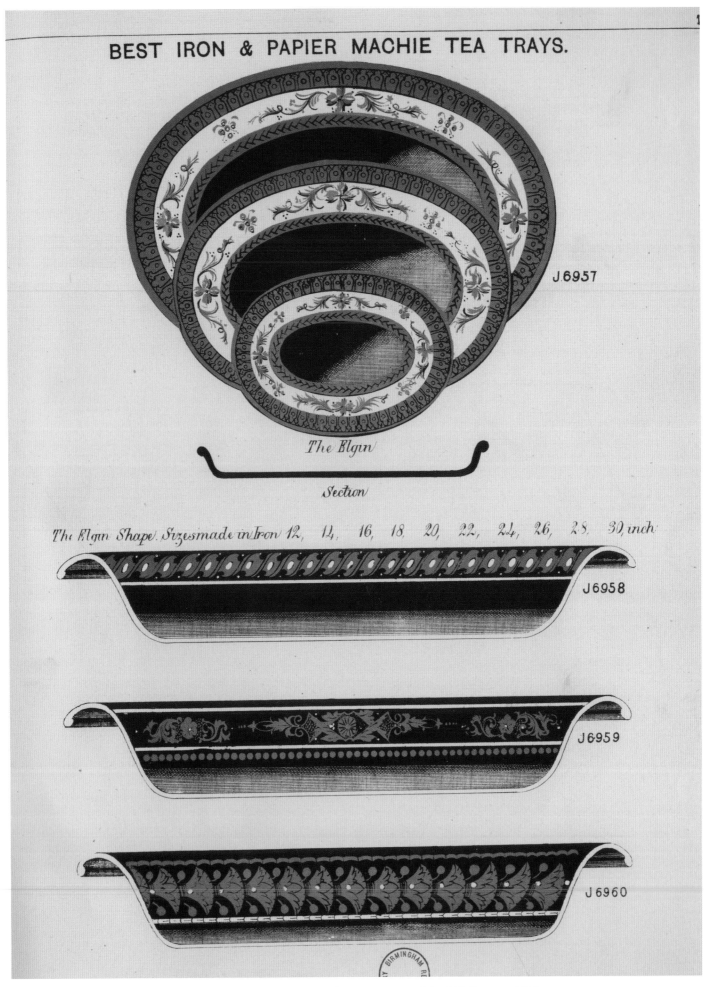

228. A page of tea trays from Jones Brothers' *Price List of Steel Holloware*, 1882.

His reception at the next warehouse was scarcely more friendly, but he managed to sell eighteen sets of trays of varying qualities, and at another, apart from 'a little trouble with an officious Clerk',[7] he was treated with civility and given an order for 'ten setts [sic] of this, and the other two patterns'[8] and three further sets of small trays. When these orders were delivered and paid for, Jones successfully approached the Birmingham merchants.

It continued to be difficult to find experienced japanners prepared to risk working for so new a business, but as trade increased, Jones selected two boys from a nearby school to help in the workshop. They remained with him for the rest of his business life, one rising to become foreman of the tinplate shop, and the other, foreman of the japan shop.

In 1854, with his brothers Harry (1833–1871) and Benjamin (1830/1–1877) eager to become partners, and assisted by a loan of £40 from his mother, Jones purchased a larger factory which had fallen vacant on the death of Thomas Wellings, a japanner. Situated in Ablow Street and surrounded by gardens, it lay just outside the town. His few belongings 'looked rediculas [sic] … in such a large room', but with some boards laid across two empty crates to form a table, he thought it 'made quite a show'.[9] As a further improvment, and to the amusement of his brothers, he arranged a row of large empty varnish bottles, left by Mr Wellings, along the back wall. From these modest beginnings, the flourishing firm of Jones Brothers & Co. would develop.

Soon after the move, William Jones was joined by his brother Harry, and they painted, on the front of their factory, in letters thirty inches high:

Graisley Works
W. & H. Jones, Japanners[10]

Within a year, when they had been joined by their brother, Benjamin, the firm was re-named 'Jones Brothers'. Benjamin had been employed at the Old Hall in about 1845, working first as a warehose boy, then rising to become a commercial traveller and, finally, head of the office. It was he, therefore, who undertook most of the travelling for Jones Brothers, while William and Harry continued to design and decorate many of their trays themselves.

Working from early morning until 10 o'clock at night, the brothers built up a steady trade, taking on the manufacture of tin- and iron-plate goods in addition to japanning. It says much for the firm that it attracted decorators of the calibre of John Thomas (qv), even though 'the ink of [his] agreement was hardly dry'[11] when he accepted a more tempting job elsewhere. Among those who did stay, were the japanners Thomas and Alfred Orme, although they too left in the 1870s to set up their own japan works.

Benjamin's sons, William (1861–1919) and Benjamin (1862–1949), joined the business in about 1880 and accordingly, it was re-styled 'Jones Brothers & Co.'. They greatly extended sales by travelling to India, China and South Africa – countries where japanned iron deed boxes and trunks withstood the climate and resisted damage from insects better than any other material then available.

229. Engravings of an Etruscan Toilet Set, from Jones Brothers' *Price List of Steel Holloware*, 1882.

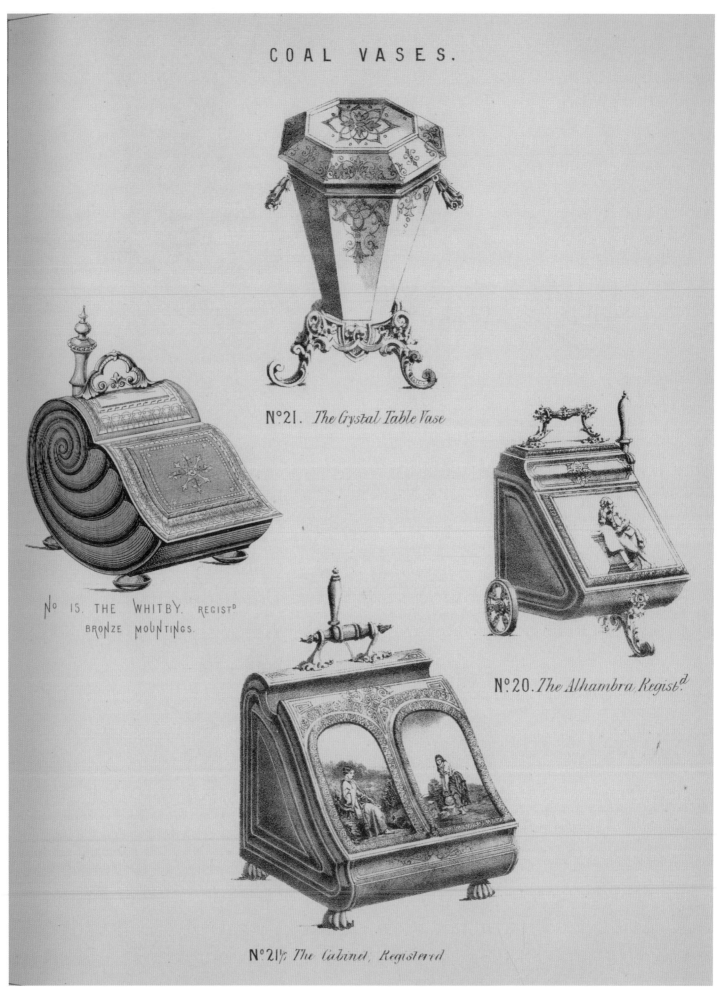

COAL VASES.

Nº 21. *The Crystal Table Vase*

No 15. THE WHITBY. REGISTD BRONZE MOUNTINGS.

Nº 20. *The Alhambra Registd*

Nº 21½ *The Cabinet, Registered*

230. A page of coal vases from Jones Brothers' *Price List of Steel Holloware*, 1882.

In 1882, the publication of their twelfth catalogue showed the extent to which their lines had increased. By then, they described themselves as:

> *General Japanners, iron, copper, zinc and tinplate workers, Manufacturers of Papier Mâché and iron trays, Wrought iron enamelled holloware, sole makers of Registered Bankers Safety Deed, Cash and bullion boxes; Toilet Ware, baths and wash-stands in great variety. Coal Scoops and vases with crystal lids, general enamelled [ware?]; registered Overland steel travelling boxes, lanterns etc.[12] (plates 228-30)*

After William Highfield Jones retired from active involvement in 1896, the business became a limited liability company. The inside lid of a japanned tin trunk from this period shows an oval transferred label printed with two hands encircled by the legend 'The Two Brothers', the mark of Jones Brothers & Co. Ltd. W.H. Jones continued as senior director until his death in 1903 having written, three years earlier, one of the standard histories of the trade, *Story of the Japan Tin-plate Working and Bicycle & Galvanising Trades in Wolverhampton.* The business finally came to be owned by Phillip Highfield Jones (1893–1951), great-nephew of the founder, who wound it up in the 1920s against competition from newer materials.

SELLMAN & HILL
c.1900–1915
Talbot, Ionian and Albert Works
Stewart Street, Wolverhampton

The firm of Sellman & Hill occupied three large factories for the manufacture of 'all kinds of tin and japan wares, pressed hollow-ware &c., &c., for home and export.' A 'breakfast tray' illustrated in their trade catalogue, is indicative of the type of goods they made (plate 231).

BREAKFAST TRAY. **No. B327.**

							14	18	22	27 inch.
As Engraved, Pattern No. T565	...	...	...				3/1	4/7	6/6	9/4 each.
Metal Borders, from	...	...	...	...	...		2/7	3/11	5/1	7 8 „
Gold „ „	...	...	...	...	...		4/3	5/10	8/3	11 6 „
Art Colours „	...	...	...	...	...		2/4	3 3	4/6	6/10 „
Art Colours, Clouded, and Hand Painted Designs, from							3/6	5/-	7/8	11 1 „

231. A tin breakfast tray from a catalogue issued by Sellman & Hill, of Wolverhampton, c.1900.

232. Round tin waiter made by Wilkes & Co., Wolverhampton, c.1910. Dia: 25cm

CHAPTER X

THE BILSTON JAPANNERS
(in chronological order)

JOHN HARTILL
fl. c.1750–c.1815
Priest Fields, Bilston

John Hartill began as a tray-maker in Bilston in about 1750, and according to a local historian, he was the first japanner in the town. From this it must be deduced that he was the first decorative japanner, for records show there were japanners in Bilston as early as 1719 (p. 18). Although no examples of Hartill's work are known today, there are clues which point to the fact that he ran a successful workshop and could have made some of the early tin-ware which is so admired by collectors today. The first of these clues is his inclusion in the Staffordshire Game Duty List published in the Wolverhampton Chronicle in 1789,[1] indicating that he was a man of some financial standing. The second is an advertisement the following year, and in the same newspaper, for several stovers and spotters which points to a serious level of business.[2] Most telling of all, however, is that when George, Prince of Wales (later George IV) visited Bilston in 1810, apparently incognito, he left with 'several samples of Bilston Industry ... among them ... specimens of Japan ware from the shop of Mr Hartill.'[3] The Prince's known extravagance and love of luxury make it unlikely that he returned to London with anything less than fine examples of japanning, possibly including a tray or, perhaps, given his renowned weakness for collecting such articles, a japanned tin snuff box.

John Hartill's name does not appear in a local directory of 1818; instead one, William Hartill, japanner, is to be found.

GERRARD BARBER *fl.* 1761–1830s
Market Street, Bilston
(later) **R. LAWLEY 1862–c.1870, and**
G. & J. LAWLEY c.1870–1900s
Reliance Works, 2 & 3 Market Street, Bilston

This, the longest-operating Bilston japan factory, can be traced back to Gerrard Barber who had been a japanner in the town since 1761. It must therefore have been he who had supplied japanned bread baskets to Ryton's of Wolverhampton in 1810 (p. 93).

However, it was his son, also Gerrard, who first appeared in a local directory in 1818.[1] Barber junior, had been apprenticed to John Hartill (*qv*) with whom he is reputed to have introduced cork-stencilling as a quick means of decorating. There is no record of when Barber branched out on his own, but in 1834, he built a factory in Bilston market-place where he operated as a japanner, tin- and iron-plate worker, and blank tray maker. There, he pursued his interest in producing good quality objects at the fastest rate possible and with his son-in-law, Richard Lawley (c.1800–1871), adapted the transfer-printing process for use by japanners. Barber was the designer, while Lawley undertook the actual transfer-printing.

Richard Lawley, whose family had been associated with japanning, iron- and tinplate working in Bilston since at least the early nineteenth century, became sole proprietor in about 1862 and continued to japan trays, waiters and baskets for the 'Home & Foreign Trade'.[2]

Opposite: 233. Tin teapot with a hinged lid and gold-leaf border; made by J.W. Baker at the Batchcroft Works, Bilston, in the second half of the nineteenth century. H: 24cm

234. Tin snuffbox, its hinged and 'cushioned' lid is mounted with a facsimile of a George IV half-sovereign, and bordered by a naïve imitation of cross-banding; Bilston, c.1825. 3.5 x 5.2 x 2.5cm
© WOLVERHAMPTON ARTS AND MUSEUMS SERVICE, www.blackcountryhistory.org

235. An advertisement for Froggat & Tyler, showing a popular utilitarian tray-type which has survived in huge quantities, from *Bilston, its Present Industries*, an official handbook published by Bilston Urban District Council, c.1925.
© WOLVERHAMPTON ARTS AND HERITAGE (BANTOCK HOUSE MUSEUM)

The firm passed from Richard Lawley to his sons, some time before 1871, and continued as G. & J. Lawley in a similar vein to its parent company, making blank trays for wholesale, in addition to japanning. It was thus through its descendancy via the Barber family that G.T. Lawley in his *A History of Bilston* (1893), described the firm of G. & J. Lawley as Bilston's oldest existing firm in the trade.

In the early twentieth century, the anonymous author of an unpublished typescript *Commercial & Industrial Notes of Nineteenth Century Bilston*, was shown a set of pattern books then in the possession of the Lawley family. Old and worn through constant use in the factory, the books showed various dates, for example, 1761, 1784, and 1791, and included 'some very beautiful Japanese and other designs'.[3] Whether these books belonged originally to the Lawley or Barber family of japanners will remain a mystery until such time as, hopefully, they resurface.

J DEAN & Son
1805–c.1880
Temple Street & Oxford Street, Bilston
(later) FROGGATT & TYLER
c.1880–1936+
Crown Tin & Japan Works, Oxford Street, Bilston

John Dean, who commenced as a japanner in 1805, was later joined by his son. As J. Dean & Son, the emphasis of their trade shifted towards galvanising, but they nevertheless continued to produce japanned goods. An advertisement of 1862 shows them to have produced the usual run of Bilston goods: utilitarian 'iron, tin and galvanised wares',[1] including tea trays and waiters, and a later advertisement of 1871[2]

showed them also to have made papier mâché trays. 'After one or two changes',[3] their business was taken over by Froggatt & Tyler in the early 1880s.

Under Froggatt & Tyler, the factory was said to have been considerable, and 'all kinds of japanned goods and tin-wares, such as coal vases, trunks, toilets [ie. toilet-sets], bowls baskets &c.' were made there, 'the machinery employed being of the newest and most adequate kind.'[4]

In recognition of John Dean's date of foundation, Froggatt & Tyler's trade mark was a profile of Admiral Lord Nelson's sailing ship, *The Victory*. They exhibited japanned goods and tinware at the Wolverhampton Exhibition in 1884, became a limited liability company in 1901 and were still producing japanned ware in 1936 (plate 235).

S & S CADDICK (sometimes Caddock)
fl. c.1818–1822
Greencroft, Bilston

The Caddick family had been japanning in Bilston since at least 1818 when Simeon & Samuel Caddick of Green Croft, Bilston, were listed as tin-plate workers and tray- and waiter-makers.[1] They were by then blank-makers and their workshop was situated behind the Blank-makers' Arms which was licensed in the name of one of the partners, Samuel Caddick. Samuel's sons, Daniel and Thomas, were employed in the blank-making shop, but their copious drinking in their father's tavern caused the down-fall of his business. In January 1823, 'the stock in trade of the late Simeon and Samuel Caddick of Bilston, tray and waiter makers, and tin-plate workers',[2] was sold by auction.

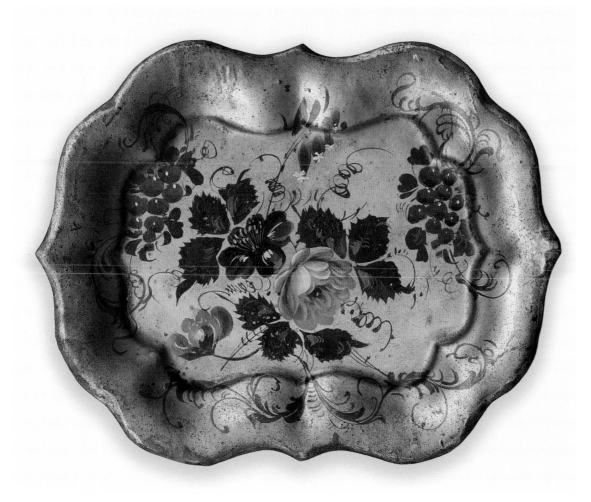

236. A gothic tin waiter with an unwired edge, deftly painted against a bronze ground; second half of the nineteenth century. 17 x 21.5cm

COLLECTION SHIRLEY BAER

237. Convex-edge tin tray, the blue ground naively painted, and the border stencilled with four 'principal' motifs interspersed with 'mapwork'; c.1830. 23 x 30.5cm

COLLECTION SARA TIFFANY, PHOTOGRAPH BY DON NELSON

238. Large iron tray painted with a scene entitled *Jerusalem Hath Sinned* and made by J. Sankey & Co. to demonstrate their supreme skill in evenly rolling so large a sheet of metal; mid nineteenth century. 99.5cm

© WOLVERHAMPTON ARTS AND HERITAGE (BANTOCK HOUSE MUSEUM)

HARTILL & JACKSON
fl. 1830s
(later) **HARTILL & SANKEY, 1848–1854**
Middlefield Lane, Bilston
(then) **JACKSON & SANKEY, 1854–1867**
High Street, Bilston

Charles Hartill[i] (1811–1854), Samuel Jackson (b. about 1808) and, from 1846, Joseph Sankey (c.1826–1886), were all employed by Mrs Birch, alongside her two sons, in her japanning and tin-plate workshops behind the Golden Cup tavern of which she was licensee. Her sons, more interested in her alehouse than in her japanning concern, brought about the closure of her workshop in about 1848.

Hartill and Jackson set up on their own as japanners, tin- and iron-plate workers, and blank tray manufacturers, and took Sankey with them to the premises they had acquired on Dudley Lane. One of their employees recalled that by 1850, Hartill & Jackson employed about twelve blank-makers.[1] The quality of their products may be judged by the huge tray – over 1m in diameter – which they made as a demonstration piece for their stand at the Great Exhibition in 1851. Believed to have been made by Sankey himself, and with no trace of a hammer-mark

on its vast rolled surface, the tray was justly admired for its craftsmanship. It was painted by an unknown hand with *The Finding of Moses in the Bullrushes*, and is testimony to the high standard of work of which the often derided Bilston japanners were capable (*cf.* plate 238).

In 1853, notwithstanding their success at the Great Exhibition, the firm was found to be £800 in debt to one, John Bate, its principal creditor and supplier of rolled sheet iron. To save the business and thereby ensure he got paid, Bate agreed to resume supplies only if Hartill retired and Jackson took Sankey into partnership. Jackson & Sankey commenced business in 1854 cementing the foundations of what is today, a major international conglomerate (see below). Under Sankey's management, japanning was abandoned in favour of making blank-trays which they soon supplied to all the japanners in Bilston, and many in Birmingham and Wolverhampton also. In the 1861 Census, Sankey described himself, and his responsibilities as a 'master blank-maker employing 8 men and 7 boys [and] ironmaster employing 6 men and 2 boys';[ii] in addition, he had a secondary occupation as a grocer. Jackson sold his business interest to Sankey in 1867 but continued as foreman of the blank-tray shop until his death in 1884.

JOSEPH SANKEY
1867–c.1902
(later) JOSEPH SANKEY & Sons Ltd.

Joseph Sankey was orphaned at the age of nine, when his parents are believed to have died following the Bilston cholera epidemic of 1835. Prior to being employed by Mrs Birch, Sankey was apprenticed, aged fourteen, to John Duncalf, a blank-tray maker of Hall Street, Bilston, under whose guidance he mastered not only manual dexterity but was taught the principles of design and mechanical drawing. The letter written by Duncalf to Sankey on completion of his apprenticeship in 1846 shows a remarkable degree of mutual respect between master and pupil, and a generosity of spirit on Duncalf's part which surely underpinned Sankey's future success:

> To Joseph Sankey,
> In consideration of your Faithfulness to me, and your good conduct in my house, it is my desire to mark such attention by presenting you with my Case of Instruments, drawing Board and T Square as a Token of regard for your Faithfulness towards me and which I hope you may be enabled to use to your own improvement and to the benefit to those who may hereafter employ you to accept them with the same sincerity as they are are given to you and believe me your Friend and well wisher
> John Duncalf [1]

In 1867, Samuel Jackson sold his business interest to Sankey who, soon after, purchased some land in Albert Street where he erected new workshops equipped with steam-operated stamps. Jackson continued as foreman of the blank-tray shop until his death in 1884, and under his supervision it became the largest factory in Bilston for the manufacture of blank-trays. Sankey, however, had greater ambitions. He extended his product range to include frying pans, tin trunks and all manner of iron-plate holloware, and built up a large export trade, particularly in the sale of shallow pans (known as Cassada pans) to Brazil where they were used in drying coffee, rice-bowls to Ceylon (now Sri Lanka), and cash-bowls to China. Nevertheless, in 1870 when the firm's total output yielded £6,500, almost £4000 of this was from the sale of tray blanks.[2] Between then and 1874, its workforce almost trebled, increasing from twenty-four to sixty-five men.

The first of Sankey's sons, John (b.1856), became a partner in 1878, after which the firm became Joseph Sankey & Son, and went from strength to strength. Joseph died in 1886, but the firm continued to expand, purchasing the business of blank-tray maker J.P. Whitehead of Bilston, and diversifying into electrical laminations, steel for electrical purposes, and pressed steel for car bodies. By 1891, two further sons had become partners, and

as Joseph Sankey & Sons, they increased their output of holloware: in 1893 they acquired James Motlow's Providence Works (*qv*) and then in 1899, they purchased J.H. Hopkins' business in Birmingham (*qv*) together with the rights to the 'Sphinx' trade-mark which Hopkins had used on a range of decorative japanned ware (plate 177). The supply of blanks was becoming less important to Sankey's business, but in about 1900, they were still supplying tray blanks to a London client, for example, 12in. (30.5cm) round trays at 2/9d per dozen, and 'New Oblong' trays with rounded corners of 16½in. x 12½in. (42 x 32cm) at 3/3d per dozen.[3]

Joseph Sankey & Sons became a limited liability company in 1902. The works had grown into five factories and the original line of manufacture into many more, though by then the name Sankey was no longer associated with japanning and blank-making but with pressed-steel.

JAMES ROWLEY
c.1833–early 1860s
(later) Thomas Farmer

Rowley (b. about 1801) had commenced trade in Gozzard Street, Bilston, as a japanner and blank tea-tray maker by 1833. He soon branched into the allied trades of iron- and tinplate working and built up a large and successful business producing, it was said, some very beautiful work. His work was not purely decorative for in 1849 he advertised as patentee of the 'Olmstead Stove' and by 1851, with a workforce of 238, he had added varnish-making to his various trades. Rowley moved his works to Caledonia Street, where he remained until the early 1860s when he was declared bankrupt. Rowley may have expanded too quickly for the 1861 and 1871 censuses, show him to have been no longer an employer but a tin-plate worker and japanner respectively. His business, and the Caledonia Works passed to Thomas Farmer (*qv*).

THE BEEHIVE WORKS
1850–1930s
Tame Street, Bilston

This concern had its roots in the factory begun in Gozzard Street, Bilston by James Jones (japanner, tin-plate worker and blank-maker), and flourished under various partnerships. By 1862, Jones had been joined by two men with whom he had previously trained: James Bird and George Smith. They are known to have made cash and deed boxes amongst other articles. When their partnership ended in the mid-1870s, their premises were taken over by Seager & Co. (*qv*) and the three men went their separate ways (plate 241).

---

i. There is no evidence of any direct link with the earlier workshop run by John Hartill (*qv*), but to judge from their respective dates, they may have been father and son.
ii. Jackson, in the same Census, was also described as a 'blank tray maker employing 8 men and 7 boys'; thus it is evident that these were the employment figures for the Jackson & Sankey partnership.

Jones moved to the Beehive Works, where he was succeeded by a man named Robert Lewis, who then sold out to Julius Krause in 1892. Krause took his son into partnership in 1919, and trading as J. Krause & Son, made the type of objects which have survived in plenty: japanned iron tea-trays and waiters in many shapes and designs, crumb trays and brushes, hot water and toilet cans, cash and deed boxes. Examples of their trays can be seen in an advertisement of c.1930 in which they also advertise more utilitarian goods such as oil cans and feeders (plate 239). They ceased japanning in the 1940s.

James Bird moved to the Britannia Works and was subsequently taken over by Smith Armstrong (*qv*).

George Smith, together with two men named Keay and Liddington, moved into a newly built factory, the Earl Street Works, where they made a standard range of cash and deed boxes and traveller's trunks. Smith & Liddington, as the firm was styled from about 1872, closed when it ran into financial difficulties, and George Smith went to work for Sankey.

THOMAS FARMER
fl. c.1851–1879
Oxford Street, Bilston
(later) FARMER & CHAPMAN
1879–1936+
Caledonian Japan & Hollow-ware Works, Bilston

Thomas Farmer (1814–1885) commenced as a japanner, tin- and iron-plate worker in about 1851 having taken over the Bissell family's business (est. c.1818) of tin-plate-working, japanning and blank-tray making, in about 1850. It was evidently a substantial concern, for the 1851 Census shows that he employed twenty men and twenty-nine women; an advertisement of the same year also described Farmer as a manufacturer of japan goods for the home and export trade.[1] In the early 1860s, Farmer absorbed James Rowley's trade (see above) and moved part of his own business to the Caledonian Works, expanding but not changing his output: at the 1869 South Staffordshire Exhibition in Wolverhampton, for example, Rowley exhibited 'some specimens of japanned goods for the usual home and foreign markets'.[2] By 1879, he had been joined by a man named Chapman; as Farmer & Chapman, their workforce expanded to seventy-three (twenty-four men, six youths, and forty-three females). They continued to make considerable quantities of high class goods – both tin and iron – and to export world-wide. The firm exhibited at the 1884 Exhibition in Wolverhampton where they showed iron tea-trays, waiters and other japanned goods, and 'all kinds of stamped holloware, both tinned and enamelled'.[3] Farmer & Chapman were still japanning in the 1930s, but by then they were also making enamelled ware and signs, as well as general iron hollow-ware such as cooking pans. The firm was taken over, and its product-range greatly extended, by the Lee Brothers who themselves had succeeded to the factory of Edward Perry (*qv*).

J. & W.H. BAKER
fl. 1851–1901+
Batchcroft Works
Hartshorn Street, Bilston
London offices: 4 Newgate Street

This firm was founded in 1851 by two former apprentice tin-plate-workers, James Baker (1826–1909) and his brother William Humpage Baker (1828–1918) in 1851. They were the sons of James Baker (b. between 1794 and 1801, d.1868), a journeyman painter of japanned ware.

The brothers set up in a newly-built factory and conducted 'a very brisk and prosperous business'[1] as japanners and iron- and tin-plate workers. This did not prevent them from buying in ready-made blanks and they were said to have done some very good work using the 'best quality of blanks from Joseph Sankey & Sons'.[2] They made military equipment during the Crimean War (1854–5) and were reputed to have been the first to introduce bright block-tin goods to Bilston. The Bakers kept pace with demand, expanding their product range accordingly, and steadily increasing the number they employed, from forty-five in 1851, to sixty-three in 1881.

Their display at the Wolverhampton Exhibition in 1884 included:

> *All qualities of Japanned trays, waiters etc., Coal vases, Cash Boxes, Travelling Trunks, Cabin Trunks, Picnic and other Boxes, Sitz[iii] Shower and Sponge Baths, Imp[d] Hip Baths, Cabinet and Folding Wash Stands, Oak and Fancy Toilet Ware, Tea and Coffee Pots, Lanterns, Dish Covers, Ewers and Basins, Sole manufacturers of the "Portable" Travelling Trunks.[3] (plate 233)*

The partnership was dissolved in 1891 on the retirement of James Baker, and W.H. Baker continued as sole proprietor assisted by his two sons, Willis (b.1858) and James Baker (b.1868) who acted as manager and foreman respectively, and by James' wife, Kate, who served in an administrative capacity. It was thus a close-knit family firm. However, finding it impossible to withstand 'the falling off in the fashion of using iron Tea Trays',[4] the firm finally closed down in the early twentieth century.

JOHN MARSTON
fl. 1859– c.1900 (as a japanner)
London Works
Bilston

On receiving his indentures as a japanner from Edward Perry of Wolverhampton in 1859, John Marston (b. Ludlow, 1836–1918) purchased the japanning business of the late Daniel Lester of Bilston; this allowed him to claim that his firm was established in 1790. Within two years, and aged only twenty-four, he had a workforce which numbered twenty men, twenty-seven women and twenty-four girls – an early indication of his entrepreneurial skills. Marston exhibited 'various japanned and other goods'[1] at the 1862 exhibition in London for which he received an Honorable Mention. A clearer idea of the type of goods he produced is given by the articles which he showed, seven years later, at the Wolverhampton and South Staffordshire Fine Art & Industrial Exhibition. These included trays, coal vases, cash boxes, travelling boxes, baths and toilet ware etc., all of which were considered suitable for both home and colonial markets.

In 1871, after his Bilston workshops had been destroyed by fire, Marston bought the Jeddo Works in Paul Street, Wolverhampton, which had fallen vacant following the death of his former master, Edward Perry. He transferred his business there and continued to expand so quickly that by 1881, he had a workforce of 141. As japanned articles began to lose public favour, Marston saw how the japanning and metal-working skills among his workers could be readily transferred to bicycle-making, and in 1888, he listed this among his trades. By 1891, having been joined in partnership by his son, Charles (b.1868), he began the manufacture of 'Sunbeam' cycles for which their firm would become so famous. Although they took 'a selection of goods in papier mâché, japanned tin, brass, copper and nickel plate'[2] to the 1884 Wolverhampton Exhibition, these branches of their trade were soon completely overshadowed by the success of their bicycles.

SEAGER & Co.
1876–c.1932
Carlton Works, Gozzard Street, Bilston

Christopher Seager & Co., japanners and tin-plate workers, acceded to the business of Jones & Bird (see pl. 241). They were makers of hand-painted iron tea trays, waiters, bread baskets and coal vases, as well as toilet wares, trunks, and hat and bonnet-boxes for the home and foreign markets (plate 233). In 1881, Seager (1840–1908) is known to have employed six men, two boys, eight girls, and seven women.

JAMES MOTLOW
fl. 1866–1893
Providence Works
Dudley Street, Bilston

James Motlow (b.1831) was a maker of tray blanks and frying pans, and a japanner and galvaniser, with a large business in Dudley Street where, in 1871, he is known to have employed twenty men and twenty young people. To judge from his display at the 1884 Wolverhampton Exhibition, he made the usual range of Bilston goods: 'dished sheets, fry

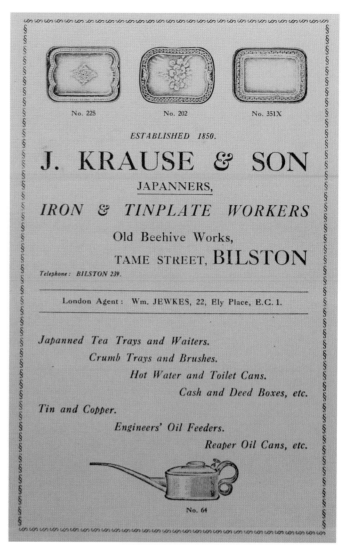

239. An advertisement for J. Krause & Son, makers of popular utilitarian trays, from *Bilston, its Present Industries*, c.1925 (for details see pl. 235).

© WOLVERHAMPTON ARTS AND HERITAGE (BANTOCK HOUSE MUSEUM)

pans, rice bowls, bake plates. Iron tray blanks, galvanised buckets of every description. Chamber pails, foot tubs, water bowls and basins, milk pans etc.'[1] Having fallen on hard times, he became an insurance agent, and his works were acquired by Sankeys in 1893 (*qv*).

STAR JAPAN CO.
c.1866–c.1916
Railway Street, and later Brook Street, Bilston

John Scott, proprietor of the Star Japan Co., was formerly employed in the stamping department of Josiah Sankey & Sons Ltd. He began with little funding, but persuaded shop-keepers to grant him a year's credit for provisions. After taking John Bacon, a Birmingham clerk, into partnership, the firm traded as Scott & Bacon. In 1869, and styling themselves the Star Japan Company, they showed a 'large oval iron tray 6' [183cm] in length, japanned and ornamented',[1] at the Wolverhampton Exhibition. Bacon

iii. A therapeutic hip bath (Chambers).

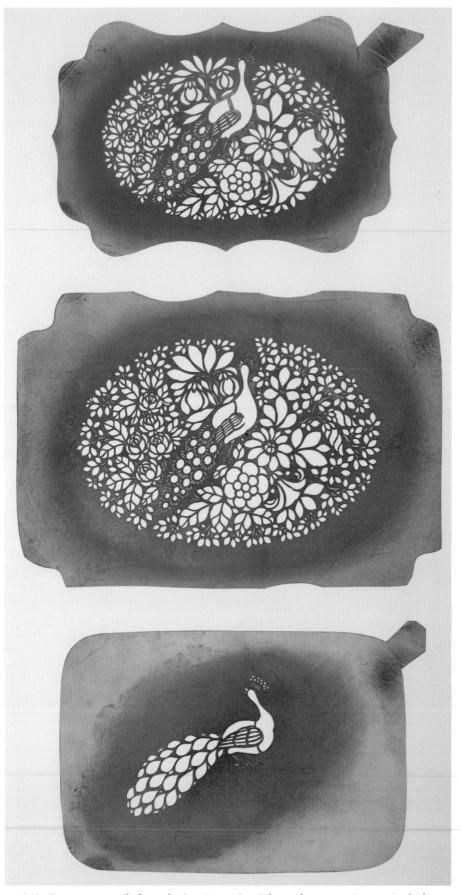

240. Cut-paper stencils from the Star Japan Co., Bilston, for use on tin trays in the late nineteenth/early twentieth century; other stencils from the same source incorporate the design registration mark for 1866.

© WOLVERHAMPTON ARTS AND MUSEUMS SERVICE, www.blackcountryhistory.org

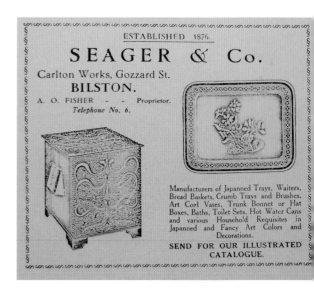

241. An advertisement for Seager & Co., from *Bilston, its Present Industries*, c.1925 (see pl. 235).

© WOLVERHAMPTON ARTS AND HERITAGE (BANTOCK HOUSE MUSEUM)

242. An advertisement for Armstrong Stamping Works Ltd, showing a Unique tray – a name frequently used from the mid nineteenth century, but its significance is not clear – from *Bilston, its Present Industries*, c.1925 (see pl. 235).

© WOLVERHAMPTON ARTS AND HERITAGE (BANTOCK HOUSE MUSEUM)

243. Queen-gothic tin tray with painted and stencilled decoration, made by *Period Art*,
the trade name of the Star Japan Co., Bilston, late nineteenth/early twentieth century.
50.5 x 64.5cm

© WOLVERHAMPTON ARTS AND HERITAGE (BANTOCK HOUSE MUSEUM)

withdrew and by 1884, Scott had been joined by Joseph
Harris; bouyed up by the production of a special line of milk
pans, their business flourished. They made a large variety of
japanned goods, both 'best and common qualities to suit all
markets,'[2] many of which were printed with their trade-
name, *Period Art* (plate 243). A large collection of cut-paper
stencils used by this firm (now in the collection of
Wolverhampton Arts and Museums) includes designs for
trays and tea canisters in a wide range of styles and of
varying complexity. Some of the stencils are for geometric
patterns, some are cut in the form of flower sprays, fruit, or
birds, and others combine all these elements (plate 240). In
addition, there are stencils cut as advertisements for various
firms both at home and abroad. Some of the smaller stencils
incorporate a design registration mark for 1866.

The Star Japan Company continued into the early twentieth
century under the management of Sidney & Ernest Harris.

SMITH & ARMSTRONG
c.1900–1940+
Britannia Works
Bissell Street, Bilston

The Britannia Works was an important Bilston landmark in
the early twentieth century. Tucked behind a row of shops, its
narrow approach alongside the factory stoves was popularly
known as 'the warm entry', as many passers-by sought
comfort there in cold weather. Smith & Armstrong, like other
Bilston japanners, made trays and waiters which were painted
or stencilled with flowers or with 'Greek-key' borders.

On the death of Josiah Smith in 1920, the firm continued as
Armstrong Stamping Works Ltd., and made mainly utilitarian
burnished steel hollow-ware, as well as japanned trays, as
shown by an advertisement of c.1930 (plate 242). These were
variously painted or stencilled.

CHAPTER XI

JAPANNERS in LONDON and OXFORD

LONDON

The Clerkenwell district of East London, home to clock-makers, working jewellers and scientific instrument makers, was also the centre of London's early japanning trade. Local clock-makers would call upon the Clerkenwell japanners to make fashionable chinoiserie-style clock-cases, and similarly, cabinet-makers in nearby Shoreditch and Bethnal Green, both long-established furniture-making centres, as well as those from further afield, would send chairs, tables, cabinets, chests and other items to be decorated in the style of imported lacquered furniture.

It is surprising, therefore, that it was not until the late 1780s, when Edward Strickland opened his factory just off Tottenham Court Road, that japanned tin and papier mâché began to be produced to any significant extent in London.[i] This was considerably later than in the Midlands, some seventy years after the development of Pontypool japanned ware, and almost fifty years later than the introduction of japanned papier mâché in France.

There were relatively few japanners of tinware and papier mâché in London, and in consequence, the industry developed on a far smaller scale than in the Midlands. From the profiles of the leading exponents described below, it will be seen that the London makers focused on high quality papier mâché, but like their counterparts in the Midlands, not exclusively so.

The firm of Henry Clay was revived in London in 1832, and took a display of goods to the Great Exhibition in 1851; it compared favourably in every way with those exhibited by leading Midlands japanners. Amongst other London japanners at the Exhibition, the most noteworthy were Charles Steedman, and Thomas Gushlow. Steedman, a japanner and ornamental painter, showed 'slate tablets japanned and ornamented, adapted for churches and other buildings';[1] his firm appears to have been of longstanding since a James Steedman, also a 'japanner and ornamental painter', was listed in a London directory of 1805–7.[2] Gushlow also exhibited articles in slate although of a very different nature; his were said to be 'in imitation of china, adapted for table-tops',[3] alongside which he also showed tea trays in iron, papier mâché and other materials.

J.H. Scroxton of Bishopsgate exhibited a range of 'show goods, used by tea-dealers and grocers for decorating shops. Vases in tin, ornamented and japanned [and] Octagon stands, inlaid with pearl.'[4] And finally, Charles Bray, an 'inventor' displayed, amongst other things, a 'square pedestal wash-stand of papier mâché, japanned and ornamented with gold mouldings',[5] and a japanned tin crumb tray.

---

i. The Midlands style of japanning had obviously been adopted in London a few years prior. Aris's Birmingham Gazette (30 Mar., 1772), for example, carried an advertisement for a japanner who was seeking 'a woman that has been used to a stove and can polish; likewise a Person that can Japan, to reside in London'.

Opposite: 244. A tilt-top centre table, with a japanned iron top and papier mâché frieze, above a japanned turned wood support. This style is popularly attributed to John & Frederick Crace (see also pl. 251); c.1810. 70 x 87 x 104cm
COURTESY OF MALLETT, LONDON

In general, however, by the mid nineteenth century, this branch of the japanning trade had ceased to be of any great significance in London.

STRICKLAND & Co.
fl. **1788–1801**
London Street
From 1790: **3 Corporation Row**
Tottenham Court Road, St John Street, Smithfield

Although no marked examples made by this firm are known, their several advertisements are indicative of the quality of their wares.

From the outset, Strickland (d.1800) was obviously intent upon emulating Midlands japanned ware and sought to attract workmen trained in that region. This is evident from the advertisement he placed in Aris's Birmingham Gazette in 1788, the year in which he opened his factory: 'WANTED immediately, some … Fruit and Flower Painters'.[1] Moreover, his assurance not only that 'good Workmen or Women, may have constant place and good Encouragement', but that letters of application 'will be attended to',[2] and their postage paid, leads to the conclusion that Strickland operated a well-run and serious concern.

This is further endorsed by another advertisement in the same newspaper in 1790. Then, as Strickland & Wilton, and describing themselves as 'Japanners and transparent painters to their Royal Highnesses, the Prince of Wales, and Dukes of York and Clarence',[3] they sought further workmen. Their advertisement on that occasion, again sheds light on the well-finished nature of their manufactures: 'WANTED several Workmen in the Painting, Japanning, and Varnishing, also Pasters and Cabinet-makers, who understand turning and finishing of Paper Work in general, each in their own and separate Branch.'[4] On the evidence of the announcement of his marriage in Aris's Gazette, Stickland was himself a painter, as well as a japanner.[5]

Later that year, Edward Strickland and his partner, Wilton, moved to larger, newly built premises at 3 Corporation Row, St John Street in Smithfield, from where they were soon seeking more japanners and polishers. That they once again advertised these posts in Birmingham, shows that it was worth-while to do so, and that men and women from Birmingham were prepared to re-locate to London.

Some time in the early 1790s, the firm became known as Strickland & Richardson. In 1797, they supplied two items: 'One 30 inch [76cm] oval paper tray. No298 £2/4/- [and] one 18 inch [46cm] waiter to match 16/-,'[6] to Chamberlain's of Worcester – prices which suggest that Strickland & Richardson were in competition with the likes of Henry Clay.

Between 1794 and 1799, Edward Strickland was listed as a japanner in his own right at the same address. This may have been in anticipation of his partner, Robert Richardson, being declared bankrupt in 1800. Strickland & Richardson's remaining stock was sold by auction, and advertisements for the 3-day sale, printed in *The Times* newspaper, provide a clear picture of the nature of their business:

> To JAPANNERS, HARDWAREMEN, TOYMEN, STOVE-GRATE MAKERS &c.
>
> The First Part of the very extensive valuable and prime finished STOCK in TRADE of Mr. ROBERT RICHARDSON, Japanner, a Bankrupt, late Partner with Mr. EDWARD STRICKLAND (carrying on trade under the firm of STRICKLAND and RICHARDSON); comprising a very large assortment of paper and iron trays and waiters, japanned and finished with beautiful painted and Chinese centers [*sic*] and rich gold borders; plate warmers, knife trays, decanter stands, wine coolers, tea and coffee pots, cannisters [*sic*], snuffer trays, clock and time pieces … and various other articles of japan ware, executed in the first stile [*sic*] of workmanship and in the most fashionable patterns and which [*are*] in lots suitable for private Families as well as the Trade.[7]

A little over a month later, they placed another advertisement in the same newspaper for the remaining stock and, again, it makes interesting reading. Together with articles of the type detailed above, the second day's sale included 'a quantity of unfinished work, oils, varnish, &c.', followed by:

> Valuable Fixtures and Utensils in Trade, consisting of 11 capital drying stoves, with wrought-iron doors, sliders and bars, work-benches and tables, turning lathes, lead cisterns, counters, shelves, presses, iron repository, mahogany desks, and numerous other articles.[8]

Amongst other things sold on the third day, were '2 Single Horse Chairs', and '3 bass's [?] of aspaltom [*sic*], a pipe of linseed, a cask of dip and other oils; varnishes, gold size, and numerous other articles.'[9]

Bidding would, surely, have been keenly competetive at the sale of such an evidently prestigious concern, and it is tempting to imagine that Messrs Wontner & Benson (see below) whose commencement as japanners coincided with the closure of Strickland & Richardson, in 1801, were among those who attended the sale.

WONTNER & BENSON 1801–1805
St John's Street, Clerkenwell

The workshops of Wontner & Benson were first listed as a 'Royal Japan Manufactory', in Kent's Directory of London in 1801, and last appeared in Holden's *Triennial Directory* for the

245. Octagonal straight-edge papier mâché tea-board; impressed Wontner & Benson, London, c.1801–1805. 86 x 62cm. Reproduced from *Marked London Furniture 1700-1840* (C. Gilbert, 1996).

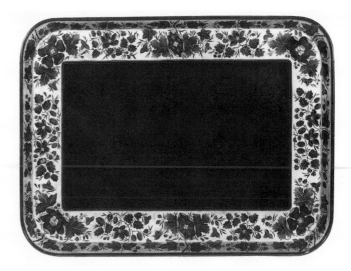

246. A straight-edge papier mâché tray with a gold leaf and painted border; impressed 'DYSON & BENSON/LONDON', c.1815. Measurements not known.

years 1805–1807. Little is known of this very short partnership, save that Joseph Benson had been employed by Edward Strickland, and that objects marked for Wontner & Benson, mostly tea trays and counter trays, are always of a high order (plate 245). It is possible that Wontner and Benson took over from Strickland & Co. (for further details see Dyson & Benson).

DYSON & BENSON 1802–1826
St John's Street, Clerkenwell

On 27 August, 1823, the following announcement appeared in the *Wolverhampton Chronicle*:

> To Ironmongers, Japanners, Tin Plate Workers and the
> Public in General
> By Mr Stewart
> on Tuesday, 2d [*sic*] of September next, and four
> following days ... [*at*]
> 132, St John Street, Clerkenwell, by Order of the
> Proprietors

The whole of the superb and interesting STOCK IN TRADE of the oldest JAPAN TIN, and PAPER TRAY MANUFACTORY in London, Many Years established, and carried on under the Firm of DYSON & BENSON, afterwards Joseph Benson & Co., and recently by Mr. HENRY SWINBURN. – The Stock comprises highly finished painted Salvers, Trays, and Waiters, in Sizes; Bread Baskets, Knife and Spoon Trays, Plate Warmers, Lamps, Candlesticks, Decanter Stands, Snuffer Trays, &c.; a superbly painted Iron Table Top, 4 Feet 6 Inches Diameter; a large Assortment of black japanned Paper Panels, Skreens, Quadrille Pools, Match Boxes, &c.
Lease, good will & utensils in trade also sold.[1]

The advertisement is interesting on several counts. First, there is the claim that it was the oldest manufactory of its type in London. Since there is no reason to doubt the claim, it must be supposed that their predecessors, Wontner & Benson, had succeeded to the business of Strickland & Richardson, which thus entitled them to cite 1788 as the date of their foundation. Certainly, this is borne out both by Dyson & Benson's address, and that of Wontner & Benson, in St John's Street, where Strickland & Richardson had also been situated, and by their respective closing and opening dates. Similarly, since they advertised from the start as 'Royal Japan Manufacturers', this privilege also appears to have been inherited from the founding firm.

Second, Joseph Benson was listed as a 'Royal Japan Manufacturer' at the same address from 1817 – 1826, along with a James Benson, 'japan manufacturer', in 1817. It was not until 1820, that the firm became known as Joseph Benson & Co., whilst at the same time continuing to be listed as Dyson & Benson.

Next, the advertisement lists some of their products[ii] which, together with their status as suppliers to the royal family, confirm the quality of objects they produced – a fact endorsed by surviving, marked examples (plate 246).

And finally, the sale of 'black japanned Paper Panels, Skreens, Quadrille Pools, Match Boxes, &c.', suggests that a number of undecorated articles would have been bought up by other japanners, not just in London, but also in the Midlands, to be decorated in their own workshops – a factor which has already been shown to be a problem when attempting the attribution of unmarked pieces.

---

ii. See also 'Tables' p. 240.

247. Gothic-shaped papier mâché bread basket with bronze and painted decoration; impressed CLAY/KING S^T/COV^T GARDEN, c.1830. 6.5 x 23 x 34cm
COLLECTION SARA TIFFANY

248. Sandwich-edge round papier mâché card tray with gilt metal swing-handle and edge; impressed CLAY/KING S^T/COV^T GARDEN, c.1830. 28.5cm
PRIVATE COLLECTION

VALENTINE & HALL (later Charles Valentine)
c.1804–c.1825
1 St James' Place, Clerkenwell

Valentine & Hall were 'Paper Tea Tray Manufacturers'[1] who, between 1804 and 1806, occupied workshops at 22 Aylesbury Street, off St John's Street, not far from Dyson & Benson. By 1807, Hall had left the firm, and Charles Valentine, who had

been apprenticed as a japanner to Strickland & Wilton in 1791, became sole proprietor of the firm. It was he, who in 1809, successfully applied for a patent for 'A New Mode of Ornamenting and Painting all Kinds of Japanned and Varnished wares of Metal, Paper, or any other Compositions and Various other Articles', (#3219) which has been described earlier (p. 65).

There follows an unaccountable gap in this firm's history, for it is not until 1815, that Charles Valentine is again listed in London directories as a tea-tray manufacturer. He had moved to premises nearby, at 1 St James' Place, where he continued until c.1825, and where, from 1817–1820, a Frederick Valentine, was also operating as a japanner.

As yet, none of Valentine's products have been identified, but it is to be assumed that some, at least, would have been decorated, according to his patent, with gold transfer prints.

HENRY CLAY & CO.
18 King Street, Covent Garden

From c.1773, Henry Clay (see p. 126) had displayed his wares at the premises of a sedan-chair maker in Coventry Street, Piccadilly, and at a coach-maker's in Long Acre – firms with which he may have had links as a supplier of papier mâché coach panels.[iii] In 1783, he also opened his own showroom in King Street, Covent Garden.

Many of Henry Clay's paper wares were stamped with his name together with his address in Covent Garden, and this has lead to the mistaken belief that he operated a manufactory there. It was in fact a 'Birmingham Warehouse', in other words a London showroom for Birmingham made goods. Between 1802 and 1804, the premises were also listed in the name of T. Clay who may have been managing the showroom on behalf of Henry Clay, to whom, presumably, he was related. At this time the property was shared with a laceman.

Although Henry Clay's Birmingham factory was closed following his death in 1812, the business was continued in his name at the King Street address until 1823, but by whom remains a mystery.[iv] Also at this address from 1821, was T.F. Eagles, 'Makers of Paper Tea Trays to their Majesties and the Royal Family.'[1]

---

iii. There was a coach-maker named Clay, situated close to Henry Clay's Birmingham workshops, but no link has yet been established.
iv. W. Clay & Son of Fenchurch Street was a London Agent for H. Clay & Co. (Thrale or Johnson, *qv.*). He was still listed in 1820, but at 5 Lawrence Lane, Cheapside.

v. Intriguingly, the notice advised anyone interested in the 'returns of business, &c', to contact either Jennens & Bettridge, or Shoolbred, Loveridge & Co. (*The Times*, 10 Mar., 1855, p. 3, col. D).

249. Gothic-shaped papier mâché counters tray with painted and bronzed decoration; impressed mark: 'CLAY' beneath a crown, 1830s. 10 x 12.5cm

After a gap of seven years, the firm was revived as Henry Clay & Co. in the same premises in King Street. This time, the buildings were shared with the Birmingham japanner T. Small & Co. (qv); both firms were described as 'Tea Tray Makers'.[2] By 1841, the two firms were styled 'manufacturers of paper tea trays to the Queen and the royal family.'[3] In 1851, they had been joined at King Street by William James Cheshire, another maker of paper tea trays (plates 247-9).

In 1851, and calling themselves 'designers', Henry Clay & Co., exhibited at the Great Exhibition, where they showed a range of papier mâché typical of the period. The *Art Journal*, in 1852, selected three of Clay's exhibits for illustration. The first was a work-table 'of somewhat new form, and ... in many respects good', but it suffered from what the writer considered 'a not unfrequent fault, in this class of articles – too much weight in the centre.'[4] In addition they selected a writing case and one of several ink-stands, both of which were deemed praiseworthy (plate 250). Their other exhibits included a chiffonier decorated in colour, pearl and gold leaf with panels of fruit and flowers; a toilet-table and glass with matching chair and footstool; a table, multiformias of 'classical design', and firescreens incorporating needle-work panels; pot-pourri jars; a so-called 'Regency' writing desk; a chess-table with a glass centre 'enamelled' with mother-of-pearl, as well as the usual tea-caddies and trays of various types and sizes.

By 1852/3, both H. Clay & Co., and W.J. Cheshire, had moved to premises at 20 Pall Mall. These premises were advertised for sale in March, 1855,[v] and the firm finally closed its door. (See also the main entry for Henry Clay, p. 125ff.)

250. Engravings of a work-table, stationery case and inkstand made by Henry Clay & Co., from the *Art Journal*, 1852 (p. 223).

From the establishment of Mr. CLAY—an establishment famous for productions in *papier mâché* since the application of the material to purposes of household art—we have selected three objects, exhibiting novelties and some improvements. The WORK-TABLE is of somewhat new

form, and is in many respects good. It has, however, the not unfrequent fault in this class of articles—too much weight in the centre. The case for letters, paper, and their accessories, is a very pretty and pleasing

work, designed with due regard to convenience, excellent in character and in ornamentation. The INK-STAND is one of several which Mr. Clay has recently introduced—all being elegant in style and well arranged.

There are few branches of Art-Manufacture more important than that under notice. It is one in which we have arrived at great excellence, far surpassing the best manufacturers of the Continent, where the material is but little used for the purposes to which it is here largely applied.

251. Side cabinet, attributed to John & Frederick Crace, though its japanned iron top and door-panels may have been undertaken by a London, or Midlands, japanner; c.1810–1815. 93 x 95 x 48cm

THOMAS HUBBALL & SON
c.1805–c.1832
10 Clerkenwell Green/Close

Thomas Hubball commenced his 'Japan Manufactory' in about 1805, but his name quickly disappeared until 1812, when together with a tin-plate worker, William King, he was granted a patent (#3593) for a method of decorating japanned and other goods, with bronze powders (p. 75). The firm was next listed in 1817 as Hubball & Son, at the same premises where it continued until about 1832. Nothing is known of the goods produced by Hubball & Son, but it is likely that some, at least, would have demonstrated a form of early bronzing.

THE CRACE FIRM 1768–1899

Several pieces of early nineteenth century furniture which incorporate substantial panels of japanned papier mâché or iron are frequently attributed to John and Frederick Crace. Although not japanners themselves, they merit a place in this survey, if only for the purpose of clarification.

The Crace firm of designers and interior decorators, enjoyed royal patronage throughout its various partnerships, but it is the early generations of the family which are of concern here.[vi] Edward Crace (1725–1799), who founded the firm in 1768, received commissions from George III, while his son, John (1754–1819) and grandson, Frederick (1779–1859), famously designed much of the furniture and interior decoration for George IV's[vii] extravagant chinoiserie confection, Brighton Pavilion.[viii] On account of the latter, it is now customary to attribute all good early nineteenth-century chinoiserie furniture, made in the 'Brighton Pavilion style', to John and Frederick Crace. This, however, is misleading in relation to those pieces which contain japanned inserts – often their most striking aspect – for it is more than likely that the decoration of such panels was out-sourced (plates 244 and 251).

All three craftsmen, Edward, John and Frederick, were descended from Thomas Crace, a coachmaker in Rochester Row, London, and had themselves trained either as coach-makers or decorators, practising their trade in Long Acre – the centre of the London coach-making trade, and a district where there were many skilled craftsmen, among them japanners. By the mid eighteenth century, it was fashionable for coaches to be japanned and embellished with heraldic emblems associated with their owners, and so the Craces would have been familiar with, if not necessarily experienced in, the craft of japanning. But does this point to their having made and decorated the japanned panels found in their furniture? Almost certainly not.

They could, of course, have bought japanned iron and papier

252. The Oxford shop of Richard Spiers, retailer of papier mâché articles, from *The Adventures of Verdant Green*, written and illustrated by Cuthbert Bede (1853).

mâché blanks from specialist suppliers for decoration in their workshops and sent them to a japanner for their final varnishing, but it is unlikely. With experienced firms like Dyson & Benson (*qv*) and Valentine & Hall (*qv*) in nearby Clerkenwell, not to mention makers like Henry Clay in Birmingham, or Thomas Illidge in Wolverhampton, equipped with the necessary stoves, controlled atmospheric conditions, and artists skilled in the art of transparent painting (p. 56), it would have been scarcely worthwhile to have undertaken the work themselves; surely they would have out-sourced it, as they and subsequent Crace partnerships did for so much of their specialised work.

In the absence of any surviving records, we do not know from whom John and Frederick Crace commissioned their japanned panels, but their style of decoration is so wholly consistent with that found on contemporary tea-boards, for instance, that it could have been undertaken by any one of the leading japan houses in London or the Midlands. Japanned iron panels found in furniture attributed to John and Frederick Crace are, today, sometimes linked with Pontypool japanned ware, but stylistically, they are closer to the products of London and Midlands japanners.

OXFORD

RICHARD SPIERS & SONS
c.1850–1854/1861 (as retailers of papier mâché)
102/3 High Street, Oxford

Richard Spiers started his company in about 1830, as a perfumer, hair-dresser and stationer at his shop in High Street, Oxford. By 1847, it had become a general 'fancy repository'[1] for all manner of luxury goods, from dressing-cases to decorative glass. And, soon, it would become a significant retail outlet also for papier mâché (plate 252).

---

vi. For a full history of the Craces, see: Aldrich, Megan, ed., *The Craces, Royal Decorators 1768–1899*, The Royal Pavilion Art Gallery and Museums, Brighton, 1990.
vii. Brighton Pavilion was begun while George IV was still Prince of Wales.

viii. Aldrich, p. 25. A Mr Lambelet was said to have painted japanned panels in the Music Room at Brighton Pavilion.

The contributions in papier mâché of Messrs. Spiers & Son, of Oxford, are numerous; they consist of tables, work-tables, writing-desks, being sufficiently subdued, and regard being had, generally, to harmony of composition. They derive much of their interest and attraction

ten-trays, albums, fire-screens, portfolios, &c., all of which are in good taste; the ornamentation from the paintings with which they are embellished, consisting of some of the most pic-

turesque or celebrated edifices in Oxford, as well as sketches taken from its outskirts.

253. Papier mâché articles decorated by Spiers of Oxford, from the *Art Journal Illustrated Catalogue of the Industries of all Nations*, 1851 (p. 253).

So significant in fact, that Spiers showed some 'two – three hundred specimens' at the Great Exhibition of 1851, displayed 'in a semi-octagonal dome-shaped glass case … designed by Mr Owen Jones'.[2] Their exhibits included tables, cabinets, and a large range of smaller articles, 'ornamented with upwards of 150 different views of the colleges, public buildings, the college

walks, gardens and other objects of interest in the city and its neighbourhood'[3] (plate 253). They were, it was noticed, distinctly different in character from 'the usual subjects of birds, flowers, Chinese landscapes, arabesques or other less pleasing styles'[4] then in vogue on papier mâché goods.

Spiers & Son were not, themselves, papier mâché manufacturers. They bought japanned blanks from Birmingham – the newly established firm of Alsager & Neville being, for a time, their chief supplier – and had them decorated in Oxford (plates 254-257). The painting was done by hand, according to Robert Hunt who further explained that:

> *Many of the scenes are sketched upon the spot, and studies of details made by the persons who are employed to paint them … These remarks are made because some persons not acquainted with the executive of painting imagine, from the correctness of the architectural details, that they are done by some block-printing process.*[5]

Many views however, can be traced to contemporary prints.

The name *Spiers & Son, Oxford*, together with the name of the college or decorative subject, was lettered in small script along the lower edge of the picture, or on the underside of the article. This, and their high standard of painting, guaranteed their attraction as souvenirs for contemporary Oxford undergraduates. Moreover, articles could be decorated to order – a luxury indulged by Mr Verdant Green, the hero of Cuthbert Bede's amusing spoof on life as an Oxford student in the 1850s. Having visited the shop, and after much deliberation:

> *Mr. Verdant Green … ordered a fire-screen to be prepared with the family arms, as a present for his father; ditto, with a view of his college, for his mother; a writing-case, with the High Street view, for his aunt; a netting-box, card-case, and a model of the Martyrs' Memorial, for his three sisters; and having thus bountifully remembered his family-circle, he treated himself with a modest paper-knife.*[6]

Spiers exhibited in Dublin in 1853, and in the same year, at New York where they were awarded a prize medal. They received an Honorary Mention at the Paris Exhibition of 1855, and showed at the 'International Exhibition', held in London in 1862, but their focus at the latter had shifted to other goods.

Although the firm continued to be listed in local trade directories until c.1889, papier mâché ceased to feature in their stock-lists sometime between 1854 and 1861.[ix] Nevertheless, their popularity as souvenirs for Oxford's alumni has continued to the present time, but they are now purchased as expensive antiques.[x]

---

ix. There are no Oxfordshire directories available between these years, but Spiers' entry in Dutton Allen & Co's *Directory of Oxfordshire and Berkshire*, published in 1863, makes no mention of papier mâché, and nor do any subsequent directories.

x. Not all papier mâché decorated with views of Oxford was made by Spiers.

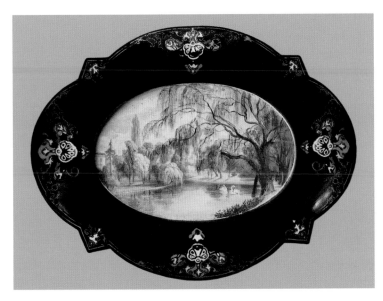

254. Papier mâché dish lettered in white on the base WORCESTER COLLEGE/GARDEN OXFORD/134[or9?]/SPIERS & SON OXFORD, c.1850–1855.
27 x 35cm

255. Papier mâché wall-pocket, painted with Oxford views: the Martyrs Memorial, and Christ Church Walk; printed mark of Spiers & Son, c.1855. 38 x 25.5cm

256. Papier mâché visiting-card tray, the painting signed at lower edge: 'Spiers and Son. 546 Magdalen Hall' [now Hertford College], c.1855. Dia: 25.5cm

257. Gothic-shape papier mâché visiting-card case with spring-release cover painted with a view of Queens College, and High Street, Oxford; signed 'Spiers and Son', c.1855. 8 x 11 x 1.5cm

CHAPTER XII

PRODUCTS

Midlands japanners rarely fought shy of attempting the seemingly impossible. There were few luxury objects or household items which they did not make. No article of furniture was too big nor too improbable; at the Great Exhibition, for instance, Jennens & Bettridge displayed not only a huge golden throne, but also an upright piano (plate 90).

It would be futile to compile a definitive list of products made during the course of the industry because there were far too many. Nevertheless, a list of 'the Principal Japan Articles' of the day, compiled by a Birmingham japanner, William Barrow, in 1794 indicates the range of products made in larger workshops and decorated during the early period, with 'every Japan pattern':

Coach pannels	Paper Quadrille Pools	Chimney Fronts
Paper Trays	dᵒ Bread Baskets	Table Candlesticks
dᵒ Waiters	dᵒ Tea Caddies	Bracket Candlesticks
dᵒ Bottle stands	Tea Urns	Chamber Candlesticks
dᵒ Tobacco Boxes	Coffee Urns	Metal Japanned Caddies
dᵒ Snuff Boxes	Japanned Buttons	Table Bells
Cups	Spice Boxes	Wine Coolers
Metal Quadrill Pools	Chestnut Dishes	Dressing Boxes
Letter Racks	Ink Stands	Tobacco Pots
Tobacco Boxes	Tea Pots	Plate Warmers
Snuff Boxes	Coffee Biggins	Knife Trays
Snuffer Trays	Bread Baskets	Cannisters [sic]
Comvoors[i]	Milk Pots	Jugs
Glass Coolers	Cheese Trays	Cruet Stands [1]

Fifty years later, the product lists compiled by large-scale japanners ran to several pages. For the present purpose, however, an overview of particular categories may be helpful, not least because some articles were produced over a far longer period than is often believed.

FURNITURE

It is customary to take Henry Clay's patent of 1772 as a marker for when furniture was first made by Midlands japanners, but records show that it was produced well before that date. The earliest known evidence for this is found in Baskerville's patent of 1742 where he proposed that japanned metal mouldings be used to veneer large pieces of furniture. It is not known how quickly he put this idea into practice, but certainly japanned tea-tables were included in his stock in the 1760s.

Mostly, however, it appears from contemporary records that furniture made by Midlands japanners in the late eighteenth century was a combination of wood and papier mâché. A patent (#1662)[ii] granted to Lewis Ducrest of Jermyn Street, London, in 1788, describes the method by which such furniture was constructed:

---

i. This may have been a misspelling of samovars.
ii. The full title of Ducrest's patent is 'Making Paper for the Bulding of Houses, Bridges, Ships, Boats, and all sorts of Wheel Carriages, Sedan Chairs, Chairs, Tables, and Book Cases, either intirely [sic] of Paper, or Wood and Iron covered with Paper.'

Opposite: 258. Papier mâché tilt-top table painted with a European townscape, the baluster painted as a stone tower, and the base with a maritime scene; stamped 'J&B Patent' for Jennens & Bettridge, c.1840 H: 63cm, Dia: 52cm
COURTESY OF AN AUCTION HOUSE IN PHILADELPHIA

The furniture for apartments is made, as [are] *carriages, of light wood covered all over with several sheets of paper pasted successively one on another; it is afterwards dryed* [sic] *in a stove or hot room and varnished. The varnish being quite dry, the furniture is painted and ornamented.*

As yet, little furniture from this early period has been identified, not, one suspects, because little has survived, but rather, because its true origin has yet to be recognised. There are three reasons why this is so. First, there is the problem of distinguishing between japanned and cold-painted decoration. Second, it is not always readily apparent whether the 'painting' was carried out on wood, metal, or papier mâché. Third, because early Midlands japanners adhered closely to contemporary and mainstream furniture design, their products cannot be recognised by style alone.

As early as 1805, the Bilston japanner Thomas Jones suggested moulding table-tops from paper-pulp and thereby opened up the possibility of a wholly new branch of furniture manufacture which lent itself to comparatively large-scale production. Notwithstanding, it was not until the 1830s that such ideas became commercially viable.

259. Side-table: gilded and painted pinewood, with japanned copper top and frieze. The top is painted with medallions of Abra and Innocence from engravings by Thomas Burke (1783), after steel-engravings by Robert Samuel Marcuard (1782), copied from paintings by Angelica Kauffman; attributed to George Brookshaw, c.1785. 81 x 116 x 53cm

Photo © Victoria and Albert Museum, London (Museum No. 349A-1871)

Even then, in form, as distinct from decoration, the transition to new furniture styles was relatively slow and japanners largely persisted with familiar models. To our eyes this seems blinkered, but in their own terms, and as Jennens & Bettridge's throne for the Great Exhibition demonstrated, japanners often rose to remarkably ambitious technical challenges.

By 1850, such ambition was already deemed foolhardy, and one contributor to the *Journal of Design and Manufactures* felt driven to remark that, while papier mâché was 'the fittest substance for a tea tray … [it was] … most unsuitable for a sofa or a wardrobe, where its peculiar characteristics are not called out.'[2] Although his voice was fairly representative, manufacturers remained undeterred by such criticism. Large items of furniture like chiffoniers and wardrobes, which did not call for the 'peculiar characteristics' of the material, and chairs and sofas, some of which just as certainly did, continued in production for many years longer.

The production of papier mâché furniture centred upon Birmingham where several factories were involved in its manufacture. Furniture was made to a lesser extent in Wolverhampton, where it was mostly constructed from iron, or from a combination of iron and papier mâché. Marked examples of japanned furniture were the exception rather than the rule.

TABLES. Until recently the reference to furniture in Baskerville's patent has been little more than a curious and tantalising fact. But, in light of new research, it raises the possibility that some mid-eighteenth century, so-called 'painted' furniture was actually japanned in Midlands workshops. The evidence is particularly compelling in relation to tables.

We have seen that, in 1759, some years after Baskerville's patent, Stephen Bedford sent a letter from Birmingham to the Society of Arts, in which he said that he japanned copper panels for coaches. Although seemingly unrelated, these details concerning Baskerville and Bedford take on greater significance if compared with tables, made in the 1780s, by the London furniture maker, and artist, George Brookshaw (1751–1823). In addition to working on gessoed wood, Brookshaw painted on thinly rolled sheets of copper which he attached, as veneers, to the tops of his tables, concealing the join between the two layers with a decorative gilt-metal band (plate 259).

Was this how Baskerville envisaged using the japanned iron veneers of his patent, and was it how he made the tea-tables which he advertised in 1767? If so, then this, together with what is known about the decoration of his japanned ware, gives some idea of how his tables might have looked. They are likely to have been japanned in black, or in imitation of mahogany or tortoiseshell, and painted with flowers, fruit, or classical subjects and, less plausibly, dead game – each of which was a ground-effect, or a subject he is known to have favoured. Like his trays, some of Baskerville's tables may have had pierced edges. As prestigious articles of manufacture, it seems not unreasonable to suppose that some of these tables may have survived and may yet be found.

But Brookshaw's use of copper has even greater relevance here, for as he said, his painting was 'burnt-in' to its surface.[3] This implies that it was baked or stoved. In other words, he japanned his tables – a process with which he would have been familiar, having served his apprenticeship in Birmingham with the japanner and painter, Samuel Troughton. It is not known whether Troughton japanned on copper, but we know for sure that two of his contemporaries, Stephen Bedford and John Taylor, did so at the time.

Similarly, it was as a veneer that papier mâché was first used in furniture-making in the 1770s. The Pembroke table made by Henry Clay for the Etruscan dressing room at Osterley Park (plate 110), was constructed in this way, as was the set of tables which he later made for Lord Bristol (plates 113-115), and to which he attached protective gilt-metal bands like those found on Brookshaw's tables. And it was the method adopted for the corner cupboard shown here (plate 264 and frontispiece).

The advantage of painting on japanned metal and papier mâché was that, unlike wood, neither surface required filling, nor did it crack in normal use. Brookshaw's work is proof of this. The surfaces of the cabinets and commodes which he painted on gessoed wood have tended to split along the grain of the underlying wood, while his painting on copper has remained relatively stable, developing only a surface craquelure. This craquelure, or map-like pattern of crazing, is wholly characteristic of early japanned iron and papier mâché surfaces.

With this in mind, a crazed surface, or the presence of gilt-metal edging, and both these characteristics in combination, may signify that the table has been veneered with a thin layer of japanned iron, copper, or papier mâché. But unless an object is damaged, how is it possible to be sure of its construction? Apart from scientific analysis or, in the case of iron, the use of a metal detector, the one means of checking is by inspecting the back of the table where the edge may not be concealed by a decorative metal strip. If this is not possible, and touch alone yields no clue, then the chances of the table having been painted or japanned are equally balanced.

260. Papier mâché tilt-top table with gilt-metal edge, decorated with a chinoiserie scene in paint and pearl, outlined in gold leaf; c.1835. H: 78 Dia: 66.5cm

It does not follow, of course, that all such japanned tables were made in the Midlands. Brookshaw, as we have seen, came from Birmingham but later worked in London. Also in London was Henry Swinburn, successor to the japanners Dyson & Benson, who, in 1823, sold as part of the stock-in-trade of his Clerkenwell workshop, a 'superbly painted Iron Table Top, 4 Feet 6 Inches [in] Diameter'[4] (see also, The Crace Firm, p. 235).

However, it is the small, papier mâché tables with tilt-tops which are now most closely associated with the japanning industry (plates 258, 260-263). When first introduced in the early nineteenth century, their circular tops were cut from flat sheets of pasteboard and usually mounted on japanned wooden columns and feet. After about 1825, when it became possible to mould large sheets of pasteboard into curved forms, it was only a short time before tables were made with shaped tops and their pedestals made from the same material. But papier mâché alone was too light to provide adequate stability. Consequently, an iron tube was placed inside their

261. Large papier mâché table on an octagonal flower-decorated wooden baluster and spreading foot, above a triangular, paper-covered wooden base, and scrolling wooden feet; c.1840. Dia: 122.5cm

supporting columns to make them less vulnerable, and their bases were made either of wood encased in papier mâché or, if made entirely of papier mâché, they were weighted. By the 1840s, tables with tilt-tops as large as four-feet across were made from papier mâché, but like the example seen in plate 261, these were made with wooden supports and paper-clad bases. Various brass fastenings were fitted to the undersides of the table-tops to secure them when in use, and on some of Jennens & Bettridge's best tables, these incorporated patented swivel mechanisms (plate 262).

Tables were also made from moulded pulp – a brittle material which readily chipped and fractured. They were less expensive than tables made from pasteboard and this was reflected in the inferior surface of their japan-varnish and in their decoration, which was sometimes perfunctory, clumsily pearled, and seldom incorporated pure gold leaf. At best, they were painted with a simple and redeeming charm; at worst, they were cheaply printed, of little aesthetic merit, and often their gilt decoration has deteriorated so much that only the tinted size with which it was applied now remains. Dating from about 1840, tables made from pulp continued in production until at least the 1870s (plate 263).

Less commonly found than either of the two previous types of table are those with japanned slate tops, and those which combine papier mâché with iron. A good example of the former type can be seen in plate 71, which was made in the 1840s. As an exercise in unifying the underlying materials – slate, wood and papier mâché – it is a masterpiece because, if judged by appearance, it could be mistaken for papier mâché alone. But with a slate-top, almost 1m in diameter, and about 1in. thick, it is far heavier than that material. The second type of table, constructed of papier mâché and iron, was made mainly in Wolverhampton. Frederick Walton, for instance, showed an iron and papier mâché table at the Great Exhibition in 1851. And his close rivals, Henry Loveridge & Co., included in their catalogue of 1869, a small octagonal 'work table' on a cast iron pedestal, available with either a papier mâché or japanned iron top, which could be taken to pieces for packing. Another type of cast iron table incorporated a reverse glass painting in its top, but like Walton's crystal trays, the glass was vulnerable and few have survived in good condition.

262. The swivel-mechanism connecting the column support and top of the table seen in pl. 137; stamped 'J&B PATENT' beneath a crown (ie. Jennens & Bettridge).

263. Page from the *Birmingham & Wolverhampton Illustrated Hardware Price List of 1878*; the tables shown were 9 to 10 shillings if 'middle quality', and 12 to 15 shillings when 'best quality'.

264. Corner cupboard, decorated in 'Etruscan' style with a figure-group and Sphinx, taken from Pierre d'Hancarville's engravings of William Hamilton's Greek vases (see p. 128); attributed to Henry Clay, c.1780–1790. H: 86cm, W: 65.5cm, De: 37cm (from front to rear corner)

265. Side cabinet of maplewood, with two papier mâché door panels. c.1830. W: 106.5cm. Panels marked for Jennens & Bettridge have been seen in a similar cabinet.

COURTESY OF MALLAMS, OXFORD

Nests of rectangular tables, usually comprising three tables on wooden legs, are frequently found. They appear not to have been made in the Midlands and, indeed, sets are known which bear the mark of Shoolbred,[iii] a London furniture maker. Their papier mâché tops, although often fairly thin in section, are generally decorated to a high standard. It is possible that mainstream furniture makers purchased the finished tops from specialist japanners for assembly in their own workshops, but this is mere speculation. Similar tables, made in large numbers by the French firm Adt Frères (*qv*), are sometimes mistaken for English examples.

CABINETS. These fall into three main types: the earliest, which are veneered with sheets of pasteboard, others which are inset with papier mâché or japanned iron panels, and those which, from about 1840, were made entirely of papier mâché.

A good example of the first type is a corner cabinet, made by Henry Clay, and shown in plate 264, which is likely to have been one of an original set of two or four. Like the pier tables Clay supplied to Lord Bristol at much the same time (plates 113-5), its carcase was constructed from wood and finished with a ⅛in. veneer of pasteboard, but its turned-wood legs are not paper-covered. The inside of the single door is faced with various woods, including purple heart and mahogany, while less expensive timber was used for those parts of the cabinet which are obscured from view. In common with Clay's tables, a gilt-metal band runs round the top edge of the cabinet to conceal and protect the paper veneer. Interestingly, the canted panels to left and right of the door are not faced with paper but are inlaid with ebony and boxwood – had they been veneered, then Clay would have been forced to complicate the overall design by incorporating protective wood or metal strips at their edges. The exterior is thus a combination of japanned, painted and inlaid decoration.

Stylistically, the second type of cabinet follows one of two forms. The first, introduced in about the second decade of the nineteenth century, and continued until the 1840s, was often in the style of Regency side cabinets and chiffoniers. Made from such woods as mahogany, walnut and rosewood, their doors were inset with either papier mâché or japanned iron panels. Initially, the panels were decorated with gilt chinoiseries, but by the 1830s, sprays of painted flowers became increasingly popular. The panels of such cabinets are occasionally marked for Henry Clay, or Jennens & Bettridge, but this is not to suggest that they were the sole makers (plates 265 & 266). The second form of cabinet in this category was introduced in the 1830s; it followed similar shapes, but instead of being inset into furniture of contrasting wood, they were set into japanned wooden cabinets. In line with the styles then fashionable, they were

266. Side cabinet, wood with papier mâché door panels and a top painted in imitation of Siena marble; impressed mark: 'CLAY/LONDON' beneath a crown, c.1825. 79 x 126.5 x 12cm
© CHRISTIE'S IMAGES LIMITED

267. Part of a papier mâché bedroom-suite reputed to have been purchased at the Great Exhibition, in 1851.
COURTESY OF LOTHERTON HALL, LEEDS MUSEUMS AND GALLERIES

iii. Any link between this firm and the Wolverhampton firm of Shoolbred & Loveridge has yet to be established.

usually ebulliently painted with flowers and, by mid century, they incorporated pearl decoration and landscape vignettes (pl. 270). As seen in Chapter VIII, cabinets of this type were made in Birmingham by makers such as Halbeard & Wellings, Richard Turley and, in particular, by McCallum & Hodson. Of course, there are anomalies like the cabinets-on-stands made by Jennens & Bettridge in the 1850s, which straddle both the early and late forms of the second category, but their extremely glossy surfaces, and the style of the drawer knobs (plate 158), indicate their relatively late manufacture (plate 270).

Finally, there are small cabinets made entirely of papier mâché, which were designed to stand on tables. Generally described as ladies' cabinets, they are the type most frequently found by collectors today. The majority were made in Birmingham between 1840 and 1870, and their decoration reflects the styles that were currently popular, from extravagant flower sprays to restrained Moorish motifs. However, two fine examples, seen in plates 185 & 199, were made by Frederick Walton & Co., at the Old Hall in Wolverhampton. Similar, but less expensive, cabinets were made from pulp in the 1880s by such firms as Ebeneezer Sheldon.

268. Papier mâché bonheur-du-jour, on a japanned wood stand, with painted and pearled decoration which includes a view of Windsor Castle; c.1850. 99 x 66 x 56cm

PRIVATE COLLECTION: PHOTOGRAPH COURTESY OF STEPHEN JARRETT, WITNEY ANTIQUES

269. Chiffonier with papier mâché panels and a wooden frame; c.1845. 135 x 85 x 35cm

COURTESY OF BONHAMS

270. (Opposite) Cabinet on stand, believed to have been made in Birmingham, in 1859, and painted by William Backham for his sons, Charles and Henry (*cf.* pl. 158). 137 x 89 x 53cm

COURTESY OF S. & S. TIMMS ANTIQUES LIMITED, AMPTHILL

247

271. Papier mâché 'gondola'-style chair; mid nineteenth century.
H: 84cm

272. Bedroom chair of japanned wood, made by McCallum &
Hodson, from the *Art Journal Catalogue of the Industries of all
Nations*, 1851 (p. 156).

CHAIRS. Papier mâché, in spite of its acknowledged strength,
was unsuitable for legs and frames of chairs and sofas.
Instead, these parts were constructed from wood. One firm
tried making chair-legs entirely from pasteboard and pulp
(p. 32) but there is no record of how successful they were.

The joint between wood and papier mâché was often a source of
weakness (plate 273). To some extent, this problem was
overcome by the introduction of steam-moulding. This allowed
chair-backs to be not only made in one piece, but doubly curved
both horizontally and vertically ie. the sides of the chair-back
curved around the sitter while at the same time, its edges curved
away, thereby increasing the strength of the panel.[iv] Jennens &
Bettridge took such a chair to the Manchester exhibition in
1846, and patented its method of production the following year
(plate 142). This was followed by others, constructed along
similar lines, among them the so-called 'gondola' chair, a type
which is often found to have a design registration mark on its
back for the year 1844; they are among the few designs which

273. William & Mary style chair, with a thick, papier mâché back
cut and steam-moulded to create a carved effect – such tall chairs
suffered from weakness at the joint between papier mâché and wood;
mid nineteenth century. H: 131cm

maximised the possibilities which papier mâché afforded (plate 12). The suite of chairs and sofas reputedly made for the Queen of Spain in about 1849, is a splendid example of the type (plate 141). It is testimony to their strength that chairs of this form have survived in good condition and in relatively large numbers. Interestingly, in form, if not in decoration, they foreshadow Eero Saarinen's moulded 'Tulip Chairs' of 1956.

Bedroom chairs with japanned beech frames and caned seats which became popular in the mid nineteenth century continued to be made in various forms for many years (pls. 161 and 272). They were generally decorated with pearl and gold-leaf, and some were embellished with papier mâché slats or other details. Similar chairs were made in France.

BEDSTEADS. In the 1840s, a fashion arose for japanned iron bedsteads with decorative papier mâché head- and foot-boards. They were made by bedstead-makers, as distinct from japanners, and, according to George Wallis, they were 'almost exclusively an article of British manufacture. [For] the English seem to be the only people who really understand how to make a metallic bedstead, at once ornamental and useful.'[5] 'Some of the more exquisite kinds', the *Art Journal* reported in 1848, 'have for their ornaments exquisitely painted groups of flowers, and these, accompanied by an appropriate tone of colour in the other parts, have a rich and frequently, a magnificent effect.'[6] The leading manufacturers were Messrs R.W. Winfield, and Messrs Peyton & Harlow (later Peyton & Peyton), both in Birmingham (plate 274). The name H. Schürhoff, found on a four-post bedstead is not that of its maker, but of a merchant and exporter who operated in Birmingham between the years 1880 and 1926.

Peyton & Harlow, of the Bordesley Works in Birmingham, were awarded a prize medal at the 1851 Exhibition for their display of 'metallic japanned bedsteads'. It included an 'iron four-post, with massive pillars of taper iron tubing, head and foot rail, japanned to correspond with [the] suite of papier mâché furniture exhibited by Jennens & Bettridge.'[7] Indeed, it was a feature of their bedsteads that they could be 'painted to any pattern of papier mâché furniture.'[8] Then, re-styled 'Peyton & Peyton', the firm received a further medal at the 1862 Exhibition in London, where George Wallis commended their japanned bedsteads for being 'quiet and unobtrusive in colour which [he observed] is a rarity with these articles.'[9, v] They twice exhibited at the Paris Exhibition, first in 1867, where again their articles were reported to have been 'ornamented with taste and harmony of colour,'[10] and then in 1878, where 'the novel and prominent feature' of their brass bedsteads was 'the introduction of oval japanned panels in the head and footboards.'[11] Peyton & Harlow also decorated their japanned bedsteads with lithographic prints of scrolls, wreaths and flowers in both gold and colour.

At the Cambridge Street Works, R.W. Winfield, who had 'long been famous'[12] as a maker of brass bedsteads, also made a wide range of general furnishing and ironmongery including ornate chandeliers and gasoliers; in 1849, he also made 'pier and console tables, with marble and papier machêe [*sic*] tops'.[13] In the same year, he exhibited at the Birmingham Exposition, a 'Japanned 4-post Bedstead' which featured an 'improved tester cornice',[14] alongside a cradle which, to judge from a contemporary illustration, was similar in form to that shown by Jennens & Bettridge two years later at the Great Exhibition. Although the bedsteads which Winfield showed in London in 1851 appear not to have been japanned, those which he took to Paris in 1867 almost certainly were; they were harshly judged. The larger bedsteads, richly embellished and painted with passion flowers were deemed 'not quite satisfactory', while the sprays of ivy painted on the ornamental panels of others, were considered untrue to nature 'and the[ir] repetition disagreeable'[15] and their printed flower designs were thought to have left much room for improvement. In short, the bedsteads made by R. Winfield appear to have been inferior to those of Peyton & Harlow.

Peyton & Harlow's Patent Metallic Bedstead.
Iron French bedstead, with canopy and taper tube pillars, ornamentally japanned, with brass mountings. Solid iron French, japanned. Series of pillars for bedsteads.

274. Bedstead with japanned iron posts, made by Peyton & Harlow; illustration from the *Official Descriptive and Illustrated Catalogue of the Great Exhibition*, 1851.

---

iv. Thonet, whose name is now synonymous with bent-wood chairs, had patented a method for steam-moulding wood in 1841. This may have been the stimulus for subsequent developments in English papier mâché.

v. In the same essay, Wallis condemned a bedstead exhibited by Jennens & Bettridge, for being 'unhappily based upon so decided a wooden type as to practically contradict the material of which it was made.'

275. Base of a tin tray, painted with a scene from Lawrence Sterne's *Tristam Shandy* (Book IV, ch. 43); signed and dated 'E. Bird 1793', to whom the painting is attributed. 78 x 61cm

© WOLVERHAMPTON ARTS AND MUSEUMS SERVICE, www.blackcountryhistory.org

TRAYS

In his *Letters from England*, Robert Southey wrote, in 1807:

> *The breakfast table is a cheerful sight in this country: porcelain of their own manufactory, which excels the Chinese in elegance of form and ornament, is ranged upon a Japan waiter, also of the country fabric; for here they imitate everything.*[16]

As one of the mainstays of the japanning industry from its outset until its demise, trays could be said to provide a microcosmic overview of its history in terms of both technical developments and stylistic changes. Today, however, we use the word 'tray' more loosely than our Georgian forebears.

Southey used the term 'waiter' in its early sense. In 'about 1775', according to Hutton, japanned 'tea-trays ... were then called, waiters, [they] seldom exceeded twenty to twenty-four inches in length and the only forms then made were round, square, and oval with pierced edges.'[17]

By the turn of the eighteenth century, the terminology had become more complicated and a clear distinction was made between trays, waiters and tea-boards. Trays were for carrying china, cutlery and food to the table; waiters,[vi] 'on which glasses, &c, are presented',[18] were smaller, while by contrast, papier mâché tea-boards were usually about 30in. across and, thus, much too large to have been carried when laden. The primary purpose of tea-boards was to protect fine walnut and mahogany tables from heat and spills when tea was served in the drawing room.[vii] This in no way undermined their social and monetary value. On the contrary, as a vital accoutrement to personal style and social standing, a tea-board would have cost its original purchaser perhaps as much as £5.8s 9d and would have been carefully looked after.

When not in use, tea-boards were 'usually placed upright on the side-tables of middle-class families and ... made an object of art and a room decoration by being ornamented with a well executed painting.'[19] Not only picture trays received this treatment. A small watercolour of a Yorkshire interior, painted in the 1830s by the amateur artist Mary Ellen Best, shows, for example, a large red tea-board with a broad gilt border, similarly placed on a side-table.[viii] Twenty years later, this, and even more protective measures were recommended. According to Anne Cobbett, paper trays were 'very durable if taken care of', but she advised that 'to prevent their being scratched, keep tea-boards and trays in green baize under the dresser of the pantry, or if convenient hung against the wall, to be out of the way when not in use.'[20] Today's collectors have good cause to be grateful that so many owners appear to have heeded her advice.

The paintings on Georgian trays and tea-boards were so valued by Victorian collectors that some fell victim to what now seems little short of vandalism. 'I have seen at Wolverhampton, some of [Edward] Bird's tea trays ... which were so highly prized by their possessors who in some cases,' Cuthbert Bede recalled, 'had cut out the painting and had framed it, like a picture.'[21] The oval tin tray-base, signed 'E. Bird', now in the collection of Wolverhampton Arts & Museums, (plate 275), may have been the tray in question.[ix]

The earliest trays, both iron and papier mâché, were round, oval, or rectangular with either square or canted corners. Many of the iron trays had lace-like pierced edges – a type hitherto wholly associated with Pontypool japanning, but which is now known to have been made in Birmingham also. By the 1820s, a wider range of shapes was made possible by improved production methods. Thereafter, and probably to help retailers when re-ordering, tray-shapes were given names. Generally, the names prevailed across the industry, but there were notable exceptions like the 'Victoria' tray, the shape of which varied between factories. The number of different shapes, particularly from the late 1860s onwards,[x] was too great to be listed here to any useful purpose. Nevertheless, the popularity of some shapes has ensured their survival in large numbers, and these will be discussed here.

Despite the careful distinctions which our forebears made between trays, waiters and tea-boards, it is more convenient, here, to adopt the term 'tray' as a generic description for all such articles, from snuffers- and counters-trays to tea-boards.

First, however, it is necessary to explain the trade jargon because in addition to their named shape, trays were further defined by the construction of their edges, or sides, as straight, concave, convex, or sandwich. These distinctions provide useful shorthand for collectors and catalogers.

STRAIGHT-EDGE: this refers to the deep, and near-vertical sides attached to early oval, rectangular and round trays. It finally gave way to newer styles in the 1830s, but was re-introduced in the 1860s by Henry Loveridge & Co. whose trays, with their smoother surfaces, are unlikely to be confused with earlier products (plates 276 and 363).

CONCAVE-EDGE: first used in the 1820s, it was a gentle upward curve moulded around the edge of a tray to form a rim. It was especially favoured by Henry Loveridge & Co., in the 1860s (plate 277).

CONVEX-EDGE: this first appeared on rectangular iron trays in the 1820s, and was subsequently adopted for

276. Straight-edge papier mâché tray with an early bronze border – the curious figures depicted may be pilgrims since they appear to be climbing steps on their knees; c.1815. 38 x 51.5cm
COLLECTION OF SARA TIFFANY, PHOTOGRAPH BY DON NELSON

277. Concave-edge papier mâché tray with 'raised work' and gold leaf decoration; impressed mark of H. Loveridge & Co.; c.1870. 32 x 42cm
© WOLVERHAMPTON ARTS AND HERITAGE (BANTOCK HOUSE MUSEUM)

papier mâché trays also. It was moulded in one with the tray and took the form of a broad convex rim around the tray. The convex-edges of rectangular iron trays often had 'hand-holes' to facilitate carrying (plate 89).

vi. Unlike silversmiths, japanners seldom used the term 'salver' to describe these small trays.
vii. Amanda Vickery in *The Gentleman's Daughter* (1998), wrote of a 'genteel' but not 'ultra-fashionable Lancashire lady whose 'relatives made her aware of current modes and sometimes fashion constrained her choices – the tea-tray of china she sought in 1754 could not be had anywhere because of the rage for tea-boards' (p. 169).
viii. The present whereabouts of this painting is unknown, but an illustration will be found in Caroline Davidson, *The World of Mary Ellen Best*, London 1985, plate 70, p. 69.
ix. Papier mâché panels rescued from ships prior to their being broken up, have also been framed in this way; their sometimes odd proportions help to distinguish them from tray-bases.

x. In 1866, the weekly aggregate of trays sold in sets of three was 2,000. The weekly aggregate of waiters 'manufactured', as distinct from sold (although surely there would have been some correlation) was 50,000. Larger manufacturers were said to have carried about 2,000 tray patterns.
In 1874, and in Wolverhampton alone, 'the average factory' was said to have produced '600 sets trays (ie. 3 per set) and 400 gross waiters each month.' One maker was observed to have 'not less than 1700 distinct patterns of trays and waiters', a fact borne out by contemporary pattern books.

278. Sandwich-edge papier mâché visiting-card tray with bronze, gold leaf, and painted decoration (*cf.* pl. 69); c.1840–1850. Dia: 27cm

COURTESY OF ROBERT HARMAN, ANTIQUES, AMPTHILL

279. Concave-edge king gothic papier mâché tray with bronze and painted decoration; impressed WALTON & CO, c.1845. 59 x 78cm (*cf.* pl. 68)

COLLECTION OF ASTRID DONELLAN

SANDWICH-EDGE: this was the term used to describe a straight, concave or convex section 'sandwiched' between the base and rim of a tray. First used on papier mâché trays, in the 1820s, and subsequently, also on iron trays (plate 278).

With these descriptions in place, it is now possible to consider the most frequently found tray-shapes.

Rectangular Sandwich-edge Trays. These trays, which date from the 1820s, have shallow, angled edges, broad flat rims, and rounded corners. The earliest were made of papier mâché and their surfaces often have the characteristic matt appearance of early japan-varnish, but by the 1830s, this had largely given way to smoother surfaces. They were made by all the leading firms, including Henry Clay and Jennens & Bettridge, but it is the mark of Ryton & Walton of Wolverhampton that is most often found on these trays. Although there were later iron versions, the description 'rectangular sandwich edge' has become almost synonymous with paper trays of this type (plate 136).

Gothic Trays. Trays of this shape are like elongated gothic-quatrefoils and it was presumably from these architectural features that their name derives. Jennens & Bettridge introduced the 'gothic' tray early in the 1820s. By 1823, having shrewdly presented an example to George IV, they were granted the right to describe themselves as 'Manufacturers in ordinary to the King', and within two years, the gothic tray had 'become a favourite article of sale, from its having received this particular mark of royal taste and approbation.'[22] Indeed, it was so popular that it is now one of the hallmark shapes of both papier mâché and japanned iron trays. The shape was adopted by other makers, among them B. Walton of Wolverhampton, and R. & G. Bill and Robert Winn both of Birmingham, each of whose trade cards were engraved with a gothic tray (plates 126 and 127).

In its earliest form, the gothic tray had a gently curved outline with, first, a simple concave edge and, a little later, a narrow-rimmed, so-called 'concave sandwich edge'; both types continued in production for many years. A more exaggeratedly curved version with a broader rimmed sandwich- or convex-edge, was introduced by Ryton & Walton at the Old Hall in Wolverhampton, in the mid 1830s. One who was apprenticed at the factory at the time said many years later that it was designed by George Wallis. To judge from a Ryton & Walton pattern book, the outline of the tray was described as 'new-shape gothic'[23] until, in 1837, it was re-named 'Victoria gothic' in honour of the new queen. The shape was widely adopted across the industry, and soon became known as 'queen-gothic'; the 'old shape' was re-designated 'king-gothic' (plates 279 & 280).

The fashion for gothic trays was evidently waning by the mid-1850s. This was reflected in two advertisements for 'papier mâché trays and iron waiters' placed by William S. Burton, a retailer in Oxford Street, London, inside the covers of the monthly instalments of Charles Dickens' novel *Bleak House*. Gothic trays, which featured prominently in his advert of 1853, had been replaced just four years later by what he described as a new style of 'oval papier mâché trays'.[24]

Nevertheless, it was, surely, the queen-gothic tray that inspired Lewis Carroll to famously liken a flying bat to a tea-tray:

> *Twinkle, twinkle, little bat*
> *How I wonder what you're at*
> *Up above the world you fly!*
> *Like a tea tray in the sky.*

The joke would not have been lost on middle-class readers of Carroll's *Adventures of Alice in Wonderland*, in whose homes, in 1865, such trays would still have been familiar sights. A more immediate parallel today, is the stylised promotional silhouette of Batman, the popular comic strip hero.

Although the fashion for the best gothic papier mâché trays had begun to decline, those made from pulp or iron continued to be made until the early twentieth century (see, for example, the Star Japan Co. (plate 243).

280. Queen-gothic papier mâché tray, with sandwich-edge, painted with a rustic scene; impressed mark of Jennens & Bettridge, c.1845. 60 x 81cm
PRIVATE COLLECTION

281. Octafoil sandwich-edge papier mâché tray, painted with 'Scott's Grave'
from the engraving by William Miller, after J.A. Bell, published in the *Art Union*,
vol. 9, 1847; impressed: 'B. WALTON & Cᵒ/WARRANTED', c.1850. Dia: 72cm
© WOLVERHAMPTON ARTS AND HERITAGE (BANTOCK HOUSE MUSEUM)

Victoria shaped trays: there is much confusion about the
actual shape of these trays and not least because it was the
name briefly given by Ryton & Walton to their queen-gothic
trays. There appear to be two later shapes in contention for
the name 'Victoria'. Of the first, George Dickinson wrote 'a
pattern called 'Victorian' [*sic*] was exclusively Walton's and is
the only shape that is known to have been exclusive, this was
a round tray', he continued, 'the outline of which was a series
of small semi-circles'[25, xi] (plate 281). The second tray of this
name was essentially oval in shape, and was included in an
illustrated list of tray shapes in the 1869 trade catalogue of
Henry Loveridge & Co. Thus, the shape may have been
exclusive to Walton, but not the name (plate 282).

Windsor trays: this name is generally associated with oval
iron and paper trays with integrally moulded convex edges.
The Old Hall pattern books, however, tell a different story.
Towards the end of the earliest surviving book, covering the
years 1832 to 1851, are references to 'round Windsor' trays.
To confuse matters further, not all oval trays were 'Windsors':
pattern books from the Merridale Works, for example,

variously list trays of this shape as 'oval iron', 'oval paper',
'oval common', 'fine oval paper', and only some, as 'Windsor
fine'. None of which helps narrow the definition of a Windsor
tray. In the absence of anything more concrete, it seems that
'Windsor' was the name given to a particular type of convex
edge rather than a tray shape (plate 283).

Wine, Breakfast, & Parlour-maids trays: roughly kidney-
shaped and curved to fit comfortably against the waist of the
bearer, these trays appear to have developed from the
innovative wine-tray with its integral decanter-stands which
Richard Redgrave designed for Jennens & Bettridge in 1847
(plates 148 and 149). The shape was taken up and adapted by
other manufacturers – and none more freely so than W. Harry
Rogers extraordinary 'Design for a Papier Mâché Wine-tray'
which was exhibited in Birmingham in 1848 (see p. 323).
There is no indication that Rogers' design was ever realised,
but if it were, the impracticality of its complicated outline
would almost certainly have hindered its commercial success,
despite the contemporary claim that it 'seems especially
convenient for its intended use.'[26]

xi. If, as Dickinson said, this shape was exclusive to Walton, then other, similarly-shaped
trays which bear the mark of 'Clay, London', for example, may have been purchased as

blanks at Walton's bankruptcy sale in 1847.

282. Victoria-shaped tray with convex edge, painted with a scene of Loch Achray, Perthshire, from an engraving of 1836 by J.C. Armitage, after the painting by Thomas Allom; c.1840. 39.5 x 77cm

283. Windsor tray painted with a still life; although this example is not marked, an identical tray is marked for H. Loveridge & Co.; c.1850 63 x 80cm

284. Tin breakfast tray with pearl, painted and gold leaf decoration; c.1850; probably made in Wolverhampton. W: 50cm (approx.)
Private Collection

285. Round-gothic papier mâché visiting-card tray, with the letters: Tombs of the Bereed Kings, Beeder (India), from an engraving by A. Fullarton, *Gazetteer of the World*, 1850-55. Dia: 29cm
Private collection

Trays which are known today as 'parlour-maids' trays' were at first called tea-trays or breakfast trays (plate 284). They are distinguishable from wine trays by the absence of designated spaces for decanters. Made by several manufacturers in both iron and papier mâché, they were available in various sizes, and in graduated sets. Drawings which Jennens & Bettridge proposed to submit as evidence that their registered design for a tea-tray of this type had been pirated (see p. 154) usefully show not only the outline of their parlour-maid's tray, but also that of their rival. If the so-called pirated copy,[xi] is compared with a near-contemporary engraving of McCallum & Hodson's 'new-fashioned breakfast-tray',[27] there is little doubt that they were the perpetrators of the offence (see plate 174).

Cake/Card Trays: Small round trays with, or without ormolu handles, are generally called 'card trays', thus denoting their use in entrance halls as receptacles for visiting-cards. George Dickinson certainly describes these trays as such, but nowhere in the pattern books in the collection of Wolverhampton Arts and Museums, for example, are any articles so-called. The only specific reference found, so far, is to an 8in. card tray in the Sheldon Collection (*qv*). Instead, there are references to cake baskets of various shapes: Victorian, oval, gothic, fluted, shell, scalloped, and so on, including a 'round gothic tin cake basket with handle.' It is possible that the shallower trays were for cards, and the deeper ones for cakes, but like so many things, cake baskets and card trays were probably interchangeable according to the whims of their owners. Whatever their original purpose, these small trays, first introduced in the 1830s, were made by many manufacturers during the middle third of the nineteenth century, and their shapes coincided with those of tea-trays. They were made by most leading manufacturers and their decoration was often of the highest order (plate 285).

Trays, 1855 onwards: Although, firms like McCallum & Hodson, Walton & Co. and Henry Loveridge continued to make the type of trays upon which they had built their reputations, the demand for large papier mâché trays was in decline in the 1860s. They, and smaller manufacturers, began to add many new, less expensive trays to their catalogues. These were mostly of japanned metal and, from the similarity of their outlines and names – Elgin, Canton, Unique and so on – it appears that many were bought as blanks from specialist suppliers. Some of these trays were painted by hand, some were decorated with coloured transfer prints, but the majority, particularly towards the end of the industry, were ornamented with transfer-printed borders and centres in either gold-leaf, Dutch gold or some other inexpensive alloy. Today, without a maker's mark, it is unlikely the products of one factory can be distinguished from those of another.

Crystal Trays: Patented by Walton & Co. at the Old Hall in Wolverhampton in 1855, the bases of these trays were entirely protected by a sheet of glass set within their iron or papier mâché edges – rather like a framed picture. Although generally round or oval, crystal trays were made in various shapes, and ranged in size from small teapot stands to breakfast trays and large, oval, urn stands (plate 200).

Club Fine: This term appears to have been exclusive to Henry Loveridge & Co., and was used to describe a range of moulded rectangular trays with rounded corners, the design of which was registered in 1875. Their decoration was usually of a high standard (*cf.* plate 226).

Union Trays: A contemporary red paper label attached to the underside of a late and large oval tray with a black japanned ground and a transferred gold leaf border, was printed with the following description:

> *The Union Trays combine the best qualities of both Paper and Iron Trays; they are produced by coating the front and back with the same description of Paper as used in the manufacture of real Papier Mâché Trays, and hence possessing a better surface, they are more pleasant to handle and are quite free from rusting:– they have all the stiffness and lightness of Iron Trays, and are sold at a very moderate price.*

Clearly, then, 'Union Trays' were made of iron which had been covered with paper. There were no other marks or labels on this tray by which to identify its maker, and neither was there any indication that its method of construction was protected by patent, although it sounds very similar to the one granted to William Sheldon in 1844 (p. 35). It is likely, therefore, that the manufacture of union trays was not confined to one maker.

Combination Trays: On the evidence of trays which have this printed on their bases, 'combination trays' were exclusive to Henry Loveridge & Co. Their rectangular bases with rounded corners were cut from sheets of pasteboard and mounted with decorative, pierced and vertical metal galleries which sometimes had a handle at each end. Their design was registered in 1882 (plate 286).

286. Papier mâché tray (on later stand); red-printed mark: 'THE COMBINATION TRAY/HENRY LOVERIDGE & C⁰/SOLE MAKERS', encircling a diamond registration mark for 1 October, 1882. Tray: 45 x 34cm
NB. The 'table' edge is original to the tray.
COURTESY OF NEAME ANTIQUES, LONDON

xi. See *Journal of Design and Manufacture*, vol.I, p.32, 1849.

BOTTLE-STANDS

Better-known today as coasters, these articles were first called 'bottle-stands', and then, when bottles gave way to decanters, they were named either bottle- or 'decanter-stands'.[xiii] The majority were made of papier mâché, but some were of japanned tin. The simple, straight-sided and fluted styles can be difficult to date because they were made over a wide period from the late eighteenth century until at least 1870, but the surfaces of both the japan-varnish and the gilding on earlier examples will be less smooth and glossy. Other shapes were introduced in the mid-1820s, which, following the lines of new tray designs, are less of a problem to date. Nevertheless, they can be much later than their styles suggest; for example, silver-pattern bottle stands, together with gothic, straight-edge, 'O.G.' [ogée], and fluted stands, were all featured in Loveridge's 1869 catalogue.

Bottle-stands came in various sizes, usually in pairs, and sometimes to match tea-trays, bread-baskets and snuffers-trays, like those given by Henry Clay to his friend, Mrs Papendiek. Their bases were covered with green baize to allow them to be shunted across a polished table without scratching its surface. Some early nineteenth century bottle-stands were mounted with Sheffield-plate rims, and occasionally these were linked to allow them to be pulled together across a table. A contemporary variant of this type took the form of a boat-shaped tray fitted with two fixed bottle-holders, but these are now extremely scarce. Bottle-stands were seldom marked, the small one shown in plate 122, is a rare exception, the name 'CLAY' being prominently impressed on the interior base. Equally as rare, is the large set of matching bottle-stands obviously made for formal occasions (plate 287). Bottle stands were also pressed into service as cruet stands (plate 288).

287. Several from an unusually large set of straight-sided papier mâché bottle stands with early bronze decoration; c.1835
COURTESY OF DAVID WEBB

288. Papier mâché cruet with contemporary bottles, their silver caps hall-marked 'Birmingham 1797'. H: 27cm
COURTESY EASTBOURNE AUCTION ROOMS

289. One from a pair of large papier mâché picture frames impressed on the reverse:
'W. HILL/& Cᴼ/ BIRMᴹ beneath a crown, c.1815-20. 56 x 61cm
COURTESY OF WITNEY ANTIQUES

MINIATURE FRAMES, WINE-WAGONS , CRUET & LIQUER STANDS

There is, in fact, a homogeneity to this apparently random group of objects. They were all made from pasteboard, or button-board (see glossary), which could be purchased from specialist suppliers, and assembled, mostly, in workshops not primarily devoted to japanning. Cutting such articles from ready-made boards required precision but little specialist skill, and their relatively small size meant that they needed only the smallest of stoves in which to dry the japan varnish. Thus, many papier mâché miniature frames, wine wagons, cruet and liquor stands, were made by men generally engaged in trades like silver- and gilt-plating, ivory-, bone-, or wood-turning – men who would have supplied silver or gilt-metal mounts, handles, knobs and other finishing articles to japanners and other manufacturers of small decorative articles. With few exceptions, their involvement with papier mâché was generally shortlived and coincided with the period when these articles were most popular. When demand dwindled, they simply continued with their main trade, or like

Thomas Wharton, they looked to new fashions in household taste and added such goods as lamps, glass-lustres for oil lamps, and bronze ornaments, as well as newly available photographic apparatus, to their lists of products.

MINIATURE & PICTURE FRAMES: The best-known makers of papier mâché frames for miniatures and small pictures were Hill, Green & Co. who were operative between c.1812–c.1835, at 10 Great Charles Street, Birmingham.

William Hill had been working in Suffolk Street, Birmingham, as a gilt and plated button-maker for some time when, in 1812, he added miniature-frames to his list of manufactures. There is no record of what these early frames were made from, but to judge from a later advertisement, he was certainly making black japanned papier mâché frames for miniature portraits and small pictures by the 1820s. As a button-maker, it is unlikely that Hill, himself, made papier mâché but, rather, made his frames from ready-made button-board (qv) bought from a specialist supplier.

---

xiii. Jabez Maud Fisher was a notable exception to this rule, when he called them 'decanter stands' in 1776 (see p. 127).

290. Papier mâché miniature frame, impressed W. HILL/&
Cᴼ/BIRMᴹ beneath a crown, c.1815-20. 7 x 5cm
COURTESY CLEVEDON SALEROOMS

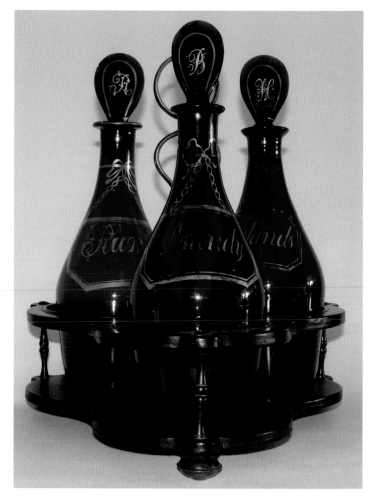

291. Papier mâché liquor stand with gilt metal mounts, early
nineteenth century. H: 13cm (approx)
COURTESY OF HALCYON DAYS, LONDON

Hill's frames were invariably rectangular and inset with either
rectangular or oval gilt mounts to surround the miniatures.
The earliest were impressed 'W. HILL' beneath a crown, but
this was soon replaced by 'W. HILL & Cᴼ / BIRMᴹ', also
below a crown (plate 290), and then by 'HILL & GREEN /
Bᴴᴬᴹ' impressed beneath a crown and the Prince of Wales'
feathers. Hill had been joined by Green in about 1822, and by
1825, they had moved to Great Charles Street from where
they advertised as brass founders and makers of 'patent paper
miniature and large Picture Frames';[28] the 'large' frames
generally measured no more than approximately 19 x 14cm,
although a pair, stamped for W. HILL & Co., measures
56 x 61cm (plate 289). Hill, Green & Co. also had premises
in London at 1 Ely Place, Holborn.

There may have been a connection between this firm and that
of Samuel W. Hill, also of Great Charles Street, who from
1835, was listed as a manufacturer of papier mâché buttons.

Others who made papier mâché frames in Birmingham
included Henry Clay (qv), Obadiah Westwood (qv), Samuel
Buggins (1808-1811), Robert Winn (qv), Thomas Wharton
(1818–1850), and William Leeson (1839-1844). Similar
frames were made in Germany.

CRUET AND LIQUOR STANDS: These tiered papier mâché stands
were made to hold two or more bottles. The earliest examples,
which date from the late eighteenth century, have gently curved
serpentine edges, while later examples, dating from the 1820s,
have almost gothic-shaped outlines. They were made by several
firms, including John Moore, a silversmith, plater and glass
cutter, who added them to his trade in 1808, and Samuel
Buggins, a plater and maker of pencil cases, muffineer, ink and
caster tops, etc., who made papier mâché cruet and liquor
frames between 1808 and 1811. They were also made, from
1812–1815, by John Clark, a manufacturer of cut-glass, and by
Joseph Hardy & Co., a silver plater, between the years 1818
and 1820. One of the longest to be involved in their
manufacture was Thomas Wharton (see above) who
commenced in business as a gilt-toy maker in 1816, added
cruet and liquor stands to his products in 1818 and only ceased
making them in about 1850 (plate 291). Stands of this type
continued to be made until the 1870s.

(See also, Bottle Stands, above)

WINE WAGONS: These were similar in construction to cruet and
liquor stands but fitted with four brass wheels and a handle at
each end to facilitate their navigation across a table. They were

260

generally plain black, but some were painted with flowers and ornamented with gold leaf. The name 'Leeson' is sometimes found impressed on wagons of this type (plate 292).

William Leeson & Son, of Little Hampton Street, were tool-chest makers and turners in ivory and bone who, in 1835, added japanning and the manufacture of pasteboard, to their list of trades. In 1835, with additional premises in New Street, they advertised as makers of 'cruet stands &c.', and by 1839, also as miniature frame makers. The Leesons were involved in making these articles for only five or six years, for in 1845, having ceased all manufacture, George Leeson is next found at the Star & Garter Inn where, one year later, he was described as a victualler.

BUTTONS, BEADS and ROSARIES

Birmingham had long been renowned as a button-making centre when Henry Clay introduced japanned papier mâché buttons in the 1770s. As we have seen, he made them in huge quantities, but because of difficulties in recognising them, none of his buttons, nor indeed, any eighteenth-century papier mâché buttons, have so far been identified – a possible exception being the example shown in plate 293. The types of button that Clay produced, both common black, and extraordinarily richly decorated ones, were described earlier, but for purposes of identification, it is useful to look more closely at their construction since this will shed further light on their appearance.

For buttons made according to his patent of 1778, Clay used sheets of pasteboard (*qv*), or 'plates of paper' as he called them, and cut them 'into round, oval, or other bitts with a common piercing-press, or other machine'.[29] From these, he made two types of button. The first was made by drilling a hole to receive a metal or cat-gut shank, then filing its top surface and attaching, with glue, another piece of layered paper – for less expensive buttons, this second layer was omitted. The button was afterwards shaped on a lathe, japanned and, if required, painted

and gilded. The second style of button was made by inserting ready-japanned and decorated 'bitts', into metal cups, or cavities cut into discs of pearl. Thus, it may be imagined how difficult it would be to identify the underlying fabric by eye alone.

Six years later, in 1786, Clay successfully filed the second of his patents for paper buttons. To make these, he took various natural fibres, dyed them to the required colour, and ground or beat them to a pulp in a paper-engine. The pulp was then bound with a paste made from glue and wheat flour, or from isinglass, gum-Arabic or other strong glue, and mixed with a drying oil such as linseed. Clay spread this mixture on a board which had slightly raised sides, covered it with flannel, and rolled it to expel any excess pulp. On removal from the mould, the pulp was stoved, and cut into round or other shapes.

293. Papier mâché button with a thick wire shank; late eighteenth/early nineteenth century. 3.5cm
COURTESY OF TENDER BUTTONS, NEW YORK

According to the patent, the shanks were 'forced into the button by the power of the screw and lever.'[30] If, after all this, the colour was not as required, the buttons could be re-dyed. They were then 'compleat and ready for sale.'[31] Thus, they were neither polished nor japanned. It may have been this type of button that Clay is seen wearing in his portrait (plate 106).

In addition, Clay made buttons from slate which when japanned, would have closely resembled those made according to his first patent. In fact, to judge from contemporary accounts, Henry Clay's button output was enormous, and more important to his business than is generally realised.

However, in spite of his patents, Clay was not without rival button-makers, one of whom, found imitation none too easy. For example, William Cheshire, writing to Matthew Boulton some time later, in 1796, lamented that the 'remarkable flatness ... which most people consider highly recommendatory of [Clay's buttons] ... has given me much trouble to imitate.'[32] Cheshire, here, was making the distinction between more easily made, and inferior, round-topped buttons. Nevertheless, having overcome the difficulty by grinding the tops of his buttons, he assured Boulton that he could considerably undercut Clay's prices for both plain black coat and waistcoat buttons, in some cases, by as much as half, and by offering merchants 20% discount against Clay's 15%.

Another of Clay's early rivals, and certainly the most frequently named, was Obadiah Westwood (*qv*). Like Clay, Westwood proposed to mould some of his pulp buttons with 'different designs engraved or made thereon'.[33] Once japanned, painted and gilded, it is unlikely that they could now be distinguished from those made by Clay or any other maker.

Alongside Obadiah Westwood and William Cheshire, contemporary japanners like Thomas Ashwin, Thomas Small and others, also made japanned papier mâché buttons. Thomas Watson (*qv*), a former apprentice of Henry Clay, who was listed in local directories as a japanner and paper button-maker, described himself as a 'Royal Patent, Paper Button manufacturer', but since there is no record of him as a patentee, he may have been operating under license from his former employer. Other papier mâché manufacturers included buttons in their various patents, but since they were no more than passing references, we cannot be sure that the patentee ever produced them.

The first known reference to japanned metal buttons is found in the second of the inventories compiled for Boulton & Fothergill's japanning department in 1782. They were mainly of solid wrought iron, and variously japanned in green, yellow or black; less expensive types were simply described as 'Tin Plates painted blue.'[34] That metal buttons are less frequently mentioned in contemporary records, may reflect their relatively low status for, in the early nineteenth century, it was said that japanned metal buttons were made 'for slopsellers, military work, or export'.[35]

In the 1850s, Jennens & Bettridge, while not known to have made buttons, manufactured papier mâché rosaries which looked like jet, but had the advantage of being stronger and less vulnerable; when, almost twenty years later, their successors, J. Bettridge & Co., closed their factory and sold their remaining stock, it included forty-two plain black neck chains.

Generally, by the nineteenth century, the production of papier mâché buttons, or their equivalent, was largely confined to specialist makers like 'Messrs. Twigg, Souter, Mrs. Hewison, &c.'[36, xiv] who in 1853, were said to have been very extensive producers. Sadly, and with few exceptions, nothing is known about the buttons they each made. Among these specialist makers, however, was Davenport & Cole, in Birmingham which, in 1861, patented a method for making japanned buttons, beads and their like, in imitation of jet – possibly in anticipation of a demand for black buttons following the death, one month later, of Queen Victoria's consort, Prince Albert. Notwithstanding their appearance, Davenport & Cole's buttons were not really papier mâché but a compound of varnish, gutta percha, resin, linseed oil, and black pigment. In addition, Davenport & Cole made brooches and bracelets, though for these, and for chain-link, they preferred to use papier mâché, made from a mixture of flour, glue, ground papier mâché, pulped paper, and black pigment, on account of its strength and pliability. In spite of their small size, some of their beads were stamped with their name.

As was seen in Chapter III, a duty was levied on paper mills, and on all goods made from paper. This included ready-prepared button-board. Inevitably, and wherever possible, ways were found to avoid payment. If sheets of button-board were cut into button-blanks at the paper mill, then the papier mâché button-makers were not liable for tax. This ruse so increased the demand for button-blanks, that their makers had to introduce steam presses in order to keep up – a move which reduced costs yet further. The savings were so great that the blanks cost the button-makers less than the duty they would have had to pay on the boards. But so happy an outcome was unusual.

The levy was lifted in 1861, but until then it had caused much resentment. The rancour among button-makers was exacerbated by the number of French papier mâché buttons which had begun to appear on the English market, and not least because in France, papier mâché makers were allowed, unlike those in England, to use any type of paper. Indeed, most of the papier mâché buttons which are found today were made in France (plate 315). They are usually round, of various sizes, generally japanned in black, and decorated, mostly, in one of three styles: with mother-of-pearl floral motifs, with so-called scrap-pearl ornament, or transfer printed in gilt and colour with Japanese figures and landscapes. Many of these buttons were made in Paris by Albert Parent & Company which from 1825 until the early twentieth century, was the leading maker of luxury buttons in France. Similar buttons were made by Adt Freres (*qv*).

296. Tin snuff box with hinged lid, and incised decoration in imitation of bright-cut silver; probably made in Bilston; c.1810. L: 9cm
PRIVATE COLLECTION

294. (far left) Tin snuff box with 'cushion top' hinged lid, painted with transformation portraits of the Duke of York and his mistress, Mary Anne Clarke; probably made in Bilston, c.1810.
COURTESY OF CAPES DUNN, MANCHESTER

295. Tin snuff box with hinged cover, deftly painted with a stylised swan; probably made in Bilston, c.1820.
COLLECTION OF SHIRLEY BAER

Papier mâché buttons were also made between 1895 and 1900, by Daniel Cooksley, proprietor of the Bird Japanning Company in Boston, Massachusetts (see p. 307).

SNUFF & TOBACCO BOXES

TIN SNUFF BOXES: Tin snuff boxes were among the first articles to be japanned in the Midlands. John Taylor was probably the first to have made them on a commercial scale, but in 1742, George Orton, of Temple Street, Birmingham, advertised in Aris's *Birmingham Gazette* that 'any person may be served, wholesale or retail with a variety of the best japanned snuff-boxes etc. upon the shortest warning.'[37] It cannot, of course, be concluded from this that Orton, himself, made the boxes, but as a painter of coaches, escutcheons and signs, it is possible to imagine that some, at least, of his snuff-boxes might have been decorated with the crests and armorial bearings of his clients.

The earliest boxes were round or oval with detachable lids, and with japanned black, or imitation tortoise-shell grounds – a type which continued to be made for many years. Another early type of japanned snuff box is now more closely associated with Birmingham's enamelling industry than with japanning. This is because of their decorative enamel lids.

Made in about 1755-1760, these small round boxes with attractively painted or printed enamel lids and, occasionally, fitted with Sheffield plate mounts, had japanned copper sides and bases. Now rare, they are remarkable as early examples of brightly coloured japanned grounds for, in addition to black, some were vermilion for example, whilst others were japanned in imitation of semi-precious stones.

These enamel boxes apart, tin snuff-boxes possessed an everyday practicality which set them apart socially. The painter, Sir Joshua Reynolds, perhaps mindful of this, carried two snuff boxes, one gold and one tin. When asked by Fanny Burney 'why he made use of such a vile and shabby tin one', he jovially, and tellingly, replied 'because I naturally love a little of the blackguard.'[38] Demand for the humble tin snuff-box lasted until well into the nineteenth century.

It was for this popular market that the small, tin pocket snuff-boxes with hinged lids, were made, in Bilston, in the 1820s. Like the bases made for the enamel boxes, they, too, were brightly coloured: red, green, yellow, and various shades of blue, and some were japanned in imitation of marble. Although mostly oval, rectangular or octagonal, other shapes were made, like the manufacturer's sample which is in the form of a closed book (plate 44). Their decoration was, at once, both naïve and charming (plates 294 & 295). The majority was quickly and deftly painted in styles reminiscent of narrow boat painting (plate 44). Others, however, looked to a more sophisticated source and imitated the effects of bright-cut silver (plate 296). Both types of decoration: painted and incised, may be found with applied gilt-metal facsimiles of half-sovereign coins stamped with a profile head of George IV (plate 234).

---

xiv. After the partnership of George Souter & Son was dissolved in 1851, they continued alone: George as a japanner, and his son as a button-maker. It is likely that this was the same George Souter who devised the pearl-working methods which Jennens & Bettridge patented in 1825.

297. Papier mâché snuff box, painted with a portrait of George IV, signed 'S. Raven', after Sir Thomas Lawrence; lettered in red, inside the lid: 'J. Machin Union Commercial Room, S. Raven Pinxᵗ', c.1825–1830, Dia: 13.5cm. Machin, was landlord of the Union Inn, Cherry Street, Birmingham from 1825-c.1856.

© BIRMINGHAM MUSEUMS & ART GALLERY (1944 f 264)

As the nineteenth century progressed, the social cachet attached to snuff-taking declined and with it, the need for a special container for the pocket.

PAPIER MÂCHÉ SNUFF BOXES: In 1761, when Parson Woodforde exchanged his 'Paper Snuff Box with Miss Nancy Rooke for one of hers by way of Remembrance of her',[39] he relinquished a very early example of its type, for unless it had been imported from France, papier mâché snuff boxes had, at that date, been made for only a few years in England. They were among the first articles to be made commercially in the Midlands from papier mâché. The earliest were round, made from layered paper, and had lift-off lids painted with flower sprigs and other contemporary motifs. In all but their styles of decoration, they were precursors of the more highly finished boxes which superceded them in the late eighteenth century, and which, like the earlier examples, were intended for the table rather than the pocket. Elizabeth Papendiek told how Henry Clay made papier mâché boxes with hinged lids, a feature which points to their having been rectangular, but the majority of English papier mâché boxes made in the eighteenth century, and later, were round. At their best, the painted lids of those made in the early nineteenth century are among the finest examples of the japanners art.

The English boxes most prized by collectors today are those painted by Samuel Raven, not least because he was the only snuff-box artist who consistently signed his work (plate 297). Other signatures, like that of George Bullock of Birmingham, found on a fine early nineteenth century box, are, therefore, extremely rare. Similarly, the large box decorated for William Pickin, licensee of the George Hotel, Stafford, is a rare example of a snuff-box made by Jennens & Bettridge (plate 134).

Searching for a signature is part of the fun of the chase for collectors, and finding one can add greatly to our knowledge of the japanning industry, but the absence of a signature does not diminish the quality of a snuff box. Many finely-painted boxes were not signed, either by the artist, or the manufacturer. As a result, they are possibly one of the most troublesome of all papier mâché products in terms of attribution. Since they are frequently decorated with topical subjects, it is sometimes possible to date a box precisely, but it is with less certainty that English boxes can be distinguished from similar Continental examples. German firms like Stobwasser (qv), Stockmann (qv), and Meyer & Wried (qv), all made exquisite boxes to which they mostly applied their factory mark, but in that country, as in England, many were unmarked.

Similarly-shaped boxes with printed decoration on their lids are equally as problematic and for the same reasons. Made between 1820 and the middle of the nineteenth century, they have transfer-printed paper discs attached to their lids. Some prints were left in their monochrome state and simply coated with copal varnish, others were lightly hand-coloured and varnished, while others were so extensively coloured as to make it difficult for the naked eye to see whether they were printed or not. Moreover, the prints were so discreetly attached to the lids that, after several coats of clear copal varnish were applied, no visible sign remained of the edge of the printed paper.

Curators and collectors have given much consideration to the profile shapes of these paper boxes, to their measurements, the quality of their japanned surfaces, and their interior finish, in fact to every aspect which might provide a rule of thumb which would allow for a clear distinction to be made between English, German and Russian snuff-boxes. But still, they defy classification. Even boxes painted with British subjects could have been made in Germany, where both Stobwasser and Stockmann are known to have copied pictures by Wilkie, Lawrence and other popular artists, or made at the Lukutin factory in Russia (qv). To judge from marked examples, the one factor which may separate the one from the other, is that boxes with hard, glossy, almost glasslike surfaces which date from the 1820s and later, appear to be German in origin. But this is no more than an academic debate for the finest boxes, regardless of origin, are very fine indeed.

There is another type of papier mâché snuff box which, although often described as English, is, in fact, French or German. These are the small rectangular, hinged boxes decorated with mother-of-pearl flower-sprigs, or with scrap-pearl borders contained within pewter metal strips; a number, generally printed as advertisements for British manufacturing companies, had flute-moulded sides. Some of these boxes are clearly lettered 'Made in Germany' (plate 314).

In short, snuff-boxes with their fine paintings and the frequent topicality of their subjects, are a fascinating, if tantalising branch of papier mâché manufacture.

PLATE & VEGETABLE WARMERS

In spite of their being customarily labelled as 'Regency' when offered for sale today, these useful objects were among the standard items which most large factories made, uninterruptedly and with few modifications, from about 1820 until the late nineteenth century. Thus, for example, Henry Loveridge & Co. included in their catalogue of 1869, four plate-warming cabinets in 'gothic', square, cushion- and arch-topped styles, two small plate-warmers, and a vegetable warmer which was available in widths ranging from 24 to 42in. Williamson of Worcester carried similar stock into the 1880s and possibly later. They defy dating on grounds of style alone: the method of construction, texture of the japan varnish, and type of gilding have all to be taken into account (plates 298 & 177).

COAL VASES etc.

Contemporary inventories show that japanned receptacles for coal date from the eighteenth century. Inventories made following the Birmingham Riots in 1791, recorded that William Hutton, the Birmingham historian, possessed '1 japand coalhod', in the kitchen of one of his two houses,[40] and that in the home of the scientist, Joseph Priestley, there was '1 Japan'd Coal Scope'.[41] However, the majority of so-called coal-vases[xv] which appear on the market today, date from the mid nineteenth century and later. Until the 1840s, most of these vessels had lift-off lids: thereafter, their lids were mostly hinged. There were several types. In addition to vases, there were purdoniums and scoops, as well as utilitarian hods and boxes, within which there was a myriad of shapes and styles of decoration. Even allowing for their seasonal sales-pattern, coal vases etc. were one of the staples of the industry, from about 1840 until the close of the nineteenth century, particularly in Wolverhampton where firms like Walton & Co., Henry Loveridge & Co., Edward Perry, and Henry Fearncombe are all known to have made them in large numbers. If contemporary trade catalogues may be used as measures, then demand for these seasonal articles was huge – Edward Perry illustrated a wide range in his catalogue of 1860, and Henry Loveridge obviously considered it worthwhile to include no fewer than forty-five different containers for coal in his 1869 catalogue.[xvi]

Few articles divided critical opinion as much. While Charles Eastlake considered 'delicate tints, and

patterns of flowers etc., utterly unsuitable in such a place', and believed the insertion of photographs in their lids and sides to be an 'absurdity',[42] there were others who welcomed their new forms and decorative styles. Those displayed by Edward Perry at the Great Exhibition for example, elicited a polar response: 'the coal scuttle is invariably thrust into some obscure corner, as unworthy of filling a place among the apartment', but Perry's versions 'have the effect of drawing them from that obscurity, and assigning them an honorable post, even in the drawing room'[43] (plate 215).

298. 'Cushion top' plate warmer, tin, with cast iron legs and brass ring handles; mid nineteenth century. H: 71cm

© WOLVERHAMPTON ARTS AND HERITAGE (BANTOCK HOUSE MUSEUM)

---

xv. Commenting on a helmet-shaped receptacle for coal, George Wallis preferred to call it a 'coal casket [for] we cannot call it a vase'.

xvi. The duties of an apprentice at Henry Loveridge & Co., in the early twentieth century, included keeping each department supplied with coal. Although the factory made coal hods etc., he often had to carry the coal, up three flights of stairs, on an old tin tray.

DISPLAY CANISTERS

When a Wolverhampton grocer and druggist retired from business in 1821, the auction of his household effects included twenty-four japanned canisters.[44] Thirty years later, it seems that they had not been superceded by anything better, for we find Anne Cobbett recommending them for storing 'tea, sugar, coffee, cocoa' and other dry food-stuffs.[45] The canisters in question are likely to have been those which were so thinly-coated with japan varnish that the silver colour of their tinned surfaces shone through creating a treacle-coloured finish (plate 28).

Fig. 104.

NEW SHAPE OCTAGON CANISTER.

With leaf gold fronts.

10	12	14 lbs.
12/-	13/-	15/-

If in burnished gold, 2/- each extra.

299. Tin tea canister from the catalogue of W.H.B. Wood, of Birmingham, c.1880

Collection of David and Rosemary Temperley

The canisters and 'show bowls' in which grocers displayed their stock, were altogether different: they were properly japanned and many were highly decorative. During their period of production, from about 1840 until the early twentieth century, their shapes changed little, if at all. They were made by many factories, not only in Birmingham and Wolverhampton, but in Worcester, Bristol and many other places. It is possible that what appear to be makers' names impressed or attached to these canisters are, in fact, the names of their suppliers and not their makers. For example, a set of grocers' display vases richly ornamented with Chinese figures, which were illustrated in a catalogue issued by the Birmingham firm of Griffiths & Browett in the 1880s, were identical, in every way save in price, to a set included in the catalogue of W.H.B. Wood – a firm listed in Birmingham directories, as japanners and 'Grocers' Canister Makers' (plate 299). If purchased from Griffiths & Browett, the set cost £9.10s, if bought from Woods, it was £10. These so-called 'show goods' were sometimes further decorated with pearl, like the octagon stands 'inlaid' with pearl, shown at the Great Exhibition by J.H. Scroxton of Bishopsgate Street, Manchester.

BELLOWS

Two Birmingham bellows-makers exhibited japanned examples of their trade at the Great Exhibition: William Allday (b.1797) and John Collingwood Onions. Neither maker was a japanner and so possibly these bellows were japanned by outside decorators. It is unlikely that they were alone in producing such articles, but they are the only makers whose names are known.

Allday, a manufacturer of all kinds of bellows, exhibited two examples. The first, ornamented with pearl, showed a view of the cathedral of Notre Dame, Antwerp; the second were gothic-shaped dust-bellows decorated with pearl flowers.

J.C. Onions, whose family had been making bellows in Birmingham since 1787, exhibited, amongst other articles, 'japanned bellows, [of] different patterns.'[46]

Some time between 1880 and 1885 these two firms were joined in partnership (*cf.* plate 300).

ALBUM, BOOK, & BLOTTER COVERS

The papier mâché book-covers or, more accurately, boards, made by Jennens & Bettridge, and Alsager & Neville have already been discussed. It is unlikely that they were without rivals; making book-covers was, after all, only a short remove from making covers for blotters, notebooks and other small articles like needle-cases, which, surely, were included in the product-lists of most leading firms in the 1840s to 1860s (plate 302).

However, a series of books published by Paul Jerrard (1810-1888) of 111 Fleet Street, London, with their decorative papier mâché covers, sheds an interesting sidelight on the subject and demands attention here (plate 301).

With titles such as *Garden Beauties*, or *The Book of Exotic Birds*, they were mostly illustrated and/or their covers designed by (Henry) Noel Humphreys (1807-1879). 'We ... went to Mr Jerrards' wrote Humphrey's son, also called Noel, in November 1852, 'and saw his new book which papa designed and drew for him entitled *Flowers from Stratford*; the cover which is a novel Idea being a gold design stamped upon Japan. I liked it exceedingly. It looks so chaste and striking.'[47]

The cover he saw was evidently produced according to Jerrard's patent of 1852 (#604) for 'Certain improvements in ornamenting japanned and papier mâché surfaces. As also the surfaces of varnished and polished woods'. Clearly, Jerrard was concerned only with their decoration:

My improvements in ornamenting these surfaces consist in the application of gilding to their surfaces. This I effect by the application of such tools as are usually used by bookbinders and embossers. The intended design is engraved upon the surface of the tool as usual, and the gold leaf, bronze, or other medium of ornament placed between the tool and the article to be ornamented; considerable pressure is then applied and the impression is indented or embossed upon the surface. Heat may be applied should it be found requisite.

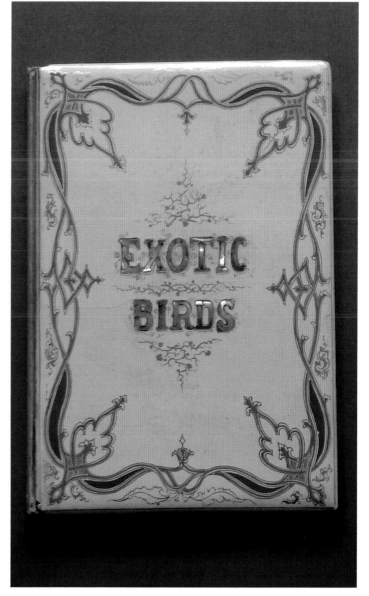

300. Bellows, wood, with brass-studs and leather fittings, painted on the front with a view of Killarney against a bronze ground; mid nineteenth century. 39 x 12.5cm

© WOLVERHAMPTON ARTS AND HERITAGE (BANTOCK HOUSE MUSEUM)

301. Papier mâché book cover by Paul Jerrard; 1852. 28 x 19cm

COLLECTION OF DAVID AND ROSEMARY TEMPERLEY

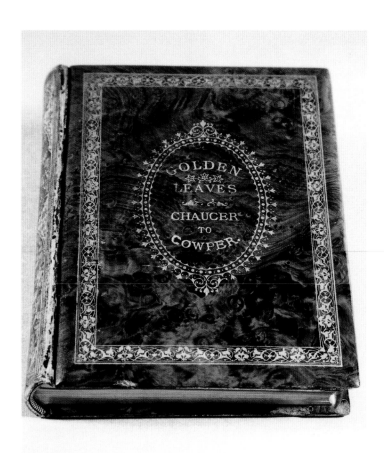

302. Papier mâché boards for a book edited by Robert Bell, and published by Charles Griffin and Company, London, 1865. (Boards) 23.5 x 16.5cm

<small>COLLECTION OF DAVID AND ROSEMARY TEMPERLEY</small>

By implication then, Jerrard bought boards which had already been japanned from specialist suppliers, and when pearl formed part of the decoration, he embedded it into the surface by means of heat (to soften the varnish) and applied pressure; once the varnish had hardened, the pearl would be firmly attached. Could it be that Humphreys, born and educated in Birmingham, had introduced Jerrard not only to the idea of using papier mâché, but also introduced him to a supplier of ready-japanned board in that town?

With their luxury bindings, and at a cost of at least £1.11s.6d., Jerrard produced these books as 'Special Presents'. Their front covers are stamped 'Paul Jerrard patentee' and, sometimes, also 'Patent Binding'.[xvii]

There were, besides, other publishers of books with japanned papier mâché covers. For example, *The Book of Gems*, edited by S.C. Hall (3rd edn) in imitation walnut covers embellished with gold leaf, and published by Bell & Daldy who, in the same year, 1866, also issued Evangeline by Longfellow, with illustrations by Birkett Foster, in a simulated malachite binding.

With notable exceptions, such as the book-covers painted by John Thomas (see p. 177), the indications are that Midlands japanners supplied publishers with japanned covers which they, the publishers, then decorated and bound into books.

HATS

Brindley's patent of 1848 (p. 35) included a method of making hats with brims from papier mâché. These were made in one operation by pressing sheets of wet pulp over a mould of the appropriate shape. Once dry, they were trimmed, oiled and stoved, and then either japanned or painted. It was said in a newspaper article that these shiny hats were worn by London drivers of horse-drawn cabs.[48] However, there is no evidence to suggest that they were made by Midlands japanners.

This patent also included details for making papier mâché basins, but for reasons which he did not explain, instead of japanning them, Brindley preferred to paint their interior surfaces with white paint and bake them at about 200°F.

LAWYERS' WIG BOXES

Although wig boxes were traditionally made of japanned tin, no japanners in Birmingham, Wolverhampton or Bilston appear to have made them. The majority of such boxes were made, in the twentieth century, by Williamson & Sons of Worcester, until the firm was taken over by the Metal Box Company which continues the tradition to the present day.

A CURIOUS SIDELIGHT

In addition to the products described above, there are other japanned tin and papier mâché objects which defy classification, or fall into the category of curiosities.

A good example is the tea-caddy shown here, which commemorates Nelson's victory at Trafalgar, in 1805 (plate 303). Made of tin, it is clad with a layer of japanned lead or pewter and decorated in the manner of 'bright-cut' silver or other metals. Where or by whom such objects were made remains a mystery.

The surface decoration on the above caddy is similar to that found on tinware made in both Wolverhampton and Bilston in the early nineteenth century, but there is no evidence that Midlands japanners ever clad their smaller goods in this way; nor, it should be said, is there any evidence that they did not.

xvii. The author is indebted to Howard Leathlean, author of 'Paul Jerrard Publisher of Special Presents' (*The Book Collector*, Vol. 40, no. 2, Summer 1991), from which much of the above is taken, and to the editor of *The Book Collector* for permission to quote from it.

It should not be forgotten, however, that manufacturers like John Baskerville in Birmingham, and George Brookshaw in London, veneered articles of furniture with metal, although neither is known to have engraved or cut their surfaces in this manner.

However, a patent (# 1065) granted in 1774, to Joseph Jacob the younger, a coachmaker of Saint Mary Ax, London, may hold a clue. It is short on detail but it is worth quoting the relevant part, not least because it provides a context for such objects. The patent, was for 'A METHOD OF ORNAMENTING CARRIAGES, SEDAN CHAIRS, BUILDINGS, FURNITURE, MUSICAL INSTRUMENTS, BOOKS, AND TOYS', which consists:

In painting, gilding, japanning, lacquering, high varnishing, engine cutting, stamping, printing, engraving, inlaying, and piercing the metals commonly called tin foil. Lead, and pewter, beat or roll'd out into thin sheets and fixed on to the parts of the aforesaid subjects designed to be ornamented.

By drawing attention to these unusually decorated objects, it is hoped that others will come to light and allow a proper study to be made.

303. Tin tea caddy clad with a layer of japanned lead or pewter, incised in the manner of bright-cut silver, and made to commemorate Nelson's victory at Trafalgar; c.1805.
10.5 x 13 x 8cm
COURTESY OF RICHARD DEAKIN

CHAPTER XIII

OTHER WESTERN JAPANNING CENTRES

Collectors, when attempting to identify the origins of eighteenth- or nineteenth-century papier mâché and tinware, should be mindful of two things: the fashion for amateur japanning, and that much which is now popularly described as English was, in fact, made elsewhere in Europe or, indeed, in America.

AMATEUR JAPANNING

Japanning was a popular pastime and an admired accomplishment for young ladies in England in the seventeenth and eighteenth centuries. This, and its expense, are highlighted in a letter from Edmund Verney to his eight-year old daughter Molly, a pupil at 'Mrs. Priests School at Great Chelsey':

I find you have a desire to learn to Jappan [sic], as you call it, and I approve of it; and so I shall of any thing that is Good and virtuous ... for I admire all accomplishments that will render you considerable and lovely in the Sight of God and man ... I hope you perform yr Part according to yʳ word... To learn this art costs a Guiney entrance and some 40s more buy materials to work upon.[1]

John Stalker and George Parker wrote their *Treatise of Japanning and Varnishing* (1688) in part, to 'put a stop to all cheats and cousenage of those whiffling, impotent fellows who pretend to teach young Ladies that Art, in which they themselves have need to be instructed, and to the disgrace of the Title lurk and shelter themselves under the notion of Japanners, Painters, Guilders &c.'[2] Their treatise covered the subject so thoroughly that it became a standard handbook for professionals.

But to imagine that Miss Verney, or the many genteel ladies who followed in her footsteps, undertook japanning in the same way as commercial manufacturers, would be far of the mark. Amateur japanners worked on ready-varnished articles which they decorated in imitation of imported Japanese, Chinese or Indian lacquer.

'Everybody is mad about japan work', said the intrepid Mrs Pendarves – later Mrs Delaney – in a letter to Mrs Anne Granville, in 1729, and 'I hope to be a dab at it by the time I see you.'[3] The Countess of Bristol, in her Will of 1741, left to her son, Lord Hervey, 'my cabinet chest, large screen and small screen being white japan of my own work in confidence that he will preserve them for my sake.'[4] It is to be hoped he was more appreciative than would have been Sir Horace Walpole who railed against the craft, describing 'Two vile jars that look like the modern Japanning by ladies'[5] – a comment which makes his mother's attempts all the more remarkable; Lady Walpole is known to have japanned a cabinet which stood in the Blue Bedchamber at Strawberry Hill, her son's house in Twickenham.

Opposite: 304. Tinware from a set comprising a tin swing-handled cake basket, one round, and two oval boxes, and two oval trays; marked with the label of van J. Burgers, Amsterdam, c.1845. Basket: 6 x 26 x 33.5cm
COURTESY OF THE MUSEUM FÜR LACKKUNST, MÜNSTER

An idea of what this furniture may have looked like can be found in Robert Dossie's *Handmaid to the Arts* (1758). There, he gave instructions for those 'who may practise japanning ... for their amusement only, and consequently may not find it worth their while to encumber themselves with the preparations necessary for the other methods.'[6] As long as cabinets or other articles had been undercoated, and were not intended for extensive use, they could, Dossie said, be painted with watercolours which, if 'tempered with the strongest isinglass size and hony [sic], instead of gum water, and laid on very flat and even', would be almost equal in appearance and durability to 'old Japan.'[7] In a later edition of his book, published in 1764, he described how 'Japan work' could also be imitated by gluing hand-coloured prints onto furniture, and varnishing them – a method known as *lacca povera*.[8]

By 1835, B.F. Gandee in *The Young Ladies Instructor* – an epistolary guide to ornamenting a variety of 'articles for fancy fairs' – wrote of japanning, that 'Any things that are made in papier mâché will be best for the purpose, although wooden articles can be prepared for it.'[9] And it appears that 'fancy shops, both in town and country,' could supply not only patterns, but 'work-boxes, card racks, netting boxes, match-cups, memorandum books, watch-stands, letter racks, bellows, screens,' and much else besides, 'all ready for the work.'[10] According to Gandee, the only equipment needed was a tea-tray, a jug of water, a pipkin, some vinegar, a pair of scissors, an old newspaper, and 2–3 sheets blotting paper. If any young lady was deterred by the smell of turpentine, then she need only mix 'some essence of lemons with it',[11] and similarly, her fears about any possible messiness could be overcome by 'simply wearing an old glove during the process of polishing the varnish,' or, if she preferred, and provided she fully understood the process herself, her 'servant may be employed to do it'.[12] Otherwise, there were commercial japanners who were prepared to varnish and polish amateur work; one such was E. Brown, in Long Acre, who advertised in *The Times* in 1850 that he gave lessons and provided materials at trade price.[13]

The extent to which amateurs experimented with japanning cannot now be calculated, but on the evidence of the number of how-to-do-it guides, there was no falling off in interest. Indeed things appear to have become more serious. In 1850, for example, the anonymous author of *The Book of Papier Mâché & Japanning*, acquainted readers with how to stove-dry papier mâché:

> *Small articles may, with great care, be dried in a good oven; but so much exactness must be used in regulating the heat, that it becomes very wearisome. In fact, beautiful as is the result, the means by which it is achieved are anything but pleasing. To stand all day rubbing the surface of a table or a chair with wet pumice stone can scarcely be deemed either a lady-like or gentlemanly occupation, whatever the advertisements may choose to assert to the contrary; nor is the odour of varnish much more agreeable than patchouli itself.*[14]

In spite of these reservations, it was still possible in 1878 for 'those who like to try their hands at the decoration of papier mâché [to] purchase blanks ... for the purpose.'[15] And in the early twentieth century, amateur decorators could buy blank papier mâché trays and other small articles from the Patent Pulp Manufacturing Company (*qv*) which gave rise to a small cottage industry in and around the town of Thetford, in Norfolk, where the firm was situated.

JAPANNING CENTRES OUTSIDE THE ENGLISH MIDLANDS

Since the form and decoration of japanned ware was largely driven by fashion and popular taste, the products of various countries were sometimes so similar that attribution can be difficult. The intention here is to highlight the most significant of the japanning centres outside Birmingham, Wolverhampton and Bilston, and to flag potential areas of confusion in distinguishing the products of one from another.

As may be expected, patriotic allegiances skewed many a contemporary reporter's comments on their respective home industries, but occasionally their criticisms were fairly balanced. Thomas Archer, for instance, a juror at the Paris exhibition of 1867, while on the one hand maintaining the superiority of English papier mâché, had to admit that England was 'not superior in all branches. In most of the small goods exhibited, such as snuff and cigar boxes, brush backs, and other articles of a similar class', he conceded that 'the superiority of the foreign work is incontestable.'[16] Archer was particularly impressed by articles which were 'inlaid with pearl, metal or wirework' and by examples of inexpensive 'painted woodwork';[17] whilst requiring no stoving and possessing great strength, he considered these successful competitors to papier mâché.[i]

This is the one point in this book where secondary sources of information have been largely relied upon. For readers wishing for further information, these sources are given at the foot of each relevant section.

GREAT BRITAIN

PONTYPOOL, South Wales

Pontypool in South Wales has the distinction of being the first place in the world where tinware was successfully japanned, for it was there, at John Hanbury's iron-works, that his manager, Thomas Allgood (c.1640–1716) devised a satisfactory method of tin-plating sheet-metal and where, with his master's encouragement, he began work on a varnish suitable for finishing articles made therefrom (see p. 14). By adapting the so-called japan varnish used by Western cabinet-makers to imitate and compete with imported Eastern lacquered goods,

Allgood laid the foundations for the japanning industry – a wholly new branch of decorative arts manufacture which soon spread to the English Midlands and into Europe.

The name Pontypool has become a by-word for finely painted, early japanned tinware, often regardless of both origin and date. Midlands manufacturers themselves used terms like 'Fine Pontipool Work' to advertise their best japanned metal ware and continued to do so long after the closure of the Pontypool Japan Works.[ii] To some extent this was understandable: Pontypool had led the way, and as this book has shown, by the mid eighteenth century, there was little to distinguish between the majority of Welsh and English japanned tin-ware. But this generic use of the term 'Pontypool' has created a misunderstanding. Objects which are now traditionally attributed to that factory, particularly japanned sheet-iron trays with pierced edges, and oval trays with deep, near-vertical sides and all-over painted decoration, were as likely to have been made in Birmingham or Wolverhampton as in Pontypool.

Contemporary records hint at differences between Welsh and English products but, generally, without documentary evidence, there are no rules to assist collectors in making reliable attributions. A further complication arises from a disagreement among the third generation of Allgoods which led some of them to set up a rival workshop in nearby Usk. For almost forty years, the products of the Pontypool and Usk factories were so similar as to be indistinguishable.

The Pontypool Japan Works c.1716/20–1822

Notwithstanding Thomas Allgood's pioneering work, none of his early experiments are known to have survived, and it was only after his death that japanning was developed on a commercial scale by his two sons John (b. pre-1681) and Edward (1681–1763).

Thus, it is Edward who, having succeeded his father as manager at the iron works, is generally credited with having 'Invented ye Pontypool Japan and also ye Art of Tinning Iron Sheets'[18] for it was he who, between 1716 and 1720, perfected

305. Tin tray with pierced edge and tortoiseshell ground, gilded with a view of Kelmarsh Hall, Northamptonshire, home of the Hanbury family; Pontypool c.1760–1765. 38 x 52.5 x 4cm
© National Museum of Wales (NMW A 50239)

both processes and ensured their success. Albeit with Hanbury's encouragement, Allgood is thought to have pursued his varnish experiments at home and in his own time, using blank articles made by his elder brother, John. At the outset, therefore, it was very much a cottage industry.

They were joined in business by Edward's sons, Thomas (c.1707–1770) and Edward (1712–1801), and by John's son, Thomas (1727–1779), who oversaw the practical work. Together, they founded the Pontypool Japan Works in about 1730. Already, by 1734, one of Hanbury's sons, Sir Charles Hanbury-Williams[iii] (1708–1759), a man of fashion, could enthuse in a letter to his wife that 'Tom Allgood has found a new way of japanning which I think so beautiful that I'll send you a couple of pieces of it'.[19]

Trays represented the major part of the output at Pontypool as they would in the Midlands. The earliest Pontypool trays were round or rectangular and mostly edged with decorative pierced rims, ½in. to 1½in. deep. The round trays and waiters ranging from 6–24in. in diameter were more popular than the rectangular trays which came in only three sizes; their costs in 1754 ranged from 4–18 shillings each (plate 305).

Candlesticks were also a successful line and in addition to those they made themselves, the Allgood's japanned

i. These were most likely French, and Belgian respectively.
ii. Not surprisingly, this was greatly resented in Pontypool and drove the Allgoods to issue a statement in *The Gloucester Journal*, on 8 August 1763, quoted here on p. 276.

iii. Sir Charles Hanbury Williams was Ambassador to the Court of St Petersburg, and it was probably he who presented several pieces of Pontypool ware to Catherine the Great.

306. Tin counters trays with pierced edges and gilt chinoiseries on a tortoiseshell ground; Welsh or English, c.1800. 3 x 11 x 14cm

COURTESY OF ASTRID DONELLAN

307. Oval pierced tin dessert basket; Pontypool c.1770. 4.5 x 30.5 x 33cm

© NATIONAL MUSEUM OF WALES (NMW A 50214)

ordinary snuffbox with a golden flower painted on it is sold', he said, 'for 2 shillings, and a smaller version for 18 pence [ie. old pence].'[20] They were decorated in one of two styles: at first with gilt designs, and from some time after 1756 (see below), with delicately painted flower sprays, fruit, and birds, distributed across the surface of the object (plates 307 & 308). These motifs, and the presence of a pierced edge, have been widely adopted as defining characteristics of Pontypool japanned ware, but since they were quickly adopted by japanners in the Midlands, they are not – as popularly believed – a reliable guide to attribution (see plate 103). The fact remains, however, that these decorative styles were first used at Pontypool and were produced there until the end of the eighteenth century (pl. 306). Therefore, other distinguishing factors have to be considered.

In the early years, and according to Dr Richard Pococke who visited Pontypool in 1756, the main differences between Allgoods' japanned wares and those made in the Midlands, lay in their gilding methods, and in the absence of coloured decoration. In addition, he noted the yellow/brown hue of Welsh tortoiseshell finishes as distinct from the reddish tinge of those produced in the Midlands – but this was a short-lived distinction, for Pontypool soon adopted the less expensive Midlands technique for imitating tortoiseshell.

The Pontypool Japan Works suffered serious disruption in 1763 when, on the death of Edward Allgood senior, his successors failed to agree among themselves. His sons (Thomas and Edward) withdrew, taking with them some of the firm's best decorators, to set up rival workshops in nearby Usk (see below). The Pontypool concern was continued by their cousin, Thomas Allgood, who, with financial support from two local attorneys, traded as Allgood, Davies and Edwards.

John Stockham, one of the chief decorators, stayed on at Pontypool, and was joined by the artist, Benjamin Barker who specialised in painting animals and armorial bearings. Many specially commissioned Pontypool articles decorated with coats-of-arms, are attributed to him. The firm also accepted requests for trays to be painted with portraits or landscapes, like the one listed in their account book for the period 1765–1777: 'An oval Tray with a Landskipp made for Sir Charles Morgan: 15 guineas'.[21] Although Barker lacked the talent of those decorators who had moved to Usk, the new partnership prospered and considerably expanded its market by exporting to America. They added blue to their range of japanned background

candlesticks brought in by their customers – a service which explains the existence of brass candlesticks decorated in Pontypool style. Coffee pots, either pear-shaped or with inward-sloping straight-sides, and cane-insulated handles, were also amongst early products, but tea-pots were rarely/never made at Pontypool (plate 29).

These, and other early domestic articles like tobacco boxes and small copper boxes were generally japanned in black or deep crimson and, from about 1750, also in imitation of tortoiseshell. One described by Angerstein in 1754 as 'an

colours, but otherwise continued to make the type of goods with which Pontypool had made its name. An advertisement placed by one of their agents in Felix Farley's *Bristol Journal*, in 1764, for example, described them as makers of a 'Great variety of Snuff-Boxes, Japan'd Waiters, Bread Baskets, Tea-Kitchens [urns], Tea Kettles, and Lamps, [and] Coffee Pots'.[22] The following year, tea-chests and dressing-boxes were added to this list.

Of Thomas's five children, only two entered the trade: Henry and William (d.1811). They inherited the Japan Works in 1779, but like their forebears, they failed to agree. Henry left for Birmingham to work for John Taylor (*qv*), the industrial entrepreneur and japanner. William carried on alone with continued financial backing from Davies and Edwards, and the business was moved into two larger premises: one to serve as a manufactory and stoving-shop, and the other as a retail shop and dwelling house.

Benjamin Barker had left for Bath by 1782, and new decorators were engaged, among them William (Ned) Pemberton[iv] from Birmingham who, en route, had worked at the japanning factory at Usk, and Anne and Hannah Walker, also from the Midlands. Sadly, there are no known surviving examples of work by either Pemberton or the Walkers.

New products were introduced: letter-racks, plate warmers, candle-snuffers, and chestnut urns,[v] and fewer commissions were accepted. William Allgood, known locally as 'Billy the Bagman' on account of his selling skills, extended his market to include France and Holland. But in 1795, William Edwards relinquished his interest in the business, leaving Billy the sole proprietor, and their remaining stock was sold without reserve.[vi] While in the 1770s the manufactory was observed to have been 'in a decline',[23] by 1800, Pontypool japanned ware was, once again,

308. Knife box, japanned sheet iron over a wooden carcase, with brass fittings; English or Welsh, c.1765. 43 x 25 x 24cm
THE COLONIAL WILLIAMSBURG FOUNDATION (1966–2,1)

'everywhere seen and everywhere admired'.[24] Indeed, many surviving Pontypool articles date from William Allgood's period of ownership. His success lasted another decade or so, but in order to compete with the large japanning factories in Birmingham and Wolverhampton, less time-consuming styles of decoration, like the meandering lines of the Stormont pattern (*cf.* plate 309), were increasingly introduced.[vii]

---

iv. G. Bernard Hughes, in 'The Japanners of Wolverhampton' (*Staffordshire Life & County Pictorial*, Winter, 1956, vol. 7 no. 4, p. 13), writes of 'Thomas Pemberton who had worked as a painter and copyist for the Rytons [of Wolverhampton].' The source of this information is not known.
v. The majority of chestnut urns, particularly those which are richly gilded and painted on brightly coloured grounds, are continental in origin. W.D. John said that, by contrast,

Pontypool chestnut urns were of 'rugged workmanship and sombre colourings'.
vi. Davies had relinquished his partnership some years previously. For details of the sale of the remaining stock of Messrs Allgood and Edwards, see *The Times*, 15 April, 1795 p4 col.c
vii. This derives from a pattern used first on French wallpaper and, later, on English marbled paper. It was also adopted by Midlands japanners who referred to it, more prosaically, as 'mapwork'.

309. Round, gothic tin waiter, decorated in red with the Stormont pattern (*cf.* 'mapwork' pl. 122) and sprigged with gilt; Usk, early nineteenth century. 30.5cm

© National Museum of Wales (NMW A 50072)

Billy the Bagman died in 1811, leaving the works to his son William. Within two years, through lack of interest and increasing competition from Midlands japanners, the younger William allowed the business to decline 'exceedingly'. [25] He emigrated to America in 1817, and japanning came to an end in Pontypool. His mother, Mary, and her nephew, John Hughes, struggled on, presumably by selling the remaining stock, but when she died, in 1822, the Pontypool Japan Works finally closed. An ignominious end but, ironically, the fine reputation earned by the Pontypool Japan Works lived on, by default, in the contemporary products of their rivals at Usk which, by virtue of their similarity, continued to be widely known as 'Pontypool'.

Allgoods & Co., Usk
1763–1860

When the third generation of Allgoods inherited the Pontypool Japan Works in 1763 (see above), the disagreement between them was such that Edward Allgood's two sons, Thomas and Edward, withdrew their capital from the firm, secured the support of their retail agents, and took the younger members of the Stockham family, and other skilled decorators, to set up rival workshops in Usk. Unable to obtain supplies from Pontypool, they purchased their sheet-iron from Monmouth, and their tinplate mainly from Caerleon, both in South Wales.

Thomas and Edward Allgood, trading as Allgoods & Co., continued to make finely painted trays and waiters with pierced edges and, indeed, all the other products they had made at Pontypool. Just how similar their wares were may be judged from the embittered advertisements each firm placed in *The Gloucester*

Journal in July, 1763. Messrs Allgood, Davies and Edwards were first to enter the fray with the announcement that 'all Sorts of the real and most durable Japan Ware is continued to be made and sold at the Manufactory at Pont-y-pool.'[26]

Not to be outdone, the Allgoods at Usk responded, a month later, by describing themselves as 'the original JAPAN MANUFACTURERS' who would supply:

Every Article in the JAPAN WAY, well known and allowed by Judges far to excel any Performance of the Kind in the known World. And whereas great quantities of Japan Goods made in Birmingham and elsewhere (vastly inferior for Beauty and Duration to the original Manufacturers) are sold under the Sanction of our Names, to the great Imposition of the Public, and Discredit of our Business.[27]

And, thus, their grievances continued to be publicly aired over the ensuing weeks.

Between c.1799 and 1811, the Usk firm was owned by John Hughes, a relative of the Allgoods, but run largely by Morgan Davies (d.1837), its 'chief designer and ornamental painter',[28] and Richard Stockham, son of Pontypool's leading japanner and decorator, John Stockham. Hughes' wife is believed to have mixed the pigments. A record in the journal of A.M. Cuyler, who visited Usk in 1807, shows, yet again, its similarity with Pontypool in terms of both its products and customer-service. 'In an upper room is a large apartment of japanned Articles', Cuyler noted, in which the objects ranged:

From the handsomest Trays and Tea Urns, to common candlesticks and Nut-crackers, and it is very reasonably expected that the visitor should make a purchase, as a recompense for the indulgence which has been shown him. Any person wishing for a particular pattern – to have his Arms emblazoned – or a view of his house or grounds painted and japanned upon a tray or other article, upon sending a drawing, may have it executed to his wishes ... Old worn out things are also re-japanned and made as good as new.[29]

Cuyler's reference to 'common candlesticks' somewhat underplayed Usk's reputation for making excellent articles of the sort.

Thereafter, from 1814 to 1826, under the ownership of John Pyrke, a former employee, Usk's reputation for high quality workmanship continued, but fashions had changed, and demand for old-style Pontypool-ware had declined against increased competition from Midlands manufacturers. Gothic-shaped trays were introduced, with brown or black grounds decorated all-over with the 'Stormont pattern' in red, and small rectangular tea-canisters with lift-off round lids, decorated with delicate flower-sprigs in gold against brown, black or crimson grounds, were particularly characteristic of the Usk factory during this period (plate 309).

Evan Jones, a brick, tile and pipe manufacturer, took control of the factory in 1826. The factory had lost its earliest rival with the closure of the Pontypool Works four years earlier, but that did little to reduce the effects of the large-scale development of japanning in the Midlands. And when electro-plating was introduced in the late 1830s, the Usk factory, in no shape to seriously counter its effects, witnessed a rapid downturn in trade. Jones died in 1860 and the factory was closed down; its stock was sold by auction two years later.

Further Reading

Babbidge, Adrian, *A Short History of Pontypool Japanware*, Torfaen Museum Trust, 1984.

Berg, Torsten & Peter (Transl.), *R.R. Angerstein's Illustrated Travel Diary*, 1753–1755, Science Museum, London, 2001

John, W.D., and Simcox, Anne, *Pontypool and Usk Japanned Wares*, Newport, England, reprint 1966.

Kyrle Fletcher, John, 'The Painted Tray', *Apollo*, vol. XXVI, no. 152, Aug. 1937, pp. 87-92.

Nichols, Reginald, *Pontypool and Usk Japan Ware*, Pontypool, 1981

Sanderson, Patricia, & Wildgust, Deborah, *The Story of Pontypool & Usk Japanware*, Torfaen Museum Trust & Usk Rural Life Museum, 2009

THETFORD
The Patent Pulp Manufacturing Company 1879–c.1939
Thetford, Norfolk

The Patent Pulp Manufacturing Company of Thetford in Norfolk began making japanned pulp goods in 1879, the year of its foundation.

A list of their more decorative products reads like those of many Midlands japanners, but where the Thetford company differed noticeably was in the range of bowls they made. The factory was perhaps best known for its oval baby-baths, but they also made powder bowls for the dressing table, bowls to serve as plant holders, and display bowls for shopkeepers and manufacturers who, if they ordered more than two gross, could have them printed with their names. Those made for tea-merchants were often decorated with Japanese-style prints.

This Eastern style of decoration, used on many of their products, is the cause of much confusion among collectors today as similar prints are found on contemporary French work. Introduced in Thetford in about 1890, it took the form of Japanese figures which were transfer-printed in gold and colour, initially on black grounds, but from the early 1900s, also on scarlet, orange, light green, or cream (plate 310). The Thetford decorators never embellished the printed

310. Papier mâché dish with transfer-printed decoration; printed mark of Thetford Patent Steel Pulpware; late nineteenth/early twentieth century. Dia: 19.5cm

© WOLVERHAMPTON ARTS AND HERITAGE (BANTOCK HOUSE MUSEUM)

figures with hand-painted impasto faces as was customary in France, but since the French had dropped this practice by the early twentieth century, this rule of thumb for distinguishing the products has its limitations.

Thetford Fibre was made from various raw materials: jute bagging, imported wood-pulp, waste paper and rags, boiled with lime to remove impurities, and milled for up to forty-eight hours until a fine pulp. Articles were then made in much the same way as Midland pulp goods: shaped in moulds, stove dried and steeped in linseed oil and resin to make them damp-proof, and japanned with several coats of varnish. As on some Midlands pulp-ware, the pattern of the mesh-moulds in which the articles were formed often shows in the surface of the varnish.

The resulting material, though light, was so strong that it was used to make safety helmets for cyclists and miners. In fact, it was marketed as 'Thetford Patent Steel Pulpware', and some goods, like the bowl seen here were marked, in gold, to this effect. The factory used several marks during the course of its history, but only this, and a circular mark, also printed in gold, and lettered '150 useful articles made in England' encircled by the name 'Thetford Norfolk Pulpware', are of relevance here.

After the second World War, pulp-ware gave way to newer materials like polythene and polpropylene. Today, the company specialises in the manufacture of safety helmets.

Further Reading

Durbin, Gail, 'Thetford Pulpware', *Antique Collecting*, vol. 19, no. 9, Feb. 1985, pp. 27-9.

EUROPE

FRANCE

It is not known precisely when japan varnishes were first used in France, but on the evidence of 'two tables on pedestals varnished in red', listed in the royal inventory, in 1661,[30] it is generally believed to have been before then. The craft was evidently well established by 1713, when Jacques Dagly (1655–1728)[viii] was granted a patent as a varnisher, and appointed director of lacquer at the Gobelins workshops in Paris. By 1738, japanning was sufficiently noteworthy to have provoked a public debate on its technique in the June and August issues of the French journal, *Mercure*.

Under the influence of Louis XIV (1638–1714) and his taste for high fashion, many leading French furniture makers began to produce japanned furniture, among them, Sieur Jean-Félix Watin whose later treatise, *The Art of Painting, Gilding & Varnishing* (1772), became a classic work on the subject. Japanning was in demand throughout the courts of Europe: Dagly's chinoiserie designs, for example, so impressed Tsar Peter the Great, during his visit to his workshops in 1717, that he had Russian craftsmen decorate a hall in similar style in his summer palace, Montplaisir, and thus triggered the start of japanning in Russia (see below).

The commercial development of japanning in France, took a different course from that in Britain insofar as the process was first carried out on papier mâché as distinct from metal. It was not until twenty or so years later that the French applied the technique to metal. This was partly because paper-making had begun earlier in France, and papier mâché had been used, since the sixteenth century, for making architectural ornaments. But it was also due to the foresight of four Parisians, who, as *vernisseurs* to the royal court, saw the combined potential of japan varnish and papier mâché. They were the Martin brothers and they gave their name to a style of decoration which came to be known as *vernis Martin*.

Robert Dossie criticised French japanners for priming the surfaces of their papier mâché coaches and snuff-boxes with size because, he said, it made the 'japan coats of the Parisian boxes crack and fly off in flakes whenever any knock or fall, particularly near the edges, exposes them to be injured.' In his estimation, similar products made by 'the Birmingham manufacturers [wore] greatly better than the French.'[31] In spite of such an apparent shortcoming, French papier mâché ware was admired throughout Europe – a success grudgingly acknowledged, as we have seen, in a Birmingham trade directory in 1780. But, the anonymous author added, somewhat defensively, 'whatever goods the French may have made of this composition for use, seems to have been confined to their own kingdom; those which have come to England from thence, having been of less consequence.'[32]

Certainly, this would explain the ignorance of the older and highly successful French papier mâché industry, displayed by a correspondent to the *Notes and Queries* column of a Birmingham newspaper, over one hundred years later. The letter also gives an indication of the wide range of uses for which papier mâché was employed in France in the late eighteenth century:

> In the 'Journal de Paris' for June 1778, there is an account of a papier mâché carriage used by a certain M de Montfort, in his travels in Africa some years before the above date. It appears that doubts were expressed as to the truth of De Montfort's story, and to set them at rest he made a similar carriage in Paris, and the editor of the 'Journal' states that he saw at De Montfort's house examples of 'cabinets, Salons portatif, furniture for the richest apartments, vases, boats, gondolas, and baths.' The material is said to be capable of being cut like wood, and the sheets of which the carriage was made were two lines thick. Is it possible that these could have been some of Clay's manufactures imported into France? I never heard that the French made papier mâché articles at that time. RPB.[33, ix]

In the nineteenth century, the French papier mâché industry developed along lines so similar to those in England that it can be difficult to distinguish the products of one country from another. Styles of decoration are not always useful guides, for as David Sarjeant noted in his report on the papier mâché shown at the Paris Universal Exhibition, in 1867, 'English workmen are highly esteemed in Paris', and 'many have been employed here'[34] (plate 311).

Tôle Peinte[x]

The japanning of metal did not seriously begin in France until about 1760–65. In Horace Walpole's inventory of *China in the Waiting Room at Strawberry Hill*, compiled in 1784, for example, it was still possible for him to describe 'Two monteiths of Tolle [*sic*]' as 'a *new* French metal japanned' [author's italics].[35]

Early French japanners generally worked on articles made from tin-plate or pewter, and finished their goods with a varnish made from linseed oil, driers, and gum copal, which by contrast with the quick-drying spirit varnish used in Wales and the English Midlands, had a tendency to crack.

Initially, French manufacturers made mainly chimney garnitures, but the range increased during the course of the next sixty years and included the brightly coloured and finely decorated chestnut urns which are now so frequently mistaken for Pontypool japan ware. In fact, the majority of surviving chestnut urns were made in France and not in Pontypool. However, some of the best French japanned tinware, painted in the style of Sevres porcelain, dates from the early nineteenth century.

Writing of the tin-ware shown at the Paris Exhibition in 1867, Archer commented that 'tea trays appear to be articles not much used in France and the grocers do not adopt the same methods of showing their goods'[36] as grocers in Britain. Nevertheless, trays with coloured grounds, similar to light coloured wood, and decorated with topographical engravings of France, were made c.1860. They were varnished to preserve them from damage. And it was noted that 'Baths, toilet wares &c, always japanned [in England] are here generally left in the bright metal.'[37]

It is possible here, only to dwell on the best-known manufacturers, and upon those makers who attracted the attention of English reporters at major exhibitions. 'There were other exhibitors of French japanning but as their products showed neither novelty of shape nor decoration',[38] Archer chose to ignore them.

311. Part of the display of English and French papier mâché furniture in the Museum of Decorative Art, Paris.

viii. Brother of the celebrated japanner Gerhard Dagly (*fl.* 1687–1714), of Spa.
ix. 'RPB' was evidently mindful of later French papier mâché. At the time of his writing, the English market was flooded by inexpensive articles made by one of the leading French papier mâché manufacturers, Adt Frères (*qv*).

x. Although *tôle-vernis* (japanned sheet iron) is the more accurate term for the type of goods under discussion, it has been superseded by tôle (sheet iron) and tôle peinte (painted sheet iron).

Vernis Martin
Paris

In 1753, Simon Etienne Martin (d.1770), patented a copal-based varnish which, in combination with papier mâché, would play an important part in the development of the European japanning industry. Indeed, Martin's varnish was acknowledged by the *Birmingham Gazette* in 1767, for having been 'for some Years ... the Admiration of all Europe in the Beauty of [Martins'] Coaches, Snuff Boxes, &c. and appears equal to glass itself.'[39] Moreover, it was the varnish for which the Royal Society had so anxiously sought an English equivalent in 1759 (p. 118). The French varnish came to be known as *vernis Martin* – a term which has been adopted as a generic name for a wide range of French products decorated in the style of the Martin workshop in Paris.

First, however, it is necessary to provide the context in which this varnish was developed.

The Martin workshop had been founded, some years before, in about 1730, by Guillaume Martin, a distinguished carriage painter (d.1749), whose three younger brothers: Simon Etienne, Robert (1706–1765/6), and Julien (d.1752), soon joined him in business. Among Guillaume Martin's clients was Louis XIV's ambassador in Vienna, for whom he made a carriage with panels japanned in imitation of aventurine glass[xi] – opulence of an order mocked by Voltaire in his comedy Nanine, and which later prompted the reactionary Gabriel Mirabeau (1749–1791) to rail against ostentatious vernis Martin carriages.[40] The varnish which Guillaume employed was not of his own invention, but he brought it to such perfection, that, in 1730, Louis XV (1710–1774) granted him a patent, and appointed him varnisher to the royal household – a highly influential position, which he held until 1749.

Under royal patronage, the Martin brothers forged a reputation across Europe as creators of fine furniture inset with chinoiserie panels in extravagantly scrolling gilt rococo mounts, and lacquer rooms, decorated with impasto ornament in imitation of Eastern lacquer – a technique for which they were granted a second patent in 1744.

However, it is as pioneer makers of japanned papier mâché that the Martin Brothers are of concern here, for they can be said to have kick-started the development of an entirely new industry in Europe.

Guillaume Martin first japanned papier mâché in about 1740 – more than ten years before similar experiments were begun in England – and so successfully, that within five years, Paris was flooded by less expensive imitations. The novelty of Martin's invention, and its curiosity value in England, can be gauged from a short notice which appeared in The London

Tradesman, in 1747:

I must inform the Reader of a late French invention of Snuff-Boxes, which however absurd it may seem at first sight ... are made of the same Materials as Paper; are to be had at Paris of any Colour, but are most commonly Black, as Ebony, and are actually as hard and durable as any made of Wood, Horn, or Tortoiseshell. They are made of Linen-Rags, beat to a Pulp, as if intended for Paper. A large Quantity of Pulp is put into a Vessel, and the Water allowed to drain off; the Pulp is dried, and coheres together in a hard uniform Lump, out of which they turn upon the Leath, Boxes or any other kind of Toys, which for their Novelty fetch a large price.[41] (plate 312)

A later, more detailed description by Jerome le Français de Lalande, published in France, in 1762, shows that, by then, the Martins' made their papier mâché boxes by the layered method – the method which was soon to have such an influence first upon English manufacturers, and then upon other European makers.

In 1748, the factory was appointed a 'Manufacture Royale'. Guillaume Martin died the following year, but the continued success of his papier mâché was ensured when, in 1753, his brother, Simon-Etienne, patented his famous copal-based varnish which was described by Sieur Jean-Félix Watin in *The Art of Painting, Gilding & Varnishing* (1772), his seminal work on the subject, as '*vernis blanc au copal*'. There were, he said, five essential steps in its application: a light rubbing with pumice and a damp cloth; another with a cloth soaked in rottenstone and olive oil; rubbing the surface dry; cleaning with starch or chalk powder to remove all traces of oil; and, finally, polishing with a clean linen cloth. This was the varnish which the Royal Society in London, and Stephen Bedford in Birmingham, were so keen to rival.

Also in 1753, the Martins were exempted from all taxes in recognition of their significance to the national economy. The official declaration to this effect provided the first known record of the vernis Martin process, and it is from this that we know the Martins primed their wares with a paste of whiting and size – a practice criticised by Dossie, who thought it was likely to cause the overlying varnish to crack. Prior to varnishing, the article was rasped and filed and the coloured decoration added. Green grounds were the most highly prized, but blue and yellow were also popular. Powdered gold was sometimes added to the base colour in imitation of Japanese lacquer.

At Scone Palace, near Perth in Scotland, are displayed seventy pieces of papier mâché, made by the Martins, from a set of one hundred and twenty,[xii] originally designed for Louis XVI's palaces at Fontainebleu and Versailles. They include mainly vases and urns, painted with classical scenes in a restricted palette of black and gold powders on crimson grounds, all exuberantly mounted in gilt-metal by London goldsmiths. They are remarkable, not least as early examples of papier mâché hollow-ware. The collection was presented to the 2nd Earl of Mansfield (d.1796) who, earlier in his career and as the 7th Viscount Stormont, had been ambassador, first to Vienna, and later to Paris. He was a friend of Marie Antoinette whom he first met when she was a young girl in Vienna, and again in Paris as Queen of France. The gift was made in 1793, the year in which her husband, Louis XVI, was executed.

The Martins' shops were fashionably situated in Faubourg St-Martin, rue St-Denis, and rue St-Magloire, from where, in addition to furniture and coaches, they supplied the French royal family and other prestigious clients – including the famously extravagant Mme de Pompadour – with snuff-boxes, bowls, goblets, necessaires, and other trifles, many of which were mounted in gold. They were japanned in various colours: red, green, blue, yellow, white and, of course, black, and often given aventurine-effects by scattering coloured metal powders such as brass or copper, on to the wet varnish. These formed the backgrounds for finely painted flowers, or copies of celebrated paintings framed within delicate gilt borders of wavy or reticulated lines, or for the coats of arms of their noble and aristocratic clients. Since such flagrant displays of wealth and status were unwise in the turbulent climate of pre-Revolutionary France, it is said that some aristocrats had the insignia on their boxes painted over.

Jean-Alexandre Martin, the last member of the family to be involved with the factory, ceased trading in 1787.

None of the Martin brothers marked their work, and few surviving examples can be reliably attributed to them. This, and the use of *vernis Martin* as a generic term, means not only that many products so described were made by other makers, but that these makers are likely to have been greater in number than is generally credited. Unless the quality of a French papier mâché box, for example, is outstandingly high, it is unlikely to have been made in the Martin workshops.

Adt Frères 1839–1950s
Ensheim, Germany
From 1844 also at Forbach, and from 1871, at Pont à Mousson, France

There is a very distinctive range of mid/late papier mâché goods which have survived in huge numbers. They come in the form of inexpensively produced items such as snuff-boxes, tea-trays, crumb-trays and other articles for the dining table which, contrary to popular belief, were made, not in England, but in France, by Adt Frères.

312. Papier mâché box with silver, and chased gilded metal fittings, containing a lift-out tray with two compartments; French, possibly made by the Martin brothers, c.1740–1770. 5.5 x 13.5 x 7cm

PHOTO © VICTORIA AND ALBERT MUSEUM, LONDON (Museum No. W.44+A – 1923)

The history of the Adt factory is entangled in the politics of the Franco-Prussian War, for having begun as a German firm in 1839, it became a French company in 1871. Whether their products are German or French, therefore, depends upon when they were made.

The firm originated in Ensheim, a small German town near Sarreguemines on the border with France. There, Mathias Adt (b.1715), a miller, carved wooden figures and snuff-boxes as a hobby, which he sold to Michael Stein, the abbot of nearby Wadgassen who, in turn, sold them in local abbeys and convents where, in the mid eighteenth century, snuff-taking was widespread.

Stein had purchased, in Paris, some vernis Martin boxes of papier mâché which he instructed Adt to copy. The resulting rectangular, black varnished boxes with painted lids were so successful that in about 1770, Stein set up a workshop for their manufacture under the direction of Johann-Peter Adt (1751–1806), one of Mathias' sons.

Rival makers soon followed, and by 1800, the area around Ensheim and Sarreguemines was renowned for the production of snuff-boxes. About 250 families were involved, making over 100,000 dozen boxes per year for the home market and for Italy, Russia and Turkey. Adt's workshop was the only one of any significance to survive both the economic effects of the Napoleonic Wars and increasing competition from other German papier mâché manufacturers such as Stobwasser (*qv*) in Brunswick.

xi. Now in the Musee Cluny, Paris.
xii. The remainder were bought by the Tsar and housed at The Hermitage until their disappearance in 1917.

PAPIER MACHE PUFF BOXES.

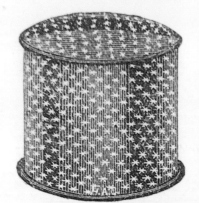

Best Star Pattern.

	Per doz.	
	s.	d.
$3\frac{1}{8}$ inch diameter ...	3	0
$3\frac{1}{2}$,, ,, ...	3	6

Best Chinese Pattern.

	Per doz.	
	s.	d.
$2\frac{7}{8}$ inch diameter ...	3	6
$3\frac{1}{8}$,, ,, ...	4	0
$3\frac{1}{2}$,, ,, ...	5	0

Daisy Pattern

	Per doz.	
	s.	d.
$2\frac{7}{8}$ inch Diameter...	3	6
$3\frac{1}{8}$,, ,, ...	4	0
$3\frac{1}{2}$,, ,, ...	5	0

Rose Pattern.

Black Ground, sprays of Coloured Roses.

	Per doz.	
	s.	d.
$2\frac{7}{8}$ inch diameter ..	3	6
$3\frac{1}{8}$,, ,, ..	4	0
$3\frac{1}{2}$,, ,, ..	5	0

Gold Ground, sprays of Coloured Roses. Will not tarnish.

	Per doz.	
	s.	d.
$2\frac{7}{8}$ inch diameter ..	4	9
$3\frac{1}{8}$,, ,, ..	5	9
$3\frac{1}{2}$,, ,, ..	7	0

Oval, sprays of Coloured Roses on black ground.

5/6 per dozen.

Oval, spray of Coloured Roses on gold ground. Will not tarnish.

7/- per dozen.

Oval Daisy Pattern.

5/6 per dozen.

The "Cylinder."

$3\frac{1}{4}$ in. high.

	Per doz.	
	s.	d.
Rose patt. Black Ground	5	6
,, ,, Gold ,,	7	0

Oval "Louis XVI" Pattern.

Very elegant.

9/- per dozen.

313. Page showing papier mâché boxes made by Adt Frères, from the 1893 catalogue of H.A. Goodall & Co., London, 'Merchants & Dealers in Sundries for the Brush and Hardware Trades'.

By the third generation, and under the guidance of Peter Adt III (1798–1879), the company had become a major producer of papier mâché goods, showing regularly at fairs and exhibitions, and winning medals at Munich in 1835, and at Spire in 1837. A new factory was built at Ensheim in 1839, the year in which Adt's sons named the business 'Gebrüder Adt'.

Ensheim continued to be their leading factory but, in order to evade French import duties, Adt built two factories in the French town of Forbach in Lorraine, one in 1844, and another in 1853, and it was as 'Adt Brothers of Ensheim', that they showed a range of papier mâché cigar cases, glove boxes, work boxes and cash boxes at the Great Exhibition in London. Their manufactures, however, were more varied than this list would suggest for, by then, their products ranged from trays to pedestal tables, and from utilitarian goods to decorative panels for the salons and boudoirs of fashionable Parisiennes.

The German origins of Pierre Adt IV (1820–1900) placed him in an invidious position at the outbreak of the Franco-Prussian War, when France was forced to cede Alsace and part of Lorraine to Germany. In 1871, with 200 loyal employees from Forbach, he built a new factory at Pont-à-Mousson in the French part of Lorraine, restyled the company 'Adt Frères' and, thenceforward, looked upon this as his main factory. It was there, and at Forbach, that the wares decorated with flowers which have survived in such large numbers were made from the late 1870s until about the First World War (plate 313). The factory at Forbach supplied mostly the Russian, UK, Balkan, and North American markets, while the one at Pont-a-Mousson focused upon France and her colonies.

Adt sometimes marked their wares with an impressed pattern number or, very occasionally, with an impressed or printed trade mark. Generally, however, goods left the factory without any permanent form of identification. Their product list was too extensive to enumerate here and their shapes and decorative styles too varied. There are, however, certain characteristics of form and decoration which may help in their identification.

Adt made many of the small papier mâché articles which are decorated only with mother of pearl, or with delicate pewter motifs arranged to form either border patterns, or bold check-effects for the centres of small trays and other flat-ware. Often, pearl and pewter were used in combination. It is a sign of their competitive prices, and the declining state of the papier mâché trade in England in the 1860s, that Adt made souvenir wares

in these styles for the English popular market. Since these inevitably featured names of English resorts and towns, they can, if unmarked, deceive today's collectors (plate 314).

Today, the most commonly found objects made by this firm are square boxes for handkerchiefs and rectangular glove boxes with brightly coloured interiors, powder-boxes, wall-pockets, hanging shelf brackets, pen trays, and crumb trays with matching brushes. In addition there are small round dishes with plain or scalloped edges, round waiters, and

314. Papier mâché snuffbox with hinged lid, decorated with scrap-pearl and pewter in typical Adt Frères style; c.1860. 4 x 2.5 x 7.5cm
© WOLVERHAMPTON ARTS AND HERITAGE (BANTOCK HOUSE MUSEUM)

315. Papier mâché buttons with metal shanks; French, second half of the nineteenth century. Av. dia: 3cm
© WOLVERHAMPTON ARTS AND HERITAGE (BANTOCK HOUSE MUSEUM)

316. Concave-rectangular papier mâché tray with transfer printed decoration; made by Adt Frères, impressed pattern no. 6202; late nieteenth/early twentiech century. 18.8 x 25.6cm

rectangular trays with rounded corners (plate 316). Other frequently found small articles are snuff-boxes with hinged lids, spill vases, and spectacles cases. Larger objects include nests of tables, huge cylindrical umbrella stands, and variously shaped tables constructed from trays of equal or graduated sizes, arranged in tiers and fixed to simulated bamboo legs.

Hand-screens with pierced or fretted edges are among less frequently found but distinctive objects (plate 317). Equally distinctive, and again less common, are liqueur cabinets. These took the form of small, often oval cabinets, with two doors and hinged lids which opened to reveal glass decanters and a set of liqueur glasses. Cabinets of this type, which appear always to have been painted with flower sprays and ornamented with gold leaf and pearl, are sometimes mistakenly believed to be English.

From about 1880, however, it is by their decoration that Adt products are most readily identified. The various styles of ornament were used across all their products and not confined to any particular article. The most popular floral motifs at Adt were daisies, sunflowers, and lilies of the valley. Other much-used designs were Japanese scenes transfer-printed in gold and colour with the flesh-tints of the figures on early examples, so thickly painted, by hand, that they stand in relief on the surface. It is this over-painting which distinguishes them from similar articles made in England by Thetford Pulp Ware (*qv*), although, for reasons of economy, Adt, also, dispensed with these hand-painted additions on later wares.

Finally, in terms of decoration, the simplest of Adt's ornaments was a transfer printed pattern of all-over bronze or

317. Papier mâché handscreens with die-cut edges, and painted decoration; French, last quarter of the nineteenth century. Screens: 23.5 x 24cm

318. Letter rack, papier mâché with transfer printed decoration; Adt Frères, late nineteenth/early twentieth century. 21.5 x 17 x 4.5cm

320. Papier mâché snuff boxes with hinged lids, transfer-printed for the English market; made by Adt (see p. 281), c.1880s. Av. W: 7.5cm
COURTESY OF BRIGHTWELLS, LEOMINSTER

319. Vase made from papier mâche and jute, with transfer-printed decoration; Adt Freres, c.1880–1900. H: 70cm (Similar vases from this factory exceeded 1m in height).
COURTESY OF LE MUSÉE DE PONT-À-MOUSSON

silver stars against black and coloured grounds. To judge from the many examples which have survived, this pattern was produced in large numbers over many years (plate 313).

A pen-tray by Adt, decorated with the star pattern and lettered for the *Gouvernemente Egyptienne*, was almost certainly part of a large and official order. Such orders, and the production of advertising and souvenir goods for both French and foreign markets, constituted an important branch of Adt Frères' business. It is not uncommon, for instance, to find snuff-boxes, trays, and small desk-items printed in gilt with varying designs, and named for various companies, or to find others decorated with Islamic symbols for export to Turkey, or with subjects suitable for North Africa, a former French colony.

Much of Adt Brothers' success was due to their shrewd marketing. In addition to the exhibitions already mentioned, they showed at every Leipzig fair between 1835 and 1939, and won medals at the Paris Exhibitions of 1878 and 1889. In addition to outlets in Berlin, Nuremburg, and Milan, they opened one in London in 1860 – mindful perhaps of the declining trade of the English papier mâché makers – and another in Brussels in 1880. Alongside England and Russia, it appears that their stiffest competition came from American papier mâché manufacturers. Accordingly, they opened a showroom in New York in 1888 but, on account of the McKinley Tariff, introduced in America two years later to

control imported goods, it was less successful than their other overseas outlets. By 1889, their trade catalogues were published in English as well as in French and German. Adt Fréres became a limited liability company in 1901 with registered offices in Paris where they also had a large warehouse with shop-windows for the display of their goods.

Together with their popular ranges, Adt made high quality goods for their wealthier clients. Among them were a number of very large vases decorated, by hand, in oriental style, of which some very fine examples are on show at the museum in Pont-à-Mousson (plate 319).

By the early twentieth century, the thrust of their industry was changing, and in 1904, the Pont-à-Mousson factory diversified into making insulation sheaths for electric cables. When war broke out in 1914, the factory at Forbach was seized by the French authorities and continued under state ownership until 1923 when, together with the other factories, it became the Socièté Nouvelles des Etablissements Adt. They began to make *Fibrolaque*, a form of japanned, compressed paper, for the production of inexpensive advertising materials, and for bobbins and spindles for the textile industry. The company was bought out in 1927 and continued to make decorative papier mâché until the 1930s, but by then, it was largely overshadowed by newer branches of business. It finally closed in the 1950s.

C.A. Gallais
Paris

Furniture featured prominently among the japanned goods at the Paris Exhibition in 1867, and one of the leading makers was C.A. Gallais who specialised in its production.

To judge from contemporary reports, the furniture made at Gallais' large factory in Paris seriously rivalled that made by English japanners. The firm exhibited at both the 1862 Exhibition in London, and at the Paris Exhibition of 1867, and on both occasions, English commentators praised the quality of Gallais' products.

In London, where he focused on imitations 'of Chinese lacker-work' [sic], his exhibits included a wooden cabinet decorated in this style, and others made of papier mâché, which were all considered 'excellent in form, and very carefully executed'.[42]

A visitor to his Paris showroom in 1867 saw a 'large assortment of goods in every style of decoration common in England', together with 'imitations of Japan lac and ebonised woodwork [both] decorated and plain'.[43] Light coloured or neutral grounds were a feature of the Gallais factory. For example, at the Paris exhibition in the same year, he showed part of a suite of furniture 'decorated with Watteau subjects and Italian ornaments on a white ground' and with 'no gold' – it was considered 'very chaste'.[44] The seats and backs of chairs and couches were generally covered with tapestry. Gallais' foreman said 'I will sell lots of these in your country'[45] which his English visitor believed was probably true.

David Sarjeant's report, following his visit to the Gallais factory, is especially interesting in relation to the differences between the French and English trades. Most of the gilding was carried out as in Birmingham, for example, but there were two notable differences: Gallais did not employ bright gilding, and he used another technique 'similar, if not identical, with picture frame gilding';[46] in other words, it was left unvarnished. Another difference was remarked upon by Gallais' foreman who said to Sarjeant:

> *"You English can beat us in landscape and gold work, but you cannot touch our flowers." He commissioned me [Sarjeant] to send a landscape painter, offering to pay him 10 francs per day. If it is true as some assert, that living is cheaper here, this is better pay than can be got in England.*[47]

The flower and ornamental painting were done in the workman's home and, Sarjeant added, 'judging by the price paid for flower painting, I think a good workman may earn £3 per week'.[48] Another important difference was that Gallais employed a designer. 'With us', Sarjeant noted, 'this part is ovelooked, one man making, the other finishing, each according to his own taste'.[49]

Thus, while Gallais made few small articles, his products would have provided serious competition for English firms like McCallum & Hodson, who exported much furniture to France. As one of the jurors at the London Exhibition, in 1862, observed: 'To M. Gallais belongs the honour of having given a great impulse to this neglected industry in France and to have restored it to the domain of progress and good taste.'[50]

Other French Exhibitors at the Paris Exhibition of 1867

In their reports on French japanned ware shown at the Paris Exhibition of 1867, the English jurors – David Sarjeant and Thomas Archer – singled out only those manufacturers who showed new designs or commendable skill. Of those named, Adt Frères, and C.A. Gallais, have already been discussed. Although they had less to say about the Parisian firms of Trouchon and Germain, it may be helpful to draw them to the attention of collectors today, and particularly so in the case of the latter, because some of his products appear to have closely resembled earlier English examples.

Trouchon was one of several japanners whose exhibits included japanned iron chairs and tables, garden seats, and japanned and gilded bird-cages. He also showed japanned zinc flower-pot stands, which were thought both 'tasteful and cheap'.[51] Other exhibitors of this category of goods showed japanned iron clock fronts, bedsteads and candelabra.

The papier mâché exhibits made by Germain, whilst focussing on furniture, also included trays and the usual array of goods made from this material. Decorated with pearl 'and finished in a style made popular some years ago by a well-known firm in Birmingham',[xiii] their effect was 'dazzling' and the 'finish of flowers shows a study of nature usually wanting in that class of work'.[52] The comparison with an earlier Birmingham style hinted at their lack of novelty, and Germain's goods were further criticised for showing the 'unevenness of surface usual in inferior papier mâché.[53]

Further Reading:
Bourne, Jonathan, et al, *Lacquer, An International History and Collector's Guide,* London 1984
de Dampierre, Florence, *Les Plus Beaux Meubles Peints,* Suresnes, 1991
Huth, Hans, *Lacquer of the West,* Chicago, 1971
Kopplin, Monika, *European Lacquer,* Museum fur Lackkunst, 2010
Lallemand, Pierre, *Le Papier Mâché,* Editions Pierron, 57206 Sarreguemines, France, 1999

GERMANY

Although Hamburg was the first German town to be associated with japanning in the late seventeenth century, it was later developments in Brunswick that are of relevance here. For it was there, in the eighteenth and nineteenth centuries, that some of the finest japanned papier mâché and tin-ware was made.

That German japanned ware is often confused with products made in the English midlands is not entirely surprising. The English king, George I, was of German nationality and a member of the house of Brunswick-Lüneberg. Under his influence, Brunswick society looked to English workshops for their japanned furniture, and to such an extent that it caused local craftsmen to fear for their livelihoods.

Two of them, Georg Siegmund Stobwasser, and his son, Johann Heinrich, opened a factory in Brunswick for the manufacture of japanned goods. It not only established Brunswick as a major japanning centre, but it quickly proved a serious rival to japanners in the English midlands, in Pontypool, and in France.

Georg Siegmund Stobwasser & Son
1763–1870s
Brunswick & Berlin

Johann Heinrich Stobwasser (1740–1829) became interested in black japan varnish through his father, Georg Siegmund Stobwasser (1686–1776), a dealer in Ansbach lacquered goods. By 1757, Johann had discovered how to make the varnish, and, with his father, used it on small decorative articles like boxes, trays and papier mâché cups, which they sold at Bayreuth market. They sold so well, and to such prestigious clients as the Margrave of Bayreuth, that soon the Stobwassers had to employ help.

In 1763, the Stobwasser family moved to Brunswick where, under the patronage of Carl, Duke of Brunswick (1735–1780), they opened a japanning factory. There, they japanned decorative domestic wares made from tin-plate (which they purchased from Wales), brass, and wood, but mainly they japanned papier mâché.

Some of their papier mâché articles were moulded from paper pulp, but when strength and durability were required they, like the English, adopted the layered method devised by Guillaume Martin (*qv*) in Paris. Clearly, the Stobwassers worked with much thinner paper than papier mâché makers in England, for it is said they used as many as sixty to seventy sheets to make only a small box, but otherwise, their respective processes appear to have been similar. The boxes were given twenty to twenty-four coats of japan varnish, their surfaces being

polished on a lathe after every fourth coat. There then followed five to six coats of varnish made from amber and copal, after which the article was soaked in oil, baked, and polished prior to decoration. An idea of how important amber was to his commercial success, is provided by a portrait[xiv] of Johann Heinrich Stobwasser, which shows him with his hand resting on a drawer marked 'Bernstein' (amber). As in France and England, the painting was carried out with pigment suspended in varnish to ensure a completely smooth surface. When completed, the painting was protected by ten to twenty layers of copal varnish and it was this thick coating which gave German snuff-boxes their characteristic high gloss.

The Stobwasser factory soon earned a reputation for finely painted tables and supplied one to the Duke of Brunswick in 1764. Since this was the year in which the Duke had married the English princess, Augusta, a sister of George III, it may have been the table which Stobwasser is reported to have made in response to her arrogant claim that no German japanner could make anything to compare with English japanned goods. To prove her wrong, he made a table in English style. It had a sheet-iron top with a pierced rim, similar to the edges of contemporary Welsh and English trays, which Stobwasser, himself, japanned in green with red etched decoration, and on which he had one of his leading artists, Johann C.A. Schwarz (1756–1814) paint a central medallion. The Princess was unable to distinguish it from English japanned ware; Stobwasser had made his point and, in future, she ordered all such goods from him.

Among Stobwasser's earliest employees, was Jean Guerin (d.1797), a skilled cabinet-maker. Because of Guerin's considerable experience of the trade and his French ancestry, he has been linked with the Martin workshops in Paris, but there is no evidence for this. He gained his knowledge from Sebastian Chevalier, a japanner, with whom he had worked on several 'lacquered' rooms in the grand houses of Berlin and its environs. This brought Guerin to the attention of Frederick the Great who appointed him Second Court Lacquerer.

Guerin introduced imitation tortoiseshell grounds at the Stobwasser factory. It is especially apt, therefore, that one of his personal snuff-boxes which has survived, is lettered in gilt 'Jean. Guerin Vernisseur, Brunswick' on a tortoiseshell ground. His name is now mostly associated with papier mâché table-tops decorated in this manner, generally as a background to further painting.

Other early Stobwasser articles included tobacco boxes, walking sticks, cups and coffee pots, but it was the panels they made for state coaches which, in 1768, led Frederick the Great, King of Prussia (1712–1786), to invite the Stobwassers to open a factory in Berlin – an invitation which they declined.

---

xiii. This was, surely, a reference to Jennens & Bettridge.
xiv. The portrait is by F.G. Weitsch (1758–1828), a landscape painter and teacher at Stobwasser's school of painting, who was responsible for the decoration of many

Stobwasser wares prior to 1784 when he left for Italy. He was a former pupil of Tischbein, and son of Pascha Johann Friedrich Weitsch (1723–1803).

The Stobwassers preferred to stay in Brunswick where, the following year, they were granted a Ducal Concession to make, amongst other things, tables, coffee-boards (*cf.* Teaboards p. 250), waiters, games- and other boxes, mugs, cups and dressing tables, and, in addition, given the right to use a trade mark. This was a privilege rather like Henry Clay's status as 'Japanner in Ordinary to the King' but with the added benefit of providing twenty years protection against anyone setting up a rival establishment in the same town; it thus served as a type of patent. With such backing, the firm of Georg Siegmund Stobwasser & Son became not only the most celebrated japanning factory in Germany, but renowned throughout Europe for the quality of its wares – a reputation which remains undiminished among collectors today.

Stobwasser's eldest sister, Louise, married Guerin in 1767, and five years later, they moved to Berlin to open a Stobwasser factory in Wilhelmestrasse, and a retail shop in nearby Unter-den-Linden.

The extent to which Stobwasser products were influenced by contemporary English and French japanned wares is evident in the Concession which King Frederick granted the Guerins in 1773. It gave them sole right, in Berlin, to produce japanned papier mâché in English style – '*nach Englischer-Art*' – and copper, iron, leather and wooden goods, in both French and English styles, exactly as they had in Brunswick. The similarity of their tinned iron trays to their Welsh and English counterparts, is borne out by an accusation made by Ludweig Kraegelius, (*qv*) who, much to Stobwasser's chagrin, had established a rival workshop in Berlin in about 1791 – more-or-less the time that Stobwasser's royal concession expired. Kraegelius argued that Stobwasser purchased sheet-iron tray blanks with pierced edges from England – an accusation he vehemently denied. If the style of piercing may serve as a guide, then all surviving evidence is in Stobwasser's favour, for although the overall construction of his trays was similar, the pierced patterns at their edges are distinctly different from those made in Birmingham and Pontypool (plate 321).

321. Oval tin tray painted with a scene entitled *Die Lesestunde* (The Reading-hour), on a contemporary japanned wood stand. Made by Stobwasser, Berlin c.1790. 81 x 67 x 87.5cm

BRAUNSCHWEIG STADTISCHES MUSEUM (INV. NR. ST 465)

An advertisement for the Brunswick factory in 1755 shows its products to have included all that would be expected of contemporary major Midlands japanners. Where Stobwasser's output differed significantly was in the papier mâché pipe-bowls that he produced. Made in huge numbers, they were available with either finely painted black japanned bowls or moulded in imitation of Meerschaum pipes. Similar goods were made at the Berlin factory.

Johann Heinrich Stobwasser became sole proprietor of the Brunswick and Berlin factories upon the death of his father in 1776. Retaining the firm's name, 'Georg Siegmund Stobwasser & Son', he extended the firm's market into Turkey, Hungary and Russia and, in order to maintain the firm's reputation for high standards of decoration, he established a factory school of painting. By 1780, in Brunswick alone, he had sufficient business to maintain a staff of thirty-one, including two cabinet-makers, two turners, eight painters, two gilders, two japanners, one cutter, two polishers, and two further polishers who worked solely on pipe-bowls, in addition to a number of outworkers. Within six years, this number had risen to about eighty. The main thrust

322. Papier mâché snuffbox painted with a young woman in a feathered hat; made by Stobwasser, Brunswick, c.1820. Dia: 10cm
BRAUNSCHWEIG STADTISCHES MUSEUM

323. Papier mâché spectacles case painted with a portrait of *Isabel*; made by Stobwasser, Brunswick, c.1820.
14 x 7.5cm
BRAUNSCHWEIG STADTISCHES MUSEUM (INV.NR.ST141)

of his trade at this time is evident from a surviving stock-book of the same year. In terms of papier mâché, for instance, the warehouse stock included over 50 tables, 39 coffee trays, 366 waiters, close on 700 boxes of various types including tea caddies, quadrille, tobacco and other such boxes, 3 toilet cases, 5 dozen small cases, 9 dozen cups, and 200 dozen pipe bowls. Among the stock of japanned metal-ware were various types of boxes, coffee pots, and snuff-boxes. He also manufactured a successful range of japanned walking-sticks.

There was a period of unrest in the 1790s when Johann's son, Christian Heinrich Stobwasser (1780–1848), joined the business and thereby dashed the hopes of a man named Schultze, the son of Stobwasser's book-keeper in Brunswick, who had set his sights on taking over the Berlin factory. Schultze resigned and opened a factory in Breslau, taking with him not only Stobwasser's painting supervisor, but also other leading workmen. To counter this threat to his market, Johann Stobwasser successfully sought a concession from King Frederick to open a second, and larger, factory in Berlin. Leaving the Brunswick factory in charge of Ehlers, a trusted employee, Stobwasser and his son went to Berlin where, in spite of the loss of some of their best men, and the death of Guerin in 1797, their second factory prospered. Within four years the Stobwassers were able to return to Brunswick, transferring Ehlers to Berlin to manage the new factory.

Christian Heinrich took full control of the company in 1810. Having visited factories in England some years before – though there is no record of which – he implemented some of the ideas he had picked up there. In 1812, when trade between Germany and England was re-opened following the lifting of Napoleon's blockade, many English landcapes, portraits and topical subjects were introduced into his decorative repertoire copied

from engravings after Angelica Kauffmann, or Reynolds, Hogarth and other English painters. It was during this period also, that articles were painted with copies of works by Italian and Dutch old masters, or of French eighteenth and early nineteenth century painters like Fragonard, David, and Ingres.

In fact, the majority of Stobwasser's snuff- and tobacco-boxes, cigar- and spectacles-cases, which are now almost synonymous with his name, were made in in the nineteenth century in the years leading up to, and during, the 1820s. Today, these articles, with their finely painted decoration, are perhaps the most collected of all Stobwasser products (plates 322 and 323). It also appears they were equally prized by contemporary connoisseurs, for as Jurgen Glanz observed in the catalogue of his collection, so many that are found today, seem never to have been used. Such deference is hardly surprising since, often, they represent some of the finest painting ever carried out on papier mâché. As in England, however, the decoration was rarely signed, but details of the artists concerned, and of the painters employed in the earlier years of the factory, can be found in Detlev Richter's book *Stobwasser Lackkunst aus Braunschweig & Berlin* (vol. II).

Christian Heinrich returned to Berlin in 1818 and sold the Brunswick branch of his business to Meyer & Wried (*qv*) in 1832. After the sale, the Berlin factory was re-named 'C.H. Stobwasser & Co.', and its focus shifted to making lamps and bronze articles. Japanning took on a lesser importance at the Stobwasser factory, leaving the path clear for Meyer & Wried to assume an unrivalled position in Germany.

Following Christian Heinrich's death in 1848, the firm became a stock company and traded as 'Berlin Lamp & Bronze Goods Factory of Stobwasser & Co.'

Notwithstanding, the firm took part in the Great Exhibition in London in 1851, where, besides showing 'Lamps in German silver, bronze, brass and composition, gilt, &c.',[54] they also exhibited 'a large assortment of japanned articles, ornamented with paintings, in imitation of agate, malachite, tortoiseshell, &c. Tea boards, caskets, bread baskets, &c.'[55]

In 1863, the management of the company was taken over by Gustav Stobwasser (1816–1898). A cheval screen which he sent to the Paris Exhibition in 1867 upheld the firm's high standards, being remarkably well painted with figure subjects and framed in imitation of malachite and ormolu – a combination much in vogue at the time. But, sadly, the goods made towards the end of his short tenure, with their impasto decoration, or glued-on engravings, were a far cry from the fine articles made by his forebears, and no match for the inexpensive oriental imports which were beginning to infiltrate the European markets. The firm finally closed in the 1870s.

The Stobwassers fiercely guarded their pre-eminence but, inevitably, they were not without rivals, the most significant of whom are listed below.

Ludwig Kraegelius
1791–1841
Wenden Gate, Brunswick

Ludwig Kraegelius was a tin-caster who in 1791, took the bold step of setting up a japanning factory in Brunswick in opposition to Stobwasser. Moreover, he had the temerity to poach one of Stobwasser's workmen, together with a painter and two apprentice-painters. In a predictably litigious outburst, Stobwasser objected and accused Kraegelius not only of taking his men, but of opening a factory without 'concession or sample'.[56]

The episode shows how ruthlessly Stobwasser guarded his position, but also it underscores Kraegelius's determination to break the Stobwasser monopoly on the manufacture of japanned ware in Brunswick. He was granted a Concession to make japanned tin-ware provided he made no further overtures to Stobwasser's employees and that he mark all his products with his name, thus avoiding any confusion with articles made by Stobwasser – a commitment which he may have failed to uphold since no marked pieces of Kraegelius japanned tin-ware have been found.

The quality of the Kraegelius products was obviously a matter of real concern to Stobwasser, for in 1792, he lodged a further complaint. This time, he accused his rival of ignoring the bounds of his concession by making sheet-metal ware, and of continuing to poach his painters. In his defence, Kraegelius pointed out that the goods in question – boxes, candlesticks, and other sheet-metal goods – were not made in his factory, but ordered from Leipzig and, furthermore, that he japanned

them himself only because Stobwasser had failed in his promise to japan them for him. As for having poached two painters, one had never worked for Kraegelius, and the other was, anyway, freelance. And so the spat continued with each side making counter-accusations (see above), until eventually the Duke of Brunswick was forced to settle the matter by complimenting Kraegelius's products but at the same time reinforcing the terms of his Concession, and stipulating that painters could move between the two factories only after two years.

Although Kraegelius did not japan wood or papier mâché, a list of products which he exhibited in 1808 shows the extent to which his tin-plate and sheet-metal wares overlapped with those made by Stobwasser. It included tables, trays, coffee-services, kettles, candlesticks, tobacco- and snuff-boxes, and much else besides. In fact, Kraegelius's goods – commended for their 'delicacy, ornamentation, and gilding'[57] – were so similar to Stobwasser's, that they were difficult to tell apart.

The firm closed in 1841 through falling demand.

Heinrich Ludwig Evers (later **Ludwig Evers Nachfolger**)
1791–1838
Brunswick

Heinrich Evers, a master wig-maker, established a small japanning workshop in Brunswick in 1791, where he focussed entirely on wood and papier mâché articles. He is associated with a fine white japan varnish which, like all the varnishes he used, he made himself. Just as Stobwasser had undermined Kraegelius, so he took Evers to task for making and selling japanned goods, and for allegedly using his decorators. The complaint was upheld and Evers was forbidden to continue, but later in the same year, Stobwasser made further allegations, and accused him of attempting to poach his customers, and of having sold japanned mirror frames. On receipt of another ban, and in exasperation, Evers applied to the Duke of Brunswick for a Concession permitting him to continue in Brunswick.

Stobwasser argued that such a Concession would so greatly affect his own trade that he would have to dismiss staff. In the event, Evers was instructed to paint only to order, and to simply varnish, rather than japan, his work, but again, he ignored the directive. Commended for the tastefulness of their painting and the inventiveness of their forms, Evers' factory was capable of producing work of a similar standard to Stobwasser, but mostly his products were inferior. His snuff-boxes, for example, were less well-painted and finished and, according to a report sent to the Duke in 1792, the decoration of Ever's other wares generally took the form of bright colours on imitation porphyry grounds which rarely equalled the heights reached by similar decoration found on

Stobwasser's products. And, unlike the better-known firm, Evers never identified, on the box-lids, the well-known paintings from which some of them were copied.

The relentlessness of Stobwasser's attack drove Evers to move to Wolfenbüttel in 1792. Upon Ever's death in 1822, the firm passed to his son-in-law who traded as 'Ludwig Evers Nachfolger [successor]' until 1838.

Evers' round snuff-boxes were usually shallower than those made by Stobwasser, and were signed on their inner rims with an 'E' and two numerals. His successor generally signed his boxes 'EvN' in a small oval.

J.H. Wilhelm Stockmann
1811–1869
Steingraben (later Wilhelmstrasse), Brunswick

Johann Heinrich Wilhelm Stockmann (1788–1866), the son of a painter and japanner, was the best-known and most successful of all Stobwasser's German competitors. He began by showing japanned tin and sheet-iron goods at Brunswick Fair in 1811, and by 1819 had built up a product list comparable to Stobwasser's. It included various boxes, baskets, plates, lamps, lamp-shades, and clock casings as well as japanned tin figures. Stockmann used the same decorative subjects as Stobwasser but his trays were always japanned in black. He also produced fine copies of famous paintings on tin-plate, thereby bringing such pictures within reach of a wider market.

When Stockmann's brother, Johann Heinrich August Stockmann, joined him in 1820, the firm was re-designated 'Wilhelm Stockmann & Co.' It must have been about then that they began to produce papier mâché because in 1821 they advertised in a local newspaper as makers of finely painted paper snuff-boxes. Stockmann's snuff boxes were of such a high order that it is difficult to distinguish unmarked examples from those made by Stobwasser, but as a general rule, the former's boxes tended to be smaller. Differences between their cigar cases are easier to detect. For example, although in cross-section, both took the form of an elongated oval, the bases of Stockmann's cases are generally flat and they are invariably japanned in black, both inside and out. He signed his boxes with the letters 'St' or 'St/st' (plate 324).

324. Papier mâché snuffbox painted with a deer-hunt and lettered, in orange, inside the lid *Ein Treibjagen nach Rysdael*, and numbered in red 460 (or 400); the inside base painted in red 'St/St' for W. Stockmann of Brunswick, c.1820. Dia: 9.5cm

© WOLVERHAMPTON ARTS AND MUSEUMS SERVICE. www.blackcountryhistory.org

The firm was granted a Ducal Privilege, and in 1836 was appointed Lacquer Manufacturers to the court of William, Duke of Brunswick (1806–1884).

Johann Stockmann took sole charge of the company in 1845 and, soon after, the firm of W. Stockmann & Co., had achieved the status that once belonged to Stobwasser. It was represented at the Dublin Exhibition, in 1853, by a range of paintings on metal. The firm closed on the death of Johann Stockmann, in 1869.

Schaaffhausen & Dietz
1815–1914
Koblenz

This firm began as Fink, Dietz and Schaafhausen, in 1806, but following Fink's death in 1815, it traded as Schaaffhausen & Dietz. By the 1840s, if not before, it was producing a typical range of decorative and utilitarian japanned goods, not only for the German market, but also for export, especially to Greece and Turkey. Like other contemporary japanners, they looked to long-established design traditions: gothic, rococo, and, of course, eastern motifs. The firm changed hands in

325. Tinware typical of the products of Schaaffhausen & Dietz, Koblenz; mid nineteenth century. W: 59cm (tray)

1893, and continued to trade under the same name, but failing to keep pace with new technology, it finally closed in 1914. Its products are often mistakenly believed to have been made in England, or Wales (plates 325 & 327).

Meyer & Wried
1832–1856
Brunswick

In 1832, Christian H. Stobwasser sold his Brunswick japanning factory to A.W. Meyer and Carl Wried. It appears they also bought the firm's Ducal Privilege, for one of several ways in which they styled themselves was 'Stobwasser's Successors Meyer & Wried, Ducal Court Lacquer Factory'. Although relatively short-lived, Meyer & Wried were renowned for the superior quality of their japanned tin and papier mâché wares, which, in every way, matched those of their predecessors (see pl. 326). At the Mainze Fair in 1842,[xv] for instance, they showed a range of sheet-iron panels painted with copies of famous old master paintings, together with various iron trays – some of which were rectangular with rounded corners – similarly decorated with copies of popular paintings. In addition, they exhibited a table which incorporated a papier mâché panel decorated in imitation of lapz-lazuli and painted

with 'Family Friends' after a painter named Drummond. They also showed a tea-caddy and several boxes, including a papier mâché glove box, tin and papier mâché cigar cases, and twelve papier mâché snuff boxes, a sheet-metal writing set, a toy box, and what were described as 'papier mâché tool chests'.[xvi] Like the Stobwasser factory, this firm often left visible the brass screws with which they attached lids to boxes.

Meyer & Wried also exhibited at the Great Exhibition in London in 1851, where their display included japanned trays painted with *The Summer's Evening* after Nickoll, and *The Tinker* after Mieris, and what they described as 'varnished paintings with gilt frames',[58] among them one painted with *The Blind Fiddler* after David Wilkie. They appear to have shown similarly decorated trays at the New York Exhibition in 1853, and in the same year, they exhibited in Dublin.

They exported to England, France, Holland and elsewhere.

The firm closed in 1856 against stiff competition from manufacturers of cheaper goods, and a fall in demand for tobacco boxes, cigar cases, and snuff boxes, due to the new fashion for cigarettes. Meyer & Wried sometimes attached printed paper labels inside the lids of their metal boxes.

---

xv. A more detailed list will be found in Richter p. 57.

xvi. These may have been needlework boxes or manicure cases.

326. Papier mâché spectacles case painted with a portrait of Lt Colonel Kessel; made by Meyer & Wried, Brunswick, after 1831 – the year when Kessel commanded the Belgian artillery in the Battle for Kermt. 15.5 x 8cm
COURTESY OF THE MUSEUM FÜR LACKKUNST, MÜNSTER
(INV. NR. EU-ſ-d-Î)

Sandauer Boxes

Sandau, a town near the German-Austrian border, gave its name to the huge number of snuff-boxes produced in the region. Although best-known for these small boxes, other articles such as coffee pots, drinking cups, jewellery, boxes and bottles, were also japanned in the region.

Sandauer boxes were made of wood or papier mâché, and were typically round or rectangular, although star-shaped boxes with inlaid silver name-plates are also known. They were generally less sophisticated than boxes made in Brunswick but, neverthe-less, possessed a charm which made them popular with tourists from all over Europe who flocked to Marienbad, Franzenbad, and other fashionable spa resorts. An advertisement in a German newspaper in 1869, for example, reported sales to French, English, Dutch, and Russian visitors.

Their decoration varied from delightfully naïve to extremely competent, but the subjects depicted were much like those found on Brunswick and Berlin boxes, namely landscapes, portraits, and humorous scenes, the titles of which were often lettered in gold script on the painting itself. Some of the most innocuous scenes found on Sandauer boxes served as foils for erotic scenes concealed within double lids. Interestingly, these scenes are often painted with a crudity matched only by their subject, and are completely at odds with their usually better-painted exteriors.

The absence of protective raised rims on their lids and bases, their gently domed lids, and their flat bases, make the round Sandauer snuff-boxes more like some of their English counterparts than those made in Brunswick and Berlin.

Other German snuff-box-makers

From 1808, **Johann Paul Hahn** of Nurnberg-Gostenhof, made small rectangular papier mâché snuff-boxes with hinged lids. Very

little is known about this firm save that its boxes were smaller than those made by Stobwasser, and were naively painted with various subjects or, occasionally, decorated with silver inlays, or with mother-of-pearl. Hahn was granted a Ducal Privilege and marked his boxes accordingly, 'I.P.H.priv' under a running fox.

There are in existence a few signed and painted snuff boxes made by **Meyer & Kreller,** of Freiberg, Saxony, a firm which, it is believed used mother-of-pearl in their decoration.

In addition there was the firm of **N. Fleisch** of Ensheim, near Zweybrücken, which made and exhibited various snuff boxes, needle and cigar cases in papier mâché at the Great Exhibition in London in 1851. Also there, was **Hupfer & Wolfermann** of Schmölln, Saxe Altenburg, whose exhibits included a 'variety of fancy and ornamented snuff boxes etc., in papier mâché, tortoiseshell etc.',[59] in addition to a small papier mâché writing desk with a view of Heidelberg. **Abele & Co.** of Stuttgart took to the exhibition japanned papier mâché snuff-boxes decorated with ornamental drawings, mother-of-pearl, or gold and silver.

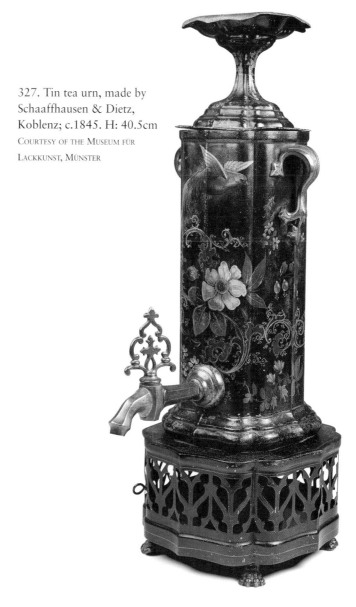

327. Tin tea urn, made by Schaaffhausen & Dietz, Koblenz; c.1845. H: 40.5cm
COURTESY OF THE MUSEUM FÜR LACKKUNST, MÜNSTER

German japanners who exhibited at the Great Exhibition

Besides the snuff-box makers named above, there were other German japanners who exhibited at the Great Exhibition. The **Directors of the Herford Prison**, Westphalia, displayed a papier mâché case decorated with straws, while the Göpingen firm of **Rau & Co.** (plate 328), showed both japanned tin-plate and papier mâché articles, some of which were decorated with mother-of-pearl. Rau claimed that the application of pearl to japanned tin-ware was new. Other German exhibits included various cast and japanned metal articles such as pedestal lamps, candle-sticks, baskets, a sugar box, covered pails, water receivers for pipes, and writing desks, made in Frankfort am Oder by **Lewy Bros.**

Further Reading

Glanz, Jurgen, *Historisches und Frivoles auf Lackdosen*, Museum of Art & Industry, Hamburg, 1999

Huth, Hans, *Lacquer of the West*, Chicago & London, 1971

Kleber, Peter, 'Koblenzer Beiträge zur Geschichte und Kulture', Neve Folge 13, 2003,*Von der Feinblechwarenfabrik zum Schweinestall: das unrühmliche Ende der Koblenzer Blechwarenfabrik Schaaffhausen & Dietz*, pp. 107–114

Kopplin, Monika, *European Lacquer,* Hirmer Verlag, Münster, 2010

Richter, Detlev, *Lacquered Boxes*, Schiffer Publishing Ltd, Pennsylvania, 1989

Richter, Detlev, with Schroeder, Susanne, (vol.I) and Lacher, Reimer F, (vol.II), *Stobwasser Lackkunst aus Braunschweig & Berlin*, Museum für Lackkunst, Münster 2005, (Vol.I p. 146ff. provides a list of German manufacturers)

RUSSIA

The commercial development of japanning in Russia began in response to a State initiative to invigorate the national economy. Landowners were encouraged to divert profits from farming to set up workshops and factories on their estates. The first to do so was the Demidov family of iron-masters when they established workshops in the Ural Mountains, in 1769, for the japanning of sheet-metal (see below). With their knowledge of ironworking, and the artistic skills among their serfs, many of whom came from families long associated with icon painting, japanning was a natural progression for the Demidovs.

328. Bird-cage and flower stand made by Rau & Co., Göpingen, from the *Official Descriptive & Illustrated Catalogue*, of the Great Exhibition (Vol. III, p. 1118)

However, it is the later factories of Pyotr Lukutin, and Filipp Nikitich Vishniakov, both situated near Moscow, and begun in 1795 and 1803 respectively, which are best-known today, particularly for their finely painted papier mâché snuff boxes and cigar cases.

At first, the Russian industry was influenced by japanned goods made in Western Europe, both in shape and decoration. Many early Russian iron trays are mistakenly attributed to Welsh or German makers and, similarly, any unmarked but well-painted papier mâché snuffbox is, today, more likely to be attributed to Germany than to Russia. Like the snuff-boxes made in Germany, the interiors of Russian snuff-boxes might be japanned in brown, or in imitation of tortoiseshell. As David Archer, a juror at the Paris Exhibition of 1867, observed of the Russian papier mâché displayed there, it differed 'in no essential respect from similar work in Germany'.[60] Moreover, gothic-shaped iron trays made in St Petersburg and decorated with flower sprays and trailing gilt tendrils often bear a remarkable likeness to contemporary English examples (plate 337). But alongside these influences, Russian japanners began to look to their own history and artistic traditions and, by the early nineteenth century, patriotic scenes from Russian history, views of Moscow and, to a lesser extent, of St Petersburg, had become popular subjects, particularly on Lukutin's boxes.

These themes took on greater importance under the new social and political order in Russia, and they heralded one of the most significant of all decorative innovations. Romanticised views of times past, showing idyllic scenes of troika speeding through snowy landscapes, or of tea-drinkers convivially seated around a samovar, became so popular that some of Lukutin's artists painted nothing else; the interiors of small boxes decorated in this way were often brightly japanned in cinnabar red, like Oriental lacquered ware. It may have been this focus on national interest that enabled the japanning industry to continue in Russia, largely uninterrupted, to the present day. Similar scenes are still painted on boxes made today and such is their popularity, and high cost, that inexpensive Chinese copies are now available which are sufficiently convincing for an example to have been exhibited as 'old' at a prestigious antiques fair.

329. Papier mâché pot-pourri
with metal beaded edge,
probably Russian; late
eighteenth/early nineteenth
century. 29 x 39 x 54cm
© CHRISTIE'S IMAGES LIMITED

Distinguishing Russian from Western European
japanned ware can, therefore, be problematic
(plate 329). After 1830, Russian japanned ware
was required by law to be marked with both the
maker's initials and the Imperial eagle – extra
eagles being added to the mark on the accession
of each successive Tsar. A mark can thus be a
useful guide to when an article was made.
Nevertheless, since many pieces escaped marking,
other distinguishing factors need to be
considered.

Besides traditional folk themes, the characteristic
styles of decoration used by both Lukutin and
Vishniakov, and probably by lesser-known
Russian makers also, were as follows:

CHINOISERIE ORNAMENT. This was
introduced in the 1820s or 1830s, and
especially popular during the 1840s and
1850s. It often incorporated raised work
but the overall style is bolder than
chinoiseries found on wares made by more
westerly japanners (plate 330).

'FILIGREE' WORK. Introduced in the 1850s,
this had the appearance of intricately
inlaid silver. It was achieved by pressing
tiny shapes of white metal into still-wet
black japan varnish. Filigree decoration
sometimes stood alone, or it was used on
snuff-boxes to border painted portraits or
traditional Russian scenes (cf. pewter
motifs used by French and German
japanners) (plate 331).

330. Papier mâché snuffbox with chinoiserie decoration; made by Lukutin, 1830s.
3.5 x 7.5cm
© 2003 STATE HERMITAGE MUSEUM, ST PETERSBURG

331. Papier mâché snuffbox with hinged lid painted with a troika within a silver
filigree border, the interior painted in imitation of tortoiseshell, and marked for
Lukutin; mid nineteenth century. L: 9.5cm
COURTESY OF BONHAMS

THE POSKVOZNOMU TECHNIQUE in which thin glazes of colour were applied over mother-of pearl to create luminous and iridescent effects. It is found mainly on small objects which lent themselves more readily to being entirely faced with one piece of pearl; the shell was either glued to the object, or it was attached with small brass screws which were allowed to remain visible on the finished article.

THE ZIEROVKA TECHNIQUE. This was a process by which surfaces were thinly covered with tin- or other metal-foil and japanned all-over. The design was then lightly scratched into the varnish revealing the metallic layer beneath. The whole was then coated with a golden varnish to give the appearance of an intricate gold pattern on a black ground. For increased effect, variously tinted varnishes were used together as on the example shown here (plate 332).

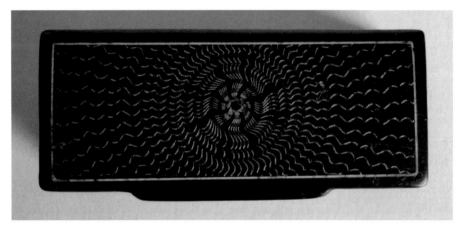

332. Papier mâché snuffbox with hinged lid decorated by the *zierovka* method; made in Fedoskino, Russia, mid nineteenth century. 2 x 9 x 3.5cm
PRIVATE COLLECTION

333. Papier mâché bottle-stand decorated with a so-called 'tartan' pattern; made in Fedoskino, Russia, mid nineteenth century. Dia: 12cm
PRIVATE COLLECTION

TARTAN PATTERNS. This is a misleading description since the designs more closely resembled simple lattices than a Scottish tartan. However, that they should have been so-called may reflect the extent of contemporary trade links between the Baltic and Scotland (plate 333).

SIMULATED EFFECTS. These included tortoiseshell effects (created by smoking a light-coloured surface while it was still wet), and imitations of marble and other semi-precious hard-stones. They were used mostly on small boxes, although tortoiseshell later became a popular ground pattern for sheet iron trays.

Finally, there is often a subtle stylistic difference in the gilding on some Russian papier mâché and tin-ware. It is difficult to pin-point precisely what this is, and mentioning it comes close to saying that you can tell hard- from soft-paste porcelain because the former chips concoidally – useless information unless the object is chipped. Nevertheless, and eagle motifs apart, comparison between the gilding on the tray shown in plate 334, and that on English specimens illustrated earlier in this book, may show the difference in question.

David Sarjeant, another juror at the 1867 Paris Exhibition, noted among the Russian displays of japanned ware 'an assortment of fancy articles some with landscapes others with Landseer's favourite dog subjects such as "Dignity and Impudence"', which he thought had 'a German look about them.'[61] But his description of a papier mâché table-top, inlaid with wood and japanned, in what would appear to be typically English style, demonstrates the caution required when attempting attributions. It was, Sarjeant said, 'the most beautiful specimen of its kind', he had seen. The design incorporated:

Aquatic plants, two flowers of the Victoria Regia being the principal objects; from one side of these rises an exotic plant with gigantic bell-shaped flowers upon which is seated a parrot with gorgeous plumage, small water-weeds are trailed about the bottom among which lizards and other small reptiles disport themselves. Pearl is used for the principal objects and gold, artistically coloured or stained, for the stems and leaves.[62]

It is evident then, that the production of papier mâché and tinware was far more significant in Russia than is often believed, and that much that was made there is now frequently mis-attributed to makers elsewhere.

334. Papier mâché tray painted with a view of the Panins' Estate, the home of Nikita Petrovich Panin, at Dugino, Smolensk; made at the Lukutin factory in the first half of the nineteenth century. 30.5 x 44cm

Over the years, and because the Russian industry received encouragement from the Soviet state in terms of tax-exemption on exports, considerable quantities of its products filtered into Western European and American markets.

The industry was based, mainly, in three centres: in Nizhny Tagil in the Ural Mountains; in a cluster of villages about twenty-five miles north of Moscow now known collectively as Fedoskino; and in fashionable St Petersburg. As will be seen, each centre had its defining characteristics.

Nizhny Tagil

In about 1769, the Demidov family set up two japanning workshops on their estates in Nizhni Tagil and Nevyansk near Ekaterinburg (now called Sverdlovsk), in the Ural Mountains. They were important as the first workshops of their type in Russia.

At first, they varnished domestic wares made of brass and iron, but when Peter Pallas, a Berlin scientist visited Nizhny Tagil in 1769, the Demidovs were seen also to be varnishing and painting wooden bowls, tumblers and trays, finely-rolled tin articles and panels for carriages. They set up an apprentice scheme by which to train their workmen, and the standard of their painting was considered high.

Other japanning workshops were established in the area and it soon became important as a centre for the manufacture of sheet-iron trays. Early production focused mainly upon four styles of tray.

The earliest trays were oval, with almost vertical sides into which D-shaped holes were sometimes cut to form handles. They were decorated with subjects copied from famous European or popular Russian paintings. Unlike English trays of the period, the pictures did not fill the base of the tray, but were framed by the surrounding ground colour in the manner of Welsh and German trays.

A particularly distinctive style of Nizhny Tagil tray had pierced or fretted sides with prominently beaded edges. Such trays were variously rectangular, octagonal, or twelve-sided, and always had either cut-out handles or separately attached 'swan-neck' brass handles. Occasionally, their surfaces were covered with flower sprigs or trailing garlands, but mostly they were painted with scenes similar to those on the oval trays described above, and edged with floral and foliate gilt borders.

Equally as peculiar to Nizhny Tagil were trays on which the decoration of the flat surface was quartered, or further subdivided, by gilt bands radiating from a central roundel, or segmented in the manner of the tray shown here (plate 335).

335. Tin tray with pierced sides and beaded gilt-metal edge decorated in a style typical of Nizhny Tagil tray-painters; early nineteenth century. 72.5cm

Each segment was painted with flowers or fruit against differently coloured grounds. Trays with four segments were generally round, but others were hexagonal, or octagonal, depending upon the number of divisions.

The fourth style of tray, introduced in the early nineteenth century, is easily confused with similarly shaped English and French trays. The trays in question were rectangular with rounded corners, convex rims, and sometimes they had cut-out handles. They were painted or stencilled (or decorated with both techniques in combination) with figurative subjects, biblical or historical themes, topical events, or formal patterns and, always, there were decorative gilt borders around their rims and framing the main decoration on their bases. These trays appear to have survived in large numbers, particularly in the United States to where many were exported.

The Demidov factory closed in the mid nineteenth century, having lost its market position to rival factories like Vishniakov (qv) in Zhostovo. Other japanners continued in Nizhny Tagil but, being so far from their main markets – Moscow, for example, was over 1,000 miles away – they had to sell through middle-men, and this resulted in demands for increased production and inferior work. Nevertheless, in the early twentieth century, Nizhny Tagil was still producing up to seventy-five trays per day, though by then, painted decoration had given way to glued-on prints and quickly stencilled designs.

Fedoskino

Fedoskino, some twenty-five miles north of Moscow, was home to two of the best-known japanning factories in Russia. The first was started by Pyotr Korobov and later taken over by Pyotr Lukutin; the other was founded a few years later by Filipp Vishniakov.

Japanning methods in Fedoskino were much like those in the English midlands, the main difference being the application of a putty-based primer prior to the several layers of japan varnish.

P Korobov
fl. 1798(?)–1819

Pavel/Pyotr Ivanovitch Korobov (1752–1819) was a merchant who established a small workshop on his estate in the village of Danilkovo in about 1795. He quickly achieved commercial success by japanning the peaks of shako caps for the military. Under Korobov and his successors, the Lukutins, the factory became the largest and most successful producer of japanned ware in Russia.

In 1798, Korobov visited Brunswick, where he enticed ten of Stobwasser's workmen to join him in Russia to japan iron trays and also to enable him to become the first commercial producer of papier mâché in that country. At first, he made papier mâché snuff-boxes to which he affixed printed paper portraits of leading statesmen, events associated with the Napoleonic War of 1812, or other historical scenes. The venture was so successful that in 1804, and with a workforce of twenty-eight, Korobov was said to have made almost 10,000 of the 13,429 snuff-boxes produced in Russia that year.[xvii] Painted papier mâché snuff-boxes were introduced in Korobov's lifetime and he is also known to have made papier mâché trays; in the Hermitage Museum in St Petersburg, for example, there is a round paper tray from his factory which, commemorating Russia's alliance with Austria and Prussia, can almost certainly be dated to c.1815.

The Lukutin Factory
fl. 1819–1904

Korobov was succeeded by his son-in-law, Pyotr Vasielievich Lukutin (1784–1863), an enterprising man, who considerably developed the business. He shrewdly established an apprenticeship scheme under which to train his decorators, and with twenty apprentices at a time, the factory quickly earned a reputation for the high standard of its painting. In 1821, Lukutin guaranteed that his varnish was chip-resistant, and such confidence in the quality of his goods was not misplaced, for in 1828, his factory won first prize at the Milan exhibition. Until then, he had marked his products only with his monogram 'FPL' – which stood for Factory Pyotr Lukutin. Thereafter Tsar Nicholas allowed him the privilege of adding the Imperial eagle – two years before it became a legal requirement.

336. Gothic-shape papier mâché tray made at the Lukutin factory in the mid nineteenth century. 65 x 82.5cm

© 2003 STATE HERMITAGE MUSEUM, ST PETERSBURG

In Russia, the name Lukutin became a synonym for japanned snuff-boxes. And to judge from a number of such boxes bearing French inscriptions, and made by Lukutin in the 1830s and 1840s, they were evidently popular in France also. Although snuff-taking began to decline among fashionable society in the 1820s, Lukutin continued to make round snuff-boxes with lift-off lids until at least the 1860s, but new shapes evolved alongside them. Oval, square, and elongated 'gothic' shapes became popular, and rectangular boxes were given rounded corners and a gentle curve along the front edge of their hinged lids. Small snuff-boxes with flute-moulded sides, and borders with similar mouldings on their lids were also introduced.

In the 1830s, Lukutin extended his product range by introducing papier mâché needlework boxes, tea-caddies, visiting-card cases, and so on, and he introduced several papier mâché tray-forms new to Russia, including the 'gothic' shape which was so popular in England (plate 336). In addition, Lukutin made high quality cigar cases of tall oval section, similar to those made by Stobwasser[xviii] and pencil cases which closely followed the shape of early Indian and Persian brush boxes. Also, at about this time, Lukutin introduced a wholly distinctive and characteristically Russian range of goods like nests of tea-cups for travel purposes, small panels intended for the sides of money-purses and, in the 1860s, Easter eggs decorated with Russian themes.

---

xvii. A number of round paper snuff-boxes with monochrome engravings glued to their lids, have been associated with Korobov's factory although this is now in doubt. See Jurgen Glanz, *Historisches und Frivoles auf Lackdosen*, Hamburg, 1999, p. 23.

xviii. The ends of Lukutin's papier mâché cigar cases are often flattened, rather than rounded as in some German examples, and the painted decoration on these, and on Russian snuff-boxes, was rarely copied from famous masters, and never erotic as in Germany.

At one time, Lukutin's factory made over 600 different articles of japanned tin and papier mâché, and provided for every sector of the market. For example, it was said that, depending upon its quality, the cost of a Lukutin box ranged from 2–300 roubles. The finest wares were painted with allegorical subjects, or with historical or genre scenes, still-life groups, or heroic portraits, copied largely from famous Russian and Western art. Or Lukutin's wealthier clients commissioned articles painted with their portraits, or with scenes of their houses and parks which, if requested in later years,[xix] were fitted with sumptuous silver mounts made by Fabergé in St Petersburg. Less expensive, but nevertheless good quality wares were decorated with traditional folk festivals, with troika and other distinctly Russian subjects.

In 1843, Lukutin was joined by his son Alexander (1818/19–1888) and their wares were marked accordingly: 'P&AL'. Alexander raised the firm's products to yet higher artistic standards, equalling the quality, though not the high cost, of those made in Germany and France. When he took sole charge in about 1863/4, his firm almost monopolised papier mâché manufacture in Russia, having absorbed a number of smaller workshops in Danilkovo. The so-called 'airy' style of painting, with thin glazes over mother of pearl, and filigree decoration, were especially popular at this time, as were boxes painted in imitation of tortoiseshell, birch-bark, or mahogany, or painted in tartan patterns. Lukutin won gold medals at every Russian exhibition in which he took part, and he showed at major international exhibitions, including the Paris World Fair in 1867. He exported on a large scale to Italy, France, Germany, Sweden, America, and other foreign markets.
Nikolai Alexander Lukutin (1853–1902), grandson of the founder, took over in 1888, and in 1894 was allowed to mark his goods with four Imperial eagles signifying the four tsars under whom the factory had prospered. He was a physician, and kept the firm going only in honour of his forebears. Artistic standards fell as talented workmen left to take jobs with Filipp Vishniakov (*qv*) in nearby Zhostovo, or to work in other, newly emergent industries. His widow continued until the economic effects of the Russo-Japanese War forced her to close down in 1904.

A co-operative of former Lukutin workers was formed in 1910 to ensure the continuation of their craft, but its products never equalled those of the earlier period and it ended in 1917, shortly before the Revolution.

The Vishniakov Factory
fl. **1803–c.1917**

In 1803, Filipp Nikitich Vishniakov and his brother, Taras Vishniakov, opened factories for the manufacture of iron trays in Moscow and Zhostovo respectively, and they soon rivalled Korobov in Danilkovo. Another member of the family, Yegor Vishniakov began a similar business in Ostashkovo in 1815. By

the 1840s, other japanning factories had been set up in the Zhostovo area and at least one, the factory of Yegor [?] Belyayov, was almost as big as Taras Vishniakov's, employing fifty-one men to his fifty-nine. Nevertheless, the two Vishniakov enterprises in Moscow and Zhostovo were pre-eminent and the firm eventually overtook Lukutin as leading tray-makers in Russia.

The earliest Vishniakov trays were similar to those made in Nizhny Tagil: rectangular in form, with rounded corners, and with hand-holes cut into their broad convex edges. And they, too, were painted with mythological and historical subjects such as Hector taking leave of Andromache, or dramatic scenes from the lives of Napoleon or Peter the Great which were copied from engravings, often with scant regard for the original.

Today, however, the Vishniakov factory is best-known, for its straight-sided, round tobacco- and snuff-boxes made from papier mâché, often with reed-moulded bands around their lids and bases, and painted with scenes of Russian folk-lore; they generally have bright red interiors. Vishniakov also painted trays in this style. And, like Lukutin, the declining popularity of snuff-taking led Vishniakov to expand his product range to include papier mâché caskets, purses, cigar cases, tea caddies, albums, and larger objects such as tables. Along with the styles already described, a favourite decorative technique in Zhostovo involved the use of Dutch gold as a ground beneath translucent colours (*cf.* English bronze decoration p. 74*ff*). Vishniakov's decoration was generally less accomplished than the best from Lukutin's workshops, but they, too, accepted the occasional commission.

The Vishniakov firm closed shortly before the Revolution of 1917.

Zhostovo Trays

From the mid nineteenth century, tray-making developed as an independent industry in several of the villages around Moscow, especially in Zhostovo. Tray forms that were currently popular at Nizhny Tagil, like the oblong, round, oval, and octagonal, and the so-called 'guitar'-shapes, were copied or adapted, as were gothic-shape iron trays with flower painted centres and pendant gilt foliage, similar to those made by Labutin, and Kondreyev, in St Petersburg (*qv*).

The lively decoration on trays made by Vishniakov and others in Zhostovo in the second half of the nineteenth century was rooted in traditional folk-motifs, and this, combined with their brightly coloured grounds, led to their being bought not only as functional items but as decorative art-objects. This may be seen in contemporary paintings of Russian interiors where, in particular, guitar-shaped trays are attractively grouped together and hung on walls.

By the 1870s and 1880s, Zhostovo had taken the lead in the manufacture of japanned sheet-iron trays in Russia. This was due to several factors: Zhostovo was closer to the markets than Nizhny Tagil; Russia's expanding hotel, restaurant and bar trade had created a new demand for popularly priced trays; and several rival tray-makers in St Petersburg had closed down. In the 1880s, flowers had begun to dominate the decoration of these trays which, regardless of the village where they were made, have all come to be known as 'Zhostovo trays'.

ST PETERSBURG

Situated about 500 miles north-west of Moscow, St Petersburg was a newer and more stylish cosmopolitan centre. It was strongly influenced by Western Europe and this was reflected in its japanned ware.

Lacquered chinoiserie panels had been made there since the early eighteenth century, and round papier mâché snuff-boxes with glued-on engravings were certainly made at the factory of Eck in 1812. But it was not until about 1830 that japanned iron articles such as tea-trays, snuffer trays, bread and cake baskets, began to be produced in St Petersburg.

The leading factories were those of **Jakov Labutin** and **Yegor Kondratyev**, and by the mid nineteenth century, both had overtaken Demidov as makers of high quality japanned goods. Some of their shapes and designs were distinctly English in character, and none more so than the black japanned gothic-shaped iron trays with their finely pearled and painted flowers and exotic birds, as well as their scrolling, pendant gilt foliage (plate 337).

The japanning industry was fairly short-lived in St Petersburg and its factories had already begun to close down in the 1870s.

JAPANNING in POST-REVOLUTIONARY RUSSIA

The Russian japanning industry had all but ended by the start of the Revolution in 1917, but in the 1920s, a revived interest in traditional crafts triggered the setting up of new co-operatives, several of which merged in 1928, to form the *Metallopodnos Artel*. Its history was a troubled one, as

337. Gothic-shaped tin tray; made by Jakov Labutin, St Petersburg, 1840–1860s. 52 x 70cm

© 2003 State Hermitage Museum, St Petersburg

338. Tin tray, with painted decoration, made in Zhostovo, printed mark: MADE IN USSR/Apt HX?-M?/090-3092A, c.1990. 23.5 X 32cm

Private collection

member-artists were under pressure from the State to copy from easel paintings, or to paint in styles alien to their own. They resisted, and eventually, in 1960, their artel was renamed *The Zhostovo Decorative Painting Factory*.

---

xix. Gustav Fabergé, jeweller and silversmith, opened a shop in St Petersburg in 1842; his son, Peter Carl Fabergé, would later be appointed as Imperial Goldsmith, making the fabulous Easter eggs for both Alexander III and Nicholas II for which they are best remembered today.

Today, the old Fedoskino-style boxes and Zhostovo trays continue to be painted with traditional motifs, but individual painters are encouraged to develop them in their own styles; to paraphrase B.V. Grafov (a tray-painter himself), tradition should not be seen as an end in itself, but rather as a stimulus for developing new shapes and styles of decoration (plate 338).[63]

Similar foresight underpinned the thinking behind what has come to be known as 'Russian Lacquer Miniature Painting'. In all but their styles of decoration, these exquisitely painted papier mâché boxes, brooches, and other small articles appear to have much in common with earlier Russian japanned ware. Yet their origins lie in the icon-painting traditions of the villages of Palekh, Mstiora, and Kholui, near Ivanovo, some 250 miles north-east of Moscow. With no call for religious icons after the Revolution, painters had to find new ways of employing their skills. Art schools were set up in the three villages, and each developed its own style of painting.

Instead of the varnish colours used by japanners, the lacquer miniaturists use tempera colours – pigment mixed with egg-yolk, vinegar and water. They begin with the lightest hues, slowly adding darker colours layer by layer, before the work is gilded and given seven to twelve coats of lacquer. The miniatures are therefore lacquered and not japanned.

However, it is Fedoskino – the largest and most important of the modern centres – which, in terms of technique, if not necessarily subject-matter, continues to be closely aligned with japanning. This link allows it to be said that Russia is the only European country where japanning has continued, almost uninterrupted, from the eighteenth century to the present day. Nevertheless, because of their superficial similarity, Fedoskino japanned ware, along with the modern products of Palekh, Mstiora, and Kholui, are marketed as 'Russian lacquered miniature painting'.

Further Reading

Boguslavskaya, I, *Zhostovo Painted Trays*, Moscow, 1994
Gilchrist, Cherry, *Russian Lacquer Miniatures, a Collector's Guide*, Bristol, 1999
Glanz, Jürgen, *Historisches und Frivoles auf Lackdosen des 18. & 19. Jahrhunderts*, Museum für Kunst und Gewerbe, Hamburg, 1999
Guliayev, Vladimir, *The Fine Art of Russian Lacquered Miniatures*, London, 1989
Huth, Hans, *Lacquer of the West*, Chicago & London, 1971
Kopplin, Monika (ed.), *Russische Lackkunst. Von Peter dem Grossen bis zur Grossen Revolution*, Museum für Lackkunst, Münster, 2002
Kopplin, Monika, *European Lacquer*, Hirmer Verlag, Münster, 2010
Krapivina, Irina, *Russian Hand-painted Trays*, Leningrad 1981
Lea, Zilla Rider, *The Ornamented Tray*, Vermont 1971
Malakov, Nikolai, *Fedoskino*, Moscow, 1990, (trans. Butkova, Tatyana)
Richter, Detlev, *Stobwasser, Lackkunst aus Braunschweig & Berlin*, Museum für Lackkunst, Münster, 2005
Richter, Detlev, *Lacquered Boxes*, Pennsylvania,1989

HOLLAND

The Dutch held a virtual monopoly on European imports of Japanese lacquer for close on 300 years, but even so, as elsewhere, the high cost of such goods prompted a home market for less expensive imitations and, already, by 1610, Willem Kick of Amsterdam, had begun to make objects in imitation of Eastern lacquer. By 1741, and also in Amsterdam, H. Cocq not only varnished and decorated metal-ware, but wrote a treatise on the subject which was published posthumously in 1771.

Nevertheless, it was not until about 1780, and with a view to competing with what were considered superior English goods, that the japanning of metals was begun on a commercial scale in Holland. In 1780, for example, Henrik van Temming, a japanner from Leeuwarden, submitted a specimen of japanned tin to the Dutch Society for Industry and Trade (DSIT), which besides being heat-resistant, was thought to excel the English product (*cf.* plate 339).

339. Navette-shaped tin cruet frame with integral caster; Dutch, early nineteenth century. W: 25cm, De: 10cm
COURTESY OF NEW ORLEANS AUCTION GALLERIES

The English influence was, at first, so strong that japanners like Jan Klinkman and Jocobus Carmignac advertised as makers of 'English Lacquerware [sic]'. Examples of copper articles, japanned in various colours, and decorated with Chinese and other borders, which Klinkman sent to the DSIT in 1807, are shown in plate 304. Not only did Dutch japanners employ English methods, but to judge from contemporary household inventories, the range of articles they japanned was also similar: inkwells, bread-baskets, washing bowls, coffee pots, chafing dishes, chestnut baskets, trays and candlesticks (plate 341). Interestingly, however, papier mâché was not as widely produced in Holland as elsewhere, and the few who did make it, were subject to criticism (see L.J. Nooyen, below).

After the Haarlem Exhibition in 1825, at which several Dutch contributors had shown japanned wooden tables decorated in Oriental style, furniture became a significant feature of the Dutch japanning industry. W.A. Franse, of Haarlem, for example, 'a decorator and painter of carriages', and an 'art lacquerer',[64] gained international renown as a maker of black japanned screens ornamented with birds in mother-of pearl, and G. van der Lugt from the Hague showed tables at the General Exhibition of Dutch Industry and Arts in 1866. Van der Lugt's tables, decorated with birds, flowers and landscapes, were judged among the most beautiful in the show, together with the japanned furniture exhibited by two of Holland's leading japanners – Zeegers, and Nooyen (plate 344).

F. Zeegers, of Amsterdam was widely known, both at home and abroad. He was the only Dutch japanner to be represented at the 1851 Exhibition in London where, besides a red lacquered table, and a fire-screen, he displayed an eight-fold screen decorated in oriental style, for which he was awarded a medal, and which an English observer described as 'the most remarkable object among the furniture exhibited'.[65] Zeegers showed it again, at Arnhem, in 1852.

Zeegers won many awards and commendations for his work. He received a prize for a bonheur du jour and four small tables, shown at the Paris Exhibition, in 1855, and a bronze medal at the Haarlem Exhibition in 1861, where a ladies' secretaire, a tea-table and some sewing tables were singled out for praise. And five years later, at the General Exhibition of Dutch Industry & Arts, he was awarded another bronze medal, and his goods were much praised along with those of Nooyen and van der Lugt.

One of five Dutch japanners to take part in the Amsterdam Exhibition in 1877, Zeegers showed again in 1879, at the Exhibition of National & Colonial Applied Art – the last to involve all of Holland's leading japanners. There, he exhibited a bonheur du jour which, although decorated in Japanese style, was criticised for not being constructed according to Japanese principles.

340. Two from a set of eight tin candlesticks and a matching biscuit box with gilt chinoiserie decoration; made by Jan Klinkman, Haarlem, Holland, early nineteenth century. H: approx. 20cm
COURTESY OF TEYLERS MUSEUM, HAARLEM

341. Tin tray with painted decoration, highlighted with gold leaf; Dutch, first half of the nineteenth century. 57 x 76cm
COURTESY OF DAVID FOORD-BROWN ANTIQUES, CUCKFIELD, SUSSEX

342. Tin box and matching stand, with pearl decoration; made by L.J. Nooyen, Rotterdam, c.1865–1875. Box 6.5 x 13cm, Tray 19.5cm
MUSEUM ROTTERDAM (11373-A-C)

The most famous Dutch japanner was L.J. Nooyen, who had commenced business in Rotterdam, in 1858 (plate 342). Some of his wooden furniture, made from pine and other softwoods, was painted either red or black in imitation of oriental lacquer, and decorated in gold raised work which he afterwards polished, varnished and covered in bees-wax. However, like both van der Lugt and Zeegers, he also produced papier mâché, and despite being criticised for doing so on the grounds that it yielded a cloudy and imperfect surface compared with wood or tin, it was for that material that he was best known (plate 343).

Nooyens' papier mâché was characteristically decorated with sun- or moon-lit landscapes. A silver medallist at the General Exhibition of Dutch Industry in 1866, he sent 'a large and attractive assortment' of both iron and papier mâché goods to the Paris Exhibition a year later. It included folding screens – defining products for Nooyens – baskets and trays which, in Thomas Archer's opinion, were well-made but of the 'time-honoured ... oval, Gothic, Victoria, elliptic, and convex patterns [which] went out of fashion in England years ago'.[66]

Archer was similarly dismissive of a large, folding japanned wooden screen, which incorporated twelve large pearl-glass panels painted with views and figure subjects (plate 344). While acknowledging that it was pleasing and skilful, he observed that its style was 'introduced and patented by Thomas Lane about 20 years ago',[67] and, furthermore, implied that it was the work of a former employee at Lane's Birmingham factory. David Sarjeant was more emphatic, saying that it was 'the work of an Englishman, who was apprenticed to Mr. Lane.'[68]

Reporting on the Philadelphia Exhibition of 1876, a contemporary Dutch newspaper noted that trays decorated with moonlit effects in mother-of-pearl accounted for much of Nooyens' profit. That it was copied by many of his rivals was a cause of regret in aesthetic circles where it was thought to have hindered artistic development.

With regard to japanned tin-ware, J. Bekkers, (later Widow J. Bekkers & Son) of Dordrecht, who began japanning c.1845, was the largest metal-ware manufacturer in nineteenth-century Holland. He won many awards at major international exhibitions where his exhibits included japanned tin lampshades, bird-cages, firescreens and tea trays. A fire-screen and some trays decorated with Faustian scenes and shown at the Arnhem Exhibition in 1879 were thought distasteful.

However, for collectors of English papier mâché and tin-ware, the products of J. Burgers of Amsterdam are perhaps the most perplexing. If it were not clearly marked 'J. Burgers', the set of tin-plated iron trays and matching boxes with their rich fruiting vine borders in gold leaf and painted colours, would almost certainly be described as English (plate 304). Burgers exhibited at major exhibitions in Holland: in Ghent in 1830, Utrecht in 1847, and at Delft, in 1849, where he showed a gothic-shaped papier mâché tea tray decorated with a Chinese landscape. And finally, he showed at Arnhem in 1852. Burger's work was admired both in Holland where, from 1830, he was privileged to advertise as 'Purveyor to the Court', and abroad. He ceased trading in about 1862.

In all, there were about forty Dutch japanners who, during the nineteenth century, regularly took part in exhibitions both at home and abroad, and whose goods were, therefore, widely exported. By 1864, not only did Holland's exhibition jurors think Dutch japanned ware was unsurpassed, but the visiting Chinese envoy was much impressed by what he had seen.

343. Papier mâché tray with painted and gold leaf decoration, signed 'L J Nooijen, Rotterdam'; c.1858–1865. Dia: 60.5cm
MUSEUM ROTTERDAM (63819)

344. Japanned ware exhibited by L. J. Nooyen, of Rotterdam, at the *General Exhibition of Dutch Industry*, held in Amsterdam, in 1866.

345. Papier mâché work basket by A Renel, Vienna, from the *Illustrated London News*, 4 October, 1851 (p. 427).

LADY'S WORK-BASKET, PAPIER MACHE.—BY A. RENEL, OF VIENNA.

The *papier korb*, or paper basket, from the Zollverein, is a good specimen of the *papier mâché* manufactures which have been sent in such variety from that quarter.

Further Reading

Kopplin, Monika, *European Lacquer*, Hirmer Verlag, Münster, 2010

Raay, Stefan van (ed.): *Imitation and Inspiration. Japanese Influence on Dutch Art,* Amsterdam, 1989, Chapter Seven: Dutch Lacquerwork in the Nineteenth Century, Titus Eliens, pp. 85–97

AUSTRIA

According to the *Art Journal*, japanned papier mâché was first made in Vienna towards the end of the eighteenth century and by 1851 was 'carried on upon a large scale'.[69] This expansion of the industry may have been due, in part, to an influx of German japanners setting up factories in Austria following Meyer & Wried's take-over of Christian Stobwasser's factory in Brunswick.

While producing well-made and well-decorated articles, it appears that Austrian japanners were not especially innovative. Writing generally about the Austrian displays of japanned ware at the Paris Exhibition in 1867, David Sarjeant noted 'excellent figure painting and pencilling of the good old sort – bronze skies and landscapes, exteriors of buildings, imitation Japan and China work'. He also asked: 'Do these old fashioned things find a market at

346. Papier mâché vase designed by B. de Bernardis, and made by Becker & Kronik, Vienna, from the *Official Descriptive & Illustrated Catalogue of the Great Exhibition* (Vol. III, p. 1041).

the present day?' Concluding that they did, he surmised that 'they may one day come back as novelties.' He noted also, that 'gigantic round trays which are only used in oriental countries, show that we [Midlands' japanners] have a rival in that quarter', and observed a 'gaudy group of pearl and stained silver flowers, with grotto border', which he conjectured was bound for American markets. However, he was not wholly critical of the Austrian exhibits and praised, unreservedly, a range of ebonised wood articles decorated with gilt bands and painted with landscapes and flowers which, he noted were 'left without varnish'.[70] At the same exhibition, there was a notable show of Austrian varnished iron bedsteads with ormolu mounts.

The Viennese firm of A. Renel took part in the Great Exhibition in London, where they showed, amongst other things, an elaborate work-basket in papier mâché, an engraving of which featured in the *Illustrated London News* (plate 345). Also from Vienna was the company Becker & Kronik (sometimes Kronig) who showed a japanned wood screen, a firescreen covered with papier mâché, papier mâché tables, a range of cups made from either tin or papier mâché, and two enormous vases designed by M. de Bernardis, an architect (plate 346). At the 1867 Paris Exhibition, and under the name of Kronik, this firm showed many 'expensively decorated' iron trays, some of which were 'tipped [or edged] with white metal a plan which', according to an exhibition juror, 'though not unknown in England is little practised'.[71] In addition, Kronik showed screens, cabinets, chairs and a table. Though lacking in originality, Kronig was judged to have mounted a worthy display.

Another Austrian company with a stand at the 1851 Exhibition was Zofferty. This firm mounted a display of chairs, tables and screens decorated 'in imitation of japanned work', but they were judged inferior to the real thing.

Further Reading
Austen, Brian, *Tunbridge Ware*, London, 2001, ch. 14
Huth, Hans, *Lacquer of the West*, 1971
Kopplin, Monika, *European Lacquer*, Hirmer Verlag, Münster, 2010

ELSEWHERE IN EUROPE

There were other European countries where, from the sixteenth century, japanning had been carried out on an equally sophisticated level as those described above, Italy and Spain being just two examples. As elsewhere, they took their early leads from imported oriental lacquer, devising substitute varnishes with which to imitate eastern originals, and then branched out into more commercial manufactures. They operated outside the influences and rivalries so far described here and looked more to their own design traditions. As such, their products pose no problems of attribution for today's collectors of Midlands japanned ware and thus they fall outside the scope of this book.

Further Reading
Bourne, Jonathan, et al, *Lacquer, an International History and Collector's Guide*, 1984
Huth, Hans, *Lacquer of the West*, 1971
Kopplin, Monika, *European Lacquer*, Hirmer Verlag, Münster, 2010

USA

English japanned furniture was first imported into Massachussetts in about 1690, and by 1700, American imitations had begun to be made in Boston. Some of the earliest were made by English emigrées and, indeed, advertisements for workmen in a wide range of decorative manufactures to take up work in America, had appeared in the English press. An announcement placed in the *Birmingham Gazette* by a Mr George Watson junior, of Bristol, Somerset in the mid 1760s, promised that he would 'give great Encouragement to Handicrafts and Servants who will chuse ... to go to Pennsylvania for some years'. In New York, between 1735 and 1772, less sophisticated furniture than that produced in Boston was made by two japanners who, as father and son, shared the name of Gerardus Duyckinck, and a more rustic line in japanning was developed in Connecticut, particularly in

the town of Taunton. Amongst these early goods, long-case clocks, japanned and decorated with chinoiserie in the English manner were especially popular.

It is not surprising, therefore, that when papier mâché began to be made in America, somewhat belatedly in 1849/50, its earliest manufacturer – The Litchfield Manufacturing Company – specialised in making clock-cases. But, as in England, japanned tinware had a longer history in America than japanned papier mâché.

American Painted Tinware

The manufacture of domestic tinware had begun in Connecticut in about 1740, and from there, it spread throughout the the East Coast states of Maine, New York, New Jersey, Pennsylvania, Maryland and Virginia. Since there were no rolling-mills of any significance in their own country, American tinsmiths imported their tinplate from Pontypool and it was via this route that, towards the end of the eighteenth century, they are believed to have become familiar with the practice of decorating domestic tinware. By 1810, painted tinware had become an important offshoot in the trade of many American tinsmiths.

The colourful painted tin boxes (or 'trunks', as they are called in America), trays, bread baskets, canisters, and the many other small, domestic articles made by local tinsmiths, are known as American Painted Tinware, or as 'country painted tin'. In the UK, they are popularly referred to as 'Pennsylvanian Dutch' – but that is to generalise and to overlook the subtleties of their designs.

Recent research into methods of construction and styles of painting have shown there to be regional differences, and that within these, each tinsmith developed his or her own distinct characteristics. In Connecticut for example, where it had all begun, Welsh and English decorative influences were strong, but in Pennsylvania where there was a large migrant German community, the traditional decorative styles of their country prevailed – the corruption of 'Deutsch' into 'Dutch', once again skewing our understanding of the country of origin. The appeal of 'Crystallised tin' for Pennsylvania decorators, for example, probably stems from its earlier use in Germany, where Stobwasser is known to have used the technique in the early nineteenth century.

Inevitably, these styles merged and developed, so that to the untrained eye, they are now difficult to disentangle. Moreover, they are now seen as so characteristically American that they are unlikely to be confused with Welsh, English or German products. The number of tinsmiths and decorators, and the nuances of their styles, are too great to cover here, but they are fully discussed by Lois Tucker and the late Gina Martin in their pioneering and definitive work on the subject (see below).

American Papier Mâché

The Litchfield Manufacturing Co.
1849/50–1854
Connecticut

This company was founded by Dr Josiah G. Bechwith, a druggist and importer of English varnishes, following an exhibition of English papier mâché on his premises. On display was a typical range of contemporary products, from tables and chairs to small boxes and card cases. The exhibition provided the stimulus for the company to start making its own card trays, bowls, and clock-cases from papier mâché in 1851, and from then on, they sold their products alongside the English imports.

The company devised ingenious methods of construction. For example, an octagonal card tray was formed from one sheet of pasteboard by cutting out 'v'-shapes at each corner of a central octagon, removing the excess board and folding the the remaining parts upwards to the required angle to create the sides of the tray. The sides were held in place by staples and the joins concealed by strips of paper; the edges of the trays were sometimes cut with a jig-saw for added decorative effect. They may have lacked the finesse of their English counterparts but they were very strong.

The articles were then black-japanned and painted, gilded and pearled by young girls who had been trained in the company workshops by japanners brought over, for that purpose, from Wolverhampton, Oxford, and Germany.

The Litchfield Manufacturing Company was situated in an area long associated with clock-making. Thus, in 1851, a policy decision was made to focus on that branch of their trade. They produced fifty-five clocks daily, both mantle- and wall-clocks, their wooden carcases fronted by papier mâché panels with intricately cut edges and painted, scrap-pearl and gilt decoration. The company exhibited their clocks at the New York Exhibition in 1853 where, on a stand nearby, the Ansonia Company showed some 'iron papier mâché clocks'[72] – these were, surely, iron-cased clocks clad in papier mâché.

The company merged with Terry & Barnum Manufacturing Company in 1854, and moved to East Bridgport. An economic slump brought about the closure of the factory in 1855, but like japanners in Europe, its workers were able to transfer their skills to newly emerging industries – for many of the Litchfield japanners this meant the decoration of sewing machines.

Wadhams Manufacturing Company
1851–1861
Torrington, Connecticut

Wadhams Manufacturing Company originally manufactured brass buttons and general metal-ware, but in 1851, and for reasons not known, turned its attention to making papier mâché goods. They used both panel and pulped papier mâché: panel for the sides of cases, blotters, book covers and other similarly flat surfaces, and pulp for hollowware and japanned stair-rods.

Their products were decorated in English style with painted and metal leaf ornament combined with pearl imported from England and of the type used by japanners there, namely white and great snail shells, and for more expensive work, the aurora shell. A local newspaper, *The Litchfield Republican*, said in 1852, that 'their papier mâché work is very fine and evinces an artistical finish hard to be beaten.'[73]

The company closed in 1861, at the outbreak of the American Civil War. Few of its products can be identified today and not least because they are difficult to distinguish from similar goods made in England.

The Bird Japanning Company
c.1875–1900+
Boston, Massachussetts

Established by E. Bird, in about 1875, this firm specialised in japanning wood and iron articles such as shoemakers' machinery and sewing machines. The factory was taken over by Daniel Cooksley, a japanner who was born in Birmingham, England.

Between the years 1895 and 1900, Cooksley made papier mâché buttons as a hobby, and it is these which are of most interest here. Made from thin paper-board, they were both round and oval, and fitted with metal shanks. They were mostly japanned in black, and some were edged in grey, and mainly decorated with scrap pearl and bands of painted white dots. Occasionally, Cooksley ornamented his buttons with flower motifs.

According to an article written by Shirley DeVoe in 1985, Cooksley would also decorate items such as trays, mirror frames, boxes and wire hairbrushes for his friends and family. In contrast with his buttons, it is unlikely that these could be identified today.

The Historical Society of Early American Decoration

Concern that a long tradition of decorative craft skills was fast-disappearing in America, led to the foundation, in 1946, of the Esther Stevens Brazer Guild.

When Esther Stevens Brazer (1898–1945) embarked on a mission to preserve her heritage, it is unlikely that she would have foreseen its outcome. A descendant of Zachariah Stevens, tinsmith, of Stevens Plain near Portland, Maine, Mrs Brazer studied first at Portland School of Art, and then, as a student of interior decoration, at Columbia University, before becoming involved in the restoration of historic buildings. It was in the course of her work as a restorer that she developed

347. Tin tray painted in 1984, by Deborah Lambeth, Master Craftsman and accredited teacher of the HSEAD. 34 x 46cm

COURTESY OF DEBORAH LAMBETH; PHOTOGRAPH BY LYNNE RICHARDS

348. Tin tray with stencilled decoration by Astrid Donnellan; 1979 (see also pl. 350). 53.5 x 76cm

COURTESY OF ASTRID DONNELLAN

349. King-gothic wooden tray decorated in 1991, by Phyllis Sherman, Master Craftsman and accredited teacher of the HSEAD. 46 x 63.5cm

COURTESY OF PHYLLIS SHERMAN

350. Round-gothic tin card tray painted and gilded in 2000, by Astrid Donnellan, who, as Master Teacher, holds the highest accreditation within the HSEAD. (*cf.* pl. 223) Dia: 23cm

COURTESY OF ASTRID DONNELLAN

351. Queen-gothic tin tray, decorated in 1989, by Roberta Edrington, Master Craftsman and accredited teacher of the HSEAD. 48 x 63.5cm

COURTESY OF ROBERTA EDRINGTON, PHOTOGRAPH BY JOHN COLLIGAN

an interest in decorative techniques and became aware of the importance of sharing her newly-acquired practical knowledge. She gave her first class in tray painting and stencilling in 1931, and quickly built up a loyal following of talented students, eighty of whom, after her death, decided to commemorate and perpetuate her important contribution to the study and preservation of American decorative crafts by establishing a guild in her memory. Today, renamed *The Historical Society of Early American Decoration* (HSEAD), and with Chapters across America, and members in Canada, Australia, the UK and Japan, the organisation is dedicated to ensuring the practical survival of these skills.

In order to become a guild member, an applicant must first satisfy the society's artistic standards. Then, through careful study of eighteenth- and nineteenth-century originals,[xx] and classes in practical techniques, they progress through various achievement levels until their work is on a par with, and in some cases superior to, the very best examples of antique japanned ware. With regard to japanning, which is only one facet of its interest,[xxi] the Society focuses on the decoration of both Welsh and English products, with particular emphasis on five decorative categories: Pontypool-work; stencilling on tin; free-hand bronze decoration; Victorian flower painting; and the application of metal leaf. This British focus may seem an anomaly in a programme devoted to early American decoration, until it is remembered that it was Welsh and English imports which provided the original stimulus for early American manufacturers of japanned tin and papier mâché. The fine examples seen here are the work of the one Master Teacher and five Master Craftsmen, each of whom achieved their status by having met exactly high standards not only in japanning, but in every other branch of the Society's decorative interests. To become a Master takes many years (plates 347–353).

HSEAD members work mostly on old-style blank tin trays and boxes which they purchase from specialist suppliers. But as these become increasingly difficult to obtain, they hunt for badly worn and rusted antique specimens on which to work. Any traces of original decoration that may remain, are fastidiously traced or otherwise recorded, and stored in the Society's design library,[xxii] and may, indeed, be replicated on the article on which it was found. Before any decorative work can begin on old and damaged surfaces, the articles have to be thoroughly rubbed down to the bare metal and primed in readiness to receive as many coats of base colour and varnish, as are necessary to provide the density of colour and the silky smooth lustrous surface that are essential to the Society's work. The only concession to modern times is the use of modern resins which, by-passing the need for stove-drying, can be safely employed in the home environment. The methods used by HSEAD members are, therefore, equally as labour-intensive as those used by Georgian and Victorian japanners.

As may be expected from such attention to detail, the articles they produce are exquisite, and it is not surprising that their work is in demand, not only by collectors, but for restoration purposes also. In order to ensure anonymity, members sign their work only after it has been assessed by the Society's judging committee. In the past, however, members were curiously reluctant to name their work. While this may not present a problem today, it could become an issue when articles crafted by HSEAD members have acquired the patina of age for, with their expert decoration, the naked eye may be unable to distinguish them from the finest originals – a testimony to the consummate artistry and talent that the Society nurtures and encourages.

352. Queen-gothic tin tray, decorated in 2002 by Carolyn Hedge, HSEAD Master Craftsman. 62 x 79cm
COURTESY OF CAROLYN HEDGE

353. Queen-gothic tin tray, decoration in 2009 by Carol Heinz, Master Craftsman and accredited teacher of the HSEAD. 49.5 x 63.5cm
COURTESY OF CAROL HEINZ

Further Reading

Baer, Shirley S., and Gearin, M. Jeanne (eds): *Decorative Arts: 18th & 19th Century. Research and Writings of Shirley Spaulding DeVoe*, Historical Society of Early American Decoration, 1999
DeVoe, Shirley Spaulding, *The Art of the Tinsmith*, Pennsylvania, 1981
Martin, Gina, and Tucker, Lois, *American Painted Tinware*, vols. 1–4

xx. The HSEAD study collection of eighteenth- and nineteenth-century japanned ware is now housed in the American Folk Art Museum, New York.
xxi. The Society also teaches the histories and techniques of reverse-glass painting, the painting of clock-dials, wall-stencilling, theorem painting, and penwork.
xxii. The library of patterns is deposited at the David Wight House, Old Sturbridge Village, Sturbridge, MA.

CHAPTER XIV

NOTES FOR COLLECTORS

Papier mâché versus tinplated iron

Pontypool japanned ware enjoys an elevated status among collectors whereas japanned metal-ware made in the Midlands, and particularly that produced in the nineteenth century, is often seen as a poor relation to similar articles made from papier mâché. This is a mistake. Tinware was often decorated in the same workshops, and by the same workmen, as papier mâché, and at its best, there is little to choose between the two. Indeed, japanned tin trays produced for the popular market, have a naïve charm which is generally wanting at the lower end of papier mâché production.

Attributions

The majority of japanned papier mâché and tinware was unmarked. It has been customary for the best of these unmarked specimens to be attributed to Henry Clay if they are pre-Victorian, and to Jennens & Bettridge if they are later. If this book serves no other purpose, it will demonstrate not only the number of other manufacturers equally as worthy of consideration, but the futility, in most cases, of even attempting attribution. Wherever possible, marked examples have been used to illustrate this book, but to have been bound by such limitation would have resulted in the omission of some very fine objects (plates 354-359). In short, collectors should not hope to be able to attribute everything, nor believe that failure to do so in any way lessens the intrinsic value of a good example.

Marks

MANUFACTURERS' MARKS. Marked examples of japanned ware are the exception rather than the rule. The marks are mostly impressed, but sometimes painted or printed, and they are generally found on the back, underside or inside (in the case of snuff-boxes) of objects. If an item is not obviously marked by its maker, close scrutiny will sometimes be rewarded by the discovery of an impressed mark visible only in certain lights.

Generally, if papier mâché or tinware is marked for a firm not mentioned in this book, then it is more likely to be the name of the original retailer rather than the maker (see below).

See also, 'Restoration', below.

PATTERN NUMBERS. Objects often have numbers, occasionally prefixed by letters, painted on their bases, as for example, B922 or L8517. These are pattern numbers (plate 360). Unfortunately, they serve no practical purpose for collectors today; Wolverhampton Arts & Museums has several pattern books from the factories of Walton & Co., and Henry Loveridge in Wolverhampton, and from Scott Harris, of Bilston, but to date, it has never been possible to match a number painted on the underside of an object with any number written alongside the patterns in these books.

Opposite: 354. Papier mâché tea-poy with hinged lid, containing four caddies; pearled, painted and gold-leaf decoration, c.1850. 79 x 35 x 44cm
COURTESY OF BONHAMS

355. Oval papier mâché tea caddy with hinged lid and two compartments, painted all-over with a maritime scene; late eighteenth century. H: 15, W: 16.5cm

COURTESY OF RICHARD GARDNER ANTIQUES

356. Papier mâché writing slope, the top decorated with an abbey ruin in paint, pearl and gold leaf; mid nineteenth century. 32 x 41cm

PRIVATE COLLECTION

RETAILERS' MARKS. The practice of shopkeepers demanding that their own names be used in place of those of the maker, was deplored by Matthew Davenport Hill QC, in his paper on the industrial history of Birmingham, in 1867. It was, he said:

A very objectionable not to say fraudulent practice as regards the public, and most oppressive on the manufacturer, whose means of acquiring a just reputation were thus usurped by mere pretenders. Many Birmingham men (to their honour) resisted this demand, and thence incurred serious losses which pressed hardly upon them for years while slowly obtaining recognition of their merits in other quarters. Not a few, for want of capital to enable them to persevere to the end, must have sunk under the trial.[1]

It is to be assumed that a firm like Jennens & Bettridge, with their careful marking policy, was among those able to resist such demands without detriment.

A name printed on a paper label and attached to the underside of an article is most likely to be that of a retailer, but not invariably so (see plate 83). Retailers' names can be helpful in dating articles, and sometimes very precisely, if the merchant in question was in business for only a very short time. Retailers whose names are most commonly met with, and often mistaken as manufacturers, are John Joseph Mechi, Mapplebeck & Lowe, and Edwin Alderman (plate 362).

John Joseph Mechi
1828–1881 (retailed papier mâché from c.1839–1850s)
4 Leadenhall Street, London

John Joseph Mechi started business as a 'pencil maker' at 130 Leadenhall Street, in 1828, but by the early1830s, he was described also as a cutler and had expanded his trade to include 'Mechi's Famous-razors, Scientific Strops & Paste, Desk and Dressing Cases &c.' He appears to have

357. Pole screens, turned and japanned wood, and papier mâché; c.1835.

COURTESY OF HOLLY JOHNSON ANTIQUES

commenced selling papier mâché in about 1839, when he was listed in a London trade directory under 'Paper Tray & Papier Mâché Manufacturers' and took a full-page advertisement announcing:

Mechi's Novel & Splendid
Papier maché [*sic*] Articles
Consisting of Tea Trays, tea caddies, Ladies' work, cake and note baskets, card cases, card pools, fruit plates, fruit baskets, netting boxes, hand screens, card racks, chess boards[2]

By 1848, he was boasting a display of papier mâché tea trays which, as 'unrivalled specimens of japan work, infinitely surpassing the Chinese', varied in price 'from a very low figure up to 20 guineas the set.' Mechi thought them 'brilliant specimens of art, in figures, landscapes, flowers and birds, with buhl and gold.' Alongside these, he stocked the usual range of papier mâché products of the period, from pole screens and chess tables, to glove boxes and cake baskets, all 'very cheap, say from 13s. up to £20'.[3]

It was to Mechi's warehouse that the anonymous author of *The Book of Papier Mâché and Japanning*, which has frequently been referred to in these pages, went to study specimens of papier mâché. The articles s/he selected for illustration were all made by McCallum & Hodson, but the implication was that Mechi also stocked goods made by other firms.

A gothic shaped papier mâché tray, painted with a bird's eye view of Tiptree Farm in Essex, is especially interesting. Mechi was noted for his advanced farming methods and opened his model farm, at Tiptree, to the public in 1852; the event was reported in 'The Farmer of Tiptree Hall' in the weekly journal *Household Words*.[4]

Mechi's concern with papier mâché was relatively shortlived, having all but ceased by the mid-1850s.

Mapplebeck & Lowe
c.1835–1888
6 & 7 Bull Ring, Birmingham
Mapplebeck & Lowe commenced as 'furnishing ironmongers, cutlers and factors',[5] and by 1855, described themselves also as silversmiths, and manufacturers of lamps, stoves, stove grates, fenders and fire irons, and as a repository of

358. Papier mâché handscreens with turned wood sticks; c.1840

359. Oval papier mâché bread basket with early bronze decoration; c.1835, 30 x 37cm

agricultural and horticultural implements. They were not manufacturers in the sense in which that term is understood today, and certainly, they were not japanners. They used the term, probably, to mean that they had exclusive rights to a particular line from a specific japanning factory. For example, the name 'Mapplebeck & Lowe' is frequently found on crystallised tin trays for candle snuffers; these may have been made in Wolverhampton, where Mapplebeck & Lowe are believed to have purchased articles from the sale of Walton's stock-in-trade, in 1845.[6] Occasionally, however, an article will show both their name and that of its manufacturer (plates 362 and see p. 48).

Mapplebeck & Lowe, ceased trading in 1888.

4314 — Chinese Blue Ground
do Green Tip

4315 — Blue Ground
Pink Tip

4316 Grey Ground
Blue tip

4317 Grey Ground Pink tip

4318 White Ground Gold
Pink tip

4319 White Ground
Pink tip
Gold

Bronze

4320 Blue Ground
Blue tip

4321 Blue Ground Blue tip

4322 White Ground
Blue tip

360. Page of border designs in a pattern book from the factory of Henry Loveridge &
Co., mid nineteenth century onwards.

Edwin Alderman (fl. 1820s)
41 & 42 Barbican, London

The name 'Alderman', which is occasionally found, stamped on the underside of early trays, is for Edwin Alderman, a jeweller, silversmith and hardwareman. In an advertisement in *The Times* in 1825, he announced that he had considerably added to his stock of paper trays 'a great variety of new and elegant shapes, including Gothic or King's pattern, Sandwich edge, silver form, &c.'[7] They were, he said, the result, of an arrangement 'with a first rate manufacturer of papier mâché [*sic*]',[8] which allowed him to sell at very advantageous prices: a thirty-inch tray with gold borders, for example was twenty-five shillings. Alderman also stocked 'superior quality' japanned iron trays for supply to 'Proprietors of hotels and large establishments'. 'Shipping orders', he maintained, were 'executed at the manufacturers' prices.'[9]

PAPER LABELS. Old paper labels should not be removed from objects, for by so doing, important documentary evidence could be destroyed. For instance, a very fine graduated trio of straight-edge trays which appeared on the market in 1998, with their formal gilt borders and matt surfaces, could easily have been mistaken as Regency-period by the unwary, if it were not for a white paper care-label gummed to the underside of one of the set; printed in black, in sans serif typeface, it read:

> To PRESERVE THE GOLD
> Do not use HOT or even
> WARM water, nor let any
> water remain longer than necessary

Sadly, by the next sighting of these trays, the label had been removed. A more richly-decorated tray, with a similar care-label attached, is shown here (plate 363).

It would be naïve to overlook the financial benefits of this action, but along with its removal went one of the most interesting features of the trays. Certainly, the paper label found on the underside of the 'union tray' described on p. 257, lends importance to an otherwise unremarkable tray.

Manufacturers also attached paper labels to their travellers' samples. Like the example in plate 83, these are generally printed with the name of the manufacturer, the pattern name and/or number, and with the prices of the various sizes in which the article was available – these are given either in code or in sterling.

Restoration

Few would attempt to restore antique ceramics themselves, and the same should be true of japanned ware. The skills required are several and include re-shaping, varnishing, gilding, inlaying (the term is used advisedly here), and painting. Rusted tin-ware is an even greater problem for not only has the visible rust to be treated but also that which may have extended beneath the

361. Purchasing a japanned tray, an engraved illustration from *Scenes of British Wealth*, by Rev. I Taylor (2nd edn, 1825)
PRIVATE COLLECTION

surrounding varnish; this can be a very costly procedure when expertly undertaken. Save in the hands of a skilled restorer, papier mâché and tin-ware are best left alone.

Condition

As with most antiques, it is advisable to avoid purchasing damaged articles, but this is not always possible, either for financial reasons, or because the object in question is a particularly rare and interesting example.

Nevertheless, the purchase of over-painted articles should be avoided at all costs. It has been shown how japanners achieved the smooth finish and transparent colours which are

362. Papier mâché visiting-card tray, the base printed only with the mark of its retailer, Mapplebeck & Lowe; mid nineteenth century. Dia: 25.5cm
PRIVATE COLLECTION

so characteristic of the best papier mâché and tinware. To imagine that oil colours, cold-painted on old japanned surfaces, no matter how competently executed, will suffice, can lead only to disappointment – they will will sit heavily on the surface, and lack the vibrancy of original decoration. Unfortunately, this has not deterred amateur attempts at either restoration or mis-guided enhancement.

There are three types of over-painting that are to be met with, and they are all equally questionable. The first is the touching-up of small damaged areas. The second involves 'enhancing' the original decoration – this is most commonly found on early trays, or tea-boards with restrained border patterns, to which often inappropriate scenes or motifs have been added to their once undecorated centres. And the third is usually carried out to give new life to an object in generally poor condition – trays with prestigious marks, like that of Henry Clay, are the most likely objects to receive such treatment.

It is a mistake to scrape damaged varnish from the surface of pearl, for in removing one evil, another more unsightly one is introduced, namely harsh shapes of almost white pearl which detract from the overall design and create disharmony. Pearl which was intended to be painted over was chosen for its capacity to intensify any colours laid over it; it was not intended to stand alone, and is thus quite different from the types of pearl which, with their distinctive markings and colours, were selected to form decorative elements in their own right.

Care of papier mâché and tinware

The care of japanned papier mâché and tinware is fairly straightforward, but it may be worth highlighting what will seem, to many, to be obvious. Papier mâché should be kept away from sources of direct heat or sunlight, and any objects which have damaged surfaces – whether papier mâché or japanned metal – should be protected from damp.

Neither paper nor metal trays should be hung on plate stretchers as these will bruise their edges. If trays are to be displayed on a wall, then their hanging devices should not put any stress on the edge of the tray, and the points at which they make contact with the object should be protected with acid-free cushioning.

One of the contemporary selling points of japanned ware was the ease with which it could be cleaned. As Anne Cobbett assured her readers in 1851:

> *Paper trays are very durable if taken care of. They will seldom require washing; but when they do, the water should only be lukewarm, for if hot water be poured on them the paper will blister. Wipe clean with a wet cloth, and when dry, dust a little flour over, and wipe that off with a soft cloth.*[10]

The method for cleaning japanned iron trays was similar, and to remove stains on both these and papier mâché trays, it was recommended that a little sweet oil be rubbed in. However, this advice was given when such articles were new and their surfaces flawless; it would be unwise to press it into service today.

Thus, the warning issued by Harriet Martineau is as relevant today as it was when she was writing in 1850: 'those who cho[o]se to have their trays kept bright and clean, must make up their minds to see the gilding rub off in patches, leaving a dull surface which no "elbow grease" could polish.'[11] In short, over-zealous cleaning should be avoided as it will almost certainly damage any gold leaf and may lift any loose or projecting pieces of pearl, particularly if anything other than a lint-free cloth is used. Collectors, as distinct from conservators or restorers, will find it preferable to treat japanned ware with a little good quality beeswax furniture cream rather than wax polish – it requires less buffing and thus is less likely to cause damage.

Sticky labels and japanned surfaces

Gummed paper labels, attached to the underside or inside of objects, are preferable to sticky labels since they can be gently moistened, and lifted off.

Ideally, neither self-adhesive labels, nor sticky tape, should be used on japanned ware, for their removal is likely to damage the surface. This, of course, is difficult to avoid when numbering lots for auction, or pricing them for sale, but better the inconvenience of having labels attached to the underside or inside of objects, than having their outer surfaces and decoration damaged.

Confusing look-alikes

Mauchline Ware
Ayrshire and Lanarkshire, Scotland
Between 1878 and 1892, three of the leading makers of Scottish Mauchline-ware: W. & A. Smith; Wilson & Amphlet; and Archibald Brown, all made what they described as 'ebonised goods'. Today, collectors of Mauchline Ware describe these ebonised articles as 'black lacquered goods', and it is for this reason that they are included here.

The objects in question, mainly boxes, note-books and sewing tools, were all made from sycamore, and given a shiny black surface prior to being decorated with transfer prints or photographs. In spite of superficial similarities, the means by which these glossy surfaces were achieved was wholly different from the processes described elsewhere in this book.

The exterior surfaces of the articles were simply stained, or thinly painted, in black, and given several coats of copal varnish; the grain of the underlying wood can usually be seen with the aid of a magnifying lens. Their interior surfaces were

363. Straight-edge papier mâché tray with 'raised-work' decoration; a printed paper label attached to its base, directs: 'To Preserve The Gold – Do Not Use Hot or Even Warm Water nor let any water remain longer than necessary'; probably made by H. Loveridge & Co., c.1875. 46 x 60cm

COURTESY OF BONHAMS

left in their natural state, or tin-lined, and their bases were usually covered with paper in imitation of morocco leather.

Each of the three makers named above had warehouses in Birmingham which, with its central position, was an ideal distribution point for their products. It would be tempting to speculate that the town's japanning industry had some bearing on their decision to introduce 'ebonised' goods, but for the fact that japanning itself was in decline in the 1880s. A more likely explanation is that the dwindling fashion for their mainstream 'white wares',[i] led Mauchline Ware manufactures, like japanners, to compete with the inexpensive Eastern lacquered goods which were then flooding the British market.

Further Reading (Great Britain)
Baker, John, *Mauchline Ware*, Shire Publications (#140), 2004
Trachtenberg, David, & Keith, Thomas, *Mauchline Ware*, Woodbridge, 2002

Spa, Belgium

The town of Spa, near Liège, is one of the oldest lacquer centres in Europe. In the seventeenth century, it was home to the Dagly family of japanners, and birthplace of Gerard Dagly (fl. 1687–1714), the most celebrated japanner of his day, who became court-lacquer-master to Frederick the Great, in Berlin. His brother, Jacques Dagly, also took up an appointment as lacquer-master at the Gobelins factory in Paris in 1713.

As a fashionable watering-place, Spa attracted rich and aristocratic visitors from across Europe and became an important venue in their social calendars. Recognising a market for souvenirs, japanners began to make suitably small articles, and by 1689, the physician, Edmond Nessel observed: 'it is a pleasure to see thousands of niceties made in lacquer,

done à la façon des Indes',[12] which he said were decorated in both flat and raised work, in gilt and many colours, and also with pearl, and imitation boulle-work.

Forty years later, in 1729, another visitor, Baron Pöllnitz, marvelled at how japanners in Spa 'mimick Japan so exactly that it is difficult to find the difference.'[13] Nevertheless, it is the small lacquered souvenir boxes, or boites de Spa, and other trinkets, made from the mid-eighteenth century and through the nineteenth century, which are of concern here, since a few could, at first, be mistaken for japanned papier mâché.

Their likeness, however, is superficial, for Spa boxes were made from the wood of the plane, alder, or lime trees, but they were so finely turned, as to be as light as paper. Their ground colours were mixed with glue and painted directly onto the bare wood, and their surfaces decorated either with pen and ink drawings, or with gouache colours the earliest examples of which were en grisaille. After receiving several coats of sandarac varnish, the article was polished.

Thus, Spa-ware was neither papier mâché, nor in later years was it japanned, but as the Birmingham japanner, David Archer, noted about Belgian goods shown at the Paris Exhibition in 1867, 'all the class of goods usually made in papier mâché, are made of this material'. He also remarked that 'altogether, the variety and gaiety of this class of goods, with moderate prices, make it a formidable rival to papier mâché.'[14]

Further reading (Belgium)
Austen, Brian, *Tunbridge Ware*, 2001, pp. 196ff
Bourne, Jonathan, et al, *Lacquer, an International History and Collector's Guide*, 1984
Huth, Hans, *Lacquer of the West*, 1971
Kopplin, Monika, *European Lacquer*, Hirmer Verlag, Münster, 2010

i. Souvenir wares made from sycamore. The earliest were decorated with penwork vignettes; these gave way to transfer-printed views, and later, photographic images were employed.

DIRECTORY OF KNOWN ARTISTS AND DECORATORS

George Dickinson's pioneering research and conversations with 'two or three old workers in papier mâché factories,' in the early twentieth century, enabled him to link some Victorian artists and decorators with their painting specialisms: Luke Amner with tulips, Thomas Hanson with parrots and so on. Over the years, these links have assumed the status of a checklist against which collectors hope to identify decorators of tin-ware and, more particularly, papier mâché. But these names have endured at the whim of the elderly workmen with whom Dickinson spoke, and at the expense of other talented artists and decorators. John Thomas, for example (see below), who Dickinson mentioned only in passing, was sufficiently distinguished in his time to be the subject of an article in a contemporary journal – possibly the only japan artist to be so honoured. Thomas had worked with Charles Neville, one of Dickinson's interviewees, but he was a loose cannon and not an endearing character about whom to fondly reminisce. As such, he stands today as a sobering reminder that in spite of their talents, such individuals are sometimes air-brushed out of history.

It is possible to add names to Dickinson's list, particularly from the earlier period, but these, like those he provided, do not enable reliable attributions of workmanship. Nevertheless, the following roll-call of artists and decorators, though far from complete, serves to show the overwhelming influence that the larger firms had by acting as training grounds for the wider industry. In addition, it indicates the extent to which artists and decorators moved between factories. Together, these factors make it impossible, without documentary evidence, to make attributions to either artist or decorator or, indeed, manufacturer, on grounds of painted styles alone.

Hopefully, publication of this incomplete list will elicit further details about not only the artists and decorators named, but about the many who have escaped mention.

Alsager, John (1805–1870): apprenticed to Jennens & Bettridge where he began producing the 'Indian' and 'Chinese' designs in mother-of-pearl with which he became identified. Most of his work in this style was undertaken in his own workshops at Alsager & Neville (qv).

Amner, Luke (fl. c.1840+). Amner had a reputation as 'A fantastic character among flower painters' in Birmingham, with a particular fondness and skill for painting tulips. He led a 'vagabond' lifestyle painting during the winter 'but on the first sign of Spring he was off on the tramp' seeking any work he could so long as it was not 'regular'. A contemporary of both Edwin Haselar (qv) and George Neville (qv), Dickinson estimated Amner to be an old man by c.1895.

Archer, Thomas (b. about 1826) A japanner and designer who contributed an artisan's report, *On Japanning in General*, in the Paris Universal Exhibition, 1867.

Barney, Joseph. There were two men of this name, both native to Wolverhampton, whose histories have become confused; they were father and son. The elder Barney is known to have been a japanner in the town in the 1750s, prior to becoming a partner in the firm of Barney & Ryton (qv) in 1761, but there is no evidence of him being either an artist or decorator. It was the younger Barney (1751–1827) who distinguished himself as a painter and who, at the age of sixteen, studied in London under Angelica Kauffman before being appointed drawing master at the Royal Military Academy at Woolwich. After painting classical subjects, Barney jnr. turned to religious themes and later, to domestic scenes and, by the end of his life, was described as a 'painter in fruit and flowers to His Majesty' George IV. The younger Barney is believed to have undertaken occasional work as a japan artist and, according to his father's Will, inherited his stock-in-trade, etc.

Berks (fl.1850s +) A figure painter employed by McCallum & Hodson for whom he painted a number of royal portraits.

Bettridge, Thomas (fl. 1840s) A sewing box, painted with a view of Warwick Castle, is signed for this artist, about whom nothing more is known.

Bird, Edward (1772–1819). Bird is one of the best-known of the early japan artists. He was apprenticed, in about 1785, to Taylor & Jones (qv) at the Old Hall in Wolverhampton where, under their master-painter, Mr Gower, he honed his painting skills and learnt to copy from engravings. He 'soon stood out among his fellow workmen', and began to paint pictures for which he found a ready sale. After his apprenticeship, and despite inducements to remain in the 'trade', Bird moved to Bristol in 1794 to pursue his ambition to become an easel painter. He took work as an artist at the Japan and Pontypool Manufactory on Temple Back, and in 1797, established an evening drawing academy. It is likely that to begin with, he juggled all three activities simultaneously: easel painting, japanning, and teaching.

The purchase of his painting *The Country Choristers* by the Prince Regent, in 1810, placed him briefly in rivalry with David Wilkie (1785–1841) and, in 1813, following the success of his painting *The Day after the Battle of Chevy Chase*, he was appointed historical painter to Princess Charlotte. He became an Academician in 1817. Disappointed that the Prince Regent bought no further works, Bird turned to painting religious subjects. After more than two years of ill-health, Bird died in poverty – a sad end for an artist whose japanned ware would, in a little over fifty years, be in such demand in Wolverhampton, as to fetch 'extravagant prices'.

Of the few japanned works attributed to Bird, it is tempting to say that those in the collection of Wolverhampton Arts & Museums (plates 185 and 271) are representative of the period when he worked in that town, just as a tray, held by Bristol City Museum & Art Gallery, is believed to have been painted when he was domiciled there. The probable dates of the relevant pieces would support the notion, but on that basis, what should be made of an oval tin panel, a *Study for a Memorial to Earl Howe* which, although in the collections at Wolverhampton, was painted on Lord Howe's death in 1799 when Bird is believed to have been firmly established in Bristol. It is unlikely that any reliable distinction can now be made.

Bond, Daniel (1725–1803) A landscape painter whose work was likened to that of Richard Wilson, Bond was awarded the first prize of £25 by the London Academy in 1764, and £50 the following year for the best 'landscape in oil.' The Birmingham historian, William Hutton, owned a large teaboard and matching waiter, both painted with a landscape by Bond. William

Shenstone considered him 'an Artist of great Taste and Ability.' He lived and worked at 15 Colmore Row, Birmingham where, by 1777, he was operating also as a japanner; this may have been for Henry Clay by whom, at some point, he is believed to have been employed to paint papier mâché.[i] Thus, he came to japanning by way of his painting skills. When made a freeman of the city of Gloucester in 1789, Bond was described as a painter and japanner of Birmingham.

Booth, Edwin (*fl.* 1820+) Known for delicate gilding in the Indian style, Booth was employed at the Old Hall, alongside Joseph Booth (*qv*) who is believed to have been his brother. Considered by colleagues to be 'overbearing' but otherwise 'unremarkable'. In earlier accounts of the japanning industry, Booth has been confused with the American tragic-actor of the same name whose brother, John Wilkes Booth, assassinated President Lincoln in 1865

Booth, Joseph (*fl.* 1820+) Booth was employed by Jennens & Bettridge between 1821 and 1835, where his fine pencilling skills were admired throughout the trade, and where, in 1824, he is said to have decorated a tray for King George IV. He afterwards worked at the Old Hall in Wolverhampton. Joseph Booth is popularly credited with the introduction of formal Chinese and Japanese styles of decoration on papier mâché, and is now most closely associated with this type of ornament. The designs were carried out in gold leaf and often included so-called 'raised work' and bronzed-gold. Booth is reputed to have given Western features to the 'oriental' figures in his work, and the conventionality of his early work was said to have given way to greater freedom. He decorated mostly trays, pole-screens and other panels with such skill that he was reputed to have earned as much as £8–10 per week; by 1866, his works had already become sought-after rarities. The style became so popular that 'There was probably no shop of importance engaged in decorating japan and papier-mâché ware, that did not copy Booth's Chinese patterns with variations of their own.'[ii]

George Dickinson, who told a story about Booth's attempt to sell a tray, probably as a pattern, to Ryton & Walton at the Old Hall in Wolverhampton (p. 187), recalled being shown this tray by a descendant of the young copyist. It was he said, identical to a tray, dating from the 1830s or 1840s, decorated with a scene of *The Rushcutters* in pearl and gilt, which he illustrated in his article in *The Connoisseur* in 1925. The copy was included in the RBSA Exhibition of Papier Mâché in 1926 (cat. no. 128).

Bourne, William (*fl.* 1840s+) Bourne was a pottery painter who transferred his skills to the japanning industry. He worked at various japanning factories in Wolverhampton, including the Old Hall, before moving to Birmingham. Considered 'a good, natural artist', he took to painting 'nothing but verbenas' for which he apparently achieved a particular personal style. A contemporary of Breakspear (*qv*), he was said to have been middle-aged in 1850,

Breakspear, John (1828–1918). Apprenticed, in about 1840, to Halbeard & Wellings (*qv*). Although distinguished as a flower-painter, examples of his work – a tray painted with dead bird and fruit, and a blotter ornamented with sea-birds – show his range to have been wider. A verbena-painted panel, by Breakspear, was said to have been influenced by Bourne. All these examples are illustrated in George Dickinson's book *English Papier Mâché*.

Breakspear[e], W A. (*fl.* 1865+) Apprenticed, like his father John Breakspear (*qv*), to Halbeard & Wellings. He went on to study painting in Paris, afterwards establishing a reputation as an easel painter specialising in figures and eastern scenes. His work may be seen in Birmingham City Art Gallery. It is not clear whether the 'Panel, by W. Breakspeare', included in the Royal Birmingham Society of Artists *Exhibition of Papier Mâché* (cat.no.33), in 1926, was papier mâché.

Brookshaw, George (1751–1823) Apprenticed to the Birmingham japanner, Samuel Troughton from whom he absconded in May, 1767. An announcement to this effect, in Birmingham's *Aris's Gazette* (25 May, 1767), provides a rare, and vivid portrayal of an apprentice japanner. Troughton described Brookshaw as 'a thin Youth, about 17 Years of Age, 5 Feet 8 Inches high, smooth Face, his own Hair light, which is very short; had on a light drab colour Coat and Waistcoat with a red Collar to the Coat, and dark brown Breeches.' The following month, his employer, of the opinion that Brookshaw was 'employed by some Milliners at Nottingham, Derby, Ashby-de-la-Zouch, and Towns adjacent, in Painting of Gauze, Ribbons &c.', offered a reward of 2 guineas (AG. 27 July, 1767). Whether Brookshaw ever returned to Troughton, is not known, but the incident seems not to have hindered his career. By 1777, he had moved to London where he worked as a decorator of high quality furniture (see p. 240), and where, from 1804–1808, his major work, the *Pomona Britannica* – a sumptuous collection of 103 plates showing the 'Most Esteemed Fruits at present cultivated in this country; together with the Blossoms and Leaves' – was published in parts. Examples of his painted furniture can be seen in the Victoria & Albert Museum in London, and in the Lady Lever Art Gallery at Port Sunlight. (For further details, see Lucy Wood, *George Brookshaw*, parts I and II, *Apollo*, May and June, 1991)

Brown (*fl.* c.1850) A borderer at the Old Hall, renowned for bronzed borders, usually incorporating roses and convolvulus, which took his name.

Clayton, Samuel (*fl.* 1765+) Apprenticed as a painter to John Baskerville from whom he twice absconded, once in 1766, and again in1767.

Coleman, Edward (*fl.* 1838–1848; d.1867) Son of a portrait painter, James Coleman, he painted portraits, dead game etc., and also decorated papier mâché.

Cooper, Albert. (c.1820–c.1910) Employed by McCallum & Hodson, 'A very fair artist' who, driven by necessity, worked into very old age undertaking repairs and other miscellaneous work.

Davis, William (*fl.* 1820s+) Davis 'a painter of some merit', is now wholly associated with rustic scenes carried out in bronze powders, many of them painted after the popular works of George Morland. After working in Wolverhampton, Davis went to Birmingham where, living to a very great age, he died in McCallum & Hodson's workshop. Two allegorical bronze pictures are attributed to him: *Daniel in the Lions' Den*, and *The Goddess of Earth*.

Dixon, Alfred (*fl.* 1840+) A Wolverhampton flower-painter who is believed to have purchased blank trays from James Fellows which he employed copyists to decorate. He appeared in a local directory of 1855 as a 'portrait and landscape artist' at Pipers Row, Wolverhampton.

Egington, Francis (1737–1805) A talented and versatile decorative artist. Born in Bilston, Egington would have been familiar with, if not trained in one or both of the decorative trades of his home-town: enamelling and japanning. He is known to have been living in Birmingham by 1759, and to have been employed at Matthew Boulton's Soho Works (*qv*) by 1764 where, with his skills as an enameller, japanner, modeller and chaser, he was involved in the manufacture of some of the firm's most prestigious products. Japanned ware was introduced at Soho soon after Egington joined the firm and, in about 1778, when such goods were extremely fashionable, he entered into partnership with Boulton & Fothergill for the production of both those and mechanical painting – a process of his own invention for copying and transferring paintings onto canvas or decorative panels. Briefly, this involved rubbing an engraved copper plate with a mixture of ink and honey, transferring it to a thin film of paper which he then attached to a prepared

---

i. *Catalogue of Paintings*, City of Birmingham Art Gallery, 1930, p. 16.

ii. Dickinson, George, *English Papier Mâché*, London, 1925, p. 69.

canvas before exposing it to sunlight in order for the ink to solidify, hence their alternative name 'sun prints'; once the ink had dried, the print was coloured with oil pigments to resemble an original easel painting. Large paintings could be reproduced in this way by printing small sections of the work to be copied, and piecing them together to form a whole.[iii] Although not wholly successful, it is possible that Egington applied this technique in the decoration of japanned wares (p. 65). His partnership with Boulton was shortlived (see p. 122*ff*), but Egington continued, in his own right, at his former workshops at Soho until, in 1784, having shifted his focus to glass-painting, he set up his own establishment nearby, and soon became the leading exponent of his day; his first major commission was for three heraldic windows for St George's Chapel, Windsor.

Precise details of Egington's process remained unclear until very recently, when it was found that a patent, granted to the japanner, Charles Valentine, in 1809, in respect of transfer printing, appeared to unravel the mystery.

AE (*fl.* c.1835+) A flower-painter who is known only by his intials hidden in the detail of an exquisitely painted table-top which is stamped for Jennens & Bettridge (plate 137). Whether regularly employed by Jennens & Bettridge, or one of their journeyman painters, this table shows him to have been one of their best painters.

Finnie, John, c.1829–1907 This artist is listed in the *Dictionary of Biography*, as a landscape painter and print-maker, who was apprenticed to a japanner at Wolverhampton, before becoming a glass-pianter at Newcastle-upon-Tyne.

Franklin, Mr/s (*fl.* early 1900s) A decorator at the japanning factory of Smith Armstrong, Bilston.

Finley, Alfred (*fl.* 1850s), designer of trays, toilet ware etc., for Frederick Walton at the Old Hall, Wolverhampton.

Goodman, George. (*fl.* 1840+) Somewhat confusingly, Dickinson states that Goodman was 'apprenticed' to Jennens & Bettridge in Birmingham, and 'trained' at the Old Hall in Wolverhampton. Wherever he trained, he worked subsequently for Alsager & Neville; a cabinet made by Charles Neville with panels painted by Goodman is illustrated in Dickinson's book. However, he is best remembered for his patent of 1852, for transferring designs onto japanned surfaces (p. 65). It was said that Goodman's paintings of church interiors were 'among the most noteworthy of that style', but it is unclear whether these featured in his decorative work, in his later easel-paintings (which he signed 'Foley), or both.

Goodman, John (*fl.*1840+) Brother of George Goodman (*qv*), he was apprenticed to Jennens & Bettridge, and employed by Tearne & Richardson, of Birmingham.

Green, Amos (1735–1807) Born Halesowen in Worcestershire. A painter and japanner who, specialising in flowers and still-life, decorated boxes and other 'trifles' for both Matthew Boulton (*qv*) and John Baskerville (*qv*). He received much encouragement from the aesthete William Shenstone who, in 1760, declared him 'inferior to no one for fruit [painting]' and noted that 'He also paints flowers, insects and dead-game *very* well.' Alongside his japanned work, Green built a successful career as an easel painter and was said to have worked for Lord Lyttleton among others, and been much admired in Oxford. He exhibited at the Society of Art between 1760 and 1765, and later moved to Bath and then, on his marriage in 1796, to Yorkshire where, with his wife, he made northern sketching tours, and painted watercolours. He died in York in 1807.

Grimes ? A decorator of this name is said to have painted hawthorn blossom and snowdrops.

Hamson, Thomas (*fl.* late 1830s and 1840s). Apprenticed to Jennens & Bettridge where he worked under George Neville (*qv*). His only distinction when he became a decorator was that he always included one or more parrots in his designs. An example of his work is illustrated in Dickinson's book. It may have been he who was nick-named 'Peacock Hempson'.

Hanson, George (*fl.* mid nineteenth century) Hanson had 'no particular gift for ordinary work', but was remembered by fellow workmen for drawing and painting mice – a subject which he never introduced into his work as a decorator.

Harper, George (*fl.* c.1850) A decorator at Alsager & Neville, where he introduced malachite grounds (*qv*) – a style of decoration which was much copied by other firms.

Harvey, Alfred (*fl.* 1840+) Although illiterate, Harvey was considered 'a genius at realistic flower painting.' He painted extremely slowly, sometimes studying a flower for an hour before beginning work, and constantly wiping away his painting until he was satisfied – a method which some colleagues mistook for laziness. By this process, a pole-screen panel which Harvey painted with flowers against a white ground, must have taken days, if not weeks, to complete. Paid sixpence per flower, Harvey sometimes received only two shillings and sixpence for a week's work which, as Dickinson observed, would have been insufficient to keep his family had it not been for his wife who earned fifteen shillings a week in the varnishing shop. He spent his last years with McCallum & Hodson (*qv*), but it is not known where he had worked previously. A pole screen,which Harvey painted with flowers, was shown in the Royal Birmingham Society of Artists *Exhibition of Papier Mâché* (cat.no.113) in 1926.

Haselar/Haseler, Edwin (b. c.1812–1901) Haselar was born in Pontypool, but apprenticed, as a japanner, to Jennens & Bettridge in Birmingham. A scrap of paper painted with morning glory and other flowers, found among a small collection of surviving art-work from Jennens & Bettridge, bears the name 'Mr Haseler' (p. 58). Described in the 1841 Census as a 'japanner journeyman', Haslelar remained with Jennens & Bettridge until 1845 or 1846 when he became principal painter for Walton & Co. at the Old Hall in Wolverhampton. There, he had the honour of decorating a tray for presentation to Queen Victoria (plate 198). Tradition favours Haselar over his close rival George Neville (*qv*), for having introduced realistic flower painting on papier mâché; together, they were said to have raised this style of decoration to a level which was never excelled. In 1858, Haselar was described as an artist and photographer, and many local *cartes de visites* bear his name. It is unclear whether he continued to paint japanned ware, but by 1891, when he had returned to live in Birmingham, he was still said to be an artist painter.

Haughton (also **Horton**), **Moses** (1734–1804) Born in Wednesbury, Haughton was apprenticed to the enameller Hyla Holden, before moving to Birmingham in about 1761, where he is known to have painted for the japanners John Baskerville, and Henry Clay. An inventory of the Japan Shop at the 'Soho Works', compiled for Boulton & Fothergill (*qv*) in 1779, included 'Two Turkish heads done by Haughton', which were valued, together, at £1.11.6. This, alone, is insufficient evidence from which to conclude that Haughton was employed to decorate japanned ware at Soho but, nevertheless, it raises the possibility. A picture of an owl, painted on one of Clay's papier mâché panels, and the only known example of Haughton's japanned work, shows him to have been a very fine decorative painter (plate 107). By the 1780s Haughton appears to have abandoned japanning in favour of still-life painting in oils and became best known for his fish and game subjects. He exhibited regularly at the Royal Academy from 1788 until his death in 1804, and won criticical acclaim from Sir Joshua Reynolds for 'the most firm and off-hand execution of any works he was acquainted with'.

Haughton's achievements and unassuming character were vividly captured on his memorial tablet in what is now Birmingham Cathedral:

He excelled in every branch of his profession; more particularly in his Paintings of Still Life. Plain in his manners, and frank in his disposition, he neither sought popularity, nor courted patronage, but passed his days in obscurity; contented with the merit of distinguished excellence, though not enriched by its rewards

Henshall, Harry (*fl.* 1840–1850) Said to have been a flower-painter who purchased tray blanks from James Fellows which he employed copyists to decorate, and of whom nothing else is known.

Hicken, George (*fl.* 1840s+) Apprenticed to Jennens & Bettridge where, from about 1852, he continued as a decorator. He specialised in landscapes and rustic scenes, an example of which may be seen on a pole-screen panel, painted in the style of Birkett Foster and illustrated by Dickinson in his book. He was later employed by Frederick Walton (*qv*) at the Old Hall in Wolverhampton where he painted mostly landscapes on tea-trays. Hicken also painted on canvas.

Hinks, James. (*fl.* 1840s+) A decorator at McCallum & Hodson, who painted landscapes and copies of well-known pictures such as '*The Deestalkers*' by Sir Edwin Landseer. A sheet of designs for folios found among a collection of artefacts from Ebeneezer Sheldon's factory (*qv*), and dated 1879, suggest that James Hinks, or his brother John (see below), later worked for that factory.

Hinks, John. (b. 1808, *fl.* 1840s+) Like his brother, James Hinks (*qv*), John Hinks was a decorator at McCallum & Hodson. He was associated with the 'Persian style' of decoration which he is said to have created in about 1855, when painting an album cover; he divided, and subdivided, its surface with broad gold lines and scrolls, and filled the spaces with colour as he went along. The result was likened to the pattern of a Turkey carpet or Persian rug and, for the next four or five years, the 'Persian style' became so popular that McCallum & Hodson, and other workshops, sometimes struggled to meet demand. Described in the 1851 Census as a journeyman japanner, he may later have worked for Ebeneezer Sheldon (see James Hinks, above)

Hobson, (John Henry ?) (*fl.* 1820+) A journeyman gilder with Jennens & Bettridge (p. 72).

Holland, James[iv] (*fl.* 1830s) A painter at Jennens & Bettridge. His name was shown alongside a painting of a passion flower included among art work from Jennens & Bettridge (see p. 59). Some of his 'Studies for papier mâché', were exhibited in the Royal Birmingham Society of Artists *Exhibition of Papier Mâché*, held in Birmingham in 1926 (Cat. Nos. 11–14)

Horton, Moses see Moses Haughton

Jackson, Samuel (*fl.* 1766+) Apprenticed as a painter to John Baskerville for the sum of £21, and from whom he absconded in 1767. By 1797, he was listed in a local directory, in his own right, as a 'tortoiseshell-worker and japanner', and continued as such until about 1812.

Jackson, William (*fl.* 1840s+) Although not specifically a flower-painter, Jackson is remembered today for blotters, bellows and other small articles which he decorated with lilies of the valley, usually on black and, less effectively, on pale or white grounds. The style was widely copied with varying degrees of success. He also designed borders.

Jones, Edward (1799–1847) A decorator at the Old Hall, Wolverhampton. Two of his trays were exhibited at the Wolverhampton Exhibition in 1884. The first, a 'very fine specimen of Indian work … date 1820' measured 14 x

11in. (35.5 x 28cm), while the other, a 'sandwich shape Japan tray, 30 x 24in. (76 x 61cm) [was a] fine specimen of transparent coloured ground work with Chinese figures worked in bronze … date 1825'.

Jones, Peter (*fl.* 1840s+) After completing his apprenticeship at Jennens & Bettridge, Jones found employment at a slate-marbling works. From there, he went to work for Alsager & Neville where he decorated japanned goods with marbled-effects. He is not known to have been related to the Jones family of japanners in Wolverhampton.

Lane, (Joseph?) (*fl.*1850+) painted pictures on tea-trays, tables and other flat surfaces, at Woodward & Midgeley. 'A work box with bronze landscape [and] a companion case with a painting of *Feeding the Robins*' were thought to have been painted by an artist named Lane. This may have been Thomas Lane's son who, in the mid 1840s, was a student at Birmingham School of design.

Leigh, J (*fl.* 1830s+) A painter at Jennens & Bettridge, whose name was found on a painting of morning glory, from the Jennens & Bettridge factory (p. 59).

Lewis, Charles (*fl.* 1765+) from Gloucester; apprenticed to John Baskerville in 1765, for the sum of £21, from whom he absconded in 1767. Pardoe described him as a painter.

Lines, Samuel (b. 1778) Apprenticed, in 1794, to Thomas Keeling, a Birmingham japanner, clock dial enameller and decorator. According to the local historian, Joseph Hill, Lines 'made decorative designs' for Henry Clay, and also for die-sinkers and makers of sword blades. He began teaching in 1807 and among his pupils was Thomas Creswick RA.

Martin, Thomas Described by George Bernard Hughes as a tray-painter but nothing more is known of him.

Martland, John (*fl.*1840–1850) Said to have been one of several Wolverhapton flower-painters who purchased tray blanks from James Fellows and who employed a copyist to decorate them.

McCallum, James (b.1811) Apprenticed as a decorator at Jennens & Bettridge, he joined in partnership with Edward Hodson to form the Birmingham firm of McCallum & Hodson (*qv*).

McCallum, Philip (b. about 1800, *fl.* c.1847+) Journeyman japanner, designer and artist. In about 1854, after serving an apprenticeship with Jennens & Bettridge, Philip McCallum set up in business with another of their apprentices, Philip Nock; the partnership lasted only two or three years. McCallum was considered a good painter but his work lacked spontaneity. He appears to have returned to work for Jennens & Bettridge where his three sons were all apprenticed: Philip (b.1825), the eldest, worked with his father and became his equal as an artist: William, the second son (b.1831, *fl.* 1875+) went to work for Walton's at the Old Hall, and Robert, known as the 'soldier', volunteered for the Army before joining Alsager & Neville as a decorator.

McCallum, Robert see Philip McCallum

McCallum, William[v] see Philip McCallum

Midgley, Charles (*fl.* 1840+) A decorator at Alsager & Neville who devised a means of attaching silver foil beneath glass in imitation of Jennens & Bettridge's patent for 'inlaid gem' ornament (see p. 83). Some of his 'Studies for papier mâché', were exhibited in the Royal Birmingham Society of Artists *Exhibition of Papier Mâché*, held in Birmingham in 1926 (Cat. Nos. 15-16).

---

iii. For a discussion of Egington's mechanical paintings, see Barbara Fogarty, *Matthew Boulton and Francis Eginton's Mechanical Paintings: Production and Consumption*, MPhil. Thesis, 2010, History of Art, University of Birmingham.
iv. Not to be confused with the watercolourist James Holland (1799–1870).

v. Alongside a painting of a fountain and exotic birds, found among material associated with Jennens & Bettridge (p. 59), is written the name 'Mr McCullum [*sic*]. It is not known to which of the above family members it refers.

Milward, Charles Apprenticed to Amos Green, painter and japanner, in 1767, though whether as a decorator we cannot be sure.

Neale, Reuben (1859–1943) Originally apprenticed to a jeweller, Neale joined McCallum & Hodson at the age of sixteen and remained with them until their closure in 1920, the last of their employees to leave. He can be seen in a photograph, taken in McCallum & Hodson's workshop around the turn of the nineteenth and twentieth centuries (p. 55). A small collection of Neale's work, held by Birmingham Museum & Art Gallery, shows him to have painted animals and historic buildings.

Neville, Charles (*fl. c.*1830s+) Trained at Jennens & Bettridge before becoming a decorator for his brother, George (see below), at Alsager & Neville. It may have been he who introduced the shell pattern, although it has also been attributed to David Sargent (*qv*). This took the form of a row of regularly spaced sea-shells in brown and gold bronze around the rims of a tray and, sometimes, around the margin of the base, or floor, of the tray.

Neville, George. (1810–1887) A distinguished flower painter and close rival of Haselar (*qv*). Neville served his apprenticeship with Jennens & Bettridge where, in about 1830, he devised his revolutionary style of 'painting down to the black' (p. 177). He was known for painting convolvulus with folded petals, parrots and birds of paradise, and especially for the 'unmistakable' transparency of his rose leaves through which you could see not only from 'one leaf to another, but even through a second to a third.' He left Jennens & Bettridge in 1846 to set up in partnership with John Alsager (*qv*). Dickinson described him as 'one of the very few Birmingham papier mâché makers who lived in comfortable circumstances and left a fair fortune'.

Newman (Frederick?)[vi] (*fl.*1840s+) Newman learnt his trade at the Old Hall where he gained a reputation as an eccentric. A general decorator, his decision to focus on painting peacocks became a joke in the workshops (p. 192). He later worked for Henry Loveridge (p. 207).

Nock, Stephen (b. 1810) An able artist who had been apprenticed to Jennens & Bettridge before joining Philip McCallum (*qv*) in a short-lived partnership.

Noyes, Robert (dates n/k) A Wolverhampton artist whose early nineteenth century paintings of coaching scenes were said to have been copied, in his 'studio workshop' on japanned trays made in Wolverhampton.

Pemberton, William (Ned) c.1761–1810 A skilled Midlands painter who was lured to Pontypool, by William Allgood, where he painted many trays. He went on to work as a decorator at Usk, but had returned to Birmingham by 1795.

Perks, Frederick (*fl.*1840s+) Perks worked for Benjamin Walton at the Old Hall. He is renowned for panels and tea-trays decorated with interiors of cathedrals, mansions, etc for which he employed the late-bronzing technique (p. 78). He later took up easel-painting.

Pettit, Charles (*fl.*1850s) After an apprenticeship with Jennens & Bettridge, Pettit turned to easel-painting. His pictures were said to have sold well in Wolverhampton.

Pinfield, James (*fl.* 1767+) Originally from Bromsgrove; apprenticed as a painter to John Baskerville from whom he absconded in 1767.

Pink, Thomas Named by George Bernard Hughes as a tray-painter; nothing more is known about him.

Raven, Samuel (1775–1847) A Birmingham-born landscape and animal painter, Raven has the distinction of being the only painter of English papier mâché snuff boxes about whom anything is known. He first appeared in the Birmingham directory of 1803 where he was described as a japanner at 27

Church Street; by 1818, he was listed as a 'painter' in Bartholomew Street. The most interesting entries of all, however, appeared in 1835 when, with an address in Stafford Street, he is recorded not only under 'artists' but also under 'tobacconists and snuff-dealers' – a shrewd commercial move for a snuff-box painter.

Raven did not personally paint every box which left his workshop, nor did he undertake all the painting on boxes required by even the most prestigious of his clients. For example, 'H.H.H.H.', who is known only by his initials and was apprenticed to Raven from 1820 until 1827, recalled how he 'painted the greater part of a copy of Wilkie's "Rent Day" upon a cigar-case for the Duke of Sussex, Mr Raven himself adding the last touches.' This may have been the cigar case which was the subject of Raven's cleverly calculated announcement in Aris's *Birmingham Gazette* in December, 1819:

> *Under the Patronage of the Duke of Sussex, S.Raven, having completed the Segar Case for which he had the Honour personally to receive the Commands of his Royal Highness the Duke of Sussex, he would be happy to shew the same to any Lady or Gentleman who may wish to inspect it, previous to its Transmission to his Royal Highness.*[vii]

Thereafter, Raven signed the inside lid of his boxes in one of two ways, and usually in red, or white, copper-plate script: 'S. Raven pnx[t]. Patronised by H.R.H. the Duke of Sussex & Prince Leopold' or 'S. Raven pnx[t]. Patronised by H.R.H the Duke of Sussex & Prince Leopold of Saxe-Coburg'.[viii] The title of the painting was, sometimes, included in the inscription and, occasionally, he signed 'S. Raven' on the painting itself (plates 102 and 297).

Raven is also known to have painted wooden panels with sporting subjects which he signed 'SR'; an oval japanned tin tray painted with a rustic scene and believed to be Raven's work, is signed in this way (plate 46).

It is unlikely that Raven made or japanned his own boxes. An 1808 directory lists one 'Richard Raven, japanner and victualler at the Golden Horse, Bartholomew Row',[ix] but if he supplied Raven with japanned boxes it was a short-lived arrangement for, by 1815, he appears to have dropped japanning in favour of victualling, sign painting and gilding on glass. More helpful, are the recollections of David Archer, written in 1886:

> *About sixty years ago I used to be sent by the firm to whom I was apprenticed, Messrs. R. and G. Bill [qv], of Summer Lane, to a person in Stafford Street with large snuffboxes to be painted on the top. I believe the artist's name was Raven. They were very cleverly done, and the artist had a great name in the trade for his productions.*

In 1840, Raven exhibited painted snuff boxes at the Halifax Exhibition where, significantly, the firm of R & G Bill also exhibited.

There are no records which show that Samuel Raven received any formal training. This perhaps, was why he seldom, if ever, originated a picture. H.H.H.H. confirmed that all the boxes and cigar cases painted in Raven's workshops were copied from engravings of well-known paintings and named the most popularly copied subjects:

> *Wilkie's earliest works, engraved by Burnet and Raimbach, such as the 'Blind Fiddler', 'Rent Day', Blind Man's Buff', 'The Cut Finger', 'Village Politicians', also Burnet's 'Young Bird', 'The Poacher Detected', by Kid, 'The Beeswing', I think by the same artist, a great favourite. But perhaps no subjects were more frequently required than two by the celebrated Harley [sic], called the 'Proposal' and 'Congratulations'; these were repeated ad nauseum to his pupils tastes. Lawrence's portrait of George IV was often in demand too,*

and the portrait of the selfish and dissipated George IV and his unfortunate Queen Caroline... The works of Morland were often copied, although at this period almost out of fashion. Sometimes game pictures, or figures, after Moses Haughton were painted ... [the] mistresses of George IV, were frequently commissioned upon boxes, and also the Duke of York, after Sir T. Lawrence, amongst the few portraits. Animals also, especially two well-known bulldogs, called 'Crib' and 'Rosa', after A.Cooper R.A., and a rat-killing terrier were popular, and even designs after Etty.

Raven's work is keenly sought by collectors today and commands high prices. His snuffboxes have survived in large numbers; examples of cigar-cases, signed by Raven, are rarely found.

Rejlander, Oscar Gustav (c.1814–1875). Of Swedish descent, Oscar Rejlander, best known today as a pioneer of art-photography, originally trained as a painter. By 1841, he settled in England, working first in Lincoln, and by 1846, in Wolverhampton. It is tempting to speculate that he was attracted to Wolverhampton by Walton's search for artist-decorators, but there is no evidence that he ever worked in the japanning industry. He did, however, paint a portrait miniature, on ivory, of Frederick Walton (*qv*) in 1851 (plate 196), perhaps to mark Walton's success at the Great Exhibition held that year. Soon after, Rejlander's interest turned to photography; he became friends with Edward Bradley who shared his interest in photography and who himself, is of interest here for his scathing remarks on papier mâché and its decoration, written under his pseudonym Cuthbert Bede (p. 77).

Roberts, David (1854–1887) Described as a japanner in the 1871 Census, he is believed to have been an artist or decorator in the Wolverhampton japanning trade. There was an earlier Wolverhampton artist of the same name who worked as a 'grainer and writer' and 'painter' until at least 1874. He may have been the flower-painter whom George Bernard Hughes named among those who, between 1840 and 1850, bought tray blanks from James Fellows and employed copyists to decorate.

Rogers, W. Harry (*fl.*1840s/1850s) A papier mâché wine tray, designed by Rogers, and illustrated in the *Art Union* journal in 1848 (p. 356) was, three years later, exhibited at the Great Exhibition in London. The tray had an extraordinarily sinuous outline and was decorated with trailing stems of various fruits. Nothing more is known of this designer.

Sadler, George (*fl.*1845+) A decorator at the Old Hall, Wolverhampton, who was renowned throughout the trade for the speed with which he could paint, in one sweep of the brush, a perfect line around the edge of a large tray.

Sargent, David (b.1829) Apprenticed to Jennens & Bettridge where he designed the eponymous pattern, 'Sargent's fern' – an arrangement of fern-fronds, generally painted in vivid green, against a white, yellow or grey ground. The pattern was widely copied by others in his own workshop and elsewhere. Sargent then went to work for Footherope and Shenton (*qv*) where it is said he, personally, painted all the fern-decorated objects. This pattern was replaced, in popularity by the shell-pattern, the creation of which has been attributed to both Sargent and Charles Neville (*qv*). Sargent worked, finally, for McCallum & Hodson. He was among the 'artisans' commissioned to prepare reports on japanned goods at the International Exhibition held in Paris in 1867, which have been quoted, here, on several occasions. For the

Census of 1881 Sargent described himself as a 'designer and decorator of papier mâché'.

Sheldon, William (*fl.* 1844) Described as a 'japan painter' in his patent application of 1844 (p. 35).

Simmons ? (*fl.* 1782), a painter at Boulton & Watts' Soho factory, and named in their 1782 inventory of Egington's japan shop.

Sketchley, Samuel (*fl.* 1770) Listed in the Birmingham Directory of 1770, as a japanner and painter at 74 Bull Street, Birmingham, Sketchley was one of the artists featured by Joseph Hill in *The Artists and Art Workers of Birmingham*, his annual address as President of the Midland Arts Club in 1895. Hill described Sketchley as a 'bookseller, stationer, japanner and painter in general.'

Smart, Mary (*fl.* 1776). Mentioned in Aris's Birmingham *Gazette* (26 Aug., 1776), where she was described as a 'flower and fruit painter in the japanning trade.'

Smith, John (*fl.* 1840–1850) Among several Wolverhampton flower-painters who are supposed to have bought tray blanks from James Fellows and employed a copyist to decorate them. No more is known of him.

Smith, Richard (*fl.* 1769) A painter and japanner, with a 'warehouse of japanned goods' in Birmingham, advertised in Aris's *Gazette* (9 and 30 April, 1769), that 'A youth who understands some drawing is wanted as apprentice.'

Spilsbury, George (*fl.* 1750s)

Stainier, Harry (b.1833) One of three brothers trained at the Old Hall who all went on to work for Jennens & Bettridge. Harry, the most distinguished of the three, transferred his skill as a figure-painter on papier mâché, to easel painting and specialised in Egyptian subjects. (Henry Stanier, a Birmingham painter of historical genre, flowers, and Spanish views, who exhibited at SS from 1860 to 1864, was probably one and the same; C.Wood.)

Steele, Richard[x] (*fl.*1847+) A flower painter who made his reputation in the Staffordshire Potteries prior to moving to Wolverhampton where he was among the talented artists recruited by Frederick Walton at the Old Hall.

Stockwin, Mr. (*fl.* 1830s+) A decorator at Mander Brothers. Stockwin took second prize at an exhibition of local manufactures held at the Mechanics Institute, Wolverhampton, in 1838 (p, 197).

Stubbs, Edwin (b.1836) Son of Richard Stubbs (*qv*), and a gilder at Henry Loveridge & Co. A collection of japanned tin and papier mâché articles held at Bantock House in Wolverhampton, gives him the unique privilege of being the only gilder in the industry whose name can be linked to specific objects.

Stubbs, Richard (b.1813) An accomplished flower and landscape painter, and a competent copier of Landseer's work on both tin and papier mâché. Whilst employed at the factory of Edward Perry in Wolverhampton, Stubbs took first prize for a papier mâché table which was shown in a local exhibition in 1838. He later became a master-painter at Henry Loveridge & Co.; examples of his work from this period are held at Bantock House. He is

---

vi. This may have been *Richard* Newman (b.1812), a journeyman japanner, living in Wolverhampton at the time of the 1861 Census.
vii. As this announcement appeared in December 1819, it is possible that, sixty years later, HHHH may have misremembered the precise date of the commencement of his apprenticeship.
viii. Augustus, Duke of Sussex (1773–1843), son of George III. Prince Leopold (1790–

1865) the son of Francis Duke of Saxe-Coburg-Saalfield married Princess Charlotte, daughter of George IV, in 1816. He became first King of the Belgians in 1831 but it is likely that Raven continued to use his old title after that date.
ix. Bartholomew Row was probably a terrace of houses on Bartholomew Street, so it is likely that Richard and Samuel Raven were living at the same address.
x. Possibly 'Edwin'.

one of the few artists in the japanning industry to whom specific articles can be reliably attributed. His sons, Edwin (see above) and Richard (b.1841) were also involved in the japanning industry.

Thomas, John (c.1820–1889+) Flower, bird, figure and landscape painter. Apprenticed to Charles Mander in Wolverhampton, with whom he stayed until the firm closed in 1840 when he moved to Birmingham to complete his training with Jennens & Bettridge. Thomas, 'small and frail' and a target of fun in the factory, was so confident of his artistic ability that he carried out his oft-repeated threat to run away unless given better work. It is a measure of his worth that, even though an apprentice, he was given his own room upon his return where, 'unmolested by his comrades' he found 'an outlet for his artistic predilections.'

After his apprenticeship, he studied figure drawing and landscape painting at Birmingham School of Art, and worked briefly for Alsager & Neville before becoming a journeyman painter – a way of life which better suited his independant spirit. He found steady employment painting papier mâché table-tops for which he received up to six or seven pounds weekly. A colourful tale concerning Thomas and one of his employers, 'Mr H—', demonstrates both his wilful character and the precarious nature of the journeyman's lot. Thomas, having not been paid, refused to release any further work; he locked his workshop against Mr H— who, notwithstanding, broke in through a window, 'seized a table top' and fled, hotly pursued by John Thomas who was armed with a handsaw. A large crowd gathered as an unseemly battle ensued: Mr H— using the painted table-top as both shield and club, and Thomas, brandishing the saw. Both were taken to court where Thomas won his case.

He returned to work for Alsager & Neville where a he decorated a series of papier mâché book covers which so impressed Jennens & Bettridge they offered him a handsome sum to paint ship-panels. It is not known if he accepted but, certainly, he spent the next nine years decorating ship interiors for a Mr T. Laurie of Glasgow before returning to Wolverhampton to work for Frederick Walton – a period which, although lucrative, he considered undemanding and a waste of his talent. He signed a contract with Jones Brothers, but 'the ink of the agreement was hardly dry' when, tempted by a more attractive offer, he left the japan trade and went to Manchester. There, he took control the design room of Heywood, Higginbottom & Smith, a firm of paper stainers, before moving to Wales to focus on easel painting. His skills were spotted by John Harwood who invited him to decorate the interior of the Royal Exchange in Manchester; this led to further commissions in London and Manchester. Thomas published two books: *Bird and Flowers Studies* in two volumes, and 'a little work on Interiors'. Two plates from the former show him to have been a competent draughtsman but serve no purpose as aids to identifying his japanned work; with the possible exception of the book covers he painted for Alsager & Nevill, it is unlikely that Thomas's japanned work can now be identified.

Tibbett (or Tibbits), Joseph (*fl.* 1840–1850) A Wolverhampton flower painter who was among several believed to have purchased blank trays from James Fellows for copyists to decorate. It is possible that this was James Tibbits who was listed as an artist in a Wolverhampton directory of 1874. All that is known about this decorator is that his work was said to have been far above the average.

Tyrer, John (b. c.1817) Son of Richard Tyrer (*qv*), artist on wood, canvas and japanned ware. Described as a 'master manufacturer', he painted trays and other articles, in Bond Street – presumably for his father – until, driven by bad trade and mounting debt, he called in his creditors. As a respected Methodist minister, his assurance that he would honour his debts was

accepted. He joined the firm of Henry Fearncombe (*qv*), and his income allowed him to pay his creditors in full.

Tyrer, Richard (b.1782) Tyrer was originally from London It is unlikely that his name would be included here if it were not for a small papier mâché panel painted with a view of St John's Church, Wolverhampton, which is inscribed along its lower edge 'Bond Street, Wolverhampton March 26 1811' and initialled 'RT' (plate 85). The initials are almost certainly for Richard Tyrer who was listed in local directories as a japanner, in Bond Street. The back of the panel shows the rubbed remains of a landscape painting; this suggests that it may have been a factory 'waster', picked up by Tyrer, painted in his own time and surreptitiously stoved at the factory where he worked which is, perhaps, why it was possible for him to sign the work. Since the sign to the left of the painting is for Samuel Duncomb, a cabinet lock-smith who was first listed in Bond Street in 1811, this panel may have been painted to mark the opening of his shop. Of Tyrer's ten children, James (b. c.1803), became a japanner, and John (b. c.1817) a japan artist who worked for McCallum & Hodson.

Underhill–. Learnt to paint on papier mâché but left the japanning industry to concentrate on easel-painting.

Voss, Charles James (b. about 1815–1871) A German artist whom Frederick Walton brought from Dusseldorf in 1847, to join the team of talented artists he was assembling at the Old Hall. Voss visited popular beauty spots such as Dovedale, Llangollen and Conway Estuary for his pictures. In addition to painting, Voss taught German; he became a naturalised British subject and spent the rest of his days in Wolverhampton.

Wallis, George (1811–1891) Born in Wolverhampton, Wallis was apprenticed as a painter at the Old Hall between 1827 and 1832, where would have been contemporary with both Haseler and the Nevilles (*qv*). He left both the industry and Wolverhampton in 1832, for a period of five years, returning in 1837, briefly resuming work at the Old Hall. He oversaw an exhibition of local art and manufacture at the Wolverhampton Mechanics Institute in 1839, and in 1843, was appointed head of Manchester School of Design. He was, by then, a recognised artist and design educator, and set up his own 'Academy of Industrial and Fine Art' in 1846. Wallis regularly contributed to contemporary art journals and continued, frequently, to comment on the japanning industry. He was deputy commissioner for the Great Exhibition of 1851, and was involved also in the Paris Exhibitions of 1855 and 1867, as well as the London Exhibition of 1862. Wallis was appointed head of Birmingham School of Art in 1851 – a position which would have brought him, once again, into close contact with the japanning industry. He left this post in 1858 to become senior keeper of the art collections at South Kensington (now the Victoria & Albert Museum).

Watson, Robert (*fl.* 1840s+) An animal painter employed by Jennens & Bettridge in the decoration of picture trays during the early 1840s. He also painted in oils. Nothing more appears to be known of this artist.

Williamson, John (1751–1818) Portrait and landscape painter, b. Ripon, worked as a decorator in a Birmingham japan works before settling in Liverpool in 1783.

Worsey, Thomas RBSA (1828/9–1875) A Birmingham flower painter, trained as a japanner, but left the industry in about 1850 to focus upon easel painting.

Wylie, William (or Wiley) (*fl.*1830–1845+) Wylie was employed by Mander Brothers (see p.196) before he branched out on his own in Zoar Street, Wolverhampton.

GLOSSARY of TERMS

Amber a fossilised resin. In finely powdered form, it was an early ingredient of japan varnish.

Aquafortis concentrated nitric acid.

Aquatint a print achieved by etching a metal plate with acquafortis.

Asphaltum a black, or dark-brown, hard bituminous substance, occuring as a natural residue in petroleum distillation.

Bessemer Steel steel made from pig-iron, developed in 1856 by Sir Henry Bessemer (1813-1898).

Block Tin pure tin in the form of blocks or ingots.

Brazing the joining of metals with hard or unmolten solder.

Button Board a sheet of thin, heavily compressed pulp, which was cut into variously sized discs to form button 'blanks'.

Carton Pierre often confused with papier mâché, but stronger and much heavier. Made of pulp mixed with whiting and glue, it was poured into moulds and backed with paper; it more closely resembled plaster. It was used by firms like Jackson of London to make architectural ornaments, and was widely used in France and Germany.

Ceramic Papier Mâché a composition made of paper pulp, resin, glue, drying oil and sugar of lead, mixed and kneaded together. It was extremely plastic and could be pressed or moulded into any form. Much used for cornices, capitals, and other architectural mouldings.

Copal Varnish a fine transparent varnish made from a hard aromatic resin obtained from various tropical trees. Finely pulverised and diluted with oil of turpentine, it was used by japanners to protect those parts of the surface which were decorated, and for mixing with pigments.

Dragon's Blood an imported resinous gum obtained from various rattan trees. Dossie says of Dragon's Blood that 'The best is the brightest red …You may buy it in drops (as the Drugsters call it) which is the best. They are made up in a kind of leaf or husk.'

Drying Oils oils which harden by oxidation when exposed to air.

Ebonising a method of staining wood black to resemble ebony.

Enamel/enamelling enamelling is the application of a glaze made from powdered glass and other substances which, when quickly heated in a kiln, fuse to form a hard vitrified surface on various metals. It is thus different from japanning, which involves coating surfaces with oil-varnish and then slowly baking them dry. In the eighteenth and early nineteenth centuries, Birmingham and Bilston were among the leading centres for the manufacture of small, decorative, enamelled articles such as snuff boxes, wall-plaques, and candlesticks. John Taylor (*qv*), the earliest japanner in Birmingham, was also an enameller.

Fat Oil Concentrated linseed oil.

Fibrous Slab made of course fibre mixed with earthy matter, chemical agents to make it fireproof, and size. After being kneaded into a mass, it was repeatedly passed through iron rollers to squeeze out the excess moisture and give it a uniform thickness, and stove dried.

Foots the flaky, floating substance which appears in oil when heated to 370º.

Glue J. Barrow in his *Dictionarium Polygraphicum* (1758, 2nd edn.) gave two recipes for making glue. Of the first, made from the gelatine extracted from the skins, hooves, sinews and nerves of cattle and sheep, he said the best was made in England; it came in square pieces of a ruddy-brown colour. The second, described as 'strong and fine', was prepared from isinglass (*qv*) and spirits of wine, heated and strained. Frederick Walton, in his Patent of 1855 (# 2717), described a 'cement' made from equal parts of resin and beeswax, and a small quantity of brick dust, which he heated until liquid.

Gold size see 'size'.

Gum Animi a hard gum used in the finest varnishes.

Gum Arabic a gum obtained from some types of acacia; it is soluble in water.

Gum Lac also called seed-lac. A dark red resin found on the bark of certain trees punctured by the *Coccus lacca* insect.

Isinglass a semi-transparent gelatinous substance obtained from the air-bladders of the sturgeon and other fresh water fish.

Ivory Black a black pigment made from the dust of burnt ivory; today it is made from bone.

Lamp Black a black pigment derived from the soot of a burning lamp.

Metal Spinning the conversion of a flat piece of metal into a globular form by pressing it against a wooden chuck or mould attached to a rapidly turning lathe.

Millboard used by book-binders. It was also employed for bulk-heads and, because it was a bad conductor of sound and heat, for cabin and room partitions. It apears to have been the material shown by Mr Haddon at the Great Exhibition as suitable for railway carriage panels. The earliest was a type of pasteboard but this gave way to board made from pulp.

Moiré Metallique the French equivalent of crystallised tin.

Muriatic Acid hydrochloric acid.

Naphtha Varnish made from tar or asphaltum.

Paste a mixture of very fine flour, glue and water.

Pig or Pig Iron unforged iron ore which, when cast into bars or ingots, were known as pigs.

Pinched Glass/Glass Pincher the making of so-called 'Birmingham diamonds'; or one who prepares the glass for 'Common Glass Link Buttons and Rings' and a maker of glass buttons.

Planish to flatten sheet metal with a smooth-faced hammer.

Pounce, to a method of dusting fine powder over a perforated pattern in order to transfer a dotted outline of the design to the surface beneath.

Puddle/Puddling the conversion of pig-iron into wrought iron by the expulsion of carbon.

Rhus Vernicifera (sometimes verniciflua) a tree of the same family as the American poison ivy and poison oak, it exudes a viscous sap which is the basis of both Chinese and Japanese lacquer. The sap is highly toxic and according to Dossie could be 'fatally pernicious'.

Rosin the residue of turpentine after the oil has been distilled.

Rotten Stone a finely powdered form of limestone, used for polishing.

Russian Tallow a salt-free grease.

Sal Ammoniac ammonium chloride. Commonly used to remove the bloom from iron sheets prior to tinning.

Sarcocolla Persian gum.

Seedlac see 'gum lac'.

Sharps a type of sand.

Shellac gum-lac (*qv*), melted and strained to form thin plates, and dissolved in alcohol prior to use.

Size a water-diluted glue used as an adhesive when laying gold and other metal leaf. It had the effect of dulling or 'deadening' the brilliance of the metal.

Spirits of Wine alcohol or rectified spirit.

Spun Metal see 'Metal Spinning'.

Tripoli imported rotten-stone (*qv*).

Varnish there were three types:

fat or oily varnish (resin dissolved in fixed oil)

essential varnish (resin dissolved in volatile oil)

spirit varnish (resin dissolved in alcohol)

Virgin(s) Wax fresh bees-wax.

Whiting pure, ground chalk.

Wrought Iron a malleable material, beaten into shape and welded as distinct from cast.

SELECT BIBLIOGRAPHY

(in addition to those listed in References)

Bourne, Jonathan, et al, *Lacquer. An International History and Collector's Guide*, Bracken Books, London, 1984

DeVoe, Shirley Spaulding, *English Papier Mache of the Georgian and Victorian Periods*, Barrie & Jenkins, London, 1971

DeVoe, Shirley Spaulding, *The Art of the Tinsmith, English and American*, Schiffer Publishing Ltd., PA, 1981

Honour, Hugh, *Chinoiserie. The Vision of Cathay*, John Murray, 1973 (re-print)

Impey, Oliver, *Chinoiserie. The Imapct of Oriental Styles on Western Art and Decoration*, Charles Scribner's Sons, New York, 1977

Jacobson, Dawn, *Chinoiserie*, Phaidon Press Ltd., London, 1999

Jourdain, Margaret and R. Soames Jenyns, *Chinese Export Art in the Eighteenth Century*, Spring Books, Middlesex, 1967 (re-print)

Lea, Zilla Rider, *The Ornamented Tray ... 1720–1920*, Charles E. Tuttle Co., Vermont, for The Historical Society of Early American Decoration, Inc., 1971

Mander, Charles Nicholas, *Varnished Leaves. A Biography of the Mander Family ... 1750 – 1950*, The Owlpen Press, Glos., 2004

Toller, Jane, *Papier-mâché in Great Britain and America*, G. Bell & Sons, London, 1962

REFERENCES

ABBREVIATIONS

ABG	Aris's *Birmingham Gazette*
AJ	*The Art Journal*, London, 1847-1911:
	AJ/1 'The Birmingham Exhibition of Manufactures and Art', 1849
	AJ/2 Hunt, Robert, 'Papier Mâché Manufacture', 1851
	AJ/3 *Illustrated Catalogue of The Great Exhibition – London 1851*, facsimile edition, Newton Abbot, 1970
Angerstein	Berg, Torsten & Peter (trans.), *R.R. Angerstein's Travel Diary*, Journey 4, 1754. Science Museum, London, 2001
Archer	*Reports of Artisans* selected by a Committee Appointed by the Council for the Society of Arts to visit the Paris Universal Exhibition, p. 109 Archer, Thomas, 'On Japanning in General', Bell & Daldy, London, 1867
AU	*Art Union Monthly Journal*, London 1839-1847:
	AU/1 'Exposition of British Industrial Art at Manchester', 1846
	AU/2 'Illustrated Tour in the Manufacturing Districts. Birmingham Second Division', 1846, pp. 59-62
Bennett	Bennett, William, *John Baskerville*, Birmingham, 1939
BMI	Phillips Bevan, George (ed.), *British Manufacturing Industries*, London, 1878 (2nd edn), vol. III, pp. 165–180: George Lindsey, 'Papier Mâché'
BN	Barford Newitt, *Visitors Guide to Wolverhampton*, Wolverhampton, 1871
BOU	The Matthew Boulton Papers, Birmingham Archives and Heritage Service
BRL	Birmingham Reference Library
Burritt	Burritt, Elihu, *Walks in the Black Country & its Green Border-land*, London, 1868, (reprint, Kineton, 1976)
Cobbett	Cobbett, Anne, *The English Housekeeper or Manual of Domestic Management*, London, 1851 (6th edn)
Cornish/1	Cornish Brothers, *Stranger's Guide through Birmingham* [etc], Birmingham, 1825
	ditto 1849
	ditto 1855
Cornish/2	Cornish, William, *Visitors Handbook through Birmingham*, Birmingham, 1852
	ditto 1853 (3rd edn)
	ditto 1854
Dickinson	Dickinson, George, *English Papier Mâché*, Leamington Spa, 1925
Dir. 1780	Pearson and Rollason's *Directory of Birmingham, Wolverhampton etc.*, 1780
Dir. 1827	Smart, J., *Directory of Wolverhampton*, Wolverhampton, 1827
Dir. 1830	West, William, *The History, Topography and Directory of Warwickshire*, pub: R. Wrightson, 1830
Dir. 1855	White, Francis, *General and Commercial Directory and Topography of... Birmingham*, 2 vol., 1855
Dodd	Dodd, George, *The Curiosities of Industry and the Applied Sciences*, London, 1854
Dossie 1	Dossie, Robert, *The Handmaid to the Arts*, 1758 (1st edn)
Dossie 2	*ditto*, 1764 (2nd edn)
Exh.Cat.1849	*Catalogue of the Birmingham Exhibition of Manufactures and Art*, 1849
Exh.Cat.1869	*Catalogue of the South Staffs. Industrial & Fine Art Exhibition*, Wolverhampton, 1869
Exh.Cat.1884	*Wolverhampton Exhibition – Official Catalogue*, revised issue (1884), John Steen & Co., Wolverhampton
F&S	Finer, Anne, and Savage, George, *The Selected Letters of Wedgwood*, London, 1965
Fisher	Morgan, Kenneth (ed.), 'An American Quaker in the British Isles. The Travel Journals of Jabez Maud Fisher, 1775-1779', *Records of Social and Economic History, New Series XVI*, published by The British Academy, OUP, Oxford, 1992
Gandee	Gandee B.F., *The Artist or Young Ladies' Instructor in Ornamental Painting, Drawing etc.*, London, 1835
Gibbs	Gibbs, F.W., *Annals of Science*, Taylor and Francis, London:
	1 *The Rise of the Tinplate Industry*:
	1-i. The Tinplate workers. vol. 6 no. 4, 21 Nov. 1950, pp. 390–403
	1-ii. Early Tinplate Manufacture to 1700. vol. 7 no. 1, 28 Mar. 1951, pp. 25–42
	1-iii. John Hanbury (1664-1734), *ibid*. pp. 43–61
	1-iv. An Eighteenth Century Tinplate Mill. vol. 7 no. 2, 28 June, 1951, pp. 113–127
	1-v. Cockshutt on Tinplate Manufacture. vol. 11 no. 2, 28 June, 1955, pp. 145–153
	2 *Historical Survey of the Japanning Trade*:
	2-i. Eastern and Western Lacquer. vol. 7 no. 4, 28 Dec., 1951, pp. 401–416
	2-ii. Early British Japanning. vol. 9 no. 1, 28 Mar. 1953, pp. 88–95
	2-iii. Pontypool and Usk. vol. 9 no. 3, 28 Sept. 1953, pp. 197–213
	2-iv. The Midlands. *ibid*. pp. 214–232
Godden	Godden, Geoffrey, *The Connoisseur*, 'English Paper Trays 1780–1815', Aug. 1967, pp.250-254
Goodison	Goodison, Nicholas, *Matthew Boulton: Ormolu*, London 2002
Horton	Horton, Harry H., *Birmingham. A Poem*, 2nd ed., Birmingham and London, 1853
Huth	Huth, Hans, *Lacquer of the West*, Chicago, 1971
Hutton	Hutton, William, *An History of Birmingham*, 6th edn, Wrightson & Webb, Birmingham, 1836
ILN	*Illustrated London News*
IndBi.	Anon., 'Commercial and Industrial Notes of Nineteenth Century Bilston', typescript prepared for Mr G.H. Sankey, c.1954/60 (GKN Archives)
JDA	Anon. 'Rise and Fall of an Art Industry', *The Journal of Decorative Art*, Sept., 1889, pp. 139-140
JDM	*Journal of Design & Manufactures*, London 1849-1852
J&J	Jourdain, M, & Soame Jenyns, R., *Chinese Export Art in the Eighteenth Century*, London 1967
JRep/1	*Reports of the Juries...*, 1851 exhibition, 'Japan Ware', Class XXVI, London: Wm Clowes & Sons, 1852, pp.548-549
JRep/2	*ibid*. Supplementary Report on Design, p.723
JRep/3	*Reports of the Juries*, International Exhibition, London, 1862, London: Wm Clowes & Sons, 1863 p.6
Jurors Reports	*Reports by the Juries ...*, 1851 exhibition, W. Clowes & Sons, London, 1852
Lawley	Lawley, George T., *A History of Bilston*, Bilton, 1893
LL	Anon., *The Ladies' Library*, London, Darton & Co., 1850
Mander	Mander, Geoffrey Le M., *The History of Mander Brothers 1773-1955*, Wolverhampton, 1955
Martineau	Martineau, Harriet, 'Flower Shows in a Birmingham Hot-house', *Household Words* (ed. Charles Dickens), no. 82, vol. iv, 18 Oct., 1851
MChron	*The Morning Chronicle*
Measom	Measom, George, *The Official Illustrated Guide to the Great Western Railway*, 'Papier Mâché and Japan Works...of Mr John Bettridge...', 1862, pp. 312*ff*
Meteyard	Meteyard, Eliza, *Life & Works of Josiah Wedgwood*, vol. II, 1865
N&Q	*Local Notes and Queries*, published in the Birmingham Weekly Post, and dispersed among various bound editions, in Birmingham Reference Library
Papendiek	Papendiek, Charlotte L.H., *Court and Private Life in the time of Queen Charlotte*, vol. I, London, 1887
Pardoe	Pardoe, F.E., *John Baskerville of Birmingham Letter-Founder & Printer*, London, 1975
PM	*The Penny Magazine*, published weekly by Charles Knight, London, 1832-1844
Prosser	Prosser, R. B., *Birmingham Inventors and Inventions*, 1881, (reprint 1970)
RSA	The Royal Society of Arts
Ryton	Papers relating to the Old Hall Works, Wolverhampton.. (John Ryton, Japanning company etc., W'ton Archives & Local Studies [Access No. 2522])
Sarjeant	*Reports of Artisans* selected by a Committee Appointed by the Council for the Society of Arts to visit the Paris Universal Exhibition, p. 100 Sarjeant, David, 'On Papier Mâché'. Bell & Daldy, London, 1867
Scarfe	Scarfe, Norman, *Innocent Espionage: The La Rochefoucauld Brothers' Tour of England in 1785*, Woodbridge, 1995
SFTR	*The Stationer and Fancy Trades Register* (periodical)
SHA	Walpole, Horace, *Strawberry Hill Accounts 1747-1795*, with notes and index by Paget Toynbee, Oxford, 1927
Shelburne	'Extracts from the Diary of Lady Shelburne', *English Historical Documents 1714-1783*, Historic Mss Commission
Spicer	Spicer's *Official Descriptive & Illustrated Catalogue of the Great Exhibition*, 1851, vols I and II

S&P — Stalker J. & Parker, *A Treatise of Japaning* [sic], Oxford, 1688, title-page, (reprint Tiranti, London, 1971)

Thackrah — Thackrah C. Turner, *The Effects of Arts, Trades and Professions, and of Civic States and Habits of Living on Health and Longevity*, London, 1832, pp. 45 & 151

Timmins — Timmins, Samuel (ed.), *Birmingham and the Midland Hardware District*, 1866. Reprinted London, 1967:
Timmins/Loveridge – Loveridge, Henry, *Wolverhampton Trades*, pp. 117–121, with Addenda by Tildesley, J.E., pp. 121–123, and extracts from a Government Report of 1864, p. 124
Timmins/Aitken – Aitken, W.C., *Papier Mâché Manufacture*, pp. 566–573

Wallis 1 — *The Art Manufactures of Birmingham and the Midland Counties in the International Exhibition of 1862*, Virtue Bros., London, 1863
i. Ch. IV: Wallis, George, *Works in Brass, Bronze etc., Papier Mâché and Japanned Tinware*
ii. Ch. VI: Wallis, George, *Wolverhampton and Walsall Manufactures*

Wallis 2 — Wallis, George, 'Recent Progress in Design, as applied to Manufactures',

WB — *Journal of the Society of Arts*, IV, 14 March, 1856
Correspondence: William Barrow to Matthew Boulton, *A Statement of the Cost of the different Operations of Fine Trays & Waiters etc.*, 29 May, 1794. Birmingham Archives and Heritage [BOU/B.I./177]

WChron. — *Wolverhampton Chronicle*

WDJ/AS — John, W.D., and Simcox, Anne, *Pontypool and Usk Japanned Wares*, Newport, 1966 (2nd edn)

WHJ — Jones, William Highfield, *Story of the Japan, Tin-plate Working ... Trades in Wolverhampton*, London, 1900

WHJ/1 — Jones, William Highfield, 'Family History, 1899', unpublished ms. (Private collection)

WHJ/2 — Jones, William Highfield, 'My Mother's Family', unpublished ms., undated (post 1899). (Private collection)

YAPP — Yapp, G.W., *Art Industry: Furniture, Upholstery and House-Decoration*, London, 1878, Ch. III 'Papier Mâché, Carton-Pierre, Japan and Lacquered Ware', pp. 26–32

CHAPTER I

1. John Pollexfen, *A Discourse of Trade & Coyn*, London 1697, quoted in Gibbs 2-i, p. 406
2. S&P, title-page
3. Quoted by Hugh Honour, *Chinoiserie, the Vision of Cathay*, London 1973, p. 43
4. Pollexfen, op cit., p. 99, quoted by J&J, p. 23
5. S&P, p. 7
6. MS Records of the East India Company, quoted by J&J, p. 23
7. Petition of the Joiners Company, 1700, in J&J, p. 20
8. Quoted by Rosalind K. Marshall, *The Days of Duchess Anne*, London 1973, p. 155
9. Quoted by J&J, p. 19
10. PM, '*Japan Ware in Japan*', 1845 vol. 14, p.200
11. S&P, p. xvi
12. Dossie 2, p. 408
13. ibid. p. 408
14. S&P, p. 20
15. ibid. p. 19
16. WDJ/AS. Sir Charles Hanbury-Williams to his wife, Dec. 1734, p. 25
17. Saint Fond, B.F. de, *A Journey through England & Scotland to the Hebrides in 1784* (ed. Archibald Geikie), Glasgow, 1907, vol. II, p. 346
18. Dossie 2, vol. 1, Ch. IV, Section 1, p. 479

CHAPTER II

1. Huth, p. 125
2. *ABG*, 14 Aug. 1758, p. 4, col.3
3. Evans, Chris, and Rydén, Göran, *Baltic Iron in the Atlantic World in the Eighteenth Century*, Leiden & Boston, 2007, p. 122
4. WChron. 26 Oct. 1791, p. 1, col. 2
5. *The Official Illustrated Guide to Birmingham*, 1862, p. 266
6. *ABG*, 25 Jan., 1796, p. 2 col.3
7. ibid
8. *ABG*, 2 Mar., 1795
9. WChron., 7 April, 1813, p. 3 col.4
10. WHJ, p. 43
11. ibid. p. 44
12. ibid. p. 135
13. ibid. p. 136
14. Burritt, p. 172
15. Exh. cat. 1869, section XV
16. Exh. cat., *The Wolverhampton Art & Industrial Exhibition*, Wolverhampton, 1902, Industrial Hall, no. 63

CHAPTER III

1. Dossie (1), p. 407
2. Official Catalogue of the *Exposition des produits de l'industrie de toutes les Nations*, Paris, 1855

3. Boyle, Robert, *Of Man's Great Ignorance of the Use of Natural Things*, vol. III, quoted from the Supplement to Chamber's *Cyclopaedia*, 1753 by E.A. Entwisle, in *The Book of Wallpaper*, 1970, p.71
4. Williams, Marjorie, *The Letters of William Shenstone*, Oxford, 1939, p. 336
5. Boyle, *op cit.*, quoted by Shirley DeVoe, *English Papier Mâché etc.*, Connecticut, 1971, p. 12
6. Campbell, R., *The London Tradesman*, 1747, p. 125
7. Verulam, Earl of, 1769, quoted by Gibbs 2–iv, p. 226
8. Bedford to the RSA, 29 March 1759; *RSA Guard Book* vol. 4, no. 50
9. Fisher, pp. 252–3
10. Pearson & Rollason, *The Birmingham Directory*, 1777
11. Thomson & Wrightson, *New Triennial Directory of Birmingham*, 1808
12. Pigott & Co., *Directory of Birmingham*, 1828-9
13. William Robson & Co. *Birmingham, Coventry, Dudley, Wolverhampton & their Immediate Environs*, 1839
14. Cornish/2, 1853, p. 19
15. Quoted by Burton, Elizabeth, *The Georgians at Home*, London, 1967, p. 180
16. Cornish, William, *Corporation, General & Trades Directory of Birmingham*, 1861
17. LL, p. 1
18. Broadley, A.M. (ed.), *Dr Johnson & Mrs Thrale*, (1774) London, 1910, p. 213–4
19. Hatchett, Charles, *The Hatchett Diary: A Tour Through the Counties of England & Scotland in 1796*, ed. Arthur Raistrik, Truro, 1967, p. 55
20. Smith J., *The Panorama of Science and Art*, Liverpool, 1813, vol. I
21. Anon., *The Leisure Hour*, 'Birmingham and Her Manufactures', no. 62, 3 March, 1853, p. 154–5
22. JRep/1, p. 548
23. AU/2, pp. 59-62
24. Cobbett, p. 20
25. Dossie 2, Part VI, Ch.1, p. 397ff
26. *The Gentlemans Magazine & Historical Chronicle*, 1754, vol. xxiv, p. 207
27. Patent, #1027, 1772
28. ibid.
29. Fisher, pp. 252–3
30. Allen's *Pictorial Guide to Birmingham*, Birmingham, 1849, p. 171
31. ibid.
32. Cornish/2, 1853, p. 18

33. Dickinson, p. 9
34. Thackrah, p. 85
35. Burrit, p. 173
36. Hunt, R., *Handbook to the Official Catalogues of the Great Exhibition*, 2 vols, London, 1851, vol. II, p. 638ff
37. JDM, vol. 3, Mar.-Aug., 1850, London, p. 114
38. AU/2, p. 59
39. Pat. # 9953, 1843
40. Pat. # 2830, 1805
41. ibid.
42. Horton, Appendix, Note VIII, p. 141, also [Timmins/Aitken], p. 567
43. WB, BRL, (BOU/A/209)
44. Hutton, 1835, p. 490
45. Gandee p. 104
46. ibid.
47. Yapp, p. 27
48. Rees, Abraham, *The CYCLOPAEDIA or Universal Dictionary of Arts, Sciences, and Literature*, 1818, vol. 4, p. 85 (1972 reprint)
49. Martineau, p. 83
50. ibid.
51. ibid.
52. *Journal of the Society of Arts* 'Affects [sic] of Paper Duty on Manufacters of Papier Mâché, 8 Sept. 1854, p. 723
53. ibid.
54. ibid.
55. Hodson, E.H., *Handbook of Birmingham*, 'Papier Mâché Trade', Birmingham 1886, p. 202

CHAPTER IV

1. 'Diary of the Hon ANNE RUSHOUT', daughter of the first Lord Northwicke, Broadway, Worcs. Private Collection. Quoted in *Apollo*, May 1956, p. 163
2. LL, p. 6-7
3. ibid.
4. Thackrah, p. 54
5. WB
6. Lawley, pp. 254-5
7. Mander Archives, *Black Varnish Book*, 1849+ (Deposited with Flint Ink, Wolverhampton)
8. WB
9. LL, p. 23
10. ABG, 21 Dec., 1767, p. 1, col.3
11. Dossie 2, vol. I, p. 493
12. ibid.
13. ABG 21 Dec., 1767, p. 1, col.3
14. ibid.
15. LL, p. 6
16. AJ/2, p. 278
17. ibid.
18. IndBi. p. 2
19. Patent # 8972, 1841
20. LL p. 8
21. Archer, p. 110
22. Dodd, p. 21
23. Dossie 2, p. 494
24. ibid.
25. Pococke, Dr Richard, *Travels*

through England, 1756, Camden Society re-print, 1888-9 vol. ii, p. 210
26. ibid.
27. WB
28. Anon., N&Q, 24 Mar., 1877
29. Patent #4146, 1817
30. Ure, Andrew, *A Dictionary of Arts, Manufactures and Mines*, London 1839, p. 1253
31. Anon., N&Q, (no.24), *The Old Japan Trade*, 3 Mar. 1877
32. Patent #1576, 1786
33. Taylor, Isaac, *Map of Wolverhampton*, 1751
34. Pattern Book # LP161 patt. no.523 (Wolverhampton Arts & Museums: Bantock House)
35. LL p. 9
36. ibid.
37. Thackrah p. 55
38. Timmins/Aitken p. 569
39. LL, p. 15
40. Dickinson, p. 117
41. Meason, p. 314
42. Martineau, p. 84
43. JRep/1, pp. 548-9
44. BMI, p. 175
45 ibid., p. 175-6
46. Wallis 1-i, pp. 49-50
47. *Connoisseur Yearbook*, G.W. Beard, *Robert Adams' Craftsmen*, London,1958, p. 32
48. Warner, Rev. Richard 1801, as quoted in SHA, p. 172
49. Martineau, p. 84
50. Dodd, p. 21
51. Dugdale, Thomas, *England and Wales Delineated*, London, u.d. (c.1870s), p. 1551
52. ibid.
53. Martineau, p. 84
54. ABG, 5 Nov., 1753, p. 3, col.2
55. Wedgwood to Bentley, 19 May, 1770, quoted by F&S, p. 92
56. WHJ p. 41
57. Wallis, George, N&Q, *Replies: Paintings on Tea Trays*, 6th S.I. March 13, 1880, p. 218
58. Correspondence: Obadiah Ryton to William Ryton, 24th January, 1792 (Ryton: RY-401)
59. Mander, p. 23
60. Wallis 1-i, p. 218
61. ABG 12 Apr., 1790, p. 3 col.3
62. Martineau, p. 84
63. Anon., N&Q (note 32), *Traditions of Old Japan Trade*, 24 Mar., 1877
64. Warner, Rev. Richard, op cit. p. 172
65. Wallis 1-i, p. 218
66. BMI, p. 171
67. AJ/2, p. 277
68. Dir. 1827 p.xxvi
69. BMI, p. 171
70. Dickinson, p. 86
71. Martineau, p. 84
72. Dickinson, p. 84

73. Anon. newspaper cutting, source and date unknown
74. LL, p. 17
75. ibid.
76. Spicer vol. II, p. 588, No.91
77. LL, p. 17
78. ABG, 15 June, 1767, p. 1, col.2
79. ibid.
80. WHJ/1, p. 24
81. Cornish/2 1853, p. 19
82. Timmins/Loveridge, p. 123
83. ABG, 21 Dec., 1767, p. 1, col.3
84. Lichtenburg, Georg, *Brief 1775*, quoted by HH, p. 118
85. AJ/2, p. 277
86. Fisher, pp. 252-3
87. ABG 23 June, 1788, p. 3 col 3
88. BMI, p. 173
89. ibid.
90. LL, p. 16
91. PM, 'A Second Day at the Birmingham Factories', vol. xiii, Dec. 1844, p. 505
92. WHJ/2, p. 17
93. Lawley, G.T., *History of Bilston*, Bilston, 1868, p. 85
94. ABG 27 Nov., 1752, p. 3 col.3
95. Prosser, p. 43
96. WHJ, p. 126
97. ibid.
98. Anon., N&Q, (6th S.i., 96, 125), 21 Feb., 1880, p. 159
99. BN, p. 45
100. AJ/2, p. 278
101. Timmins p. 625. Peyton, Edward, *Manufacture of Iron and Brass Bedsteads*
102. ibid.
103. ABG, 27 May 1782, p. 4, col.2
104. Hutton, 1835, p. 490
105. LL, p. 19
106. ABG, 4 Sept. 1758, p. 3 col.c
107. Dossie 1, p 428
108. Wedgwood Archive, *Common Place Book I J W*, p. 120. (Wedgwood manuscript accumulation, Wedgwood Museum, Barlaston [E39/28408])
109. Dossie 2, p. 441
110. JDA, p. 139
111. Exh.Cat.1884, Cat. no.5, p. 54
112. JDA, p. 139
113. AJ/2, p. 278
114. Anon., *The Leisure Hour*, 'Birmingham and her Manufactures', *no. 62, 3 Mar. 1853*, p. 155
115. LL, p. 19
116. Anon., SFTR, 'Papier Mâché Manufacture', 5 May 1869, p. 269
117. Patent #3219, 1809
118. Prosser, p. 44
119. Timmins, p. 640 Browett, J. B., et al, *The Miscellaneous Trades*
120. LL, p. 18

121. Dickinson, p. 37
122. Patent #3593, 1812
123. Timmins/Aitken, p. 569
124. Gandee, p. 96
125. Timmins/Aitken p. 569
126. Anon., N&Q, (no.32), *Traditions of Old JapanTrade*, 24 Mar., 1877
127. ibid.
128. Bede, Cuthbert (alias Edward Bradley), *The Adventures of Mr. Verdant Green, an Oxford Freshman*, London, 1853, p. 91
129. AJ/2, p. 278
130. BMI, p. 173
131. ibid., p. 174
132. ibid.
133. AJ/2, p. 278
134. Dickinson, p. 123
135. ibid. p. 117
136. Anon., SFTR, *Editorial Rambles amongst the Workshops of Birmingham*, Oct. 2, 1865, p. 262
137. Timmins/Aitken, p. 570
138. Dickinson, p. 37
139. Sarjeant, p. 104
140. Dickinson, p. 89
141. Timmins/Aitken, p. 569
142. Gandee, p. 83
143. Patent #10,046, 1844
144. op. cit. N&Q (NO. 32), 24 MAR. 1877
145. ibid.
146. ibid.
147. ibid.
148. Patent #10,046, 1844
149. Patent #1552, 1786
150. ibid.
151. Patent # 11,670, 1847
152. ibid.
153. Anon., *Illustrated Birmingham Times*, 'Papier Machee [sic] Manufactures by Messrs Jennens & Bettridge', Sept. 1854, p. 1, col. 3
154. ibid.
155. ibid.
156. Martineau, pp. 84-5
157. Meason, p. 315
158. LL, p. 19
159. ibid.
160. Archer, p. 110
161. LL, p. 23
162. Cornish/2, 1854, p. 19
163. LL, p. 23
164. Wallis, G., N&Q, *Paintings on Tea Trays*, 13 Mar. 1880, (6th S. i. 96, 125, 159, 199), p. 217
165. AU/2
166. JDM, 1849-50, vol. II, p 117
167. JDM, *Piracies*, 1849-50, vol. II, p. 87
168. WHJ, p. 5
169. Hawkes Smith, W, *Birmingham and its Vicinity as a Manufacturing and Commercial District*, Birmingham, 1836, pt II, p. 21
170. ibid.
171. Exh.Cat.1884, p. 53, no.1
172. WB
173. Mander, Charles, *Regulations for a Traveller*, 1839 (a draft ms. in the archives of Flint Ink, Wolverhampton). For a full transcript of the final version, see Charles Nicholas Mander *Varnished Leaves*, 2004, pp. 54-57
174. ibid.

CHAPTER V

1. Angerstein, p. 41
2. ABG, 7 Nov. 1785, p. 3, col.2
3. Quoted by Peck, T. Whitmore, and Wilkinson, K Douglas, in *William Withering of Birmingham, MD, FRS, FLS*, Bristol, 1950, p. 16
4. ibid, 23 Jan. 1786
5. Hutton, 1819, p. 121
6. WHJ, p. 27
7. ibid, p. 28
8. IndBi. p. 6
9. Sketchley's & Adams' *Tradesman's True Guide; or an Universal Directory for the Towns of Birmingham, Wolverhampton, Walsall & Dudley*, 1770
10. Chapman, T., *Annual Directory or Alphabetical list of the Merchants, Tradesmen and Principle Inhabitants of the Town of Birmingham and its Vicinity*, Birmingham, 1808
11. IndBi. p. 3
12. Jones, Joseph, *Historical Sketch of the Literary Institutions of Wolverhampton, 1794-1897*, London, 1897, pp. 36-38
13. MChron., Letter VII, 'The Condition of Factory Women and their Families', 25 Nov. 1850, p. 5 col. 5
14. WHJ, p. 29
15. Timmins/Loveridge, p. 120
16. ABG 23 June, 1788, p. 3 col.3
17. MChron., Letter VII, 25 November, 1850, op cit
18. Martineau, p. 84
19. ibid.
20. Correspondence: A. Love to Yvonne Jones, 6th May, 1983 (Wolverhampton Arts & Museums: Bantock House)
21. *Minute Book of Birmingham School of Art*, 26 March, 1874
22. ibid.
23. WHJ/1, p. 13
24. ibid. p. 14
25. ibid.
26. Thackrah, p. 45
27. Timmins/ Loveridge, *Extracts from Government Report (1864)*, p. 124
28. English Historical Documents, vol. xi, No. 371, Arthur Young: *Tours in England & Wales (1791)*, LSE Reprints, xiv, pp. 255-258
29. Jones, W.H., *Family History 'My Great Grandfather'*, unpublished ms 1899 (Private collection)
30. Timmins/Aitken p. 572
31. Whittock, N. (& others), *The Complete Book of Trades or the Parents Guide & Youths Instructor in the choice of a Trade, Business or Profession*, London 1837, p. 486
32. ibid. p. 493
33. WHJ, p. 39
34. ABG, 17 Dec., 1759, p. 2 col.2
35. Dickinson, p. 103
36. WHJ, p. 39
37. ibid.
38. CW, p. 9
39. Dudley, T.B. (ed.), *Memoir of James Bisset (written by himself)*, Leamington Spa, 1904, p. 72
40. ibid.
41. ibid. p. 73
42. ibid. p. 72
43. ibid. p. 73
44. ibid., title page
45.WHJ/2, p. 15
46. Dickinson, p. 112
47. WHJ/2, p. 15
48. ABG, 30 June, 1788, p. 3, col.3
49. ABG 13 Dec., 1790

50. WHJ/1, p. 20
51. ABG, 26th January, 1788
52. WB
53. WHJ/2, p. 14
54. LL, p. 6
55. Anon., *The Four Trades etc. etc., some Elementary Information respecting Varnishes ...*, 1898 (Mander archive, Flint Ink, Wolverhampton)
56. Correspondence: Ashwin T. to Boulton, M., 1 April, 1778 (BRL Archives [BOU/A/209])
57. ibid.
58. Thackrah, p. 45
59. ibid. p. 151
60. ibid.
61. Martineau, p. 83
62. WHJ, p. 34
63. Timmins/Loveridge, Henry, *Extracts from Government Report (1864)*, p. 123
64. Correspondence: J.O. Smith to Y. Jones, 1971 (Wolverhampton Arts & Museums: Bantock House)

CHAPTER VI

1. JRep/1, p. 549
2. Yapp, pp. 26-7
3. AJ, 1886, p. 105
4. Martineau, pp. 82-85
5. ABG, 21 Jan.1754, p. 3 col.2
6. ibid. 3 Mar. 1760
7. Anon., N&Q, *Birmingham in 1818* (vol. R., p. 76 no. 3473)
8. ibid.
9. AU 1847, *Chairs of Papier Mâché by Jennens and Bettridge*, p. 291
10. AU/2, p. 62
11. Wallis 2, p. 297
12. JDM, 1849, vol. I, p. 134
13. Wallis 2, p. 297
14. Wallis George, 'The artistic, industrial and commercial results of the Universal Exposition', *The Exhibition of Art & Industry, Paris*, London, 1855 (Quoted by Edwards, Clive *Victorian Furniture, Technology & Design*, Manchester, 1993, p. 132)
15. JRep/2, p. 723
16. Timmins/Loveridge, p. 121
17. JRep/2, p. 723
18. AU/2, pp. 59-62
19. Sarjeant, p. 105
20. Morley, Henry, 'A House Full of Horrors', *Household Words*, vol. 6, 4 Dec., 1852, pp. 265-70
21. Archer, p. 111
22. JDM, *Birmingham & Wolverhampton – Effects of the Great Exhibition – Schools of Design*, vol. 6, Sept.1851– Feb.1852, p. 135
23. AJ, *The Exhibition of Art-Industry in Paris* 1855, Supplement, p XI
24. Sarjeant, p. 105
25. Martineau, p. 84
26. Dodd, p. 22
27. Wallis 2, p. 297
28. Timmins/Aitken, p. 571
29. ibid. p. 573
30. Sarjeant, p. 104
31. Wiley, Samuel, to the *Select Committee on Arts & Manufactures*, 1835 (quoted by Clive Edwards, op cit., p. 129)
32. Sarjeant, p. 105
33. BMI, p. 175
34. ibid, p. 177
35. ibid.
36. ibid.
37. Yapp, p. 26
38. Wallis, George, *Papier Mâché Japanned Tin and Tin Ware*, section XV of 'South Staffs. Industrial & Fine Arts Exhibition, Wolverhampton, 1869', a Special Report prepared by the Committee of Education, Science & Art Dept.
39. LL, p. 1
40. ibid.

CHAPTER VII

1. JDA, p. 140
2. Sarjeant, p. 104
3. *ibid.*
4. Sarjeant, p. 105
5. Timmins/Aitken, p. 573
6. BMI, p. 172
7. Dickinson, G., *Royal Birmingham Society of Artists*, 'Exhibition of Papier Mâché' [Foreword to the catalogue], 13-21 Sept. 1926, p. 3
8. Martineau, Caroline, *Tour to the Lakes*, 1850, ms. notebook (private collection)
9. Archer, p. 110-111
10. Spicer, vol. 2, Class 22, p. 598, no.60a
11. Allen, G. C., *The Industrial Development of Birmingham and the Black Country, 1860-1927*, London, 1929 (1966 reprint) p. 197
12. BN, p. 45
13. JDA, p. 139

CHAPTER VIII

John Taylor

1. Hutton, 1st edn, 1783, p. 102-3
2. Court W.B., *Rise of the Midland Industries 1600-1838*, Oxford University Press, 1965, p. 235
3. Boswell, James, *Life of Dr. Johnson*, (Sir Joshua Reynolds edn, London 1885) vol. I, p. 49
4. Ryland, W.H., *Reminiscences of Thomas Henry Ryland*, B'ham 1904, p. 46
5. Lloyd, Samuel, *The Lloyds of Birmingham*, Birmingham 1907 ch.5, p. 41
6. ibid.
7. Ryland, op cit.
8. Patching, Resta, *Four Topographic Letters, 1757*, Letter IV, 31 July, 1755, pub. 1760, p. 62
9. ibid., p. 63
10. Hall, Thomas, & Mulford, John, *Journey ... thro' part of Hampshire Berkshire Gloucestershire Monmouthshire, Herefordshire Worcestershire & Warwickshire*, 1-13 July 1765, ms. diary, Thurs. 11 July, 1765 (private collection)
11. Shelburne, 19 May, 1766, p. 471
12. ibid.
13. Drake, J., *Picture of Birmingham*, Birmingham 1825, quoted by Eric Hopkins, *The Rise of the Manufacturing Town*, (1998 edn) p. 84
14. Dickinson, H.W., *Matthew Boulton*, Cambridge 1937, p. 121
15. ABG 3 April, 1775, p. 3 col.2

John Baskerville

1. Baskerville to 'The President of the R.A. of Science at Paris' (2nd Dec.1773) quoted by Bennett, vol. I p. 24
2. ibid. p. 41

3. ibid. p. 42
4. ibid. p. 43
5. Baskerville's Will, 6 Jan. 1773, quoted by Pardoe, pp. 123-6
6. ibid. pp. 11-12
7. Angerstein, p. 33
8. ibid.
9. ibid., p. 163
10. Connell, Brian, *Portrait of a Whig Peer compiled from the Papers of the Second Viscount Palmerston 1739-1802*, Andre Deutsch, 1957, p. 26
11. Letter: Baskerville to Horace Walpole 2 Nov., 1762, quoted by Leonard Jay, *Letters of the Famous 18th century Printer John Baskerville*, Birmingham 1932, p. 19
12. Letter: Baskerville to Benjamin Franklin, 7 Sept. 1767, quoted by Bennett, vol. II, p. 11
13. ibid.
14. Strauss, Ralph & Dent, Robert K, *John Baskerville, A Memoir* Cambridge 1907, p. 10
15. Hutton, 4th edn, 1809, p. 121
16. Bennett op cit. vol II, pp. 115-6
17. Shelburne, 16 May, 1766, pp. 470-471
18. *Autobiography of the Rev. Dr Alexander Carlyle*, London, 2nd edn. 1860, quoted by Pardoe p. 12
19. Shelburne op cit.
20. The Papers of Benjamin Franklin, (Yale v.d.), vol. 9 pp. 258-9, quoted by Pardoe, p. 58
21. Hall, Thomas, *The Journey of Thos Hall & Jn Mulford thro' part of Hampshire Berkshire Gloucestershire Monmouthshire Herefordshire Worcestershire & Warwickshire*, 1–13 July, 1765, ms. diary. (Private collection)
22. Shelburne op cit.
23. Sketchley J., *Birmingham, Wolverhampton and Walsall Directory*, 1767
24. Derrick, Samuel, *Letters written from Leverpoole, Chester, Cork, The Lake of Killarney, Dublin, Tunbridge-Wells, and Bath*, Dublin 1767, Letter 1 p. 3, Derrick to the Rt Hon. The Earl of Corke
25. Bennett, W., op cit., p. 150: William Shenstone to Richard Graves
26. Strauss, Ralph, & Dent, Robert K, op cit., p. 8
27. Pye's *Birmingham Directory*, 1797
28. Boulton & Fothergill to Mrs Mary Stovin, 19 Jan. 1771 (BOU. Letter Book E, p. 16, BRL)
29. John Wyatt to William Matthews, 1 April 1771. (BOU. Letter Book E, p. 93, BRL)
30. Baskerville to Boulton, 20 July 1773 (BOU/B.1/206, BRL)
31. Letter: W.J. Scofield to *Birmingham Weekly Post*, 22 Nov., 1879, quoted by Pardoe, p. 151
32. Auctioneer's description of Easy Hill in 1778, quoted by Pardoe, p. 14

Stephen Bedford

1. Gibbs 2-iv p. 227
2. Premiums by the Society for the Encouragement of Arts, Manufactures, & Commerce, 1759, p. 134
3. RSA, Guard Book, vol. 4 no.50

4. Bedford, Stephen to RSA, PR/MC/105/10/543/ A 4/6, no.42
5. ibid.
6. ibid.
7. Minutes of Premium Committees, 1762-3, Dec.4, 1762, p. 14 (RSA Archives, PR/GE/112/12/4)
8. ibid. 12 March, 1763
9. ibid. 21 May, 1763, p. 54
10. ABG, 4 July, 1763, p. 3, col.2
11. Dossie, Robert, *Memoirs of Agriculture*, 1768, vol. i, p. 193
12. Historic Manuscripts Commission *Report on the Manuscripts of the Earl of Verulam*, 274, quoted by Gibbs 2-iv, p. 226
13. ABG, 20 Jan., 1772, p. 3, col.2
14. ibid.
15. ibid.
16. ABG, 3 Feb, 1772, p. 2, col.3
17. ibid., 19 April, 1773 p. 2, col.2
18. Gibbs 2-iv, p. 223

Thomas Fletcher
1. ABG, 17 Sept., 1764, p. 3, col.3
2. Boulton & Fothergill to John Shuttleworth, 19 Dec., 1772, Letter Book F, p. 120 (BOU/BRL)
3. ABG, 1791, quoted in N&Q, vol. R., 21 Nov., 1896, p. 247

Boulton & Fothergill
1. Notebook 1751-59 (BOU/BRL)
2. Goodison, p. 48
3. Wedgwood J. to Bentley, T., 25 Oct. 1776 (Wedgwood manuscsript accumulation, Wedgwood Museum, Barlaston [18707-25])
4. ibid.
5. ibid.
6. Wedgwood J. to Bentley T. 25 April, 1778 (Wedgwood manuscript accumulation, Wedgwood Museum, Barlaston [E25 18831])
7. Boulton & Fothergill to John Shuttleworth, 19 Dec., 1772, Letter Book F, pp. 203-4, (BOU/BRL)
8. J. Roveray to Boulton & Fothergill, 8 April, 1773 (BOU/D.2/342 BRL)
9. Meteyard, p. 402
10. Hodges, J.to Boulton, M., 10 May, 1778 (BOU. [MS3782/12/63/5], (BRL)
11. Keir, W. to Boulton, M., 20 Oct., 1778 (BOU. [MS 3782 12/65/24], (BRL)
12. J. Hodges to Boulton 17 April, 1780 (MB Archives MS 3782/12/63/12), (BRL Archives)
13. ibid.
14. ibid.
15. Hodges, J., to Boulton, M., 26 Sept., 1780 (BOU. [MS 3782/12/63/17] BRL)
16. Hodges, J., to Boulton, M., 10 May, 1778, (BOU. [MS 3782/12/63/5], (BRL)
17. ibid.
18. Boulton & Fothergill to the Countess of Craven, 1776, quoted by Goodison, p. 261
19. Boulton, M. to Lord Lansdown, 12 Nov., 1794 (BOU. [BOU/L.1./87] BRL)
20. Inventory of Francis Egington's japan shop at the Soho Works, 31 Dec., 1779, BOU. [E.2./10]. (BRL)
21. Inventory, June 22, 1782

(BOU [MS 3782/2/13] (BRL)
22. Lot 92, in the Sale of the produce of Messrs Boulton & Fothergill's manufactory, 16 May, 1778, quoted by Goodison, p. 469

Henry Clay
1. ABG, 29 Mar., 1790, p. 3, col.2
2. ibid.
3. ibid.
4. ibid.
5. Apprentices Records , Public Records Office (ref. 51/275 1753)
6. Sketchley, J., *Directory of Birmingham, Wolverhampton and Walsall*, 1767
7. AU, pp. 59-62
8. Sketchley, J., *Birmingham, Wolverhampton & Walsall Directory*, 1767
9. ABG, 28 Nov, 1768, p. 3 col.3
10. Boulton & Fothergill to Edward Scales, 28 Sept. 1771, (Letter Book E pp. 203-4). (BOU.BRL)
11. ABG, 3 Aug., 1772, p. 3 col.2
12. Boulton & Fothergill to Shuttleworth, J. 19 Dec.,1772, (Letter Book F, p. 120). (BOU.BRL)
13. ABG, 5 April, 1773, p. 3, col.4
14. Broadley, A.M., (ed.), *Dr Johnson and Mrs Thrale including Mrs Thrale's unpublished journal of the Welsh Tour ...*, London, 1910, p. 213-14
15. SHA, p. 172; footnote quoted from Rev. Richard Warner 1801
16. ibid.
17. ABG, 5 April, 1773, p. 3 col.4
18. Receipts for payments by Sir Thomas Ward, including a bill from Henry Clay (Warwickshire County Record Office, [CR 162/640])
19. Lichtenburg, Georg, *Brief 1775*; quoted by Huth, p. 233
20. Fisher, p. 253
21. Clay, H. to Wedgwood, J., 21 June 1781 (Wedgwood Manuscript accumulation Wedgwood Museum, Barlaston [10-9131])
22. SHA, Document 5, p. 182
23. Walpole, H., *A Description of the Villa of Mr Horace Walpole etc.*, Thomas Kirgate, 1784, p. 79
24. SHA, Note 5, 1779, p. 1735.
25. Quoted by G.W. Beard, 'Robert Adams Craftsmen', *Connoisseur Yearbook*, 1958 p. 32
26. Burlington, C. and Rees, D. L., *The Modern Universal British Traveller*, London, 1779
27. Estimate for Sir John Hussey Delaval, Bart, 22 August, 1780 (Northumberland Record Office, [ref: 2DE/23/2/24])
28. The Journal of the La Rochefoucauld Brothers, 1785. Ms p. 68 (l'Assemblée Nationale, Paris, [ref: ms. vols. 1249 bis, ter and quarter])
29. ibid. p. 69
30. ibid. p. 69
31. Clarke, E D, *A Tour through the South of England, Wales and part of Ireland ...1791*, London, 1793, p. 376-377
32. ibid.
33. Brasbridge, Joseph, *The Fruits of Experience ...*, London 1824, p. 203

34. Dir. 1780
35. ibid.
36. ABG, 29 May, 1775, p. 3, col.2
37. Meteyard, p. 402
38. ibid. quoting letter from Wedgwood to Bentley, 14 July 1776
39. ibid.
40. ibid.
41. Wedgwood to Bentley, 25 Oct.,1776 (Wedgwood Manuscript accumulation Wedgwood Museum, Barlaston [18707-25])
42. Meteyard, p. 403
43. Wedgwood to Bentley, 2 July, 1776, quoted by F&S p. 195
44. Goodison, op. cit, p. 173
45. Ward, J., *The New Birmingham Directory*, Birmingham, 1798
46. Wedgwood to Bentley, 2 July, 1776 (Wedgwood Manuscript accumulation Wedgwood Museum, Barlaston [Vol.X, 102])
47. Wedgwood to Bentley, 14 July, 1776 (E.18684-25); quoted by F&S p. 195
48. Brasbridge, op. cit., p. 131
49. Scarfe, p. 113
50. Papendiek, p. 212
51. McKechnie, Sue, *British Silhouette Artists and their work, 1760-1860*, Sotheby, Parke Bernet, 1978, p. 36
52. Papendiek, p. 212-3
53. Scarfe, p. 114 n20
54. Hatchett, Charles, *The Hatchett Diary, a tour thro' the counties of England and Scotland in 1796 ...*, ed. Arthur Raistrick, Truro, 1967, p. 55
55. 'Dairy of the Hon. Anne Rushout, 26 July, 1797': quoted by G.W. Bright, in *Apollo*, May, 1956, p. 163
56. Patent # 1778
57. Woodforde, James, *The Diary of a Country Parson, 1758-1802*, 24th May, 1793, Oxford, 1975, p. 435
58. Papendiek, p. 212
59. ibid. p. 213
60. Scarfe, p. 113
61. Patent # 1786
62. ibid.
63. Clarke, E.D., op cit., pp. 376-377
64. Patent # 1792
65. ibid.
66. ABG 27 May, 1793 p. 3, col.2
67. AU/2, pp. 59-62
68. Sale of Costly Household Furniture of 11, Sutton-Place, Hackney by direction of John Gould, 13 June, 1814. (Guildhall Library, London, ref: PAM 9703)
69. Papendiek, p. 176
70. Godden, p. 252; and Chamberlain Account Book 1802, (The Worcester Porcelain Museum)
71. ABG 18 May, 1812, p. 4 col.3
72. ABG 15 June, 1812, p. 2 col.5
73. AU/2, pp. 59-62
74. Prosser, p. 40
75. ibid.
76. Spicer, Class 26, p. 749, no. 189
77. ibid.
78. SHA, footnote p. 171 'see J.T. Smith's *Nollekens & His Times*, ed. W. Whitten, 1920, vol. I, p. 175
79. Papendiek, p. 177

R. Watson
1. ABG, 25 June, 1770, p. 2, col.4
2. ibid. 17 Mar., 1788, p. 2, col.4

Thomas Bellamy
1. ABG, 19 April, 1773, p. 2, col.2
2. Bisset, James, *Memoir of James Bissett*, ed. by T.B. Dudley, Leamington Spa, 1904
3. ibid. p. 71
4. Bisset, James, *Magnificent Directory*, 1808

Obadiah Westwood
1. Ward, J., *The New Birmingham Directory*, 1798
2. Patent # 1786
3. Prosser, p. 47
4. ABG, 25 Dec., 1786, p. 3, col.2
5. Prosser, p. 47
6. Pye's *Birmingham Directory*, 1785

Thomas Ashwin
1. Correspondence: Ashwin, T., to Boulton, M., 1 April, 1778 (BOU. [BOU/A/209], BRL)
2. Pye's *Birmingham Directory*, 1791
3. WChron. 17 Aug., 1791, p. 4, col. 3

John Waring
1. ABG, 15 Mar., 1779, p. 3, col.4
2. ABG, 22 April, 1786, p. 2 col.4
3. Goddden, p. 252; and Chamberlain Account Book, 1791, (Worcester Porcelain Museum)

Francis Byrne
1. Godden, p. 252

Thomas Small
1. Cornish/1, 1825, p. 94
2. Dir. 1830

R & G Bill
1. N&Q (note 1942), *Snuff-Box Painting: S. Raven*, 17 July, 1886, p. 262
2. Exh. cat., *Catalogue of the Wonders of Nature and Art in the Halifax Exhibition*, 1840

T Watson
1. Trade card (BRL Trade Card Collection TC/1041)

Charles Docker
1. Godden, p. 252; and Chamberlain Acct Book, 1804-6 (The Worcester Porcelain Museum)

Robert Winn
1. Wrightson, *The Directory of Birmingham*, 1833
2. Robson's *London Directory*, 1837, Appendix p. 68

Jennens & Bettridge
1. Wrightson's *Triennial Directory of Birmingham*, 1823
2. Cornish/2, 1853, p. 20
3. Measom, George, p. 312
4. AU/2, pp. 59-62
5. Allen's *Pictorial Guide to Birmingham*, 1849, p. 171
6. Martineau, p. 83
7. Dir. 1830, part I, adv. between pp. 246 and 247
8. ibid
9. Martineau, p. 82
10. Dir. 1830, part I, p 246
11. ibid.

12. ibid, adv. between pp. 246 and 247
13. PM, *Papier Mâché Trays*, vol. XIII, Dec.,1844, pp. 505-506
14. BMI, vol. 3, p. 173
15. AU/2, pp. 59-62
16. ibid.
17. ibid.
18. Exh. cat., *Catalogue of the Mechanics Institute Exhibition of ... Fine Arts, Natural History [etc]*, Dumfries, 1841, cat no. 225
19. AU/1, p. 33
20. AU, 'Chairs of Papier Mâché by Jennens and Bettridge', 1847, p. 291
21. ibid.
22. ibid.
23. ibid.
24. Jennens & Bettridge's *Visitors Book*, 1837–c.1840 (Private collection)
25. JDM, vol. I p. 60, '3rd Annual Exhibition of Arts', 1849
26. Anon. ' Progress of British Manufactured Art ... The Works of Jennens and Bettridge', AJ 1849, p. 92
27. Exh.Cat.1849, p. 47, Tables no.60 and 61, exhibit 3
28. JDM, vol. I, p. 119
29. Anon., 'Papier Mâché Easel', AJ 1849, p. 214
30. Anon. 'Progress of British Manufactured Art ... ', op, cit., AJ 1849, p. 92
31. ibid.
32. Anon., 'Progress of British Manufactures. The Papier Mâché Works of Jennens and Bettridge', AJ 1847, p. 23
33. Shadlers, Henry, *The Illustrated Birmingham Times: A record of Local Events and Literary Miscellany*, No.2, Sept. 1854, p. 1, col.3
34. ibid.
35. ibid.
36. ibid.
37. ibid.
38. JDM, Mar.-Aug. 1850, vol. III, p. 114-5
39. ibid. vol. 2, Sept.1849 - Feb.,1850, p. 87
40. ibid. vol. I, Mar.- Aug., 1849, p. 32
41. Anon., 'Papier Mâché Easel', op. cit.
42. ibid.
43. Martineau, p. 85
44. JRep/1, p. 548
45. ILN, 2nd Supp. 4 Oct. 1851, p. 433, col.3
46. JRep/1, p. 548-549
47. MChron. 24 April 1851, p. 2 col.4
48. AJ/3, p. 66
49. MChron. 'Papier Mâché', 26 May,1851, p. 2, col.1
50. Martineau, p. 85
51. ibid.
52. ibid. p. 82
53. Spicer, p. 748, no.187
54. JRep/1, p. 549
55. ibid.
56. *Official Catalogue of the New York Exhibition ...*, 1853, British Section, Class 26, Div.B, Ex.no.12, New York: Geo. Putnam & Co., 1853, p. 115
57. *Articles of Ornamental Art in the Museum of the Department of Practical Art*, 1853, p. 58
58. ibid. Cat.no. F32
59. ibid. Cat.no. F33
60. ibid. Cat.nos. F48 and F49 respectively

61. Shadlers, Henry, op. cit.
No.1, 1 Aug., 1854, p. 16, col.3
62. Martineau, p. 82
63. *The Exhibition of Art-Industry in Paris 1855*, AJ 1855, Supplement, p. 28
64. ibid., pXI
65. *Catalogue of the Second Exhibition of the Manufacture Association*, National Galleries, Edinburgh, 1857, pub: R & R Clark, 1857, p. 97, no.261
66. Jennens & Bettridge's *Visitors Book*, op. cit.
67. Martineau, p. 85
68. *Journal of the RSA*, vol. 2, 8 Sept, 1854, p. 723
69. Patent #597, 1857

John Bettridge & Co.
1. Kelly & Co., *Post Office Directory of Birmingham*, 1860, adv. p. 23
2. Measom, p. 315
3. *Illustrated Catalogue of the International Exhibition*, AJ London 1862, (1973 reprint, p. 60)
4. Wallis 1-i, p. 40
5. Measom, op cit. p. 315
6. ibid.
7. SFTR, 2 Oct., 1865, Editorial Rambles amongst the Workshops of Birmingham, 'Papier Mâché Workshops of Messrs. J. Bettridge and Co.', p. 262
8. Wallis 1-i, p. 40
9. *Post Office Directory of Birmingham*, 1867, vol. II, Court & Commercial
10. *Catalogue of the Finished Portion of the extensive and high-class stock of the PAPIER MÂCHÉ GOODS Belonging to the Estate of Messrs. J. BETTRIDGE & Co., (late Jennens & Bettridge)*, Assembly Room, Royal Hotel, Temple Row, Birmingham, 8, 9, & 10 Aug. 1870

Thomas Lane
1. Kelly, *Post Office Directory of Birmingham*, 1850
2. *Exposition of British Industrial Art at Manchester*, Art Union, 1846, p. 33
3. Kelly, op cit.
4. Quoted by Toller, J., *Papier Mâché in Great Britain and America* (London, 1962), p. 33
5. AU/2, pp. 59-62
6. ibid.
7. ibid.
8. ibid.
9. John Johnson Collection, ref. Box: Trade Cards, Bodleian Library, Oxford
10. AJ/1, p. 316
11. Exh.Cat.1849, p. 54, Table no. 65, exhibits 4-6
12. ibid.
13. Spicer vol. II, Class 26, p. 742, no.128
14. ibid.
15. ibid.

Richard Turley
1. Spicer vol. II, p. 743, no 138
2. Wallis 1-i, pp. 40-41

Woodward & Midgeley
1. N&Q, *Traditions of Old Japan Trade*, no. 32, 24 March, 1877
2. Woodward, C.J., *Papier Mâché an Extinct Industrial Art*, 1926, p. 3; a lecture delivered to the Royal Birmingham Society of Artists, 21 April, 1926

3. ibid.
4. Catalogue to the *Exhibition of Papier mâché*, with a foreword by George Dickinson, Royal, Birmingham Society of Artists, 13-21 Sept.,1926

Isherwood Sutcliffe
1. AU/2, p. 62
2. ibid.
3. Spicer vol. II, p. 743, no 137
4. WHJ p. 131

Thomas Farmer
1. AU/2 pp. 59-62
2. Exh.Cat.1849, p. 74, Table no.117, exhibit 14
3. JDM, vol. II, Sept. 1849 - Feb. 1850, p. 66

McCallum & Hodson
1. Pigot, J. & Co., *New and Complete Directory of Birmingham and its Environs*, 1841
2. AU/2, pp. 59-62
3. Dickinson, p. 62
4. AU/2, pp. 59-62
5. ibid.
6. ibid.
7. LL, p. 26
8. AJ/1, p. 309
9. ibid
10. MChron. 19 July, 1851 p. 5 col.4
11. Horton, p. 144
12. MChron. op cit.
13. Dickinson, p. 127
14. Timmins/Aitken p. 571
15. AJ/3, p. 156
16. MChron. op cit.
17. Kelly & Co., *Post Office Directory of Birmingham*, 1860
18. Jones & Proud, *Jones's Mercantile Directory of Birmingham*, London, 1865
19. Hulley, J., *Birmingham Directory*, 1870 adv. p. 51

Foothorape, Showell & Shenton
1. Cornish/1, 1849, p. 88
2. AJ *The Birmingham Exposition*, 1848, p. 349
3. JDM, vol. II, Sept. 1849-Feb.1850, p. 66

J.H. Hopkins & Sons
1. Cornish/1, 1855, adv., p I
2. ibid.
3. BMI, p. 208

Halbeard & Wellings
1. JREP/1, p. 549

Alsager & Neville
1. Dickinson, pl IX
2. ibid. p. 83
3. ibid. p. 86
4. ibid. pl. II
5. ibid. p. 90
6. Anon. *The Journal of Decorative Art*, 'Contemporary Decorative Artists. Mr. John Thomas', August, 1889, p. 123
7. ibid.
8. ibid.

Griffiths & Browett
1. *Commercial Aspect of Birmingham*, 1862, p. 269

Nock & McCallum
1. Cornish/2, 1852, p. 95
2. ibid. p. xlviii (advert)

Knight, Merry & Co.
1. Dir. 1855, part 1, p. 190
2. Catalogue of the *International

Exhibition, 1862, Art Journal, 1863, (1973 reprint), p. 282

George Davies
1. Spicer vol. II, p. 742, no.129
2. ibid.
3. ibid.

Ebeneezer Sheldon
1. Horton, Appendix p. 146
2. Woodward, C.J., *Papier Mâché an Extinct Industrial Art*, 1926, p. 12

CHAPTER IX
The Old Hall
1. BN, 1871, p. 45
2. ABG, 8 Aug. 1774, p. 2, col.2
3. Pearson & Rollason, *Wolverhampton Directory*, 1780
4. Richardson, Sarah, exh.cat. *Edward Bird 1772-1819*, Wolverhampton Art Gallery, 1982, p. 1
5. Hughes, G.B., 'Old English Picture Trays II', *Country Life*, Mar. 19, 1948, p. 82
6. Cunningham, A., *The Lives of the Most Eminent British Painters, Sculptors and Architects*, London, 1830, vol. II, p. 243
7. ABG, 2 Mar. 1789, p. 3, col. c
8. ABG, 27 July, 1795, p. 3 col. c
9. Pearson & Rollason, *Wolverhampton Directory*, 1780
10. William Ryton to his mother, 25 May, 1788, quoted by J. R. Andrews *Three Schoolboys at Barr Academy*, Shropshire FHS
11. ABG, 17 Jan. 1791, p. 3, col. c
12. WChron. 8 Dec., 1790, p. 4, col. 2
13. Statement prepared for John Barney, 7 Oct., 1791, Ryton Papers (Private Collection)
14. Obadiah Ryton to Joseph Barney 19 June 1792; notice of dissolution of partnership Ryton Papers RY-371 (Private Collection)
15. WChron. 11 Mar., 1812, p. 3, col. 3
16. Pigot, James, *The Commercial Directory of Wolverhampton*, Manchester, 1818-19-20
17. Hughes G.B., 'Old English Picture Trays II', *Country Life*, 19 Mar., 1948 p-83
18. Burritt, p. 172
19. *Visitors Guide to Wolverhampton*, Barford Newitt, 1871, p. 45
20. Obadiah Ryton to William Ryton, from Warrington, 24 Jan., 1792, Ryton Papers RY-401 (Private Collection)
21. WChron. 11 Mar., 1812, p. 3, col. 3
22. WHJ, p. 13
23. Smart, J. *Directory of Wolverhampton*, Wolverhampton, 1827
24. WHJ, p. 41
25. ibid. pp. 43-4
26. WChron. 24 Mar., 1847, p. 3, col. 1
27. ibid.
28. AU/1, p. 33
29. WHJ, p. 48
30. Jones, Joseph, *Historical Sketch of the Literary Institutions of Wolverhampton, 1794-1897*, London, 1897, p. 41
31. WHJ, p. 51
32. WHJ, p. 52
33. Jones, Joseph, op cit. p. 41

34. WHJ, p. 52
35. *Illustrated London News* (supplement), 20 Sept., 1851, p. 364
36. Yapp, pl. LXVIII (Furniture)
37. ibid.
38. AJ, 1848, 'Society of Arts Exposition of British Manufactures', p. 129
39. AJ/1 p. 317
40. ibid.
41. JDM, vol. II, 1849, p. 67
42. *Morning Chronicle*, 19 July, 1851, p. 5 col.4
43. Dickinson, p. 121
44. ibid.
45. ibid. pp. 121-2
46. WChron. 21 May, 1851, p. 3, col. 2
47. 1851 Ex. Cat. vol. II, Class 22, p. 668 no. 701
48. Dickinson, op cit. p. 108
49. ibid. pp. 43-44
50. ibid. p. 44
51. ibid. p. 108
52. ibid.
53. ibid. p. 85
54. WHJ/2, p. 15
55. Patent #2717
56. WHJ, p. 112
57. Burritt, p. 171
58. JDA, p. 139

Mander Brothers
1. WChron. 21 Mar. 1792, p. 6, col. 3
2. Quoted by Mander, C.N., *Varnished Leaves*, Dursley, Glos., 2004, p. 32
3. Godden, Geoffrey, 'English Paper Trays 1790-1815', *The Connoisseur*, Aug, 1967, pp. 250-254, pl.3
4. Mander, Geoffrey Le M., *The History of Mander Brothers, 1773-1955*, Wolverhampton, 1955, p. 8
5. Mander, G. Le M., op cit. p. 101
6. ibid. p. 11
7. *The Narrative of Jemima Cox*, 1871, quoted by both G. Le M. Mander, op cit., p. 19ff, and C.N. Mander, op cit., p. 81ff
8. *Varnish Carriage Book*, 1838, manuscript ledger, held by 'Flint Ink', Wolverhampton

Thomas Illidge
1. Chamberlain's Order Book, 1813 (Worcester Porcelain Museum)
2. WChron. 11 Mar. 1812, p. 3, col. 3

Evans & Cartwright
1. Wardle, Pratt & Pigot, *The Commercial Directory of Wolverhampton for 1816-17*
2. Langford, *History of Staffordshire & Warwickshire*, 1884
3. Dickens, Charles, 'The Christmas Tree', 1850; reprinted in Michael Slater, *A Christmas Carol and other Christmas Writings*, Penguin, 2003, p. 231

James Pedley
1. Chamberlain's Order Book, 1813 (Worcester Porcelain Museum)
2. Matthew Boulton Archives (MS 3782/13/14/118 James Pedley to Matthew Boulton, 22 Nov. 1814)
3. ibid.
4. ibid.

Henry Fearncombe
1. WHJ, p. 90
2. White, F & Co., *New Commercial Directory & Topography of the Borough of Birmingham ... including Wolverhampton*, Sheffield, 1855
3. Dickinson, p. 110

Richard, George & Edward Perry
1. Smart, J., *Directory of Wolverhampton*, Wolverhampton, 1827
2. Bridgen, J., *Directory of the Borough of Wolverhampton etc...*, Wolverhampton, 1833
3. WHJ, p. 81
4. *The Times*, 18 May, 1836
5. Bridgen, J., *Directory of Wolverhampton*, 1838
6. Mander, G. Le M., *The History of the Mander Brothers 1773-1955*, p. 12
7. WHJ, p. 61
8. ibid. p. 62
9. ibid. p. 77
10. Bridgen, J., *Directory of Wolverhampton*, Wolverhampton, 1838
11. Bridgen, J., *Wolverhampton Post Office Directory*, 1847, Wolverhampton [1846]
12. Spicer II, p. 667, Class no. 22, no. 691a
13. White, F., & Co., *New Commercial Directory & Topography of the Borough of Birmingham ... including Wolverhampton*, Sheffield, 1855
14. Exh.Cat.1869
15. ibid.
16. *Industrial Great Britain* (Anon.), Historical Publishing Co., London 1891, p. 167

Henry Loveridge & Co.
1. WHJ, p. 85
2. ibid.
3. Trade Catalogue of Shoolbred, Loveridge & Shoolbred, Bridgen's, Wolverhampton, 1848
4. ibid.
5. JDM, vol. II, p. 96
6. Spicer II, p. 611, Class no. 22, no.160a
7. WHJ, p. 87
8. *Medals & Honorable Mentions awarded by the International Juries*, London 1862, Class 31, Section C
9. Archer, p. 109
10. ibid.
11. Archer, p. 111

Jones Brothers
1. WHJ/1 and WHJ/2
2. WHJ/2
3. ibid.
4. ibid.
5. ibid.
6. ibid.
7. ibid.
8. ibid.
9. ibid.
10. ibid.
11. Anon. *The Journal of Decorative Art*, 'Contemporary Decorative Artists. Mr. John Thomas', Aug. 1889, p. 123
12. Catalogue: Jones Brothers & Co., *Tin & Japan Goods*, 12th edition, c.1882

CHAPTER X

John Hartill
1. WChron. 23 Sept., 1789, p. 3

cols. 1-3
2. ibid. 31 May, 1790
3. Lawley, G., *History of Bilston*, 1868, p. 85

Gerrard Barber
1. Pigot, J., *The Commercial Directory of Wolverhampton*, 1818-19-20, Manchester
2. undated trade-card, BRL/TC1178
3. IndBi, p. 1

J. Dean & Son
1. Jones & Co. *Trades Directory of Wolverhampton*, 1862-3, London
2. Steen & Blackett, *Original Illustrated Wolverhampton Guide*, 1871, Wolverhampton
3. [IndBi], p.4
4. Lawley, G.T., *A History of Bilston*, Bilston, 1893, p. 256

S & S Caddick
1. Pigot, J., *The Commercial Directory of Wolverhampton*, 1818-19-20, Manchester
2. WChron. 1 Jan. 1823, p. 3, col.3

Hartill & Jackson etc.
1. Sankey, J.W., typescript of his address at the coming of age of S.J. Sankey, 31 Dec., 1910, quoting recollection of Charlie Britten who joined the firm c.1850 (held by GKN)

Joseph Sankey
1. Letter: John Duncalfe to Joseph Sankey, 25 Feb. 1846 (Photostat copy held by GKN)
2. Anon., *The Sankey Story*, c.1954, p. 8 (typescript held by GKN)
3. Sankey's Order Book for 'General Stampings' 17 Oct., 1900 – 23 Nov., 1901, eg. pp. 67 and 68 (held by GKN)

Thomas Farmer
1. Melville & Co., *Directory of Wolverhampton*, 1851
2. Exh.Cat.1869, Industrial Section, ex. no. 73
3. Exh.Cat.1884, Japanned and Block Tin Goods etc. p. 14, ex. no. 113

J. & W.H. Baker
1. IndBi., p. 5
2. ibid.
3. Exh.Cat.1884, Japanned and Block Tin Goods, ex. no. 125, p. 15
4. IndBi., p. 5

John Marston
1. Truscott, Son & Simmons, *Official Catalogue of the Industrial Department*, International Exhibition, London, 1862, Class 31, sub-Class C, Exh. No. 6386, p. 98
2. Exh.Cat.1884, Industrial Section Exh. no. 230

James Motlow
1. Exh.Cat.1884 Industrial Section, Japanned Goods, 232a

Star Japan Company
1. Exh.Cat.1869, Industrial Section, ex. no. 121
2. Lawley, George T., *A History of Bilston*, Bilston 1893, p. 257

CHAPTER XI

London
1. Spicer II, p. 759, no.346
2. Holden's *Triennial London Directory*, 1805-7
3. Spicer II, p. 732, no.37a
4. ibid. p. 755, no.271
5. ibid. p. 651, no.500

Strickland & Co.
1. ABG, 17 Mar. 1788, p. 3, col.3
2. ibid.
3. ibid. 12 Apr. 1790, p. 3 col.4
4. ibid. 4 Oct. 1790
5. ibid. 26 April, 1790
6. Chamberlain Account Books (Worcester Porcelain Museum)
7. *The Times*, 3 May, 1800, 4c
8. ibid. 9 June, 1800, 4a
9. ibid. 14 June, 1800, 4d

Dyson & Benson
1. WChron. 27 Aug., 1823, p. 3 col.4

Valentine & Hall
1. Kent's *London Directory*, 1804

Henry Clay (II)
1. Critchett & Wood's *Post Office London Directory*, 1821
2. *London Post Office Directory*, 1830
3. Kelly's *Post Office London Directory*, 1841
4. 'The Progress of Art Manufactures', AJ 1852, p. 223

Spiers, Oxford
1. Hunt's *Oxford Directory*, 1846
2. *Morning Chronicle*, 19 July, 1851, p. 5, col. 4
3. ibid.
4. ibid.
5. AJ/2, p. 278
6. Bradley, Edward (alias Cuthbert Bede), *The Adventures of Mr. Verdant Green ...*, London, 1853, p. 91

CHAPTER XII

1. WB
2. JDM, 'Tea-tray, Knitting Box and Inkstand by Jennens & Bettridge', Mar.-Aug., 1850, p. 114
3. Lucy Wood, 'George Brookshaw 'Peintre Ébéniste par Extraordinaire'. The case of the vanishing cabinet-maker: Part 2', *Apollo*, June, 1991, p. 384
4. WChron. 27 Aug., 1823, p. 3, col.4
5. Wallis, 1-i, p. 35
6. Anon. 'The Birmingham Exposition', *AJ* 1848, p. 349
7. 1851 Cat. Class 22, no. 371, vol. II, p. 639
8. Cornish/1, p. 77
9. Wallis 1-i, p. 35
10. Archer, p. 111
11. *Illustrated London News*, 'The Illustrated Paris Universal Exhibition', 1878, p. 341
12. *Illustrated Catalogue of the International Exhibition*, AJ London, 1862, (reprinted by EP Publishing, 1973, p. 118)
13. Cornish 1, op cit.
14. Exh.Cat.1849, Table no. 48, p. 19
15. Archer, p. 111
16. Robert Southey, *Letters from England by Don Manuel Alvarez Espriella*, 1807, ed. J. Simmons, 1951

17. Hutton, p. 488
18. Fenning, D., *Royal English Dictionary*, London, 1771
19. N&Q, Cuthbert Bede (Edward Bradley), *Paintings on Tea-Trays*, (6th S. i. 96, 125), p. 159
20. Cobbett, p. 20
21. N&Q C.Bede, op cit.
22. Birmingham Stangers Guide, *Jennens & Bettridge's Show Room and Manufactory of Japan Wares*, 1825, p. 97
23. Pattern Book, dated Sept. 1832-Oct. 1851 (Wolverhampton Art Galleries & Museums, Access. no. LP-151)
24. Quoted by Shirley deVoe, *English Papier Mâché of the Georgian and Victorian Periods*, Wesleyan Uni. Press, 1971, p. 151
25. Dickinson, p. 96
26. Anon. 'The Birmingham Exposition', AJ 1848, p. 356
27. LL, p. 25
28. Trade Card Collection, Birmingham Reference Library (ref: BRL/TC/647)
29. Patent # 1572, 1786
30. ibid.
31. ibid.
32. William Cheshire to Matthew Boulton [?], MS 3782/12/59/158, 11 Feb., 1796
33. Patent # 1576, 1786
34. MS 3782/2/13 Inventory, 22 June 1782
35. Timmins p. 439. Turner, John P., *The Birmingham Button Trade*
36. Horton, Appendix, p. 115
37. ABG, 3 May, 1742, p. 4, col. 1
38. *Diary and Letters of Madame D'Arblay* [Fanny Burney], ed. by her niece, London 1842, vol. II, 1781-1786, 28 Dec., 1782, p. 218
39. Woodforde, James, *The Diary of a Country Parson*, (ed. John Beresford), 3 Oct., 1761, Oxford, 1975
40. Inventory: William Hutton, Bennett's Hill, Saltley, in the parish of Aston, Birmingham, 25 Feb. 1792 (BRL 145428)
41. Inventory: Joseph Priestley, Birmingham 21 Feb.1792 (BRL 399801)
42. Eastlake, Charles, *Hints on Household Taste* (1878), Dover reprint, 1969, pp. 92-3
43. AJ/3, p. 32
44. WChron. 12 Dec., 1821, p. 3, col. 3
45. Cobbett, p. 15
46. Spicer II p. 620, no. 249
47. Quoted by Leathlean, Howard, 'Paul Jerrard Publisher of 'Special Presents'', *The Book Collector*, vol. 40, no. 2, Summer 1991, p. 185
48. *The Daily Telegraph*, 'Papier Mâché', 17 Nov., 1925

CHAPTER XIII

1. Verney, Margaret M., *Memoirs of the Verney Family*, London, 1899, p. 221
2. S&P, *Epistle to the Reader and Practitioner*, p. xvi
3. Llanover, Lady A. (ed.) *Autobiography and Correspondence of Mary Granville Mrs Delaney*, 6 vols. London, 1861-2, vol. I, p. 213
4. Quoted by Oliver Impey, in *Chinoiserie, The Impact of*

Oriental Styles on Western Art and Decoration, New York, 1977, p. 116
5. Quoted by Huth p. 31
6. Dossie (1) p. 409
7. ibid. p. 410
8. Dossie (2), p. 483
9. Gandee p. 104
10. ibid.
11. ibid. p. 75
12. ibid. p. 107
13. *The Times*, 5 July, 1850, p. 11, col. c
14. LL, p. 20
15. Yapp, p. 27
16. Archer, p. 115
17. ibid.
18. Inscription on tombstone of Edward Allgood, formerly in the Baptist burial ground at Penygarn, but now missing; for illustration see Nichols, Reginald, *Pontypool and Usk Japan Ware*, Pontypool, 1981, p. 36
19. Quoted by WDJ/AS p. 35
20. Angerstein vol. I, journey 5d, p. 163
21. WDJ, p. 38
22. Quoted by WDJ/AS, p. 36
23. Wyndham, H.P., *A Tour through Monmouthshire & Wales*, Salisbury, 1781. Quoted in Gibbs 1-iv, p. 127
24. Quoted by WDJ/AS, p. 39
25. ibid., from the *Cambrian Travellers* Guide, 1813
26. Quoted from the *Gloucester Journal*, 4 July, 1763, by John & Simcox, op cit, p. 35
27. Quoted from the *Gloucester Journal*, 8 Aug., 1763, by R. Nichols, op cit, p. 27
28. *The Usk Gleaner*, quoted by Nichols, Reginald, *Pontypool and Usk Japan Ware*, Pontypool 1981, p. 30
29. Cuyler, A.M., unpublished letter in The National Library of Wales, Aberystwyth, quoted by WDJ/AS, p. 47
30. Quoted by Dampierre, Florence, *Les Plus Beaux Meubles Peints*, Suresnes, 1991, p. 21
31. Dossie (2), vol. I, pp. 481-2
32. Pearson & Rollason, *Birmingham Directory...*, 1780
33. N&Q vol. Q, article no. 2938, 25 May, 1892, p. 210
34. Sarjeant, p. 106
35. *A Description of the Villa of Mr Horace Walpole ... with an Inventory &c*, 1784, p. 15
36. Archer, p. 109
37. ibid.
38. ibid., p. 112
39. ABG, 21 Dec., 1767 p. 1, col.3
40. Voltaire, F-M A, The Dramatic Works, (trans. Rev. Mr Francklin), London, 1771, vol. IV, *Nanine*, p. 173
41. Campbell, R, *The London Tradesman*, 1747, p. 125
42. *Reports by the Juries*, International Exhibition, London, 1862, p. 6
43. Sarjeant, p. 106
44. ibid.
45. ibid.
46. ibid.
47. ibid.
48. ibid.
49. ibid.
50. *Reports by the Juries*, International Exhibition London 1862, London, 1863, p. 6
51. Archer, p. 109
52. ibid. p. 112

53. ibid.
54. Spicer II p. 1058, no199
55. ibid.
56. Quoted by Richter, Detlev, *Lacquered Boxes*, Pennsylvania, 1989, p. 46
57. Hassel, G, and Bege, K *Principalities of Wolfenbüttel and Blankenburg*, quoted by Richter, Detlev, op cit. p. 49
58. Spicer II, p. 1092, no.764
59. Spicer 2, p. 1093 no.744 and p. 1072 no. 390
60. Archer, p. 114
61. Sarjeant, p. 108
62. ibid.
63. Boguslavskaya, I, *Zhostovo Painted Trays*, Moscow, 1994 (unpaginated: final paragraph of Introduction)
64. Raay, Stefan van (ed.) *Imitation and Inspiration. Japanese Influence on Dutch Art*, quoted by Titus M Eliëns, 'Dutch Lacquerwork in the Nineteenth Century', p. 92
65. ibid. p. 91, see note 29
66. Archer, p. 112
67. ibid.
68. Sarjeant, pp. 106-7
69. Sarjeant, p. 107
70. Archer, p. 112-113
71. ibid.
72. Shirley DeVoe, 'The Litchfield Manufacturing Company 1850-1854', first published in *The Connecticut Historical Society Bulletin*, vol. 37-3, and reprinted in Shirley S. Baer and M. Jeanne Gearin: *Decorative Arts: 18th & 19th Century, Research and Writings of Shirley Spaulding DeVoe*, HSEAD, 1999, p. 122
73. Shirley DeVoe, 'Papier mâché in Wolcottville, Connecticut', first published in The Connecticut Historical Society Bulletin, vol. 34-1, 1969, and reprinted in Shirley S. Baer and M. Jeanne Gearin: *Decorative Arts: 18th & 19th Century, Research and Writings of Shirley Spaulding DeVoe*, HSEAD, 1999, p. 34

CHAPTER XIV

1. Hill QC, Matthew Davenport, *Address delivered at the Birmingham & Midland Institute*, 30 Sept. 1867. London, Longmans & Co., 1867, p. 12
2. Pigot & Co., *Directory of London*, 1839, adv.9
3. *The Times*, 6 Mar., 1848, 11a
4. 'The Farmer of Tiptree Hall,' *Household Words*, vol. 5, 7 Aug., 1852, pp. 477-482
5. Wrightson, *The Directory of Birmingham*, 1835
6. DeVoe, Shirley Spaulding, *English Papier Mâché of the Georgian and Victorian Periods*, London, Barrie & Jenkins, 1971, p. 72
7. *The Times*, 4 Jan., 1825, 4b
8. ibid.
9. ibid.
10. Cobbett, p. 20
11. Martineau, p. 82
12. Quoted by Huth p. 107
13. ibid. p. 108
14. Archer, p. 112

INDEX

Page numbers referring to plates and captions are shown in **bold**.

Abele & Co., 293
Adam, Robert (*see also*: Derby House; Kedleston Hall; Osterley Park House), 9, 15, 53, 61, 125, 128, 130
Adt Frères, 78, 109, 244, 262, 281, 282-6; **284, 285**
Aitken, William, 76
Albert, Prince Consort, 52, 83, 145, 146, 151, 152, 165, 167, 170, 171, 195, 207, 262
Albert Parent & Company, 262
albums, 78, 158, 162, 170, 179, 266, 300
Alderman, Edwin, 312, 315
Allen, Joseph, 18
Allen & Moore, 181
Allgood & Edwards of Pontypool, 95
Allgood, Edward (jnr), 273, 274, 276
Allgood, Edward (snr), 14, 17, 115, 273, 274, 276
Allgood, Henry, 115
Allgood, John, 152, 273
Allgood, Thomas, 14, 17, 115, 272-4, 276
Allgood, William ('Billy the Bagman'), 115, 275
Allgood, Davies & Edwards, 274
Allgoods, the, 17, 18, 115, 273, 274, 276
Allgoods & Co., 276
Alsager & Neville (*see also*: Harper, George), 36, 46, 57, 95, 168, 174, 176-8, 180, 192, 197, 236, 266
amateur japanners, 36, 69, 75, 79, 271-2
Angerstein, Reinhold Rücker, 89, 115, 117, 274, 277
apprentices, 56-60, 76, 84, 89, 92-5, 102-3, 125, 138-9, 142, 168, 176-7, 183, 299
Archer, Thomas, 43, 83, 108, 152, 166, 272, 279, 286, 304
Aris, Samuel (see also *Birmingham Gazette*), 134
Art Journal, 41, 154, 159, 162, 170, 174, 208, 233, 249, 305; **27, 153, 154, 157, 162, 169, 171, 175, 176, 181, 191, 202, 204, 208, 233, 236, 248**
Art Union, 27, 84, 85, 102, 103, 125, 149, 152, 155, 165, 168, 169, 170; **151, 171, 254**
Artist or Young Ladies Instructor, The (Gandee, B.F., 1835), 66, 75
Artist's Assistant, The, see: Robinson & Swinney
Ashwin, Thomas, 25, 96, 140, 262
aurum mosaicum, 70

Baker, J. & W.H., 224; **219**
Baker, James, 224
Baker, W.H., 224
Barber, Gerrard, 41, 65, 93, 184, 186, 197, 219, 220
Barker, Benjamin, 274-5
Barker, Thomas, 62
Barney, Joseph, 57
Barney & Ryton, 97, 183-6
Barrow, William, 36, 40, 45-6, 62, 86, 96, 122, 239
Baskerville, John, 9, 18, 24, 43, 60, 61, 90, 113, 114, 115-18, 120, 123, 125, 140, 183, 239, 240, 241, 269
beads, 261-2
Becker & Kronik, 305; **305**
Bede, Cuthbert *see*: Bradley, Edward

Bedford, Stephen, 9, 24, 64, 65, 114, 117, 118-20, 123, 138, 240, 241, 280
beds and bedsteads, 41, 162, 173, 188, 200, 249, 286, 305; **162, 245, 249**
Beehive Works, The, 223-4
Bekkers, J & Son, 304
Bell, John, 104, 154, 157
Bell, Robert, 268
Bellamy, Thomas, 94, 120, 138-9; **139**
bellows, 266; **267**
Bennett, 117
Bernardis, M. de, 305
Bessemer steel, 21
Bettridge, John (*see also*: John Bettridge & Co.), 83, 144, 149, 161, 174
Bettridge, Joseph, 42, 162-3
bicycle industry, 21, 41, 111, 205, 212, 217, 225
Bielefeld, Charles, 24, 152
Bill, R. & G., 142, 252
"Billy the Bagman" *see*: Allgood, William
Bird, Edward, 57, 72, 183-6, 250, 307; **185, 250**
Bird, James, 223-4
Bird Japanning Co., 263, 307
Birmingham Gazette, 40, 54, 56, 59, 64, 89, 94, 95, 114, 120, 134, 137, 139, 138, 140, 183, 229, 230, 263
Birmingham School of Design, 58, 148, 165
blanks, 19, 26, 31, 33-4, 36, 45, 91, 96, 108, 110, 117, 123, 170, 178, 186, 202, 223, 224, 225, 235, 236, 254, 256, 262, 272, 288
blank-makers *see*: Barber, Gerrard; Caddick, James; Fellows, Enoch
blotters, 52, 266, 307
book-covers, 266, 268
Booth, Edwin, 186
Booth, John, 36
Booth, Joseph, 79, 145-6, 168, 187
bottle stands/coasters, 34, 36, 48, 124, 137, 139, 140-1, 206-7, 211, 239, 258; **137, 258, 296**
Boulle, Charles André, 43
boulle-work, 43, 46, 317
Boulton, Matthew, 9, 26-7, 36, 40, 46, 62, 86, 89, 96, 114, 117, 120, 133-4, 138, 140, 146, 200, 262
Boulton & Fothergill, 117, 120-4, 126, 262; **120**
Boyle, Robert, 24, 28
Bradley, Edward (alias Cuthbert Bede), 66, 77, 236, 250; **235**
Brasbridge, Joseph, 125, 133, 135
Bray, Charles, 229
bread baskets, 20-1, 60, 93, 115-7, 123, 126, 135, 137-8, 141, 164, 178, 180, 186-7, 200, 206, 211, 219, 225, 231-2, 239, 258, 275, 290, 303, 306; **92, 137, 141, 211, 213, 313**
Breese, Charles (Breese & Hayward), 74
Brindley, William, 34-6, 268; **37**
Bristol, 4th Earl of, 133
bronze decoration, 68, 75, 76, 78, 300, 309; **73, 102, 141, 198, 199, 258, 313**
Brooks, John, 64, 139
Brookshaw, George, 123, 130, 133, 240-1; **240, 269**
Brown, E., 272
Brown, W.N., 41

buckles, 18, 116
Burgers, J. van, 271, 304
button makers *see*: Adt Frères; Albert Parent & Company; Ashwin, Thomas; Boulton & Fothergill; Clay, Henry; Cheshire, William; Davenport & Cole; Watson, Thomas; Westwood, Obadiah
buttons, 26, 27, 35, 49, 80, 120, 123, 125, 135, 136, 139, 140, 239, 260, 261-3, 307; **261, 283**
Byrne, Francis, 140, 143

cabinets, 11, 12, 24, 28, 40, 82, 123, 126, 133, 134, 141, 143, 148-9, 156, 165-7, 169, 170-1, 173-4, 176-7, 179-80, 191, 200, 224, 229, 236, 241, 244, 246, 265, 271-2, 278, 284, 286, 306; **11, 50, 156, 160, 172, 173, 182, 194, 234, 244, 245, 246/7**
Caddick, Isaac, 40
Caddick, James, 91
Caddick, S. & S., 220
cake trays and baskets *see*: tray shapes
cameos (and intaglios), 84, 134, 136
candle snuffers (*see also*: snuffers trays), 27, 117, 275, 313
candlesticks, 17, 20, 32, 45, 46, 56, 109, 116, 117, 125, 166, 174, 183, 186, 231, 239, 273, 274, 276, 290, 303; **303**
card trays *see*: tray shapes
Careless, Edward, 40
Carlyle, Dr Alexander, 116
Carmignac, Jocobus, 303
Catalogue of Etruscan, Greek and Roman Antiquities (D'Hancarville, Pierre Francois), 61
Catherine the Great, 133, 273
ceremonial ware, 52
chairs, 26-8, 32-3, 35, 42, 96, 103, 126, 133, 138, 149, 150, 152, 154-5, 157-9, 161-4, 168-9, 173-4, 200, 229, 230, 232-3, 239, 240, 249, 269, 272, 286, 306-7; **25, 26, 34, 152, 157, 163, 248**
Chamberlains, Worcester, 137, 140, 196
Charlotte, Queen, 57, 133, 135
Cheshire W.J., 233
Cheshire, William, 262
chestnut urns, 275, 278
chimney pieces, 28, 80, 82, 123, 126, 130, 133, 139, 143, 148, 168, 239, 278; **130**
chinoiserie(s), 60, 70, 146, 187, 196, 212, 229, 244, 255, 278, 280, 295, 301, 306; **101, 113, 136, 187, 189, 202, 241, 274, 295, 303**
Chopping & Bill, 137, 138, 140, 142
Christopher Seager & Co. *see*: Seager & Co.
chromo-lithography, 64, 66
Cipriani, Giovanni Battista, 62
Clay, Henry (*see also*: Henry Clay & Co.), 9, 24, 26-9, 31-3, 36, 39, 49, 53, 56-7, 61-2, 65-6, 69, 70, 75, 77, 85, 89, 90, 97, 99, 100, 108, 116-7, 120, 121, 122, 123, 124-38, 139, 140, 141, 142, 143, 152-3, 212, 219, 230, 233, 235, 239, 241, 244, 252, 254, 258, 260-2, 264, 278, 288, 311, 316; **2, 27, 29, 31, 62, 63, 68, 71, 76, 125, 127, 128, 129, 130, 131, 135, 136, 137, 232, 244, 245**

clock dials, 25, 139, 140, 141, 143, 309
coaches, 15, 28, 82, 118, 119, 126
coal receptacles, 20, 42, 46, 81, 104, 109, 110, 162, 164, 178, 181, 191, 192, 195, 203, 202, 205-9, 211, 212, 217; **178, 188, 191, 202, 204, 205, 208, 213, 216**
Cobbett, Anne, 27, 250, 266, 316
Cocq, H., 302
coffins, 24, 35
cold painting, 123
combination trays, 124, 212, 257; **257**
Cooksley, Daniel, 307; **263**
Copley, John Singleton, 62
copper panels, japanned, 118, 123, 240; **130**
cork-stencilling, 66, 219; **59**
Corke, Earl of, 116, 117
Corn Laws, 91, 189
counters/quadrille trays, 46, 124, 175, 186, 230, 251; **84, 199, 233, 274**
Court, William H.B., 113
Crace, the firm of 235; **229, 234**
Craven, Lord & Lady, 122, 123, 126, 134
Crimean War, 224
Crompton, T.R., 35
Crompton, T.B. 29
Cronstedt, Count Otto, 89
cruet stands, 143, 239, 258, 259, 260-1; **258, 302**
crystallised tinware, 48, 178, 187, 200, 306, 313; **48, 49, 178**
cutlery urns, 121; **121**
Cyclopaedia (Chambers), 24
Cyclopaedia of Useful Arts (Tomlinson, Charles), 49

D'Hancarville, Pierre Francois, 61, 62, 128; **62, 244**
Darwin, Charles,
Davenport, Matthew, 312
Davenport & Cole, 262
David, Edmund, 36
Davies, George, 180, 275
Davies, Morgan, 276
Davis, William, 58, 76, 187
Dean, J., & Son, 220
Dean, John (*see also*: Dean, J., & Son), 120
Demidov family, 294, 297, 298, 301
Department of Practical Art, 105, 158
Derby House, 128; **130, frontispiece**
Derrick, Samuel, 116
Dewson & Sons, 181
Dickinson, George, 9, 29, 52, 56, 59, 69, 74, 78, 89, 97, 157, 176, 181, 187, 202, 252, 256; **98/99**
display canisters, 266
Docker, Charles 41, 75, 143
Dodd, George, 43, 104
dolls house furniture, 200; **200**
door panels, 53, 130, 153; **160, 234, 244, 245, frontispiece**
Dossie, Robert, 13, 15, 23, 24, 28, 41, 43, 69, 119, 272, 278, 280
Dresser, Christopher, 104, 164, 205
Ducrest, Lewis, 239
Dutch metal *see*: gilding
Dyke, Joseph, 20
Dyson & Benson, 231-232, 235, 241; **231**

Eagles, T.F., 232
East India Co., 11, 12, 186, 198
East India Co., Dutch, 12

Eastlake, Charles, 265
Easy Hill, 115, 116, 117, 118
Education Act (1870), 93
Egington, Francis, 65, 122, 123, 124, 126, 134
electro-plating, 74, 85, 103, 104, 108, 109, 110, 161, 196
Elkington (& Mason), 108, 152
embossing (*see* gilding)
enamel/enamelling 14, 21, 54, 55, 60, 64, 65, 73, 78, 82, 84, 90, 108, 110, 113, 114, 121, 124, 125, 138, 159, 161, 178, 179, 180, 191, 192, 195, 202, 203, 217, 224, 233, 263; **124**
enamel, vitreous, 21, 110
enamelling, gem, 152
English Papier Mâché, see Dickinson, George
Esher Stevens Brazer Guild, 307
Evans & Cartwright, 199-200
Evers, Heinrich Ludwig (Ludwig Euus Nachfolger), 290-1; **199, 200**
exhibitions:
    Arnhem (1852), 303, 304
    Arnhem (1879), 304
    Birmingham (1849), 166, 174, 179
    Edinburgh (1857), 159
    General Exhibition of Dutch Industry (1866), 303, 304; **305**
    Ghent (1830), 304
    Glasgow (1840), 149
    Great Exhibition (1851), 21, 27, 32, 52, 58, 81, 85, 99, 104, 107, 138, 151, 156, 157, 158, 159, 163, 166, 167, 168, 170, 174, 179, 180, 181, 192, 204, 207, 213, 222, 229, 233, 236, 239, 240, 242, 249, 265, 266, 283, 290, 292, 293, 294, 305; **27, 81, 99/100, 157, 158, 172/3, 194, 205, 207, 249, 267, 294, 305**
    Haarlem (1861), 303; **303**
    Halifax (Yorks.) (1840), 142
    London (1862)83, 162, 173, 286
    Manchester (1846), 248
    New York (1853), 144, 158, 168, 208, 236, 292, 306, 307
    New Zealand (1865), 208
    Nottingham (1840), 149
    Paris (1855), 23, 159, 163, 166, 174, 175, 195, 208, 236, 303
    Paris (1867), 21, 43, 78, 83, 152, 162, 166, 209, 249, 272, 279, 286, 290, 294, 296, 304, 305, 317
    Paris (1878, 1889), 285
    Philadelphia (1876), 304
    Society of Artists (1847), 151
    Society of Artists (1848), 151, 152, 191
    Society of Artists (1849), 151, 152
    South Staffordshire (1869), 21, 195, 205, 209, 224, 225; **46, 209, 210**
    Utrecht (1847), 304
    Wolverhampton (1884), 72, 85, 186, 220, 224, 225
export (*see also:* McKinley Tariff; Morrill Tariff Act), 17, 29, 64, 65, 66, 85, 104, 109, 120, 145, 159, 173, 196, 198, 200, 217, 223, 224, 262, 274, 285, 286, 291, 292, 297, 298, 300, 304

Farmer, Thomas, 18, 73, 78, 168-9, 223, 224
Farmer & Chapman, 224
Farmer & Rogers, 108
Farnworth Mills, 29
Fearncombe, Henry, 41, 95, 183, 197, 200-2, 203, 265; **201, 202, 203**
Fellows, Enoch, 91

Fellows, James, 21, 95, 213
Fellows, S.J. & E., 21
Fenn, Charles, 113
firescreens, 80, 138, 141, 148-9, 165, 187, 196, 233, 236, 303-5; **82**
Fitz-Cook, Hugh, 154, 157, 162; **162**
Fletcher, Thomas, 120, 121, 122, 126, 133
Fletcher & Sons, 120
fold screens *see:* screens
Foothorape, Frederick, 175
Foothorape, Showell & Shenton, 174, 175; **175**
Fothergill, John, 120, 121
frames (miniature and picture), 24, 28, 34, 43, 47, 82, 115, 126, 135, 139, 143, 153, 159, 179, 212, 251, 259-61, 281, 286, 290, 292; **50, 61, 81, 259, 260**
Francis & Guest, 62
Franklin, Benjamin, 116
Franse, W.A., 303
Frederick the Great, 287, 317
Froggatt & Tyler, 47, 220

Gallais, C.A., 286
Gandee, B.F., 36, 66, 75, 79, 272
Gebrüder Adt *see:* Adt Frères
gem enamelling (*see:* enamelling, gem)
gems, inlaid, 82-83, 152, 153, 159, 164, 166, 168, 177, 180; **82, 83, 152, 153, 162**
George III, King, 135, 136, 145, 235, 287
George, Prince of Wales (later King George IV), 219, 235, 252, 263; **220, 264**
Gerrard Barber (*see* Barber, Gerrard)
Gibbons, John, 61, 125, 126
Gibbons & Clay, 125, 133
gilding (incl. bright gilding, dead gold, embossing, metal leaf, metal leaf powders, oil gilding, stencilled gilding, water-gilding), 39, 40, 43, 56, 66-74, 75, 80, 135, 136, 180, 186, 192, 193, 205, 258, 265, 267, 269, 274, 278, 280, 286, 290, 296, 307, 309, 315, 316; **68, 71**
Giles, Benjamin, 82, 83
Giles, John 116
Gillray, James, 63
Gittins & Boothby, 40
glass, japanned, 53, 84, 130, 138, 152
Goodman, George, 65, 66, 177, 180
Goodman Method, the (*see also:* transfer printing), 65
Graiseley, Works, 212
Great Depression, The (1878-1879), 110
Great Strike of Tinplate Workers, The (1851), 203
Green, Amos, 116, 124
Griffiths, Samuel, 190
Griffiths & Browett, 104, 178-179, 189, 266; **188**
Gruner, Ludwig, 83, 150, 151, 152, 154
Guerin, Jean, 287, 288, 289
Guest, John, 140
gum Arabic, 28, 261
Gushlow, Thomas, 229

Haddan, John, 33, 35
Hahn, J.P., 293
Halbeard & Wellings, 176; **176, 246**
Hall, T., & Mulford, J., 117
Hall, Thomas, 114, 116
Hamilton, Duke of, 12
Hamilton, Sir William, 61, 128, 133, 244; **62**
Handbook on Japanning, A (W.N. Brown, 1913), 41

Handmaid to the Arts (Dossie, Robert), 13, 23, 41, 272
handscreens 53, 153; **42, 65, 73, 77, 284, 313**
Harris, Charles Restall, 179
Harris, Henry, 67
Harris, Joseph, 227
Harris & Crick, 179; **179**
Harper, George (*see also:* Alsager & Neville), 46, 177
Harthill, Charles, 222
Harthill & Sankey, 222
Hartill, John, 219, 223
Hartill & Jackson, 222
Haselar, Edwin, 58, 64, 77, 193, 195; **193**
Haselar, George, 73
hat-boxes, 46
hats, 34, 35, 58, 265
Haughton, Moses, 124, 126; **127**
Heaviside, John, 58
helmets, 24, 91, 277
Henry Clay, & Co. (*see also:* Clay, Henry), 138, 232-233; **232, 333**
Hertford, Lady, 73, 79, 146, 148; **146**
Hill, W. & Co., 260; **259, 260**
Hill, Willliam, 259, 260
Hill & Green, 259, 260
Hinks, James, 173, 180
Hipkiss, John, 141
Hipkiss, Richard, 25, 141
Hipkiss & Harrold, 141
Historical Society of Early American Decoration (HSEAD), 8, 307, 308; **308, 309**
Hobson, 47, 72, 73, 74
holloware, 31, 41, 217, 223, 224; **214, 215, 216**
Hopkins, Alfred, 175
Hopkins, J. H. , 174-175, 223; **111, 175**
Hopkins, John, 174
Horsley, John Callcott, 85, 192
HSEAD *see:* Historical Society of Early American Decoration
Hubball, Thomas, 75, 235
Hubball, Thomas & Son, 235
Hunt, Robert, 32, 41, 62, 78, 236
Hunt, William Holman, 55
Hupfer & Wolfermann, 293
Hutton, William, 36, 69, 75, 107, 113, 115, 116, 250, 265

Illidge, Thomas, 25, 31, 75, 80, 186, 189-199, 200, 235; **75, 198-199**
imitative effects (*see also:* lapis lazuli; makii; malachite; tortoiseshell; wood-grain), 43, 46, 53, 212
impasto, 63, 78, 79, 145, 277, 280, 290; **63**
imports, 12, 37, 109, 111, 290, 302, 307, 309
incised/bright-cut decoration, 48, 263, 268; **49, 87, 263, 269**
ink-stands, 84, 149, 158, 233
inlays, 68, 78, 80, 82, 162, 168, 269, 293, 315
intaglios (*see:* cameos)
iron (incl. black iron plate, hammered sheet iron, sheet iron, wrought iron) 14, 17, 18, 19, 20, 21, 29, 30, 35, 36, 39, 41, 42, 52, 54, 57, 58, 64, 74, 75, 78, 96, 99, 102, 103, 109, 110, 111, 115, 116, 118, 121, 123, 124, 125, 126, 127, 138, 140, 143, 161, 162, 164, 165, 168, 173, 174, 178, 179, 180, 187, 188, 191, 193, 195, 202, 204, 205, 206, 207, 208, 211, 212, 215, 217, 219, 220, 222, 223, 224, 225, 229, 230, 231,

235, 239, 240-241, 244, 249, 251, 252, 253, 254, 256, 257, 262, 272, 273, 276, 279, 281, 286, 288, 291, 292, 294, 296, 297, 299, 300, 301, 304, 305, 307, 322, 315, 316; **30, 121, 162, 178, 188, 191, 202, 203, 204, 205, 206, 208, 209, 222, 228/9, 234, 249, 265, 275**
Isabella II, Queen of Spain, 151, 152

Jackson, Rev H., 150
Jackson, Samuel, 116, 222, 223
Jackson, William, 59
Jackson & Graham, 24
Jackson & Sankey (*see also:* Sankey, 93, 222
Jacob, Joseph, 269
Japan varnish (*see also:* varnish), 13, 14, 18, 27, 36, 39, 40, 42, 52, 53, 59, 77, 79, 83, 115, 123, 211, 242, 252, 258, 259, 265, 266, 272, 275, 287, 290, 295, 298; **13, 43**
Japonisme, 109
Jeddo Works, 203, 205, 225
Jennens & Bettridge, 9, 28, 29, 32, 33, 36, 37, 41, 42, 46, 51, 52, 54, 55, 56, 57, 58, 59, 60, 63, 64, 72, 73, 78, 79, 82, 83, 90, 92, 95, 102, 103, 104, 108, 137, 144-161, 162, 163, 164, 165, 166, 167, 168, 170, 173, 176, 177, 180, 183, 187, 191, 192, 197, 232, 239, 240, 242, 244, 246, 248, 249, 252, 254, 256, 262, 263, 264, 266, 287, 311, 312; **25, 27, 32, 46, 53, 76, 77, 82, 83, 99, 105, 144-161, 239, 242, 244, 253**
Jerrard, Paul, 267, 268; **267**
John Bettridge & Co. (*see also:* Bettridge, John), 34, 35, 36, 42, 46, 78, 161, 162, 163, 164, 262; **162, 163**
Jones, Edward, 64, 85, 93, 213
Jones, Evan, 277
Jones, James, 223-224
Jones, John, 72, 85
Jones, Joseph, **194**
Jones, Owen, 58, 104, 192, 236
Jones, Peter, 62, 177
Jones, Phillip Highfield, 217
Jones, Thomas, 26, 33-35, 240
Jones, William Highfield, 9, 20, 59, 64, 90, 94-96, 168, 187, 200, 212-16
Jones & Bird, 225
Jones & Taylor, 183, 184
Jones Brothers, 212-217; **214, 215, 216**
Josiah Sankey & Co., 225
Journal of Design & Manufactures, 33, 85, 151, 154, 196, 174, 192, 240
Journeyman decorators, 168, 177, 224

Kauffman, Angelica, 62, 124, 130, 289; **130, 240**
Kedleston Hall, **23/4, title page**
Kick Wilhelm/Willem, 14, 302
King, William, 75, 235
Klinkman, Jan, 303; **303**
knife trays, 20, 110, 124, 141, 200, 230, 239
Knight, Merry & Co. (Davies), 180
Kondratyev, Yegor, 30
Korobov, P., 298-300
Kraegelius, Ludweig, 285, 290
Kunckel, Johannes, 43

La Rochefoucauld brothers, 57, 130, 133, 135
Labutin, Jakov, 300, 301; **301**

lacquer (incl. lac, rhus vernicifera, resin lacquer, seed lac, shellac, stick lac, true lacquer), 11, 12, 13, 14, 15, 17, 42, 49, 66, 69, 70, 77, 78, 109, 198, 271, 278, 280, 302, 304, 306, 314; **11, 15**
Ladies Amusement, The, 60, 113; **61**
Landseer, Edwin, 63, 84, 85, 103, 148, 159, 164, 170, 211, 296; **105**
Lane, Thomas, 41, 80, 102, 144, 163, 164, 165, 166, 168, 180, 197, 304
Lane's Patent, 166, 168
lapis lazuli, 46, 168, 292
Lawley, G.& J., 219-20
Lawley, R., 219-220
layered paper, 23, 24, 28, 31, 261, 264, 280, 287
Leeson, George, 261
Leeson, William (inc. Leeson & Son), 260-1; **261**
Lichtenberg, Georg Christof, 61, 126
Light iron ware, 191
Lindsay, George, 56
Lindsay, W.S., 153
liquor stands, 259, 260; **260**
Litchfield Manufacturing Co., 306, 307
Loveridge, Henry & Co., 21, 42, 47, 54, 68, 74, 80, 84, 90, 91, 103, 104, 109, 124, 192, 195, 196, 203, 205-12, 242, 251, 254, 256, 257, 258, 265, 311; **30, 68, 74, 80, 87, 97, 108, 109, 208, 209, 210, 211, 212, 213, 251, 255, 257, 314, 317**
Loveridge & Shoolbred (*see also:* Schoolbred & Loveridge), 190, 205-12, 232, 245; **72, 206, 207**
Ludwig Evers Nachfolger *see:* Evers, Ludwig
Lugt, G. van der, 303, 304
Lukutin factory, 264, 294-5, 298, 299-300; **295, 297, 299**
Lunar Society, 26
Luxborough, Lady, 23

Maclise, Daniel, 57
makii effect, 49
making paper, 28-9, 35, 37, 59, 153, 161, 239; **30**
malachite, 46, 161, 164, 176-8, 180, 212, 268, 290; **46**
Mander, Benjamin, 55, 91, 196; **196**
Mander, Charles, 9, 31, 40, 42, 87, 90, 176, 177, 198, 205, 206, 213; **197**
Mander, John, 196
Mander, Nicholas, 198
Mander & Son, 196; **196**
Mander Brothers, 40, 196-8
Manders Inc., 198
Mapplebeck & Lowe, 48, 312-3; **315**
Marston, John, 205, 212, 224-5
Martin, Gina, 306
Martin, Guillaume, 24, 280-1, 287
Martin, Jean-Alexandre, 281
Martin, Simon Etienne, 118-9, 280-1
Martin Brothers, Paris, 99, 278, 280-1, 287; **281**
Martineau, Caroline, 108
Martineau, Harriet, 31, 37, 53, 82, 96, 100, 104, 316
Mauchline Ware, 316-7
McCallum & Hodson, 9, 29, 33, 39, 51, 55, 58-9, 72, 74, 95, 96, 102-4, 109, 144, 162, 169-74, 176, 177, 178, 202, 246, 256, 286, 313; **76, 95, 171, 172/3, 173, 174**
McKinley Tariff, 111, 285
mechanical painting, 63, 123, 124, 126
Mechi, J.J., 312-3
Merridale Works, 25, 74, 144, 197, 203, 206-8, 212, 254

metal leaf *see:* gilding
Meteyard, Eliza, 122, 133, 134
Meyer & Kreller, 293
Meyer & Wried, 264, 289, 292, 305; **293**
Midgely, Charles (*see also:* Woodward & Midgely), 167
Millar, James, 116
Morland, George, 59, 63, 76, 187; **57, 58**
Morrill Tariff Act, 104, 109
Motlow, James, 223, 225
moulds/cores, 28-35, 36, 138-9, 152, 192, 203, 211, 277; **34, 60, 163**
Mulford, John, 114, 116
'Mystery' process, 114

Napoleonic Wars, 18, 25, 91, 281, 299
Nasmyth, James (incl. Nasmyth's hammer), 20, 188
Neale, Reuben, 140, 174
Neville, Charles, 78, 176-7
Neville, George (*see also:* Alsager & Neville), 57, 64, 176, 178
Neville, James, 178
Noble, Mark, 115
Nock & McCallum, 179
Nollekens & his Times (Smith, J.T.), 23
Nooyen, L.J., 166, 303-4; **304, 305**

Oakamoor Tinplate Works, Cheadle, 18
Old Hall/Old Hall Japan Works, 20, 25, 36, 46, 55, 56, 57, 58, 59, 64, 72, 74, 78, 86, 90, 91, 93, 94, 95, 96, 144, 168, 183, 184, 185, 186, 187, 188, 189, 190, 192, 195, 196, 200, 202, 203, 206, 207, 209, 213, 215, 246, 252, 254, 257; **48, 88/9, 184, 187, 192**
Osterley Park House, 62, 128, 136-7, 241; **128**

Palmerston, Lord, 116
Papendiek, Elizabeth, 135, 137, 138, 258, 264
paper, chewed, 23
paper duty, 36-7
paper ware, 24-5, 29, 212, 232
Parent, Albert, & Companie, 262
paste and glue, 28, 29, 30, 33, 35, 82-3, 168, 261, 280
pasteboard, 24, 29, 30, 31, 32, 33, 34-5, 36, 90, 99, 123, 124, 161, 202, 212, 241, 242, 244, 248, 257, 259, 261, 307
Patent Pearl Glass, 80, 164-5, 166, 168; **50, 81, 165**
Patent Pulp Manufacturing Company, 272, 277, 284; **277**
pattern books/nos, 40, 46, 50, 104, 159, 190, 198, 206, 220, 251, 253, 254, 256, 283, 311, 315; **31, 284, 314**
pearl decoration, 24, 40, 49-53, 56, 64, 77, 84, 99, 103, 104, 105, 107, 135, 138, 139, 142, 146, 148, 151, 154, 156, 157, 158, 159, 161, 163, 164, 165, 166, 167, 168, 169, 170, 173, 174, 176, 177, 179, 180, 191, 229, 233, 242, 246, 249, 261, 262, 264, 266, 268, 272, 283, 284, 286, 293, 294, 296, 300, 301, 303, 304, 305, 307, 316; **33, 49, 50, 51, 52, 53, 77, 81, 134, 159, 165, 173, 194, 241, 246, 256, 283, 304, 311, 312, 317**
Pedley, James, 200
Period Art Ware, 227; **227**

Perry, Edward, 91, 95, 109, 183, 197, 202-5, 206-7, 209, 224, 225, 265; **204, 205**
Perry, George, 202-5
Perry, Richard, 202-5
Perry, Richard & Son, 205, 207
Peyton & Harlow (incl. Peyton & Peyton), 66, 104, 249; **249**
Phoenix Works, 200, 202
piano stools, **179**
pianos, 52, 104, 156-7, 162, 239; **98/99, 162**
Piozzi, Mrs (formerly Thrale, Hester), 135
plate and vegetable warmers, 20, 110, 117, 196, 211, 230-1, 239, 265, 275; **175, 265**
pocket coin-balances, 46
Pococke, Richard, 45, 60, 274
pole screens *see:* screens
polishing, 39, 40, 45, 53-4, 84, 92, 123, 180, 272, 280
Pontypool *see:* Allgood, Edward; Allgood, Thomas; Hanbury, John
Pontypool Iron Works, 14, 18
Pontypool Japan Works, 14, 17, 115, 118, 273-6, 277
Postans, 40
presses (incl. fly, hydraulic, pressure, power, stamp, steam), 20-1, 33, 34, 96, 110, 114, 178, 204, 230, 261, 262
Priestley, Joseph, 26, 265
Prosser, Richard, 65, 73, 74, 118, 138-9
Pugin A.W.N., 145
pulp, 13, 23, 24, 26, 28-9, 32-7, 53, 104, 108, 109, 111, 135, 139, 145, 153, 168, 169, 240, 242, 246, 248, 253, 261, 262, 268, 280, 287, 307
Pyrke, John, 276

railway carriages, 35, 37, 161, 179
railway wheels, 35
Raven, Samuel, 57, 116, 142, 264; **117, 264**
Redgrave, Richard, 154-5, 158, 164, 254; **154, 155**
Rees' *Cyclopedia*, 41
relief-moulded decoration, 35, 51, 74, 79, 103, 135, 153, 209, 284
Renel, A., 305; **305**
restoration, 315, 316
Richard Spiers & Son *see:* Spiers
Robinson & Swinney *The Artists's Assistant*, 41
Rochefoucauld brothers *see:* La Rochefoucauld brothers
rosaries, 159, 163, 261-2
Rowlandson, Thomas, 63
Rowley, James, 223, 224
Royal Society of Arts (Royal Society for the Encouragement of Arts, Manufacturers and Commerce), 25, 26, 37, 100, 119, 280
Rushout, Anne, 39, 96, 126, 135
Russia *see:* Demidov family; Kondratyev, Yegor; Korobov, P.; Labutin, Jakov; Lukutins factory; Tagil, Nizhny; Vishniakov factory; Zhostovo trays
Ryland, Thomas Henry, 113
Ryton, Benjamin, 36, 186
Ryton, John, 184, 187; **184**
Ryton, Obadiah, 55, 56, 86, 97, 184, 185, 186, 196; **185, 187**
Ryton, Richard, 187
Ryton, William Lott, 36, 56, 184, 185, 186, 188, 196; **187**
Ryton & Walton, 46, 48, 55, 168, 186, 187, 188, 219, 252-4, 275; **187, 189**

Sadler, George, 56, 207
Sandauer boxes, 293
Sankey, J., & Son(s), 223-4
Sankey, Joseph, 91, 175, 222-3
Sankey & Co., 21, 224-5; **222**
Sarjeant, David, 78, 103-4, 107, 278, 286, 296, 304-5
Sayer, Robert, 113
Schaaffhausen & Dietz, 291-2, 294; **292, 293**
Schools of Design *see:* Birmingham; Somerset House (Govt School of Art); Wolverhampton
Schürhoff, H. 249
Scone Palace, 280
Scott, John, 225, 227
Scott & Bacon, 225
Scott Harris, 92, 93, 227, 311
screens (incl. fold screens and pole screens; *see also:* firescreens; hand screens), 12, 28, 36, 83, 108, 110, 126, 143, 146, 148, 152, 155, 158, 160, 164-7, 174, 180, 195, 200, 271-2, 290, 303-6, 312; **143, 312**
Scroxton, J.H ., 229, 266
Seager & Co. (Christopher Seager & Co.), 223, 225; **226**
Sellman & Hill, 217; **217**
Shelburne, Lady, 65, 113, 114, 116
Shelburne, Lord, 114
Sheldon, Ebeneezer, 34, 40, 109, 180-1, 246
Sheldon, William, 34, 40
Shenstone, William, 23, 117
ship panels, japanned, 28, 55, 64, 82, 126, 152, 153, 162, 164, 166, 177, 239, 251
Shoolbred (unknown), 244
Shoolbred, William, 197, 205-8, 245
Shoolbred & Loveridge (*see also:* Loveridge & Shoolbred), 90-1, 190, 197, 206, 232; **206**
Shoolbred, Loveridge & Shoolbred, 207-8; **72, 207**
slate, japanned, 39, 136, 229, 242, 262; **77**
Small, T., & Son, 41, 137-8, 140-2
Small, Thomas, 138, 141, 233, 262
Small(s) & Hipkiss, 141; **141**
Smith, George, 223-4
Smith, J.T., 23, 27
Smith, Mary, 91
Smith, W. & A., 316
Smith, William, 18
Smith & Liddington, 224
Smith Armstrong, 60, 224, 227
Smith Hawkes, 85
snuffboxes (*see also:* tobacco boxes), 13-5, 23-5, 27-8, 32, 43, 46, 48, 54, 63-4, 66, 99, 113-6, 120-1, 125, 127, 133, 138-9, 141-3, 148, 159, 174, 186, 199, 219, 239, 263, 272, 274-5, 278, 280-1, 284-5, 287, 289-95, 299, 302, 311; **45, 55, 87, 146, 199, 220, 263-4, 283, 285, 289, 291, 295-6**
snuffers, *see:* candle snuffers
snuffers trays (pans/stands), 46, 48, 86, 110, 123, 124, 137, 140-1, 198, 200, 206, 230-1, 239, 251, 258, 301, 313; **26, 48**
Society for the Encouragement of Arts, Manufactures and Commerce *see:* Royal Society
Soho Works *see:* Boulton, M.
sofas, 26, 32-3, 104, 151, 155, 162, 240, 248-9; **150**
Sollom, Benjamin, 19; **18**
Somerset House (Govt School of Art), 102

Spa boxes (boites de Spa), 317
spectacle cases, 190, 284; **289**, **293**
Sphinx Ware (*see also*: Hopkins, J.H.), 174-5, 223
Spiers, (Richard) of Oxford, 178, 235-6; **235**, **236**, **237**
Spiers & Son, 236, 237; **237**
St Fond, Faujas de, 14
Stalker, John, 11, 12, 271
Stalker & Parker, 11-14, 271; **13**
Star Japan Co., 66, 225, 227, 253; **59**, **226**, **227**
steam moulding, 27, 33, 149, 152, 163, 180, 248-9; **34**, **245**
Steedman, Charles, 229
Steedman, James, 229
Stencilling, 64, 66, 74-8, 175, 219, 227, 298, 308-9; **59**, **62**, **67**, **102**, **221**, **226-7**, **308**
Stobwasser/Stobwasser & Son (*see also individual listings below*), 46, 78, 152, 179, 264, 281, 287-3, 291, 299, 306; **288**, **289**
Stobwasser, Christian Heinrich (C.H. Stobwasser & Co.), 289, 292, 305
Stobwasser, Georg Siegmund, & Son, 287-9
Stobwasser, Gustav, 290-3
Stobwasser, Johann, 287-9
Stobwasser, Louise, 289
Stockham, John and Richard, 274, 276
Stockmann, J.H. August, 291
Stockmann, J.H. Wilhelm, 264, 291; **291**
Stockmann, W. & Co., 291
Stone, Samuel, 18
stomach warmers, 205
stoving/baking *see*: cold-painting
Strickland, Edward, 56, 229, 230-1
Strickland & Co., 95, 230-1
Strickland & Richardson, 230-1
Strickland & Wilton, 93, 230, 232
Stubbs, Edwin, 211; **72**, **211**
Stubbs, Richard, 203, 211; **72**, **211**
Summerly, Felix, 155; **154**
Sutcliffe, Isherwood, 168; **169**
Swedish wood-pulp, 35, 109

tables, 29, 31, 41, 54, 58, 62-3, 66, 77, 80, 85, 100, 103, 104, 110, 116, 123, 126-8, 131, 133, 136-8, 141-3, 146, 148, 151, 155-9, 161-3, 165-71, 173-4, 176, 179-80, 183, 192-3, 195, 200, 203, 211, 229-31, 233, 236, 239, 240-2, 244, 246, 249, 260, 272, 278, 283-4, 286-8, 290, 292, 296, 300, 303, 305-7, 313; **38/9**, **77**, **119**, **128**, **131**, **132**, **133**, **146/7**, **148**, **175**, **176**, **182/3**, **228/9**, **233**, **240**, **241**, **242**, **243**, **257**
Tagil, Nizhny, 297-8, 300-1; **298**
Taylor, H.F.W., 212
Taylor, John, 14, 18, 54, 60, 65, 113-5, 117, 241, 263, 275
Taylor, Jones & Badger, 183-4
Taylor, Law & Co., **106**, **181**
Taylor, Rev. I., 11; **315**
Taylor, Thomas (*see also*: Jones & Taylor), 183-4
Taylor & Jones *see*: Jones & Taylor
Taylor & Lloyd, 115
Taylor & Pemberton, 113-5
tea boards, 70, 108, 116, 136-7, 145, 198, 212, 235, 250-1, 290, 316; **75**, **101**, **136**, **198**
tea caddies, 18, 26, 29, 32, 34, 48-9, 62, 64, 66, 69, 86, 100, 110, 113-4, 121-4, 126, 133-5, 138-9, 143,

148, 158, 164, 174, 178-9, 187, 205, 233, 239, 268, 289, 292, 299, 300, 312; **19**, **20**, **29**, **32**, **45**, **48**, **49**, **62**, **69**, **72**, **85**, **124**, **134**, **149**, **158**, **269**, **310/11**, **312**
tea/coffee urns, 123, 125, 126, 139, 188, 239, 276; **293**
teapots, 14, 20, 36, 103, 174, 178, 189, 195, 207, 239, 259, 274; **218/9**
Temming, Henrik van, 302
Temple Street Works (R. Perry, Son & Co.), 202, 204-5
Thackrah, Charles, 39, 51, 93, 96-7
Thetford Patent pulp (incl. Thetford fibre, Thetford pulp ware), 35, 109, 272, 277, 294; **277**
Thornley & Knight, 40-1, 144
Thrale, Hester (later Mrs Piozzi), 126, 135, 232
Tin-Plate Workers Union, 91
tobacco boxes (*see also*: snuffboxes), 46, 198, 239, 263, 274, 287, 292
tôle (incl. tôle ware, tôle peinte), 17, 278-9
Tomlinson, Charles, 49; **16/7**
tortoiseshell effect, 14, 43, 45, 46, 62, 115, 121, 124, 241, 263, 274, 289, 291, 295, 296, 300; **44**, **199**, **273**, **274**, **295**
trade embargoes, 25
transfer printing (*see also*: Goodman Method), 64-6, 73-4, 80, 105, 109, 113, 118, 162, 175, 178, 219, 232, 259, 262, 264, 284, 316-7; **85**, **109**, **206**, **277**, **284**, **285**
travellers' samples, 85-7, 188, 213, 219, 315; **55**, **86**, **87**
travelling trunks, 12, 47, 110, 203, 210, 215, 217, 220, 223-5
tray forms
    club fine, 212, 257
    combination tray, 124, 212, 257; **257**
    concave-edge, 141, 251, 252; **68**, **71**, **105**, **141**, **145**, **207**, **213**, **251**, **252**, **284**
    convex-edge, 141, 251, 252, 254, 298, 300; **47**, **67**, **97**, **102**, **211**, **221**, **255**
    sandwich edge, 30-1, 34, 141, 187, 189, 251, 252-3, 315; **68**, **76**, **86**, **101**, **136**, **148**, **189**, **198**, **232**, **252**, **253**, **254**
    straight-edge, 31, 212, 251, 315; **63**, **70**, **75**, **80**, **128**, **136**, **145**, **185**, **196**, **198**, **199**, **203**, **231**, **251**, **317**
    teaboards, 31, 70, 75, 80, 116, 136, 138, 250, 288
    waiters, 20, 26, 28, 30, 34, 36, 40, 43, 45, 46, 54, 56, 60, 62, 64, 65, 75, 85, 91, 94, 110, 111, 115, 116, 122, 123, 124, 126, 127, 136, 137, 138, 139, 140, 143, 168, 178, 187, 192, 193, 196, 200, 205, 206, 219, 220, 224, 225, 227, 230, 231, 239, 250, 251, 253, 273, 275, 276, 283, 288, 289; **56**, **59**, **178**, **211**, **217**, **221**, **276**
tray shapes
    breakfast, 205, 216, 254, 256-7; **166**, **174**, **217**, **256**
    cake (inc. baskets), 80, 109, 188, 205, 256, 301, 313; **108**, **271**
    card, 78, 170, 256, 307; **80**, **232**, **237**, **252**, **256**, **308**, **315**
    Crystal, 80, 83, 195, 242, 257; **195**
    gothic, 31, 78, 85, 141, 142, 145, 157, 189, 206, 207, 252-3, 256,

258, 265, 276, 294, 299, 301, 300, 304, 315; **59**, **76**, **77**, **80**, **108**, **142**, **211**, **221**, **232**, **233**, **237**, **256**, **299**, **301**, **308**, **309**, **313**
    king gothic, 253, 315; **46**, **53**, **71**, **79**, **105**, **141**, **145**, **155**, **159**, **188**, **207**, **252**
    parlour-maid's, 154, 254, 256; **166**
    queen gothic (*see also*: Victoria), 188, 253, 254; **227**, **253**
    rectangular sandwich-edge, 187, 252
    Union, 257, 315
    Victoria (*see also*: queen gothic), 251, 253, 254, 304; **255**
    Windsor, 254; **255**
    Wine, 154, 155, 158, 169, 170, 179, 230, 254, 256; **154**, **155**
trays (incl. iron, paper mâché, tin; *see also*: teaboards), 14, 17, 18-21, 25-8, 30-1, 33-7, 40, 45-6, 48-9, 53-9, 61-4, 66, 72, 74-6, 78, 80, 84-7, 90, 94, 99-100, 103, 105, 107-10, 115-7, 120-2, 124, 126-7, 133-46, 149, 154-9, 161-4, 166-70, 174-5, 178-81, 183-4, 186-7, 191-3, 195-6, 198, 200, 202-3, 205-9, 211-3, 215, 217, 219-20, 222-5, 227, 229-33, 239-42, 250-8, 265, 272-4, 276-7, 279, 281, 283-92, 294, 296-9, 300-9, 311, 313, 315-6; **26**, **30**, **37**, **46**, **48**, **53**, **56-8**, **63**, **67-8**, **70**, **71**, **74**, **76**, **80**, **84**, **86**, **87**, **97**, **101**, **102**, **105**, **105**, **109**, **119**, **128**, **139**, **141**, **145**, **148**, **155**, **159**, **166**, **169**, **174**, **181**, **185**, **188**, **189**, **193**, **195**, **196**, **198**, **199**, **201**, **203**, **207-9**, **213**, **214**, **217**, **220**, **221**, **222**, **225**, **226**, **227**, **231**, **233**, **237**, **250-7**, **271**, **273**, **274**, **284**, **288**, **292**, **298**, **299**, **301**, **303**, **304**, **308**, **309**, **315**, **317**
Troughton, Samuel, 241
Turley, Richard, 104, 166-7, 248; **167**
Two Brothers, The, 217

Ure, Andrew, 48
urn stands, 195, 257
urns (*see also*: chestnut urns; cutlery urns; tea/coffee urns), 14, 280

Valentine, Charles, 65, 73, 93, 232
Valentine, Frederick, 232
Valentine & Hall, 232, 235
varnish (incl. asphaltum varnish, black tar varnish, brown tar varnish, Brunswick black, mixing varnish, spirit varnish, tar varnish) 11-14, 17, 24, 27-8, 36, 39-43, 45-8, 51-3, 55, 58-9, 64-5, 69-70, 72-3, 75, 77-80, 82-4, 87, 90, 92, 94, 96-7, 111, 115, 118-9, 121, 123, 126-7, 130, 134, 136, 138-40, 144, 168, 170, 176, 192, 196-8, 211-3, 215, 223, 230, 232, 235, 240, 242, 252, 258-9, 262, 264-5, 266-9, 271-3, 277-81, 286-7, 290, 292, 295-9, 302, 304-7, 309, 315-7; **13**, **43**, **56**
vases, 26, 31, 32, 54, 62, 73, 79, 83, 121, 123, 126, 128, 133, 135, 143, 146, 148-9, 152, 159, 166, 168, 178-9, 191, 192, 195, 197, 205, 229, 266, 278, 280, 284, 285, 305; **31**, **146**, **151**, **153**, **159**, **171**, **187**, **190**, **193**, **204**, **244**, **285**, **305**
vernis martin, 24, 60, 100, 120, 278, 280-1
Verulam, Earl of, 24, 120
Victoria, Queen, 142, 150, 152, 163,

170, 171, 188, 193, 195, 209, 262; **193**
Vishniakov factory, 295, 298, 300
Vishniakov, Filipp Nikitich, 294, 295, 298, 300
Vishniakov, Tara, 300
vitreous enamel *see*: enamel

Wadhams Manufacturing Co., 307
Wallis, George, 53, 55, 56, 58, 62, 84, 85, 102-4, 162, 167, 170, 186-8, 204, 249, 253, 265
Walpole, Horace, 116, 127, 271, 278
Walton, B., & Co., 66, 85, 91; **79**
Walton, Benjamin (*see also*: Walton, B., & Co.), 20, 78, 91, 93, 178, 186, 188, 190
Walton, F., & Co., 191-3, 195, 196
Walton, Frederick (*see also*: Walton, F., & Co.) 191-3, 195, 196, 203, 207, 213, 242; **192**, **194**, **195**
Walton & Co. (*see also*: Walton, B., & Co., Walton, F., & Co.), 31, 58, 104, 191, 192, 195, 209, 254, 256-7, 265, 311, 313; **197**, **252**, 203, 207, 213, 242; **192**, **194**, **195**
Waring, John, 140
Warner, Richard, 53, 126
Warner, Robert, 69
Warner, William, 193
Watson, Robert (incl. Watson & Kindon; Watson & Rayney), 138
Watson, Thomas, 143, 262
Watt, James, 26, 114, 120, 122, 134
'Watteau' style, 148, 156, 166, 192, 286
Wedgwood, Josiah, 26, 54, 61, 69, 121, 122, 125, 127, 133, 134, 153, 163
Westwood, Obadiah, 33, 49, 139, 260, 262
Wheatley, Francis, 62
wig-boxes, 268
Wilkes & Co., **217**
Wilton (London) (*see also*: Strickland & Wilton), 24, 93, 230
wine coolers, 196, 207, 230, 239
wine wagons, 259, 260-1; **261**
Winfield, R.W., 41, 102, 249
Winn, Robert, 143, 252, 260; **142**, **143**
Wolverhampton School of Design, 103
Wolverhampton School of Practical Art, 208
'Wolverhampton style' decoration, 78, 189
Wontner & Benson, 230-1; **231**
Wood, W.H.B., 179, 266; **266**
wood-grain effect, 46, 47, 178; **38/39**, **47**
Woodforde, Parson, 135, 264
Woodward, Charles Joshua, 72, 81, 168
Woodward, Josiah, 46, 72, 81, 167, 168
Woodward & Midgely (*see also*: Woodward, Josiah; Midgely, Charles), 32, 35, 41, 51, 55, 72, 76, 81, 83, 166-167, 168, 177, 197
work-boxes, 36, 52, 135, 152, 187, 272
workshops *see*: Ch. V
wrought iron *see*: iron

Yapp, G.W., 36, 104, 105
Yarranton, Andrew, 17

Zeegers, F., 303, 304
Zhostovo trays, 298, 300-2; **301**
Zofferty, 306
Zucchi, Antonio, 130; **130/131**